D1596073

AFRICAN HISTORICAL DICTIONARIES
Edited by Jon Woronoff

32. *Ethiopia,* by Chris Prouty and Eugene Rosenfeld. 1981. *Out of print. See No. 56.*

33. *Libya,* 2nd ed., by Ronald Bruce St. John. 1991.

34. *Mauritius,* by Lindsay Rivire. 1982. *Out of print. See No. 49.*

35. *Western Sahara,* by Tony Hodges. 1982. *Out of print. See No. 55.*

36. *Egypt,* by Joan Wucher King. 1984. *Out of print. See No. 67.*

37. *South Africa,* by Christopher Saunders. 1983.

38. *Liberia,* by D. Elwood Dunn and Svend E. Holsoe. 1985.

39. *Ghana,* by Daniel Miles McFarland. 1985. *Out of print. See No. 63.*

40. *Nigeria,* by Anthony Oyewole. 1997.

41. *Côte d'Ivoire (The Ivory Coast),* 2nd ed., by Robert J. Mundt. 1995.

42. *Cape Verde,* 2nd ed., by Richard Lobban and Marilyn Halter. 1988. *Out of print. See No. 62.*

43. *Zaire,* by F. Scott Bobb. 1988.

44. *Botswana,* 2nd ed., by Fred Morton, Andrew Murray, and Jeff Ramsay. 1989. *Out of print. See No. 70.*

45. *Tunisia,* 2nd ed., by Kenneth J. Perkins. 1997.

46. *Zimbabwe,* 2nd ed., by R. Kent Rasmussen and Steven L. Rubert. 1990.

47. *Mozambique,* by Mario Azevedo. 1991.

48. *Cameroon,* 2nd ed., by Mark W. DeLancey and H. Mbella Mokeba. 1990.

49. *Mauritius,* 2nd ed., by Sydney Selvon. 1991.

50. *Madagascar,* by Maureen Covell. 1995.

51. *The Central African Republic,* 2nd ed., by Pierre Kalck; translated by Thomas O'Toole. 1992.

52. *Angola,* 2nd ed., by Susan H. Broadhead. 1992.

53. *Sudan,* 2nd ed., by Carolyn Fluehr-Lobban, Richard A. Lobban, Jr., and John Obert Voll. 1992.

54. *Malawi,* 2nd ed., by Cynthia A. Crosby. 1993.

55. *Western Sahara,* 2nd ed., by Anthony Pazzanita and Tony Hodges. 1994.

56. *Ethiopia and Eritrea,* 2nd ed., by Chris Prouty and Eugene Rosenfeld. 1994.

57. *Namibia,* by John J. Grotpeter. 1994.

58. *Gabon,* 2nd ed., by David Gardinier. 1994.

59. *Comoro Islands,* by Martin Ottenheimer and Harriet Ottenheimer. 1994.

60. *Rwanda,* by Learthen Dorsey. 1994.

61. *Benin,* 3rd ed., by Samuel Decalo. 1995.

62. *Republic of Cape Verde,* 3rd ed., by Richard Lobban and Marlene Lopes. 1995.
63. *Ghana,* 2nd ed., by David Owusu-Ansah and Daniel Miles McFarland. 1995.
64. *Uganda,* by M. Louise Pirouet. 1995.
65. *Senegal,* 2nd ed., by Andrew F. Clark and Lucie Colvin Phillips. 1994.
66. *Algeria,* 2nd ed., by Phillip Chiviges Naylor and Alf Andrew Heggoy. 1994.
67. *Egypt,* 2nd ed., by Arthur Goldschmidt, Jr. 1994.
68. *Mauritania,* 2nd ed., by Anthony G. Pazzanita. 1996.
69. *Congo,* 3rd ed., by Samuel Decalo, Virginia Thompson, and Richard Adloff. 1996.
70. *Botswana,* 3rd ed., by Jeff Ramsay, Barry Morton, and Fred Morton. 1996.
71. *Morocco,* 2nd ed., by Thomas K. Park. 1996.
72. *Tanzania,* 2nd ed., by Thomas P. Ofcansky and Rodger Yeager. 1997.
73. *Burundi,* 2nd ed., by Ellen K. Eggers. 1997.
74. *Burkina Faso (former Upper Volta),* 2nd ed., by Lawrence Rupley and Daniel Miles McFarland. 1998.
75. *Eritrea,* by Tom Killion. 1998.

Historical Dictionary
of
Eritrea

Tom Killion

African Historical Dictionaries, No. 75

The Scarecrow Press, Inc.
Lanham, Md., & London
1998

SCARECROW PRESS, INC.

Published in the United States of America
by Scarecrow Press, Inc.
4720 Boston Way
Lanham, Maryland 20706

4 Pleydell Gardens
Kent CT20 2DN, England

British Library Cataloguing in Publication Information Available

Library of Congress Cataloging-in-Publication Data

Killion, Tom.
    Historical dictionary of Eritrea / Tom Killion.
        p.   cm.. — (African historical dictionaries : no. 75)
    Includes biographical references.
    ISBN 0-8108-3437-5 (cloth : alk. paper)
    1. Eritrea—History—Dictionaries.   I. Title.   II. Series.
DT394.K55   1998
963.5'003—dc21   97-30018
                                                              CIP
ISBN 0-8108-3437-5 (cloth : alk. paper)

CONTENTS

EDITOR'S FOREWORD

Back in the 1960s, new states were being created every few months in Africa. Since then, newcomers have been few and far between. The latest is Eritrea. Its birth pangs were exceptionally acute because the imperial power it escaped was not European, but African: the Ethiopian empire. In a continent known for artificial borders, borders have nonetheless become sacrosanct. The only example of a scission so far is Eritrea. This was partly because it was attached to Ethiopia only at the beginning of the decolonization period (in 1952) and partly because it enjoyed a brief period of internal autonomy (1952-62), when it began to form as a state. But it will have to work hard, and enjoy some good luck, to succeed. From all appearances, the people and leaders are willing to work hard, as they fought hard in the past. Let us wish them good luck!

Writing an African historical dictionary is not like writing one on Europe, Latin America, or much of Asia. You do not just look up the information and fill in any blanks. In Africa, the blanks are often bigger than what has been written. So you must go out and collect the data yourself. For Eritrea, the blanks were unusually large, both for the earlier and recent periods. And information was hard to come by. That is why Tom Killion deserves special praise for all the research and legwork he accomplished. Part of this was done during a stay in Eritrea in 1993-94, when he taught an Introduction to Eritrean History course at Asmara University, while his earlier work with Eritrean refugees in Sudan and visits to guerrilla-controlled parts of Eritrea during 1987-88 laid the foundations for his understanding of the contemporary nation. Dr. Killion has lectured and

written extensively on Eritrea, with a special interest in the
nationalist movement. Presently, he teaches in the Humanities Department at San Francisco State University.

Henceforth students, teachers, journalists, diplomats
and others seeking information on Eritrea will have a much
easier time. They can consult this *Historical Dictionary of
Eritrea* and find numerous entries on persons, places,
events, institutions and various political, economic, social,
and cultural features. The chronology fits this information
together historically, and the introduction provides a broad
overview. The inevitable remaining blanks may be filled by
consulting the specialized works in the exhaustive bibliography. All this makes the following historical dictionary a
particularly welcome addition to the series.

Jon Woronoff
Series Editor

ACKNOWLEDGMENTS

This volume is based in large part on research under- taken in Eritrea while the author was on a Fulbright Fellow- ship, teaching history at the University of Asmara. Later work was facilitated by the resources of the History De- partment at Bowdoin College, Maine; the Humanities De- partment at San Francisco State University; and a research fellowship at Stanford University, generously arranged by Richard Roberts. Much of the recent historical material comes from oral interviews conducted with the enthusiastic aid of Zemhret Yohannes of the PFDJ, Takeste Baire, Em- manuel Kahsai and others at the National Confederation of Eritrean Workers, and Arefaine Berhe at RICE (Rome, 1983). In Asmara, Azieb Tewolde of the Research Center on Eritrea provided access to EPLF publications; Brother Ezio Tonini of the Pavoni Center Library provided unfailing assistance with rare Italian publications and manuscripts; and in Washington, D.C., Veronica Rentmeesters of the Eritrean Embassy answered my questions whenever possible.

Important assistance on specific matters was further provided by Abdelkader Saleh Mohammed, Alemseged Tes- fai, Angela Winn, Anghesom Yisaak, Azien Yassin, Bereket Habte Selassie, Betty La Duke, Chris Connery, Chris Datta, Chu-Chu Woldemariam, Dani Duflah, Donald Crummey, Fouad Makki, Francis Anfray, Gebre-Yohannes Tesfamariam, Gebru Tareke, Girmai Yohannes, Goitom Berhane, Hagos Gebrehiwet, Hamed Ahmed, Hamid Nur Hussein, Harold Marcus, Hiroui Tedla Bairu, Hugh and Marty Downey, Idris M. Galadewos, Irma Taddia, Jaber Saad Mohamed, James McCann, Jonathan Bascom, Kahsai Wad Libby, Karen Hauser,

Kawsir Abdurahman, Megdelawit Kidane, Mohamed Said Nawad, Neil Kotler, Pam DeLargy, Phillipe Bourgois, Robert Van Buskirk, Roland Marchal, Ruth Iyob, Saleh Meky, Salome Iyob, Selamawit Arefaine, Senait Iyob, Sewit Bocrezion, Simon Iyob, Steve Brandt, Taha M. Nur, Tekeste Habtu, Tekie Fissehatzion, Tekle M. Woldemikael, Tewolde Beyene, Thomas Kane, Trish Silkin, Wolde-Ab Wolde-Mariam, Wolde-Mika'el Abraha, Wolde-Yesus Ammar, Yemane Gebre-Ab, Yohannes Haile and Yohannes Tseggai. The author is, of course, responsible for all errors and omissions.

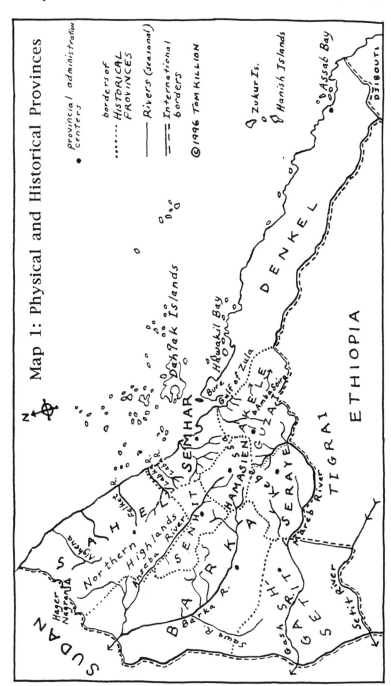

Map 1: Physical and Historical Provinces

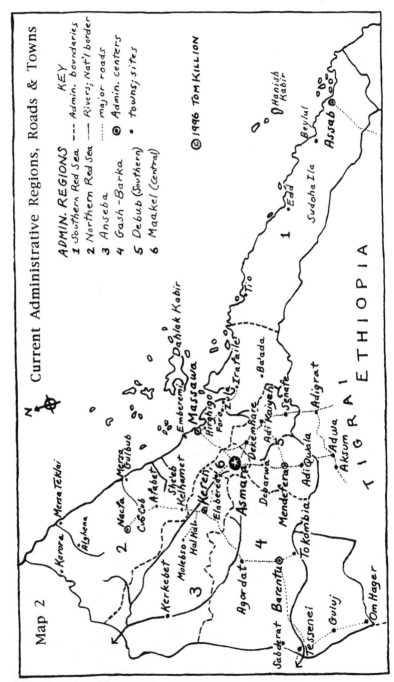

Map 2   Current Administrative Regions, Roads & Towns

ADMIN. REGIONS   KEY
1 Southern Red Sea   --- Admin. boundaries
2 Northern Red Sea   — Rivers; Nat'l border
3 Anseba   ..... major roads
4 Gash-Barka   ◎ Admin. centers
5 Debub (Southern)   • towns; sites
6 Maakel (Central)

© 1996 TOM KILLION

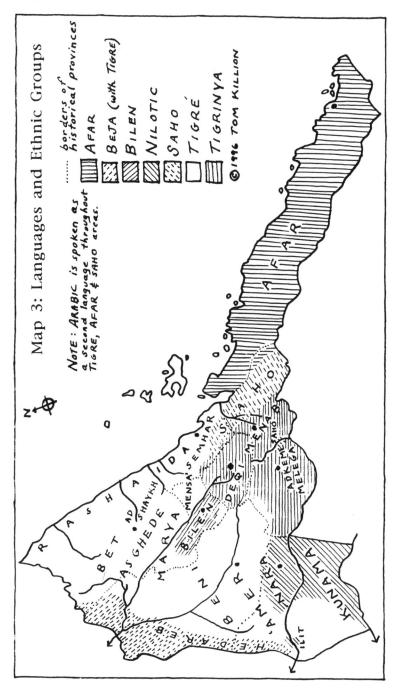

Map 3: Languages and Ethnic Groups

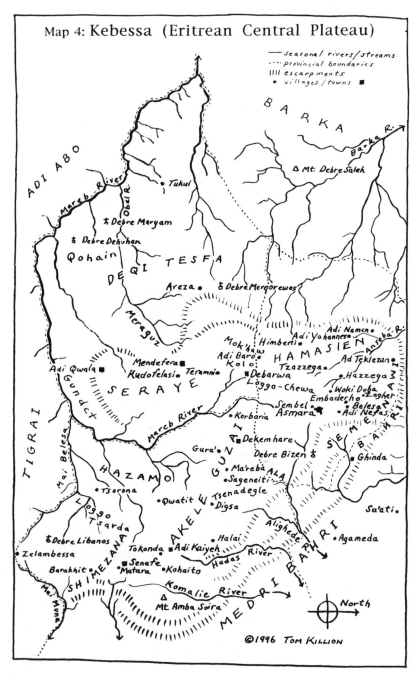

Map 4: **Kebessa (Eritrean Central Plateau)**

— seasonal rivers/streams
··· provincial boundaries
|||| escarpments
• villages/towns ∎

BARKA

ADI ABO

Mareb River

Obel R.

△ Mt. Debre Saleh

Barka R.

• Tukul

⸸ Debre Maryam

⸸ Debre Dehuhan

Qohain

DEQI TESFA

Meraguz

Areza •   ⸸ Debre Mergorewos

Ansəba R.

Adi Namen •

Himberti •   Adi Yohannes •

Mok'haw

Adi Baro •   HAMASIEN   Ad Teklezan

Kolo

Tzazzega •   • Hazzega

Mendefera ∎

Adi Qwala ∎   Kudofelasio   Teramni •   ∎ Debarwa   • Woki Duba   Zagher

Loggo-Chewa   Embaderho •   • Belesa

SERAYE   Sembel •   • Adi Nefas

Gundet   Asmara ∎

Mareb River   • Korbaria

TIGRAI   Ma. Belesa   ⍦ Dekemhare

Gura' •   Debre Bizen ⸸   • Ghinda

HAZAMO   G U N A   Ma'reba

• Tserona   • Sageneiti   ALA

Loggo   • Qwatit ⍦ Tsenadegle

Tsarda   • Digsa

⸸ Debre Libanos   Tokonda ∎   • Halai   Alighede   • Agameda

• Zelambessa   ∎ Adi Kaiyeh   Hadas River   Sa'ati •

Barakhit •   ∎ Senafe • Kohaito

SHIMEZANT   • Matara   Komalie River   North

Ma. Muna   △ Mt. Amba Soira

MEDRI BAHRI

SEMENAWI BAHRI

AKELE

©1996 TOM KILLION

ERITREA: Basic Information

POPULATION:

1984 (Ethiopian government) census = 2,703,998.
1997 (estimate) = 2.8 million.

Population density per/square kilometer = 22.3.

HEALTH:

Life expectancy = 46 years

Population per/doctor (1992) = 1:48,000;
    (1994) = 1:28,000.
Population per/nurse (1994) =   1:8,393.

Infant mortality (1992 est.) = 135:1,000 live births.

EDUCATION:

Literacy (1994) = 20% overall; women = less than 10%.

ECONOMY:

GDP (1992) = $400 million.

GDP per/capita (1992) = $115.

Annual average income (1992) = approx. $75 per/capita.

NOTE TO READER

Cross-Referencing in Text

All words that appear in FULL CAPITALS in the text are cross-references to other Dictionary entries, to which the reader may refer for further information.

Money

All monetary figures preceded by $ are in current U.S. dollars.

Spelling

Eritrea has yet to adopt a uniform system of transliterating the Ge'ez syllabary ("alphabet") of Tigrinya and Tigre into Roman characters. Consequently, three overlapping systems of transliterating Eritrean names and words into English remain in general use. The first relies on Italian letter values and is largely used for colonial era subjects; the second is an ad hoc British system dating from the 1940s; the third is the complex transliteration system adopted in Ethiopia after 1966, which unfortunately produces widespread mispronunciations by the uninitiated and loses most of its usefulness when shorn of its unwieldy diacritical marks. While the last of these systems has been definitively rejected by the present Eritrean government, the other two remain in widespread use. To add to the confusion, there is no standard system of transliterating Eritrean Arabic names.

In this volume I have adopted the spellings of Eritrean personal and place names most commonly used in the contemporary Eritrean English-language press. Eritrean words, where they appear, are direct phonetic transliterations of Ge'ez. Where alternative spellings for Dictionary entries, may be encountered by the reader, I have indicated them in parentheses, preceded by "alt." In general I have represented Ge'ez sounds with letter combinations that best represent the way an English-speaker would pronounce the Eritrean word; for example, I have represented the Ge'ez diphthong vowel-sound "ay" with the English letters "ai," and the Ge'ez diphthong "gn" (like the "n" in canyon) with the English letters "ny."

A special note must be added concerning the spelling of "Tigrai," "Tigre," "Tigrean," and "Tigrinya." Throughout this volume "Tigrai" will refer to the Ethiopian province and "Tigrean" will refer to its inhabitants (as opposed to Eritreans). "Tigre" will refer to lowland Eritreans who speak the "Tigre" language, and "Tigrinya" will refer to highland Eritreans who speak the "Tigrinya" language (which is also spoken by the "Tigreans" of Ethiopia's "Tigrai" province). I have adopted these spellings not because they represent the best transliteration of Ge'ez spelling (which is largely the same for all these different peoples, places, and languages), but to differentiate them from one another as clearly as possible.

ABBREVIATIONS & ACRONYMS

AAU	Addis Ababa University (formerly Haile Selassie I University).
A.D.	After Christ (Common Era).
AES	Association of Eritrean Students
AESNA	Association of Eritrean Students in North America
A.H.	After Hejira (Muslim calendar, c.620 years behind Gregorian).
ALF	Afar Liberation Front.
alt.	alternate spelling.
Amh.	Amharic language.
AOI	Africa Orientale Italiana (Italian East African Empire).
Arab.	Arabic language.
ARDU	Afar Revolutionary Democratic Union.
ARDUF	Afar Revolutionary Democratic Unity Front.
ARF	Afar Revolutionary Forces.
AUDF	Afar National Democratic Front.
BA	British Administration (1949-52).
B.C.	Before Christ (Before Common Era).
BMA	British Military Administration (1941-49).
c.	circa (around).
Cav.	Cavaliere (Italian title).
CC	Central Committee (EPLF).
CELU	Confederation of Ethiopian Labor Unions.
CERA	Commission for Eritrean Refugee Affairs.
Dej.	Dejazmatch (Amh./Tigrn. military title).
EAL	Ethiopian Airlines.

E.C.	Ethiopian Calendar (7-8 years behind Gregorian).
EDM	Eritrean Democratic Movement.
EDU	Ethiopian Democratic Union.
EFLNA	Eritreans for Liberation in North America.
ELF	Eritrean Liberation Front.
ELF-CC	Eritrean Liberation Front-Central Committee.
ELF-NC	Eritrean Liberation Front-National Council.
ELF-PLF	Eritrean Liberation Forces-People's Liberation Forces.
ELF-RC	Eritrean Liberation Front-Revolutionary Council.
ELF-UO	Eritrean Liberation Front-United Organization
ELM	Eritrean Liberation Movement.
EPDM	Ethiopian People's Democratic Movement.
EPLA	Eritrean People's Liberation Army.
EPLF	Eritrean People's Liberation Front.
EPRDF	Ethiopian People's Revolutionary Democratic Front.
ERA	Eritrean Relief Association.
ERD	Eritrean Relief Desk.
ErOC	Eritrean Orthodox Church.
ERRA	Eritrean Relief and Rehabilitation Association.
ERRAC	Eritrean Relief and Refugees Affairs Commission.
FAO	Food and Agriculture Organization (United Nations).
Fit.	Fitiwari (Amh./Tigrn. military title).
FWP	Food for Work Program.
IGADD	International Group to Advise on Drought and Development.
LWR	Lutheran World Relief (Council).
MFH	Mahaber Feqri Hager (Tigrn.: "Patriotic Society").
MLWP	Marxist-Leninist Workers' Party.
MTT	Maria Theresa thaler (Austrian silver dollar).
NGO	Nongovernmental Organization.
PDRY	People's Democratic Republic of Yemen.
PFDJ	People's Front for Democracy and Justice.
PLF	People's (Popular) Liberation Forces.

PLO	Palestine Liberation Organization.
PROFERI	Program for Refugee Reintegration and Rehabilitation of Resettlement Areas in Eritrea.
RC	Revolutionary Council (ELF).
RICE	Research and Information Center on Eritrea.
SATAE	S.A. Transporti Automobilisti Eritrei (Eritean Automobile Transport Company).
SAVA	S. A. Vetreria di Asmara (Asmara Glassworks Company).
SCP	Sudan Communist Party.
SDF	Sudan Defense Force.
SEDAO	Sede Electrica dell'Africa Orientale (East African Electric Company).
SEM	Swedish Evangelical Mission.
Tigrn.	Tigrinya language.
TPLF	Tigrean People's Liberation Front.
UKCC	United Kingdom Commercial Corporation (1941-46).
UN	United Nations.
UNDP	United Nations Development Program.
UNESCO	United Nations Educational, Scientific, and Cultural Organization.
UNHCR	United Nations High Commission for Refugees.
U of A	University of Asmara.
U.S.	United States of America.
USSR	Union of Soviet Socialist Republics.

CHRONOLOGY of ERITREAN HISTORY

c. 6000 B.C.   Earliest cave paintings in Akele Guzai and Sahel.

c. 2500-1500 B.C.   Egyptian trading expeditions to Eritrean coast.

c. 1500-1200 B.C.   Earliest evidence of South Arabian contacts with Eritrean coast.

c. 700-500 B.C.   Strong South Arabian influence on central Eritrea; development of "Pre-Aksumite" civilization in highlands.

c. 500-300 B.C.   Urban civilization in eastern Akele Guzai.

c. 230 B.C.   Port of Adulis founded by Ptolemy Euergetes.

c. 100 A.D.   Rise of Aksumite control over network of urban trade centers connecting Tigrai with Akele Guzai and Adulis.

c. 200-225   *Periplus of the Erythraen Sea* describes power and wealth of Aksumite empire and Adulis.

c. 325-60   Rule of Aksumite Emperor Ezana, who converts to Monophysite Christianity.

525   Emperor Kaleb conquers South Arabia.

615-29   Emperor Armah aids Muslim refugees from
                    Arabia.

c. 702-03   Muslim expedition sacks Adulis, seizes
                    Dahlak Islands.

c. 750-850   Beja expand into highlands and found new
                    ministates on ruins of Aksumite empire,
                    now called "Kingdom of the Habesha" by
                    Arabs.

c. 900-1100   Agaw and Saho peoples move into central
                    Eritrea.

c. 950-1200   Dahlak and Massawa islands become base for
                    spread of Islam on coast.

c.1200s   Eritrean highlands ruled by Zagwe governor
                    of Ma'ikele Bahre.

c. 1320-37   Ewostatewos preaches Christian doctrine
                    with strong regionalist political content.

c. 1325-28   Ethiopian Emperor Amde Siyon deposes
                    rulers of Ma'ikele Bahre and creates
                    military colonies.

c. 1350-60   Filipos founds Debre Bizen, center of
                    Ewostatean reform movement.

1450-68   Emperor Zara Ya'qob accepts Ewostatean
                    doctrine, imposes governorship of Bahre
                    Negashi over central Eritrea.

1520-26   Portuguese expedition meets Bahre Negashi
                    at Debarwa.

c. 1520s   Bet Asghede move to northern highlands.

1533-35   Ahmed "Gragn" al-Ghazali's Muslim
                  warriors conquer Eritrea despite resistance
                  of Adkeme Melega and Bahre Negashi
                  Yesh'aq.

1541   Portuguese land at Massawa and join Yesh'aq
                  to defeat Ahmed's forces in Akele Guzai.

c. 1550s-   Sudanese Funj control Western Eritrea and
   1600s   Beni 'Amer tribal confederacy is formed.

1557   Turks fortify Massawa and attempt to
                  conquer highlands.

1578   Yesh'aq and Turks are defeated by Ethiopian
                  Emperor in Tigrai.

1589   Turks appoint Na'ib to govern coast, while
                  Ethiopian-supported Bahre Negashi rules
                  Mareb Mellash highlands, reinforcing
                  cultural division of region.

c. 1660s-   Bahre Negashi Habsullus of Tsazzega rules
   1700s   Mareb Mellash.

c. 1700s-40s   Gebre-Kristos of Tsazzega and sons rule
                  Mareb Mellash and Tigrai: apogee of Bahre
                  Negashis' independent power.

1768-71   Bahre Negashi Bokru deposed by Ras Mika'el
                  Sehul, marking rise of Tigrean power in
                  highlands.

1770s-1831   Struggle for control of Mareb Mellash
                  between rival houses of Tsazzega and
                  Hazzega .

c. 1800s-40s   Conversion of Bet Asghede and other Tigre-
               speaking Christians to Islam under
               influence of Ad Shaykh.

1813-23   Egyptian occupation of Massawa and Eastern
               Sudan.

1831-39   Wube, governor of Tigrai, dominates Mareb
               Mellash.

1832-36   Egyptians raid Western Eritrea.

1837   Italian Catholic missionaries begin activity.

1840   Egyptians fortify Kassala and impose
               authority over Beni 'Amer. Wube imprisons
               Hailu of Tsazzega.

1844-50   Wube imposes military administration on
               highlands and raids lowlands. French and
               British establish consuls at Massawa.

1846-49   Second Egyptian occupation of Massawa.

1856-60   Struggle between Hailu of Tsazzega and
               Wolde-Mika'el of Hazzega for control of
               Hamasien.

1865   Egyptians occupy Massawa and subdue
               Na'ib. Final spread of Islam throughout
               northeast Eritrea.

1868   British Napier expedition uses Zula and
               Senafe as bases.

1869   Italian shipping company purchases Assab.

1872   Egyptians fortify Massawa, Hirghigo and
                Keren under Munzinger's administration;
                Tigrean Emperor Yohannes IV imposes
                direct rule over highlands.

1875-76   Egyptian invasions of highlands defeated by
                Yohannes IV at Goda-Gudi and Gura'.

1877   Wolde-Mika'el defeats Hailu at Woki Duba.

1878   Wolde-Mika'el defeats Yohannes' governor at
                Bet Maka'.

1879   Wolde-Mika'el arrested and imprisoned; Ras
                Alula appointed Tigrean military governor
                of central Eritrea.

1882   Assab transferred to Italian state; Sudanese
                Mahdiyya threatens Egyptian regional
                control.

1884   Hewett Treaty provides British recognition
                of Yohannes IV's control over central
                Eritrea, excluding Massawa.

1885   (Feb.) Italians occupy Massawa.
                (Nov.) Egyptians evacuate Eritrea.

1887   (Jan.) Ras Alula defeats Italians at Dogali.

1889   (Aug.) Italians occupy Asmara and advance
                to Mareb. Highlands devastated by famine.

1890   (Jan. 1) Italians formally create colony of
                Eritrea.

1891-93   Italians begin policy of agricultural
                colonization in central highlands.

1894   (Dec.) Bahta Hagos leads rebellion against
                Italians.

1895   (Jan.) Tigrean invasion of Akele Guzai
                defeated by Italians, who then invade Tigrai.

1896   (Mar. 1) Italians defeated at Battle of Adwa.
                (Oct.) Addis Ababa Treaty confirms Italian
                sovereignty over Eritrea.

1897   Fernando Martini becomes first civil
                governor of Eritrea.

1900   Asmara becomes official colonial capital.

1909   Colonial Land Law declares lowlands "state
                land" and ends further colonization in
                highlands.

1911   Massawa-Asmara railroad completed.

1912-32   Over sixty thousand Eritrean soldiers serve
                in Italian colonial wars in Libya.

1921   Earthquake destroys much of Massawa.

1923-26   Construction of irrigated cotton plantation
                at Tessenei.

1935   (Oct. 3) Italians invade Ethiopia.
                Massive military recruitment and
                infrastructure construction; Fascists
                promulgate race laws.

1936   (May) Italians occupy Addis Ababa.
                Eritrean governate enlarged to include
                Tigrai.

1936-37   Urban and industrial growth of Asmara and
               Dekemhare, spurred by Italian immigration.

1941   (Apr. 1) British occupy Asmara, create
               military administration but retain Italian
               civil service.
               (May 5) Eritreans organize Mahaber Feqri
               Hager (MFH) movement for self-
               determination. Emperor Haile Selassie
               begins campaign for unification of Eritrea
               with Ethiopia.

1942-44   U.S. and British military bases flourish;
               Italians develop industry and agriculture
               for wartime markets.

1943   Ibrahim Sultan founds serf-emancipation
               movement in north and west.

1944   Eritrean police strike supported by pro-
               Ethiopian Unionists.

1945   Beginning of postwar economic depression
               and *shiftanet* anti-Italian banditry. British
               begin to decontstruct military and transport
               infrastructure.

1946   (Aug. 28) Sudanese troops in British
               garrison massacre Christian Eritreans in
               Asmara, provoking widespread Muslim-
               Christian fighting.
               (Nov. 22-23) Wa'la Bet Gherghis meeting of
               MFH fails to reunite self-determination
               movement; Unionist and Independence
               groups organize separately.
               (Dec. 3) Ibrahim Sultan founds Muslim
               League.

1947   (Jan. 1) Tedla Bairu forms Unionist Party.
(Feb. 10) Paris Peace Treaty charges Four
Powers with deciding Eritrea's political
future.
(Nov. 12) Four Powers commission arrives to
find the population largely divided between
Christians favoring union and Muslims
favoring independence.

1948   (Sept. 15) Four Powers turn over decision on
political future to UN. Pro-Ethiopian
terrorist attacks on Independence leaders
increase.

1949   (May 17) UN fails to adopt Bevin-Sforza plan
for partitioning Eritrea between Ethiopia
and Sudan.
(June) Independence Bloc formed.

1950   (Feb. 21-23) Bloody Christian-Muslim
rioting in Asmara accompanies arrival of UN
commission of inquiry, which is unable to
agree on Eritrea's future.
(Dec. 2) UN adopts U.S.-sponsored
compromise, Resolution 390 A (V),
federating Eritrea with Ethiopia.

1951   (Feb.) UN Commissioner Anze Matienzo
arrives to oversee transition to federation.
(June) British anti-*shifta* campaign ends
most political violence.

1952   (Mar.) First Eritrean Assembly elected.
(June 10) UN-drafted constitution adopted;

Unionist leader Tedla Bairu elected chief
executive.
(Sept. 15) Ethio-Eritrean Federation takes
effect. Ethiopian military occupies key
towns and ports.
(Nov.) Wolde-Ab Wolde-Mariam organizes
the Confederation of Free Eritrean Labor
Unions.

1953   (Feb.) Wolde-Ab wounded in seventh
assassination attempt, followed by exile.
(May 22) U.S. signs twenty-five year lease
with Ethiopian government for communications base at Kagnew Station, Asmara.

1955   (July 23) Fall of Chief Executive Tedla
Bairu; replaced by Asfaha Wolde-Mika'el.

1956   (Sept.) Second Assembly elected, resulting
in Unionist majority. Wolde-Ab makes
nationalist radio broadcasts from Cairo.

1958   (Mar. 10-14) General strike in Asmara
against Unionist labor laws.
(Nov.) Eritrean flag banned; Eritrean
Liberation Movement (ELM) formed in Port
Sudan.

1960   (July 10) Eritrean Liberation Front (ELF)
founded in Cairo by Idris M. Adem and
others.
(Sept.) Third Assembly elected in Unionist-
controlled voting; Amharic declared official
language.

1961   (Sept. 1) Hamid Idris Awate battles police
                on Mt. Adal, initiating armed struggle for
                independence.
                (Nov.) ELF begins military campaign in
                west.

1962   (Nov. 14) Ethiopian annexation of Eritrea
                accepted by Assembly without a vote. End of
                federation.

1963-64   ELF expands operations to northern
                highlands and coast; receives growing Arab
                support.

1965   (May) ELF leaders divide Eritrea into four
                Zonal   commands based on ethnic/geographic
                divisions, and   eliminate ELM attempt to
                field its own guerrilla force.

1966   (Sept.) Isaias Afwerki joins ELF. "Christian"
                fifth zone created in central highlands.

1967   (Mar.) First major Ethiopian military
                operations in western lowlands, 28,000
                refugees flee to Sudan. Isaias and Ramadan
                M. Nur sent to China for training.

1968   (June 16) Reform of ELF discussed at
                Aredaib meeting.
                (Sept. 5) Omer Ezaz defeated at Hal-Hal.
                (Sept. 19) ELF reformists hold Anseba
                Conference and form Tripartite Unity
                Forces.

1969   (Aug.) ELF restructured at Adobaha
                Conference.

1970   (Mar.) ELF Christian recruits massacred;
                many Christian fighters withdraw to Ala
                with Isaias.
                (June) Osman S. Sabbe transports ELF
                reformists to Denkel, where they organize
                People's Liberation Forces at Sudoha Ila.
                (Nov.) Obel group formed by Beni 'Amer
                dissidents.
                (Dec. 1) Ethiopians massacre over six
                hundred villagers at Ona.
                (Dec. 16) Martial law and "free fire" zones
                declared on Sudanese border and coastal
                regions; 10,000 more refugees flee to Sudan.

1971   (Oct.-Nov.) ELF National Congress at Are
                restructures ELF leadership under
                Executive Committee and Revolutionary
                Council, which are dominated by
                clandestine Labor Party; Military Committee
                under Abdullah Idris reorganizes army.
                (Dec.) Obel group forms the Eritrean
                Liberation Forces.

1972   (Jan.) ELF-PLF formed in Beirut by Obel
                (ELF), PLF, and Ala groups.
                (Feb.) ELF leaders decide to "liquidate"
                ELF-PLF, beginning first civil war (1972-
                74).
                (Sept.) Anti-Ethiopian student demon-
                strations close Eritrean schools.

1973   (Feb.) Battle of Ghirghir; ELF fails to defeat
                proto-EPLF forces.
                (Sept.) PLF and Ala groups merge to form
                basis of Eritrean People's Liberation Front.

1974   (Feb.-Sept.) Ethiopian revolution; military
               mutinies in Eritrea.
               (June) EPLF leadership eliminates Menka
               group.
               (Sept.-Nov.) Gen. Aman Andom, an Eritrean,
               heads Ethiopian Derg and attempts political
               settlement in Eritrea but is killed by
               Mengistu Haile-Mariam's faction.
               (Oct. 13) ELF and EPLF declare truce at
               Zagher.
               (Dec.) Ethiopian *afegn* death squads operate
               in Asmara.

1975   (Jan. 31-Feb. 11) Heavy fighting and
               Ethiopian reprisals around Asmara kill
               4,000 civilians, followed by exodus to
               liberation fronts and defection of most
               Eritrean police.
               (Feb. 15) Martial law applied to entire
               country; massacres of civilians at Woki
               Duba, Om Hager, etc.
               (May) Second ELF Congress elects Ahmed
               Nasser to leadership.
               (Aug.-Sept.) ELF and Sabbe negotiate merger
               of fronts.
               (Nov. 12) EPLF field leadership rejects
               merger and repudiates Sabbe.
               (Dec.) 220,000 Eritrean refugees now in
               Sudan.

1976   (Mar.) EPLF formally splits from ELF-PLF.
               (May) Ethiopian Peasant March defeated at
               Zelambessa.
               (Dec.) EPLF defeats Ethiopians in Battle of
               Anseba.

1977   (Jan.-July) EPLF liberates towns from
               Karora to Keren.
               (Jan.-Aug.) ELF liberates west and Seraye.

(June) ELF leaders purge Falul movement.
(Oct. 20) ELF-EPLF unity agreement
reached in Khartoum.
(Dec. 21-23) EPLF captures Massawa
mainland but suffers heavy losses in attack
on naval base. Major USSR military support
for Ethiopia begins.

1978   (Jan.) Liberation fronts control 95 percent
of Eritrea, surround Asmara.
(Mar.-Apr.) EPLF and ELF implement unity
agreement and announce joint leadership.
Battles of Adi Hawesha and Woki Duba
outside Asmara.
(May) ELF-EPLF joint offensive on Barentu
fails.
(June-July) Ethiopian first offensive from
Tigrai defeats ELF in western lowlands and
Seraye.
(July) EPLF defeated at Mai Aini,withdraws
from Akele Guzai and Massawa.
(Nov. 20) Second offensive breaks through
EPLF lines at Adi Yaqob, followed by Battle
of Elabered and EPLF's strategic
withdrawal to Sahel.
(Dec.) 400,000 Eritrean refugees are now in
Sudan.

1979   (Feb. 6-9) Ethiopian third offensive
stopped by EPLF and ELF on trenchline
around Nakfa.
(Mar. 30-Apr. 11) Fourth offensive fails to
outflank EPLF lines around Alghena.
(July 14-26) Fifth offensive defeated along
front line stretching 400 kilometers from
northeast Sahel through Nakfa to Barka.
(Dec.) First EPLF counteroffensive around
Nakfa.

1980   (Jan.) EPLF counteroffensive in northeast
             Sahel.
             (Apr.-May) ELF opens secret negotiations
             with USSR.
             (July 7) ELF withdraws units on northeast
             Sahel Front.
             (Aug. 17) Ethiopians attack northeast Sahel.
             (Aug. 28-Nov. 27) EPLF drives ELF units
             from most of Eritrea during second civil
             war, while Ahmed Nasser negotiates with
             Derg through USSR.
             (Nov. 23) EPLF proposes referendum to
             decide Eritrea's future.

1981   (Mar. 24) Tunis Agreement for unity of
             liberation fronts remains unimplemented.
             Saudia Arabia supports formation of an
             Islamist movement in former ELF.
             (Aug.-Sept.) EPLF drives remaining ELF
             units over border into Sudan.
             (Dec.) 500,000 Eritreans refugees are now
             in Sudan.

1982   (Jan.-Mar.) Derg moves Ethiopian
             government to Asmara to implement multi-
             faceted Red Star campaign intended as "final
             solution" to Eritrean war.
             (Feb. 15) Sixth Offensive launched on three
             fronts: Barka, Nakfa, and northeast Sahel.
             (June) Offensive defeated with heavy losses
             on both sides.
             (Dec.) Ethiopian attack defeated north of
             Hal-Hal.

1983   (Mar. 23-June) Seventh ("stealth") offensive
             around Hal-Hal defeated after heavy
             fighting north of Molebso.

(Mar.) Former ELF fighters of Saghem return
to Eritrea in agreement with EPLF.
(Dec.) EPLF offensive in Barka begins.

1984   (Jan. 15) EPLF liberates Tessenei.
(Mar. 19-21) EPLF defeats Derg in northeast
Sahel.
(May 22) EPLF commando raid on Asmara
airport.
(July-Dec.) Severe famine sends 140,000
Eritreans to Sudan in search of food.

1985   (Jul. 6) EPLF occupies Barentu.
(Aug. 25) Ethiopians recapture Barentu and
Tessenei.
(Oct. 10-Nov. 29) Ethiopian Red Sea
offensive against Nakfa and the Anseba
Valley fails.

1987   (Mar. 12-19) EPLF Second and Unity
Congress marks development of broad
national political organization.
(Dec. 8-11) EPLF surprise attack on Nakfa
front.

1988   (Mar. 17-19) EPLF destroys northern
Ethiopian army in Battle of Afabet; Derg
abandons northern and western Eritrea.
(Apr. 1) EPLF breaks through Hal-Hal
Front.
(May 10-11) EPLF assault on Keren fails.
(May 12) Ethiopians massacre over 400
civilians at She'eb.
(May 13-23) Ethiopian counteroffensive
defeated outside Afabet.
(May 14) Martial law declared throughout
country by Ethiopians; bombing of towns
begins.
(Dec.) Approximately 600,000 internally
displaced Eritreans.

1989   (Jan. 17-Feb. 3) Ethiopian armored forces
              defeated in Battle of Semenawi Bahri.
              (Feb. 15-22) EPLF brigade supports TPLF at
              Battle of Shire in Tigrai.
              (Mar. 15-19) EPLF liberates southwestern
              Seraye.
              (Mar. 22-30) Ethiopians fail to break out of
              Keren.
              (May 16-18) Ethiopian military coup fails
              after fighting in Asmara.
              (Sept. 7; Nov. 20) Inconclusive Ethio-
              Eritrean peace negotiations sponsored by
              former U.S. president Carter.
              (Dec.) Nearly two million Eritreans
              threatened with famine.

1990   (Feb. 8-16) EPLF offensive seizes coastal
              plain and Massawa.
              (Mar.-Apr.) Ethiopians bomb Massawa;
              heavy fighting below Ghinda.
              (Apr. 24-30) EPLF liberates southern Akele
              Guzai.
              (May 28-June 3) EPLF offensive around
              Sagenieti.
              (Aug. 6-15; Sept. 30) Heavy fighting on
              Dekemhare front.

1991   (Jan. 14) UN begins relief shipments to
              Massawa.
              (Feb. 27-Apr. 4) EPLF Denkel offensive
              drives from Tio to Beylul.
              (May 19-21) EPLF breaks through
              Dekemhare front.
              (May 24) Asmara liberated, Ethiopian army
              flees towards Sudan.
              (May 25) Assab liberated.
              (May 28) EPRDF occupies central Addis
              Ababa.

(May 29) EPLF forms Provisional
Government of Eritrea (PGE). (June-July)
EPLF deports 83,000 Ethiopian prisoners of
war and 44,000 Ethiopian civilians.
(July 1-5) Addis Ababa Conference on
Ethiopia's political future accepts plan for
Eritrean referendum on self-determination.
(Nov.) EPLF Political Committee announces
programs for national service, demo-
bilization of fighters, foreign investment
and labor organization.
(Dec.) About 80 percent of Eritrean popula-
tion remains dependent on food aid.

1992
(Mar.) UNHCR and Eritrean CERA disagree
over resources needed to repatriate
estimated 500,000 refugees in Sudan.
(Apr. 7) Referendum Commission created.
(June 20) First Martyr's Day marks
announcement of over 65,000 war dead.
(Dec.) By now some 70,000 refugees have
voluntarily repatriated from Sudan.

1993
(Jan. 6-17) Isaias Afwerki, critically ill
with cerebral malaria, is airlifted by U.S. to
hospital in Israel.
(Apr. 23-25) UN-observed national
referendum approves independence by 99.8
percent majority.
(May 19) National Assembly formed.
(May 20) Disgruntled EPLF fighters stage
protest in Asmara over continuing unpaid
service.
(May 24) Formal independence celebrated.
Isaias Afwerki becomes first president of
the Government of the State of Eritrea.
(May 28) Eritrea takes seat at UN.

(June 7) State Council appointed as executive branch of transitional government.
(July 14) Demobilization plan for army announced.
(Dec. 16) Islamic jihad guerrillas based in Sudan battle Eritrean army in Barka.

1994

(Feb. 10-17) EPLF Third Congress in Nakfa forms the People's Front for Democracy and Justice (PFDJ) as an autonomous political party and approves a National Charter for future constitutional government.
(Mar. 15) Constitutional Commission created.
(May 16) National Service Law promulgated.
(July 11) War-disabled fighters protest demobilization at Mai Habar training center; three die.
(July-Sept.) First good rainy season in a decade.
(Aug. 1) First group of national service military trainees goes to Sawa in Barka.
(Aug. 12) Joint ministerial meeting with Sudan attempts to improve relations based on mutual noninterference.
(Sept.) Eritrea, UNHCR and Sudan sign agreements on refugee repatriation pilot project.
(Dec. 5) Eritrea breaks diplomatic relations with Sudan over Sudanese support for Islamic Jihad.

1995

(June 17) Sudanese opposition parties begin meeting in Asmara to form National Democratic Alliance.
(Dec. 15-18) Eritrean forces defeat Yemen army in battle over Hanish Islands.

1996   (Jan.) Sudanese opposition leaders meet in
                        Asmara.
                        (June 21) Yemen and Eritrea agree to send
                        Hanish Islands dispute to arbitration.

1997   (May 24) Draft constitution approved by
                        Constituent Assembly.
                        (Nov. 8) Eritrea's new currency, the nakfa,
                        begins circulating.

INTRODUCTION

The Land

Eritrea is situated on the Red Sea coast of Africa, sharing a border with Sudan to the west, Ethiopia to the south and southeast, and Djibouti on its southeastern tip (*see* map 1). It covers 124,300 square kilometers (45,754 square miles), stretching from roughly 18 to 13 degrees north latitude and 36 to 43 degrees longitude. Eritrea's coastline extends about twelve hundred kilometers, flanked by coral reefs and 354 islands, including the important Dahlak archipelago.

Today Eritrea is divided into six administrative regions (*see* map 2), but its historical division into the nine provinces of Akele Guzai, Barka, Denkel, Gash-Setit, Hamasien, Sahel, Semhar, Senhit, and Seraye will be used throughout this volume for all geographical references.

Eritrea's geography is dominated by its division between the hot and arid lowlands of its coastal and western plains, and the cooler and better-watered highlands of the central plateau (or "Kebessa") and northern highlands. Rainfall is the key to human population density in the country, with the densely settled Kebessa receiving an average of 61 centimeters per year (rising to almost 100 centimeters in the Semenawi Bahri lands of the eastern escarpment), while Keren in the northern highlands receives an average of only 45 centimeters and Agordat in the western lowlands receives only 35 centimeters. In the Denkel desert along the southern coast, rainfall drops below 10 centimeters, and the temperature can rise to 50 degrees centigrade, while the temperature averages 30 degrees in the western lowlands and 17 degrees in the Kebessa. These climatic and topographical variations have formed four distinct ecological regions in Eritrea: the coastal plain, central highlands, northern highlands, and western lowlands.

The Coastal Plain

It was around the coastal plain that modern Eritrea was formed, and Eritrea's geographical relation to the sea is what gives its people their unique identity, including their tragic history of armed occupation by a succession of colonizers bent on controlling the coast. The coastal plain itself, however, is a sparsely inhabited desert whose waterways are usually dry and whose temperatures are among the hottest in the world. The northern coastal plain averages 35 kilometers in width, with sandy soils punctuated by seasonal watercourses, the most important being the Felket, Lebka, and Laba. This coast has few natural harbors and has been inhabited historically by seasonal nomads.

The central coast, including Semhar province and extending south from Massawa to the Bure peninsula, is more favored. Here the mountains come almost to the sea, and watercourses are numerous. Along the western shore of the Gulf of Zula is a fertile plain, watered by the Alighede, Hadas and Komalie rivers, which drain the central highlands. Ports and fishing villages have been located in this region since ancient times, and it has a large and diverse population centered around Eritrea's principal port of Massawa.

The southern coast is the most barren, merging with the volcanic hills and alkaline wastes of Dankalia, which together comprise the entirety of Denkel province. Assab, Eritrea's busiest port, is located at the southern end of this coast, but its land connections and economy are tied completely to Ethiopia in one of the many ironies of Eritrea's colonial history.

The Kebessa

The Kebessa, or central plateau, forms the physical and political-economic center of Eritrea. It comprises a

northward pointing triangle of land averaging 2,000-3,000
meters (7,000-9,000 feet) in height, and includes the historical provinces of Akele Guzai, Hamasien and Seraye (*see
map 4*). It receives enough rainfall during its brief spring
rainy season and longer *krimti* summer rainy season to
sustain cereal agriculture, and has been a center of
civilization since antiquity. Consequently, despite its small
area (about 8 percent of Eritrea), the Kebessa is home to
more than half of the country's population.

The eastern edge of the Kebessa is an abrupt escarpment that rises from the northern end of the East African
rift valley and abuts the Denkel deserts and coastal plain in
a series of steep canyons and ridges, whose northern slopes,
the Semenawi Bahri lands, are well forested and enjoy two
rainy seasons. From the edge of this eastern escarpment the
highlands tilt gradually westward in a plateau that is broken by numerous river valleys. The most important river is
the Mareb, which rises in Hamasien and flows south through
the Hazamo plain, where it forms the boundary between
Akele Guzai and Seraye. It then turns westward to form the
southern border of the highlands, dividing the Eritrean
plateau from Ethiopia. The western boundary of the Kebessa
is less distinct, as here it descends toward the lowlands in a
maze of ravines and ridges some thirty to fifty kilometers in
width.

The Northern Highlands

The northern highlands are an extension of the
Kebessa, whose high plateau continues northward in a narrow band of mountains parallel to the coast all the way into
Sudan. Although they reach 2,500 meters in places, the
northern highlands are broken into many small ranges by
numerous passes and river valleys. The most important
river here is the Anseba, which rises in Hamasien and flows
northward through Senhit and Sahel to join the Barka at the
Sudanese border. Along the river valleys and the narrow
ridge tops, people have grown cereals and pastured animals
for thousands of years. In modern times the strategic importance of the passes between the coast and western lowlands,

and the rugged redoubts of the Sahel mountains, have made this region the site of many of Eritrea's bloodiest battles.

The Western Lowlands

The western lowlands comprise almost half of Eritrea's land area. The hills and plains of the west average about 800 meters in height, with isolated outliers of the highlands projecting to as much as 1,500 meters in striking horns of granite. In the north, the lowlands are dry and thinly covered with grass and thorn brush that can only support seasonal grazing, except along the valley of the Barka river. The Barka rises along the western edge of the Kebessa and runs northward across a wide plain to the Sudanese border.

South of the Barka, the Mareb runs out into the lowlands, where it is called the Gash, and waters the rich cotton lands along the Sudanese border at Tessenei. Between the Barka and the Gash, southwest of Agordat, the summer rains become heavier, and sedentary agriculture is possible. South of the Gash, the great Ethiopian river Takezze flows across the lowlands, where it is called the Setit, and forms Eritrea's southwestern border with Ethiopia. Between the Gash and Setit the land is relatively rich and thickly forested in places, and the whole Gash-Setit province has been populated since ancient times by Nilotic farmers. This is a region for which modern Eritrea has great hopes: for irrigated agriculture around Tessenei, rain-fed tractor farming between Guluj and Om Hager, and hydroelectric power from a proposed dam on the Setit.

The People

Like most African countries, the borders of modern Eritrea were drawn by European colonial powers (specifically Britain and Italy) at the end of the nineteenth century. These borders took little account of existing ethnic and cultural unities, and divided many precolonial peoples, while joining others who had little previous political interaction, under a single administration. The result was Eritrea's cultural mosaic of nine distinct ethno-linguistic groups (*see* map 3). Fortunately for modern Eritrea, many of these groups have a long history of commercial and political interaction, intermarriage, and shared cultural characteristics. This is particularly true of the two largest   linguistic groups: the Tigrinya and Tigre, who together make up over 80 percent of the population.

The ecological divide between the coastal and western lowlands, on one hand, and the highlands, on the other, is reflected in the economy and culture of Eritrea's peoples, who may be roughly divided today between largely pastoralist and Muslim lowlanders and largely agricultural and Christian highlanders. In contrast to this general lowland/highland division, which reached its height during the colonial period, within the ethnically diverse lowland population, Islam has provided a framework for increasing cultural unity, which has been reflected in the adoption of the Tigre language by many of these peoples in the last few centuries and the spread of Islam among the formerly Christian peoples of the northern highlands.

Population and Ethnicity

Although no census is currently available, in 1997 Eritrean government figures on regional populations provided an overall figure of about 2.8 million. Perhaps as many as half a million additional people of Eritrean descent reside outside the country, giving a total "Eritrean" population of well over three million. Based on census material from the colonial period and incomplete data from the 1993 referendum, it appears that the division of Eritrea's population between ethno-linguistic groups (by percentage of total population) is roughly:

Ethnicity	Appx. %	Language	Religion(s)*
Tigrinya	50%	Tigrinya	Christ./Mslm.
Tigre	30%	Tigre	Muslim
Saho	7%	Saho	Mslm./Christ.
Bilen	5%	Bilen	Mslm./Christ.

Afar	3%	Afar	Muslim
Kunama	3%	Kunama	Traditional/
			Mslm./Christ.
Nara	+1%	Nara	Muslim
Hedareb	-1%	To-Bedawe	Muslim
Rashaida	-1%	Arabic	Muslim

*The predominant religion of each group is cited first.

In terms of religious divisions, the number of Muslims and Christians is almost equal, with the great majority of Tigrinya people being Christians and the great majority of Tigre being Muslims. The details of religious and linguistic affiliation will be discussed below, but here we should caution that these ethno-linguistic divisions are quite porous and have been the subject of continual historical transformation. Furthermore, many Eritreans are multi-lingual, with fluency in Tigrinya, Tigre, and Arabic spreading rapidly throughout the smaller linguistic groups. In particular, many Muslim Eritreans speak Arabic, although it is the "mother tongue" of only the tiny Rashaida ethnic group, and Arabic, together with widespread use of Tigre, has provided a lingua franca throughout all the lowlands. Since 1991 there has also been a rapid spread of Tigrinya in the lowlands, as it has become the de facto language of government service.

Peoples of the Lowlands and Northern Highlands

The lowland peoples contain members of three linguistic families: the Nilo-Saharan (Nilotic), Cushitic, and Semitic. Moving in a clockwise direction from the southwest corner of Eritrea, the eight lowland ethno-linguistic groups who encircle the Kebessa are, first, the Kunama, a Nilotic people with an ancient and quite distinct language who farm the Gash-Setit. To their immediate north, between Barentu and Agordat, is another Nilotic group, the Nara, who have adopted much of the Islamic culture of their Beja and Tigre neighbors. Further north again, along the western edge of the Barka plains, are the Hedareb pastoralists, who are the last linguistic remnant of the great Beja-speaking popula-

tion whose blood and culture were so important in the formation of the Tigre people.

In the northern provinces of Barka and Sahel, the most
important linguistic group are speakers of the Semitic
tongue, Tigre, whose territory extends from the western
fringes of Gash-Setit, across all of Barka and the northern
highlands to the Red Sea, where Tigre speakers form the
major coastal population from the Sudanese border to the
Massawa area. The Tigre are divided into a number of tribes
and tribal confederations, the most important being the Beni
'Amer, Marya and Bet Asghede. Today most Tigre speakers
are Muslim, though some Christian elements remain among
the Mensa'; and most are agro-pastoralists, though some also
are involved in commerce. Another Semitic-speaking people
are the Rashaida, a pure Arab tribe that has migrated to the
northern Eritrean and Sudanese coast in the last 150 years.

In the Senhit area of the northern highlands, around
Keren, the Bilen people have retained their ancient Central
Cushitic language, despite widespread bilingualism in Tigre
and Tigrinya. The Bilen are mostly agriculturalists, and
have both Muslim and Christian subgroups, with Islam pre-
dominating. Further south, along the coast and eastern escarpment south of Massawa, live the Saho people, whose language is an Eastern Cushitic relative of Afar. Over the last
millenium, Saho people moved into the central highland
province of Akele Guzai, where some have adopted
Tigrinya/Christian culture, but the great majority are Muslim agro-pastoralists. The last of the lowland peoples are
the Afar, who speak an Eastern Cushitic tongue and inhabit
the coastal desert of Denkel province. They are all Muslim,
and the majority are pastoralists, although the coastal population includes many fishermen and merchants.

People of the Central Plateau

The ninth Eritrean ethno-linguistic group, and by far
the largest, are those speaking the Semitic language,
Tigrinya. The Tigrinyas inhabit the central plateau, or
Kebessa, and are the cultural heirs of the Christian civilization that flourished in this area beginning in the fourth

century. They are sedentary agriculturalists and have
maintained close cultural and economic ties with their col-
inguists in Ethiopia's Tigrai province. These ties have had
an important impact on Eritrea's history, as it is this longstanding ethno-cultural relationship that Ethiopian rulers
have manipulated in their attempts to control and annex
Eritrea in modern times. Today the Tigrinya make up the
majority of Eritrea's internal population and dominate the
new nation's political and intellectual life. Most Tigrinya
speakers are Christian, but a significant minority of them,
known as Jiberti, are Muslims.

Historical Overview

Although it was an Italian colonial administration that
created the modern territory of Eritrea and gave it its name
in 1890, the Greek name *Erythreus* (red) has a long association with the region, extending back at least to the fifth
century B.C., when Aeschylus mentioned the "Erythrean
Sea." Perhaps it was natural for Italian imperialists, se-
duced by their project of recreating the glories of ancient
Rome, to resurrect the name "Eritrea" for their Red Sea
colony. And the name is fitting, for it recalls the ancient
commercial and cultural links between present-day Eritrea
and the Mediterranean, Egyptian, and Arabian worlds. But
we must be careful to remember that "Eritrea" is a modern
creation and that "Eritrean" as a national identity is of even
more recent provenance. The projection of the terms
"Eritrea" and "Eritreans" back onto the pre-colonial past in
this book is, therefore, merely a matter of literary convenience and in no way implies that this particular identity
existed prior to 1890.

Ancient and Medieval Periods

The lack of sustained archaeological research in Eritrea has made its early human history a subject of almost
pure speculation. Drawing on evidence from neighboring areas, scholars hypothesize that the earliest human population may have been small-statured hunter-gatherers similar

to the "bushmen" who once lived throughout East Africa.
Linguistic evidence indicates the next group to inhabit the
area were Nilotic people akin to today's Kunama and Barya.
Place names suggest these people first occupied the highlands and then were slowly driven back to their present
homes in the southwest by a third population group:
Cushitic-speakers coming perhaps from the southern areas
of the African Horn. By c. 5000 B.C. there is evidence for
both agriculture and livestock rearing in Eritrea, and by the
second millennium B.C. the Eritrean coast was almost certainly visited by Egyptian trading expeditions.

Sometime after the Egyptians, perhaps by 1200 B.C.,
Semitic-speaking peoples from South Arabia (present-day
Yemen) also began to trade along the Eritrean coast, and
their influence became so strong by the eighth century B.C.
that most scholars believe South Arabians migrated to the
Eritrean coast and settled in the central highlands. During
the period 700-300 B.C. an urban, agricultural civilization
developed in the Eritrean highlands and northern Tigrai
(Ethiopia). Writing, architecture, and artifacts all attest to
a close relationship between this civilization and the South
Arabian kingdom of Sab'a, although lately scholars have emphasized the political independence of a local state, Da'a-
mat. What is certain is that a fusion occurred between
Cushitic and Semitic peoples in the Eritrean highlands, and
from this fusion was born the distinct civilization of the
Habesha (Abyssinians).

Around 100 A.D. a new Habesha political and economic power arose to dominate the Eritrean region: the Aksumite empire. The rise of Aksum, centered in northern
Tigrai, was closely associated with the development of a lucrative overseas trade in ivory and gold from the port of
Adulis (Zula) on the central Eritrean coast. The dominant
external influence on this trade were Greek-speaking merchants from the Eastern Mediterranean. From Adulis an
important trade route ran through Akele Guzai to Tigrai,
and along this route developed the centers of Habesha civilization in Eritrea. Inscriptions and coinage give us an indi-
cation of a close political relationship between Aksum and
central Eritrea, and it seems fair to assert that during 300-

600 A.D. most of Eritrea was part of an Aksumite empire
that included Tigrai and extended at times across the Red
Sea into South Arabia and westward into contemporary Sudan. During this period Monophysite Christianity spread in
Eritrea, and Christian centers extended from Hager Nagran
in the far north to Ba'da in southeastern Akele Guzai.

The Christian Habesha civilization went into a period
of decline with the breakup of the Aksumite empire in the
late seventh century, and the Eritrean region was fragmented between a variety of immigrant and indigenous
ethno-linguistic and tribal groups. By the ninth century
Beja immigrants from present-day Sudan had created a con-
stellation of small states in north-central Eritrea, some of
which adopted the Christian culture of the Habesha people
with whom they mixed. During the eighth through tenth
centuries Muslim Arab civilization influenced commercial
and urban development on the Dahlak Islands and around
Massawa, while during the eleventh through thirteenth
centuries the struggles accompanying the southward movement of Habesha political power to the Amhara region of
Ethiopia sent waves of Cushitic-speaking refugees into the
Eritrean highlands, including ancestors of the Bilen and
various Tigrinya clans. During the same period Saho speakers moved into both Akele Guzai and the northern highlands, where they formed aristocratic ruling classes over
the Tigre-speaking Marya and Mensa' peoples. In the fifteenth through sixteenth centuries a similar process occurred as Tigrinya-speaking immigrants formed ruling
castes over the Tigre-speaking Bet Asghede and others,
further reinforcing the typical social division of all Tigre-
speaking peoples between aristocratic *(shumagulle)* and serf
(tigre) elements.

After the fall of the Aksumite empire, the Eritrean
region ceased to be the center of a dominant Habesha civilization and instead became a multicultural periphery of
more distant political centers in present-day Ethiopia, Sudan, and Yemen. Ethiopian Amhara political control over
central Eritrea reached its high point during the fourteenth
through fifteentm centuries, under the emperors Amde
Siyon and Zara Ya'qob, the first of whom asserted direct

military control over central Eritrea while the second settled the Ewostatean religious controversy, which had taken
on regionalist political overtones in the Tigrinya-speaking
areas. In the early sixteenth century Ethiopian authority
was eroded first by the Muslim Somali/Afar invasion of the
highlands led by Imam Ahmed al-Ghazali ("Gragn"), and
then by the Ottoman Turkish occupation of the coast and invasion of the Kebessa. By the end of the century present-day
Eritrea was divided between a Muslim coast whose Afar,
Saho and Tigre peoples were under the nominal rule of the
Turkish-appointed Na'ib of Hirghigo, while the Christian
Kebessa was under the nominal rule of the Ethiopian governors of Tigrai, and the western lowlands had come under the
nominal rule of the Funj empire of Sudan, whose political
appointees, the Nabtabs, welded the Tigre-Beja population of
Barka into the Beni 'Amer tribal confederacy.

The early modern history of the Kebessa is dominated
by the rise of the Tigrinya Christian clans of Tsazzega and
Hazzega in Hamasien, whose leaders eventually shook off
Ethiopian political control in the early eighteenth century
and briefly ruled northern Tigrai, before the lords of Tigrai
reimposed their authority over the Kebessa in mid-century.
After this, the precolonial history of the highlands is
largely the story of increasingly powerful Tigrean rulers
manipulating the rivalries of Tsazzega and Hazzega to impose their authority ever more effectively, reaching a highpoint during the reign of the Tigrean Emperor Yohannes IV
(1872-89). In the lowlands and northern highlands the weak
authority of the Turks and Funj was overshadowed by the
rise of Egyptian power in the early nineteenth century.
During the period 1820-65 Egyptian authorities promoted
the spread of Islam through Mirghaniyya and Ad-Shaykh
missionaries, and by the time the Egyptians departed in
1885, the religious unity of the Muslim lowlands was essentially complete.

Colonial Period

During the period 1865-85 direct Egyptian colonial
rule over the coastal and western lowlands and the northern

highlands ushered in the modern era, as a communications infrastructure was created and the foundations of the colonial Eritrean state were laid. In a pattern of political alliances with outside forces that continued into the early Italian period, both lowland and highland Eritrean political leaders turned to the Egyptians for aid in the stuggle to maintain their independence from Tigrai and Ethiopia. For similar reasons, some Eritreans also welcomed European missionaries, who during the mid-nineteenth century laid the foundations for both Catholic and Protestant congregations among the Bilen, Kunama, Mensa', and Tigrinya.

Before 1885 the European power most concerned with Eritrea was Britain, which sought to block French control over the increasingly strategic Red Sea coast following the opening of the Suez Canal in 1869. To this end Britain supported first Egyptian and then Italian "sub-imperialism" in the region, although the British briefly toyed with the idea of supporting the independent Tigrean power of Yohannes IV in 1884, when Admiral Hewett negotiated an agreement recognizing Yohannes's authority over all Eritrea, with the exception of Massawa. But in 1885 "perfidious Albion" allowed the Italians to seize Massawa and the former Egyptian colony, fulfilling Italian territorial designs that had begun with the purchase of Assab in 1869.

Following their seizure of Massawa, the Italians embarked on a full-scale colonization of Eritrea, part and parcel of the "scramble for Africa" set off by the Conference of Berlin. Yohannes IV's defense of the highlands ended with his death in 1889, and the Italians, aided by thousands of Eritrean auxiliaries, quickly occupied the highlands. This occupation was accepted by the new Ethiopian emperor, Menelik II, and on January 1, 1890, the Italian king declared the formation of the colony of Eritrea.

The Italians then turned on their erstwhile Eritrean allies, sending many to prison and death, and seized huge swaths of agricultural land in the highlands, which they planned to settle with Italian farmers. This sparked an anticolonial revolt led by Bahta Hagos in 1894, which directly precipitated the Italian invasion of Tigrai and the disastrous Italian defeat by the Ethiopians at Adwa in 1896. Emperor Menelik did not pursue his victory with an invasion of Eritrea, however, but instead confirmed Italian occupation in the peace treaty that followed, renouncing Ethiopian claims to the colony.

Although the Italians, like most colonial powers, manipulated Eritrea's ethnic and religious divisions to reinforce their own power, their most important legacy was the administrative and economic integration of the territory, which laid the foundations for the modern Eritrean nation. During the first three decades of the twentieth century the Italians built an infrastructure of ports, railroads, roads, telecommunications, administrative centers, and police posts that tied the colony together under a single centralized government and enabled Eritreans to move from one region to another in pursuit of commerce, employment, and social activities. The effect of this on shaping an Eritrean national consciousness was reinforced by large-scale military recruitment from all sections of the colony during the years 1911-32 for Italy's colonial wars in Libya. At the same time the provocative policy of European agricultural colonization of the Kebessa was abandoned in favor of a far less conflict laden development of lowland plantation agriculture.

Despite the integrative effects of the policies outlined above, Italian educational and state employment practices were designed specifically to limit the development of an Eritrean intelligentsia. Beginning in 1932, the Fascist government expelled Protestant missionaries, the only source of Eritrean education beyond grade four, and racial segregation was introduced in urban areas. During 1935 hundreds of thousands of Italian workers and soldiers poured into the colony in preparation for the invasion of Ethiopia, and central Eritrea was transformed into a vast military supply base. Forty percent of working age male Eritreans were conscripted into the army while tens of thousands of others found employment in the mushrooming cities and the network of airfields, garages, workshops, and military stores connecting Massawa with the Ethiopian border. By 1941, 20 percent of Eritreans lived in urban areas, where most worked as poorly paid soldiers, servants, laborers, and prostitutes.

The Italian colonial project collapsed abruptly in 1941, when the British defeated them at Keren and occupied Asmara. Eritreans expected the British to overturn the Italian colonial regime and set them on the road to self-government, which had been promised in a number of leaflets dropped over the colony. But the British retained much of the Italian administration and encouraged Italian farmers and entrepreneurs to increase production. American contractors took over Italian military facilities, and Eritreans experienced a second "war boom" that created much of the colony's industrial base in metalworking, glass, ceramics, chemicals, and food processing. With the end of the war came a depression, however, as much of the Italian population repatriated and industries lost their markets to revived overseas competition. The economic strains of this depression, coinciding with uncertainty over Eritrea's political future and a relaxation of British controls on public discussion and organization, produced the beginnings of the Eritrean nationalist movement.

The Early Nationalist Movement

The development of Eritrean nationalism is the most important issue in modern Eritrean history because it is this movement that created the independent nation of Eritrea in a fifty-year struggle that dominated Eritrean life and profoundly altered every aspect of Eritrea's society, economy and even physical landscape. The nationalist movement, however, was never a monolithic bloc with a common purpose. Instead, it was divided into a number of competing factions whose main cleavages followed the great regional and religious divide that we have already noted between the predominantly Muslim lowlands and the predominantly Christian highlands. From the beginning, numerous external forces attempted, with frequent success, to manipulate these historical groupings to achieve their own ends, and it was only after years of horrendous warfare that a real degree of national unity was achieved.

The nationalist movement began with the formation of the Mahaber Feqri Hager ("Patriotic Society") in April 1941, among whose original members may be found all the leading figures of the first two decades of nationalist politics. The Patriotic Society was originally concerned with ending Italian domination of Eritrean civil life, but a second, irredentist, wing that campaigned for Eritrea's union with Ethiopia was soon formed in Addis Ababa. Anti-Italian feeling ran high in the mid-1940s, and this was channeled by the pro-Ethiopian faction into a growing terrorist movement of anticolonial *shifta* (bandits). After the allied victors in the world war decided that Italy could not regain its African colonies, however, the Patriotic Society began to split into two camps. One camp, led by the Tigre political organizer Ibrahim Sultan and representing the vast majority of Eritrean Muslims, called for independence or a UN trusteeship; the other camp, led by the Tigrinya intellectual Tedla Bairu, called for union with Ethiopia. Between these camps were a number of Muslim and Christian intellectuals, most notably Wolde-Ab Wolde-Mariam, who called for some form of autonomous federation with Ethiopia as a compromise to keep the nationalist movement unified. The unionists, however, mobilized Tigrinya/Christian irredentist sentiment through the Orthodox Church, *shifta* attacks on Muslim leaders, and intercommunal violence.

By the end of 1946 the federalist compromise was abandoned as Eritrean political parties formed along sectarian lines: Ibrahim Sultan led the Muslim League; Tedla Bairu led the Unionist Party; and Wolde-Ab led the only nonsectarian independence party, popularly called "Eritrea for Eritreans." The aim of these parties initially was to lobby the allied victors' Four Powers investigation commission, which was charged with ascertaining Eritrean views on their political future. In 1947 the commission found a divided population and was itself divided on Eritrea's disposal. In 1948 the Four Powers turned the matter over to the UN, which also failed to find a solution to the "Eritrean Question," although it came very close to partitioning Eritrea between Ethiopia and Sudan. Fear of partition inspired the pro-independence forces to form the "Independence

Bloc" in 1949 to lobby the UN, by which time they clearly represented a majority of Eritreans and threatened to derail the Unionist program. The Ethiopian government responded with a terrorist campaign against all pro-independence forces that reached a crescendo of intercommunal violence in early 1950, when the UN sent its own investigation commission to Eritrea.

The UN commission was just as divided as the earlier commission, however, and the Eritrean dilemma was finally resolved by a U.S. brokered return to the compromise solution of autonomous federation. The U.S. was determined to retain and develop the former Italian military communications base at Asmara, and Emperor Haile Selassie, fearful of losing Eritrea altogether, accepted the federal compromise and guaranteed U.S. access to the communications base. The U.S. then pushed through the federation of Eritrea with Ethiopia in UN Resolution 390 A (V) on December 2, 1950.

Federation with Ethiopia

Although few Eritreans had wanted this compromise, the majority accepted it and expected the UN to guarantee Eritrea's autonomy. A democratic constitution was drafted, providing Eritrea with an independent parliamentary government, its own flag, school system, police force, and national languages. Federation took place September 15, 1952, but it soon proved unworkable. The autocratic regime of Haile Selassie had no desire to coexist with a democratic Eritrea, and the emperor quickly made use of provisions in the federal agreement to gain control over the Eritrean economy, depriving the Eritrean administration of much of its budgetary revenue. Tedla Bairu, the Unionist chief executive, was caught in a contradictory position and forced from office in 1955. He was replaced by the emperor's representative, Asfaha Wolde-Mika'el, who proceeded to push through the Unionist-dominated Assembly legislation that ended Eritrea's independent labor movement, abolished its flag, replaced Tigrinya and Arabic with Amharic, and reduced autonomy to an empty cipher. When the old nationalist leaders attempted to organize opposition or appeal to the

UN, they were driven into exile. But a new, grassroots, nationalist movement emerged among urban workers and students. In 1957 student strikes shut down Eritrean secondary schools, and in March 1958 a four-day general strike paralyzed Asmara. After the repression of these movements, nationalists went underground and formed the Eritrean Liberation Movement (ELM) in 1959, in preparation for a mass uprising.

During the 1950s many Muslim Eritreans left for education in the Arab world, and in 1958 students in Cairo formed a nationalist association. Inspired by the Algerian revolution, in July 1960 Idris Mohamed Adem and some students formed the Eritrean Liberation Front (ELF), committed to beginning an immediate armed struggle against Ethiopian rule in Eritrea. The initial ELF leaders were all Muslim, and many of them subscribed to a Pan-Arabist ideology that saw Eritrea as part of the Arab world. This ideology was reinforced when Osman Saleh Sabbe joined the movement and quickly rose to prominence as a fund-raiser. In addition to its sectarian orientation, the ELF program of immediate armed struggle brought it into conflict with the more secular and multiethnic ELM, and as the two movements competed for supporters, the Ethiopian security services were alerted to their existence. Both movements attempted to recruit Hamid Idris Awate, an experienced guerrilla leader, and in August 1961 he fled into the mountains from an Ethiopian police raid. He took a small band of fighters with him, and on September 1, 1961, the first shots of the Eritrean independence war were fired. Awate's force was recruited into the ELF, out of which a small guerrilla army developed during 1961-65.

The Early Armed Struggle for Independence

The Ethiopian government, meanwhile, pushed on with its policy of annexing Eritrea as an integral province of the empire, achieving this goal on November 14, 1962, when the emperor declared Eritrea to be Ethiopia's "fourteenth province." Student protests and a growing number of guerrilla attacks in the lowlands were met by increasing

Ethiopian repression and a cynical but somewhat successful policy of divide and rule in which the emperor played on Christian religio-cultural sentiments to pit them against a largely Muslim-led insurgency.

In 1966 the first significant numbers of Christian Eritreans, including the future president, Isaias Afwerki, joined the ELF. The Christians and other, Muslim, recruits were drawn from a new generation of former students who began to criticize the ethnocentric and sectarian tendencies of the ELF leadership. These criticisms increased after the return of Isaias, Ramadan M. Nur, and others from a training course in China, where they were exposed to Maoist doctrines of guerrilla warfare that were to have an important effect on the later development of the Eritrean People's Liberation Front (EPLF). By 1968 a reform movement had developed among the new generation, and in 1970 further power struggles among the leadership, the persecution of Christian recruits, and the failure of successive unity conferences led the reformist groups to withdraw from the ELF. This break was formalized in 1971, when the ELF held its First National Congress, but failed to reincorporate the dissidents, who created their own Eritrean Libertaion Front-People's Liberation Forces (ELF-PLF) organization funded by Osman S. Sabbe and led in the field by Isaias and Ramadan. The newly elected ELF leadership then declared war on the ELF-PLF, and a civil war between the fronts lasted until 1974. During this period the majority faction (PLF) of the ELF-PLF formed a new organization, the EPLF, which soon became the leading force in the nationalist movement.

Despite its internal struggles, the ELF greatly expanded its military operations during the late 1960s, and in 1967 the Ethiopians, with U.S. support, launched their first large-scale counterinsurgency campaign in the western lowlands, burning villages, massacring civilians, and provoking the first exodus of Eritrean refugees into the Sudan. Simultaneously, the Ethiopians increased their anti-Arab propaganda campaign and began to force peasants into fortified "strategic hamlets." But as the war became increasingly brutal, more and more Christian Eritreans joined the nationalist movement. The Ethiopian army became increasingly demoralized, and the Asmara garrison was a leading force in the 1974 mutiny that sparked the Ethiopian revolution and led directly to Haile Selassie's overthrow by a group of junior officers, the Derg ("Committee").

Total War

As the Ethiopian government collapsed, the competing liberation fronts were able to gain control of most of rural Eritrea, and by the summer of 1974 they were fighting each other in the central highlands, a few miles outside Asmara. A bloody battle between the fronts at Zagher provoked Eritrean civilians to intervene and force the two fronts to negotiate a cease-fire in October, after which they divided the country between them and organized joint military operations. But despite a series of negotiations and attempted mergers, the issue of unity between the ELF and EPLF was to plague the nationalist movement throughout the next seven years, and its complexities frequently baffled Eritreans as well as foreigners. Neither front had a particular ethnic constituency, and both drew their recruits from every sector of Eritrea. The EPLF was better organized and more successful both politically and militarily, and it consequently expanded tremendously during the "first liberation" of Eritrea (1975-78).

In January 1975 the two fronts launched a joint attack on Asmara, and in the bloody fighting that followed, the Christian highland population forever turned their backs on any association with Ethiopia. Tens of thousands of young Eritreans, along with most of the Eritrean police and commandos, joined the fronts, and the nationalist military forces laid siege to all the Ethiopian garrison towns, gaining control over 95 percent of the country by late 1977. But the Derg's acquisition of massive USSR military aid, combined with the fronts' failure to create a unified political and military organization, led to the loss of much of the highlands and the west in mid-1978. The ELF was decimated in the first offensives, and in November the EPLF was forced to make a "strategic withdrawal" into the rugged mountains around Nakfa in Sahel province.

The Ethiopians then launched a series of offensives against the Sahel redoubt, defended by the EPLF and remnants of the ELF. Hundreds of thousands more refugees fled across the border into Sudan, and tens of thousands of Ethiopians and Eritreans died along the trench lines of Sahel, which by the end of 1979 extended across a front almost 400 kilometers in length. The Ethiopians, despite an army of 120,000 equipped with hundreds of tanks, aircraft and the latest in Soviet arms, were unable to break through the Eritrean lines. From 1980 to 1981 the EPLF took advantage of the stalemate on the Sahel front to consolidate its political position in the rest of the country, first driving the remnants of the ELF into Sudan in a second civil war and then rebuilding its underground political networks in Ethiopian-controlled areas. The Sahel liberated zone provided the base from which EPLF units operated throughout the country, contesting Ethiopian attempts to impose their administration even in the central highlands, and organizing village committees, land redistribution and social services in every area without an Ethiopian garrison. It was this sustained effort that kept the revolution alive during the darkest years of the nationalist movement, when it appeared to be abandoned by all external powers and fell back on its own campaign of "self-reliance" as its only means of survival.

In 1982 the Derg launched its strongest effort to destroy the nationalist movement, combining political and economic initiatives in the towns with the huge Red Star offensive on the Sahel front. The fighting was the most intense of the war and lasted into 1983; but the EPLF repelled all attacks, even as the beginning of a terrible drought spread devastation throughout the country. The stalemate continued on the Sahel front from 1984 through 1987, but the EPLF began a shift to the offensive in other parts of the country, while it consolidated its leading position in the nationalist movement when it incorporated important elements of the ELF at its Second Congress in 1987.

Liberation

In March 1988 the EPLF permanently moved to the offensive with the smashing defeat of the main Ethiopian army around Afabet, forcing a rapid Ethiopian abandonment of all northern and western Eritrea. The huge amounts of weapons captured by the EPLF enabled it to go on to win the war not only in Eritrea, but also in Ethiopia, where EPLF units were crucial in supporting the victories of the Tigrean People's Liberation Front (TPLF) during 1988 in Tigrai. The final liberation of Eritrea by the EPLF was only achieved at the cost of tens of thousands more lives and great physical destruction. Massawa was liberated in 1990, and the final EPLF offensives came in early 1991, coordinated with an TPLF/EPRDF campaign to capture Addis Ababa. Eritrean forces fought their way down the Denkel coast to cut off the Ethiopian supply lines at Assab, and in May they broke through the Ethiopian defenses around Dekemhare in a bloody five-day battle that culminated in the liberation of Asmara on May 24, now celebrated as independence day.

The Eritrean victory coincided with the overthrow of the Ethiopian Derg by the EPLF's Tigrean allies and the establishment of an EPRDF government in Addis Ababa that accepted Eritrea's right to self-determination. This change of power in the region, combined with the collapse of the USSR and U.S. support for the new EPLF and EPRDF governments, facilitated international, and particularly UN, acceptance of a long-standing EPLF proposal to hold a referendum on Eritrean national independence. To facilitate the disentanglement of Eritrean-Ethiopian relations, the referendum was put off until 1993. During the interim the EPLF formed the "Provisional Government of Eritrea" and began the difficult process of national reconstruction and political consolidation. The lack of international recognition and financial aid during this period hindered reconstruction efforts, but voluntary national service by the EPLF army and thousands of civilians nonetheless cleared the worst of war debris and damage, and began to repair Eritrea's basic infrastructure. Finally, after the April referendum in which 99.8 percent of Eritreans voted for independence, Eritrea achieved formal sovereignty on May 24, 1993.

Independent Eritrea

Isaias Afwerki became the first president, and the EPLF provisional government was transformed into the new government of the State of Eritrea, with a mandate to oversee the transition to a multiparty, constitutional democracy. In February 1994 the EPLF dissolved itself at its Third Congress, and was reformed as the People's Front for Democracy and Justice (PFDJ), a civilian party that inherited many of the EPLF's economic assets and prepared to contest the multi-party elections that are expected by 1998. In March 1994 a constitutional commission was formed to draft a document based in large part on Western ideals of democratic government, and steps were taken to establish the basis of a free-market economy, including a land reform law designed to replace communal tenures with individual leaseholds, a liberal investment code, and independent labor and employers' federations.

These changes have been overseen by the PFDJ, whose goal is, above all, to ensure that the divisive forces of religion and regionalism that so hampered the nationalist movement will not emerge in the form of political parties in the future. This concern, together with the PFDJ's continuing commitment to promote the interests of the socially disadvantaged, and particularly women, has already set it at odds with traditionalist elements in rural society.

In the Muslim lowlands and the refugee camps of the Sudan, traditionalist elements can and have been mobilized by the growing Islamist movement, with its base across the border in Khartoum, which has challenged the EPLF-PFDJ's secularism as a disguise for Christian domination of the new Eritrean state. The most militant Islamist element is the small Eritrean jihad movement, based in Sudan. Armed clashes between the jihad and EPLF forces began in 1989, and have continued through the present, leading to a diplomatic rift and virtual state of war between Eritrea and Sudan, and threatening the repatriation of the 150,000 or more Eritreans who remain in Sudan as of 1997.

In Eritrea the government commands widespread support among the war-weary population, and its local and regional representative assemblies are providing local government in all areas. In May 1997 a draft constitution was adopted by a representative assembly, and national elections are scheduled for 1998. The successful demobilization of over half the former guerrilla army, the repatriation of over 165,000 refugees without substantial outside assistance, widespread infrastructural reconstruction and the development of education, health, and local administrative facilities all attest to the efficiency of government workers, who, although poorly paid, are widely viewed as among the least corrupt and most highly motivated in Africa. A key program in the government's effort to build national unity has been the development of a universal national service program that includes military training. Unfortunately, Eritrea's economy remains in poor shape, with much of the population still dependent on food aid and little new investment in industry. The government's economic program, modeled on the self-sufficient policies of Asian countries like Singapore, will require financing that can only come from foreign loans or the hoped-for development of offshore oil reserves and tourism along the Red Sea coast.

THE DICTIONARY

- A -

ABDALLAH IDRIS. Military commander and leading figure in the ELF. Abdallah was born c. 1944 to a BENI 'AMER family in BARKA. He received a scholarship for schooling in CAIRO during the 1950s and in 1963 tried to join the ELF but was sent back to Cairo because of his age, where he studied at Al-Azhar University. In 1966 the ELF sent him to Syria for military training. In 1968 he joined the leadership of Zone 5, where he became involved in the LABOR PARTY.

Following the ADOBAHA meeting, Abdallah emerged as a leading figure in the Military Committee of the KIADA AL-AMA, and at the first ELF National Congress he was elected both to head the Military Committee and as second vice-president of the REVOLUTIONARY COUNCIL (RC). Abdallah's control over military reorganization led to his rise as the key ELF power-broker during the 1970s, when his support was crucial for both AHMED NASSER and the Labor Party. When the ELF was driven out of Eritrea in 1981, he became an implacable enemy of the EPLF and accused Christian elements in the ELF of destroying the organization.

Abdallah was expelled from the RC in November 1981, but on March 20, 1982, he led a coup and organized his own election as head of ELF-RC, hastening the ELF's breakup (*see* ELF FACTIONS). During 1982-83, Abdallah toured Arab capitals claiming to represent the mainstream ELF and using Islamist rhetoric to gain support. But in 1984 his attempt to redeploy fighters in Eritrea was defeated by the EPLF, and after failing to gain leadership of the SAUDI ARABIAN-sponsored ELF United Organization in 1985, he was increasingly marginalized. Abdallah remains in Egypt as of 1997.

ABDELKRIM   AHMED. A leader in the early ELF, Abdelkrim was born in 1929 to SAHO parents in SENAFE, where he attended Koranic school. In 1951 he went to work at the Massawa SALT works, where he participated in political actions that led to his arrest in 1954, after which he emigrated to CAIRO, enrolling in Al-Azhar University where he joined the Eritrean student union. Abdelkrim participated in the early formation of the ELF, and in June 1960 attempted to burn the Ethiopian embassy with MOHAMED ALI OMERO. In 1962 he organized ELF cells in the KEBESSA, and in 1963 he went to Syria with the first group of military trainees.

Abdelkrim returned to Eritrea in April 1964, and in 1965 he was appointed commander of the newly created ELF Zone 3, which became a *de facto* Saho-Muslim zone under his leadership. During 1965-67 Abdelkrim and his Saho fighters alienated many Christians in AKELE GUZAI and SERAYE with extortionate taxation, the burning of villages and tactics that reignited the longstanding TOR'A-TSENADEGLE WAR. The failure of his policies led the ELF to form the "Christian" Zone 5 in 1967, but he also came into conflict with the BARKA-based leadership of Zone 1. Abdelkrim was ousted from his command in 1968, while he was getting married in Sudan. He returned to Eritrea from exile in 1992.

ABDULKADIR   KABIRE (1902-49). A leading figure in the early nationalist movement, Abdulkadir was a founding member and first vice-president (1941-46) of the MAHABER FEQRI HAGER (MFH) and a founding member and president of the Hamasien section of the MUSLIM LEAGUE

(1946-49). He was born near Massawa, and traced descent from both coastal people and JIBERTI highlanders. During the 1930s he served as a colonial government interpreter. One of his wives was Afar, and he played an important role in mobilizing Muslim Eritreans for the pro-independence camp from DENKEL, SEMHAR, and the KEBESSA. In 1946 he resigned from the MFH following the failure of the WA'LA BET GHERGHIS, where he supported WOLDE-AB WOLDE-MARIAM's compromise attempt, after which he played a leading role in the highland branch of the Muslim League. In 1949, Abdulkadir was chosen as an INDEPENDENCE BLOC delegate to the UNITED NATIONS, but he was assassinated by ANDENET terrorists on March 27, 1949, two days before his scheduled departure.

ABERRA KASA, Dejazmach. Great-grandson of Dej. HAYLU TEWOLDE-MEDHIN of TSAZZEGA, Aberra was orphaned at an early age when both his great-grandfather and father were killed by WOLDE-MIKA'EL SOLOMUN at the battle of WOKI DUBA. Aberra took refuge with the Italians in Massawa after 1885, as did many of the highland MEKWE-NENTI. He rose to be *capo* of a BANDA of fifty rifles and was a loyal Italian soldier in the campaign to conquer the highlands. But when the Italians began to reduce the privileges of their erstwhile Eritrean supporters in 1890-91, Aberra became disillusioned. Hearing that the Italians planned to disarm him, on January 31, 1892, he fled with his men to Showate Anseba. His banda was pursued by Capt. Bettini and a column of ASCARI, and on March 18 Aberra ambushed and killed Bettini and seven ascari near Wolta Medhane. He then fled to TIGRAI, losing many of his men in battle at Mogo, and eventually found refuge with Ras Sebhatu in Agame. Aberra supported the Tigrean rulers' unsuccessful invasion of Eritrea in 1895, and died in exile in Ethiopia.

ABIYE ABEBE, Lieutenant-General. Imperial Representative (Amh.: Ende-Rase) to Eritrea from late 1959 and first Governor-General. Abiye Abebe was a member of the Shewan nobility and son-in-law to Emperor HAILE

SELASSIE. He held Eritrea for the Emperor during the attempted coup of December 1960, and was consequently elevated to Minister of Interior. He retained his duties in Eritrea, however, and on July 12, 1962, narrowly escaped death in a bomb attack at AGORDAT. In November he presided over Eritrea's annexation, and served as the province's first Governor-General until 1964, when he was elevated to President of the Ethiopian Senate.

ABRAHA TESSEMA, Dejazmach. Leading figure in early nationalist politics. Dej. Abraha was born in 1901, the first son of Ras TESEMMA ASBEROM of Ma'reba (AKELE GUZAI). He attended GE'EZ and Italian schools and became an accomplished scholar, agriculturalist, and painter. He served as secretary to his father and eventually took over the administration of the Hadegti district. Under the BRITISH ADMINISTRATION he served as district chief and then political secretary from 1948-52. During this period he also founded the leading Eritrean bus company, SATAE.

   Along with his father, Abraha became deeply involved in nationalist politics during the 1940s, helping to organize the "Eritrea for Eritreans" movement, the LIBERAL PROGRESSIVE PARTY and participating in the INDEPENDENCE BLOC. But in 1950 he formed the Liberal Unionist Party in an attempt to develop a KEBESSA Christian alternative to the UNIONIST PARTY. He was elected to the ASSEMBLY in 1952 and ran against TEDLA BAIRU, his great rival, for the office of Chief Executive. Tedla had him arrested on trumped-up charges of conspiring to assassinate him in October 1953, and although he was not convicted, he was forced to retire from politics, devoting himself to business, agriculture, and community improvement.

ABRAHAM TEWOLDE. One of the earliest Christian members of the ELF, Abraham joined the guerrillas in 1964. He was assigned to Zone 5 when ZONAL COMMANDS were created in 1966, and was appointed zone commander in 1967 after the defection of Wolde Kahsai. He developed a close working relationship with ISAIAS AFWERKI, the

zone's political commissar, and participated in organizing
the TRIPARTITE UNITY FORCES. In 1970 Abraham led the
defection from the ELF of most of the old Zone 5 Christians, who gathered with him at ALA, where he died of
illness later in the year.

ABU   TAYARA (Mohamed   Omer   Abdallah).   A founding
member of the ELF guerrilla army and later leader of the
MARYA faction   of the ELF-PLF. "Abu Tayara" was born in
Marya Tselim in 1926 and joined the SUDAN DEFENSE
FORCE in 1944. He rose to the rank of Sergeant by 1961,
when he was recruited into the ELF along with two other
Marya of later importance: Omer Mohamed Ali "Damer"
and Mohamed Idris Haj. In May 1962 he went with the first
group of fighters to join HAMID IDRIS AWATE inside Eritrea, and participated in the leadership of the early
ARMED STRUGGLE, taking over field command of ELF
forces briefly in 1963. In February 1964 he went with the
first group for training in Syria, along with Omer Damer,
and when he returned in 1965 he was given command of
the reserve battalion while Omer Damer took over the
training camp. These appointments to marginal commands
reflected in some ways the outsider status of these two
Marya leaders, caught between the BILEN and BENI 'AMER
in the "tribal" politics of the ZONAL COMMANDS.
     Following the ADOBAHA Conference, he went back to
Kassala along with Omer Damer, and in 1970 he made
contact with OSMAN SALEH SABBE, helping him organize
the recruitment of disgruntled fighters for what was to
become the ELF-PLF . In June he attended the SUDOHA
ILA meeting, where he was elected to the PLF leadership,
but in 1971 he and Omer Damer led a group of Marya and
others north to Sahel, where they linked with the remnants of OBEL in early 1972. He participated in the CIVIL
WAR in the ELF-PLF leadership, but after June 1973 he
and his Marya fighters merged with the Obel group and
remained separate from the PLF until June 1974, when
there was a brief rapprochement that ended in November
1975. At that time Abu Tayara and most of his Marya
fighters left the field, joining Sabbe's "third force" (*see*

ELF-PLF), which had already attracted Omer Damer. In the
ELF FACTIONS of the 1980s, Abu Tayara was associated
with Sabbe's organizations, returning to Eritrea with the
ELF-UO in 1992.

AD SHAYKH. A TIGRE-speaking tribe of SAHEL and
SEMHAR, which claims its descent from the Muslim missionary, Shaykh Al-Amin ibn Hamad, who was of mixed
Arab-BEJA descent. Shaykh Al-Amin arrived in northern
Sahel from Sudan in the early nineteenth century, where
he preached among Muslim Tigre "serfs" of the Christian
BET ASGHEDE, and over several decades built a following
through teaching and miracle working. He is credited with
having begun the conversion of the Bet Asghede SHUMAG-
ULLE to Islam, and his descendants helped complete the
conversion of all the Tigre-speaking northeast by the
1860s. His numerous progeny and clients formed the basis
of the Ad Shaykh tribe, which amassed a wealth of livestock through religiously-inspired gifts and developed a
serf class of dependents who had sought their protection,
very much like the other Tigre tribes. A saintly cult developed around Shaykh Al-Amin in Sahel, while his
grandson, Shaykh Mohamed Shaykh Ali (d. 1879), became
an equally venerated saint in Semhar, where his tomb at
EMBEREMI is an important pilgrimage site. Shaykh Mohamed's descendants became important merchants and
plantation owners with holdings spread across Semhar in
the colonial period.
      The two main branches of the Ad Shaykh are today
centered around Emberimi and AFABET. Other smaller
sections migrated west into Barka, where they joined the
BENI 'AMER confederacy as the FAIDAB and Garabet sub-
tribes. In the 1950s the Ad-Shaykh and their dependents
numbered some fifty thousand, but much of the tribe fled
to Sudan and Arabia during the 1960s-70s. In the 1980s
the Ad Shaykh's pastures became battlefields in the most
destructive campaigns of the ARMED STRUGGLE, which, together with the drought, eliminated most of the tribe's
animals. Today the tribal leadership and its class privileges have been displaced by egalitarian local councils,

although a residue of customary and religious deference clings to the descendants of Shaykh Al-Amin.

AD SHUMA (alt.: Ad Sciuma). A Tigre-speaking tribe of central SEMHAR, who practice seasonal agriculture and pastoralism, traditionally moving into the central highlands during the summer rains. Their center is around the tombs and shrine at Ad Shuma, on the road between Ailet and Solomuna.

AD TEMARIAM *see* BET ASGHEDE.

AD TEKLES *see* BET ASGHEDE.

AD TEKLEZAN (Hamasien). An important market town on the main road from Asmara to Keren. Ad Teklezan commands the strategic northern approaches to the central highlands, and is the administrative center of the historic DEMBEZAN district. The antiquity of human settlement in the district is attested to by AKSUMITE inscription (c. 250 AD) recovered at the nearby village of Deqi-Mehare. Dembezan's location at the edge of the Hamasien plateau, where the mountains drop steeply to the Anseba valley and Keren, made the area an important stopping point on the Christian PILGRIMAGE ROUTE from TIGRAI to SUWAKIN until the late middle ages. Before the fourteenth century the inhabitants seem to have been TIGRE-speakers, whose descendants today are called "Bargele." Around the late 1400s the Bargele were subjugated by TIGRINYA-speaking immigrants, perhaps descendants of Agaw-speakers from south of the MAREB, putatively led by a Kantibai Teklezan (hence the town's name). This immigration produced a caste division between Tigrinya-speaking SHUMAGULLE clans and their Tigre-speaking subjects, similar to that of the Tigre and BILEN tribes to the north and west. Though the inequities of this division have largely disappeared, many Dembezan residents remain bilingual, and Ad Teklezan became a popular settlement for Tigre converts to PROTESTANT CHRISTIANITY during the colonial period.

During the late 1700s, rivalry between the leading
Shumagulle clans of Ad Elos and Ad Kuflom produced a
longstanding blood feud. In the 1850s Kantibai Gulbet, of
the Ad Elos, feuded with the house of HAZZEGA and
murdered ILENI HAGOS, mother of Ras WOLDE-MIKA'EL
SOLOMUN, who took revenge on Ad Teklezan in 1855,
killing 65 and burning the town. Church leaders recon-
ciled the two districts by arranging the marriage of
Wolde-Mika'el's daughter with the nephew of Kantibai
Gulbet, but the Kantibai's posthumous child, HADGU-
AMBESSA, later took revenge on Hazzega. Under
YOHANNES IV, Kantibai Nasheh of the Ad Kuflom gained
power, but in 1889 he was forced to flee by Hadgu-
Ambessa, who had joined the Italians. Nasheh died at
Massawa in 1890, but Ad Elos supremacy was short-lived
as the Italians soon arrested Hadgu-Ambessa as well.
Eventually, in the 1920s, the Italians allowed Hadgu-
Ambessa's son, Asfaha, to regain local authority.

Colonial rule and the building of the Asmara-Keren
highway in the 1920s led to Ad Teklezan's growth as a
market center and highway rest stop. During March 29-31,
1941, the Italian army made its last unsuccessful defense
of Asmara outside the town. Under the British, Asfaha
Hadgu-Ambessa continued in power and finally settled
the Ad Elos-Ad Kuflom blood feud. In the 1940s the
primary school expanded, and in the 1950s a secondary
school was built with aid from Protestant missionaries. In
December 1977 the ELF liberated the town, and in 1978 it
was garrisoned by the EPLF, who withdrew in late
November after the Ethiopian breakthrough at ADI
YAQOB. The DERG then held Ad Teklezan until the end of
the war. Today it is a rapidly growing commercial center
with an urban population of 4,000 and about 6,000 more
in surrounding agricultural villages.

ADDIS   ABABA (Ethiopia). From the 1890s onwards, the
Ethiopian capital has been an important center for Eritrean immigrants. Initially, most were highland Christians fleeing ITALIAN COLONIALISM. A community of
educated Eritreans developed under the patronage of

Emperor HAILE SELASSIE I in the 1920s-30s, including such influential figures as Lorenzo Taezaz. During the Italian occupation a number of Muslim businessmen, particularly Tigrinya-speaking JIBERTI, moved to the capital where they dominated the lower levels of import-export trade.

In the 1940s the Eritrean community continued to grow as pro-UNIONIST PARTY Christians moved to the capital and over five hundred educated Eritreans found employment in the imperial bureaucracy. Skilled Eritrean workers, particularly mechanics and drivers in the road transport sector, but many others as well, moved to Addis Ababa in growing numbers during the 1950s and 1960s, as the center of regional INDUSTRY shifted from ASMARA to Addis. In Addis, the new Eritrean immigrants formed their own mutual aid societies, centered around Orthodox Christian *mahaber* organizations. During the 1960s, as nationalist political sentiments grew among Eritreans, these *mahaber* organizations also became centers for clandestine nationalist organization and arms smuggling.

The 1960s also saw the development of a largely Christian Eritrean student population, whose alienation from the dominant Amhara culture, and experience of discrimination against their language and political aspirations, produced some of the most important leaders of the nationalist movement, including ISAIAS AFWERKI. In 1974-75, particularly after the death of AMANUEL MIKA'EL ANDOM, many of the younger members of the Eritrean community in Addis fled to join the Eritrean liberation fronts. As the DERG's hold over the Christian highlands of Eritrea was consolidated after 1978, however, a new wave of Eritrean immigrants arrived seeking economic opportunities and fleeing the war. By 1991 the Eritrean community in Addis Ababa numbered over 150,000, most of whom remain in Addis, as the economic opportunities there are greater than Eritrea. Eritreans continue to prosper in import-export, retail trade, technical and professional services, particularly associated with air and truck transport, and communications.

ADI BARO (Seraye). A village northwest of DEBARWA on
the border with HAMASIEN, Adi Baro was an important
market town in the 1400s, figuring in early European
itineraries. In the early 1500s it was the residence of
BAHRE NEGASHI, before it was eclipsed by Debarwa. Some
of the most fertile village land was expropriated by
Italian concessionaires in the early twentieth century, but
it was restored during the Federation. Today it has a
population of about five hundred.

ADI HAWESHA (Hamasien). A village on the Asmara-
Dekemhare road that was the site of heavy fighting during
August 4-13, 1977, when the EPLA fought off an Ethiopian
attempt to break the encirclement of ASMARA and retake
DEKEMHARE. More fighting followed in September and in
March 1978, when the DERG again failed to break through.
On June 20, 1994, an estimated 150,000 people walked
from Asmara to Adi Hawesha to commemorate the Eritrean
MARTYRS who died in these battles.

ADI KAIYEH (Akele Guzai; alt.: Adi Caieh, Keieh).
Provincial capital of AKELE GUZAI. Located on a ridge
commanding the intersection of the HADAS River valley
with the main highland route from Asmara to Ethiopia,
Adi Kaiyeh was essentially the creation of Italian colonialists, who constructed a fort on the site in 1890. The
name derives from a nearby hamlet of no historical significance. The Italians built up the town as a colonial administrative and market center, with a Catholic mission and
military garrison. A mixed population of TIGRINYA and
SAHO people settled around the new center, while Italian
farmers expropriated some of the best lands in the valley
below.
      In 1923 the government opened a secondary school
for Italian and mixed-race children, but Eritreans were
not admitted until the British period. By 1931 the
population had grown to about three thousand, and this
increased further during 1937-38, when the main road
from Asmara to Addis Ababa was built, making Adi

Kaiyeh an important highway stop. Growth stopped during 1947-55, however, when SHIFTA attacks drove away most Italians and intercommunal tensions between Muslims and Christians poisoned the area; by 1962 there were only 3,300 residents. In the mid-1960s the ELF began to operate from bases on the nearby KOHAITO plateau, and by the mid-1970s Adi Kayieh had been transformed into an Ethiopian garrison town. In March 1975, the garrison massacred scores of Eritrean residents, particularly Saho, who fled en masse. In 1977 the ELF besieged the town, but in September they were routed with heavy losses in a failure many blamed on the lack of coordination between ELF and nearby EPLF forces.

The DERG held Adi Kaiyeh through the 1980s, and its large military garrison made it a center for drinking and prostitution that has left a welter of postliberation social problems. The town was ringed with land mines and residents were unable to farm or graze their animals, becoming increasingly dependent on FOOD AID. Finally, in 1990, Adi Kaiyeh was liberated by the EPLF during the April 24-30 campaign in southern Akele Guzai. During the fighting, which was very bloody as EPLA fighters had to attack across minefields in the open plain south of the fort, the Derg's locally recruited wheat militia deserted to the EPLF. Following the battle residents flocked to aid the EPLA on the DEKEMHARE FRONT, and the town became a hub of military activity as the EPLF developed its new supply line up the HADAS valley. Today Adi Kaiyeh is a growing administrative and market center, with a population of 9,500. Its hospital and schools have been rebuilt and a new football stadium was recently completed. Until 1994 it was also the logistical base for an Eritrean army corps.

ADI NEFAS (Hamasien). A village on the escarpment just north of ASMARA. Adi Nefas was founded in the fourteenth century by settlers from neighboring Embaderho, according to local tradition. The village's history is an excellent example of the many links between the highland and lowland populations of Eritrea, as the former ruling strata of the BET ASGHEDE of SAHEL trace their ancestry to Adi Nefas.

Like most of the villages of KARNISHEM, the people of Adi Nefas farmed the SEMENAWI BAHRI lands of the escarpment below the village during the winter. In c. 1865 the villagers killed a relative of Ras WOLDE-MIKA'EL SOLOMUN in a dispute over their winter lands around Durfo, and Wolde-Mika'el attacked the village, burning it and killing sixty men.

Under ITALIAN COLONIALISM, village land was alienated for the reservoir system above BELEZA and for the gold MINING operation begun directly below the village in 1928. The massive growth of Asmara in the late 1930s brought the city to the edge of Adi Nefas' land, and many villagers began to work in the brickworks located near the village. By the mid-1940s the gold mine had been expanded by Nino Garbini to employ about two hundred villagers, but on March 17, 1950, it was destroyed by a band of Unionist SHIFTA.

The Swedish Protestant Church became active in the village during the 1920s, and in the early 1950s they helped build a primary school. In January 1975, as the ARMED STRUGGLE intensified in the highlands, the Ethiopian army attacked and burned the village, forcing the residents to flee to Durfo and inciting most of the young men to join the EPLF. Intense fighting continued through April, when the DERG drove the EPLF out of the area. A military garrison was stationed to control the road to Durfo, but in February 1979 it was overrun by the EPLF in a guerrilla attack. Further fighting occurred in 1989-90, when the EPLF set up its artillery in Durfo and began shelling the Asmara AIRPORT. Today the village is being rebuilt and has a population of about three thousand, many of whom commute to Asmara for work.

ADI QWALA (Seraye; alt.: Adi Quala). An important market town and subprovincial administrative center in southern SERAYE, located on the main road from ASMARA to ADWA. Its location on the southern edge of the Seraye plateau, where it drops steeply to the GUNDET lowlands

and MAREB River, is the key to Adi Qwala's history. It was
a small village of no importance before the Italians established a fort there in 1890 to defend the central plateau
against a possible attack from TIGRAI. It remained a garrison town known particularly for its massive stone
prison until the British period, when a primary and secondary school were established and its Eritrean population began to increase. By 1962 there were some 1,500
residents, and this increased as its Ethiopian garrison
grew during the ARMED STRUGGLE.

In February 1975 Eritrean prison warders released
all prisoners at Adi Qwala to the ELF, and in July 1977
the front liberated the town, which it held until July
1978. After that it never fell into Eritrean hands again
until the end of the war, although its large garrison was
attacked by guerrilla units numerous times and heavy
fighting occured around the town in March 1989 and early
1991. Today Adi Qwala is the growing commercial center
of the MAI TSADA region, one of the richest agricultural
areas in the highlands.

ADI UGRI *see* MENDEFERA (Seraye).

ADI YAQOB (Hamasien). A hamlet near HAZZEGA and site
of the 1978 Ethiopian defeat of EPLF forces on the front
north of Asmara. During 1977 EPLF fighters had fortified
Adi Yaqob as part of a defensive line encircling Asmara,
which ran from Embadhero in the east to Showate Anseba
in the west. Between Hazzega and Adi Yaqob the EPLA
trenches ran across 400 meters of open fields, and in
November 1978 the Ethiopians' Russian advisors decided
this was the weak link in the EPLA line. At dawn on
November 23 the Ethiopians launched their attack against
the 450 fighters of Haile 3 of the 8th Brigade, concentrating 68 tanks on a 500-meter front. Over 400 fighters
died and less than a dozen escaped to rejoin EPLA units.
The Ethiopians quickly pushed down the west bank of the
ANSEBA River to the Keren road near ELABERED, forcing
the EPLF to abandon AD TEKLEZAN on November 24, and
precipitating the second phase of the STRATEGIC

WITHDRAWAL. On June 20, 1993, several thousand people walked from Asmara to Adi Yaqob to commemorate the MARTYRS who died there and elsewhere in the struggle for independence.

ADKEME MELEGA (alt.: Atkeme-Lega). A TIGRINYA descent group located in central SERAYE. The origins of this important group are obscured by several overlapping genealogies, but two traditions are clear: First, at least a part of the Adkeme Melega originated from an Agaw immigration, probably during the tenth to twelfth centuries, from the Lasta region of Ethiopia, and this immigration links the Adkeme Melega with the people of Agame in TIGRAI, who trace a similar ancestry. Part of this Agaw immigration seems to have involved a power struggle between the immigrants and the previous BELEW ruling elements, who were defeated. Second, the combination of the Adkeme Melega with peoples of local origin (remembered in traditions as the children of Juda, one of the Israeli companions of Menelik I, son of Solomon and Sheba (Sab'a), but actually associated in most genealogies with the DEQI MENAB). This intermingling gave rise by the fourteenth century to the Deqi Ware Senezghi, whose principle families, the Deqi Melega, Deqi Mai and Deqi Tesfa, became the hereditary ruling families of Seraye by the sixteenth century.

Today, most of the original ENDA groups of QOHAIN and MAI TSADA trace their origins to the Adkeme Melega, as well as other families scattered through central and western Seraye. The Adkeme Melega have their own customary law, codified in the sixteenth century or earlier, that is still used to settle many questions of land and inheritance in Seraye.

ADMINISTRATION and ADMINISTRATIVE DIVISIONS. Before ITALIAN COLONIALISM, what is today Eritrea was divided among a number of local and foreign-controlled administrations, including, at various times, those of the BAHRE NEGASHI, the DIGLAL, the NA'IB, and of EGYPT, ETHIOPIA, TIGRAI and TURKEY. The present administrative system derives from Italian colonial rule, which imposed a combination of "direct" and "indirect" administrative systems over Eritrea after 1890.

Italian administrative divisions went through a number of alterations, beginning with four divisions: Massawa (the capital), Asmara (central highlands), Keren (north and west) and Assab (Denkel). In 1903 Governor MARTINI established seven *commissariati* or provincial divisions (Akele Guzai, Assab, Barka, Hamasien, Keren, Massawa, Seraye) and three *residenze* or autonomous districts (Mareb, Sahel, Shimezana), and in 1909 Gash-Setit was added as an eighth *commissariati.* These units were reduced to six *commissariati* in 1931: Akele Guzai (Adi Kaiyeh), Bassopiano Occidentale (Western Lowlands, Agordat), Bassopiano Orientale (Eastern Lowlands, Massawa), Hamasien (Asmara), Keren, Seraye (Mendefera). In 1936 Eritrea was enlarged to include TIGRAI, divided into six additional *commissariati,* including that of Dankalia, which was administered from ASSAB. In 1941, the BRITISH ADMINISTRATION returned Eritrea to its previous borders, and returned Assab to the Eastern Lowlands Division. In 1947 Keren and Agordat divisions were merged into the Western Province as part of the British plan to partition Eritrea (see BEVIN-SFORZA PLAN). Under the FEDERATION (1952-62) these divisions were maintained and staffed by an autonomous Eritrean administration, appointed and controlled by the Eritrean Chief Executive.

After 1962, when Eritrea was annexed as ETHIOIPIA's fourteenth province, these divisions became the province's *awrajas,* and the administration was placed under the control of an Ethiopian Governor-General, until a Military Administration was imposed in 1970 as the ARMED STRUGGLE for independence intensified. In 1965 the Eastern Lowlands or Red Sea Awraja was divided into two: SEMHAR and Dankalia (DENKEL). About the same time, the SAHEL district of Keren Division (SENHIT Awraja) was detached as a separate *awraja.* Finally, after the DERG came to power in 1974, and continued the Military Administration of Eritrea, the Western or

BARKA Awraja had its autonomous district of GASH-SETIT detached as a separate *awraja,* while ASMARA was also made into an *awraja.* From 1975 onwards much of northwest Eritrea, as well as many other rural areas, came under the direct administration of the ELF and EPLF, while various attempts were made to detach Dankalia administratively (*see* ASSAB).

After independence, the Eritrean government maintained these divisions as Eritrea's "provinces" through 1995. Each province had a governor appointed by the executive branch of the national government who was responsible for provincial administration down to the local level. Each province was divided into sub-provinces, districts and sub-districts, with organs of LOCAL GOVERNMENT and elected councils at each level. In addition, urban centers have neighborhood-level *(kebele)* and zonal *(zoba)* councils and administrations.

On May 19, 1995, the NATIONAL ASSEMBLY voted to redraw Eritrea's administrative boundaries, creating six administrative regions or Zobas (Tigrn.: "zone") designed to maximize economic development programs by uniting similar ecological and resource bases. As of 1996, the new regions are: (1) Debubawi Keyih Bahri (Southern Red Sea —includes Denkel from the DJIBOUTI border to the northern limits of Tio district, with Assab as its administrative center); (2) Semenawi Keyih Bahri (Northern Red Sea—includes the entire coast and coastal plain from Mersa Fatma in the south to the border of SUDAN, and inland to the edge of the central highlands and the mountain districts of SAHEL, with its center at MASSAWA); (3) Anseba (comprises a wedge of mountainous land running north from KEREN, the administrative center, and includes the lands of the MARYA along the ANSEBA River and the northern districts along the BARKA River); (4) Gash-Barka (covers GASH-SETIT and southern BARKA, including AGORDAT, with its center at BARENTU); (5) Debub ("Southern"—with its center at MENDEFERA, comprises all the highland areas of SERAYE and AKELE GUZAI, but without their former low and midelevation districts to the west and east); (6) Maakel (Central—com-

prises Asmara and its HAMASIEN suburbs). These
Zoba/regions are subdivided into fifty-five subregions
(referred to, confusingly, as "provinces" in English
publications), with the village remaining the smallest
administrative unit.

Regional administrators, equivalent to former
provincial governors, are appointed by the President. All
levels of administration are filled through appointments
made by the heads of the next administrative unit above
them, linked through an ascending hierarchy of
responsibility directly to the President, who, as chief
executive, has authority over the entire administrative
system. The parallel system of elected councils provides
the basis for provincial assemblies and the NATIONAL
ASSEMBLY, but these bodies have yet to gain independent
legislative or budgetary authority as of 1997.

ADOBAHA (Sahel). A seasonal stream that drains the interior of the northern highlands, the Adobaha is divided
into two drainages, the Adobaha Abbai ("Big") and Nish
("Little"). In August 1969, the ELF held an important conference at a seasonal camp in Adobaha Nish valley. The
Adobaha meeting was the culmination of several years of
reformist activity inside the ELF, led by ESLAH and the
TRIPARTITE UNITY FORCES. The conference was attended
by about 160 members of all five ZONAL COMMANDS, including members of the conservative Muslim leadership of
Zones 1 and 2, the reformists of Zones 3-5, and the external leadership from the Revolutionary Command in Kassala and the SUPREME COUNCIL.

At the conference the ELF was already split into two
rival blocs, whose division was to mark the fracture line
which led directly to civil war in 1972. On one side were
the leaders of Zones 1 and 2, supported by Mohamed
Ahmed Abdu of Zone 3 and their external patrons, IDRIS
MOHAMED ADEM and IDRIS OSMAN GALADEWOS. On the
other side were the leaders of Zones 4 and 5, the Marya
group of ABU TAYARA, and OSMAN SALEH SABBE from
the external leadership. After several days of negotiations
the participants agreed to abolish the old structure of the

ELF, including both the Revolutionary Command and the
five zones. In their place was created a Provisional General Command (KIADA AL-AMA), while the military organization was divided into three "regions," with regions
one and two corresponding to the old zones 1 and 2, and
region three comprising the old zones 3-5, thus further
reinforcing the existing divisions.   Consequently, the
Adobaha conference failed to resolve the ELF's fundamental problems, and in reality hastened its disintegration.

ADULIS. Foremost port of the Eritrean coast during the
period of the AKSUMITE EMPIRE, Adulis was located on
the western shore of the Gulf of Zula about four kilometers
from the sea, where its harbor of Gabaza was sited. Today
its remains are buried under a deep layer of silt, near the
village of ZULA.
     Pottery from excavations at the lowest levels of the
Adulis site indicate the area was occupied by people in
trading contact with SOUTH ARABIA at least as early as
the second millenium B.C. The classical foundations of
Adulis coincide with the occupation of the site by Greco-
Egyptian trading expeditions during the reign of Ptolemy
II "Philadelphius" (285-246 B.C.). The famous Monumen-
tum Adulitanum with its Greek inscription from the reign
of Ptolemy III "Euergetes" (246-221 B.C.) was described
by Cosmas Indicopleustes who visited Adulis in the sixth
century, but it could have been moved to Adulis from
elsewhere.
     Archaeological evidence shows that during the last
three centuries B.C., if not before, important TRADE
ROUTES climbed from the Gulf of Zula up the valleys of the
HADAS and KUMALIE Rivers to reach the highlands of
AKELE GUZAI and thence continued to TIGRAI. Adulis
seems the most likely site for the seaside emporium of
this trade route, as it lies on the coastal plain directly
below the intersection of these river valleys, in a fertile
and irrigable area.
     By the early Aksumite period (second century A.D.)
Adulis was an important trading center for merchants
from the Mediterranean and Red Sea regions, and both

Pliny the Elder's *Natural History* (c. 75 A.D.) and *The Periplus of the Erythrean Sea* (by Pseudo Arrian, c. 200 A.D.) describe it in some detail, including its commercial and political connections with Aksum. Later Aksumite inscriptions, the *Geography* of Claudius Ptolemaeus, and archaeological artifacts, including numerous Mediterranean and Indian imports, attest to its far-flung trading connections, wealth and size during the third to sixth centuries. By the reign of KALEB, Adulis was the frequent seat of Aksumite rulers, and its trade had made the Eritrean region the most prosperous part of the empire. In 525 Kaleb assembled a fleet at Adulis of some sixty vessels, including ships from India, Arabia and Egypt, for his invasion of South Arabia. But with the rise of the Muslim empire in the seventh century the port declined, as the Indian-Mediterranean trade routes were redirected through the Persian Gulf or along the Arabian coast.

In the late seventh or early eighth centuries (probably c. 702, and not c. 640 as many scholars previously suggested) Adulis was sacked by a naval expedition from Jeddah. Although its churches were rebuilt and a Muslim trading community is mentioned there in the early eighth century, the port lost importance and soon disappeared from history, to be replaced by Muslim commercial centers at DAHLAK Kebir and MASSAWA. Today the site is unoccupied, but nearby is a village named Zula whose SAHO-speaking people have several legends concerning the ancient site. The 800-meter field of ruins has been investigated and partially excavated by archaeologists, including the surveys of Salt (1809/10), Vigneaud and Petit of the Lefebvre mission (1840), Napier's British military expedition (1868), Bent's survey (1893), the excavations of Sundstrom with the Littman expedition (1906), Paribeni (1907), and, most recently, the excavations of Anfray with the Ethiopian Archaeological Institute (1961-62).

ADWA (Tigrai, Ethiopia). The principal commercial town of central TIGRAI. Located on the road from ADI QWALA, just 48 kilometers from the MAREB River, Adwa has an important place in Eritrean history. The town developed as a commercial center during the Turkish period, relying on trade between Massawa and Tigrai along the route running through SERAYE. During the seventeenth century Adwa eclipsed both DEBARWA and Aksum as a commercial center, and in the eighteenth it became the seat of the increasingly powerful governors of Tigrai and then the capital of Emperor YOHANNES IV.

ITALIAN COLONIAL forces occupied Adwa in January 1890 and again on April 1, 1895 during the invasion of Tigrai. They held the town until March 1, 1896, when an Ethiopian army led by Emperor Menelik II defeated an Italian army of 17,000, including 5,000 Eritrean ASCARI, just outside the town, ending the first Italian attempt to conquer Northern Ethiopia. Over 4,000 Italian and 2,000 Eritrean soldiers were killed, while 1,750 Italians and over 1,000 Eritreans were captured. In the aftermath of the battle Menelik's empress ordered the amputation of one hand and one foot from at least 400 Eritrean ascari.

AFABET (Sahel). A market town and administrative center on the road from KEREN to NAKFA, and the site of the single most decisive battle of the ARMED STRUGGLE. The Afabet plain has been inhabited since prehistoric times, but until the 1950s it was little more than a seasonal camp and occasional market, and the Italian administrative post in the area was located at Cub-Cub.

In the early 1960s a police post was built and American missionaries opened a clinic and school, which the government of ETHIOPIA encouraged as part of its effort to permanently settle AD SHAYKH, BET ASGHEDE and other TIGRE-speaking peoples in the area as a means of controlling their involvement with the ELF's ARMED STRUGGLE. A military garrison was established in 1968, and as its counter-insurgency actions increased many local people fled as REFUGEES. On April 6, 1977, the EPLF liberated the town and immediately set about organizing a land reform and village assembly, but met strong

resistance until May 1978 from the traditional elite
(SHUMAGULLE), organized around the local mosque.

In January 1978 Afabet was recaptured by the DERG,
the Eritrean population fled and the town became the
military base for repeated Ethiopian OFFENSIVES against
EPLF-held NAKFA. In December 1979 the EPLA drove
Ethiopian forces back to the town, but in 1980-81 the
Ethiopians regained the Hedai valley and Cub-Cub, and
the town's military installations expanded during the RED
STAR CAMPAIGN. By 1987 the town was the base for the
Nadaw (Amh.: "destroyer") army corps, comprising three
divisions and support units, including some 22,000 men,
plus thousands more Ethiopian and (newly arrived) Eritrean civilians.

In December, 1987, the EPLA again pushed the
Ethiopians back towards the town in preparation for a
battle of encirclement aimed at seizing the garrison and
all its military stores intact. On March 17, 1988, the main
EPLA offensive was launched on three fronts. The Eritrean
left wing swept down the coast, closing off the mouths of
the Felket She'eb and Azahara canyons to prevent
Ethiopian units from escaping to the east, while the center
attacked the main front along the Hedai valley, and the
right wing destroyed the Ethiopian 21st Division. The
envelopment unfolded through March 18, by which time
surviving Ethiopian units were in full retreat towards
Afabet. On the main road, the Derg's 29th Mechanized
Brigade was trapped behind burning tanks on Ashirum
pass and destroyed by Ethiopian planes to keep it from
falling into Eritrean hands. At dawn on March 19, the
EPLA stormed Afabet, capturing the garrison, fifty tanks,
a hundred trucks, sixty artillery pieces, twenty
antiaircraft guns and immense quantities of small arms
and ammunition. The retreating Ethiopians were cut-off at
Kelhamet pass and destroyed or captured in intense
fighting on March 19-20, and EPLA infantry, which
moved behind Ethiopian lines before the battle, blocked
Ethiopian reinforcements from KEREN in heavy fighting at
MES-HALIT. By March 20, the EPLA had killed or captured 18,000 Ethiopian soldiers, and the balance of

tary power in Eritrea had permanently shifted. Basil
Davidson, reporting for the British Broadcasting Company
from the battlefield on March 21, called the victory "one
of the biggest ever scored by any liberation movement
anywhere since Dien Bien Phu."
        During May 13-23, the Derg attempted to recapture
Afabet using mechanized units and para-commandos, but
failed after intense fighting. On April 3 and 21, 1990, 16
civilians were killed, 29 wounded and 168 buildings were
destroyed by Ethiopian bombing. Today the town is being
rebuilt, with a new clinic, school and livestock market.
The struggle to overcome inequality in cultural traditions
remains a primary issue in local politics, but in 1994 a
woman was elected deputy mayor.

AFAR (Arab.: Danakil). An ethno-linguistic group whose
members inhabit DENKEL. The Afar language is a branch
of Eastern Cushitic related to Somali. The Afar people
spread across the present territories of DJIBOUTI,
ETHIOPIA and Eritrea, inhabiting the desert plains and
hills of the northern Rift Valley and the seacoast between
the Gulf of Tadjura and the Gulf of Zula. Today there are
about sixty thousand Afar in Eritrea, and many thousands
more who live as refugees on the Arabian penninsula.
They are divided between a coastal population of
sedentary fishermen, seafaring merchants and SALT
miners, who live on the BURE PENNINSULA, in ASSAB,
BEYLUL, EDD, Tio and smaller coastal settlements; a
pastoralist population who inhabit the interior hills and
work the salt pans of the Danakil Depression, practising
seasonal agriculture in a few valleys and migrating across
the border into Ethiopia; and a small sedentary
agricultural population around BA'DA.
        The ancestors of the Afar have lived in Denkel since
antiquity, and they appear in inscriptions originating
from both SOUTH ARABIA and the AKSUMITE Empire.
Arabic sources cite them by name ("Danakil") from the
thirteenth century. The Afar were among the earliest
Eritrean peoples to convert to Islam, and many joined the
armies of Imam AHMED AL-GHAZALI in the early 1500s.

The current Afar political division between "Red" Asahimera "aristocratic" clans and "White" Adohimera "commoner" clans seems to have coalesced after Imam Ahmed's defeat. The political center of the Afar is the Sultanate of Awsa, about two hundred kilometers inland from ASSAB, in Ethiopia. But outside the Assab area, the "Eritrean" Afar had little political interraction with the Sultanate, and the more populous northern areas between the Endeli river and the Bure penninsula actually suffered much closer political relationships, involving tribute-payments and raiding, with the lords of TIGRAI, the TIGRINYA-speaking plateau and the NA'IBs of SEMHAR.

By the nineteenth century the Afar living in present-day Eritrea were divided between seven major subtribes and many smaller groups. Today the most important sub-tribes are the Dahimela (inhabiting the western plains of Denkel and the Ba'da area), Damoheita (inhabiting the penninsula), Hedarem or "Hadermo" (inhabiting the foothills of the Eastern Escarpment), Bellesesuwa (inhabiting the same area as the Hedarem) and the smaller Ankala and Dunna groups. The composition of these sub-tribes illustrates the way in which "aristocrat" and "commoner" divisions are mixed together among the Eritrean Afar: the Dahimela were descended from "commoners" who gained political autonomy, eventually gaining other "commoner" clients, such as the Hedarem; the Damoheita and Ankala comprised both "commoner" and "aristocratic" groups, with Asahimera controlling political offices and resource distribution; while the Hedarem, Bellesuwa and Dunna were "commoners" claiming Arab descent who eventually gained political autonomy. By the colonial period the divisions between Asahimera and Adohimera were largely distinctions of social pedigree with little material import, although some Asahimera families continued to control political office.

During the mid-1900s European, Egyptian and Ethiopian interest in the Afar territories developed, and from 1869 ITALY became increasingly involved around

Assab and Beylul. In November 1890 the Afar regions of
Eritrea were annexed to the new colony through protectorate treaties, but   early Italian attempts at imposing
political control were resisted by the AKITO family of
Beylul and Sultan Yassin Haysama. In general the colonial
administration left Afar society alone, as long as Afar
leaders acknowledged Italian authority and refrained from
intergroup warfare. Although the colonial frontier cut
across Afar territories, it had little effect on pastoral
movements, and outside of a few Italian military posts, the
development of MINING infrastructure between Mersa
Fatma and Koluli, and the building of a modern port at
Assab, Italian colonialism had little impact on Afar life.
Military recruitment brought a few Afar into the colonial
world, but there were no Italian schools in Denkel, and an
educated Afar middle-class did not develop.

One consequence of Italian laissez-faire policies
with regard to Afar territories was that an organized Afar
political movement did not develop in Eritrea until the
1970s, and then it was much more the product of
Ethiopian Afar sentiments, centered on the Sultanate of
Awsa. Eritrean Afars formed their loyalties to family and
clan groupings, though a few individuals were involved in
national politics. In the 1940s Eritrean Afars were split
between a pro-Italian group led by Mohamed Omar AKITO
in Assab and MUSLIM LEAGUE supporters led by Musa
GAAS and ABDULKADIR KABIRE. In the 1950s-60s young
Afars in CAIRO and Sudan participated in the formation of
the ELM, which attracted more Afar support than the ELF.
In the 1970s, however, several Afars rose to leadership
positions in the ELF, including Ali Mohamed Ibrahim and
Mohamed Ali Isak, while others, such as Humed Mohamed
Karikari (see NAVY), rose to leading positions in the
EPLF.

Throughout the colonial period the leading figure in
Afar "national" politics, such as they were, remained the
Sultan of Awsa. He was courted by the Italians from the
1880s, with whom he maintained good relations through
1941. The Sultan was also courted by the British, who
controlled Afar territory in both Ethiopia and Eritrea

through 1944, but he was imprisoned by HAILE SELASSIE who was intent on dominating the new ROAD TRANSPORT route from Addis Ababa to Assab. The Emperor brought to power a new Sultan, Ali Mira, who he appeased through local autonomy and imperial favors, but this strategy collapsed under the brutal policies of the DERG in 1975, leading to the formation by Ali Mira and his son Anfere of the AFAR LIBERATION FRONT (ALF).

In northern Denkel, where the bulk of Eritrean Afars live, the 1970s initially witnessed manifestations of inter-tribal politics as young Afars were recruited into the rival ELF and EPLF organizations. Damoheita initially favored the ELF, while Dahimela favored first the ELM and later the EPLF. The political allegiance of Eritrean Afars was further divided by the DERG's ambiguous policy of creating an Assab autonomous region, and Derg support for an anti-EPLF Afar military organization called Ugugumo (*see* AFAR LIBERATION FRONT).

With independence, a split developed between those Afar who supported the EPLF, mostly in the north, and those who had fled overseas during the war or remained in the Derg-controlled areas, notably the shanty-town of Assab Sahrir. Among the latter groups, there was some sympathy for a pan-Afar independence movement calling for the creation of a united, self-governing Afar territory including Eritrean Denkel. During 1991-93, this movement received some support from SAUDI ARABIA, but even among the exiles, Eritrean Afars were far from united, and at least three different Afar political organizations formed, in addition to the ALF, to oppose Afar incorporation into Eritrea. In 1993 these groups united in the Afar Revolutionary Democratic Unity Front (ARDUF), led by Mahmouda GAAS, who joined Habib Ali Mira, son of the Sultan of Awsa in calling for a "no" vote in the REFERENDUM on Eritrean independence. But on January 22, 1993, after negotiations with the Provisional Government of Eritrea (PGE), Habib Ali Mira announced his support for Eritrean independence, including Denkel, and in the April Referendum 99.658 percent of the 29,799 registered voters in Denkel (about 75-80 percent Afar)

voted for independence. The weakness of any pan-Afar nationalism is further attested to by the Islamist orientation
of the few post-Referendum anti-government protests,
which have centered on Afar support for Arabic-language
Muslim schools versus Afar-language government schools.

AFAR   LIBERATION   FRONT (ALF). The most important
AFAR nationalist organization from 1975-1992, the ALF
was founded by the Sultan Ali Mira of Awsa after the
DERG attacked his vast estates around Assaita in May,
1975. He fled to SAUDI ARABIA and contacted the ELF,
while his son, Anfere, organized a guerrilla army with
the support of SOMALIA. During 1975-77 ELF and ALF
units attacked the Assab road and southern DENKEL, but
after the Somali defeat in 1978 the ALF's armed operations all but ceased and several splinter groups formed.
        After the defeat of the ELF in the second CIVIL WAR,
some Afar former ELF members, led by Ahmed Mohamed
Ahaw (son of the Sultan of Biru), formed a new Afar movement known as Ugugumo ("Revolution") with Derg support.
Ugugumo was based in western Denkel and Ethiopian
Dankalia, where they fought both EPLF and TPLF units for
control of the Dalol SALT trade, and were known as the
Afar Revolutionary Forces (ARF) until they joined the
ARDUF in 1993. In 1984 an Afar member of the former
ELF-RC, Mohamed Ali Isak, also formed a new ALF wing
with Saudi Arabian support and landed a few fighters on
the coast, but after fighting around BA'DA, they were
driven into southern Denkel and by 1989 had come to
terms with the EPLF.
        After the EPLF victory at AFABET the main ALF
group, led by the sons of the Sultan of Awsa, negotiated an
operational alliance with the EPLF, and on February 17,
1989, ALF and EPLA units carried out a spectacular commando assault against the Ethiopian garrison at Dubte,
260 kilometers from Assab on the road to Addis Ababa.
At the end of the war the main ALF organization, led by
Habib Ali Mira, returned to Ethiopia and participated in
creating the country's new federal structure, winning
Ethiopian Afars the vast autonomous region finalized in

the territorial divisions of October 18, 1992, and accepting Eritrean control over Denkel in 1993. Other ALF splinter groups remain in exile, and the Ugugumo group of the ARDUF has been involved in armed clashed with Tigrean government forces as recently as 1996.

AFLENDA. A TIGRE-speaking tribe inhabiting northern SEMHAR, who numbered about 3,000 in the early 1960s. They have traditionally practiced seasonal cultivation and pastoralism between the Laba and Lebka rivers.

AGORDAT (Barka). The former administrative and commercial center of BARKA Province, now part of the Gash-Barka Administrative Region. Agordat is located on the main road from KEREN to TESSENEI, at the point where the Barka River debouches onto its vast plains. Because of its location astride ancient trade routes and its proximity to the river, the Agordat area has been inhabited since antiquity. A few kilometers from the present town was located the permanent camp of the DIGLAL, the leader of the BENI 'AMER, and an important regional animal market; but the town itself is a creation of ITALIAN COLONIALISM.

In June 1890 an Italian military expedition allied with the Beni 'Amer to defeat a Sudanese Mahdist army near Agordat, and built a small fort. On December 21, 1893, the Italians and their Eritrean ASCARI defeated a much larger Mahdist army in a bloody battle around the fort, after which Agordat developed as the center of Italian rule in the province of Bassopiano Occidentale, and the seat of the Residenze of Agordat, which included most of the Beni 'Amer lands. A hospital and Italian-Arabic school were built, and in 1928 the RAILROAD reached Agordat. By 1937 there were 2,000 residents, including 168 Italians, workers from other parts of Eritrea, Sudanese, Arabs, West Africans and others. By 1943 the population was 4,000, but only a few members of the Beni 'Amer elite (NABTAB) had residences in the town, while others camped on the outskirts during the winter dry season. Italian entrepreneurs such as De Ponti and Barzanti, developed banana and other fruit plantations along the river during the 1940s and 1950s, providing more economic growth, while the town's mosques and ARABIC schools, originally built by the Italian colonial regime, attracted Muslim preachers and students. By the Federation period, Agordat was a center of Beni 'Amer culture and politics and a bustling market town, whose leading figure was IDRIS MOHAMED ADEM.

During 1959-60 many of Agordat's police and government employees were organized by the ELM into "Harakat" cells; but in 1961, Idris M. Adam's political connections assured that the town became a principal center of early ELF organization. This was made apparent on July 12, 1962, when ELF operatives bombed a ceremony attended by the Imperial Representative, Gen. ABIYE ABEBE and the Eritrean Chief Executive, which killed four officials and was followed by police gunfire that wounded 60 civilians. Repression and guerrilla attacks continued through the 1960s, as Agordat developed into a major Ethiopian garrison. In 1974-75, ELF attacks around the town intensified, and on March 9, 1975 the Ethiopian army massacred 208 people, prompting the exodus to Sudan of most of the population. In September 1977 Agordat was liberated by joint ELF and ELF-PLF forces, but the town was recaptured by the Ethiopians in July 1978. It was liberated again on April 2, 1988, following the EPLF victory at AFABET. Today the town's hospital and secondary school have been refurbished and new offices opened by the Ministry of Agriculture, while many returning REFUGEES and impoverished pastoralists have settled in shantytowns around the outskirts.

AGRICULTURE. Cereal cultivation, along with PASTORAL-ISM, has formed the basis of the Eritrean economy since prehistoric times. During the colonial era a number of cash crops were introduced and today agriculture employs over 50 percent of the population, provides 50 percent of Eritrea's GNP and, together with pastoralism, 70 percent of its hard currency earnings.

The oldest evidence of cereal cultivation comes from the BARKA region, and dates to perhaps 5,000 B.C. Plough agriculture developed in the first millenium B.C. The most important ancient grain crops were varieties of sorghum, teff (the staple highland cereal) and wheat. By the AKSUMITE period these were being cultivated throughout the highlands with ox-drawn ploughs (*mehreshe*), using the same techniques of production that are still used by the majority of highland farmers today. In lowland areas, sorghum was and is grown along seasonal water courses by people who also practice seasonal pastoralism. Lowland agriculture traditionally relied on use of hoes, as well as camel-drawn scratch ploughs, with crops being planted to take advantage of seasonal rains and flooding. In all regions cereal crops are supplemented by vegetables, particularly *berbere* peppers, onions and garlic, which provide the basis for Eritrean seasonings. During the Italian colonial period two new food crops were introduced on a large scale, maize and "prickly pear" *beles* cactus, which became the FAMINE food of the highlands.

Cotton has been cultivated in Eritrea since ancient times, providing the raw material for a local textile INDUSTRY. During the colonial period large-scale cultivation of cotton was introduced around TESSENEI and ALI GHIDER, along with irrigated cereal production. Other commercial crops included fiber plants (agave), citrus trees and large-scale tomato production particularly in the KEREN and ELABERED areas. Coffee was introduced to the slopes of the SEMENAWI BAHRI, and bananas, guavas and mangos were grown in the GASH-SETIT, SENHIT and the foothills of SEMHAR. These remain the major commercial crops of Eritrea today, although the plantations and export marketing structuring developed by Italian entrepreneurs like BARATTOLO and DE NADAI in the 1950s-60s were largely destroyed in the war. The "traditional" agricultural sector of small-scale cereal production for subsistence and local-market consumption was also severely affected by the war and the terrible droughts of the 1970s and 1980s. During the 1980s there was an estimated 40 percent drop in food production and by liberation only an estimated ten percent of Eritrea's

arable land was under cultivation, while as much as 80
percent of the population was dependent on FOOD AID.
    Today the Ministry of Agriculture is headed by
Arefaine Berhe, and together with the Ministry of Land,
Water and Environment, headed by U.S.-trained
agronomist Tesfai Ghermazien (who served as Minister of
Agriculture from 1993-97), it is leading an agricultural
redevelopment program focused on the goal of food self-
sufficiency and export production. A series of irrigation
projects are planned to greatly increase grain production
in the lowlands, including a dam on the SETIT River and
expansion of the Tessenei-Ali Ghider complex on the
Gash, together with smaller projects along the Barka River
and the Wadi Project on the coastal Labka and SHE'EB
rivers. Export production of fibers, fruit and flowers have
been begun around Asmara and in Senhit, and they are expected to offset the costs of future food imports. Much of
the initial agricultural reconstruction work has been accomplished by FIGHTERS and NATIONAL SERVICE workers.
    Reconstruction has been slow, however. By 1993 only
342,000 hectares were under cultivation, and drought resulted in crop losses of up to 80 percent. Lack of
mechanized equipment and capital began to be remedied
in 1994, when the Ministry of Agriculture deployed 279
tractors and the African Development Bank provided a $8
million loan for agriculture. Cultivation expanded by 25
percent and together with a good rainy season grain
production increased to over 60 percent of food requirements in 1994. But despite funding from the World Bank
and bilateral Western loans, the development of the
western lowlands has been slow due to insecurity
resulting from Eritrea's current "cold war" with SUDAN.

AHMED AL-GHAZALI Ibrahim, Imam (AHMED "GRAGN").
The political leader of Adal, in the present-day Harar region, who organized the Muslim conquest of the Christian
highlands of Ethiopia and Eritrea from 1528-42. Imam
Ahmed was religiously inspired and received support
from TURKEY for his *jihad* against the Christian HABESHA

empire. He used Islam to unite most of the Somali and AFAR peoples of northeastern Ethiopia in his enterprise. His armies defeated those of the Shewan emperor in the 1520s and pushed into TIGRAI in the 1530s, razing Aksum in 1533. This brought his army into conflict with the Eritrean Christians, led by BAHRE NEGASHI Yesh'aq, who resisted Imam Ahmed's attempted invasion of SERAYE in 1533-34, together with the ADKEME MELEGA, led by Tesfa Leul. The defection of Tesfa's brother, Tewodros, in return for the title of Bahre Negashi, enabled Imam Ahmed to conquer the KEBESSA in 1534-35, although Seraye rebelled against him in 1536.

The years of Imam Ahmed's rule provided great opportunities for Muslim groups from the lowlands to expand onto the fringes of the Kebessa and the JIBERTI community grew at this time. In 1541 a Portuguese expedition commanded by Cristao da Gama landed at MASSAWA and allied with Bahre Negash Yesh'aq to defeat Imam Ahmed's armies at Haneza in AKELE GUZAI. Da Gama was killed in August 1542 near Makelle in Tigrai, but his men linked with Emperor Galadewos' forces and killed Imam Ahmed at a battle near Lake Tana in October, ending the Muslim occupation of the highlands.

AHMED "GRAGN" *see* AHMED AL-GHAZALI.

AHMED NASSER. Chairman of the ELF REVOLUTIONARY COUNCIL (RC), 1975-1982. Ahmed Nasser was born of SAHO parents in ADI KAIYEH in the late 1940s, and attended Haile Selassie I Secondary School in ASMARA in the 1960s. He joined the ELF in Sudan in 1967, receiving a military scholarship to IRAQ. He returned in 1971, joining the LABOR PARTY and participating in the ELF National Congress, where he was elected to the RC's Military Committee. Ahmed's secularism, multicultural background (TIGRINYA-speaking Muslim from the KEBESSA) and links with ABDALLAH IDRIS enabled him to win election as Chairman of the RC at the Second Congress in 1975.

During 1975-78, Ahmed led ELF unity negotiations with the EPLF and attempted to maintain a middle-ground in the ELF between right-wing Islamists and the left-wing Christian FALUL group, both of which he purged in 1977-78. But his effort failed in the military debacle of 1978, and his attempt to overcome internal weakness by opening separate negotiations with the USSR in 1980 led to the second CIVIL WAR with the EPLF. In 1981 he fled with other leaders to the SUDAN, but his attempt to maintain control over the organization was disputed by Abdallah Idris, who arrested him in March 1982.

In the ELF FACTIONS of 1983-85, Ahmed attempted to rebuild a secular, mainstream (Arab.: "Tayar") movement, reclaiming the title of ELF-RC and briefly working with OSMAN SALEH SABBE. During 1986-87 he negotiated with the EPLF for a new unity agreement, but rejected the EPLF's insistence on complete merger. He continued to take this stand even after most of the remaining non-Islamist factions joined the EPLF during 1991-93, and as of 1995 Ahmed remains in exile in SWEDEN leading a small, European-based ELF-RC faction highly critical of the PFDJ government.

AIRPORTS (and Air Force). Eritrea has two international airports: ASMARA (c. 3,000-meter runway) and ASSAB. These were both originally constructed by the Italian colonial administration in the 1930s, expanded by Anglo-American wartime contractors during 1941-43, and again under Ethiopian control during the 1960s-80s. The Italians also built military airfields at GURA' and MASSAWA during 1935-36, but these facilities were largely deconstructed by the BRITISH ADMINISTRATION during 1944-46, although a dirt strip remains at Massawa. Other dirt landing fields are located at KEREN, AGORDAT and TESSENEI, and a new dirt strip capable of accommodating jet aircraft has been constructed near NAKFA since liberation. Today, all airports, flight control and travel regulations are organized under the Civil Aviation Authority based at Asmara International Airport, where facilities have been extensively repaired and upgraded

during 1993-95. Eritrea is served by a number of foreign
carriers, and internal flights between Asmara and Assab
were begun in July 1994. There is, as of 1996, no Eritrean
national carrier, although a brief attempt was made in
1992 to lease a Chinese Boeing 707 by a private party.

During the ARMED STRUGGLE the Asmara airport
assumed great military significance as the base for
Ethiopia's air force in Eritrea. Air power was Ethiopia's
greatest military asset, and although it did not alter the
course of specific battles, it forced the Eritreans to use
time-consuming and force-dispersing tactics, as well as
inflicting terrible casualties on the civilian population of
the liberated areas. Beginning in 1979, the airport was the
target of increasingly destructive EPLF commando attacks.
The most important occurred on February 20, 1982, when
twelve aircraft wre destroyed in an attempt to blunt the
RED STAR CAMPAIGN; on May 22, 1984, when thirty
aircraft were destroyed or damaged and the ammunition
dump blown up; and on January 14, 1986, when forty
aircraft were destroyed, as well as fuel and munitions.
These attacks led to an increasingly large and heavily-
manned defensive perimeter around the airport and
reprisals against neighboring civilian settlements.

After the Battle of AFABET the EPLA deployed
newly-captured artillery around Durfo, below ADI NEFAS,
and on Adi Rasi mountain, which was seized in April,
1988. In May, long-range artillery bombardment of the
airport began, forcing the Ethiopian air force to move most
of its operations to Makelle in TIGRAI. The EPLA guns
were removed later in the year, following Ethiopian
counterattacks, but were reinstalled in 1990. With the
liberation of Massawa, the airport became Asmara's only
connection to Ethiopia, with an airbridge of Russian
transports and Ethiopian Airlines cargo planes bringing
in all military and civilian supplies, including food. In
March 1990 the EPLA guns at Durfo began an effective,
though desultory, shelling of the airport which reduced
the capacity of the airbridge. When Asmara was liberated
the EPLF captured five MiGs and two helicopters, as well
as some light aircraft, which today are the core of the

Eritrean national airforce. Eritrea has many skilled
pilots, aircraft technicians and flight control personnel,
as before 1975 Eritreans comprised much of the staff of
the Ethiopian national airlines and airforce, and even
today many Eritreans work in the air transport industry
in Ethiopia and overseas.

AKELE   GUZAI. The southeasternmost of Eritrea's three
historic KEBESSA provinces, now divided between the
Semenawi Keyih Bahre and Debub Regions (*s e e*
ADMINISTRATION). Akele Guzai boasts the country's
highest mountain (Amba Soira, 3018 m) and its most
important centers of ancient civilization. The name
derives from the legendary brothers, Akele and Guzai,
TIGRINYA-speaking descendants of the DEQI MENAB, who,
together with their younger relative SHIMEZANA, settled
the highlands between today's DEKEMHARE and SENAFE.
The "six sons of Akele" form the leading ENDA groups
(putative original settlers) of the northern region, while
the "five families of Guzai" form the leading endas of the
southern area, together with the "sons of" Akele-Meshal
and Akele-Akran.   Other descendants of the Deqi Menab
are said to have settled Meretta Sembene and Eghela, in
the   northwest.
       This legend demonstrates the close connections
between the Tigrinya populations of Akele Guzai and
HAMASIEN, but the origins of Akele Guzai's present
population are far more complex, including descendants of
the ancient LOGGO group in Loggo Sarda; the four SAHO
tribes of ASAWORTA, HASO-TOR'A, Irob and Miniferi;
and the mixed Saho-Tigrinya group of the "three sons of
Drar" (Tedrer) in the southwest.
       The geography of Akele Guzai has much to do with
its multi-ethnic population, and also reflects its ancient
development as a politico-economic unit. The province
comprises the region known until the fourteenth century
as "Bur" (see BURE PENINSULA), which ran from the
ancient port of ADULIS on the Gulf of Zula, down the
eastern spine of the highlands to the border of Agame,
where the present Ethiopian BORDER lies. The eastern

boundary was the Danakil depression and Gulf of Zula, and the western boundary the MAREB river. The province thus encompasses the ancient TRADE ROUTE from Adulis to TIGRAI, along which were located all the most important Eritrean towns of the SOUTH ARABIAN and AKSUMITE periods, including KOHAITO, Kaskase and MATARA. This highland spine remained the area of Tigrinya settlement through the present, but after the fall of Aksum Saho groups moved into most of the mid-elevation and lowland areas, including the coastal plains from ZULA to IRAFAILE, the eastern escarpment and the HAZAMO plains along the Mareb. By the fourteenth century Saho groups had settled the highlands as well, from Kohaito to Senafe, where they appropriated the ancient centers of civilization and intermixed with the existing population, as can be seen in the legends of the Loggo Sarda, Deqi Drar and Eghela-Hamus.

Perhaps due to the Saho presence, Akele Guzai was isolated from the rest of the central highlands, and even its Tigrinya population paid no tribute to Tigrean or Ethiopian rulers during the sixteenth to eighteenth centuries, maintaining a fierce independence and engaging in continual skirmishes with the people of SERAYE over grazing lands along the Mareb. The Tigrinya clans did unite occasionally to support their relatives in Hamasien, and particularly to fight off Tigrean invasions, such as that led by Sebagadis, lord of Tigrai, who was defeated at Adi-Da in Mereta Sembene. It was only in the mid-1840s that Dej. WUBE defeated the Akele Guzai clans at the BELESA River and forced them to pay a tribute of 1,000 MTTs per district (i.e. Akele, Guzai, Shimezana). During Wube's rule the CATHOLIC CHURCH's missionary Fr. DE JACOBIS founded a community at SAGENEITI which later made Akele Guzai the center of Catholicism in the Tigrinya highlands.

The legacy of regional independence was harnessed by Ras TESSEMA ASBEROM during the 1940s to make Akele Guzai less supportive of union with Ethiopia than other Tigrinya areas. But longstanding land conflicts between Saho and Tigrinya people, particularly the

TOR'A-TSENADEGLE and HAZAMO disputes, combined
with Muslim-Christian religious antipathies to undermine
any unity of political sentiment in the province during
the 1960s. As the ELF in Akele Guzai developed into a
Saho-dominated organization under ABDELKRIM AHMED,
Christian peasants actually increased their support for
the Ethiopian government and joined its BANDA militias.
With the rise of the EPLF, this religiously defined
cleavage became even more apparent, as the EPLF liberated
the largely Christian area from Tsenadegle north to
Dekemhare in 1977, while the ELF held the largely Saho-
Muslim southeast and Hazamo areas. This sectarian
division was most apparent in the ELF's failure to take
ADI KAIYEH, and was exploited by the Ethiopians in their
July 1978 reconquest of the province.

Years of brutal occupation and famine ruined Akele
Guzai during the 1980s, and the EPLF's second liberation
of the province during April-June 1990 was welcomed by
Muslim and Christian alike. Today, the tradition of Akele
Guzai independence lives on and is sometimes seen in in-
ter-Tigrinya rivalries, particularly with the people of
Hamasien (*see* MENKA), while continuing Muslim-Christian land disputes and the resource issues associated with
the old province's multiplicity of ecological zones were a
major factor in its division between two new administrative regions in 1995.

AKITO (Family). The AFAR descendants of Sultan Akito of
BEYLUL, whose son Mohamed ben Akito destroyed the first
Italian post left by Sapeto north of ASSAB in 1870. The
Sultan later accepted Italian rule, and one of his
grandsons, Mohamed Omar Akito became a leading member
of the Pro-ITALY Party in the 1940s, rallying much of the
Afar population of Assab first to the Italians and then to
the INDEPENDENCE BLOC. He was elected to the Eritrean
Assembly for Assab in 1952 and served until ANNEXA-
TION, when he was one of the few members to resist the
Ethiopian take-over.

AKSUMITE Empire and Civilization. A political system
and associated culture that dominated much of Eritrea
and TIGRAI during the second to eighth centuries A.D.,
centered on the city of Aksum in north-central Tigrai.
Despite many unanswered questions concerning the extent
of its formal political linkages, archaeology provides
indisputable evidence for the cultural homogeneity of a
region that extended from northern Eritrea to Amba Alagi
in Tigrai, and from the Takezze River in the west to the
Eritrean coast in the east. It is equally clear from numerous local and SOUTH ARABIAN inscriptions, coins and
foreign texts, that Aksum was the political center of this
cultural area for most of the period. Thus we may speak of
an "Aksumite" civilization in Eritrea until the early
eighth century.

At the dawn of the Aksumite period the region seems
to have been divided into a number of independent peoples
(*hezbi*) including the Aguezat, Tsireme, Agame, Gabaza,
and others. Inscriptions suggest that each of these peoples
had its own king or *negashi,* an office perhaps originally
associated with that of tax-collector during the South
Arabian period. Sometime during the first or second
centuries A.D., Aksumite political hegemony spread over
these autonomous peoples, who began to pay tribute and
provide soldiers to the *negashi negusti* or King of Kings in
Aksum.

Beside this common political organization, Aksumite
civilization was knit together by three important factors:
a flourishing COMMERCE; an official religion; and the development of a common written language. All of these seem
to have been developed by a stratum of the population who
had significant contacts with both the Semitic-Arabian
and the Greco-Egyptian civilizations of the ancient world,
both of which had important influences on the Eritrean
region in the pre-Aksumite period. These foreign influences were internalized through a process of cultural fusion with the dominant Cushitic cultural element in the
region to produce the quite original Aksumite or HABE-
SHA civilization.

The main artery of Aksumite commerce, and consequently of both external influence and political integration, ran along the TRADE ROUTE from the port of ADULIS
through the highlands of AKELE GUZAI to Tigrai, and
along this route we find the most important Aksumite
sites in Eritrea, including Tokonda, KOHAITO, Kaskase,
Adi Galamo and MATARA (see ARCHAEOLOGY). Another
trade route probably extended northwards through the
Rora area to present-day Sudan, because along this route
we find sites near ASMARA, at Deqemahare in DEMBEZAN,
and at Arotukh just outside HAL-HAL, Rora BAQLA and
HAGER NAGRAN. Aksumite exports were primarily elephant ivory, incense and gold; while imports were mostly
manufactured goods such as metalware, glassware and
textiles. This exchange of "raw materials" for "luxury
goods," indicates the existence of a wealthy and relatively
large urban population in the Aksumite region, for whom
commerce was important enough to induce Aksumite
rulers to mint their own coins (gold, silver, bronze) from
the third to eighth centuries. Aksum's commercial position was enhanced by the growth of maritime commerce
between India and the Mediterranean during the Roman
period, but its most important external links were with
EGYPT and the eastern Mediterranean.

Ideologically, the Aksumite empire was held
together before the introduction of Christianity by a
religion representing a fusion of the earlier South
Arabian pantheon with some distinctly Cushitic elements.
The main gods were Mahrem, the Aksumite dynastic god;
Aster, an ancient Sabean god associated with the evening
star; and the agricultural-fertility gods, Beher and Meder
(see MEDRI). In the late third century CHRISTIANITY
began to penetrate the region, and during the fourth
century the emperor EZANA officially converted, making
the ORTHODOX CHURCH the ideological bulwark of the
empire by the reign of KALEB (sixth century).

In a 1974 archaeological study, Anfray has
suggested that the Aksumite Empire was divided between
two cultural regions: a western region, containing Aksum
itself and most of northern Tigrai; and an eastern region

centered on Akele Guzai. During the early period, Anfray argues the western region was the most prosperous and powerful component of the empire, but during the later period (sixth to eighth centuries) the eastern ("Eritrean") region became the wealthiest and most urbanized. Thus, the high point of Aksumite civilization in Eritrea came between the 6th-8th centuries, after the empire's rulers had converted to Christianity, and during a period when Aksum dominated the southern Red Sea, even conquering YEMEN during the reign of Kaleb, and engaging in commercial and political alliances with the Byzantine Empire.

Soon after Kaleb the empire began to decline, beginning with the Sasanid Persian conquest of South Arabia (577-90), which spurred BEJA invasions of Aksum's northern territories and disrupted the foreign commerce on which Aksum's wealth depended. The rise of the Muslim-Arab empire along the Red Sea during the 630s, and their conquest of Egypt in 640-42, spelled the end of Aksum's vital commercial links with the Mediterranean, despite Aksum's initially cordial relations with ISLAM. From the mid-600s onwards a desultory naval war was fought between the Aksumite and Muslim fleets in the Red Sea, and around 702/3 Adulis was sacked by an Arab naval expedition, which also occupied the DAHLAK islands, effectively ending Aksumite naval power and curtailing its foreign trade. Finally, it appears that powerful Beja groups occupied or gained control over most of the Eritrean highlands during the eighth through ninth centuries, pushing the old Aksumite civilization further south into present-day Ethiopia.

By the mid-700s Aksumite coinage had ceased and historical evidence of the commercially based, urbanized Aksumite civilization in Eritrea disappears. Arab chronicles, our only available evidence, no longer mention Aksum; but Al-Yaqu'bi (c. 872) does cite a Habesha kingdom with its capital at Ku'bar, near the coast (the site is unknown, but is most likely in Eritrea). A regional political center certainly was preserved around Aksum in Tigrai, but there is little evidence of a political connection between it and present-day Eritrea. On the other hand, the Aksumite cultural heritage was preserved throughout the Eritrean highlands, including Monophysite Christianity, Ge'ez script and Byzantine-influenced art. The centers of this post-Aksumite culture were Christian monastic communities, the oldest of which seem to have developed in Eritrea around Hager Nagran, Debre Sina and DEBRE LIBANOS (Ham) between the sixth and ninth centuries.

AL-AMIN   MOHAMMED   SAID. A leading figure in the EPLF from its inception and currently secretary of the PEOPLE'S FRONT FOR DEMOCRACY AND JUSTICE (PFDJ). Al-Amin is from the Massawa area, and studied at the KEKIYA school where he was influenced by OSMAN SALEH SABBE. In the late 1950s he studied in Saudi Arabia, and joined the ELF in 1964. He went for military and medical training to Syria during 1965, and on his return he was attached to Zone 4, where he participated in the organization of the TRIPARTITE UNITY FORCES. In 1970 he went with Ali Mohamed Omero to Denkel, where he was elected to the leadership of the first PLF group at SUDOHA ILA. He was a member of the EPLF CENTRAL COMMITTEE from its inception, and after the break with Osman S. Sabbe, Al-Amin took over EPLF foreign relations, traveling extensively in the Arab world during the 1970s-80s, and even negotiating for freedom of transportation of FOOD AID with the DERG in 1985. He was a member of the EPLF Political Committee from 1975, and after liberation he was appointed to head the Department (later Ministry) of Culture and Information. At the EPLF's Third Congress he was the only member of the old Political Committee besides ISAIAS AFWERKI to be elected to the new PFDJ Executive Council, which then elected him Secretary, responsible for organizing the new party.

ALA. A broad valley east of the DEKEMHARE-Nefasit road, located near the border of HAMASIEN and AKELE GUZAI. During the 1940s it became a base for SHIFTA activities, and during March-November 1970, Ala was the base for a

group of some seventy dissident Christian ELF fighters
under the leadership of ABRAHAM TEWOLDE and ISAIAS
AFWERKI, who eventually joined the ELF-PLF. Again, in
June, 1977, several hundred Christian dissidents from the
FALUL group of the ELF retreated to Ala before joining
the EPLF. Ala remained an EPLF guerrilla base after the
STRATEGIC WITHDRAWAL, but was occupied by an
Ethiopian battalion from 1985 through November 15,
1987, when the battalion was destroyed by the EPLA.

ALGHEDEN. A small TIGRE-speaking ethnic group of
southwestern BARKA, who trace their origins to the
mounted warriors of the FUNJ empire. Some scholars believe they may also be remnants of an ancient Nilotic
population similar to the KUNAMA, ILLIT and Bitama. The
Algheden were incorporated into the BENI 'AMER under
Italian administration.

ALGHENA (Sahel). A village in northeastern SAHEL, located at the mouth of the canyon of the Felket river, where
this strategic valley opens onto the northern coastal plain.
The village developed after the Italians built a dirt road
from NAKFA along the Felket valley, which divided at Alghena with one branch heading northeast along the Felket
to Mersa Teklai on the coast, and the other running along
the base of the northern highlands to the Sudanese border
at KARORA.
  Because of its strategic location, Alghena was the
site of heavy fighting between Eritrean and Ethiopian
forces from 1979 through 1987 on what became known as
the Alghena or Northeast Sahel Front. The fighting began
with the fourth of Ethiopia's OFFENSIVES, when the DERG
landed troops at Mersa Teklai on March 30, 1979, and
pushed up the Felket valley with the aim of taking NAKFA
from the north. The EPLA counterattacked and drove the
Ethiopians back to Alghena by April 11. Further fighting
occurred in the area during July 14-26, and in January
1980 the EPLA counterattacked, driving the Ethiopians
back to Mersa Teklai with heavy losses, and capturing
much of their supplies. After this, the Eritreans retired

to the mountains and the Derg reoccupied Alghena, which
was built-up as a base for the Northeast Sahel. The next
serious fighting came when the Derg's RED STAR
CAMPAIGN failed to break through at Alghena.

In 1984 the EPLA launched a major offensive in
Northeast Sahel, using armor for the first time to sweep
across the coastal plain from Alghena to Mersa Teklai on
February 22, overrunning the Ethiopian bases and
eliminating 1500 Ethiopian soldiers and 25 armored
vehicles by March 21. The Eritreans then held Alghena
until October, 1985, when they withdrew to the mountains
during the Ethiopian Red Sea Offensive. The Derg
reoccupied Alghena and held it until March 1988, when
they were outflanked in the opening phase of the Battle of
AFABET. Today Alghena has a district administration
post and a small population of recently repatriated
REFUGEES.

ALI BEKHIT. A village in BARKA, west of AGORDAT, and
center of one of largest of the BENI 'AMER subtribes, the
TIGRE-speaking Ad Ali Bekhit. The Ad Ali Bekhit are one
of the four core sub-tribes of the Beni 'Amer and claim
close ties to the paramount DAGA sub-tribe. Because of
their favored location, most of the group became settled
agriculturists during the colonial period. Most fled as
REFUGEES to Sudan in the 1970s, where many remain, especially around Wad el-Hileau.

ALI GHIDER. The administrative and residential center of
the irrigated plantations developed by the Italians around
TESSENEI in the 1920s. The irrigation scheme using the
Gash river was first proposed in 1906, and in 1913 plans
for a dam and canals were completed. But disputes with
the British in neighboring SUDAN, together with the world
war, delayed the project until 1924. In 1926 cotton and
grain cultivation began, and when the dam was completed
in 1928 some 15,000 hectares came under production. The
plantation was managed by the parastatal Italian agency,
Societa Imprese Africane (SIA), which coordinated the
work of hundreds of tenant farmers who were provided

with loans, seeds, tools and water in return for a share of profits and SIA control over crops and marketing. Ali Ghider was created as a "company town" with housing for SIA managers and skilled employees, while the tenant farmers who worked the fields lived in neighboring "native" villages.

At Ali Ghider SIA built a school and clinic, which together with secure employment, attracted a multi-ethnic population from Eritrea and Eastern Sudan. Most of the Eritrean population was drawn from outside the western lowlands, and particularly from Senhit. The extended family of Shaykh Ad-Din, from the BET JUK, exemplifies the importance of this new multi-ethnic and educated community in creating the intellectual leadership of the western lowlands that was to play such an important role in the rise of the nationalist movement. Shaykh Ad-Din's daughters married SIA employees, including the fathers of IDRIS OSMAN GALADEWOS, Jaber Said and Omer Jaber, while his son Yasin, also employed by SIA, fathered AZIEN YASSIN, leader of the ELF LABOR PARTY. By the mid-1950s SIA employed 2,000 Eritreans, 15 Italians, and provided a residence for another 12,000 part-time workers and family members.

In 1965 the textile magnate, Roberto BARATTOLO, bought SIA and expanded cotton production using seasonal migrants from Sudan and TIGRAI. During the early ARMED STRUGGLE Barattolo paid protection money to the ELF, sparing Ali Ghider from attack until the plantations were nationalized by the DERG in 1975. After this, production ceased and much of the population fled to Sudan. Both the ELF (1977-78) and the EPLF (1984-85) attempted to organize cereal production on the plantations, but lost their crops top the Derg. In 1988 Ali Ghider came under permanent EPLF control, but large-scale production was made impossible by Ethiopian air raids.

In 1993 the Ministry of AGRICULTURE created the state-managed Ali-Ghider Agricultural Development Project to reconstruct the plantation with worker-shareholders farming the irrigated land in an arrangement similar to the SIA tenancy scheme. Canals were repaired

and the damaged reservoir reconstructed. The German
agency GTZ provided tractors and other equipment, and an
initial 735 hectares produced experimental crops of
cotton and sorghum. By 1995 production had expanded to
almost 6,000 hectares and most of the 1800 tenant-
farmers were demobilized FIGHTERS, along with a smaller
number of repatriated REFUGEES. Although state
agricultural workers operate much of the heavy
equipment, including new cotton ginning machinery, the
project is plagued by problems and tenant dissatisfaction,
and as of 1997 it has yet to produce an economically
viable crop.

ALI MOHAMED MUSA REDAI (1913-1974). Leader of
the MUSLIM LEAGUE of the Western Province and first
President of the Eritrean ASSEMBLY. Ali Musa was born in
KEREN, where he attended colonial school and became a
merchant. He was elected Secretary of the Keren branch of
the MUSLIM LEAGUE in 1946, becoming an influential
figure in the organization until he clashed with IBRAHIM
SULTAN ALI in 1950 in a personal conflict apparently
abetted by the BRITISH ADMINISTRATION, which had won
Ali Musa's tacit support for their plan to partition Eritrea
between SUDAN and ETHIOPIA. Ali Musa then formed the
Muslim League of the Western Province, which called for a
British trusteeship over the western lowlands, SAHEL and
SENHIT, pending their eventual merger with Sudan. Outright partition was never publicly advocated, because of
the recent war between the BENI 'AMER and their Hadendowa kinsmen in Sudan, but the new party captured four-
teen seats in the first Assembly, and formed a coalition
with TEDLA BAIRU's UNIONIST PARTY to insure pro-
Ethiopian control over Eritrea's autonomous government.
For this, Ali Musa was despised by his fellow Muslims,
and in July 1955 he was forced to resign along with Tedla
Bairu. The new Chief Executive, ASFAHA WOLDE-
MIKA'EL, gave him a cabinet post and he served the
Ethiopian government until 1974, when he was assassinated by the ELF.

ALI SAID ABDELLA. Founding member of the EPLF and one of the inner circle of the Eritrean government. Ali was born in 1951 in HIRGHIGO, the son of a SAHO shepherd. He attended the KEKIYA school through 11th grade and began working with the ELF in the mid-1960s as an underground organizer. In February 1967 he joined a field unit in Zone 4, where he worked with MOHAMED ALI OMERO and the TRIPARTITE UNITY FORCES. In 1969 he was recruited into the Akab ("Punishment") unit trained in Lebanon by the PLO to retaliate through international terrorism against the Ethiopian "scorched earth" campaign. In June his group bombed an EAL plane in Karachi, where they were caught and imprisoned for one year. When Ali was released in 1970 he rejoined OSMAN SALEH SABBE and went by sea to join the PLF group at SUDOHA ILA. He participated in the PLF field leadership's negotiations with Osman S. Sabbe in 1971-72, and when the various forces merged to form the ELF-PLF he was placed in charge of arms and other materials being delivered from Aden.

Ali supported ISAIAS AFWERKI during the MENKA dissidence in 1974, and by 1975 he was in charge of the EPLF security service. His position at the core of the EPLF was emphasized by his membership in the CENTRAL COMMITTEE through liberation, and his assignment to fill the position of IBRAHIM AFA as head of the Military Committee in 1985. He served in the military command, working particularly with military intelligence and security through liberation, when he was appointed to run the Department of Internal Affairs in the Provisional Government, becoming Minister of Internal Affairs after independence. He held this post until 1997, when he was appointed Minister of Trade and Industry.

ALULA Engda Qubi, Ras   (1827-1906). Born the son of a poor farmer in Tembien, TIGRAI, Alula "Wad Qubi" rose to become the most powerful military figure in the MAREB MELLASH during the reign of Emperor YOHANNES IV. In 1875 he distinguished himself against the forces of EGYPT at the Battle of GUNDET, and again in 1876 at the battle of

GURA', after which he led an expedition against Ras
WOLDE-MIKA'EL SOLOMUN in SENHIT. In August 1879,
Emperor Yohannes appointed Ras Alula military governor
(Tigrn.: "Shum Negarit") of Mareb Mellash, which he ruled
for a decade with a garrison of Tigrean troops. His first
act was to appease and then arrest Ras Wolde-Mika'el,
after which he consolidated his administrative control
over the highlands from his base at Adi Tekle, HAMASIEN.
In 1884 Ras Alula moved his capital to the village of AS-
MARA.

　　　After 1885, Ras Alula led Tigrean resistance to
ITALIAN COLONIALISM's encroachment on the highlands,
wiping out an Italian column at DOGALI in 1887. He
campaigned with Yohannes against the Mahdists in
western Eritrea, participated in the battle of KUFIT, and
led numerous raids on Senhit, Semhar, Barka and Gash-
Setit. In 1889, he took most of his soldiers to fight with
Yohannes at Metemma and the Italians took advantage of
his absence to occupy the highlands. When he attempted to
regain the territory in August his weak forces were no
match for the Italians and Eritreans under Maj. De Maio
and BAHTA HAGOS, who confronted Alula at Gura' and
forced him to retreat to Tigrai. The new Tigrean ruler, Ras
Mengesha, confirmed Alula's governorship of Mareb
Mellash until 1892, when he signed the Mareb Accord
relinquishing Tigrean claims to Eritrea. But Alula
continued to be a fierce opponent of the Italians, fighting
against them one last time at ADWA in 1896.

AMANUEL MIKA'EL ANDOM (1924-1974). Ethiopian
general and first Chairman of the Provisional Military
Advisory Council or DERG. Aman Andom was born in
Khartoum to parents who had recently moved from
TSAZZEGA to escape Italian discrimination. Aman obtained an English education in Khartoum, and in 1941
marched with Emperor HAILE SELASSIE I's forces into
Ethiopia. He attended a military staff college in England
in 1950, and served with the Ethiopian army in Korea,
rising to the rank of Lieutenant General in command of the
Third Division. In the 1964 war with Somalia his victories

earned him the sobriquet "Desert Lion," but his popularity, combined with liberal ideas and Eritrean background, disturbed the emperor, who retired him to the Senate in 1965. Aman was recalled to power in 1974 by the revolutionary Derg, who saw him as a useful figurehead, first obtaining his appointment as Chief of Staff on July 3, Minister of Defense on July 22, and electing him Chairman on September 12, the day they deposed the Emperor.

Aman's ideas concerning Eritrea remain a matter of dispute, but it is clear that although he proposed a negotiated political settlement to the ARMED STRUGGLE, he never supported Eritrean independence. He began to tour Eritrea in August-September, addressing mass meetings in ASMARA and KEREN, speaking in TIGRINYA and ARABIC, but calling for Ethiopian unity. In September he proposed a program of amnesty and administrative reform, including the appointment of Eritreans as governor and police commander, but all within the context of a united Ethiopia. His proposals were rejected by the liberation fronts after their cease-fire negotiations at ZAGHER, and on October 6 Aman returned to Asmara to hold a public assembly at the stadium, where he proposed a federal solution for Eritrea. This idea was rejected by both fronts on October 13, and thereafter Aman was reduced to attempting to block the movement of the Ethiopian First Division, which included his own supporters, to Eritrea. He opposed a "military solution" in Eritrea to the end, but clearly his Ethiopian nationalist sentiments were out of touch with the majority of Eritreans. On November 15 he resigned and retired to his home in ADDIS ABABA, where he was killed on November 23 in a shoot-out with soldiers attempting to arrest him.

AMDE SIYON (Emperor, 1314-44). The first of ETHIOPIA's Amhara or "Solomonic" Emperors to assert direct control over the Eritrean region, Amde Siyon occupied the central highlands and the coast around MASSAWA in 1325 as part of an expedition against the previously autonomous governor of Enderta in TIGRAI. In 1328 he revived the Zagwe title of MA'IKELE BAHRE for the governor of the region between the Takezze river and the Red Sea, appointing his son to the office, from which he attempted to control the Eritrean highlands and coast with a mixed force of Amhara and Tigrayan soldiers. The extent of imperial authority over the Eritrean region is unclear, however, as the coast was dominated by the Muslim Sultanate of the DAHLAK islands, and the highlands were relatively autonomous under the clans of ADKEME MELEGA and DEQI MENAB.

AMHARIC (Amharinya). A Semitic language related to GE'EZ and TIGRINYA, and the language of the dominant ethnic group in Christian ETHIOPIA, Amharic was the official administrative and educational language of Eritrea from 1959 through 1991. During the precolonial period, before the literary development of Tigrinya, Amharic was widely used alongside Ge'ez by literates in the Eritrean highlands. This led to the adoption of many Amharicisms in literary Tigrinya, which then penetrated popular speech after the FEDERATION with Ethiopia and the growing use of Amharic in government, education and business. An Amharic PRESS was developed by the UNIONIST PARTY in the 1940s, and Amharic weekly newspapers, including the official *Etiopiya* and *Zemen* were published until 1991.

Resistance to the use of Amharic was an important symbolic issue for Eritrean nationalists during the struggle for independence, while Ethiopian officials attempted to impose it at every opportunity. On May 9, 1960, the Eritrean ASSEMBLY made Amharic Eritrea's official language, after which an all Amharic curriculum was adopted in Eritrean schools during 1960-63, sparking numerous student protests. Students refused to study Amharic and often failed their exams as a consequence, but by the 1970s many highland Christians spoke Amharic in addition to their own languages, and Amharic literature, including popular novels, became the principal literary medium. Since liberation every vestige of Amharic has been expunged from Eritrea as a matter of national pride, but most highlanders are able to speak it and Amharic literature is still more widely read than Tigrinya.

ANDENET (Amh.: "Unity"). Originally the Youth League of the UNIONIST PARTY, Mahaber Andenet became the terrorist wing of the party operating under Ethiopian control during 1947-50. Also known as Mahaber Menze'e (Society for Breaking Free [from colonialism]), Andenet was organized in the summer of 1946 by the unionist faction of the MAHABER FEQRI HAGER, abetted by ETHIOPIA's liason officer, Col. Negga Haile Selassie. Andenet's president and vice-president were, respectively, Habtom Araia and Gebre-Selassie Garza, and its membership was recruited largely from unemployed Tigrinya/Christian school-leavers.

In July 1947 three Andenet members were arrested for terrorist attacks on anti-unionist Eritreans, including WOLDE-AB WOLDE-MARIAM. In November 1947 the SERAYE branch organized an attack on Muslim and LIBERAL PROGRESSIVE PARTY representatives at Teramni in Seraye, where the independents were waiting to address the FOUR POWERS COMMISSION of Inquiry. Following a number of terrorist actions against Italians and independents, culminating in the assassination of ABDULKADIR KABIRE, the BRITISH ADMINISTRATION outlawed Andenet and seized its offices on April 6, 1949. Its leaders were imprisoned and Col. Negga returned to Ethiopia for a short period, but Andenet continued as an underground organization, and was implicated in many more assassination attempts during 1950-51, including four on Wolde-Ab. Its imprisoned members were pardoned and released in late 1952, following the Ethio-Eritrean FEDERATION.

The name survived in Eritrean descriptions of any form of organized, pro-Ethiopian political actions or terrorism in the Federation and post-Federation periods. As late as 1968 the Ethiopian-organized anti-Arab riots, which led to the flight of most of the Yemeni merchant community, were popularly attributed to "Andenet."

ANDERGATCHEW   MESSAI, Bitwoded. Son-in-law of Emperor HAILE SELASSIE I, Andergatchew served as Imperial
Representative in Eritrea from 1952 to 1959. His office
was intended to represent the interests of the Ethiopian
crown within the Ethio-Eritrean FEDERATION, but Andergatchew from the beginning acted more as "Governor-General" than figurehead, moving into the colonial governor's
palace or Ghebbi, and delivering his first speech to the
Eritrean ASSEMBLY in AMHARIC, to the dismay of his au-
dience. He asserted Federal (Ethiopian) control over many
of Eritrea's assets, and in his third address to the
Assembly, on March 20, 1955, he made the Ethiopian
position on Eritrea's supposed internal autonomy explicit
by stating that, "as far the Office of His Imperial
Majesty's Representative is concerned, no internal or external affairs of Eritrea do exist or will in the future."

     Andergatchew was instrumental in destroying
Eritrea's autonomy in the Federation, but by 1959 his
arrogant manner was deemed counter-productive by the
Emperor, who replaced him with another son-in-law,
ABIYE ABEBE.

ANNEXATION (by Ethiopia). Eritrea's UNITED NATIONS-
mandated FEDERATION with Ethiopia was formally dissolved, and the territory was directly incorporated into
ETHIOPIA on November 15, 1962, following an
announcement in the Eritrean ASSEMBLY on the preceding
day that the Federation was "null and void."

     The formal annexation of Eritrea took place after a
decade-long Ethiopian campaign to dismantle the territory's autonomous institutions, culminating in a number
of attempts to bring the dissolution to a vote in the
Assembly, thus placing a cloak of decency over the coercive Ethiopian strategy. But nationalist pressure on the
members of the Assembly made such a vote impossible,
and not even the often claimed "acclamation" took place on
November 14. Instead, the Assembly was called to order
while Ethiopian soldiers paraded on the street outside and
the Chief Executive, ASFAHA WOLDE-MIKA'EL, read a
prepared speech announcing the Federation's dissolution

to the members, after which they were instructed to attend a reception celebrating "reunion with their motherland" at the palace of the Imperial Representative, ABIYE ABEBE, who became the province's new Governor-General. There they heard a radio speech by the emperor welcoming the Assembly's "vote" and "accepting" Eritrea's full union, which was made official the following day.

ANSEBA (River and Region). The most important river of northern Eritrea, the Anseba rises around Asmara and flows north through SENHIT and along the western side of the SAHEL mountains, joining the BARKA at the Sudanese border. The name derives from Ain-Saba ("fountain of Saba"), and is tied to the legends about Azieb, Queen of Sab'a. In 1995 the Anseba Administrative Region was created, comprising most of the northern highlands through which the river runs, with its capital in KEREN.

The Anseba valley forms an important route linking the central highlands with Sahel, and its fertile soil has been farmed for millennia. A number of ITALIAN COLONIAL agricultural concessions were developed in the valley, including those of the CASCIANI family around ELABERED and KEREN. The valley also saw a number battles during the war, including the Battle of Anseba in late December 1976, when EPLF forces defeated the Israeli-trained Ethiopian Nebalbal ("Flame") Division in the valley north of Keren, blocking the DERG's last attempt to relieve their garrisons in Sahel.

ANSEBA CONFERENCE (1968). A meeting of ELF representatives of ZONAL COMMANDS 3, 4, and 5 held along the northern Anseba on September 19, 1968. The meeting was an outgrowth of the AREDAIB meeting of July, in which the reformist or ESLAH elements criticized the existing leadership and called for a general meeting to reorganize the front. This threatened the position of the leaders of Zones 1 and 2, and the external offices, who postponed the meeting. In the end, it was only attended by representatives of the reformists, who used the meeting to create the TRIPARTITE UNITY FORCES.

ANTHEM. The Eritrean national anthem, "Eritrea," was composed in 1985/86 by Isaq Abraham, a noted organist and member of the EPLF cultural troupe.

ARABIC. One of Eritrea's nine indigenous languages, Arabic is spoken by the RASHAIDA people, but also by large numbers of Eritrean Muslims from other ethnic groups, and some Christians. Arabic has flourished along the coast and in the western lowlands as a language of COMMERCE and EDUCATION since at least the eleventh century. As late as the 1840s the English traveler Plowden noted that a "corrupt Arabic" was the language of most of the BENI 'AMER people. The traditional Muslim education system emphasizes the study of Arabic, and in the Eritrean lowlands literacy and knowledge of Arabic were largely synonymous until the colonial period. Arabic literature was generally imported until the development of a national PRESS in the twentieth century, and even then the focus of Arabic education was outside Eritrea.

Arabic was used in Muslim religious schools during the Italian period, but it was only in 1942, when the BRITISH ADMINISTRATION introduced a religiously divided educational system, that Muslim children were required to attend school in Arabic, instructed largely by Sudanese teachers, through Grade 4. Even in Asmara, where Muslims spoke TIGRINYA, this separation by religion was imposed, and the sectarian divisions which it reinforced exacerbated existing tensions between religious communities. In 1952 Arabic was designated one of Eritrea's official languages, and the linguistically segregated school system continued, although a standard curriculum was introduced in both Arabic and Tigrinya. The official use of Arabic was an important symbolic issue for the Muslim wing of the Eritrean nationalist movement, and Ethiopian disestablishment of Arabic's official status in 1959, followed by the imposition of all-AMHARIC school curriculums, reinforced Muslim support for the ELF's ARMED STRUGGLE.

In the ELF, the Arabic language issue became entangled in the wider politics of pan-ARABISM, with its concomitant, though largely unstated, corollary of pan-Islamism. Arabic was the ELF's official language until 1971, when Tigrinya was elevated to equal status, although Arabic remained the predominant language of the leadership. In the EPLF, on the other hand, Tigrinya was used predominantly, though the issue of "official" languages was left undecided in favor of a multi-linguistic policy emphasizing basic literacy in people's native languages, which for most Eritrean Muslims was not Arabic. This emphasis had two rationales, it appears. The first was that people learn most quickly in their own language; the second was to defuse the Arabic-Tigrinya polarization that had proved so damaging in the ELF by elevating other Eritrean languages, particularly TIGRE (the language most widely-spoken by lowland Eritreans), to literate mediums which had none of the external political associations of Arabic. This second emphasis was attacked by the rising Islamist forces among the ELF FACTIONS as an anti-Muslim policy, and the issue has been misrepresented for political ends by dissident groups like the Islamic JIHAD since liberation.

Since 1992 the government has asked each community to choose the language in which primary education is given. Many lowland communities have chosen Arabic, as it is still considered the language of education by the great majority of Muslims. Furthermore, the long residence of many Eritreans (c. 700,000) in Arabic-speaking countries during the war has led to a great increase in the use of Arabic, and for many returning REFUGEES, Arabic is their first language. The problem the government faces in terms of Arabic education is now a lack of trained teachers, as most of the Arabic-speaking intelligentsia remains abroad, and the majority of EPLF-trained teachers speak Tigrinya.

Another field in which the issue of the use of Arabic has been raised as a political grievance by Muslim dissidents is the ADMINISTRATION, whose middle levels are staffed disproportionately by Tigrinya speakers

drawn from the old EPLF. As many Arabic speakers as
possible have been assigned to lowland areas, but Tigrinya
remains de facto the language of administration even
there, and at the higher levels of national government this
mono-linguism is even more pronounced, despite the fact
that most senior officials are bilingual. Again, the major
problem is not a political policy by the government, which
is doing everything in its power to promote the use of
Arabic in all official and public mediums and functions,
but a lack of trained, Arabic-speaking cadres. An unfor-
tunate consequence of the rise of pan-Islamist politics in
the region, and particularly in Sudan, has been a reluctance on the part of many Arabic-speaking, educated Eritreans to repatriate, and this has been played on by the
misleading and inflammatory rhetoric of the Islamic Jihad
and other dissident groups concerning the status of Arabic in independent Eritrea.

The reality of current government policy is a
widespread campaign to promote the use Arabic, along
with other languages, in a multilinguistic and multi-
cultural state. Arabic is now taught as a subject in the
primary schools of the Tigrinya-speaking highlands. All
news media have broadcasts and publications in Arabic
parallel to and of equal status with Tigrinya. A national
conference on languages held in the summer of 1996 recommended that the government refrain from adopting any
official language as a means of defusing the tensions surrounding the issue of Arabic versus Tigrinya, and this
will almost certainly remain government policy for the
foreseeable future.

ARABISM (Pan-Arabism). The concept that Eritreans, or at
least the Muslim half of the population, are integral members of the "Arab world" rests, albeit somewhat
tenuously, on the historical use of ARABIC in the Eritrean
lowlands and longstanding economic and cultural links
between Eritrea and the Arab countries of the Red Sea
region. But the concept of Arabism as an Eritrean political
identity emerged only in the late 1950s, when some
Muslim Eritreans sought an ideology that could legitimate

their nationalist aspirations and provide them with external support against Ethiopian hegemony. In the largely secular, leftist and explicitly anticolonial pan-Arabist politics that were sweeping the Arab world at the time, IDRIS MOHAMED ADEM, OSMAN SALEH SABBE and CAIRO student leaders all believed they had found a bulwark for their Eritrean nationalism.

Both Idris Adem and Osman Sabbe were able to use their pan-Arabist slogans to obtain military training and support for the ELF from Arab countries, but their stress on Eritreans' Arab identity, which is found throughout their writing and speeches to the early 1970s, actually played into the hands of HAILE SELASSIE I's government. The Ethiopians resurrected ancient fears among highland Christians, dating to the days of Imam AHMED AL-GHAZ-ALI, of an Arab-Muslim invasion of the highlands, and used these fears to divide Christian and Muslim Eritreans. The DERG continued this ploy, and as late as 1991 Ethiopian soldiers were told they were fighting an Arab conspiracy to take their land. The divisive effects of this propaganda were heightened by the explicit strategy of EGYPT and SAUDI ARABIA to make the Red Sea an "Arab Lake" in the mid-1970s, following the reopening of the Suez Canal. Misunderstandings and animosities generated by both ELF pan-Arabist and Ethiopian anti-Arab propaganda campaigns still plague Eritrean political discourse to this day.

Within the ELF itself, the early leaders' pan-Arabism also proved divisive, as it alienated Christian recruits who became leading figures in the explicitly secular reform movement that generated the EPLF. After 1975, as the ELF became increasingly multi-cultural, pan-Arabist rhetoric was dropped by its new leadership. But it was resurrected again among some of the ELF FACTIONS following their defeat by the EPLF in 1981, which some blamed explicitly on the Christians in the front. At this point, however, the largely secular pan-Arabism of the 1960s was replaced with a more religio-centric pan-Islamic line (*see* ISLAMIST MOVEMENTS), reflecting the changing political climate of the Arab world. The debate over Eritrea's Arab identity was resurrected after independence around the question of membership in the Arab League, but the present government has given more weight to Eritreans' laregely non-Arab historic identity, rather than the pragmatic material advantages offered by membership in the League.

ARCHAEOLOGY. Despite its rich pre-historic, SOUTH ARABIAN and AKSUMITE sites, Eritrea has received relatively little attention from professional archaeologists. The only serious pre-historic work was done by Arkell around AGORDAT in 1942 and by Franchini and Tringalli in the highlands (especially AKELE GUZAI) during the 1950s. These, and a few less professional studies, including some recently undertaken by Eritreans attached to the Ministry of Culture, have uncovered many stone tools and cave paintings dating as far back as 5,000 B.C.

During the colonial era a number of larger expeditions investigated remains dating from the South Arabian and Aksumite periods, including the preliminary excavations around ADULIS undertaken by the Napier expedition (1868), Dainelli and Marinelli (1905), Littman and Sundstrom (1906), and Paribeni (1907). In addition to these expeditions, a number of amateur archaeologists surveyed sites and collected surface remains during the colonial period, including important inscriptions and statues from Adi Gramaten, Aratukh and Deqi-Mehare (Dembezan). Nonetheless, the only serious excavations yet to be carried out were those of the French-funded Ethiopian Archaeological Institute, led by Anfray, between 1959-72, concentrating on the MATARA site near SENAFE and, to a lesser extent, Adulis.

The excavations at Matara provide us with our most detailed evidence for the ancient history of Eritrea, together with the surveys produced by contemporary archaeologists such as Fattovich (1979) and Munro-Hay (1982), which are based on studies of earlier fieldwork, coinage and ancient texts; but the record requires much more field work. Extensive ancient sites remain entirely

unexcavated, including many in AKELE GUZAI (Adi
Gramaten, BA'DA, Fekya, Kaskase, KOHAITO, Tokonda,
Zala-Kesadmai, Zala Betmek'a), Aratukh in SENHIT, HAGER
NAGRAN and RORA Baqla in SAHEL, and Raheita on the
DENKEL coast south of ASSAB. Many early Christian sites
also require investigation, including DEBRE LIBANOS at
Ham (Akele Guzai), Debre Sina (Senhit), Enda Abba Garima
(SERAYE) and Enda Sadqan at Beraknaha (Akele Guzai).
Early Muslim sites in SEMHAR also need investigation,
and particularly the ancient and medieval remains on the
DAHLAK islands whose numerous gravestones have been
largely removed to museums (Massawa, Asmara and Europe). Basset (1893), Rosso (1937), Oman (1976) and others have sketched out aspects of Dahlak archaeology, but
systematic fieldwork is still required.

Many of Eritrea's recovered archaeological artifacts
were removed to the Ethiopian National Museum before
1975, but a quite extensive collection remained in the
Italian-curated Fernando Martini Museum in Asmara until
it was seized by the DERG. Most of the artifacts were
placed in storage, and after liberation they were put on
display at the new National Museum in the colonial Governor's Palace. During 1994, UNESCO funded Anfray to train
the Museum staff and prepare a report on "Preservation
and Presentation of [Eritrea's] Cultural Heritage," which
outlines needs and methods for protecting and investigat-
ing Eritrea's archaeological heritage, now overseen by the
Ministry of Culture.

AREDAIB (Meeting). On June 16, 1968, the commanders of
all five ELF ZONAL COMMANDS met at Aredaib in northern BARKA to discuss the problems raised by the reformist leaders of Zones 3-5 (*see* ESLAH). At Aredaib the
ELF commanders agreed to unify the guerrilla army, make
it autonomous from the much-criticized SUPREME COUN-
CIL, and promote correct behavior towards civilians. A
further meeting with broader participation and a mandate
to effect organizational restructuring was planned, resulting in the ANSEBA CONFERENCE of September. But the

changes outlined at Aredaib were resisted by the leaders of Zones 1 and 2, and the Supreme Council.

AREZA (Seraye). A market town and administrative center of Areza sub-province, located in west-central Seraye on the important road from MENDEFERA to TOKOMBIA. In the pre-colonial period Areza was the home of the rulers of Deqi Tesfa, the vast western district of SERAYE, occupying the broken mountain country that decends from the head-waters of the Obel River to the Dobene area along the Mai Ambessa and the foothills bordering eastern BARKA. This was a frontier region and refuge for HABESHA settlers from the central highlands during the thirteenth through sixteenth centuries, as the story of Areza's settlement by Tesfa, son of Senesghi, indicates.

By the eighteenth century Deqi Tesfa was ruled from Areza by hereditary chiefs (Shum-Gulti), who spread their authority over much of Seraye during the reign of Dej. WUBE. Areza suffered in the internecine wars of the mid-19th century, and was burned several times by the warlords of Seraye. During the reigns of emperors Tewodros and YOHANNES IV, the chiefs of Deqi Tesfa attempted to expand their power through marriage alliances with the leading families of TSAZZEGA and HAZZEGA. The Tsazzega union produced Dej. ABERRA KASA, while the Hazzega alliance involved Barambras KAFLE-YESUS, whose fortunes as shum-gulti rose and fell with those of his father-in-law, Ras WOLDE-MIKA'EL SOLOMUN. In the 1880s, both of these men lost political authority under the government of Ras ALULA and joined the Italians, who occupied Areza in 1890.

The town developed as a colonial post connected by road and telephone to MENDEFERA. The completion of a dirt road to Barentu increased its importance as a market town in the 1940s, but Deqi Tesfa remained remote from the more developed economy of the central highlands. Consequently, Deqi Tesfa became a corridor for early ELF penetration of the highlands during the 1960s; but tensions between Christian peasants and Muslim fighters led to a number of ELF attacks on villages west of Areza. This allowed the Ethiopian government to form BANDA of Christian villagers and construct a defensive chain of fortified posts across western Deqi Tesfa, supported by a garrison of COMMANDOS at Areza. Support for the ELF was never strong in Areza until large numbers of young Christians joined the front in the mid-1970s. The ELF liberated the town in 1977 and held it until July 1978, when it was retaken by the DERG, who made it an important garrison.

The EPLF occupied the area in 1981, and in June the first in a series of battles occurred around Mai Duma on the road to Tokombia. During 1984-85 heavy fighting occurred in the area as part of the EPLA campaign to liberate Barentu. On March 15-19, 1989, the EPLA overran Areza and drove the Ethiopian garrison back to Mendefera, but counterattacks followed and the town was not completely liberated until 1990. Today Areza is a growing commercial center, serving the cattle markets at Mai Duma and Tokombia, that provide much of the livestock for the highlands. The projected all-weather road from Areza to Tokombia will certainly increase its importance.

ARMED FORCES *see* ERITREAN PEOPLE'S LIBERATION ARMY (EPLA).

ARMED STRUGGLE (1961-91). The thirty-year war for Eritrean independence from Ethiopia is commonly referred to as "the armed struggle," a name which echoes the revolutionary ideology of the liberation fronts that led it. This war was the most important event in Eritrea's modern history, shaping the lives of every Eritrean who survived it. Almost 70,000 Eritrean FIGHTERS died in the war, and an estimated 100,000 Eritrean civilians perished. Ethiopian military casualties have been estimated at up to 150,000 dead. The Eritrean economy was largely destroyed during the war and almost one third of the population fled the country as REFUGEES.

Although the first shots of the armed struggle were fired by former SHIFTA leader, HAMID IDRIS AWATE, on September 1, 1961, the ELF was the driving force in beginning the armed struggle, as this was the centerpiece of their political strategy. ELF military strategy owed much to the Algerian revolution, whose organizational models it followed, and to the counseling of the aged Moroccan guerrilla leader Mohamed Abdel-Krim, who told Eritrean students in CAIRO that they had to begin the war on their own if they were ever to receive Arab support. During 1957-61, students participated in military training sessions on the outskirts of Cairo. The main thrust of ELF strategy was to gain control of the rural areas through guerrilla actions, and eventually isolate the Ethiopians in their urban bases, at the same time relying on external (Arab) support to provide weapons and training for a conventional army capable of finally defeating the Ethiopians. The ELF organized its campaign from KASSALA in the SUDAN, which provided a vital, though politically insecure, staging area for the Eritreans throughout the war.

From 1961 to 1974 the ELF fought against HAILE SE-LASSIE I's government in the first or "Guerrilla" phase of the war. During this phase the Eritreans employed hit-and-run tactics against police and military targets, from whom they sought to capture weapons. The guerrillas sustained themselves through raids and robberies of government property, "revolutionary taxes" and contributions from Eritreans, and external military aid provided by Arab sources (notably IRAQ and Syria) and CHINA. Beginning with a core of former SUDAN DEFENSE FORCE soldiers, the ELF grew to some 250 fighters by 1963, when the external leadership obtained its first outside arms supplies and the war spread across the western lowlands. By 1965 the ELF army numbered about 2,000 and the leadership reorganized it into regionally-based ZONAL COMMANDS. Fighters were initially recruited from lowland Muslims, but as the war spread a small number of Christians joined the front, along with many educated youths. The most promising of the new recruits were trained overseas, and they contributed substantially to the increased effectiveness of the ELF in the late 1960s, when the war spread to central Eritrea. At the same time, the incorporation of these better-educated youths led to internal struggles over strategy and ideology that resulted in the fragmentation of the ELF and the first of two CIVIL WARS between it and what was to become the EPLF.

Confronted with this widening guerrilla war, the Ethiopian government pursued a twin strategy of increasingly large-scale military sweeps of the Muslim lowlands and a divide and rule policy of propaganda and incentives designed to win the loyalty of Christian highlanders. Ethiopian counter-insurgency strategy was supported by arms and training from ISRAEL and the UNITED STATES, and was most effective under Governor ASRATE KASSA, who developed the Eritrean police COMMANDOS. His strategy was undermined, however, by the brutality of the Ethiopian army's Second Division, whose Vietnam-style "pacification" campaigns across the western lowlands in 1967, and through SENHIT and BARKA in 1970, further alienated the Eritrean population, including the Christians. By 1974, despite the fronts' civil war, the Ethiopian army was largely confined to its garrisons, could only travel in convoys, and was so demoralized that it led the February mutiny against the old regime.

The Ethiopian revolution marked a new phase in the war. Instead of leading to a political solution, it brought to power, by late November 1974, a militantly nationalist faction of the Ethiopian DERG committed to destroying the Eritrean guerrillas militarily; while on the Eritrean side a popular rallying to the nationalist movement in the Christian highlands ended the civil war and mobilized tens of thousands of youths to serve in the fronts. The hardening of political positions on both sides, combined with a rapid increase in military forces and a massive influx of new weapons to the Ethiopian side, produced a new phase of "Total War" which lasted from 1975 to 1991. This new phase, beginning with a joint ELF/EPLF attack around ASMARA in January 1975, can be divided into four periods from the Eritrean perspective: "First Liberation of Eritrea" (1975-77); "Ethiopian Counter-Offensive" (1978-83); "Stalemate" (1984-87); and "Second Liberation" (1988-91).

The Eritrean armies during the 1970s were increasingly dominated and directed by reformist elements in both the ELF and EPLF, but the two organizations had different degrees of military effectiveness. Beginning with a much larger fighting force (c. 5,000 in 1974), the less well organized and disciplined ELF failed to expand as rapidly as the EPLF as the two fronts vied to seize territory from the demoralized and outnumbered Ethiopian army during 1975-77. By late 1977, when 95 percent of Eritrea was liberated, the EPLF held all the major towns along the eastern escarpment and coastal plain, from NAKFA and KEREN south to DEKEMHARE, with the exception of ASMARA and the islands of MASSAWA. The string of victories that marked the EPLF's progress swelled its ranks to about 30,000 fighters. The ELF, which had liberated much of SERAYE, GASH-SETIT and all of BARKA, had only about 15,000 fighters. Disputes between conservative and reformist factions in the ELF sapped its strength and discipline, while rivalries between the two fronts kept them from forming a unified command. Thus, even as Eritrean nationalists seemed poised to win their armed struggle in late 1977, they were vulnerable to any shift in the military balance towards Ethiopia, which was in the process of defeating its Somali enemies and building a huge new army with massive support from the USSR.

An inkling of this growing threat came to the EPLF in December, when they suffered their first serious defeat in a bloody frontal assault on the Massawa naval base (*see* MASSAWA, BATTLES). As the next phase of the war opened in 1978, the differences in political and military strategy between the EPLF and ELF were exemplified by their response to a massive Ethiopian Counter-Offensive. Politically, the reformists who formed the EPLF attempted to build a strong popular base of support by providing rural Eritreans with HEALTH CARE, EDUCATION and reforms in LAND TENURE and women's rights that contrasted with the often coercive and rapacious methods of the early ELF. Militarily, EPLF strategy drew on the writings of Mao Zedong concerning guerrilla warfare, which they had encountered in their studies or through training courses in China. EPLF leaders planned a three-stage military strategy of "protracted people's war": beginning with hit-and-run guerrilla attacks and the development of rural bases; then moving to the "strategic defensive" in which a secure "liberated zone" is created and defended by larger military units; and finally moving to the "strategic offensive" in which conventional armies are created to surround and attack the enemy's urban bases, liberating them one by one. In 1977 the Eritreans believed they were well on their way to winning the last stage of the struggle; but as events proved, they were about to enter stage two: the "strategic defensive." The ability of the EPLF leadership to recognize this, and to conduct what Mao had called a STRATEGIC WITHDRAWAL to their liberated zone in northern SAHEL, enabled their organization to survive a Soviet-supported offensive deploying 120,000 Ethiopian soldiers and hundreds of tanks in the second half of 1978, while the ELF was all but destroyed.

The Ethiopian offensive hit the ELF first, in July, in Gash-Setit, Barka and Seraye, driving the remnants of ELF battalions back into the mountains of Sahel, and away from their supply routes in eastern Sudan. The EPLF evacuated Dekemhare as the Ethiopians rolled into AKELE GUZAI from TIGRAI, and made its first "strategic withdrawal" to strengthen its defenses north of Asmara, which held until the Ethiopian breakthrough at ADI YAQOB in November. Then the EPLF hurriedly retreated northwards into Sahel, fighting rear-guard actions at ELABERED, MES-HALIT and Kelhamet, until the fighters constructed a new defensive line on the rugged mountain tops around NAKFA, where they were joined by the remnants of the ELF in a desperate defense of their Sahel base area throughout 1979.

The stages of the Ethiopian Counter-Offensive were marked by a series of seven OFFENSIVES between 1978 and 1983, in which almost 30,000 Eritreans and over 50,000 Ethiopians died. The EPLF beat back the Ethiopian assaults, seized large supplies of Russian weapons in a December 1979 counterattack, eliminated its ELF rivals in

a second civil war (1980-81), defeated the Derg's massive
RED STAR CAMPAIGN in 1982 and emerged by mid-1983
as a unified, battle-hardened and politically-skilled nationalist organization which relied almost entirely on its
own resources and had no significant foreign supporters.
The ability of the EPLF to survive this period of international isolation and sustained military confrontation
along a 400-kilometer front where it faced the largest
army in sub-Saharan Africa backed by the might of the
USSR is one of the great feats of modern warfare, and it
instilled a confidence in the Eritrean fighters that enabled them to move to the offensive in the mid-1980s, despite the overwhelming military power of the Ethiopians.
By the same token, the Derg's inability to defeat the Eritreans demoralized their army, even as they deployed increasingly sophisticated weapons and strategies, including helicopter gunships, night bombers, airborne assaults
and para-commandos, as well as ever more armor and firepower. The seasoned Ethiopian regulars of the 1970s were
decimated in human-wave assaults around NAKFA, and
they were replaced by ever younger conscripts.
Commanding officers were executed when their attacks
failed, and the personal meddling of Mengistu Haile-
Mariam produced growing resentment amongst the Derg's
generals.
    The EPLF took advantage of these weaknesses during
the next, "Stalemate," phase of the war, as it continued to
follow Maoist tactics by deploying conventional forces to
defend its base area, while using guerrilla forces to attack
Ethiopian bases throughout the rest of the country, destroying aircraft, ammunition dumps and fuel supplies
even in Asmara and Massawa. Most of the population supported the EPLF, and the guerrillas had spies and sabo-
teurs at every level of the Ethiopian administration. Once
a stalemate had been achieved, Mao argued that the people's army should form "Mobile Forces" to attack key garrisons and provoke battles in which the enemy forces
could be worn down. During 1984-85 the EPLF engaged in
"Mobile Warfare" in the north and west, using armor and
mechanized units to overrun the ALGHEDEN Front and

liberate much of Barka, including TESSENEI and BAR-
ENTU, which were held until mid-1985. The stalemate
continued until December 1986, when the EPLA overran
Ethiopian positions below NAKFA in preparation for its
overwhelming victory at AFABET in March, 1987, where
the Eritreans destroyed an Ethiopian army corps and
captured enough heavy weapons to completely alter the
military balance.

The final phase of the war followed, in which the
EPLA switched to the "Strategic Offensive," liberating all
the northern and western parts of the country and nearly
seizing Keren in a fierce battle in May. The Derg, meanwhile, hastily negotiated a peace agreement with
SOMALIA, and rushed its divisions from Ogaden to Keren,
counterattacking in mid-May in a powerful offensive that
almost broke through to Afabet. A new front-line then
developed in the north, running from HAL-HAL along the
eastern escarpment to the coastal plain north of Massawa,
where the next Eritrean offensives were launched. The
Derg responded to its defeats with large-scale bombing of
civilian targets in the liberated areas and the execution of
more commanding officers. The EPLF leadership meanwhile pursued another of their long-term strategies by
supporting the growing dissident movements inside
Ethiopia led by the TPLF. In February 1989 EPLA armor
and artillery stiffened TPLF forces in the decisive battle
of Shire, which drove the Derg out of Tigrai province and
eliminated the Ethiopians' land connections to central
Eritrea.

As the EPLF gained control over more territory its
army expanded tremendously through recruiting drives in
the newly liberated areas, until by 1991 there were some
100,000 Eritreans under arms. The last battles of the war
were fought on a huge scale, involving hundreds of tanks,
artillery and rocket launchers and tens of thousands of
soldiers. In January 1990, after extensive preparations,
the EPLA launched its biggest offensive of the war, overrunning the Ethiopian defenses in Semhar and liberating
Massawa. The Ethiopian garrison in the central highlands,
which numbered at least 140,000 soldiers, was now

surrounded and only resupplied through Asmara airport, which came under Eritrean shellfire. In April and May the noose was tightened further as the EPLA liberated most of Akele Guzai and pushed the Ethiopians back to a new front between SAGENEITI and Dekemhare.

In early 1991 the DENKEL CAMPAIGN was launched along the eastern coast to seize ASSAB and cut off the last Ethiopian access to the sea. Eritrean units also accompanied the largely Tigrean EPRDF forces that were fighting their way towards Addis Ababa. On May 19, the EPLA launched its final assault on the DEKEMHARE FRONT, and after a bloody three day battle around GURA', Dekemhare was liberated on May 21, Mengistu fled from Addis Ababa, and the Ethiopian army disintegrated as its highest officers fled to DJIBOUTI by helicopter. On May 24, Eritrean forces rolled into Asmara on the heels of the Ethiopian forces in full retreat towards the Sudanese border. Assab was liberated the following day, and a last series of actions were fought around Barentu as EPLA units cut off the Ethiopian retreat and captured most of the garrison and their heavy weapons. The armed struggle was over.

ASAWORTA (alt.: Asaorta) The largest of the SAHO tribes, inhabiting the eastern escarpment of AKELE GUZAI and the foothills and coastal plain from the HADAS River to the vicinity of HIRGHIGO. The origins of the Asaworta seem to lie in a fusion between Arab immigrants and local Saho-speakers, and the tribe already dominated the caravan routes from the coast to the highlands in the fifteenth century. Taxes and raids on caravans, combined with agro-pastoralism, formed the basis of the Asaworta economy until the colonial period. The Asaworta were long allied with the NA'IBs of Hirghigo, and they were involved in continual border warfare with the TIGRINYA population of the highlands and the Tigrean governors of the MAREB MELLASH.

The Asaworta supported the Italians from the beginning, and consequently were allowed a large degree of internal autonomy until 1933, when the colonial government

united the five main Asaworta subtribes and their six
affiliate or "client" tribes under a single paramount chief.
The client tribes included the TOR'A Bet Sarah, the Idda,
Beradotta and Rezamare, all of which inhabited the northern fringes of Saho territory. By 1952 the Asaworta and
their affiliates numbered some 35,000 according to
British administrators. Their numbers and long association with the urban center of Hirghigo made the Asaworta
one of the most important Muslim groups supporting the
ELF during the early years of the ARMED STRUGGLE, and
they suffered from repeated Ethiopian attacks which
forced much of the population to flee to the Arab world as
refugees.

ASCARI. Eritrean soldiers serving in the regular Italian
colonial army were known as *ascari* (Arab.: "soldier"),
while irregular forces were called BANDA. Military recruitment was a key aspect of ITALIAN COLONIALISM in
Eritrea, leading some contemporaries to describe colonial
soldiers as Eritrea's "principal product." Between 1890
and 1941 over 130,000 Eritrean men served as ascaris.
This massive military recruitment had a significant impact on the Eritrean economy as it removed an average of
ten percent of the active male labor force from their homes
and injected a relatively large infusion of cash wages into
the colonial economy.

Recruitment began in 1890, when the first regular
Eritrean battalions were formed to replace the irregular
"bandas." By 1896 there were over 5,000 Eritreans
serving in the army which invaded Ethiopia, 2,000 of
whom died at the battle of ADWA. Eritrean ascari served
in the Italian occupation of SOMALIA, and during 1911-
32 a total of 60,000 ascari served in Italy's colonial
conquest of Libya. Until 1935 ascari were recruited
voluntarily, for the wages and chance to serve overseas
attracted many young men from every ethnic group and
region of Eritrea, but particularly from the military-
oriented precolonial aristocratic families. Ascari schools
were created to train soldiers in basic Italian and math.
Although Eritreans were not allowed to rise above the

rank of sergeant ("mumtaz"), many veterans were
appointed to positions in the colonial ADMINISTRATION
as orderlies and local chiefs, which added to the
attractions of military service within the constricted
world of colonial opportunities.

In 1935 conscription was introduced through quotas
set at the district level to raise an army of over 60,000 ascaris to serve alongside European troops in Mussolini's
invasion of Ethiopia. This represented close to forty percent of the active male labor force of Eritrea. The
attractions of military service lessened considerably as
the Fascists imposed a strict racial discrimination that
made life bitter for the ascari, and, combined with their
feeling of solidarity with Ethiopia, impelled several
thousand to desert to the Ethiopian side in the early days
of the war, including 904 on a single night on the Ogaden
front, and over a hundred with Andom Tesfazien on the
northern front. Many deserters, including Andom, went on
to become anti-Italian guerrillas in the "Patriot" army
that fought until 1941. The Italians attempted to offset the
possible military repercussions of desertion and sabotage
by segregating many of the ascari in separate Muslim and
Christian units. Many Muslims, who had little sympathy
for the Ethiopians, were assigned to the more sensitive
positions, such as artillery, while Christians were often
put in front line infantry units where they were used as
shock troops and sustained high casualties in the battles
around Tembien, where about 1,500 ascaris died.

After the occupation of Ethiopia many ascaris stayed
on to train and lead Ethiopian native units, while others
found low-level positions in the new colonial government.
When war broke out with BRITAIN in 1940, further recruitment and call-ups of veterans brought the number of
Eritrean ascaris again to over 60,000, but the defeat of
the Italians at KEREN in March 1941, in which several
thousand Eritrean soldiers lost their lives, ended the
colonial army. Over 9,000 ascari prisoners of war were
interned in SUDAN, where many worked on the British
cotton plantations; while the rest were demobilized without compensation, leading to widespread unemployment, a

rise in SHIFTA activities and the formation of the Pro-
Italy political party in 1947, led by ex-ascaris who hoped
to obtain pensions from a reinstated Italian trusteeship
government. In the 1950s a number of ascari did obtain
pensions, and in 1995 they were still collected in Asmara
by a dwindling group of aged veterans.

ASFAHA   WOLDE-MIKA'EL, Bitwoded (b.1914). The second Eritrean Chief Executive and key figure in the dis-
memberment of the Ethio-Eritrean FEDERATION, Asfaha's
career symbolizes HAILE SELASSIE I's recruitment of former Italian colonial functionaries during the 1940s, and
their rise to high political positions. Born in Akrur,
AKELE GUZAI, Asfaha was a devout Catholic who attended
the Italian primary school in SAGENEITI and served the
colonial government as an interpreter (1932-41).
        When Haile Selassie returned to power, Asfaha was
in Addis Ababa, where he joined the Ethiopian Ministry of
Foreign Affairs' team working to gain control over Eritrea,
becoming President of the government-sponsored Association for Uniting Eritrea with Ethiopia. Upon Eritrea's
federation with Ethiopia, Asfaha was appointed Imperial
Vice-Representative under ANDERGATCHEW MESSAI, and
retained this position evena after he was elected Chief
Executive by the Eritrean ASSEMBLY on August 8, 1955,
following the resignation of TEDLA BAIRU. Despite the
fact he had never held an elective position, he served as
Chief Executive until Eritrea's ANNEXATION in 1962,
which he helped to organize, and presided over the
dismantling of Eritrean political and social institutions.
He played a leading role suppressing the 1958 General
Strike and other early nationalist actions and organizations. After annexation he returned to government service
in Addis Ababa.

ASKALU   MENKERIOS. General Secretary of the National
Union of Eritrean Women (NUEWmn). Askalu left college
to join the EPLF in 1974 and was elected to the CENTRAL
COMMITTEE in 1977. She headed the administration of the
ERA's refugee camps in SAHEL and later the organization

and development of the NUEWmn (*see* WOMEN'S ORGANI-
ZATIONS). At the EPLF's Third Congress she was elected
to the Executive Committee, and she currently is one of
the most important women in the PFDJ.

ASMARA. Capital of Eritrea and largest city in the country, Asmara and its suburbs today form the separate Central (Tigrn.: "Maakel") Administrative Region. The city
has a population of approximately 460,000 and contains
80 percent of Eritrea's manufacturing INDUSTRY and most
of its modern service sector. It is the center of transport
services, informational media, telecommunications and
many government ministries.

   Asmara has been settled since the pre-AKSUMITE
period, but the Christian village around which the modern
city developed seems to have been founded in the tenth to
eleventh centuries, according to the records of its church,
Kediste Maryam (St. Mary's), which now stands at the
center of the city. The name "Asmara" is said to derive
from the consolidation of four Christian villages, whose
inhabitants fought amongst themselves. Legend recalls
that the women of the villages, reduced to misery by the
fighting and threatened with outside raids, forced the men
of the villages to unite, forming the new village of Arbate
Asmara ("the four [villages] of those [women] who brought
harmony"). The traditional date for this is Sene (June) 21,
1515, which is still celebrated in an annual ceremony at
Kediste Maryam Church; but the name Asmara certainly
predates this, as it is mentioned in an Italian itinerary as
early as 1411.

   Asmara developed as a market center, caravan stop
and "great city" by 1519, according to another Italian
source. It was located at the intersection of the growing
TRADE ROUTES between MASSAWA, DEBRE BIZEN and the
highlands, and the PILGRIMAGE ROUTES to SUWAKIN.
Because of its commercial importance, it formed a separate
RISTI-GULTI tribute unit of the Takle-Agaba district of
DEQI TESHIM, paying its tribute (GEBRI) directly to the
governor of MAREB MELLASH. The town was sacked and
the church burned by Imam AHMED AL-GHAZALI's

warriors in 1534, and the village seems to have declined after this, for European travelers make no mention of it before 1830, when the population was reported at 150. The modern development of Asmara dates to the Tigrean military governorship of Ras ALULA, who in 1884 built his residence on a fortified hill now crowned by water towers above the office of the Eritrean Mufti. Alula appointed as his *negadras* (commercial tax collector) an Eritrean merchant, Berhanu Hagos, who settled near Asmara (present Geza Berhanu quarter) where caravans coming from Massawa stopped to rest along the banks of the Mai Bel'a stream. Here a thriving market developed at what is now the commercial center of the city, and the village grew to some two thousand permanent residents by 1885, when Ras Alula also transferred his government and residence to Asmara.

The Italians occupied Asmara on August 3, 1889, and constructed several forts on hills around the town, with the largest, Forto Baldissera, on the former site of BET MAK'A. Barracks, offices and a European residential quarter developed to the south of Mai Bel'a as Asmara became the administrative and commercial center of the highlands. In 1900, when Gov. MARTINI transferred the capital of the colony to Asmara, it had a population of 5,500 Eritreans and 910 Europeans, roughly divided by the Mai Bel'a and commercial district, with Eritreans to the north, where the "native quarters" of the colonial city developed, and Europeans to the south. To the east, demobilized Eritrean BANDA settled in Geza Banda, while former ASCARI settled around the military hospital and stores ("Deposito"). The colonial city grew from 7,000 Eritreans and 1,500 Europeans in 1905 to 20,638 Eritreans and 3,101 Europeans in 1931. Its population was heterogeneous, with Muslims, Christians and foreigners from many lands, but the largest number of residents has always been TIGRINYA-speaking Christians from the surrounding highlands. This heterogeneity is today exemplified by the city's eleven mosques and over forty churches.

In 1935 the invasion of Ethiopia prompted a massive
building boom as tens of thousands of Italians moved to
the colony and Asmara became the transport and supply
center for a colonial army of 350,000. This influx, which
produced an Italian population of 55,000 by 1941, was
paralleled by a new Fascist policy of strict racial segregation, leading to the displacement of Eritreans from Geza
Banda and other neighborhoods, and a great expansion of
the European city southwards and eastwards. The Eritrean
population also increased to 120,000 by 1941, despite
overcrowding and racial discrimination, for the war boom
and light industrialization   produced a great demand for
Eritrean workers, servants and prostitutes. The Italian
defeat was followed by Eritrean political organization to
overturn the racial laws, and the growth of Italian-owned
manufacturing INDUSTRY and military employment during
the early part of the   BRITISH ADMINISTRATION. After
the Second World War, however, much of the Italian population began to repatriate and industrial employment
declined, curtailing further in-migration.

Asmara   experienced   serious   inter-communal
violence during the British period, most of it fostered by
the xenophobic policies of the pro-Ethiopian Unionist
movement and its terrorist wing, ANDENET. Anti-Arab
rioting by unionists in July 1946 was followed by the
death of four Christians, and then, on August 28, soldiers
of the Sudanese (see SDF) garrison massacred forty-six
Christians. Assassinations of Italians, Muslims and
Independents by Andenet followed during 1948-49, and
during February 21-23, 1950, bloody Muslim-Christian
rioting killed forty-seven during the visit of a UNITED
NATIONS investigation commission. Fortunately, much of
the bitterness created by these events was laid to rest by
religious and political leaders on December 31, 1950,
when they held a successful reconciliation conference
(Tigrn.: "Wa'la Selama") at Cinema Impero.

Unemployment increased during the FEDERATION,
as many businesses moved or closed, and the frustrations
of the population led to a General Strike against the
Ethiopian-controlled government in 1958 (see LABOR OR-

GANIZATIONS). By 1962 there were less than 10,000 Italians in a total population of some 150,000, but they continued to own most of the industries in the city, while the upper levels of the commercial sector were controlled by Europeans and Yemeni Arabs, together with some Eritrean Muslims. The UNITED STATES military communications base, KAGNEW STATION, provided one growing source of employment, as did the Eritreanization of the administration and municipal services. Middle-class Eritreans and Ethiopian officials moved into the villas of the former "European" quarter, and in 1968 business opportunities for Christians improved as Yemeni merchants were driven out in a government-orchestrated pogrom. Textile manufacturing provided low-wage employment to recent rural immigrants, particularly women, but economic growth could not keep up with job demands, and many skilled and educated Asmarans emigrated to Ethiopia and abroad, from where they sent back remittances to their relatives.

In 1974 the population was estimated at 200,000, but in January 1975 heavy fighting and Ethiopian massacres prompted the exodus of the remaining Italians and other foreigners, more of the skilled workforce, and tens of thousands of young people who left to join the liberation fronts. By 1977 the population was only 90,000. After 1979, when the DERG regained control of much of Eritrea, the population swelled to some 300,000, as rural families fled the devastating effects of FAMINES and war, and impoverished Tigrean immigrants came, with Ethiopian encouragement, to take advantage of wartime opportunities. Under the Derg the city was divided into nine zones and 36 subzones or *kebelles* ("neighborhoods"), and every aspect of daily life was controlled by ubiquitous Ethiopian security and party organs. Most of the population lived on FOOD AID and remittances from relatives in Ethiopia or abroad, or on their participation in the flourishing black market, bars and prostitution that catered to the huge garrison. Crime by soldiers was rampant, and houses were surrounded by barbed wire and iron sheets.

After 1988 the city was increasingly besieged, and
for the sixteen months before May 1991 it was cut-off
from all but air supplies, while the AIRPORT itself was
under shellfire. This was a particularly grim period for
the 280,000 Eritreans in Asmara, as food was scarce,
industrial and commercial activity virtually ceased and
curfews, shelling and Ethiopian killings kept people
locked in their houses. The outpouring of joy when EPLA
tanks rolled into the city on May 24, 1991, was
overwhelming, as hundreds of thousands of people
thronged the city center, mobbing the liberation army and
dancing for three days.

Since liberation a massive campaign of reconstruction has changed the dilapidated face of the city.
The municipal government has made it a matter of pride
that streets are repaired, buildings are painted and every
area is kept scrupulously clean. Automobile traffic, which
scarcely existed in 1991, has swollen, as has the number
of bicycles, Asmara's principal mode of transport.
Infrastructure repair, particularly of the water system,
has taken longer, and in 1993 pipes were still leaking 35
percent of the municipal water supply. The
nationalization of urban housing, carried out by the Derg
in 1975, was repealed in 1992, and the process of housing
reclamation and reconstruction began, including a major
high-rise apartment complex near the airport, completed
in 1996. But housing remains the city's biggest problem,
with an extreme shortage driving up prices while title-
disputes hinder new construction. As of 1996, urban
unemployment remains high, as the old and inefficient
industries nationalized by the Derg are slowly sold to
private investors and new ones have not been developed,
while the government's decentralization policy encourages
investment elsewhere.

ASRATE KASSA, Ras (1918-1974). Ethiopian Governor-
General of Eritrea from 1964 to 1970, Asrate, like his
predecessor ABIYE ABEBE, was a son-in-law of HAILE SE-
LASSIE I and member of the Shewan nobility. He attempted
to woo Christian Eritrean support for Ethiopian rule and

developed the Eritrean POLICE and COMMANDOS, introducing counter-guerrilla strategies, such as resettling Muslim pastoralists in fortified villages, and the use of economic incentives and psychological warfare. Asrate's policies were resisted by the military and a rival faction in the Ethiopian court, led by Prime Minister Aklilu Habte-Wold. Following the assassination of General Teshome Ergetu in November 1970, Asrate was recalled to Addis Ababa and removed from office, as the military gained control of the administration and declared Martial Law.

ASSAB (Denkel). The busiest port in Eritrea and most important foreign outlet for ETHIOPIA, Assab is located at the southern end of the DENKEL coast, facing the strategically important Straits of Bab al-Mandeb, the entrance to the Red Sea. Separated from the main population centers of Eritrea by over 400 kilometers of an almost roadless, desert coast, Assab developed closer economic connections with central Ethiopia than it did with the rest of Eritrea during the period 1938-91. Consequently, Assab symbolizes the issue of Ethiopian access to the sea, which drove Ethiopia's long struggle to gain and retain control over Eritrea. Today it is a free-port, used almost exclusively for the import-export trade of the ADDIS ABABA region. It also has Eritrea's only oil refinery, a modern SALT industry that largely supplies the Ethiopian market and a growing FISHING industry.

Because of Assab's proximity, voyagers from SOUTH ARABIA have visited the area since prehistoric times. Its name seems related to the ancient kingdom of SABA, and South Arabian settlements existed on the coast during the pre-AKSUMITE period. The trade route linking Assab with the highlands of central Ethiopia also seems to have been pioneered by merchants seeking ivory, gold and slaves in ancient times. By the fourteenth century Arabic sources mention the existence of an AFAR Sultanate of Assab, which continued until colonial times, although the neighboring Sultanate of BEYLUL was more powerful.

The attractions of Assab's strategic and commercial location were evident to early European explorers, and following the inauguration of the Suez Canal in 1869, the Italian missionary and colonial propagandist, Giuseppe Sapeto, purchased rights to the port and an offshore island in two agreements concluded with the co-sultans Hassan and Ibrahim in November 1869 and March 1870, for a total of 14,100 MTTs. On July 5, 1882, Assab was ceded to the ITALY, but it remained a colonial backwater, with a population of 136 Italians and 1,000 Eritreans in 1905, and only 58 Italians and 1,500 Eritreans by 1931.

The main Italian interest in Assab was to develop it as a port for central Ethiopia, rivaling France's virtual monopoly on the lucrative export trade of the region via the DJIBOUTI-Addis Ababa railroad. In 1924 Mussolini offered HAILE SELASSIE I a 99 year duty-free concession at Assab and the right to build a road linking it with central Ethiopia. The offer was reinforced in the 1928 Italo-Ethiopian Treaty of Friendship and Commerce, but was never implemented. Mussolini used this as one of his pretexts for invading Ethiopia, and after the conquest, in 1936, construction of a road from Assab to Desse and central Ethiopia became a priority project for the Fascists, who were literally bankrupting Italy by paying exorbitant tariffs on the Djibouti railroad to move the masses of goods their new empire required. Assab port was enlarged to accommodate modern shipping during 1938, and in July 1939 the road to Desse was completed. But the port's development as a major outlet for Ethiopian commerce had to wait another decade as Italy entered the Second World War and Assab was first blockaded, and then had its military airport and some of its port facilities dismantled and sold by the new BRITISH ADMINIS-TRATION.

By 1949, the Aden-based merchant, Anton Besse, was developing Assab as an alternative to the Djibouti railroad, and during the UNITED NATIONS debate on Eritrea's future several nations raised the idea of giving the port to Ethiopia even if Eritrea remained independent (*see* USSR). Assab came under Federal (i.e. Ethiopian) jurisdiction according to the Federal Act of 1952, but Haile Selassie took this a step further in 1953 when he made it a separate administrative unit under an Ethiopian military officer. In January 1954, when Muslim dock workers attempted to resist new Ethiopian labor regulations they were fired on by Ethiopian troops, killing three. Thereafter, Assab was developed as an appendage of the central Ethiopian economy, disconnected from Eritrea in all but name, and its commercial ties to Addis Ababa were reinforced by low customs duties, Yugoslavian-aided port expansion (1958-61), and U.S.-funded road construction (early 1960s).

By the time of full Ethiopian annexation in 1962, when Assab's population had grown to 10,727 and it was Ethiopia's busiest port, over 57 percent of its residents were Christians, and 44 percent were AMHARIC-speakers. The Afar population lived in a squalid shanty-town, Assab Sahrir, on the outskirts of the modern Ethiopian city. In 1965 Haile Selassie considered combining Assab with Wello Province, but relented under Eritrean pressure. In 1967 the importance of Assab was further increased by the construction, with aid from the USSR, of Ethiopia's only PETROLEUM refinery. The DERG was even more eager than Haile Selassie to detach Assab from Eritrea administratively, particularly as nationalist sentiments began to spread among the Afar population in the 1970s. By 1978 the closure of the Djibouti railroad had increased Assab's share of Ethiopian commerce to over 60 percent, and the Ethiopian government was studying ways to attach it to Wello province or a separate Afar political unit. In 1987 the Derg finally created an Assab Autonomous Region comprising most of Eritrean Denkel and parts of Ethiopian Dankalia, but it had little practical impact on the longstanding military administration of the port, which had grown into a major garrison and naval base.

EPLF assaults on the oil refinery began in 1977, culminating in a naval attack on April 23, 1988. Assab was liberated by the EPLA on May 25, 1991, at the end of its DENKEL CAMPAIGN. During the summer Ethiopian prisoners-of-war and 40,000 civilians were repatriated, many of whom took shelter in a refugee camp outside ADDIS ABABA, where they roused anti-Eritrean sentiments. These sentiments were exacerbated by problems in the movement of goods and petroleum products through Assab during the rest of the year, resulting in serious shortages in Addis. The EPLF administration in Assab had to grapple with a number of technical problems, a shortage of trained personnel, and uncertainties concerning the distribution of goods between the Eritrean and Ethiopian economies. In June 1992 a comprehensive agreement was concluded with the Ethiopian government making Assab a free port through which all Ethiopian imports/exports pass duty free. Ethiopian customs agents collect their own duties at the port, where Eritrean authorities levy transit and port fees to pay operating costs. Since independence, roughly 95 percent of the goods passing through Assab have gone to Ethiopia.

ASSEMBLY, Eritrean (1952-62). The legislative body of the autonomous Eritrean government under the Ethio-Eritrean FEDERATION. The Assembly came into existence under UNITED NATIONS' supervision through a series of elections in March, 1952, which chose representatives for a constitutional assembly. Only the cities of ASMARA and MASSAWA had direct, secret elections, while the rural areas chose their representatives through electoral colleges of local notables. The elections were held under a BRITISH ADMINISTRATION Electoral Proclamation (121) which remained the basis for electing the Assembly throughout its existence, as the Ethiopians blocked ratification of the organic Electoral Law envisioned by the UN.

The 68 members of the First Assembly were evenly divided between Muslims and Christians, with 32 members of the UNIONIST PARTY, 18 members of the Eritrean Democratic Front (*see* INDEPENDENCE BLOC), 15 members of the MUSLIM LEAGUE of the western Province (MLWP), and 3 others. The Unionists dominated the Assembly through an alliance with MLWP, which enabled these two parties to elect their leaders, TEDLA BAIRU and

ALI MOHAMED MUSA REDAI, to the offices of Chief Executive and President ("Speaker") of the Assembly. In May the Assembly began to debate the draft CONSTITUTION prepared by the UN Commissioner, Anze MATIENZO. The Eritreans succeeded in retaining some symbols of autonomy, but the real power in the FEDERATION devolved to the Ethiopian government. In July the Assembly ratified the Constitution, transforming itself into Eritrea's legislature.

The First Assembly contained a number of leading nationalists, including IBRAHIM SULTAN ALI and IDRIS MOHAMED ADEM. The Chief Executive's dictatorial methods, combined with growing Ethiopian interference, led to a revolt in the Assembly in 1955, which forced the resignation of Tedla and Ali Musa Redai. Although Idris M. Adem was elected speaker, he was powerless to block increasing Ethiopian domination under the new Chief Executive, ASFAHA WOLDE-MIKA'EL, and was removed in June 1956 during a heated fight over implementation of an Electoral Law. Without such a law, Asfaha was able to pack the Second Assembly with pro-Ethiopian candidates in the elections of September 1956.

The Second Assembly was led by its Unionist Vice-President, Aba DIMETROS GEBREMARIAM, who overshadowed the new President, Shaykh Hamid Farej Hamid of the MLWP. Aba Dimetros allied with Asfaha to push through legislation further weakening Eritrea's autonomous status, including the anti-labor "Employment Act" of March 1958; the annulment of the "Eritrean Flag, Seal and Arms Act" which replaced Eritrea's symbols of sovereignty with those of Ethiopia on November 14, 1958; and the replacement of Eritrea's official languages with AMHARIC on May 9, 1960. Other acts concerning law enforcement further relinquished Eritrean autonomy.

The Third Assembly, elected in August 1960, was even more subservient to the Ethiopian crown, but nonetheless obstructed attempts by Aba Dimetros to bring to a vote the dissolution of the Federation during 1961-62, when members adjourned the Assembly or failed to attend in numbers sufficient for a quorum. Finally, in late

1962 Gen. ABIYE ABEBE's regime began a campaign of intimidation and bribery, including the promise of payment of their salaries for life, to force the members into accepting complete union with Ethiopia. Although a formal vote was never taken, on November 14, 1962, all but three members attended the final session in which the Assembly was dissolved and Eritrea formally annexed (*see* ANNEXATION). Among those absent was the Assembly's President, Hamid Farej Hamid, who feigned sickness. One member, Osman Hamed Hindi of Massawa, attempted to speak against annexation, but was silenced.

AZIEN   YASSIN. A leader of the intellectual left-wing of the ELF, Azien was born into the prominent BET JUK family of Shaykh Ad-Din in ALI GHIDER in 1941. He attended high school in Sudan and entered Khartoum University in 1960, where he established ties with the SUDAN Communist Party (SCP) through the student movement. He graduated in 1965 and joined the ELF, who appointed him to head the Information Department of the Revolutionary Command in KASSALA. Here he developed the Marxist ideology of the reformist movement and was instrumental in forming the clandestine LABOR PARTY.

In 1971 he was elected to the ELF Executive Committee, and led the ELF Information Department through 1980. Azien participated in negotiations with the EPLF (1977), East Germany (1978) and the USSR (1980), with the latter two facilitated by his ties to the SCP. He remained a member of the mainstream ELF-RC (Revolutionary Command) led by AHMED NASSER until the United Organization was formed in 1984, after which he was associated with continued efforts at unity. Suffering from diabetes, Azien moved to SAUDI ARABIA to work as a journalist, where he currently resides. He was appointed vice-chairman of the Eritrean Constitutional Commission in March 1994.

- B -

BAB   JANGEREN (Senhit) *see* JANGEREN.

BA'DA (Denkel). Located on the edge of the DENKEL desert at the foot of the eastern escarpment of AKELE GUZAI, Ba'da is inhabited by the Dahimela AFAR. Its permanent water supply has made Ba'da a site of human settlement since ancient times, with remnants from the SOUTH ARABIAN, AKSUMITE and medieval Christian periods scattered through the area. Its remoteness and water led the ELF to use it as a base, and it was the scene of fighting between the ELF and EPLF in 1980, and between the EPLF and a faction of the AFAR LIBERATION FRONT in 1984. Since liberation an irrigation canal has been built and agricultural production has increased.

BAHRE NEGASHI (Tigrn.: "Lord of the Sea"). Title of the governor of the central Eritrean area from the coast around MASSAWA and ZULA to the MAREB River, being the district often referred to as MAREB MELLASH. The title first appears during the reign of ZARA YA'QOB in the late 1440s, when it superseded the earlier title MA'IKELE BAHRE. The Bahre Negashi was initially an imperial appointee, dependent for his office on the Ethiopian Emperor and the governor of TIGRAI. By the early 1500s the Bahre Negashi's capital was located at DEBARWA. With the destruction of the Ethiopian state by Imam AHMED AL-GHAZALI in the 1530s, the Bahre Negashi Yesh'aq became autonomous, and from this time onwards the title usually was held by the leading MEKWENENTI families of the central highlands, either through their own autonomous power or in alliance with the rulers of Tigrai. The attempts of the Eritrean Bahre Negashis to maintain their autonomous rule over the Mareb Mellash, centered on HAMASIEN, is the main theme of highland Eritreans' history through the early nineteenth century.

   Often the Bahre Negashi sought foreign allies to buttress his power vis-à-vis the rulers of Ethiopia and Tigrai. Both Bahre Negashi Yesh'aq (1559) and Bahre Negashi Yohannes Akai (1632) protected Jesuit priests who had been expelled from Ethiopia (*see* CATHOLIC CHURCH). The independence achieved by the Bahre Negashi's of

TSAZZEGA in the seventeenth century was undermined in
the mid-1700s by the rise of Tigrean power under Ras
Mika'el Sehul, who deposed Bahre Negashi Bokru of
Tsazzega in favor of a candidate from the rival house of
HAZZEGA, initiating a power struggle for the office
between the rival mekwennenti families that sapped their
resources and facilitated the consolidation of Tigrean
control over the highlands in the nineteenth century. This
struggle reached its high point during the leadership of
Dej. HAYLU TEWOLDE-MEDHIN and Ras WOLDE-MIKA'EL
SOLOMUN, by which time EGYPT was attempting to appoint
its own Bahre Negashis in rivalry with the Tigreans, and
the title had depreciated to the point that several Bahre
Negashis held office simultaneously, with very localized
and limited political authority. The last Bahre Negashi
was Ras Wolde-Mika'el, who died in exile in Ethiopia.

BAHTA HAGOS, Dejazmach. Leader of the most important
rebellion against ITALIAN COLONIALISM, Bahta Hagos
today symbolizes the tradition of resistance to outside occupation that has united Eritreans from the highlands
and lowlands, but he also represents the contradictions
faced by nineteenth-century Eritrean leaders squeezed
between far stronger powers on the coast and in
ETHIOPIA.
      Bahta was born in SAGENEITI during the mid-1800s,
when Bishop DE JACOBIS was building the CATHOLIC
CHURCH in AKELE GUZAI. Bahta converted to Catholicism,
and he rose to prominence in 1875 when he killed the son
of a Tigrean lord, Ras Araya, whose soldiers were raiding
the area. He and his two brothers fled from Tigrean
reprisals to Agameda in the adjoining lowlands, where
they became SHIFTA (bandits) and allied with the
ASAWORTA to raid Tigrean caravans. Bahta grew famous
for his military skills and sense of justice, and made an
alliance of convenience with the Egyptians at Massawa. In
1880, after Ras ALULA consolidated his power by
eliminating Bahta's supporter Ras WOLDE-MIKA'EL
SOLOMUN, Bahta and his followers fled to northern SEN-

HIT, where they were welcomed by the BET ASGHEDE, whom they protected from raids.

In 1885, Bahta, like many Eritrean leaders, joined the Italians at Massawa, where he was appointed Capo di BANDA. In 1889 his banda formed the left flank of the Italian invasion of the highlands, occupying Akele Guzai, over which the Italians appointed him chief with the title of Dejazmach. Because of his Catholicism and record of service, he was considered the most loyal of Eritrean chiefs; but Italian land confiscations, womanizing, arrests of other leaders and failure to uphold his paramount claims against the traditional democratic institutions of Akele Guzai, all pushed Bahta towards rebellion. He secretly co,ntacted the rulers of TIGRAI, and on December 14, 1894 he led his banda of 1,600 men in open revolt, seizing the Italian Resident. Some Akele Guzai chiefs supported him, while others (notably TESSEMA ASBEROM) supported the Italian force which immediately marched against him. After releasing his captive and abandoning Sageneiti to the oncoming column, Bahta attacked the Italian post at Halai, where he was killed on December 17. His brother Sengal and 400 men retreated to QWATIT where they continued the rebellion, precipitating the Italian invasion of Tigrai in 1895 and their debacle at ADWA in 1896.

BAITO (Tigrn.: "assembly" or "council") *see* NATIONAL ASSEMBLY; LOCAL GOVERNMENT.

BANDA. Irregular Eritrean militia units from the colonial era. In 1885 the Italian colonial army began to recruit and arm irregular Eritrean forces known as "banda" under their own leaders, such as ABERRA KASA, BAHTA HAGOS, HADGU-AMBESSA and KAFLE-YESUS. The banda were housed and trained on the plains of Otumlo, outside MASSAWA, and participated in the occupation of KEREN (1888) and the highlands (1889). Initially banda leaders were given positions of authority over their home districts; but in 1890 the Italians began to arrest the banda leaders and disperse their followers. By 1895 the banda

were dissolved, and many of their soldiers were incorporated into Italian-officered units that fought in the ADWA
campaign.
    During the 1960s the Ethiopian government revived
the formation of local "banda" militia units composed of
armed Christian peasants in an attempt to block ELF
infiltration into the highlands and to further their policy
of supporting Christians against Muslims in a strategy of
"divide and rule." Banda forces were mobilized
particularly on the eastern and western fringes of the
highlands, against SAHO pastoralists in the TSENADEGLE
and HAZAMO areas of AKELE GUZAI, and across the Deqi
Tesfa and QOHAIN districts of SERAYE, where banda were
recruited to man a cordon of fortified Christian villages
during the late 1960s. With the politicization of the highlands in 1974-75, however, many of the banda deserted to
the liberation fronts. The DERG tried to revive the banda
strategy in the 1980s using FOOD AID to recruit a "wheat
militia."

BAQLA (Sahel). RORA Baqla in SAHEL is an area of the
Rora Habab plateau, that, together with neighboring Rora
Laba, is rich in artifacts from the AKSUMITE period, including stone lions and GE'EZ inscriptions. The remains of
churches at Rora Endlal and Rora Baqla attest to the importance of the region as a market center and way-station
on the Christian PILGRIMAGE ROUTE to SUWAKIN. By the
9th century the name Baqla figures in Arabic descriptions
of the BEJA kingdoms of the region, and travelers' accounts note it through the medieval period. During the
following centuries the mixed Beja-TIGRE population
seems to have adopted PASTORALISM as its dominant mode
of existence, and the HABAB people of today seem to be
the direct descendants of the TIGRE-speaking Baqla
culture.

BARATTOLO, Roberto (b. 1909). A leading figure in the
Eritrean textile INDUSTRY, Barattolo came to Eritrea in
1934 and developed a commercial agency. Unlike many
Italians, after the Second World War he amassed capital in

Eritrea and took advantage of the economic opportunities presented by the FEDERATION to build ASMARA's first cotton textile factory, relying on a silent partnership with the family of HAILE SELASSIE to smooth any political difficulties. Production began in 1956 and Barattolo was successful in gaining a large share of the Ethiopian market. In 1965 he bought the SIA cotton plantation at ALI GHIDER and also began exporting knitwear to Europe and the Middle East. The factory employed almost three thousand workers, 70 percent of whom were women. Barattolo was able to keep wages low and overcome the workers' LABOR ORGANIZATION through his political connections, but in 1975 the factory was nationalized by the DERG and Baratollo departed, eventually receiving compensation from the Italian government.

Although it was renamed Asmara Textile Co., the factory is still called "Baratollo" by Eritreans. It was the site of one of the bravest civilian acts of the ARMED STRUGGLE during February-March 1982, when workers struck against the Ethiopian management's demand for unpaid labor. The military intervened and seventy-five workers were taken to the notorious MARYAM GHIMBI prison. During the 1980s production declined as machinery deteriorated, and today the state-owned factory is in need of refitting and large-scale investment. The government turned-down Baratollo's offer to buy it back at a discount in 1992, but it is still scheduled for privatization.

BARENTU (Gash-Setit). The administrative center of Gash-Barka region (and formerly of GASH-SETIT province) and the commercial center of southwestern Eritrea, serving the KUNAMA and NARA peoples, Barentu is situated on the main road from AGORDAT to TESSENEI. The site was called Bia Ara by its Kunama inhabitants, but its modern development began in the early 1890s, when an Italian fort was built nearby, along with a CATHOLIC CHURCH and the administrative post of the colonial Residenze. By the late 1930s, agriculture and gold MINING in the district had encouraged local commerce, and the town had over a thousand residents, including 75 Italians. Continued economic growth and a school attracted 5,000 residents by 1962, when the beginning of the ARMED STRUGGLE led to Barentu's development as a garrison for Eritrean police COMMANDOS, some of whom were locally recruited, and Ethiopian army units. Animosity between the Kunama and the ELF was encouraged by the growing Ethiopian military presence, and during early 1978 a combined ELF-EPLF siege failed to take the town, which was ringed with Ethiopian fortifications.

The EPLF returned to the area in 1984, and on July 6, 1985, captured the town, killing over 2,000 Ethiopian soldiers. Fourteen Ethiopian counterattacks followed until the EPLF was forced to withdraw on August 25, 1985. The DERG retained Barentu until March 31, 1988, when they abandoned it, taking many of the residents with them to Asmara, where they settled around HAZ-HAZ. The town was held by the EPLA until liberation, but in May 1991 there was a final battle on its eastern outskirts as the Ethiopian army fled towards Sudan. Today Barentu is a lively commercial center housing the offices of several agricultural programs, and its growing population includes many repatriated REFUGEES.

BARKA, River (Arab.: *baraka,* "blessing"). The name of the major river (Khor Barka) of northwestern Eritrea, which rises on the western edge of the central highlands and flows north into SUDAN, where it feeds the cotton plantations of the Tokar inland "delta." The river gives its name to the vast plains in the northwestern region of the country through which it flows, and to the Barka sub-region of the Gash-Barka Administrative Region.

The Barka region forms a natural route from the Nile Valley to the Eritrean/Ethiopian highlands, and has been settled since prehistoric times. Its location accounts for its mixed population of TIGRE-speakers, descended from Semiticized highlanders, and BEJA-speakers from northeastern Sudan. The BENI 'AMER, who represent a fusion of these peoples, make up the bulk of the agro-pastoralist population, along with smaller groups of NARA

and HEDAREB. During the fifteenth to nineteenth
centuries these groups all converted to ISLAM under the
influence of Arabic-speaking tribes and individuals from
eastern Sudan. Barka came under the rule of EGYPT during
the mid-1800s, and after a brief penetration by Mahdists
from the SUDAN, it was occupied by the Italians in 1890-
94, who administered it as the Residenze of AGORDAT.

Barka remained a separate administrative region or
province until 1995, and it was a center of early resistance to Eritrea's annexation by Ethiopia. Its people were
staunch supporters of the ELF, who controlled much of the
province from 1962-81, and whose FACTIONS continued to
operate in the province even after it was occupied by the
EPLF during 1984-85. Much of the province's population
fled as REFUGEES during the war, and today there are perhaps 150,000 residents, most of whom live in the southeastern corner between Agordat and Bishia. This is the
only area of the province with any modern infrastructure,
and the potential for irrigated agriculture along the river
valley remains largely undeveloped, though plans are being made to build roads and small dams in the remote
central and northern regions. In January 1993 a Barka
provincial assembly was elected with 73 members, which
advised the new provincial governor, Alamin Sheikh Saleh.
In June 1994 elections were held for local councils in the
province's eighteen districts, which in 1995 were incorporated into the new Gash-Barka Region.

BARYA. (alt.: Baria). The commonly-used TIGRINYA and
TIGRE name for Eritrea's NARA ethnic group. The name
was once synonymous with "slave," and retains a
pejorative connotation today. Nonetheless, the name is of
great antiquity, appearing first in a tenth century
description of one of the BEJA kingdoms of the western
lowlands.

BAZA (alt. Bazen). The commonly-used ARABIC and
TIGRINYA name for the KUNAMA ethnic group. Like
BARYA, the name has a pejorative connotation because of
the enslavement of Kunama people by Arabs and

highlanders, although it does not literally mean "slave" in either of these areas.

BEJA. An ethno-linguistic group of great antiquity originating in Northeastern Sudan, between the Nile and Red Sea. The Beja language belongs to the Northern Cushitic branch of the Afro-Asiatic language family. Over the centuries, Beja divided into a number of regional dialects, or sub-languages, of which HEDAREB is currently spoken in Eritrea.

The Beja people played an important role in the history of the Eritrean region during the late AKSUMITE/early medieval period, when they conquered much of the area and created a new cultural fusion that in some ways set the region apart from the lands south of the MAREB River. At the beginning of the Aksumite period Beja people, organized into a number of matriarchal tribes and worshipping a pagan pantheon, seem to have already long occupied parts of the SAHEL mountains and lower BARKA valley. Towards the end of the seventh century one tribe, the Zanafadj, moved up the Barka valley into SERAYE, and from that point on the Beja expanded across the Eritrean plateau, apparently seizing (and perhaps destroying) centers of Aksumite civilization.

By the ninth century Beja immigrants seem to have occupied the main Aksumite centers of AKELE GUZAI and the coastal plain of SEMHAR, and they apparently formed a ruling strata over the existing population. In 872 Al-Ya'qubi described the Beja kingdoms and tribes between the Nile and Red Sea, several of which contain names clearly related to modern Eritrean peoples and regions, including Hedareb, Manasa (*see* MENSA'), Baqlin (*see* BAQLA), Bazin (*see* BAZA). Jarin apparently covered much of Senhit and SEMHAR, while Qat'a was described as Christian and subject to the Aksumite king. The many traces of Beja place names in the central highlands indicate a mixed Beja/HABESHA culture developed there during the ninth through eleventh centuries, while in the northern highlands the Beja dominated TIGRE-speaking tribes.

By the twelfth century the politically dominant Beja element in the region were the BELEW. After the sixteenth century the BENI 'AMER confederacy of the Western lowlands incorporated most of the Beja-speaking groups in present-day Eritrea. ISLAM spread among the Beja peoples from the tenth century, but many traditional Beja religious beliefs and practices were retained far into the nineteenth century, and a significant degree of syncretism remains among some of the Beni 'Amer and other originally Beja groups to this day. Over the last two centuries an accelerating process of linguistic "semiticization" and Islamization has resulted in the eclipse of the Beja language in Eritrea, until at present only the Hedareb ethnic group retains its To-Bedawe tongue, although many Beni 'Amer are bi-lingual in Beja and Tigre, and also ARABIC.

BELESA River. A tributary of the MAREB in southern AKELE GUZAI, the Mai Belesa forms the Eritrean border with Ethiopia as far as its headwaters near ZELAMBESSA, after which the border is defined by the Mai Muna as far as the DENKEL depression.

BELEW (alt.: Bellou, Balau, Belo). An important historical group of mixed BEJA-Arab origin. The Belew dominated much of Eritrea during the twelfth through fourteenth centuries, and continued to form an important component of the BENI 'AMER people and the NA'IBs of Semhar. The origins of the Belew are often traced to pre-Islamic Arab immigrants from the Yemen area. According to the Sudanese historian Amarar, the name "Belew" stems from the Beja word for speakers of a foreign language, "Belaweit." The original immigrants intermarried with Beja people and eventually seem to have divided into two tribal groups, the more northerly HEDAREB in the Red Sea Hills of Sudan, and the more southerly Belew in the present Eritrean-Sudanese border area and northern Eritrea.

The historical development of a Belew kingdom in Eritrea is poorly documented, but by the fourteenth century there is evidence of a Christian Belew state in the

area from northern SEMHAR west to BARKA. During the
fifteenth century these Belew rulers, who seem to have
formed an aristocratic stratum over TIGRE-speaking
clients, converted to Islam. In the sixteenth century Belew
domination of what is now northwestern Eritrea was
overthrown by the FUNJ and their Sudanese Arab allies,
who incorporated some of the Belew into the Beni 'Amer
tribal confederation as an "intermediate class." At the
same time as TURKEY occupied the coast, some Belew
families regrouped in HIRGHIGO and by the late 1500s
their leading family had obtained appointment as the
Turks' local political representative, the NA'IB. From this
point on the ethnic name Belew is associated with the
family of the Na'ib in Eritrean history, and during the
seventeenth to eighteenth centuries some Belew moved into
the eastern highlands under the Na'ib's patronage. The
name "Belew" also has lingered in a number of Eritrean
place names, sometimes indicating an earlier Beja presence (but not historically Belew) as when it is associated
with the other Beja tribal name, Kelew, which, according to
A. Paul, originally indicated a Beja tribe from the Gash
and Barka valleys.

BELEZA (Hamasien). A village in KARNISHEM, north of
ASMARA and site of the city's major reservoir and electric power station. The village was of little importance
until its people befriended Protestant missionaries from
SWEDEN in the 1860s, and allowed them to build a
mission there in 1872. The mission was persecuted and
abandoned during the reign of Ras ALULA, but reopened
in 1890 and soon started the first girl's school in the
highlands. Beleza became the center of the Swedish Evangelical Mission's (SEM) highland parish and in 1897 the
center for translating Christian literature into TIGRINYA.
In 1900 a seminary was opened that evolved into a
teacher's training college providing the highest level of
EDUCATION available to native Eritreans before its closure by government order in 1935.

       In 1918-19 the Italian SEDAO company built three
reservoirs on land taken from the village and neighboring

ADI NEFAS. A hydroelectric plant was added in 1920, and expanded several times as a power source for Asmara. The strategic importance of the village made it a site of several battles in 1975, when the Ethiopian garrison lost it for several months to the EPLF. Today its school provides intermediate level education for Karnishem district, and the reservoir has become a popular picnic site for Asmara residents.

BENI 'AMER. The largest tribal confederation in Eritrea, dominating BARKA province, and spilling into Eastern SUDAN north of KASSALA. Composed of BEJA and TIGRE-speaking peoples inhabiting Barka, northern GASH-SETIT and western SAHEL and SENHIT, the Beni 'Amer polity came into existence in the sixteenth century, when the FUNJ and their Sudanese Arab allies, the Ja'alin, defeated the BELEW rulers of the area.

The legendary founder of the confederation was 'Amer Kunu, said to be the son of a Muslim holy man of mixed Beja-Ja'alin descent and a granddaughter of the last Belew king. His father was killed by the Belew, but 'Amer returned with a Funj-Ja'alin army to defeat them. According to tradition, 'Amer's descendants (Arab.: Beni 'Amer) formed a new ruling class, the NABTABS, each of whom created their own autonomous sub-tribe, loosely allied in the Beni 'Amer confederacy under the rule of the DIGLAL, the paramount chief who collected and paid tribute to the Funj sultan in Sennar.

The most striking aspect of the traditional Beni 'Amer political system was its inequality. The Nabtabs monopolized all political power and formed a ruling caste who never made up more than ten percent of the confederation's population. The remainder of the people came from the Beja and Tigre-speaking population of the conquered area, who were attached to each of the Beni 'Amer clan unit as "serfs" owing labor, livestock and animal products to their masters, to whom they and their descendants were bound for life. Because the majority of the Beni 'Amer practice PASTORALISM, the "serfs" were able to own property, such as livestock, and they received military protection from the Nabtabs. Over the centuries, a number of impoverished people from neighboring ethnic groups also became enserfed in return for Beni 'Amer protection.

The Beni 'Amer remained nominally tributary to the Funj until their defeat by EGYPT in 1821, after which Egyptian rule and a more orthodox ISLAM slowly spread through the mid-1800s, encouraged by the MIRGANIYYA Sufi brotherhood. The Beni 'Amer fought against the Sudanese Mahdiyya in the 1880s, and allied with ITALIAN COLONIALISM to defeat the Mahdists at AGORDAT. The Nabtabs were able to retain their influence under Italian rule as salaried chiefs, but by the late 1930s their power was being challenged by a rising group of merchants and civil servants of "serf" or "Tigre" origins.

The Beni 'Amer were shaken by the events of the Second World War, when they supported the Italians while their traditional rivals across the Sudanese border, the Hadendowa, supported victorious BRITAIN, setting off a series of cattle raids and an inter-tribal war that lasted until 1945. At the same time, the "serf" class challenged the continuation of their status under the new BRITISH ADMINISTRATION, and IBRAHIM SULTAN ALI led a serf emancipation movement that soon formed the base for the MUSLIM LEAGUE in western Eritrea. The Nabtabs consequently turned to the UNIONIST PARTY to assure their traditional positions, and a political split developed that spilled over into the pro-Ethiopian politics of the MUSLIM LEAGUE of the Western Province during the FEDERATION period. Nonetheless, the majority of Beni 'Amer were firmly opposed to Ethiopian annexation, and it was among the Beni 'Amer of Barka that the ELF formed its first underground networks and guerrilla bases at the beginning of the ARMED STRUGGLE. The Beni 'Amer consequently suffered increasing Ethiopian reprisals during the 1960s, and fled as REFUGEES to Sudan from 1967 onwards. The Beni 'Amer also provided much of the leadership of the ELF, including IDRIS MOHAMED ADEM and ABDALLAH IDRIS, and tribal connections were important in the patronage networks they constructed. Neither of these men returned to Eritrea after 1991, and today many Beni 'Amer remain in Sudan.

The traditional "serf" system was finally ended during the armed struggle by the actions of the liberation fronts, although its manifestations linger in issues of prestige among some groups. Today the major Beni 'Amer constituent sub-tribes ("badana") are the DAGA (the DIGLAL's badana), the Ad ALI BEKHIT, Ad Gultana, Ad Ibrahim, Ad Omar, Ad Sheraf (reputed descendants of the Prophet Muhamad), Ad 'Umr, Ad 'Uqud (composed of five sections), Beit Awat, FAIDAB and LABAT, along with smaller badana, some of which have separated from other sub-tribes in the last century, and others which are related to neighboring tribes, such as the AD SHAYKH. Although the formal political structure of the confederacy no longer exists, the Beni 'Amer identity persists, even among former "serf" peoples.

BEREKET HABTE-SELASSIE. Chairman of the recent Constitutional Commission and a leading figure in the wartime campaign to draw world attention to Eritrean claims to sovereignty. Bereket was born in ADI NEFAS in 1932, the son of Protestant preacher Keshi Habte-Selassie Gulbet, who was a leading Unionist during the 1940s. In 1948 Bereket obtained a scholarship to attend the University of London, where he won a degree in Law in 1956 (and a Ph.D. in 1967). He returned to Ethiopia to work in the Ministry of Justice, rising to Attorney General in 1962. He was instrumental in aiding Ethiopian (and Eritrean) LABOR ORGANIZATION and in other attempts to build the institutions of civil society in the empire, but resigned his position in 1964 to protest the emperor's policy in Eritrea. He was banished to Harar in 1967, but in 1968 was appointed mayor of the city. He then served in the Interior Ministry, until he took a job with the World Bank in 1972.

Bereket participated in the early phase of the Ethiopian revolution along with General AMANUEL MIKA'EL ANDOM, but fled to join the EPLF in late 1974, where he helped to organize the ERITREAN RELIEF

ASSOCIATION (ERA), and served as its first chairman.
During 1975 he also helped broker negotiations between
the ELF and EPLF, but in early 1977 he moved to the U.S.,
where he became a professor at Howard University and began publishing a number of books and articles, organizing
conferences and enlisting the aid of a growing community
of foreign scholars in publicizing the Eritrean struggle.
His writings cover most of the legal history of the Eritrean
FEDERATION and Eritrea's place in world politics. During
1985-91 he represented the EPLF before the UN. In March
1994 Bereket was appointed Chairman of the Commission
to draft Eritrea's CONSTITUTION. He holds an endowed
chair in African Studies at the University of North
Carolina, Chapel Hill.

BET ASGHEDE. The three SAHEL tribes of HABAB, Ad
Tekles and Ad Temaryam form the Bet ("House of") Asghede, an historical figure who migrated from ADI NEFAS,
to the RORA of Sahel in the sixteenth century. Though
there are many legends about Asghede, it seems most
likely that he was the leader of a military contingent sent
from the TIGRINYA highlands to secure control of the
historical Christian PILGRIMAGE ROUTES through the
northern highlands. He and his Christian followers settled
around Rora BAQLA and formed a military aristocracy,
the SHUMAGULLE class, who ruled the indigenous TIGRE-
speaking people. The Tigre, who were already Muslim pastoralists, became "serfs" required to provide the
Shumagulle with livestock, labor obligations and even,
according to legend, the "first night's right" to their
virgin daughters.
    Over time the descendants of Asghede divided into
the three tribes mentioned above, with the Habab forming
the largest and most powerful group. By the mid-
nineteenth century the ruling class, which already had
adopted the language of their Tigre "serfs," also converted
to Islam under the influence of the AD SHAYKH. The
disabilities of the "serf" class were eroded with time, and
during the ARMED STRUGGLE, when the EPLF controlled
the area, the old social divisions were ended and the

tribal system replaced with village and district councils elected by all the people. The Ad Temaryam remain pastoralists who move from the coast through the mountains to the BARKA plains in seasonal migrations; while the Ad Tekles are largely sedentary agriculturists in the valleys of southern Sahel. By the early 1950s the Bet Asghede numbered some 42,000, with the Ad Temaryam numbering 7,000 and the Ad Tekles 10,000. Today their herds are greatly reduced from the years of war, fought largely in their homeland, and many are REFUGEES in Sudan.

BET JUK. A small tribe living in the ANSEBA valley of southern SENHIT, centered around the village of Wasentet, just north of KEREN. The Bet Juk claim descent from Christian TIGRINYA-speaking settlers from the village of Qwanduba in HAMASIEN, who settled the area in the 1600s and formed a military aristocracy or SHUMAGULLE class over the indigenous TIGRE people, who were known as Seb-Medir ("people of the land") and became "serfs" owing services and livestock to the Shumagulle.

Like the neighboring MENSA', the Bet Juk were Christians until the mid-1800s, when they converted to ISLAM under Egyptian rule. During the colonial period they produced some Islamic scholars who founded the Bet Juk Institute in KEREN, a leading theological school. At the time of Federation the tribe numbered some 4,000 people, most of whom were farmers. The ARMED STRUGGLE took a heavy toll on the Bet Juk, as the people supported the ELF from the beginning, and the Ethiopian front-line passed through their lands from 1988-91. At the time of independence many of their villages were in ruins, and as of 1996 many Bet Juk remain REFUGEES in Sudan.

BET MA'LA. A small tribe of SAHEL province, who once belonged to the BENI 'AMER confederation and speak both TIGRE and the BEJA language, To-Bedawe. They are pastoralists who traditionally migrated from the SUWAKIN area in the north to the Bab JANGEREN area of SENHIT, but

during the ARMED STRUGGLE they fled as REFUGEES to
Sudan.

BET   MAK'A (Asmara). A suburb of ASMARA located on
the northwestern edge of the city, behind the hill on
which the "Forto" military base is located. Bet Ma'ka was
originally a   village of about a hundred inhabitants
located on Forto hill, but it was relocated to its present
site when the Italian military seized the hill in 1890 to
build Forto Baldiserra. The village was founded by
Muslims loyal to the NA'IB of HIRGHIGO during the
eighteenth century, when the Na'ib obtained title to
grazing lands in the area from the lords of TIGRAI. In
1878 it was the site of an important battle in which Ras
WOLDE-MIKA'EL SOLOMUN defeated and killed Ras Bairu,
the Tigrean governor of MAREB MELLASH.

BEVIN-SFORZA   PLAN (1949). A plan presented to the
UNITED NATIONS to settle the political future of ITALY's
African colonies, including Eritrea, which was drawn up
during early 1949 in secret negotiations between the
British Foreign Secretary, Ernest Bevin, and his Italian
counterpart, Count Sforza. It involved partitioning both
Libya and Eritrea, with Eritrea to be divided between
Ethiopia and the Anglo-Egyptian SUDAN, which was to
gain the western lowlands (BARKA and GASH-SETIT). The
plan was approved by the Third General Assembly's First
Committee in May, but anti-Italian riots in Libya changed
the delegates' minds by the time it was brought to the Assembly for a final vote on May 17. Although the partition
of Eritrea *was* approved by 37 to 11, in separate voting,
the proposal as a whole, including Libya, was rejected by
37 to 14, with abstentions in both cases. Thus, only the
Libyan riots saved Eritrea from partition, in which the
major part of the territory would have come under direct
Ethiopian rule.

BEYLUL (Denkel). A fishing village north of ASSAB, Beylul
was the most important port on the southern DENKEL coast
through the mid-1800s, serving the central Ethiopian

caravan trade from at least the sixteenth century. It was the seat of an important AFAR Sultanate, later ruled by the AKITO family; but with Italian colonization and development of Assab, Beylul was eclipsed and stagnated during the twentieth century. In the 1980s it was an Ethiopian military base, and during the EPLA's DENKEL CAMPAIGN it was the scene of heavy fighting before the village was liberated on April 4, 1991. Today its Afar inhabitants make their living from fishing, trade with the Arabian coast and working the nearby SALT pans.

BILEN (alt.: Blen, Bileni). An ethno-linguistic group and one of Eritrea's nine "nationalities," the Bilen, sometimes called BOGOS, inhabit south-central SENHIT from HAL-HAL to Halib Mentai. They speak Bilen, a Central Cushitic language, which probably derives from a fusion between local Cushitic-speaking peoples and Agaw-speaking immigrants from central Ethiopia, who displaced or gained control over TIGRE, BEJA and NARA peoples in the area. Bilen legends indicate that two waves of Agaw immigration took place, one in the tenth century and one after the fall of the Zagwe dynasty in the thirteenth century, and these immigrations seem to have produced the ruling classes of the two Bilen tribes, the Bet Tarqe and Bet Tawqe, respectively. Later, the Tigre-speaking people around Bab JAN-GEREN also adopted the Bilen language, though they were not of Agaw blood.

The Bet Tarqe occupy the district around KEREN and include the important Bet Gebru clan; while the Bet Tawqe, whose traditions assert they lived many years in DEM-BEZAN, eventually occupied the Hal-Hal area. The original Agaw immigrants formed an aristocracy (*simager*) over earlier groups, who became their vassals (*mikeru*). The Bilen first appear in historical chronicles from the early fourteenth century, and until the mid-nineteenth century they were Orthodox Christians. Although they sometimes paid tribute to the rulers of MAREB MELLASH, they became increasingly autonomous, with their own legal system and a merely nominal connection to the ORTHODOX CHURCH. As settled agriculturists they were the targets of

raids by neighboring peoples, for slaves and cattle, and
these raids grew worse during the struggle between the
Tigreans and Egyptians for control of SENHIT. The raids of
WUBE (1844-49), EGYPT (1850, 1854) and Ras ALULA
(1879-87) are still remembered.

Seeking protection from outside powers during this
period, many Bilen changed their religious affiliations.
Around KEREN some Bet Tarqe converted to the Roman
CATHOLIC CHURCH under the influence of Father Stella,
while most Bet Tawqe converted to Islam under Egyptian
influence. The process of Islamization spread among both
tribes after Egypt occupied Senhit in 1872, and by the
time of Italian occupation (1888) the Bet Tarqe were
roughly divided between Christians and Muslims, and the
Bet Tawqe were almost entirely Muslim—a division that
continues to the present. During the colonial period, due
to the proximity of Keren, many Bilen became involved in
commerce and modern education, and settled in other areas of Eritrea. Their religious divisions led to political
divisions   in the 1940s, when   Christians generally supported the UNIONIST PARTY, while Muslims joined the
MUSLIM LEAGUE and independence movement.

These religious division continued into the 1960s,
when some Bet Tarqe Christians joined the COMMANDOS,
while Muslims supported the ELF, led by OMER EZAZ, a
Bet Tawqe. But Ethiopian counterinsurgency warfare and
the forced relocation of Bilen in "strategic hamlets"
during 1967-71 alienated all sectors of the population,
particularly after the ONA massacre. Muslims tended to
flee to Sudan, and Christians into Keren or Asmara during
the fighting of 1974-77, and with the intense local
fighting of 1978 and 1988-89, many more fled as
REFUGEES. Since liberation many refugees have returned
and the Bilen have reestablished themselves in Eritrean
commerce and education.

BOGOS (Senhit). Another name for the BILEN people, said to
derive from a Bet Tarqe ancestor named Boas or Bokuste.
The name was frequently applied to the Bilen area,
including most of present SENHIT province, from the

fourteenth century to the end of the colonial period. Today Bogos is the name for the north-central sub-province of Senhit, containing the districts of BET JUK, Beyar and HAL-HAL, with a total population of about 20,000.

BORDERS, National. Eritrea's boundaries were defined by a series of agreements negotiated between Italy and surrounding states during the period 1890-1908. The long boundary with ETHIOPIA was the main source of dispute, as Ethiopian rulers had claimed most of Eritrea before Italian occupation. In the Treaty of Wichale (Ucciali) of May 2, 1889, Menelik II agreed to an initial Italian occupation of central Eritrea along a line running from IRAFAILE to Halai, SAGENEITI, ASMARA, ADI NEFAS, Adi Yohannes and thence along the BARKA River, enclosing eastern HAMASIEN and all of northwestern Eritrea. But the Italians proceeded to occupy the entire MAREB MELLASH to the line of the MAREB-BELESA-Mai Muna. This highland boundary was not officially recognized until the Addis Ababa agreement of July 10, 1900, and even this awaited a final delimitation of the border in DENKEL on May 16, 1908, when it was defined by a line paralleling the coast some sixty kilometers inland.

The border with the Anglo-Egyptian SUDAN was delimited in a series of agreements with BRITAIN and EGYPT during 1891, 1898-99 and 1901, and by a final tripartite treaty signed between Britain, Ethiopia, and Italy on May 15, 1902, in Addis Ababa. Initially, the Italians had claimed and occupied KASSALA, and the final boundary cut quite unnaturally through the northernmost end of Eritrea's northern highlands, dividing some traditional grazing areas of the BET ASGHEDE tribes; but the British were determined to gain control of the fertile Gash and Barka deltas for their cotton growing schemes around Kassala and Tokar. The border with the French territory of DJIBOUTI was defined in two protocols during 1900-1.

These boundaries remained undisturbed until the end of the colonial period, when some of their vaguer points re-emerged as sources of dispute, particularly between Ethiopia and Sudan over the agricultural land

west of OM HAGER, where both sides claimed territory in
1968, and around ZELAMBESSA after Eritrean independence. The Sudan border dispute was resolved by the 1971
Addis Ababa agreement between HAILE SELASSIE I and
Nimeiri. New disputes concerning the HANISH ISLANDS
and the border with DJIBOUTI emerged during 1995-96.

BRITAIN. Britain long entertained commercial and political interests in the Eritrean region, and ruled Eritrea
from 1941-52. British interest in the region began with a
series of explorers and adventurers, all of whom saw Eritrea as a gateway to contact and commerce with the rulers
of ETHIOPIA. James Bruce landed at DAHLAK in 1769,
followed by Lord Valentia and Henry Salt's explorations of
the coast during 1805-9. British interest in Eritrea focused on the strategic importance of the coast as it bor-
dered the Red Sea route to their Indian colony, and in the
possibilities of spreading PROTESTANT CHRISTIANITY,
which was pursued by the Church Missionary Society from
1830 to 1843.

In 1848 Plowden became the first British Counsul in
MASSAWA, where he arranged a commercial treaty between Britain and Ethiopia, and sought to counter the
growing influence of FRANCE. He continued to oversee
British affairs in Ethiopia and Eritrea through 1861, when
he was killed and replaced by Charles Cameron, who led
Britain into the dispute with Emperor Tewodros that
ended with the Anglo-Indian military expedition of Lord
Napier. The expedition of some 42,000 men (including
over 4,000 British soldiers) landed at ZULA in early 1868
and constructed a railroad to the mountains and a road up
the KUMALIE River valley to SENAFE, where a supply base
was built. The expedition returned from Ethiopia after
defeating Tewodros, and departed from Eritrea in July.

British interest in Eritrea increased with the
opening of the Suez Canal in 1869, and the growing
importance of the Red Sea steamship route to India. During
the 1870s the British supported EGYPT in its occupation
of the coast as a means of assuring their interests, and in
1879 they supported Gordon's his attempt to negotiate a

settlement between Egypt and YOHANNES IV. This failed, but with the rise of the Sudanese Mahdiyya in 1881, and the British occupation of Egypt in 1882, the British tried again to enlist Yohannes's aid, this time recognizing his control over all Eritrea outside Massawa in the 1884 HEWETT TREATY. Later in the year, however, the London government secretly encouraged its ally ITALY to occupy Massawa and the Eritrean coast.

The British supported Italian control of Eritrea, and recognized its BORDERS with Sudan, up through the entry of Italy into the Second World War, in June 1940, when British and Italian armies faced each other on the Sudanese border. The British eventually assembled an army of over 30,000, spearheaded by two Indian divisions, and invaded Eritrea in January, 1941, defeating the main Italian forces in a bloody battle outside KEREN and occupying ASMARA on April 1. This was followed by the BRITISH ADMINISTRATION of Eritrea. During this period British commercial interest in Eritrea increased, particularly in the import-export trade dominated by the firms of Mitchell Cotts and Andre Besse.

After Eritrea's FEDERATION with Ethiopia, which the British Administration supported, British interest in Eritrea declined, although a British Consulate remained in Asmara until 1975, and a British Council Library continued to operate throughout the war. Despite its long ties with Eritrea, Britain played no official role in trying to end the Eritrean war, although the Labor Party called for Eritrean self-determination from the mid-1980s and a number of British NGOs delivered important support to the ERA. Britain established diplomatic relations with the Eritrean government immediately after independence. Today the British government has provided several small development loans and the aid of its Voluntary Service Overseas (VSO) program, which supplies teachers and technicians for the Ministry of EDUCATION.

BRITISH ADMINISTRATION, Military (1941-49) and Civil (1949-52). The British conquered Eritrea and began administering the colony in March-April 1941. From

1941 to 1949 the government was the British Military
Administration (BMA), headed by a military officer with a
military staff overseeing all government offices. The chief
administrators were Kennedy-Cooke (1941-42), S. H.
Longrigg (1942-44), C. D. McCarthy (1944-45), J. M.
Benoy (1945-46) and F. G. Drew (1946-51).

The first priority of the British was to demobilize
the large Eritrean colonial army and disband the Fascist
militia and   paramilitary police, replacing them with a
new British-officered Eritrean POLICE force that included
some Italian civil police. Most of the Italian civil service
was kept on, with the exception of Fascist party members
and sympathizers, who were interned along with the military. Italian civil laws were retained, except for the more
discriminatory racial laws. By late 1941 a new ADMINIS-
TRATION was in place that contained an upper level of
British officers, a lower level of Italian civil servants, and
for the first time in the colony's history, a significant
number of Eritreans in the lower and even middle levels of
the bureaucracy, most of whom were recruited from the
ranks of former interpreters and teachers. Security was
maintained by units of the SUDAN DEFENSE FORCE (SDF)
until 1946, when British military units returned.

The next priority of the BMA was to utilize Eritrea's
resources to prosecute the Allied war effort. British and
UNITED STATES contractors took over Italian military installations and developed the MASSAWA naval base, GU-
RA' and Asmara AIRPORTS, GHINDA hospitals and depots,
and Asmara radio communications base (see KAGNEW
STATION). The British also encouraged Italian entrepreneurs to develop AGRICULTURE and INDUSTRY to
supply local and regional markets that were cut off by the
war from their European and Asian sources. Italian agricultural concessions were expanded by ten thousand
hectares of land alienated from Eritrean villages, and the
basic industrial infrastructure of Eritrea was created or
expanded, mostly centered around ASMARA. Wartime
services and production helped alleviate widespread unemployment resulting from the DEMOBILIZATION of over
thirty thousand Eritrean ASCARI, and employed much of

the ITALIAN POPULATION in the colony, but in 1944 the British and American military installations began to close down and by 1946 the regional markets for Eritrean products were being lost to renewed competition from overseas.

Post-war economic recession was exacerbated by the BMA's austere policies of "care and maintenance," the administration's attempt to make the colony self-supporting in revenue, and the dismantling and sale of most of Eritrea's military installations and some of its transport infrastructure in an attempt to pay off the UK's huge war debts (*see* MASSAWA; GURA'; GHINDA). BMA social policy did little to alleviate Eritrean suffering, as a racially-defined employment hierarchy remained in place. Pensions, unemployment benefits and HEALTH CARE services were unavailable to the vast majority of Eritreans, and under the BMA, Eritreans' right to LABOR ORGANIZATIONS was severely restricted. On the other hand, the British did encourage widespread development of the EDUCATION facilities that had been denied Eritreans under Italian rule, and schools proliferated throughout the country. The use of local languages and English in the upper levels encouraged a growing intellectual life, and Eritrea's first secular newspapers in TIGRINYA and ARABIC were sponsored by the BMA.

In 1947 the BMA allowed Eritreans to form POLITICAL PARTIES, but the London government vacillated on its own political agenda for Eritrea's future. Initially, one segment of the British government sought to achieve some form of colonial control over all the former Italian East African empire (AOI), including Ethiopia, and, failing this, in 1944 some officers favored the recreation of a "Greater TIGRAI" under British trusteeship. By 1945 the BMA's political program focused on partitioning Eritrea between the Anglo-Egyptian SUDAN, to which they envisioned annexing the Western Lowlands Province, and ETHIOPIA. BMA policy consequently focused on dividing the population into Muslim and Christian blocs, to be associated with Sudan and Ethiopia respectively. This policy was not entirely Machiavellian, though it certainly contained this element,

but it was also driven by the idiosyncratic projects of
local British officers whose ideas were often at odds with
the policies of the London government.

Contradictions in British policy were exacerbated
by the government's post-war retreat from colonialism, on
one hand, and the retention of administrators schooled in
colonial power politics, on the other. Vacillation at higher
levels apparently enabled a few advocates of Ethiopian annexation and Sudanese partition to intercede clandestinely in local affairs, helping to sow the already existing
seeds of intercommunal violence that broke out in bloody
rioting in Asmara in 1946 and the sectarian factionaliza-
tion of Eritrean politics between the MUSLIM LEAGUE and
UNIONIST PARTY in 1947, giving the impression to both
the FOUR POWERS COMMISSION (1947) and UNITED
NATIONS investigative commission (1950) that the colony
was hopelessly divided on its political future. The London
government used these apparent divisions to buttress its
partition scheme contained in the 1949 BEVIN-SFORZA
PLAN, despite the lack of support for it from any Eritrean
political party.

With the failure of the partition plan, London turned
to their increasingly dominant and pro-Ethiopian ally, the
United States, to take a stronger lead in deciding what was
now known as the "Eritrean Question." By 1949 it was
clear the British were to be a caretaker administration
preparing Eritrea for the end of European colonial rule,
and the BMA was therefore replaced by a civilian British
Administration (BA) on April 1, 1949. The main task of
the BA was to Eritreanize the economy and civil service,
whose higher levels and technical positions were still almost entirely in Italian hands (*see* LABOR   ORGANIZA-
TIONS).

The BA was also faced with the increasing violence
of an anti-Italian and pro-Ethiopian terrorist SHIFTA
campaign in the KEBESSA, but their police measures were
ineffective during 1949-50, which led many Eritreans to
speculate that the administration was in collusion with
Ethiopia. In 1951, however, after the UN decision on FED-
ERATION had been made and the UN High Commissioner

arrived, the BA finally responded with military force and legal sanctions that quickly ended the *shiftanet*. The BA, headed by D.C. Cummings (1951-52), oversaw the final transition to internal self-government, issuing the legal proclamations that enabled the first ASSEMBLY to be elected, and the formation of labor unions, press freedom and other crucial aspects of democratic civil society. On September 15, 1952, the British flag was lowered and government turned over, not to Eritreans, but to the Imperial Representative of Emperor Haile Selassie.

BURE PENINSULA and Bur (Denkel). The northernmost extension of the DENKEL coast, separated from the mainland by the Gulf of ZULA and inhabited by AFAR-speaking peoples of the Ankala, Belesewa and Damoheita subtribes. The main settlements are the fishing villages of Genfrore, Ingal and Doleh, and the inland villages of Bordele and Makagnile. The coast is surrounded by spectacular coral reefs with abundant fish, while the interior is semi-desert grazed by pastoralists and a rich variety of wildlife.

The name Bure derives from the ancient province of Bur, which included the AKELE GUZAI highlands ("Upper Bur") and the coastal plains of northern Denkel ("Lower Bur"). The volcanoes at the base of the penninsula were mined for obsidian in ancient times, and the area was an elephant hunting ground for the port of ADULIS. From the sixteenth century Bure was nominally ruled by the NA'IBs of HIRGHIGO, who governed for the Turks in MASSAWA, which is a few hours sailing away. But the Na'ib could not protect the local population from raids by highland peoples, including Azebu Oromo in the 1660s, and Tigrean Christians in the 1700s and early 1800s.

In 1868 EGYPT attempted to exercise more direct control and built an impressive stone fort near Bordele, but under ITALIAN COLONIALISM Bure's administration reverted to Massawa. Government presence was negligible until the ARMED STRUGGLE, and Afar shaykhs continued to oversee local justice, tax collection and traditional Muslim schools. The peninsula's physical isolation, but

proximity to Massawa, made it an ideal guerrilla base for
the ELF from the mid-1960s. In 1976 the EPLF also gained
a foothold through its local commander, Ali Koubeni. In
1978 the EPLF occupied Bordele, and a desultory civil war
began, escalating into full-scale fighting in 1980, when
the EPLF drove the ELF out of Denkel. Ethiopian air and
sea patrols made fishing and trade across the Red Sea
quite difficult, and many Afar moved to Saudi Arabia and
Yemen, while others joined the EPLF, providing important
recruits for the NAVY.

Ethiopian naval actions around the peninsula
intensified in the late 1980s, and after the fall of
Massawa, in 1990, the EPLF NAVY hid its speedboats in
the mangroves near Genfrore for night attacks on the
Ethiopian base at DAHLAK. The area was bombed
repeatedly and a number of boats were destroyed. Today
the Bure fishing villages are regaining their prosperity,
engaging in boat building, trade with the Arabian coast
and smuggling. The government currently promotes
TOURISM around the reefs and offshore islands.

- C -

CAIRO (Egypt). As the center of commercial, religious and
political institutions spanning the Red Sea region, Cairo
has always been a pole of attraction for Eritreans,
particularly Muslims. Since medieval times a portico of
Al-Azhar University has been reserved for JIBERTI, and
with the rise of Egyptian power in Eritrea and the SUDAN
during the nineteenth century, Eritreans traveled to Cairo
for study and trade in growing numbers. In the 1920s a
few Eritreans attended Al-Azhar University, including
the future Mufti, IBRAHIM AL-MUKHTAR. By the 1950s
there were about 150 Eritreans studying at Al-Azhar, and
in 1951 the Egyptian government began providing secular
scholarships for Eritrean secondary students, including
IDRIS OSMAN GALADEWOS, Safi Imam Musa and Taha
Mohamed Nur. Beginning in 1953, with the arrival of
WOLDE-AB WOLDE-MARIAM, Cairo became a center of
exiled Eritrean political leaders, and with the arrival of

IBRAHIM SULTAN ALI and IDRIS MOHAMED ADEM in 1959, connections between Muslim students and the nationalist movement increased.

In 1955 the Egyptian government subsidized the formation of an Eritrean Students' Club, which was transformed into the Eritrean Student Union in 1959, with Cairo-born Mohamed Saleh Hamed as president. By 1960 there were four hundred students in Cairo, including ABDELKRIM AHMED, Idris Galadewos, MOHAMED ALI OMERO, Mohamed "Gezir," Said Hamid M. Hashim, Seid Hussein and Taha M. Nur, many of whom participated in the formation of the ERITREAN LIBERATION FRONT, whose first meeting was held at the Fish Garden (Hadiqat al-Asmak) in July 1961, and whose "Foreign Office" remained in Cairo through 1970.

CAMEL. Eritrea's national symbol from May 1993, signifying the importance of camel transport for the liberation fronts during the ARMED STRUGGLE and the patience of Eritreans in the face of adversity. Today there are about a hundred thousand camels in Eritrea, and they constitute the most valuable livestock in country, as they are used for transport, milk and even plough AGRICULTURE in the lowlands.

CASCIANI. Prominent Italian colonial family, founded by Pietro Casciani (1869-1942) who arrived in Eritrea in 1899 with the Ministry of War and returned in 1901 to open a business in lowland AGRICULTURE. In 1908 he began planting sisal at ELABERED and took full control of the plantation in 1911, which he developed into a leading INDUSTRY producing rope fibers. With his sons he expanded into cotton and tobacco planting around Keren. His son Filippo also was a leader of the Italian community in the 1940s, becoming president of the Italo-Eritrean Association and addressing the UN in 1950. He merged the Elabered estate with the Fratelli DE NADAI company in 1958 and remained in Eritrea through the 1960s.

CATHOLIC   CHURCH (Roman Catholic Christianity). Roman
Christianity was first introduced to the Eritrean region
by the Portuguese mission of Father Alvarez (1520-26), a
member of which, Joao Bermudez, attempted to return to
area in the 1530s with false claims to be the Roman patriarch. No conversions were made until the first Jesuit missionary, Andrea da Oveida, was appointed Bishop of
Ethiopia (1557-77). The Jesuits established themselves at
Fremona,   near ADWA, and most of their converts were in
TIGRAI, although some may have been from the Eritrean
region. Pedro Paez (1603-23) managed to convert the
Ethiopian emperor, Susenyos, but his successor, Alphonse
Mendez, was an anti-Orthodox bigot who provoked civil
war between Catholics and indigenous Christians. In 1632
Susenyos' son, Fasilidas, expelled the Jesuits, who briefly
obtained refuge in Eritrea from the BAHRE NEGASHI, who
hoped to use them to preserve his own autonomy against
Ethiopia, but in 1634   turned them over to Turks at Massawa, who deported them under extreme hardship.

   Jesuits who returned to the Eritrean coast during
the seventeenth and eighteenth centuries were executed on
the orders of Ethiopian rulers, and it was not until 1837
that Catholic missionaries re-established themselves, led
by the Lazzarists, Giuseppe Sapeto, and, in 1839, the
newly ordained Bishop of Ethiopia, Giustino DE JACOBIS.
De Jacobis focused his activities on Agame and AKELE
GUZAI, where he evangelized the first Catholic
congregation in Eritrea, adapting Catholic liturgy to the
Alexandrine rite of the Orthodox Church, ordaining
Eritrean clergy and translating Christian texts into
TIGRINYA. The ORTHODOX CHURCH, led by Aba Salama of
Tigrai, responded with persecution, which Ethiopian
rulers pursued as state policy, including Dej. WUBE
(1844-51), Emperor Tewodros (1860-61) and YOHANNES
IV. This forced the Catholic missionaries to spend much of
their time in the relative protection of the MASSAWA
area, where a printing PRESS and seminary were
established at Monkulo.

   In 1846 another Catholic order arrived on the scene,
the Capuchins, whose leading figure, Guglielmo Massaia,

was appointed Bishop of Massawa in 1846, while awaiting
the opportunity to evangelize the Oromo. In 1851 Sapeto
and another Lazzarist, Giovani Stella, travelled to SENHIT,
where Stella established himself near KEREN and
remained until his death in 1869. Stella founded a
Catholic community among the BILEN, who he tried to
protect from Egyptian raids, but his rivalries with
MUNZINGER and his intimate relations with Bilen women
led to his falling out with the Church, which he left in
1866.

By the 1870s the Catholic Church was firmly established in both Senhit (where a school was opened in 1872)
and Akele Guzai (where a school was opened in the 1880s),
and Yohannes IV's persecution and military incursions
only increased Eritrean Catholic's animosity to Tigrean
rule, as witnessed in the career of the devout Catholic,
BAHTA HAGOS. Consequently, Eritrean Catholics at first
welcomed ITALIAN COLONIALISM, but following Bahta
Hagos' revolt, in 1895, the Italian authorities expelled the
Lazzarists who had been so important in indigenizing
Catholicism. The French-based Lazzarists were suspected
of having incited Bahta's revolt, although the records of
the order show this to be untrue. Instead, the colonial government promoted the Italian-based Capuchins, who proceeded to evangelize the KUNAMA area.

As Italian colonists settled in Eritrea the Church
became increasingly divided between a largely European
and mixed-race Latin Rite congregation, and the
indigenous Alexandrine Rite congregation. The Roman
Church and the Capuchins oversaw many of the colony's
schools and its seminary in Asmara. By 1950 there were
about 35,000 Eritrean Catholics. The Church ran orphan-
ages, schools (including the UNIVERSITY OF ASMARA)
and acquired substantial properties before 1975, when its
holdings and schools were nationalized by the DERG.
Nonetheless, the Eritrean Catholic Secretariat was the
main coordinating agency for foreign relief and
particularly FOOD AID in Derg-controlled areas during
the war. A number of Catholic priests and intellectuals

also joined the EPLF, including the noted historian Aba
Yeshaq Gebre-Yesus.

  After liberation there was some friction between the
Church and the new government over property. By 1992,
however, the Catholic Secretariat was deeply involved in
the reconstruction effort throughout the country, including some Muslim areas, where the Church financed the
construction of clinics and secular schools. In 1996,
however, the government barred the church, along with all
religious organizations, from participating in development
projects, citing the danger of reviving sectarian political
sentiments in the country. In 1991 there were 67,825
Eritreans in the Alexandrian Rite congregations and
29,622 in the Latin Rite Apostolic Vicarate of Asmara.

CENTRAL COMMITTEE (EPLF and PFDJ). The main organ
  of the democratic-centralist political structure of the
  EPLF. A Central Committee (CC) was first formed by the
  leaders of the EPLF's various political, military and other
  committees in 1975 to coordinate the activities of the
  rapidly expanding front. But the first formal CC was
  elected in January 1977 by the EPLF's First Congress. It
  comprised thirty-seven members and six alternates, who
  in turn elected a Political Committee (Politbureau) of
  thirteen, including the Secretary-General, vice Secretary-
  General and the members of the eleven new EPLF
  departments. These men were to form the central
  leadership of the front for the next decade, with day-to-
  day decisions largely in the hands of a smaller four man
  group composed of the two Secretary-Generals and the
  heads of the military and political committees.

  A new CC was elected in May 1987 by the EPLF's
  Second Congress. It comprised seventy-one members,
  including six women, and seven alternates, who in turn
  elected a new Political Committee of nine men, including
  the Secretary-General, who oversaw day-to-day activities
  of the much expanded Front. The new CC played a more
  formal role in decision making as the EPLF developed its
  democratic base, and a series of seven regular CC sessions
  were held before the Third Congress. In these sessions

major decisions were made concerning future military and political policies, and CC members acted as liaisons between the central leadership in the Political Bureau and their departments, units and mass organizations. At the fifth meeting (May 1992) the CC, which had been transformed into the "legislative body" of the new PGE (May 1991), restructured the executive of the GOVERNMENT OF THE STATE OF ERITREA, creating a formal Advisory Council to oversee day-to-day affairs. At the sixth meeting (February 1993), plans were approved for the EPLF's Third Congress, for the formation of a NATIONAL ASSEMBLY including the current CC's members, and for the drafting of a National Charter (*see* CONSTITUTION).

The EPLF CC was disbanded at the Third Congress in February 1994, and a new 75-member body, the Central Council of the PFDJ, was elected by the Congress to continue the political work of the former CC. Most of its members were the same as the previous EPLF CC; but the new 19-member Executive Council of the PFDJ, elected by the Central Council and in organizational terms the successor to the EPLF Political Committee, contained many new members. The Central Council of the PFDJ remains an important political organization in the transitional government, as its members comprise half of the National Assembly.

CHEWA (Amh.: "good manners," i.e., "gentlemen"). Ethiopian military colonists and their descendants, forming their own distinct clans, who settled in the Eritrean highlands from the reigns of Emperors AMDE SIYON and ZARA YA'QOB. The most important Chewa community developed in central HAMASIEN, where they fought for control of land with indigenous LOGGO people during the fourteenth and fifteenth centuries. Eventually the two communities divided the land and developed a common legal system to organize their district, known today as Loggo-Chewa, between Asmara and DEBARWA.

CHINA. The People's Republic of China was an early supporter of Eritrean independence and provided an important model for the EPLF's social and military strategies
during the ARMED STRUGGLE. The ELF first established
relations with China through SOMALIA in 1966, when
OSMAN SALEH SABBE and IDRIS MOHAMED ADEM visited
the People's Republic and obtained a small amount of
money, arms and a scholarship for military training. The
first group of five ELF trainees were sent in 1967: ISAIAS
AFWERKI, RAMADAN MOHAMED NUR, Ahmed Adem
Omer, Mohamed Ahmed Ibrahim and Mahmud Chekini.
Their nine months of training during the height of the
Cultural Revolution had a profound impact on Eritrea's
nationalist revolution, as they returned with a
commitment to implementing Mao Zedong's principles of
guerrilla warfare and peasant-based social revolution.
Five hundred Chinese automatic weapons were received in
1967, and a second group of twenty-five fighters attended
Nanking Military Academy later in the year; but after
China attained ETHIOPIAN diplomatic recognition in
1970, this aid ended.

     Nonetheless, the younger generation of Eritrean
revolutionaries who formed the EPLF continued to model
their strategies and programs to a large extent on the
ideas of Mao, and changes in Chinese thinking about
capitalist economic development in the late 1980s were
also closely followed. As the Ethiopian DERG relied
increasingly on aid from the USSR, the EPLF again
received Chinese overtures, but the Eritreans refused "to
mouth Chinese ideological slogans" and no aid was
forthcoming. After liberation, however, China quickly
moved to establish diplomatic relations, and was one of
the first nations to open an embassy after independence in
1993. In December the Eritrean Defense Minister visited
Beijing and obtained agreements for military aid, followed
by a visit from President Isaias in April 1994, in which a
$4.3 million interest-free loan was obtained. A Chinese
trade exhibition also was held in Asmara, highlighting the
importance of Chinese manufactures which account for a
substantial portion of Eritrea's imported finished goods.

CHRISTIANITY *see* CATHOLIC CHURCH; ORTHODOX CHURCH; PROTESTANT CHRISTIANITY.

CIRCUMCISION (Genital Mutilation). The widespread practice of male and female "circumcision" in Eritrea is but one aspect of the fundamental cultural unity of the country, despite its varying religious and linguistic traditions. Male circumcision is practiced among all Eritrean nationalities. Female genital mutilation (FGM), erroneously also called "circumcision," is traditionally practiced among all Eritrean nationalities except the KUNAMA and NARA (although most Nara have adopted it today along with Islam). The practice seems to be of great antiquity, probably pre-dating both CHRISTIANITY and ISLAM in the region, and is associated with patriarchal forms of social control which focus particularly on women's premarital chastity. It is not specifically condoned by either the ORTHODOX CHURCH or Muslim religious texts, but is a customary practice associated with ideas of ritual "cleanliness" in both religions.

The operation is a women's affair, usually performed on infants or young girls by female specialists in unsanitary conditions. FGM ranges in severity from partial excision of the clitoris in TIGRINYA and BILEN Christian areas, to full excision of clitoris and labia minora, partial removal of labia majora and infibulation (near-complete closure of vaginal orifice through sewing and scarring) among many AFAR, SAHO, HEDAREB and TIGRE-speaking groups. FGM was condemned by the EPLF before liberation as part of the campaign of its WOMEN'S ORGANIZATIONS, and today the Eritrean government and the National Union of Eritrean Women are working to educate the public about its severe impact on women's health and childbirth. Since the 1960s FGM has been declining among the educated urban population, but it continues to be widely practiced in rural areas, amongst recent urban immigrants, and among REFUGEES in SUDAN.

CIVIL   WARS (1972-74, 1980-81). The Eritrean ARMED
STRUGGLE against Ethiopian rule was punctuated by two
open civil wars between the rival ELF and EPLF guerrilla
armies. These wars developed out of the tensions in the
ELF generated by the reform movement of the late 1960s
(*see* ESLAH), and by different approaches to the key issue
of building national unity. While regional, tribal,
religious and personal conflicts played a role in the
specific unfolding of events in the civil wars, the wars
themselves cannot be attributed to these causes. Rather,
they were above all conflicts between rival organizations
whose ethnic make-up and ideology were quite similar,
but each of which saw itself as the true vanguard of the
nationalist revolution. The key issues in conflict were
actually the organizational structures and strategies of
the fronts themselves.

The ELF remained a loosely-organized, poorly disciplined coalition of forces with strong personal, regional
and ethnic-based cliques; the EPLF emerged out of a critique of the weaknesses of this organization and so it
evolved as a tightly-disciplined, centralized organization
capable of carrying out the strategy of protracted guerrilla warfare that its leaders believed would be necessary
to win independence. The two civil wars between the ELF
and EPLF essentially bracketed the emergence of the EPLF
out of the ELF, with the first civil war (1972-74) initiated
and prosecuted by the much larger ELF against the tiny
coalition of forces that later formed the EPLF, and the second civil war (1980-81) prosecuted by the EPLF to eliminate the remnants of the ELF. The period between these
two "hot" wars was merely a "cease-fire" marked by
continual political maneuvering punctuated by small-
scale military encounters, during which the balance of
power shifted decisively from the ELF to the EPLF.

The first civil war began in February 1972, when
ELF leaders decided to "liquidate" the PLF and OBEL
forces associated with OSMAN SALEH SABBE. The fighting
spread along the Red Sea coast into SAHEL and climaxed in
battles around Ghirghir in February 1973, after which the
undefeated proto-EPLF coalition moved south to the edge

of the central highlands, where they began to organize and augment their forces. The ELF followed them and during 1974 the civil war spread into the highlands, even as the Ethiopian revolution seemed to present an opportune moment for a united Eritrean push for independence. Fighting around ZAGHER in September 1974 led to a strong civilian movement to end the civil war, and on October 13 a first truce was negotiated between the two fronts, which was extended and made more effective by another agreement on January 16, 1975.

Rivalry and occasional fighting continued, however, as a series of negotiations on forming a united national front took place. The first unity agreement was reached between Osman Sabbe and the ELF during August-September 1975, but it was repudiated on November 12 by the EPLF field leadership, who had not been consulted. There followed two years of wrangling over the actual means of integrating the two fronts, with the EPLF arguing for progressive integration and the ELF arguing for coordination of two separate commands (a "mini-civil war" even broke out in DENKEL during 1977). Finally, on October 20, 1977, the leaders of the ELF and EPLF signed an agreement in Khartoum calling for joint command of a united front, which was symbolically established in April 1978. The October 20 agreement was acclaimed by all sides, but remained unimplemented before the Ethiopian OFFENSIVES of 1978 decimated the ELF and forced the EPLF into Sahel, where the two fronts fought side by side in the desperate battles of 1979.

The ELF was now by far the weaker organization, and its leadership, fearing their eclipse, opened secret negotiations with the USSR in 1980, which led to increasing friction between the fronts, exacerbated by renewed fighting in northern Denkel in June. On July 7, ELF units suddenly withdrew from the joint defensive lines in northeast Sahel, and took no part in the fighting when the DERG attacked the gap on August 17. This increased inter-front friction and on August 28 the second civil war began, this time initiated and prosecuted by the EPLF, whose leaders were determined to eliminate the

ELF. On their side, ELF leaders continued to negotiate for a separate peace agreement brokered by the USSR during August-November 1980.

EPLF forces attacked ELF units in Denkel and SEMHAR and drove them across the highlands into BARKA, while others were driven from Sahel and GASH-SETIT (with TPLF aid). By November 27, when a cease-fire was arranged, most of the former ELF had been pushed across the border into Sudan. Following another failed unity agreement, signed in Tunis on March 24, 1981, further fighting occurred in August-September, when the EPLF drove remaining ELF forces over the border. The EPLF thereafter remained the only Eritrean front fighting inside the country, although a few minor clashes took place in the remaining years of the armed struggle as ELF FACTIONS, particularly those of ABDALLAH IDRIS and the new Islamic JIHAD, attempted to infiltrate anti-EPLF guerrillas into Barka.

COATIT *see* QWATIT.

COHAIN *see* QOHAIN.

COLONIALISM *see* BRITISH ADMINISTRATION; DERG; ETHIOPIA; HAILE SELASSIE I; ITALIAN COLONIALSM.

COMMANDOS (1965-75). Paramilitary units attached to the Eritrean police and recruited from the Eritrean population, the commandos, also known as 101 Force (from an earlier British anti-SHIFTA unit), began to be recruited in 1965 under Governor-General ASRATE KASSA, using a special allocation from the Eritrean budget. The recruits were from rural areas, largely but not entirely Christian, and proud of their power and status. They were   trained and equipped by counter-insurgency experts from ISRAEL at a camp just outside DEKEMHARE, and provided shock-troops for the anti-ELF campaigns of the 1960s. In 1970, when Police General Goitom Gebrezghi assumed command, they numbered a brigade of about one thousand, organized into nine companies.

Rivalry with the Ethiopian army developed in the 1970s, and in 1974 the nationalist movement began to penetrate the commandos' ranks. General Goitom supported AMANUEL MIKA'EL ANDOM's negotiations in October-November, and in December the commandos stationed at SEMBEL barracks near Asmara were disarmed by the Ethiopian army. In January 1975 commando units from DONGOLO marched to Asmara to protect Eritrean civilians from Ethiopian persecution, and on January 15 General Goitom himself defected, followed by many commandos over the succeeding months. The remaining police commando units were dissolved later in the year, although the name lived on in the special units of the EPLA, which were used particularly in urban attacks and sabotage, such as the raids on Asmara AIRPORT.

COMMERCE. Eritrea has had a thriving import-export sector since ancient times, as well as widespread local and regional markets. Local products included grain, hides, salt, gold and other minerals, and in precolonial times ivory and slaves, as well as re-exports from ETHIOPIA. A key element in the territory's commerce was always the transit trade with northern and central Ethiopia, which used of MASSAWA, and to a lesser extent the ports of the DENKEL coast for most of their import-export trade. During the Italian colonial period, this transit trade averaged 40 percent of Eritrea's commerce, and it was probably even higher in the precolonial period. Both foreign and inter-regional trade were largely in the hands of Mulsim merchants during the precolonial period: JIBERTI in the highlands, often employed by Christian political leaders; Arabized local families and TIGRE-speakers in the lowlands; and Arabs, Indians (known as "Banyans") and a few local families on the coast. From the late-1500s to the mid-1800s the key figure in controlling foreign commerce was the NA'IB of HIRGHIGO, who could levy taxes and block caravans with relative impunity.

European merchants became increasingly involved in foreign commerce during the period of Egyptian rule on the coast, and with the Italian occupation they moved into all the more lucrative aspects of foreign commerce, dominating the import-export trade which by 1934 had been altered to benefit Italy, which sent Eritrea 78 percent of its imports and took 58 percent of its exports. Nonetheless, Eritrean Muslim merchants also prospered under the Italians, and many YEMENI small traders and shopkeepers moved into the colony during the early twentieth century. The BRITISH ADMINISTRATION somewhat altered Italy's dominant position in foreign commerce, as first the British wartime marketing board, the UKCC, took over foreign commerce, and then major British companies moved in from Aden, including A. Besse, Mitchell Cotts and several Indian firms. Exports also became more diversified with the wartime development of INDUSTRY, and the post-war expansion of fruit, vegetable, alcohol and textile exports; while transit trade with Ethiopia increased significantly after FEDERATION and particularly with the development of the port of ASSAB. Eritrea's foreign trading partners continued to multiply as well, with more exports going to the Middle East, and more imports coming from East Asia. Eritrean merchants developed their regional commercial links in Ethiopia and SUDAN during the post-Second World War period, aided by the growth of the Eritrean truck transport industry during the 1930s-40s. Following the forced emigration of most of Eritrea's Arab merchant community in the late 1960s, Christian businessman began to participate in commerce for the first time in significant numbers, including a number of immigrants from TIGRAI after 1975.

With the intensification of the ARMED STRUGGLE and the DERG's nationalization policies, Eritrean commerce declined precipitously from 1975-91, although wartime profiteering and smuggling continued in garrison towns and across military lines. The liberation fronts became involved in commerce during 1976-78, when they controlled much of the country and tried to market Eritrean products in SUDAN. They also developed important connections with Eritrean merchants in Sudan and the Arab countries to provide them with supplies, banking and fund-raising services. By the 1980s the EPLF saw the necessity of developing its own commercial company to overcome its reliance on private merchants, and in 1984 the front formed the Red Sea Corporation with $20,000 capital to purchase and import goods for the EPLF cooperative commissaries in the SAHEL liberated zone. The corporation expanded tremendously as the front liberated more territory, and in the Fall of 1990 another parastatal company was founded to invest in Eritrean development and commerce, the Nakfa Corporation, which raised $10 million by August 1991.

After liberation these two corporations worked to drive down prices for imported food and consumer goods by making bulk purchases and selling at a low profit margin (5-20 percent depending on goods) through a chain of Red Sea retail stores spread across the country. By 1994, Red Sea was grossing about $30 million per annum, with a profit of about $2 million. In June 1994 the PFDJ took over the Red Sea Corporation. Despite low prices, foreign commerce is steadily increasing, centered on Ethiopian transit trade and the import of cheap consumer goods paid for largely with remittances coming from Eritreans working abroad. Local commerce is not as well developed, as there are few local manufactures; but the inter-regional firewood, fruit, vegetable and livestock markets have been growing steadily, as have animal exports to SAUDI ARABIA.

CONSTITUTION. Eritrea's first Constitution was drafted by the UNITED NATIONS High Commissioner for Eritrea, Anze MATIENZO, as part of the implementation of Eritrea's FEDERATION with Ethiopia. The document was prepared after long consultations with the government of ETHIOPIA, the BRITISH ADMINISTRATION and Eritrean POLITICAL PARTIES during 1951, and drafted by Matienzo in early 1952. The draft provided the structure for a parliamentary democratic government within Eritrea, but it necessarily had little influence on the form of Federal government under which Eritrea's autonomous relations with Ethiopia would be developed. Consequently,

although the Constitution upheld the separation of powers
between legislative, executive and judicial branches, and
gave Eritrea jurisdictional and symbolic autonomy over
many internal institutions, numerous loopholes remained
through which Ethiopian authority could impinge on
Eritrean liberties, beginning with the Ethiopian
government's right to appoint an "imperial
representative" in Eritrea who would oversee Federal
jurisdictions. After further debate in the Eritrean
ASSEMBLY, which sought and won more symbolic autonomy, the draft was adopted on July 10, 1952, and ratified
by Emperor HAILE SELASSIE I on August 11. The
Constitution was unable to stand up to Ethiopian
encroachment on Eritrean liberties during the Federation,
however, and it was abrogated at the time of ANNEXATION.

   After independence in 1993, the new GOVERNMENT
OF THE STATE OF ERITREA drew up plans to draft a Constitution. The guiding principles for this document were
outlined in the National Charter approved by the EPLF's
Third Congress in February, 1994. The Charter called for
the establishment of a Constitutional Commission to draft
a document with maximum public participation and
consultation, cognizant of the experiences of other
nations, but taking into account Eritrea's unique
situation. The Commission was created with a two year
mandate on March 15, 1994, by proclamation 55/1994 of
the Eritrean NATIONAL ASSEMBLY, which appointed a ten
member executive committee chaired by BEREKET HABTE-
SELASSIE, with AZIEN YASSIN as vice-chair and Zemhret
Yohannes as Secretary, and a 32 member council. The
Commission, which included 20 women and members of
every ethnic group, first met on April 17, when it divided
itself into committees and established an Advisory Board
of community and religious leaders to assist in bringing
the public into the process. Educational and consultative
seminars were then held throughout the country and the
DIASPORA, and in January 1995 an International
Conference was held in Asmara to debate key issues.

   The first draft was prepared during 1995, followed
by public discussion and revision. A final draft was

submitted to the National Assembly in July 1996, and in May 1997 the completed document was ratified by a Constituent Assembly composed of all members of the NATIONAL ASSEMBLY, the six Regional Assemblies and representatives from the diaspora. The constitution is a relatively simple document which is grounded on the "realities" of contemporary Eritrean society. It forms the nation's "basic law" and provides for: the creation of a representative democracy based on electoral participation of all citizens over eighteen years and an independent judiciary; equal rights for women and all ethnic and religious groups within a secular state; basic human rights, including free speech, a free press and freedom of assembly (*see* POLITICAL PARTIES and PRESS for possible legislative restrictions of these rights); and guidelines for combining economic development with a concern for social justice, particularly regarding access to land and other resources.

CONTI ROSSINI, Carlo (1872-1948). The foremost Italian historian of the Eritrean region, Conti Rossini first came to Eritrea in 1889 as a colonial Civil Affairs officer, where he served to 1903, after which he worked for the Italian Treasury and became a professor of Ethiopian Studies at the University of Rome in 1921. He translated and published numerous manuscripts from GE'EZ, including the land charters of Eritrea's principal monasteries and the hagiographies of its principal saints, as well as the major codes of customary law of both the TIGRE and TIGRINYA-speaking peoples, and numerous collections of local history derived from oral traditions. He sketched the ancient and medieval history of Eritrea from a wealth of sources, and his work, although revised and augmented, remains the foundation for these periods. Among his numerous publications the *Principi di diritto consuetudinario dell'Eritrea* (Origins of Eritrean Customary Law) and *Storia d'Etiopia* (History of Ethiopia) are the most important.

- D -

DAGA. The largest and once the most prestigious subtribe of the BENI 'AMER, the Daga are attached to the clan of the Beni 'Amer paramount leader, the DIGLAL. They are TIGRE-speaking pastoralists who live in the area west of AGORDAT, in BARKA province. During the BRITISH ADMINISTRATION the former "serfs" of the Daga formed their own autonomous sub-tribe, the Bet Awat.

DAHLAK Archipelago (Semhar).   An archipelago of over 200 islands off the central Eritrean coast. Nine islands are inhabited, the most important being Dahlak Kebir, Debe'aluwa, Desset, Maheleg and   Nora. The island of Dahlak Kebir was settled from ancient times, when people constructed over three hundred cisterns to trap rainwater. The islands first appear in historical records as Aliaeu (alt.: Elaia or Alalaios) in Pliny's geography (79 A.D.), which, along with later Greek and Arabic accounts, mentions the islands' pearl fishery as the most important aspect of its economy. Local legends of the Furs people (probably Farsi) indicate settlement by Persian merchants during the middle of the first millenium. The present TIGRE-speaking population seems to have inhabited the islands since AKSUMITE times, with additional Afar and Arab immigrants arriving over the centuries.

In 702/03 A.D., Dahlak was seized by an Arab naval expedition from Jeddah, and it became a penal colony during the Umayyad Caliphate, as well as a base for Muslim merchants trading with the Eritrean coast. It was during this period that Dahlak's connection to the MASSAWA area developed as Arabs pioneered a new trade route into the HABESHA highlands. In the early ninth century the islands were claimed by both the Abbasid governor of Hijaz and the Negashi of the Habesha. By the tenth century Dahlak was clearly in the economic orbit of YEMEN, paying tribute to the Zabidis and forming a "Muslim bridgehead" for their caravan trade with northern and central Ethiopia. In the eleventh century

Dahlak's trade flourished as EGYPT's Fatimids revived Red Sea commerce, and its rulers became involved in Yemeni politics. About 1060 the leader of a losing faction in one of Yemen's civil wars fled to Dahlak and proclaimed himself Sultan, and from the late eleventh century through the mid-sixteenth century Dahlak formed an independent Sultanate with political connections to both shores of the Red Sea. The necropolis of elegant Kufic-script gravestones on Dahlak Kebir dates from this period, which marked the height of Dahlak's commercial and political power. Massawa came under the authority of the Dahlak Sultanate, and the sultan spent much of his year there, engaged in commerce with the rulers of TIGRAI and Ethiopia. In the mid-fifteenth century the sultan even made a trade agreement with the Christian monastery of DEBRE BIZEN; but by this period the commercial base of the Sultanate had declined and it was forced to pay tribute to powerful Ethiopian emperors.

The final disruption of Dahlak's commercial base came with the Portuguese attempt to control the Red Sea, when Dahlak was raided by Portuguese fleets (1513, 1517, 1520, 1526) and forced to pay tribute to them. A brief revival occurred under Imam AHMED AL-GHAZALI in the 1530s, but this ended with the Portugese return in 1541 and in 1557 TURKEY occupied the islands, ending the Sultanate. The fortunes of Dahlak declined under the Turks, until the islands were inhabited by only a few hundred poor fishermen whose principal commercial connections were with the Arabian coast. Under ITALIAN COLONIALISM the islands revived somewhat, as commerical FISHING was developed, limestone was exported for construction in Massawa, and a notorious political PRISON was built on the semi-detached island of Nocra. Regular ferry service with Massawa was developed, and by the 1960s the islands had 3,200 residents living in twenty villages.

The ARMED STRUGGLE renewed the islands' isolation, and in the 1970s many residents left for SAUDI ARABIA. In 1978 the USSR built a naval base at Nocra, installing a desalinization plant and prefabricated buildings and docks salvaged from its former installations in SOMALIA. The base was used by the Soviet navy and fishing vessels. When Massawa was liberated in 1990, surviving Ethiopian naval units withdrew to Dahlak, where Soviet missile launchers were used to bombard Massawa. ISRAEL also sent military equipment and advisors to the island in April 1990. The EPLF NAVY retaliated with night attacks on the Nocra base through early 1991, and the fighting induced more of the islanders to flee. Today the islands are being developed for TOURISM as a national marine park focused on preserving their beautiful coral reefs. In late 1995 a U.S. company, "Development Concept," signed a $200 million agreement to build a tourist resort on Dahlak Kebir, including a jetport, improved docks, and a 665-unit hotel and casino scheduled for completion in 1998.

DANAKIL *see* AFAR.

DANKALIA *see* DENKEL.

DAWIT WOLDE-GIORGIS. Member of the DERG and military governor of Eritrea from 1980 through early 1983, Dawit was an important architect of the RED STAR CAM-PAIGN. His strategy to win the "hearts and minds" of Eritrean Christians was similar to that advocated in the 1960s by ASRATE KASSA, but with a more socially-oriented element of economic development. During 1980-81 Dawit restricted the arbitrary actions of the army and police, and reduced the discrimination routinely practiced against Eritreans. He also began the campaign to isolate young Eritreans from their nationalist-minded elders by providing them with youth clubs, dancing and sports associations. But whatever political value these actions may have had for the Derg was undermined by the return to terrorism and Dawit's relocation to Ethiopia in 1983.

DEBARWA (Seraye). The medieval capital of central Eritrea, Debarwa is situated in the fertile Tselima district on the headwaters of the MAREB, where the TRADE ROUTE from HAMASIEN to northern TIGRAI crosses the river. This strategic location made it a caravan stop and regional market in the fifteenth century, when it was chosen as the capital of the BAHRE NEGASHI, the Ethiopian-appointed governor of MAREB MELLASH. In 1520, the Portuguese priest Alvares spent a month there and described its "fortress"-like government buildings and the richness of the surrounding agricultural land. Debarwa was looted by Imam AHMED AL-GHAZALI's armies in the 1530s, but was rebuilt by Bahre Negashi YESH'AQ, who allowed the Turks to build a stone fort at Debarwa in the 1560s, making it their highland administrative center until 1578. Debarwa remained the capital of the Bahre Negashi until the seventeenth century, when its political importance was eclipsed by the rise of TSAZZEGA; but the town continued as an important market center through the nineteenth century. Under Italian rule it developed as a district administrative center on the Asmara-Mendefera road, which bridged the Mareb at the town. It was briefly held by the ELF during 1977-78, and was the site of an Ethiopian rear-guard action against the EPLA in late May 1991. Today it has some 3,000 inhabitants.

DEBRE BIZEN (Hamasien). The most important monastery of the ORTHODOX CHURCH in Eritrea, and spiritual center of the indigenous Church, Debre Bizen was founded during the 1350s on a mountain top (2,450 m.) above the present town of Nefasit, from where it commanded the crucial TRADE ROUTES from MASSAWA to the highlands. It was founded by the great disciple of EWOSTATEWOS' religious reform movement, Aba Filipos (c.1323-1406), a native of Inyankere, SERAYE, and student of Aba Absadi (*see* DEBRE MARYAM). Filipos wandered the Eritrean plateau for many years before founding the monastery at the ultimate extremity of the highlands. Debre Bizen ("Place of Vision") grew and prospered under his leadership and by 1400 it had an estimated nine hundred monks regulated under an Ewostatian regimen completely independent of the Ethiopian church. This brought Filipos

into conflict with Emperor Dawit, who summoned Filipos
to the imperial court where he was tried for heresy and
imprisoned. In 1403/4 he was released and gained Dawit's
acceptance of Ewostatian doctrinal independence,
obtaining for his monastery the first of many imperial
land grants (GULTI). Before his death Filipos appointed
Yohannes (c. 1383-1446) as successor. Although initially
opposed by many monks, Yohannes ably continued to build
the power of Debre Bizen, as did the third abbot, Sereqa
Berhan.

By the early sixteenth century Debre Bizen was said
to have three thousand monks, most of whom were scattered on land holdings that extended along the eastern
escarpment from MENSA' to DEKEMHARE, and in rich
districts of the central plateau and TIGRAI. Debre Bizen
escaped the ravages of Imam AHMED AL-GHAZALI's
armies (1535) and continued to gain in prestige and
wealth, receiving further land grants from emperors
Galadewos, Tewodros and YOHANNES IV, all of whom
viewed the monastery as a bulwark against foreign encroachment into the highlands. The importance of Bizen
was attested to in 1889, when Emperor Menelik reserved
continued Ethiopian jurisdiction over the monastery and
its landholdings in the Treaty of Wichale (Art. 4). But
after the Ethiopian defeat in 1935, all the monastery's
lands north of Nefasit were confiscated. Italian suspicions
that the monastery harbored pro-Ethiopian SHIFTA led to
an inconclusive search of its heights by British forces in
November, 1949. In 1975 the remainder of the monastery's
landholdings were confiscated by the DERG, and they have
not been restored by the GOVERNMENT OF THE STATE OF
ERITREA.

Today, Debre Bizen continues to be the most
prestigious monastery of the Eritrean Orthodox Church,
and is the site of an annual pilgrimage to celebrate Saint
Filipos, whose tomb is there. The monastery itself is a national historical treasure, and its library contains some of
the most important GE'EZ manuscripts in the country.

DEBRE LIBANOS of Shimezana (Akele Guzai). Reputedly the oldest Christian monastery in Eritrea, Debre Libanos is supposed to have been founded in the late fifth or early sixth century by the Syrian missionary Aba Meta or Matewos (known as "Libanos"), who evangelized in BAQLA and SERAYE as well as SHIMEZANA. Originally located in the village of Ham, whose church contains ruins dating from at least AKSUMITE times, the monastery was later moved to its present inaccessible location perched on the edge of a cliff below the Ham plateau. Its church contains the "Golden Gospel," a metal-covered Bible containing copies of land charters that date back to the early thirteenth century, when Debre Libanos was an important seat of secular as well as religious power in the Shimezana region claimed as part of the MA'IKELE BAHRE by Zagwe emperors. The monastery's abbot retained a position of local secular power, based on GULTI land holdings, through the early Italian colonial period, when he functioned as chief of the Ambeset-Geleba district. The ancient churches at both Debre Libanos and Ham were rebuilt during HAILE SELASSIE I's period and in the process many important historical artifacts were lost.

DEBRE MARYAM (Seraye). Founded c. 1340-50 by Aba Absadi, the leading disciple of EWOSTATEWOS, in a wilderness area of QOHAIN, western SERAYE, above the confluence of the OBEL and MAREB rivers. Because of Aba Absadi's senior position, Debre Maryam at one time had a claim to primacy among the Ewostatian monasteries, but was surpassed by Filipos' DEBRE BIZEN in the latter 1300s. Absadi probably died before 1400, and was succeeded as abbot by Tewelde-Medhin. The monastery acquired large GULTI land holdings in succeeding centuries, and its wealth enabled its abbots to acquire the rich manuscript library and beautiful furnishings which remain today, although the land holdings have returned to the surrounding villagers.

DEBRE MERQOREWOS (Seraye). Founded in the mid-1300s by Aba Merqorewos, a disciple of EWOSTATEWOS,

in the wilds of DEMBELAS north of present-day AREZA.
Notable for its age and association with one of the leading
figures of the early Ewostatian movement, Debre Merqorewos retained large GULTI lands until the nationalizations
of the Ethiopian revolution.

DEBRE SINA (Senhit). An ancient Christian monastery located in the mountains on the edge of the MENSA' district
above present-day ELABERED, Debre Sina ("Sinai") is said
to have been founded by Frumentius in the fourth century,
and clearly dates from at least the seventh century. The
villages around Debre Sina remained Christian into the
late nineteenth century and paid tribute to the rulers of
HAMASIEN, but today are Muslim.

DEBRI-MELA. A small SAHO tribe inhabiting the escarpment edge in southeastern AKELE GUZAI. The Debri-Mela
("people of the mountain," i.e., Amba Soira) are divided
between two sections: the largely Christian Lab-hale
around Amba Soira and the Muslim Alades around Amba
Debre. Both groups are mostly sedentary agriculturalists
and the Christian Lab-hale speak both Saho and TIGRINYA.

DE JACOBIS, Giustino (1800-1860). Pioneer missionary of
the CATHOLIC CHURCH in Eritrea, De Jacobis' is credited
with having adapted the Alexandrine Rite of the ORTHO-
DOX CHURCH for use with a Catholic liturgy. He joined the
Lazzarists in 1818 and was nominated Bishop of Ethiopia
in 1839, when he journeyed to MASSAWA. De Jacobis established good relations with Dej. WUBE, which enabled
him to evangelize in AKELE GUZAI and Agame, where he
built a seminary in 1844 and translated the Bible and
other works into TIGRINYA with the aid of his disciple
Gebre-Mika'el. But Orthodox persecution forced him out of
Agame in 1846, and he spent the next few years primarily
in Massawa. Persecution continued under Emperor
Tewodros, and De Jacobis sided with Tewodros' enemies,
led by Agaw Negussie. He returned to Halai in 1859 as
Negussie's intermediary in negotiations to obtain the aid
of FRANCE, but was expelled again after the capture of

Russell, the French emissary. He died of fever at Hebo in the Alighede valley, as he attempted to return to the highlands. Today his tomb is visited by both Christians and Muslims.

DEKEMHARE (alt.: Decamare; Akele Guzai). Once a thriving center for Italian ROAD TRANSPORT, Dekemhare is located at the northern edge of AKELE GUZAI where the main roads from MASSAWA, ASMARA and the Ethiopian border intersect. The original village of Deqi-Mehari, dating from about the fifteenth century, is perched above the new colonial town, which was built on the village's traditional farmland. Little colonial development took place until 1934-35, when much of the village land was alienated for urban, industrial and agricultural concessions, and an all-weather road was built from Nefasit to Dekemhare via MAI HABAR in preparation for the Fascist invasion of Ethiopia. By 1936 Dekemhare was the main supply base and transport center for the Ethiopian campaign, filled with garages, metal shops and warehouses servicing a huge truck fleet and the military airbase at nearby GURA'.

During 1936-38 the European town was built in "moderne" style, with stuccoed homes and offices, while factories (flour, biscuits, wine, metalshops) and business agencies were added, along with vineyards and fruit orchards around the town. By 1938 there were 12,800 inhabitants, including over 6,000 permanent and 4,600 temporary Italian residents. Economic growth continued through the 1941-44 war boom (when shoe and canning factories were added), but beginning in 1945 much of the Italian population left, spurred by SHIFTA attacks after 1947. By the late 1950s the European town was largely deserted, and in 1962 the entire population of Dekemhare was only 6,000, including a few hundred Italians. For many Eritreans the decline of Dekemhare was an outstanding example of the impact of Ethiopian rule, as rumors circulated that HAILE SELASSIE I had blocked bids by Fiat and Volkswagen to develop auto plants there. Instead, during the 1960s, the Italian military camp at the

north end of town was converted into a training center for
police COMMANDOS.

Dekemhare was liberated by the EPLA in a five-hour
battle on July 6, 1977, and became a center for organizing
the southern highlands, until it was abandoned in July
1978 during the EPLF's STRATEGIC WITHDRAWAL. The
town's population remained loyal to the liberation front,
and aided guerrilla raids on the town on May 28, 1979,
and January 31, 1984. During 1990 Dekemhare was transformed into a major base for the Ethiopian army in northern Akele Guzai, and after June it was the command center
for the DEKEMHARE FRONT. The town suffered extensive
damage from bombing during 1977-78, from shellfire in
1991, and most of the population fled in 1990-91. Its
years as a military garrison led to a proliferation of bars
and prostitution. Plans to redevelop Dekemhare as a center of road transport are under way, and the Trans-Horn
trucking company moved its garages there in 1994.

DEKEMHARE FRONT (1990-91). After the EPLA liberated southern AKELE GUZAI and broke through the
SAGENEITI Front (May 28-31), the DERG reformed its defense lines between Mar'eba and Dekemhare, on the high
ridge above the plain of GURA'. This front consisted of
about thirty kilometers of trench lines and saw some of
the bloodiest fighting of the ARMED STRUGGLE. The key
position was on the high ground around Afelba, overlooking the main road, where Eritrean and Ethiopian trenches
were within fifty meters of each other. On August 6-8 and
14-15 the EPLA captured the key ridge around Afelba,
but failed to breakthrough to the plain below. Ethiopian
casualties were estimated at 11,000 and Eritrean casualties were very high. The EPLA was at a disadvantage because of its long supply lines, via the HADAS River valley.
On September 30 the Derg made an unsuccessful counterattack, losing 4,500 dead and wounded.

On May 19 the EPLA launched its second offensive,
strengthened by the withdrawal of Ethiopian units to
DENKEL and Ethiopia, and by the virtual absence of the
Ethiopian airforce, due to shelling of Asmara AIRPORT

and anti-aircraft fire. Nonetheless, the battle was extremely intense, fought with tanks, artillery and a total of close to 80,000 men. The Ethiopians were driven across the plain of Gura' and on the night of May 21/22 Dekemhare fell. Unable to reform their lines, the Ethiopian retreat became a route, leading to the liberation of Asmara on May 24.

DEMBELAS (Seraye). An historic district in the rugged mountains of western SERAYE, north of AREZA. Known for its monasteries and inaccessibility.

DEMBEZAN (Hamasien) *see* AD TEKLEZAN.

DEMOBILIZATION. Eritreans have experienced two large-scale military demobilizations in the twentieth century, the first occurring in 1941-44 when as many as 40,000 Eritrean ASCARIS returned to their homes from the disbanded Italian colonial army. No compensation or other provision was made for them, and this unplanned demobilization resulted in widespread social and economic problems.

Demobilization of the roughly 95,000 strong EPLA after liberation in 1991 was a priority of the new government, as the country could not afford to maintain such a large army. In November 1991 the government began to plan a phased military reduction of 50-60 percent and created a demobilization office. The first group of fighters to be released were those who had joined the EPLA after April, 1991. They were provided with a small cash payment, which increased with years of service, and six months of food assistance. On July 14, 1993, the first phase of planned demobilization was announced, covering over 25,000 fighters who had joined after January, 1, 1990, including 4,000 women who received special assistance.

In May 1994 the second phase was announced, to cover over 22,000 fighters, with an average of ten years service. The fighters received cash payments of 10,000 *birr* (c. $1,700), food rations if needed, job training and credit provisions to enable them to start businesses or farms. Besides the 4,000 who became civilian civil servants, it was hoped that most would take up AGRICULTURE in the lowlands, where German and UNITED STATES loans were made available for development. About 1500 ex-fighters were slated to receive cooperative farms at ALI GHIDER, but less actually took them, and the transition from military life to the war-ravaged civilian economy was difficult for many. Women, who made up 20,000 of the demobilized by 1996 (leaving only 3,000 in the national army), found the transition particularly hard, as they faced the discrimination of a still patriarchal civilian society (*see* W O M E N ' S ORGANIZATIONS). War-disabled fighters, who were released for the first time in phase two, found de-mobilization even more traumatic, as they lost the support of their comrades, and some of these fighters' discontents led directly to the tragic incidents at MAI HABAR reha-bilitation center. As of 1996, 52,000 fighters were de-mobilized, and the process continues with cash payments and loan programs available to various categories of fight-ers beyond the first two groups.

DEN-DEN Mountain (Sahel). A mountain overlooking the Hedai valley and commanding the strategic ridge line which the EPLA held in its decade-long defense of NAKFA. From 1979-86 EPLA trenches on the mountain were subjected to ferocious Ethiopian attacks, and Den-Den became a symbol of the Eritrean independence movement's survival "against all odds."

DE NADAI. Late colonial immigrants, the De Nadai broth-ers developed export fruit production in Eritrea during the 1950s-60s. Their company, Fratelli De Nadai, was fi-nanced by Italian capital and developed close connections with the Ethiopian ruling class. They took over and ex-panded Filippo CASCIANI's ELABERED concession in 1958 and began banana production along the Gash in the 1960s. Most of their exports went to Arab oil producing coun-tries, and some of their fortune was made smuggling

MELOTTI liquors along with fruit. In the late 1960s De Nadai began paying protection money to the ELF and in 1973 the elder brother was kidnapped briefly. The company was nationalized in 1975.

DENKEL. Formerly the southeastern coastal province of Eritrea, stretching from the BURE PENINSULA in the north to below ASSAB in the south, and containing the entire AFAR-speaking population of Eritrea, Denkel was divided between the new Southern and Northern Red Sea Administrative Regions in May 1995. Although it was the first part of Eritrea colonized by ITALY, geography, ethnography and commerce all worked in the past to keep Denkel, south of Bure, isolated from the rest of Eritrea. Most of Denkel is a barren desert, with its interior depressions attaining some of the hottest temperatures on earth, and pastoralist elements of the Afar have always moved across the artificial border with ETHIOPIA at will. A well-surfaced road has yet to be constructed connecting any part of Denkel with central Eritrea.

Historically, Denkel's links with the rest of Eritrea have been largely by sea, although Denkel's coastal residents trade even more frequently with the coast of Arabia than they do with MASSAWA. Although various Ethiopian rulers, Turkish governors and their NA'IBs, all claimed the small ports south of Hawakil Bay (EDD, BEYLUL, Assab) during the seventeenth to nineteenth centuries, Denkel south of Bure remained autonomous until the advent of an intermittent Egyptian authority in the late 1860s. Italian interest began in 1869, and by 1882 the Italians had usurped Egyptian authority over the coast as far north as Hawakil Bay and had sent exploratory expeditions into the interior. In 1890 Denkel was incorporated into the Italian colony of Eritrea, and in 1908 the BORDERS with Ethiopia were delimited; but Eritrean Denkel saw little colonial development outside of Assab (*see* SALT and FISHING) and the MINING of potash at Colluli, which was linked by railroad with Mersa Fatma.

After 1952 the Ethiopian government worked to detach Denkel south of Hawakil Bay from the rest of

Eritrea. In 1965 Haile Selassie planned to merge Eritrean
Denkel with Ethiopia's Wello province, and these plans,
centered on ASSAB, continued until the DERG created the
Afar autonomous region in 1987. By this time the EPLF
had grown in power in northern Denkel (*see* B U R E
PENINSULA), and after the battle of AFABET Ethiopian
units largely abandoned the area north of Hawakil Bay,
while increasing their garrisons along the southern coast.
During early 1991 all Denkel was liberated by the EPLA
in its DENKEL CAMPAIGN.

    After liberation Denkel province was restored to its
former boundaries, with its administrative center at
Assab, and its first administrator was an Afar-speaking
EPLF cadre, Mohamed Homad. The legacy of Ethiopian
political division, Afar nationalism, and an Afar-based
insurrection in neighboring DJIBOUTI all made the EPLF
cautious about Denkel's integration into an independent
Eritrea. Consequently, in preparation for the 1993
REFERENDUM, the former EPLF Secretary-General,
RAMADAN MOHAMED NUR, briefly oversaw the
administration. His encouragement of autonomous
provincial councils (elected in Denkel's five sub-
provinces on May 3, 1993) increased Afar support for the
government and REFERENDUM on independence. After a
brief stint by Mohamed Said Bareh, in February 1994,
HUMED MOHAMED KARIKARI served as governor until
Denkel was incorporated into the new Red Sea "Zobas" (*see*
ADMINISTRATION) in 1995.

DENKEL   CAMPAIGN (February-May 1991). In late 1990
the EPLF planned a military campaign to liberate the
DENKEL coastline, both to assure future political control
of the key port of ASSAB, and to create a diversionary
front from the main battles in AKELE GUZAI and central
Ethiopia. In February 1991 EPLA units pushed south from
Gelalo towards the Ethiopian base at Tio, which fell on
February 27 to a combined land-water assault, followed on
March 8 by EDD. The Derg then moved up reinforcements
and tried to hold a line just north of Berasole, known as
the Wadi Front. The EPLA attack began on March 30 and

culminated in a seven hour tank battle on April 2, in which they destroyed or captured six Ethiopian brigades and 38 tanks. EPLA units then raced south and liberated BEYLUL, only fifty kilometers from Assab. Ethiopian units were brought up from Assab and central Ethiopia, but a series of counterattacks in mid-April failed and they then dug in on the northern outskirts of the city, whose road communications with Ethiopia were cut on May 21. The EPLA held off its final assault until the Derg had collapsed, and liberated Assab after a two-day battle, on May 25.

DEQI MENAB. Largest of the original descent-groups ("deqi") of the TIGRINYA-speakers of the central highlands, the Deqi Menab claim descent from a Jewish prince of the tribe of Benjamin ("Menab") who came with Menelik I from Israel after the union of the Queen of Sab'a with Solomon (*see* SOUTH ARABIA). The actual origins of the Deqi Menab seem to be around Geshinashum in DEMBEZAN, from where they spread through KARNISHEM and most of western Hamasien, giving rise to the important descent-group of DEQI TESHIM, and mixing with the LOGGO inhabitants of central Hamasien. Other branches moved southeast into AKELE GUZAI, giving rise to the descent groups of the Meretta Kayieh, Meretta Sembene and the Akele, Guzai and SHIMEZANA, all of which share similar customary laws.

DEQI TESFA (Western Seraye) *see* AREZA.

DEQI TESHIM (Hamasien). The descendants of a legendary Aite-Shum ("Teshim") inhabiting west-central HAMASIEN gave their name to the Deqi Teshim district containing HAZZEGA, TSAZZEGA and ASMARA. By the seventeenth century the district was a feudal MEDRI divided into three GULTI for tribute purposes: Deqi-Teshim proper (centered on Tsada Kristan), Deqi-Zerai (Hazzega) and Takele-Ageba (Tsazzega), with the latter holding jurisdiction over the independent Rist-Gult of Asmara.

DERG (Amh.: "committee"). The military junta that ruled
ETHIOPIA, including much of Eritrea, from September
1974 through May 1991. First known as the Military Coordinating Committee (April 1974) and then the Provisional Military Advisory Committee (September), the Derg
was created by lower ranking officers and enlisted men to
coordinate the Ethiopian revolution, and its first chairman was an Eritrean, General AMANUEL MIKA'EL ANDOM.
But the real leader of the Derg was the vice-chairman,
Colonel Mengistu Haile Mariam, who organized Aman
Andom's fall and assumed full power as the military
dictator of Ethiopia in February 1977.

Under Mengistu the Derg became famous for its use
of terrorism to destroy its political opponents. General
Amanuel Andom was murdered in late November, and from
December 1974 to February 1975, Colonel Asfaw Zenab
ordered the murder of over 250 young Eritreans, who were
strangled with piano wire by his Afegn (Tigrn.: "Stran-
glers") urban death squads, presaging the Derg's 1977-78
"Red Terror" campaign in Ethiopia proper. The Afegn operated until 1980, while in the countryside the Derg used
Eritrean nationalist defectors and spies, known as Wedo
Gheba, to commit atrocities and sabotage, which were then
blamed on the nationalists.

During 1975-77, Mengistu moved the Derg increasingly to embrace the Marxist revolutionary program
of the student movement, while at the same time
destroying all left-wing and democratic political parties.
He attempted to co-opt calls for democratization by
forming several civilian-military committees to organize
an Ethiopian Marxist-Leninist governing structure, and in
1984 established the Workers' Party of Ethiopia (WPE),
whose leaders most Eritreans continued to refer to as "the
Derg." During 1984-91, WPE membership was usually
required of Eritrean civil servants and management level
employees in nationalized industries.

The Derg's motto was "Ethiopia First" and Mengistu
refused to countenance Eritrean independence, preferring
a "military solution" which involved increasingly violent
and costly warfare against the Eritrean liberation move-

ment. He urged the continual reinforcement of Ethiopian troops during 1975-76, and in 1977 negotiated a military alliance with the USSR that provided his greatly expanded army with massive firepower. The importance of Eritrea to the Derg was highlighted by the seniority of the Derg members who served as its military governor-generals, including the second vice-chairman, Teferi Bante, Gen. Tesfaye Gebre-Kidane and DAWIT WOLDE-GIORGIS. Mengistu promised to destroy the Eritrean movement at mass demonstrations in 1978, and toured Eritrea as the Ethiopian Second Offensive was launched. He came again in November 1981 to prepare for the RED STAR CAMPAIGN, and in early January 1982 he moved the Ethiopian government to ASMARA, where it remained for two and a half months, until it was clear the campaign had failed.

Mengistu relied on naked force to maintain his power, and his execution of rivals slowly destroyed the rest of the Derg, leaving only the most loyal or sycophantic. Although the Derg originated in the army, Mengistu's Eritrean policy slowly alienated the officer corps, as he executed commanders in the wake of military failures, beginning in July 1977 with the commander of the Eritrean army, General Getachew Nadew, followed by Gen. Tareke Taye, commander of the NAKFA front in February 1988, and the detention of the surviving AFABET commanders in March. Military failures in Eritrea also sparked a series of mutinies during the 1980s, beginning with bloody inter-Ethiopian fighting in June 1983, and culminating in an attempted coup against Mengistu on May 16, 1989. The coup was crushed in ADDIS ABABA, but in Asmara the leaders controlled the city for three days, only succumbing after a tank battle at KAGNEW STATION, following the defection of General Hussein Ahmed and two others to Mengistu's camp. In the aftermath, over 30 senior officers were killed and 250 arrested, further demoralizing the army.

Mengistu's slogans of "Unity or Death" and "Everything to the War Front" could not turn the tide, and his eleventh-hour attempts at negotiation in 1989 and

1991 were stymied by his continuing unwillingness to countenance Eritrean independence. In the face of continuing defeats the Derg/WPE maintained its power by increasingly brutal methods that further alienated its support even among its own cadres, and in May 1991 the entire military-political structure collapsed, with Mengistu fleeing to Zimbabwe on May 21, paralleled by the flight of Gen. Hussein Ahmed and other senior officers from Asmara to DJIBOUTI.

During 1991 the EPLF released Ethiopian prisoners, including officers and WPE members, at the Ethiopian border. Eritrean members of the WPE were separated according to the nature of the crimes they had committed against Eritreans, with most of them attending "re-education" courses about the value of national independence, after which they returned to their previous jobs to do their NATIONAL SERVICE. Others, who were more seriously involved in Derg/WPE activities, were assigned to road crews and similarly arduous tasks as part of their national service; while those accused of actions harming or killing Eritreans were tried and imprisoned.

DE ROSSI. A prominent Italian colonial family, founded by Giuseppe De Rossi (1867-1944) who came to Eritrea as a major in the Italian army in 1894, and worked for the colonial government in both ETHIOPIA and Eritrea until 1919. During the 1920s he pioneered the commercial use of DUM PALM and opened a button factory in KEREN that employed over a hundred women. He also developed sisal plantations in GHINDA, mineral water at DONGOLO and experimented with a brewery. He lived with an Eritrean woman, despite Italian race laws, and recognized his mixed-race son; but in the late Fascist period he left the colony.

His son, Guido (1904-53), took over his business interests around Keren and in the west, where he became a leading hides exporter and expanded the Dum Palm button factory to seven hundred workers in the 1940s. Guido was a founder and first president of the Italo-Eritrean Association, and addressed the UN in 1949 as a member of the INDEPENDENCE BLOC. Depressed by the prospects for mixed-race Italo-Eritreans in the FEDERATION with Ethiopia, he committed suicide in March 1953, deeply shocking the Italian community.

DESA (alt. diessa). The communal LAND TENURE system of the central highlands. Desa seems to have developed in the medieval period in parts of HAMASIEN and AKELE GUZAI (where it was also called *shehena).* Under the desa system the village owned all farmland in common and each household was entitled to one equal share (GEBRI). The land was graded according to fertility and a household's share consisted of several fields of varying grades. The land was periodically redistributed by a committee of village elders (SHUMAGULLE), usually every seven years. New immigrants were able to obtain shares after a certain period of time, often forty years.

The flexible and egalitarian nature of the desa system made it attractive to Italian colonial rulers as they grappled with problems of land scarcity, due to growing population and colonial land confiscations. During the 1930s, in particular, they encouraged villages to adopt desa in place of family-based RISTI tenure, as new land alienations occurred for military projects and Italian settlement. The change to desa continued under the BRITISH ADMINISTRATION, and by the 1960s it was the predominant system in Hamasien and Akele Guzai, and had spread into northern SERAYE. Land scarcity reduced the size of fields, however, and by the 1940s widows, spinsters and orphans were only given half a share. In July 1953, the Eritrean Land Tenure Act changed the redistribution of desa from a seven to a twenty-seven year cycle, freezing in place the rights of village elders who had manipulated the system under colonial rule.

During the 1970s both the ELF and EPLF viewed desa as a manifestation of indigenous socialism, but ordered new, more equitable distributions, or encouraged nondesa villages to adopt it in the highland areas they controlled. The DERG took the same view, and during the 1980s converted all of Seraye to desa tenure, as well as other

remaining non-desa highland areas. By 1991 the average
desa share was between one and half an acre, and continual use of all land had led to widespread environmental
degradation, while the threat of periodic redistribution
(although in many areas it had not taken place since Federation) was a disincentive to improvement. Although desa
did away with family land disputes, these were replaced
by disputes between villages. The new government consequently changed its attitude about desa as a viable land
tenure system, and the 1994 Draft LAND LAWS abolished
it, although full implementation may take many years.

DIASPORA (Eritrean overseas emigrants). In the early
1990s an estimated 750,000 people of Eritrean parentage
live outside the country, comprising about one-quarter of
the total Eritrean POPULATION. The diaspora began
during the colonial period, when hundreds of educated
Eritreans moved to ETHIOPIA in search of economic and
social opportunities. After the Second World War, the
diaspora grew as skilled Eritrean workers sought
employment in Ethiopia, Kenya, SUDAN and the Arab
world. By the 1960s, remittances sent home by overseas
workers were becoming an important part of the Eritrean
economy, particularly from Ethiopia and the oil-rich Arab
states.
    During the 1970s the first wave of educated, largely
Christian, Eritrean REFUGEES fled to Europe and North
America, where they laid the foundations for a prosperous
and growing diaspora community that became a key element in the financial network of the EPLF during the
1980s, with many contributing 20 to 50 percent of their
salaries. The EPLF's LABOR ORGANIZATIONS, STUDENT
ORGANIZATIONS and WOMEN'S ORGANIZATIONS were
important in organizing this community from 1974
onward, and their annual conventions developed into
important cultural events, notably the Bologna Festival
(organized by European workers from 1975 on), which
brought together the dispersed refugee communities.
Muslim refugees tended to settle in the Middle East, with
AFARs moving to SAUDI ARABIA and DJIBOUTI, while

MASSAWA townspeople settled in Port Sudan and Jeddah. Despite its longstanding ties to the ELF, the Middle Eastern diaspora, which numbered over 100,000 by the 1990s, also contributed to the EPLF's finances through fundraising and tithing.

During the decade before liberation Eritreans in the diaspora contributed at least $50 million to the EPLF. Since independence all Eritrean emigrants are required to pay two percent of net income as tax to the national government, or lose their citizenship. Remittances sent directly to relatives at home amount to much more, and make up a large proportion of Eritrea's hard-currency income. By 1993 the diaspora population included about 500,000 in Sudan, close to 100,000 in Ethiopia, 50,000 in Europe (14,000 in Germany, 8,000 in SWEDEN, 5,000 in ITALY), and 30,000 in North America (over 20,000 in the U.S.). Some of these figures are declining with REPATRIATION (Ethiopia, Sudan, Germany), but other communities are growing and becoming increasingly indigenized to their host countries (U.S., Canada, Italy).

DIGLAL. The paramount chief of the BENI 'AMER tribal confederation, the diglal is selected from the leading family of the DAGA subtribe.

DIGSA (Akele Guzai). A village of about three thousand between SAGENEITI and HALAI in the Deqi Digna district. According to tradition, Digsa was settled by the family of Weresenezghi in the fouteenth century, who drove out earlier settlers from the Liban clan. By the seventeenth century it was a fortified market town, along with Halai (founded 17th c.), on the Taranta caravan route from HIRGHIGO into AKELE GUZAI. The importance of this trade led the village to ally with the NA'IB of Hirghigo, who controlled the caravans. In 1768 Ras Mika'el Sehul, the Tigrean ruler, besieged Digsa during his war with the Na'ib, killing some seven hundred villagers. In the 1860s many Christians began to convert to Catholicism under the influence of DE JACOBIS, and in 1890 the Italians built a fort at Halai.

Residents of the two villages supported the revolt of
BAHTA HAGOS against Italian rule in 1894, and after
Bahta was killed at Halai in December, the chief of Digsa,
Sequar Bahro, buried Bahta against Italian orders. An
Italian farming concession was operated by the Gallo
family near the main road, and some economic
opportunities developed in transport and forestry, but
Italian rule is mainly remembered for Digsa's loss of a
land dispute with neighboring Hebo. During the early
liberation struggle residents of Halai, who included some
Muslim families, supported the ELF, which operated along
the escarpment, primarily among the SAHO, and briefly
controlled Digsa in 1975. On July 23, 1977, the EPLF
liberated Digsa, and many villagers joined the front. Many
others fled as refugees when the village was retaken by
the DERG in 1978. An Ethiopian garrison was built at
Digsa to protect an important microwave station; but it
was raided in March 1987 by the EPLA, and on March 19,
1990, the village was liberated.

DIMETROS GEBREMARIAM, Aba Melake Selam. A leading
figure in the UNIONIST PARTY, architect of Eritrea's 1962
ANNEXATION by Ethiopia, and important reformer in the
ORTHODOX CHURCH, Aba Dimetros was born near AREZA
in western SERAYE in 1900. He received religious
instruction in Ethiopia and in 1922 became secretary to
the leading Eritrean feudal dignitary and colonial
collaborator, Ras Kidanemariam Gebremeskel. In 1929 he
was among a select group of Eritrean clergy to be ordained
by the Coptic Patriarch in Egypt, and in 1930 he was made
responsible for his native Deqi Taes district in Seraye.
Aba Dimetros was politically ambitious, but also a
vigorous proponent of modernizing and reforming the
Orthodox Church to enable it to compete with European
Christian sects.

In 1942 he joined the MAHABER FEQRI HAGER when
his patron, Ras Kidanemariam, became its honorary
president, and he went on to play an important role in
mobilizing Eritreans to support union with Ethiopia
through the Orthodox Church. He was elected to the

ASSEMBLY for Deqi Taes in 1952, and in 1953 became its vice president. Trusted by the Emperor's representative, Aba Dimetros arranged the fall of TEDLA BAIRU and ALI MOHAMED MUSA REDAI in 1955, after which he became the most powerful figure in the Assembly, pushing through a pro-Ethiopian legislative agenda that terminated most of Eritrea's autonomous institutions. In October 1961 he was almost killed in an assassination attempt by a disgruntled former Assemblyman, Gebremedhin Hailu, who died from wounds inflicted by Aba Dimetros' bodyguards. The outpouring of mourners at Gebremedhin's funeral indicated public hatred for Aba Dimetros, who styled himself Melake Selam ("The Peacemaker"), and again narrowly escaped assassination in the 1962 grenade attack on ABIYE ABEBE. Nonetheless, he pushed through the ANNEXATION of Eritrea in November, for which he was rewarded with the prestigious ecclesiastical post of Nebur-ed of Aksum in 1963.

This office gave Aba Dimetros continued jurisdiction over Eritrean church affairs, and he was instrumental in developing the Mahaber Hawariat church printing press in Asmara, along with benevolent organizations, new church construction and the reform of church administration. In 1969 he became general administrator of the Ethiopian Orthodox Church in ADDIS ABABA. Ironically, he was imprisoned by the DERG for eleven months in 1975, and died in 1989.

DIMTSI HAFESH (Tigrn.: "Voice of the Masses") *see* RADIO.

DJIBOUTI. The former French colony is Eritrea's southern neighbor and historically was an economic rival for the entrepot trade of Ethiopia with the Eritrean ports of ASSAB and MASSAWA. Relations between Eritrea and Djibouti since 1991 have been largely cordial, despite Djibouti's neutrality during the long struggle for independence and its close ties with FRANCE, which maintains a large military presence there. When Assab fell in May 1991, about seven thousand Ethiopian soldiers fled into

northern Djibouti, where they were interned and then
repatriated; but Ethiopian NAVY vessels, claimed by
Eritrea, were retained by Djibouti. An Eritrean-
Djiboutian cooperation agreement was signed in December,
1993, but tensions between the countries were provoked
by the 1993-94 rebellion of AFAR leader Ahmed Dini, a
native of the Eritrean border region of Raheita, against
Djibouti's Somali-dominated government, and by the 1995
Eritrean claim to eleven kilometers of coast around Ras
Doumeira, based on an Italian colonial treaty with the
Afar Sultanate of Raheita. The creation of a bilateral
commission in 1997 to solve these and other issues has
led to improved relations.

DOGALI (Semhar). Crossing point of the Massawa-Asmara
road over the seasonal Hamasat River, Dogali (properly
"Teda'li") is the site of MASSAWA's principal water supply and several important battles. On the night of January
26, 1887 a battalion of Italian infantry marching to reinforce the fort at SA'ATI was ambushed and annihilated by
much superior Ethiopian forces commanded by Ras
A L U L A. The deaths of over five hundred European
soldiers provoked widespread indignation in Italy and
popularized the Italian invasion of highland Eritrea two
years later. During the colonial period a water pumping
station and bridge were built at Dogali, which made the
site strategically important as the ARMED STRUGGLE
intensified in the 1970s. An Ethiopian garrison fortified
the site and by 1977 Dogali was the rear base for the
Ethiopian positions defending the Massawa front. On
December 9 the EPLA overran Dogali, after which it became a place of refuge for civilians fleeing Ethiopian
airstrikes on Massawa. The Ethiopians returned in 1978,
and guerrilla attacks on the area continued until it was
again liberated in February 1990. Irrigated farming was
first developed in the area by the AD SHAYKH family of
EMBEREMI, and has been revived since liberation.

DONGOLO (Semhar). Two villages developed during the
Italian period along the Massawa-Asmara road around

Upper (Lalai) and Lower (Tehetai) Dongolo. Lower Dongolo
was developed as the main factory and depot for the Sabar-
guma mineral water concession in the late 1930s, and a
naval supply base was built at Upper Dongolo during the
Second World War, along with small Italian farming concessions. In 1977-78 the area was the scene of heavy
fighting as the EPLF pushed up the mountains towards
Asmara. In February 1990, during the second MASSAWA
BATTLE, the EPLF overran Ethiopian positions in Lower
Dongolo, but were unable to push past Upper Dongolo,
where extremely heavy fighting occurred during the
spring and summer of 1990 on what was known as the
GHINDA Front. After liberation the area was in ruins, but
by 1995 much of the villages had been rebuilt.

DRAMA. Despite a tradition of morality plays associated
with the ORTHODOX CHURCH, modern theater in Eritrea
owes much to European influences, beginning with the
Italian colonization of ASMARA. The first playhouse, the
Teatro di Asmara, opened in 1918 and was greatly enlarged in 1936, but its plays were all in Italian for European audiences. During the 1950s an Eritrean Cultural
Association, the Mahaber Memheyash Hagerawi, was
formed by TIGRINYA teachers who put on plays promoting
Eritrean culture, often in opposition to Ethiopian domination. In 1961 the Asmara Theater Association (MATA)
was founded, and during the 1960s it produced a number
of plays in Tigrinya with a guardedly nationalist content,
but it was dissolved in the early 1970s by Ethiopian authorities. Drama largely died out in Asmara during the
DERG period; but in the liberated zones the EPLF cultural
troupe, the Red Flowers, produced nationalist plays and
cultural shows. In October 1993 MATA was reestablished
by some of its former members and fighter-artists from
the Red Flowers, using the old the Teatro di Asmara. Its
dramatic productions include Tigrinya translations of European classics and locally written plays. The Art Lovers'
Association, founded in 1991 by fighter-artists, also
performs original plays in Asmara.

DUM PALM. The indigenous palm which is so widespread in the western lowlands that it symbolizes the BARKA region. Dum palm leaves traditionally formed an important source of fiber for clothing and construction materials, while the nut is prized by children for its sweet middle layer. Italian colonists, led by Giuseppe DE ROSSI, exploited the "vegetable ivory" of the nuts for button manufacture, which was one of Eritrea's few exports during the early colonial period. During the 1940s-60s, T. Camerino's DUMCO produced fiber for sacking from dum palms in a factory at AGORDAT. The tree trunk is also used for construction, and many were cut to fortify trenches during the ARMED STRUGGLE.

- E -

EDD (Denkel; alt.: Edi). An Afar village on the central Denkel coast, between Tio and BEYLUL. Edd was purchased in 1845 by French agents from the local Afar chief for 1,800 MTTs, but it was never developed. In 1866 EGYPT claimed it, followed in 1885 by ITALY, but no development took place beyond the appointment of traditional chiefs as salaried colonial officials. Its population was some three hundred in the late 1800s, and today is about two thousand. During the 1970s it was a stronghold of the ELF-PLF and later the EPLF, but in 1980 the Ethiopians captured it with a task force from ASSAB and held it until the DENKEL CAMPAIGN of 1991.

EDUCATION. Traditional education in Eritrea was the preserve of organized religion, either the ORTHODOX CHURCH or ISLAM. Students were almost entirely male, and study consisted of memorizing religious texts, reading and writing, for Christians in GE'EZ, for Muslims in ARABIC. Literacy was rare even among religious men, and hand-copied books were highly prized possessions. The beginnings of modern education also had a religious basis: Christian European missionaries (*see* CATHOLIC CHURCH and PROTESTANT CHRISTIANITY) who introduced a number of radical innovations from the mid-1800s onward, including female education, the literacization of indigenous languages and the printed book. While the European missionaries concentrated on the highlands, SENHIT and the KUNAMA areas, Muslim religious reformers introduced a growing interest in literacy in parts of the lowlands.

ITALIAN COLONIALISM brought the beginnings of a secular educational system, but it was extremely limited due to the conservative policies of Italian rulers, who feared the development of an educated Eritrean population that might challenge their authority. The colonialists built schools for their own children, but their objectives in educating Eritreans were limited to undermining the power of the pro-Ethiopian Orthodox Church in the highlands, promoting a state-controlled Islamic educational system in the lowlands, and producing soldiers able to understand the rudimentary commands of Italian officers, along with a few Italian-educated Eritrean interpreters. To achieve these ends the colonial Education Decree of January 31, 1909, ordered the separation of Eritrean and Italian schools, the adoption of a government-approved curriculum for all mission schools, and the limitation of Eritrean education to grade five; later reduced to grade four in 1932. Twenty-five schools were eventually established for Italian children, and only six for the entire Eritrean population. The Protestant mission schools, most of them administered by the Swedish Evangelical Mission (SEM) were phased out, and in 1935 the system was taken over by the state (*see* SWEDEN). The Catholic Church, on the other hand, took over responsibility for staffing many Italian schools.

Eritrean schools were located in Asmara, Adi Kaiyeh, Adi Ugri, Keren, Massawa and Sageneiti. Only two, the Scuola Vittorio Emanuelle in Asmara and the Scuola Salvago Raggi in Keren, gave academic classes beyond grade four, while the others provided basic literacy and vocational training. In 1923 there were 523 Eritrean students and by 1935 there were still only 2,472. The results of Italian educational policy were that a very

small group of Eritreans had any form of modern higher
education. Of these, many either emigrated to ADDIS
ABABA, particularly if they were Protestants, or joined
the colonial government as interpreters. A notable
exception was WOLDE-AB WOLDE-MARIAM, who served as
director of the former SEM school in Asmara from 1935-
41 and took a leading role in promoting TIGRINYA
language education, along with Memher ("Teacher") Yisaq
Tewoldemariam.

   After 1941 the BRITISH ADMINISTRATION encouraged modern education as part of their policy of
promoting Eritrean self-sufficiency and later to
Eritreanize the administration and economy. But the
British had few resources to invest, and most of the new
educational system was created by Eritreans. Lack of
teachers was the most limiting factor, as communities
built their own schools and the government provided basic
texts. In the lowlands, where the Italians had provided
primary instruction in Arabic, the British imported a few
Sudanese teachers and developed an Arabic-language curriculum. In the highlands, a separate Tigrinya-language
curriculum was developed for Christians, while Muslims
attended their own Arabic-language schools. Female
students attended separate schools, and in many areas
where the community could only afford one school, the
school was for males only. This fragmented school system,
developed ad hoc during the 1940s, reinforced both the
polarization between Muslim and Christian communities
and the gender gap in access to education.

   By 1951 there were 97 Eritrean schools, almost all
of which were primary schools serving grades 1-4 and
taught in either Tigrinya or Arabic, with English as a
subject and a strong emphasis on vocational training. In
1947-48 two middle schools (grades 5-8) were opened, one
in Asmara for the highlands, and one in Keren for the
lowlands. The language of instruction in these schools was
English, and they were filled by competitive examination.
To provide instructors a Teachers Training Institute (TTI)
was opened in Asmara in 1945, and textbook production
and printing was developed by the Education Department

of the administration. Thus, by the time of Federation, the basis of Eritrea's state education system had been laid. This was expanded during the Federation, when the Eritrean Department of Education continued to develop under a British and later an Indian administrator. The number of schools expanded to 126, and two high schools were opened in Asmara: the Ethiopian-funded Haile Selassie I (now Red Sea), and Prince Makonnen. Total student enrollment increased from 12,021 in 1952 to 30,936 by 1962. But during the late 1950s the Tigrinya and Arabic curriculum began to be superseded by AMHARIC language instruction, first as a subject, and then, during 1960-63, as the sole medium of instruction. This created difficulties for Eritrean students, and sparked a number of student strikes. Nonetheless, Eritrean students won a disproportionate number of seats in the Ethiopian national university and other advanced institutions. In 1958 the Catholic Church opened the College of Santa Familia, which became the UNIVERSITY OF ASMARA.

Eritrea's ANNEXATION by Ethiopia in late 1962 placed the Eritrean school system under direct Ethiopian control, and the schools were required to adopt a uniform, Amharic-language curriculum for all grades. At the same time the Ethiopian government opened a number of new schools, including five new secondary schools in Adi Kaiyeh, Dekemhare, Keren, Massawa and Mendefera. After 1964 UNITED STATES Peace Corps volunteers taught in many of the secondary schools, and U.S.-supported vocational and nursing schools expanded in Asmara. The decade preceding the Ethiopian revolution marked the high-point of Eritrean access to quality education, despite the problems created by Ethiopian rule. By 1974 there were 124,752 Eritrean students enrolled in 272 schools. But the intensification of the armed struggle and the educational policies of the DERG destroyed this system during 1974-78, reducing the number of students by 61 percent and the number of schools by 79 percent. The liberation fronts struggled to create their own alternative school system, exemplified by the EPLF's ZERO SCHOOL, but until the mid-1980s the demands of the war made this a very limited undertaking. In 1981 the Derg attempted to rebuild the school system in the areas it had recaptured, and the number of government schools increased to 220, with 104,968 students. But the standards of education were greatly reduced, the TTI teaching school was closed and then converted into a barracks and much of the teaching staff disappeared.

By 1991 the Eritrean population was 80 percent illiterate, with illiteracy among women running close to 95 percent. The EPLF, which by 1991 had some 30,000 students enrolled in its own school system, was hard pressed to take over the government school system and extend primary education to the estimated 429,000 children who needed it, as well as the 293,000 of age to attend higher grades, 85 percent of whom were not enrolled. None-theless, in September 1991 schools opened across the country, and by 1993 there were over 220,000 students enrolled in government schools, including 235 newly opened by the Provisional Government.

Eritrea's post-war educational crisis is best understood from the following statistics: the average class size is sixty, attending in separate morning and afternoon sessions; the male/female ratio averages 54/46 in all grades; 30 percent of all primary and 52 percent of all secondary schools are in Asmara; of 10,000 students who sat for the Eritrean School Leaving Certificate Exam in 1993, only 600 earned the C average required to pass. To address these problems the new Ministry of Education, headed by Osman Saleh Mohammed, has developed programs modeled on the EPLF's educational policy of providing universal primary education in the students' native language and middle-level instruction, grades 6-8, in English. Higher level education, in English, is accessed through competitive exams. The ministry's curriculum development staff produced textbooks in Arabic, TIGRE, Tigrinya and English during 1994, with plans to add instruction in other national languages. Teacher training programs are underway, augmented by NATIONAL SERVICE requirements for graduates. Foreign assistance in the form of British VSO and American Peace Corps volunteers is also increasing in the secondary schools. Besides the government schools, a number of religious schools were built before 1996 by local communities, particularly in the Muslim lowlands (*see* ARABIC), and by Eritrean-based Christian churches. But outside of the major towns, and particularly in the lowlands, education remains largely unavailable, and in 1995 among many Muslim pastoralists female enrollments were not even 20 percent of school age children.

EGYPT. As the economic center of the Red Sea region since earliest recorded history, Egypt has exercised a long-standing influence on Eritrea. The earliest written sources pertaining to Eritrea are Egyptian descriptions of their commercial expeditions to the coast in search of incense, ivory and gold during the period 2500-1500 BC. The Egyptians referred to the coast as part of the land of Punt, which was the "home of the gods" in some of their religious beliefs. In the fifteenth century B.C. Queen Hatshepsut commissioned an expedition to Punt that is depicted in a series of low-reliefs on a temple at Deir al-Bahri giving clear evidence of trade with the Eritrean coast. Egyptian trade continued through the Ptolemaic period, when Greco-Egyptian merchants founded trading posts around the BARKA rivermouth and at the site of ADULIS. Throughout the AKSUMITE period Greco-Egyptian merchants based in Alexandria dominated the foreign trade of the Eritrean coast and were among those responsible for the introduction of Orthodox Christianity, which resulted in close links between the Coptic Patriarch in Alexandria and the ORTHODOX CHURCH in Eritrea. This connection continued after the Arab conquest of Egypt, although commerce declined.

    Egyptian commercial interest in Eritrea revived during the eleventh century under the Fatimid dynasty, which was involved in trade and at times intervened politically in the DAHLAK Sultanate and the MASSAWA area. From the fourteenth century onwards the Mamluk rulers of Egypt made it increasingly difficult for the

Orthodox Church to maintain its relations with the Egyptian Patriarchate, as the Mamluks attempted to gain political control over the Sudanese coast and the lucrative PILGRIMAGE ROUTES through Suwakin. The development of ISLAM in Eritrea, on the other hand, led a growing number of Eritrean Muslims to visit CAIRO, the commercial and educational center of medieval Islam. The conquest of Egypt by Ottoman TURKEY in 1517 coincided with a renewed interest in the Eritrean coast as a battlefield in the naval contest between Islam and Portuguese Christians for control of the Indian Ocean, on which the commercial ascendancy of Egypt depended. Egyptian troops and sailors participated in the Turkish conquest of Eritrea during the mid-1500s and the Suwakin-based Turkish governate of HABESHA became in essence a dependency of the Mamluk Beys of Egypt by the eighteenth century.

Egyptian merchants played an important role in the trade of Massawa, and in the early 1800s the newly autonomous Egyptian ruler, Mohamed Ali, expanded Egyptian political influence in SUDAN and on the Red Sea coast, governing Massawa as part of his conquest of the Hejaz from 1813-22 and again, in a lease agreement with the Ottoman government, from 1846-49. Egyptian political control at Massawa underlined the dominant position of Egyptian merchants on the Eritrean coast, particularly in the lucrative SLAVE TRADE. Egyptian governors in the Sudan also sought to control and exploit the western low-lands, first through slave and cattle raiding (1823, 1832-36) and then through taxation from their new garrison at KASSALA (after 1840), from where they taxed the BENI 'AMER and raided the KUNAMA, NARA and BILEN.

After 1863, the new Egyptian ruler, Isma'il Pasha, pressed Egyptian claims to all the former Turkish province of Habesha, which he interpreted as including most of modern Eritrea. This was part of Isma'il's ambitious plan to create an Egyptian empire covering the entire Nile watershed and the African shores of the Red Sea, including present-day Sudan, Eritrea, Ethiopia and Somalia. Isma'il's development of the Suez Canal (completed 1869) changed the geopolitics of the Red Sea, making it the shortest steamship route from Europe to eastern Asia, and consequently opened an imperialist "scramble" in the region which pitted British against French interests, with Egypt playing the role of a regional imperial power. In 1865 Isma'il acquired political control over the Eritrean coast and garrisoned Massawa in return for payment of a share of tax revenue to the Ottoman Sultan. The NA'IB came under Egyptian control and fortifications were constructed at HIRGHIGO and on the Massawa mainland. In 1866-67 the Egyptian governor extended his rule down the coast of DENKEL, and in 1868 the garrison was reinforced to uphold Egyptian claims as BRITAIN invaded Ethiopia. By this time Egypt also claimed tributary authority over the Beni 'Amer, HABAB and MARYA, and in 1871 Werner MUNZINGER was appointed governor of Massawa and set about linking Egypt's western and eastern Eritrean territories by occupying SENHIT and KEREN.

In 1875-76 Khedive Isma'il attempted to occupy the KEBESSA using European and American mercenary officers and Egyptian troops. The first Egyptian expedition was defeated at GODA GUDI by the Tigrean army of YOHANNES IV on November 16, 1875; the second in a three day battle at GURA' on March 7-9, 1876. The Egyptians withdrew to the coast and a stalemate followed, with Egypt controlling the coast, Senhit and the west, and the Tigreans controlling the central highlands. Egypt employed Charles Gordon to negotiate with Yohannes IV for control of its territories, while at the same time arming Ras WOLDE-MIKA'EL SOLOMUN. But Gordon was unsuccessful in getting Yohannes to renounce his claims to Senhit, and the Egyptian position weakened in 1879, when Isma'il fell from power. In 1882 the Sudanese Mahdiyya erupted against Egyptian rule and soon threatened their position in Eritrea, just as the British occupied Egypt. In 1884 the HEWETT TREATY facilitated a final Egyptian withdrawal from Senhit, where their fortifications and supplies were turned over to Ras ALULA.

In 1885 Egyptian rule ended with ITALY's occupation of Massawa and in November the remnants of the Egyptian garrison were withdrawn. Despite their ultimate failure, the Egyptians laid the foundations of the modern colony of Eritrea, and in particular they brought a new sense of unity to much of the lowlands and northern highlands through their patronage of ISLAM, their tax and tribute policies, and their support for the MIRGHANIYYA Sufi order. Egyptian commercial and cultural connections, supported by Britain, continued through the Italian colonial period, when Cairo developed as an important pole of intellectual attraction for Eritrean Muslims.

Egyptian political ambitions were revived after 1952 by the nationalist government, which increasingly supported the claims of Eritrean Muslims to independence as part of Nasser's policy of pan-ARABISM. When Ethiopia sided with the West during Egypt's 1956 nationalization of the Suez Canal, Nasser allowed WOLDE-AB WOLDE-MARIAM to make RADIO broadcasts into Eritrea; but when HAILE SELASSIE switched his support to Nasser, the broadcasts were stopped. After this, Egyptian support for the Eritrean cause was lukewarm, as Egypt's geopolitical concern with the Nile waters dictated a conciliatory policy towards Ethiopia. Despite the presence of the ELF in Cairo from 1961-70, Egypt provided little material support for the Eritrean ARMED STRUGGLE and accepted few Eritrean REFUGEES.

Between 1991-93 Egypt was unsupportive of Eritrean independence, but after the REFERENDUM Egypt moved quickly to recognize Eritrea. In April 1992 a dispute over Egyptian fishing in Eritrean waters was settled, and in December diplomatic negotiations on future relations took place. On May 25, 1993, Egyptian President Hosni Mubarak visited Eritrea, and signed agreements providing military assistance, training and scholarships to Egyptian technical schools. Nonetheless, tensions have continued between the countries over regional issues, including the HANISH ISLANDS dispute, despite a shared interest in isolating the Islamic fundamentalist regime in Sudan.

ELABERED (Semhar). An agricultural village and extensive irrigated plantation with over 5,000 inhabitants, situated twenty kilometers south of KEREN in the ANSEBA valley on the main road to ASMARA. The area was originally known as Chindiq by its BET JUK inhabitants, but the modern village developed around the "cold well" (Tigre: Ela Beridi) on the Anseba where ITALIAN agricultural concessions were developed by the family of Giuseppe Acquisto, who first settled in the area in 1898, and Pietro CASCIANI, who received his 1,000-hectare concession in 1908. By the 1930s Casciani's sisal and grain plantation was one of the most successful in the colony, and the Acquisto brothers, Pasquale and Vincenzo, had developed irrigated fruit production.

The Second World War and repeated SHIFTA attacks during 1947-51 damaged the Italian concessions, but in 1958 the Fratelli DE NADAI bought out Casciani and developed citrus orchards for export production, adding a tomato canning plant, dairy factory, winery and other improvements, and by the late 1960s the 1200-hectare plantations were the most productive in Eritrea. The Eritrean workers were divided between permanent salaried employees who received housing and other benefits, and temporary field workers, who lived in the adjoining village. As the ARMED STRUGGLE intensified it began to affect the plantation, and on January 27, 1971, sixty elders from nearby villages accused of supporting the ELF were massacred by Ethiopian soldiers.

In 1975 the concession was nationalized by the DERG. Production declined as workers fled, and in 1977 Elabered came under EPLF control. The front tried to revive fruit and vegetable production through a village cooperative, but on November 25-26 much of the plantation was destroyed in the most important battle of the EPLF's STRATEGIC WITHDRAWAL. After the Derg broke through Eritrean lines at ADI YAQOB, they pushed an armored column along the road toward Keren through the Elabered valley, where the EPLF set an ambush. Fighters hid in the trees along the road until a long tank column filled the valley, then struck at close range. The Ethiopians counterattacked and called in air strikes that set the entire valley on fire, but the EPLA held firm and was on the

point of capturing most of the Ethiopian column when they
were forced to retreat by the Derg's movement of another
powerful force up the Red Sea coast. During the 1980s the
Derg imported Tigrean workers to harvest the remaining
fruit orchards, but the irrigation system and factory were
in ruins.

   After liberation the EPLF assigned a battalion of
FIGHTERS to rehabilitate the estate as a government-
managed cooperative. By 1994, 300 hectares were under
cultivation, the reservoir had been cleaned and repaired,
the dairy and cannery were operating and local workers
had taken over most daily operations. Labor disputes
concerning the status of temporary workers disrupted the
plantation in 1994, and the estate's administrators were
accused of mismanagement in 1995, although production
increased slightly. The government has offered the
concession to private capital on a longterm lease, but as of
1997 it remains under state management.

EMBEREMI (Semhar). A fishing village on the coast north
of MASSAWA, Emberemi is noted for the tombs of several
of the leading saints of the AD SHAYKH family and is an
important pilgrimage site for TIGRE-speaking Muslims.
The Ad Shaykh were established in Emberemi by Shaykh
Mohammed Shaykh Ali in the mid-1800s, whose grandson,
the influential   Shaykh Al-Amin Abdulkader, developed
irrigated plantations along the Desset river and elsewhere
on the coastal plain during the colonial period. The
plantations were expanded by his son Mohamed during the
FEDERATION, but in 1975 they were nationalized by the
DERG and most of Emberemi's population fled to SAUDI
ARABIA and Port Sudan. Today the village has about three
thousand residents.

ENDA (Tigrn.: "descent group"). The group of people in a
TIGRINYA-speaking village who claim descent from a
common ancestor, and through this descent also claim
usufruct rights (RISTI) to the village's land. This Enda-
based (Tigrn: enda'ba) system of LAND TENURE rests on
the rights of the descendants of putative first settlers,

who in principle claimed sole usufruct rights to the exclusion of more recent immigrants and their descendants. Out of this system developed a system of secondary leasing and even sale of usufruct rights to "newcomers," often referred to disparagingly as *makalay aylet* ("the sort who cut grass"), who had the right to farm, but not to participate in village councils (SHUMAGULLE). Some argue that the Enda system of land tenure predated the more egalitarian DESA system, but there is no proof of this, and the enda system may actually have developed later, sometime in the fifteenth to sixteenth centuries, during the period of immigration from TIGRAI and the settlement of CHEWA military colonies.

ENERGY (generation/electric power). Eritrea has a poorly developed energy-generating capacity, despite its possible wealth in PETROLEUM reserves. The most important source of household energy is still biomass (wood, dung) which supplies an estimated 82 percent of needs. The Eritrean Electric Authority (EEA), an autonomous branch of the Ministry of Energy founded in 1992, administers all electric generating plants, the most important being thermal (oil) and hydroelectric plants in ASMARA and MASSAWA, with smaller generators in the major towns. The first electric generators were installed by the Italians in 1905, and in 1913 the SEDAO (Sede Electrica dell'Africa Orientale) was formed to develop hydroelectric power from a series of three reservoirs around BELEZA. A large thermal generator was installed at Massawa in 1927, but as the Italians prepared to invade Ethiopia they added more capacity to the port by connecting it with the Beleza hydroelectric system, creating the Massawa-Asmara power grid that still exists. Smaller thermal generators were installed in ADI KAIYEH, DEKEMHARE and KEREN by the Italian Coniel company in the early 1930s, and by 1937 the other towns of Eritrea had electricity. During the succeeding years thermal capacity in urban locations was increased, and during the ARMED STRUGGLE the DERG installed a larger thermal generating station in Asmara as war and drought disrupted hydroelectric supplies.

Nonetheless, in 1991 electric capacity was below the requirements of existing industrial and urban centers.

Since liberation the Ministry of Energy and Mines, headed by Tesfai Gebreselassie, has focused on expanding power supplies as a prerequisite to industrial development. Studies of possible geothermal power from DENKEL and a large hydroelectric project at Setona on the SETIT River are underway; but immediate developments are concentrated on increasing thermal capacity and developing a power grid covering the Asmara-MENDEFERA-Keren-Dekemhare area, under a $158 million program financed by SAUDI ARABIA and the Gulf States, along with a $20 million credit from the World Bank. In 1996 the Asmara-Massawa grid had a forty megawatt potential, while ASSAB had a further twenty. In 1997 an Italian company began work on a $24.5 million extension of the Asmara-Massawa grid, and a Korean company began building a $114 million thermal plant near HIRGHIGO.

ERITREA FOR ERITREANS *see* LIBERAL PROGRESSIVE PARTY; WOLDE-AB WOLDE-MARIAM.

ERITREAN DEMOCRATIC FRONT *see* INDEPENDENCE BLOC.

ERITREAN DEMOCRATIC MOVEMENT (EDM) *see* HERUI TEDLA BAIRU.

ERITREAN ISLAMIC JIHAD *see* JIHAD.

ERITREAN LIBERATION FORCES-PEOPLE'S LIBERATION FORCES (ELF-PLF). As its name implies, the ELF-PLF was made up of several components, whose complicated mutations and divisions are one of the more bewildering aspects of recent Eritrean history; although the personality of OSMAN SALEH SABBE, the ELF-PLF's founder and "godfather," gives the organization a certain degree of continuity. The ELF-PLF developed out of the personal and ideological rivalries that were tearing apart the ELF in 1970. Osman S. Sabbe sought to create a new power-base for himself in this fluid situation by forming his own external organization, the General Secretariat (Arab.: Ama al-Oma), in January 1970. He agreed to unite his organization with the former ELM, co-opting veteran nationalists such as WOLDE-AB WOLDE-MARIAM and MAHMOUD SAID NAWD. Inside Eritrea he supported his "clients," the fighters in the Red Sea coastal districts of ELF Region 3, who depended on him for logistical support, and who he hoped would form his organization's armed wing. The Red Sea region also was the area in which the reform-minded TRIPARTITE UNITY FORCES had developed, and so Osman Sabbe was tied to the cause of reform, more by chance than by design.

As the ELF disintegrated Sabbe sponsored a number of dissident groups who were opposed to the old leadership of Regions 1 and 2, including elements of the conservative Muslim OBEL faction, the MARYA group led by ABU TAYARA, and Christian dissidents, including MESFIN HAGOS, who were fleeing persecution by Muslim military leaders. In early 1970 Sabbe brought three hundred of these fighters from SUDAN to Aden, and then to the DENKEL coast, where they were joined by several hundred more fighters from the MASSAWA area led by MOHAMED ALI OMERO and RAMADAN MOHAMED NUR. In June 1970 they all met with Sabbe at SUDOHA ILA in southern Denkel and formed the People's Liberation Forces (PLF), whose external representation would be Sabbe's General Secretariat. But disagreements between the more conservative Obeliyyun and Marya, on one hand, and the Red Sea Muslims, on the other, led the former to withdraw northwards to SAHEL in 1971. In December, after the ELF's First National Congress, the Obeliyyun decided to form their own organization, the Eritrean Liberation Forces.

The small Christian contingent in the PLF, led by Mesfin Hagos, also withdrew northwards and joined the Christian fighters who had gathered at ALA in March 1970. Osman Sabbe had contacted the Ala group and supplied them with some arms, but they had refused to join the PLF. At the end of June 1971 the PLF, which had

moved into north Denkel, met with the Ala group at Emba
Hara and the two agreed to cooperate, but rejected formal
links with Sabbe, who the reformists, led by ISAIAS AFW-
ERKI and Ramadan, did not trust. The PLF elected a new
leadership, replacing Ali Omero with Ramadan M. Nur,
and in August the Ala group elected their own leaders,
including Isaias, Mesfin and Tewolde Iyob, and published
a famous statement of their principles titled "We and Our
Objectives" in which they condemned the sectarian men-
tality of the ELF leadership. These moves laid the foundation for the merger of the two reformist groups during
1972-73 (see EPLF).

   Neither the PLF nor the Ala group attended the
ELF's National Congress. In January 1972 they sent
representatives to meet with Osman Sabbe and the Obel
leaders in Beirut, where the ELF-PLF was formed by
merging the Eritrean Liberation Forces (Obel) with the
People's Liberation Forces represented by Ramadan and
ALI SAID ABDELLA, and the Ala group represented by
Isaias and Mesfin. The ELF-PLF was to be a "national
front" in which each organization maintained its separate
structure, while Sabbe agreed to represent them
diplomatically and supply them with arms. Sabbe's
announcement of the new organization prompted the ELF-
RC's decision to liquidate them in February, sparking the
first of two CIVIL WARS, in which the ELF-PLF held out in
the mountains of Sahel, forming a joint military command
in October 1972. This broke down after the reformist PLF
groups consolidated as the "proto-EPLF" in September
1973, prompting the conservative Obel and Abu Tayara
groups to separate, after which the latter were defeated
and some of their remnants were forced to rejoin the reformists' PLF.

   By 1974, the young reformists of the proto-EPLF
were in full control of the ELF-PLF field forces, and a
break with Sabbe's external wing developed as the field
leadership attempted to gain control over external
relations and supplies. Sabbe struggled to maintain his
position by supporting a small field force of conservative-
minded ex-Obeliyyun led by Adem Saleh, Osman Agib and

Abu Tayara's group, and when the ELF offered to open
negotiations towards a merger with the ELF-PLF Sabbe
welcomed this chance to assure his position. In September
1975 a merger was negotiated in Sudan, but without the
participation of the proto-EPLF field leadership, who
rejected the agreement on November 12, and in March
1976 repudiated Sabbe and his Foreign Office completely.

This ended the first ELF-PLF, but Sabbe retained the
name and his small force of ex-Obeliyyun and other fighters, numbering some 250, who he attempted to develop as a
"Third Force" to retain his political legitimacy. Negotiations were opened with the ELF, which allowed Sabbe's token force to operate from its Sahel base area, and in March
1977 a unity agreement was concluded between the two
fronts, only to be repudiated in 1978 when the ELF-PLF
was driven into Sudan and not allowed to return due to
EPLF opposition to Sabbe.

After this the ELF-PLF became entirely
marginalized, although it retained the support of
conservative Arab governments into the 1980s. In 1979,
Ba'athist agents from IRAQ won over Osman Agib and most
of the executive committee, including Abu Tayara and
Adem Saleh, who split from Sabbe and formed the ELF-PLF
Revolutionary Council (RC) in March. In September Abu
Tayara returned to Sabbe, and on November 15, 1980, Agib
was assassinated in Khartoum. The rest of the ELF-PLF-
RC, representing almost all the former field forces, held a
congress in September 1983 and elected Abdelkadir
Jeilani, another Obeliyyun, as chairman. Sabbe continued
to control the external offices of the ELF-PLF, and
attempted to arbitrate the reunification of the ELF
FACTIONS during 1981-83, leading to the participation of
both ELF-PLF factions in the creation of the United
Organization (UO) in January 1984. Sabbe's struggles with
ABDALLAH IDRIS and others doomed the UO, however, and
the two ELF-PLF factions survived as separate organizations through 1991, although Sabbe's organization
shrank dramatically after his death in 1987, and
Abdelkadir Jeilani's faction lost most of its support after
Iraq's defeat in the Gulf War.

ERITREAN   LIBERATION   FRONT (ELF). Popularly known
as Jebbah (Arab.: "Front"), the ELF initiated the ARMED
STRUGGLE for Eritrean independence from 1961-71, when
it divided into several competing movements, the main
element of which retained the ELF name and organization
and continued to fight inside Eritrea until 1981. The
ELF's great weakness was its lack of a clear and disciplined organizational structure, for which its founders
are largely to be blamed. This weakness allowed sectarian,
ethnic and regional conflicts latent in Eritrean society to
emerge within the organization, where they were
manipulated for personal gain by leading figures, hinder-
ing the development of both a unified military organization and popular mobilization. Despite its political and
military failures, the ELF was a catalytic force in creating
the modern nation of Eritrea, and most of the leading
figures of the nationalist movement, including much of the
leadership of the EPLF, served in the ELF at one time.
Furthermore, the very diversity and factionalism of the
organization gave it a rough-and-ready democratic content, making it an early testing ground for various ideological approaches to building a unified nationalist
movement.
    The ELF was founded in CAIRO on July 10, 1960, by
IDRIS MOHAMED ADEM, IDRIS OSMAN GALADEWOS, Taha
Mohamed Nur, Seid Hussein, Mohamed Saleh Hamid and a
few others. The founders were committed to initiating an
armed struggle for liberation inside Eritrea, and were opposed to the slower-paced program of the already extant
ELM for tactical, ideological and personal reasons. All
the early ELF members were Muslims, and inside Eritrea
Idris relied on the BENI 'AMER religious leader, Sayedna
MOHAMED IBN DAWD IBN MUSTAFA, to create a network
specifically opposed to the ELM. During late 1960 Sayedna
Mohamed laid the groundwork for the ELF, and in July
1961 urged HAMID IDRIS AWATE to take up arms against
Ethiopian rule. ELF organizers also recruited Eritrean
members of the SUDAN DEFENSE FORCE (SDF), who joined

Hamid Idris's band beginning in late 1961. By 1962 a core of about twenty-five armed men was in the field.

The ELF's founders concentrated on developing external support, including arms and training. When OSMAN SALEH SABBE joined the front in late 1961, his contacts with Arab states and SOMALIA facilitated this task. External arms supplies began moving through SUDAN in 1963, and the first thirty ELF trainees also went to Syria. ELF actions began with attacks on police stations in BARKA, GASH-SETIT and SENHIT, expanded to the coastal areas in 1963, and into SERAYE and AKELE GUZAI in 1964, when the first Christian recruits began to join. The Eritrean Liberation Army (ELA) grew from four platoons in 1963, to seven in 1964, with the reorganizations taking place at annual military conferences held at Kur, in Barka. By 1965 the front had about a thousand fighters organized in small units and supported logistically from KASSALA.

The ELF's early organization was ill-defined. The original leaders elected a President, Idris Adem, and Secretary, Idris Galadewos, and in 1962 these two, plus Osman Sabbe, formed a self-appointed SUPREME COUNCIL, who directed affairs from Cairo. In May 1965 they met with field commanders in Khartoum and established a Revolutionary Command (Arab.: Kiada as-Sawriya) based in KASSALA to coordinate external and internal relations, but in reality the authority of this command was bypassed by the three leaders of the Supreme Council. Of more lasting importance was the division of military operations into four ZONAL COMMANDS, which reinforced the ethnic and regional divisions that were developing in the organization. These divisions increased during 1966-67, when large numbers of students and Christians began to join, bringing with them socialist and secular ideas that were foreign to the largely uneducated early fighters.

The Christian influx led to the formation of a separate "Christian" Fifth Zone in the highlands in late 1966, but a combination of internal conflicts and the first major Ethiopian military campaigns led to the defection of the Christian leadership under Wolde Kahsai, and the

massacre of several groups of Christian recruits by
Muslim fighters in the summer of 1967. HAILE SELASSIE
I's divide-and-rule tactics also pitted Christian peasants
against the ELF in western Seraye and Gash-Setit, where
fifty peasants were massacred by Muslim fighters in
September 1967, provoking further ethnic tensions.
Following these incidents and the front's military
failures, concerned fighters from both religions came
together to form the ESLAH reform movement which
criticized both the external leadership and the Zonal
system. In June 1968 the reformists forced the leadership
to hold a meeting at AREDAIB to discuss reorganizing the
front, but the old leadership blocked reform. In
September, Eslah leaders met in the ANSEBA valley and
formed the TRIPARTITE UNITY FORCES from the old Zones
3-5, who maintained logistical links to Osman S. Sabbe.
The leadership of Zone 1, tied to Idris M. Adem, was
opposed to the new movement, and Zone 2 had been
decimated by OMER EZAZ's disastrous attack on HAL-HAL
in August. Thus, despite its growing numerical strength
the ELF was being torn to pieces by internal crisis,
provoked in large part by the absence of an overarching
organizational structure and the gulf between the self-appointed external leadership and the military units in the
field.

An attempt was made to resolve the crisis at
ADOBAHA in August 1969, by replacing the Zonal system
with a three region system that simply reinforced the
existing divisions between the Tripartite Unity Forces
(Region 3) and the old Zones (now Regions) 1 and 2. The
Revolutionary Command was replaced by a provisional
General Command (KIADA AL-AMA) and preparations
were made for a National Congress, but the competing
forces of various ethnic and personal factions made
reconciliation unreachable, as the OBEL group split off
from Region 1, and the Red Sea coastal leadership made
common cause with the Christians in Region 3, spurred on
by the support of Osman Sabbe. Within the remaining
Kiada al-Ama, a radical Marxist underground movement,
the LABOR PARTY, emerged to challenge the authority of

the old leadership. Massacres of Christian recruits in 1969-70 and the execution of two prominent Christians in the ELF leadership, Wolde Ghiday and Kidane Kinfu, provoked the withdrawal in 1971 of many Christian fighters to ALA under the leadership of ABRAHAM TEWOLDE and ISAIAS AFWERKI. This faction was joined by Red Sea coastal forces and dissidents supported by Osman Sabbe, as well as part of the Obel faction, who formed the ELF-PLF in 1971. Eventually, the PLF sections, led by RAMADAN MOHAMED NUR and Isaias, formed the EPLF .

The majority of ELF fighters remained loyal to the old organization, which during 1970 launched a successful terrorist campaign against Ethiopian Airlines, began forming urban guerrilla cells of *fedayin,* and stepped up its military activities in central Eritrea. By 1971 the ELF had brought the war to the attention of the Ethiopian public and the international community, but the organization itself was disintegrating. The ELF's First National Congress, held at Are from October 14 to November 12, 1971, decided to restructure both its political and military organization. But the power struggle between the old leadership, led by Idris Adem, and the younger Labor Party, led by AZIEN YASSIN, ABDALLAH IDRIS, IBRAHIM IDRIS TOTIL and HERUI TEDLA BAIRU, resulted in an ineffective power-sharing agreement in which two executive bodies were created: a REVOLUTIONARY COUNCIL (RC) and an Executive Committee. The RC was intended to be the senior body, determining overall policy, and in some ways took the place of the defunct Supreme Council. Idris Adem was elected chairman and Hiroui Tedla, vice-chairman. But these leaders remained outside Eritrea most of the time, and real authority devolved to the Executive Committee, dominated by the Labor Party. Abdallah Idris, head of the powerful Military Committee, soon emerged as the leading figure in the field, and his reorganization of the ELF military structure into twelve battalion-strength sectors greatly increased the effectiveness of the ELA, which in 1972 numbered some two thousand fighters.

In February 1972 the new leadership began the first of two CIVIL WARS by attacking the ELF-PLF. This detracted from the ELF's anti-Ethiopian activities, and despite the original organization's great superiority in numbers, by 1974 the ELF-PLF (soon to be EPLF) was firmly established and beginning to seriously challenge the ELF in central Eritrea. The ELF's failure to destroy the ELF-PLF was due not only to the new organization's successful strategies, but also to the weakness of ELF military and political discipline, particularly in relation to Eritrean civilians, who were subjected to frequent taxes and requisitions by local commanders. Nonetheless, when the Ethiopian Revolution opened the way for the liberation of most of Eritrea, the ELF was still the dominant nationalist organization with some five thousand fighters.

In October 1974, following clashes with the EPLF around ZAGHER, popular pressure forced the two competing fronts to negotiate a cease-fire. Thereafter, both fronts rapidly integrated new Christian recruits, with the ELF drawing some ten thousand from the highland areas it controlled in Seraye and western HAMASIEN. The new recruits changed the cultural and regional composition of the front, and a power struggle ensued pitting the younger, largely Christian, recruits against the largely Muslim older fighters. A key issue in this power struggle was the reunification of the nationalist movement, with the new recruits largely favoring unity with the increasingly powerful EPLF, and the older leaders generally favoring Osman Sabbe's largely Muslim ELF-PLF. In May 1975 the ELF's Second National Congress was held, in which the Muslim veterans succeeded in barring the full participation of new Christian recruits, and the Labor Party finally ousted the remnants of the traditionalist leadership, marked by the removal of Idris Adem from the RC and his replacement by AHMED NASSER, with Ibrahim Totil as vice-chairman. The Labor Party leadership attempted to hold the middle ground of the diverse ELF membership, but it increasingly alienated both Christian radicals on its left and Muslim traditionalists on its right.

Immediately after his election, Ahmed Nasser opened negotiations with Osman Sabbe, who claimed to represent all the ELF-PLF and proto-EPLF forces. In August-September a unity agreement was reached in Khartoum, but it was repudiated in November by the EPLF field leadership, and in 1976 the ELF allowed Sabbe's group to join it in the field. Ahmed Nasser, pressured by the younger Christian elements, then held further negotiations with the EPLF, in which the ELF argued for a National Democratic Front to be formed in which all nationalist organizations would be fully merged, while the EPLF called for a political coalition. Even as the negotiations proceeded, the two fronts stepped up their war effort, liberating Eritrea's main towns during 1976-77. But the ELF proved far less adept than its rival, liberating only a few towns in the western lowlands and Seraye, and for the first time it began to be eclipsed by the EPLF, which by 1978 had perhaps twice as many fighters as the ELF.

This reversal coincided with internal challenges to the new ELF leadership from both "left" and "right." The leftist challenge came from the Christian dissidents of FALUL, culminating in a purge of their leaders and the defection of many of their members to the EPLF in the summer of 1977. The challenge from the right came from the new force of ISLAMISM represented by Idris Adem's son, Ibrahim, who was imprisoned in 1978, as Ahmed Nasser attempted to balance the ELF coalition by punishing both dissident groups. On October 20, 1977, as the ELF's position weakened vis-à-vis the EPLF, a unity agreement was finally negotiated that called for merger in principle, but retained the two front's separate organizations. By now an ELF "government" controlled most of western Eritrea from AGORDAT, with a transportation network that ran through Mekerka to the battle lines around Asmara. In April 1978 a joint leadership was formed with the EPLF, and in May a coordinated attempt was made to take BARENTU, but failed in the face of the DERG's counter-offensive, which struck the ELF first.

In May the ELF foiled Ethiopian attacks around Himberti and Adi Teklai, but in June-July the Ethiopians mounted a huge offensive from TIGRAI, where the ELF had operated successfully during 1975-77. By August the ELF had been driven out of most of the western lowlands and Seraye, forcing the remnants of the front's ten thousand fighters to take refuge in SUDAN or in the mountains of SAHEL, where they coordinated their resistance with the EPLF in the desperate defense of NAKFA during 1979. By 1980, the ELF was completely eclipsed by the EPLF in the field, although its external leadership continued to receive the majority of Arab and other international assistance, and projected an image of still being the senior Eritrean nationalist organization.

In an attempt to recoup its position, the RC opened negotiations with the Derg through the USSR and its Arab allies in 1980, in which terms for a separate peace were proposed. Ahmed Nasser met with Russian and Ethiopian representatives during August-November, but no agreement was reached. Nonetheless, friction grew between ELF units and EPLF forces as the ELF leadership feared its fighters would be swallowed by the larger front, and on July 7, 1980, the ELF ordered it units to withdraw from the joint defenses of Northeastern Sahel, leading directly to the Second Civil War in August. By November most ELF forces had been driven over the border into SUDAN, where they were disarmed and interned by Sudanese authorities, although fighting continued through September 1981. The remnants of the ELF entering Sudan totaled some 7,000 fighters, 3,000 dependents, 150 vehicles and some 15,000 weapons, including artillery. In Sudan, the ELF split into competing FACTIONS, and the organization as a unified, military front ceased to exist.

ERITREAN LIBERATION FRONT: FACTIONS (post-1981). After the ELF was forced into SUDAN during the Second CIVIL WAR, it split into rival factions, many of which adopted similar names and attempted a bewildering maze of abortive mergers and internecine power struggles. In Sudan, ELF members hoped to organize a third National

Congress to elect new leaders and resolve their internal divisions, followed by their return to Eritrea. But two fundamental ideological conflicts, as well as personal rivalries, prevented this. The first conflict concerned the secular versus Islamist orientation of the organization, while the second conflict was over reunification with the ELF-PLF and EPLF.

Conflict erupted in November 1981, when the RC leadership expelled ABDALLAH IDRIS, who then organized a coup against AHMED NASSER and his secular colleagues in March 1982, resulting in heavy fighting in the ELF internment camps and Abdallah's claim to chairmanship of the RC. Abdallah's faction represented an increasingly sectarian Muslim element that received substantial support from SAUDIA ARABIA and was courted by the two factions of the ELF-PLF. The secular wing of the ELF coalesced into the Tayara ("General Trend") faction led by Ahmed Nasser and Habte Tesfa-Mariam. During 1982-83 repeated attempts were made to merge these factions, sponsored by various Arab states, including SUDAN and Tunisia, and often portrayed as a necessary precondition to reunification with the EPLF. At the same time, the many ELF members who wanted to return to Eritrea and continue the ARMED STRUGGLE alongside the EPLF formed the SAGHEM faction. Most of Saghem returned to the field during 1983-87, but a small group split off and merged with the Eritrean Democratic Movement (EDM) originally founded by HERUI TEDLA BAIRU in 1977.

In November 1983, Saudi Arabia and Sudan succeeded in bringing together the two ELF-PLF factions, Tayara (which called itself ELF-RC) and Abdallah's ELF to negotiate a unity agreement in Khartoum. Disputes over the conservative, sectarian ideology of Abdallah, OSMAN SALEH SABBE and others led the former LABOR PARTY leaders, Ahmed Nasser and Habte Tesfa-Mariam to leave the negotiations, taking most of the Tayara faction with them. But the others agreed to form a United Organization (UO) in Jeddah on January 25, 1984, and elected a National Council. Power struggles between the leaders quickly undermined the UO, however, and by July 1986, when a series of rival assassinations were unleashed, the UO had divided into three main factions: Abdallah's ELF, Abdelkadir Jeilani's ELF-PLF and the main ELF-UO to which IDRIS OSMAN GALADEWOS and other early ELF leaders belonged. This marked the final disintegration of the old ELF, followed by the death of Osman Sabbe in 1987 and the rise of a strong movement towards ISLAMISM among Abdallah's faction, the newly formed Islamic JIHAD and another ELF-UO faction led by Omer Buraj. These factions were utterly opposed to the EPLF, which they regarded as their primary enemy, fielding guerrilla units against the EPLF in BARKA and even entering into negotiations with the Derg.

On the other side, the secular-oriented ELF factions of Tayara (ELF-RC) and Saghem negotiated their way towards merger with the EPLF, with the ELF-Central Leadership merging completely at the EPLF's Second National Congress. Ahmed Nasser's ELF-RC could not reach a unity agreement, however, and remained in exile, although many members joined the EPLF individually from 1988 onwards. By 1991 most of these factions, with the exception of the Jihad movement , had only a handful of fighters, and after Sudan closed their offices and expelled them in June, a number of them returned to Eritrea to work with the EPLF-controlled PROVISIONAL GOVERNMENT OF ERITREA (PGE), which on June 12 declared the dissolution of all liberation front factions and invited their members to return to work in a government of national unity. The period between liberation and the REFERENDUM (1993) saw the return of much of the ELF. In July 1992 the main ELF-UO, led by Idris Galadewos, returned en masse and transferred all its assets to the PGE, followed by many individuals from Ahmed Nasser's ELF-RC and, after the Referendum, by members of the small Christian EDM. By 1995 the only factions that maintained their political organization, out-side the Islamist movement, were the two Christian groups EDM and Saghem Qetsel operating in Ethiopia, and Ahmed Nasser's ELF-RC in northern Europe.

ERITREAN LIBERATION MOVEMENT (ELM). The first national liberation movement, and an early proponent of the secular, socialist-oriented nationalism that was later to characterize the EPLF, the ELM (Arab.: Harakat Tahrir Eritrea) succumbed to the rivalry of the ELF and Ethiopian repression before it was able to fully develop its organization or strategy. It was founded in November 1958 by MAHMOUD SAID NAWD, SALEH AHMED IYAY and several other Eritrean workers in Port Sudan. Mahmoud Nawd, its leading figure, had been a member of the Sudanese Communist Party (SCP) from 1951, and had considered developing an underground Eritrean organization on the communist cell model from 1956. When he approached IBRAHIM SULTAN ALI with the idea in 1957 the veteran nationalist was hostile, however, and in 1958 the SCP also rejected his idea of sponsoring an Eritrean liberation front. Instead, Nawd and six other Eritrean Muslims discussed forming their own organization beginning in April 1958, and by November had adopted a constitution and outline of principles.

The ELM focused on building national unity among all Eritreans on the basis of a secular, democratic government. But the organization was to be a series of seven-member secret cells, and the ELM's strategy, decided in June 1959, was to first build a country-wide network, particularly in the Eritrean government and POLICE, and then begin an armed uprising against Ethiopian rule led by a police coup. During 1959 ELM activists traveled to AGORDAT, ASMARA, ASSAB and KEREN to organize cells. Nawd contacted Eritrean Christians in Port Sudan, had the constitution translated into TIGRINYA, and in December 1959 contacted a visiting Asmara football club, recruiting its Christian players, led by student activist TUKU'E IHADOGO and manager Kahsai "Wad-Libi," who became ELM leaders in the highlands. At the same time, Tahir "Fedab" Ibrahim Suleiman went to CAIRO to contact student and nationalist leaders and publish ELM literature. The students were suspicious of the ELM, however, and IDRIS MOHAMED ADEM was already organizing his own ELF. Even WOLDE-AB WOLDE-MARIAM was equivocal, although he later agreed to join and represent the ELM in Cairo in 1962.

Recruitment was more successful in Eritrea, where cells developed among much of the police and administration, up to the highest levels, and the ELM was known to Tigrinya-speakers as Mahaber Showate ("Association of Seven"). A series of regional councils were organized to coordinate local activities, and in September forty delegates met in Asmara for the ELM's first Congress. Efforts were also made to recruit Eritreans serving in the SUDAN DEFENSE FORCE (SDF), but during late 1960 the new ELF began its own recruitment campaign in the western lowlands and SDF, undermining the ELM by accusing its leaders of being anti-Muslim Communists, afraid to take up arms and perhaps Ethiopian agents. The ELM had difficulty responding to these accusations because of its secret structure and by mid-1961 the ELF had succeeded in luring away much of the ELM's support in the west and SDF, while its defamatory campaign alerted Ethiopian authorities to the ELM's existence, provoking a police crackdown and purge that led directly to HAMID IDRIS AWATE's opening of the ARMED STRUGGLE, but destroyed much of the ELM network.

In 1962 the ELM suffered further defections to the ELF by nationalists who were frustrated with the ELM's longterm strategy. Activists in Asmara organized a protest of Eritrea's ANNEXATION in January 1963, but were quickly arrested, leading to the break-up of the highland cell organizations. By 1965 the internal network was in shambles and the Sudan-based ELM leadership decided to field its own guerrilla force of fifty fighters, who were surrounded and disarmed by the ELF at Ela Tsa'da in the Eastern lowlands in May 1965. This defeat effectively destroyed the ELM, as many militants, including Saleh Iyay, left to join the ELF and others, including Wolde-Ab and Wad Libi attempted to create a Unity Movement to reunite the nationalist groups. Mahmoud Nawd kept the core of the ELM alive, but was driven out of Sudan by the ELF in 1967, and in 1970 the organization

was formally dissolved to enable its members to join OS-
MAN SALEH SABBE's new ELF-PLF.

ERITREAN PEOPLE'S LIBERATION ARMY (EPLA). The
EPLA or Peoples Army (Tigrn.: Hezbawi Serawit), which
constitutes the armed forces of the State of Eritrea, was
officially formed in 1977 at the EPLF's First National
Congress , but its basic structure had already coalesced in
the armed units of the PLF *(see* ELF-PLF) during 1972-75.
The PLF armed forces were organized along the lines of the
Eritrean Liberation Army (ELA) of the ELF, with the basic
unit the Ganta, equivalent to a platoon, with a strength of
about thirty FIGHTERS in the mid-1970s, later increased
to about forty-five. Two Ganta form a Haile (Tigrn.:
"power"), equivalent to a company, often with heavy
weapons attached and numbering some one hundred fighters in the late 1980s. Four Hailes form a battalion, the
largest operating unit in the EPLA until the mid-1980s
when brigades consisting of three battalions were formed,
followed by the creation in the late-1980s of divisions
(four brigades) and army corps. By 1991 the EPLA had
twelve infantry brigades, a tank brigade, artillery units,
an engineering corps and a territorial militia numbering
over 20,000. But the basic organization of the army was
small-scale   and   devoid   of   insignia   or   socially
differentiated hierarchies of rank.
    The key elements of the EPLA's extraordinarily high
morale, discipline and tenaciousness under fire were developed by the PLF in the mid-1970s, including: political
education, small-unit democracy concerning certain aspects of military life, continuous training and group
bonding developed under the extremely harsh conditions
of CIVIL WAR and then total war in the ARMED STRUGGLE
against the DERG. Every recruit received six months military training before being assigned to a unit, with female
recruits training separately from men. By the mid-1980s,
women made up roughly one-third of the army and over
twenty percent of frontline units, and some women commanded companies *(see* WOMEN'S ORGANIZATIONS). An
EPLF political officer was assigned to every unit to

oversee political education and to act as a liason with the decision making structure of the EPLF .

The military leadership within the early PLF General Command was held by ISAIAS AFWERKI, while from 1975-87 a Military Committee coordinated the actions, logistics and training of the army. The first head of the committee was IBRAHIM AFA, who was succeeded in 1985 by ALI SAID ABDELLA. The EPLA grew from about five thousand fighters in 1975 to over thirty thousand in 1978, but shrank during the relentless Ethiopian OFFENSIVES of 1978-83. Though completely outgunned and outnumbered by over four to one, the people's army survived due to the willpower of the fighters, a superb intelligence network, and brilliant tactics built on an extremely flexible, radio-networked command system. During the 1980s the EPLA also built up a sophisticated arsenal of captured and reconditioned weapons, including highly effective tanks and artillery.

In 1987, a General Staff was created, led by SEBHAT EPHREM. It planned the successful campaigns of AFABET, SEMENAWI BAHRI, MASSAWA, DEKEMHARE and DENKEL. These victories were won by a flexible combination of guerrilla and conventional tactics, extremely accurate fire-control and sheer bravery against Ethiopian forces protected by superior firepower and uncontested control of the air. By 1991 the EPLA had expanded to 95,000 fighters, spread over the length of Eritrea, with heavy weapons units operating alongside the armed forces of the EPRDF deep inside Ethiopia. This expansion was facili-tated in part by the introduction of conscription after 1987 in areas under EPLF control, which produced even greater ethnic diversity, as well as problems of training and discipline for the leadership.

The EPLA, more than any other element of the nationalist movement, created the organizational and ideological foundations for Eritrean national unity. But with the end of the independence war, it was a burden on the new nation's economy that required immediate DEMOBILIZATION, reducing the army to about 45,000 by 1996. There is a large trained reserve capable of rapid mobilization, and all Eritreans between eighteen and forty-five are subject to NATIONAL SERVICE that includes six months of military training. Since 1992 the army has been administered by the Ministry of Defense, headed from 1992-95 by the former vice-chairman of the General Staff, PETROS SOLOMON. In mid-1995 Sebhat Ephrem returned to command the army, which during 1996 was reorganized along the lines of a modern, regular army, with new ranks and regulations.

ERITREAN PEOPLE'S LIBERATION FRONT (EPLF; Tigrn: Hezbawi Gunbar Harnet Ertra). Eritrea's leading nationalist movement from 1978 and the organizational foundation of the present government, the EPLF was responsible for developing the national unity and leadership necessary to win the ARMED STRUGGLE for Eritrean independence. Its leaders have stressed the importance of secular and egalitarian nationalism, social reform, modern education, self-reliance, centralized decision making and strict discipline both in winning the independence war and in rebuilding the country. Throughout its existence, the EPLF developed a unity of purpose and action, and a spirit of self-sacrifice that made its relatively small membership extremely effective in most of its activities, but resulted in outside criticism of the organization as authoritarian and undemocratic.

Although the Eritrean People's Liberation Front was not officially formed until 1977, its roots lay in the ESLAH reform movement in the ELF during the late 1960s, and the breakaway groups led by RAMADAN MOHAMED NUR and ISAIAS AFWERKI, which joined the ELF-PLF coalition in 1972. During the first CIVIL WAR, these two groups cooperated ever-more closely, uniting in September 1973 under the name People's Liberation Forces (PLF; but in Tigrn.: Hezbawi Hailetat Ertrawi), usually known as Shabiyya (Arab.: "Popular" or "People's"). The unified PLF elected a General Command to oversee field operations, with Ramadan as Secretary and Isaias as military commander, both of whom had studied

Maoist guerrilla strategy in CHINA and were committed to a Marxist-oriented program of rural social reform.

The rise of the reformist PLF as the dominant armed group in the ELF-PLF coalition dismayed OSMAN SALEH SABBE, but his arms supplies, brought by sea from YEMEN, were crucial in enabling the nearly five hundred-strong PLF to hold its own against the ELF during 1972-74. Within the PLF, a personal and ideological division developed concerning the structure of authority that pitted a radical group known as MENKA against the established leadership of Isaias, Ramadan, ALI SAID ABDELLA and MESFIN HAGOS through June 1974. After this challenge the PLF elected a CENTRAL COMMITTEE to oversee the growing organization through a democratic centralist authority structure that was tightly controlled by the leadership, who formed their own secret party to direct the broader front.

Beginning in 1972-74 the PLF developed close ties and provided training for Ethiopian (EPRP) revolutionaries and, after 1976, the TIGREAN PEOPLE'S LIBERATION FRONT (TPLF), establishing a policy of cooperation that was a key strategy in the EPLF's eventual defeat of the DERG. By mid-1974 the PLF was firmly based in eastern SAHEL and along the Red Sea coast, and was moving into the Christian highlands where its secular, multiethnic and social revolutionary political program attracted the support of many young people and peasants. The PLF's recruitment of Christians during 1974-77 dramatically changed the Eritrean independence struggle, ending ETHIOPIA's longstanding attempt to win-over the Christians and producing a numerical majority of TIGRINYA-speakers in what was soon to be the dominant nationalist organization. The success of the PLF was made clear by the return of remnants of the Obel group in mid-1974, and by the ELF's negotiation of a cease-fire in the civil war in October.

As the PLF expanded along the Bahri escarpment in HAMASIEN and AKELE GUZAI, surrounding ASMARA in early 1975, thousands of urban youths joined the front, including hundreds of women, who had been welcomed and trained as frontline fighters since 1973 in a policy that was to provide another important source of strength for the EPLF, which increasingly focused on overcoming women's oppression (*see* WOMEN'S ORGANIZATIONS). In 1974 the front created its Vanguards (Tigrn.: Fitwari) program for 14-16-year-olds who were considered too young to join in combat, but attended school, military training and provided a carrier corps during the heaviest fighting. In the cities, EPLF urban guerrillas known as the "assassinos" carried out daring attacks on Ethiopian officials and bank robberies, while in rural areas under front control, land reform was begun in 1975. During this period EPLF PEASANTS' ORGANIZATIONS were formed in villages under PLF control, along with STUDENT ORGANIZATIONS, LABOR ORGANIZATIONS and WOMEN'S ORGANIZATIONS.

The great increase in the PLF forces and its leadership's radical social programs widened the rift with Sabbe and the ELF-PLF Foreign Office. In the summer of 1975 Sabbe negotiated a unity agreement with the ELF based on its "National Democratic Front" program that would have brought the PLF under ELF control. In contrast, PLF field leaders developed a "National United Front" policy that would create a coalition with separate organizational structures and preserve the PLF's identity. This disagreement led to a complete break between the PLF field leadership now calling themselves the Eritrean People's Liberation Forces (EPLF), in March 1976. The new EPLF consequently lost access to Sabbe's external supply network, and developed instead a policy of self-reliance (Tigrn.: *res'kha me'khal)*, capturing, refurbishing and producing weapons and supplies in its own workshops. By early 1977, when the liberation of Eritrean towns began, the EPLF had expanded to about 15,000 fighters and was roughly equal to the ELF.

The EPLF's First Congress, officially forming the Front, was held in Sahel from January 23-31, 1977. The Congress elected a Central Committee, which in turn elected a Political Committee with Ramadan as Secretary-General and Isaias as vice-secretary. The Congress changed the name of the EPLF from "Forces" to "Front,"

adopted a FLAG, symbols and an eleven-point program
that stressed the creation of an independent, democratic,
secular and socially egalitarian state. The Congress also
decided to work towards unity with the ELF, but repudiated any links with Osman Sabbe. Finally, it allowed
fighters to marry, which had been previously forbidden.
With the EPLF's liberation of towns from KARORA to
DEKEMHARE during 1977, its administration and public
service departments, including HEALTH CARE and the
ERITREAN RELIEF ASSOCIATION, expanded tremendously,
and were reorganized in September. Civilian associations
also grew and held their national founding congresses in
KEREN, the EPLF's "capital," during early 1978. The EPLF
grew to some 30,000 fighters by late in the year, and its
string of military and political successes were capped by
unity agreements with the ELF in October 1977 and April
1978.

The war situation changed dramatically with Soviet
intervention in 1978, and by December the EPLF had been
forced to make a STRATEGIC WITHDRAWAL to its base in
Sahel, where it concentrated on defending NAKFA. The
year 1979 severely tested the front as it fought off
Ethiopian OFFENSIVES and the DERG annihilated much of
its urban underground political organization, while the
USSR's support for the Eritrean cause led EPLF leaders to
begin reconsidering their own Marxist ideology. These
tensions led hundreds of fighters to desert to Sudan and
exacerbated the long-simmering feud with ELF leaders,
leading to the Second Civil War in August 1980, this time
begun by the EPLF with the intention of unifying all the
Eritrean fighting forces. By late 1981 the EPLF was the
only liberation front fighting inside Eritrea, and it faced
alone, with no outside support except the TPLF's, the
largest of all the Derg's offensives, the RED STAR
CAMPAIGN, in early 1982.

The EPLF's surviving members emerged from this
test of fire supremely confident, a close-knit, battle-
hardened and politically mature organization. The EPLF's
overseas support network developed among the Eritrean
DIASPORA, and alternative sources of aid began to come

from Western non-governmental organizations (NGOs) whose role expanded greatly during the FAMINE of 1983-85. EPLF organizations were rebuilt inside the Derg-controlled towns, and guerrilla operations expanded, with the EPLA launching its first counter-offensives into the former ELF territory of the western lowlands in 1984. As the front's territorial control and operations expanded it developed its political program of creating national unity through multi-ethnic cultural programs, its powerful RADIO station, EDUCATION, rural health care, women's and peasants' organizations and the formation of democratic LOCAL GOVERNMENT. By 1987 it had quietly dropped its Marxist classification of peasants by wealth and its divisive land reform measures, and was drawing in an ever-broader cross-section of Eritrean society.

This political transformation was marked by its Second and Unity Congress, held in Sahel March 12-19, 1987, where delegates resolved to form a "broad national democratic front" of all "nationalist forces, groups and individuals." Veteran nationalists like WOLDE-AB WOLDE-MARIAM attended, and the ELF SAGHEM faction led by IBRAHIM IDRIS TOTIL joined the front. The Congress elected a new Central Committee with Isaias as Secretary-General and voted to restructure the EPLA command in preparation for a shift to offensive operations. In March 1988 the victorious AFABET offensive produced a complete change in the military balance, liberating almost all of northern and western Eritrea, and bringing an outpouring of support among Eritrean exiles, a flow of new recruits from the Ethiopian-controlled towns and a resumption of the crucial strategic alliance with the TPLF. The EPLF's victories also produced, for the first time, serious Western diplomatic interest in the Eritrean war, which led to growing relations between the EPLF and the U.S., marked by the Carter negotiations of 1989, and the London conference of May 1991, in which the EPLF was accepted as the de-facto government of an independent Eritrea.

The tremendous growth of the EPLF from 1988 to 1991, in which it almost tripled in size and broke out of

its   international   isolation,   together   with   its
administrative   and   other   responsibilities   over   an   ever-
increasing   area   of   the   country,   necessitated   expansion   and
change   in   the   formerly   tight-knit   front.   In   1990,   after   the
liberation   of   MASSAWA,   the   mass   organizations   were
suspended   and   their   staffs   transferred   to   administrative
duties.   The   leadership   also   began   to   plan   the   transition   to
independent   government,   and   in   February   1991   a
prepatory   committee   was   created   to   plan   a   Third   Congress,
where   the   EPLF's   post-independence   status   would   be
decided.   When   liberation   came   on   May   24,   the
organization   was   still   based   in   Sahel,   and   Isaias   was   in
London.   He   did   not   make   his   first   public   appearance   in
Asmara   until   June   20,   when   he   announced   the   creation   of
the   PROVISIONAL   GOVERNMENT   OF   ERITREA   (PGE),   drawn
directly   from   the   EPLF's   existing   departments   and
administrative   staff.   He   also   announced   the   decision   to
hold   a   REFERENDUM   on   Eritrea's   political   future   within
two   years.

The   EPLF's   transformation   from   a   liberation   front
into   a   national   government   was   marked   by   a   series   of
personnel   shuffles   and   difficulties   among   fighters   in
adapting   to   civilian,   urban   life   and   working   with   the   many
civil   servants   who   remained   from   the   Ethiopian
ADMINISTRATION.   On   the   other   hand,   the   selflessness,
discipline   and   honesty   of   the   EPLF   cadres,   smoothed   the
transition   in   circumstances   of   economic   devastation   and
social   dislocation.   Much   of   the   army   was   assigned   to
reconstruction,   while   EPLF   departments   such   as   health
and   education   began   the   rehabilitation   of   existing
institutions.   By   early   1993   the   preliminary   work   had
been   completed   of   transforming   the   front   into   a   national
government,   but   at   a   Central   Committee   meeting   in
February   there   was   a   heated   debate   about   the   future   of   the
EPLF.   It   was   finally   decided   to   dissolve   the   front   and
reconstitute   it   as   an   autonomous   political   party.   A
National   Charter   began   to   be   drafted   to   provide   a
statement   of   the   EPLF's   guiding   principles   as   a   basis   for
the   creation   of   a   future   democratic   government.   On
February   10-17,   1994,   the   EPLF   held   its   Third   Congress

at Nakfa, where 1,961 delegates voted to dissolve the EPLF and replace it with the PEOPLE'S FRONT FOR DEMOCRACY AND JUSTICE (PFDJ). The Congress adopted the draft National Charter and passed resolutions on the creation of a CONSTITUTION, a new administration, PRESS freedom, LAND LAWS, women's rights, refugee REPATRIATION and aid to demobilized fighters, summing up many of the issues for which the EPLF had fought so many years.

ERITREAN RELIEF ASSOCIATION (ERA and ERRA). Created in March 1975 to channel food and medical aid to Eritrean war and drought victims in the territory controlled by the EPLF and ELF, the ERA's first chairman was BEREKET HABTE-SELASSIE. A conflict immediately developed between the EPLF and ELF over political control of the organization, with the EPLF preferring autonomy, which led to the disbanding of the original board in December, 1975, and the ELF's establishment of its own Eritrean Red Cross and Crescent Society (ERCCS). A new ERA was formed in association with the EPLF under the chairmanship of Paulos Tesfa-Giorgis, but it took several years to overcome the reluctance of foreign non-governmental organizations (NGOs) to cooperate, due to competing claims from the ERCCS, the Ethiopian government and the anti-EPLF policies of most Western governments. The eventual success of the ERA in obtaining NGO support was due primarily to its own efficiency and the development of a network of international affiliates, administered by DIASPORA Eritreans in Western countries, who established cordial relations with donors. By 1983 there were 120 international agencies cooperating with ERA, including the International Committee of the Red Cross (ICRC), the Lutheran World Federation (LWF) and the World Council of Churches (WCC); but until 1981 it was the Swedish and Norwegian church agencies (SCR and NCA) that provided the vast majority of international aid.

Initially, the ERA concentrated on moving FOOD AID in a cross-border operation from SUDAN to Eritrea , where it was distributed to displaced persons in EPLF refugee camps, the most important being at Deba'at in the mountains of northern SAHEL. ERA administered the camp and began its first experiments with creating a self-sufficient refugee population under the leadership of ASKALU MENKERIOS. With the STRATEGIC WITHDRAWAL in late 1978, the number of displaced persons sheltered by ERA increased dramatically, numbering some sixty thousand in ten camps by 1981. The Deba'at camp expanded along the Sudanese border under the code-name of Solomuna, a former EPLF base area in the SEMENAWI BAHRI. As the EPLF's HEALTH CARE department expanded to provide services in liberated and semi-liberated areas, the ERA also became involved in obtaining medical supplies and training, coordinated by the administrator of the central hospital and later director of the Public Heath Project, Dr. Nerayo Tekle-Mika'el. But food aid was the ERA's principal concern, and in 1984 international contributions increased dramatically as Western donors responded to FAMINES in the African Horn.

ROAD TRANSPORT was a critical problem for the ERA's cross border operation, which initially relied on the EPLF's aging truck fleet. With the great increase in foreign donations via Lutheran World Relief (LWR) in 1985, ERA was able to purchase the first sixty-five of its fleet of Mercedes trucks, known affectionately by rural Eritreans as *adetat* (Tigrn.: "our mothers"). The intensity of the war during 1988-91 forced some 400,000 people to seek shelter in ERA camps, scattered throughout Sahel, where food and medical aid were supplied through the greatly increased cross-border operation and an ERA budget that by 1989 totaled $39 million. By 1991 ERA had 380 trucks, and supplied food aid to almost 85 percent of the population.

Peace ended the cross-border operation, but did not immediately reduce Eritrean dependency on food aid, while refugee REPATRIATION and reconstruction added immense new problems to ERA's agenda. In March 1992 ERA was transformed into the Eritrean Relief and Reha-bilitation Association (ERRA), directed by Dr. Nerayo. ERRA was mandated to coordinate all NGO relief and rehabilitation activities in the country with the overall plans of the Eritrean government. Its principal responsibility remained acquisition and distribution of food aid, but as more NGOs were registered under the government's strict 1994 guidelines, ERRA's coordinating and administrative activity in the rehabilitation field also increased. In 1995 the government's decision to phase out foreign NGOs added to the agency's responsibilities, as religious-affiliated NGOs were restricted in 1996, and even non-religious NGOs were severely curtailed in 1997. In 1996, as part of the refugee REPATRIATION effort, ERRA was merged with the Commission for Eritrean Refugee Affairs to form the ERRAC.

ERMIAS DEBESSAI. A popular EPLF military commander and leader of the elite EPLA COMMANDOS through 1991, Ermias attended high school in Asmara until 1969, when he joined the ELF. Together with MESFIN HAGOS, he was part of the Christian contingent transported by OSMAN SALEH SABBE to DENKEL in 1970, and was a founding member of the EPLF, being elected to its CENTRAL COMMITTEE from the First Congress onwards. He was appointed representative to CHINA after liberation, and in 1994 became ambassador to South Korea.

ERTOLA, Luigi. Born in KEREN in 1898, the son of the agricultural entrepeneur Carlo Ertola, Luigi rose to become a prominent business and political leader of the Italian colonial community. He built roads across Eritrea in 1935-40 and developed agricultural estates around Keren, where he led the Italo-Eritrean Association during the 1940s and narrowly escaped death in a terrorist bomb attack in 1950.

ESLAH (Arab.: "Rectification"). A reformist movement in the ELF, founded in 1967 by younger, educated fighters who criticized the divisive politics of the ZONAL COMMAND system and the absentee leadership of the SUPREME COUNCIL. Eslah grew out of a Marxist study group led by AZIEN YASSIN and attended by most of the

leading figures in the later EPLF, included ISAIAS
AFWERKI, RAMADAN MOHAMED NUR, AL-AMIN
MOHAMMED SAID, ALI SAID ABDELLA, MESFIN HAGOS
and HAILE WOLDE-TENSA'E. Eslah won over the leaders of
Zones 3-5 during 1968, and in June forced the ELF
commanders to meet at AREDAIB to discuss reform. When
they failed to gain the support of the old leadership, the
reformists held a second meeting in the ANSEBA valley in
September and formed the TRIPARTITE UNITY FORCES.

ETHIOPIA. Eritrea's longstanding cultural, economic and
political relationship with its southern neighbor,
Ethiopia, has been fraught with conflict since the colonial
period due to Ethiopian claims to all or part of Eritrean
territory. These claims were founded on the modern
Ethiopian state's professed links to the AKSUMITE Empire
and the medieval AMHARIC-speaking kingdom of
Emperors AMDE SIYON and ZARA YA'QOB, who claimed
sovereignty over central Eritrea. But from the seventeenth
to late-nineteenth centuries, Eritrea's political links with
present-day Ethiopia were almost exclusively with
TIGRAI, whose rulers often exercised sovereignty over the
Orthodox Christian population of the central highlands.
Most of the northern highlands and lowlands, with the
exception of the central coast, remained entirely
unconnected to any Amhara or Tigrean polities.
      During the early 1700s the House of TSAZZEGA had
formal political links with the emperors in Gondar, but
these were broken by the rise of Tigrean power in the
1750s. A system of Tigrean-Ethiopian military administration was briefly established over the highlands by Dej.
WUBE in the 1840s, and this system was reconstructed
and expanded after 1879 by Emperor YOHANNES IV, lord
of Tigrai, who staked modern Ethiopian claims to Eritrea
in the HEWETT TREATY of 1885. But when the Amhara
ruler, Menelik II, came to power in 1889, he accepted
Italian sovereignty over most of Eritrea, including the
eastern edge of the Christian highlands and ASMARA, in
Article 3 of the Treaty of Wichale, signed in May, 1889.
The treaty was extended to cover the Italian occupation of

all the highlands up to the Mareb-Belessa-Mai Muna BOR-DERS in a separate protocol signed in Rome by Ras Makonnen, HAILE SELASSIE I's father, on October 1, when Ethiopia agreed to recognize Italy's "present possessions" in Eritrea. Although Menelik later repudiated the treaty in a dispute over an issue unrelated to Eritrea (Article 17), he never attempted to gain control over Eritrea, even when he could have invaded the colony following the battle of ADWA. In October 1896 he formally accepted Italian sovereignty over Eritrea in the Treaty of Addis Ababa, which ended the Ethio-Italian war, and this policy was continued by his successor, Emperor Haile Selassie through 1940. At the same time, the Ethiopian government encouraged educated Eritrean highlanders to emigrate to Ethiopia, where many found successful careers in ADDIS ABABA and elsewhere, forming a large exile community that served in the highest ranks of the government, business and education, finding scope for the opportunities denied them by Italian colonialism.

After the Italian defeat, beginning in May 1941, Haile Selassie mobilized this community to participate in his campaign for Eritrea's unification with Ethiopia. Besides his multi-faceted diplomatic campaign, involving shifting alliances with BRITAIN and the UNITED STATES, the Emperor's government also subsidized the ORTHODOX CHURCH, the UNIONIST PARTY and SHIFTA leaders to pressure Eritreans through propaganda and terrorism into accepting union with Ethiopia during the period 1946-50. Many Christian Eritreans saw Ethiopian rule as a form of self-determination, freeing them from the oppressive and racist rule of Europeans. But once FEDERATION, rather than full political unification, had been mandated by the UNITED NATIONS, Eritrean nationalist sentiment grew stronger among the Christian highlanders, as well as Eritrean Muslims, and during the 1950s there was widespread opposition to the Ethiopian ANNEXATION campaign, which finally achieved its goal of making Eritrea Ethiopia's fourteenth province in November 1962.

Ethiopian rule was buttressed by military force, beginning in September 1952, when the Ethiopian Second

Brigade, later expanded to become the Second Division,
marched into the former colony. During the 1960s the
policies of Governor-Generals ABIYE ABEBE and ASRATE
KASSA were somewhat successful in dividing Christian
Eritreans from the Muslim population of the lowlands, who
overwhelmingly supported the ELF's ARMED STUGGLE for
independence. The Ethiopian government, under both
Haile Selassie and the DERG, consistently portrayed the
Eritrean nationalists as *wombede* (Amh.: "bandits") and
puppets of Arab powers bent on annexing Eritrea to the
Muslim world, playing on the ancient fears of Christian
Ethiopians, which dated to at least the time of Imam
AHMED AL-GHAZALI. By the early 1970s, however,
Ethiopian military atrocities and the coming of age of a
new generation of ardently nationalist TIGRINYA-speaking
Christians, whose leaders (including many educated in
Ethiopia) particularly resented the government's
AMHARIC language policies, had mobilized even the high-
lands against Ethiopian rule. Consequently, when the
Ethiopian revolution (February-September 1974) swept
away Haile Selassie's old regime, the Derg was faced with
the choice of granting Eritrea independence or reconquer-
ing it militarily.

    After the failure of negotiations conducted by
General AMANUEL MIKA'EL ANDOM, the DERG reinforced
its military forces but nonetheless lost control over most
of Eritrea by 1977, when it issued a nine-point peace
proposal offering Eritreans limited autonomy. After its
alliance with the USSR, however, the Ethiopian military
launched a series of OFFENSIVES that reconquered much
of central Eritrea in 1978-79, and attempted to
reintegrate the province through large-scale reconstruction and development projects during the RED STAR
CAMPAIGN, which cost Ethiopia millions. All these
campaigns and projects failed to win the war, however, and
Ethiopian military casualties were over 150,000, while its
military debt to the USSR was estimated at $8.6 billion.

    When the war ended in 1991, Eritreans were so anti-
Ethiopian that all traces of Ethiopian authority and the
Amharic language were removed from the country, over

44,000 Ethiopian civilians, most of whom were associated with the Workers' Party of Ethiopia (WPE) or the military, were expelled and during June-August all air and telephone connections with Ethiopia were severed. The new PROVISIONAL GOVERNMENT OF ERITREA (PGE) explained that this was a "necessary prelude" to rebuilding relations between the two countries. The new Ethiopian government formed by the Ethiopian People's Revolutionary Democratic Front (EPRDF), and led by the EPLF's longtime ally the TPLF, accepted the Eritrean proposal to hold a REFERENDUM on independence which the PGE announced at the July 1991 peace conference in Addis Ababa. Outside of Tigrai, most Ethiopians knew little about Eritrea, but issues such as the forced repatriation of civilians and the loss of ASSAB's port and refinery stirred resentment in Addis Ababa, leading to a student protest at the University in January 1993 in which several were killed.

Nonetheless, the two governments, both dominated by Tigrinya-speakers, worked closely to rebuild their economic links and overcome the legacy of war. Eritrea renounced any claim to reparations, and Ethiopia gave up claim to property left in Eritrea. In January 1992 a trade pact was signed and in April an agreement on transit duties was negotiated. In January 1993 agreements were reached on air travel, postal and telecommunications and the "free port" status of Assab. In July wide-ranging bilateral accords were signed covering cultural and technical exchanges, immigration and the use of transborder rivers, particularly the SETIT, as well as cooperation on monetary, security, defense and border areas. Until November 1997 Eritrea continued to use the Ethiopian *birr* as its currency, but the introduction of Eritrea's own currency may create payment transfer problems for Eritrea's important COMMERCE with Ethiopia (*see* FINANCE). As of 1997 the two governments, cooperate on a wide variety of matters, from international politics to local issues, and over 60,000 Eritrean citizens are resident in Ethiopia.

EWOSTATEWOS, Aba (c.1273-1352). A Tigrean monastic leader who spent most of his life in western SERAYE, Ewostatewos preached the observance of the Sabbath on Saturday as well as Sunday, in keeping with longstanding Ethiopian Christian traditions based on the Old Testament, but contrary to the practice of the Ethiopian and Alexandrine branches of the ORTHODOX CHURCH of his day. He was persecuted and left Seraye for Alexandria c. 1337, where he argued his doctrine to no avail before the Patriarch. He died in Armenia, from whence his followers returned to the Eritrean plateau to found a powerful regional monastic tradition. Among his disciples were Filipos, Absadi and Merqorewos, founders of the monasteries of DEBRE BIZEN, DEBRE MARYAM and DEBRE MERQOREWOS respectively.

During the 1300s the Ewostatians were persecuted by the Orthodox Church and Ethiopian state, but in 1404 Emperor Dawit negotiated a compromise with Filipos of Debre Bizen, in which the Ewostatians were allowed to continue their "Old Testament" practices and expand their monasteries throughout the MAREB MELLASH and northern TIGRAI. The initial Ewostatian "heresy" may be viewed as a medieval manifestation of Tigrean, and particularly Mareb Mellash ("Eritrean"), regional "nationalism" in opposition to the Amhara-dominated Solomonic state and its Egyptian Abuna; but the movement soon became symbolic of a general HABESHA resentment against their domination by the Alexandrine Church. During the early 1400s much of the Solomonic Empire returned to the "Old Testament" practices advocated by the House of Ewostatewos, and with the accession of ZARA YA'QOB in 1434 the Ewostatians' position was legitimized by the imperial support and confirmed as church doctrine by the Council of Debre Mitmaq in 1450.

EXPO (Asmara). A commercial exhibition ground opened in ASMARA in 1968. Expo was converted into a political prison by the DERG where some 320 Eritreans were tortured and killed during 1975-82. Today it is an exhibition ground and until 1996 it was the site of an annual national cultural festival that originated in Bologna, ITALY, in 1975, but since liberation has been held every August in Asmara and attracts many Eritreans from the DIASPORA.

EZANA. The fourth century AKSUMITE ruler credited with introducing Christianity to central Eritrea and northern TIGRAI. Some controversy exists over Ezana's dates and whether he was one or perhaps two different rulers, but most scholars agree that he reigned from c. 325/30 to 360 A.D. under the throne name Ela Abreha. His reign coincided with the Christian missionary work of Frumentius, who was reported to be his tutor and counselor. In 356 he received a letter from Byzantine Emperor Constantinus II advising him to adopt the Nicaean faith, but he remained steadfast in his Monophysite Orthodox beliefs along with his brother Sezana (Ela Atsbeha). Later inscriptions indicate that Ezana changed the official state religion from the traditional pagan pantheon to Christianity.

- F -

FAIDAB. A sub-tribe of the BENI 'AMER inhabiting south-western BARKA and northwestern GASH-SETIT near the Sudanese border. Known for their religious piety, the Faidab produced several notable Muslim leaders, including Sayedna MOHAMED IBN DAWD IBN MUSTAFA. Their camp at Himbol was an early ELF base, and the name was later used as a code word for the EPLF workshop area in northern SAHEL.

FALUL (Tigrn.: "Anarchist"). A dissident movement in the ELF begun by Christian radicals in 1976 who opposed the REVOLUTIONARY COUNCIL's (RC) agreement to merge with OSMAN SALEH SABBE's ELF-PLF, and preferred an agreement with the EPLF. The dissidents called themselves the Democratic Movement and among their leaders was HERUI TEDLA BAIRU, but the mainstream ELF labeled them "Anarchists." Several leftist members of the RC supported the Falul critique of Sabbe and ELF conservatives, and the split intensified after March 1977. In June a Falul splinter group, acting largely on its own, assassinated two conservative Muslim RC members in DENKEL, provoking a purge of the dissidents and the flight of some two thousand Christian fighters to ALA, from where they joined the EPLF.

FAMINES. The Eritrean region has been plagued by recurring famines throughout its recorded history due to lack of rainfall, locust and other infestations and cattle diseases. The central highlands, with their large agricultural population have been particularly subject to famine, with farmers often migrating down the slopes of the better-watered Bahri escarpment or into the lowlands during drought periods. Highland TIGRINYA traditions recall famines from the sixteenth century onwards, with names like Zemene Albo ("Empty Time"), Zemene Akahida ("Time of Controversy"), Zemene Sherok ("Time of Diarrhea") and Zemene Qorbet ("Time of [eating] Hides"). The worst famine in memory, the Second Akahida or Zemene Kerboni, was that of 1888-92, caused by the outbreak of rinderpest (Tigrn.: *guhlay* or *kerboni*) which killed most of the cattle in Eritrea, leaving none to plough. This famine depopulated the highlands and enabled ITALY to occupy them without resistance, as they distributed food to Eritrean soldiers who joined them.

    Despite droughts, there were no serious famines during the Italian or British periods, as the Italian introduction of the "indian fig" cactus (Tigrn.: *beles)* provided a new food source for the "hungry period" preceding each harvest, while wage labor and military service provided outside income. But in the early 1970s famine struck the rural areas of central Eritrea, now exacerbated by the economic dislocation accompanying the ARMED STRUGGLE. The drought of 1980-84, coinciding with devastating warfare, produced widespread famine, which by 1984 affected some 1.25 million Eritreans, with 600,000 remaining dependent on FOOD AID, supplied through the ERITREAN RELIEF ASSOCIATION (ERA), as late as 1987. The famine of 1980-84 also forced many more REFUGEES to flee to

SUDAN, as ERA's food supply system could not meet the needs of all the affected population and in DERG-controlled areas the distribution of food aid was tied to participation in government programs and even military service. The famine continued in the late 1980s, due primarily to the devastation and disruption of the war, and as much as 85 percent of the Eritrean population became dependent on food aid. Drought and the prospect of famine continue to haunt Eritrea since independence, although the government's emphasis on food self-sufficiency and ERRA's early warning program are greatly improving the situation.

FEDERATION (Ethio-Eritrean, 1952-62). The concept of a federation between ETHIOPIA and Eritrea was first proposed as a compromise between independence and unification at the WA'LA BET GHERGIS in 1946, but was rejected by the pro-Ethiopian UNIONIST PARTY. In May 1949 the concept was revived by a member of the Independent MUSLIM LEAGUE of Massawa, who proposed the idea of a Federation in testimony to the UNITED NATIONS General Assembly. Under pressure from the UNITED STATES and in light of its weak diplomatic position, Ethiopia accepted the idea in 1950, when it was proposed by two members of a Commission of Investigation in their report to the UN . The inability of the international community to agree on any other solution, combined with US diplomatic pressure, led the UN to vote to federate Ethiopia and Eritrea on December 2, 1950.

The Federation was intended to guarantee Eritreans an autonomous, democratic government, and a UN commissioner, Anze MATIENZO, was appointed to oversee its implementation. He drafted a constitution outlining a political structure in which Eritrea was governed by an elected ASSEMBLY, an independent judiciary and a Chief Executive who would oversee the POLICE, EDUCATION, HEALTH CARE, public services and FINANCE. Matienzo failed to create a separate Federal Government, however, other than an ill-defined Federal Council that met only once. This enabled HAILE SELASSIE I's government to gain direct control over trade, defense and all interstate communications, which meant ports, main highways and the RAILROAD, and the revenues from foreign trade. The Eritreans managed to maintain some symbols of sovereignty, such as a separate FLAG and official languages, but the Ethiopian government controlled ultimate military and financial power.

The Federation was implemented on September 15, 1953, and the Ethiopians, working through the Emperor's representative, ANDERGATCHEW MESSAI, and the Unionist Party, led by Chief Executive TEDLA BAIRU, set about dismantling Eritrea's autonomous and democratic institutions, such as opposition political parties, the free PRESS and LABOR ORGANIZATIONS. A political and economic crisis ensued, as Ethiopian interference and double (Federal and Eritrean) taxation drove out some colonial businesses while Ethiopian control over the Eritrean share of customs revenues, which made up close to 40 percent of its budget, enabled the imperial representative to manipulate the Assembly. This crisis reached its highpoint in 1955, when Tedla Bairu was forced to resign. After Ethiopian-controlled elections in 1956, the Eritrean government was in the hands of the Emperor's agents, ASFAHA WOLDE-MIKA'EL and DIMETROS GEBREMARIAM, who set about dismantling the Federation in preparation for complete unification with Ethiopia. During 1957-60 the independent British Chief JUSTICE was removed, Eritrea's official languages were replaced with AMHARIC, all symbols of autonomy were eliminated, and, despite the resistance of students, the labor movement and, after 1959, the ERITREAN LIBERATION MOVEMENT, the Emperor's government succeeded in dissolving the Federation and completing Eritrea's ANNEXATION by Ethiopia in late 1962. Despite its brief duration, the autonomous Eritrean institutions created by the Federation were crucial in establishing a sense of Eritrean national identity, particularly among the generation who grew up under them and later led the independence struggle.

FIGHTERS. The thirty year ARMED STRUGGLE for Eritrean independence created a new social group in Eritrea that quite consciously sees itself as both the embodiment of national values and the guardian of the new nation. These are "the fighters" who fought the war and today make up both the army and the government. Their name comes from the TIGRINYA word for the guerrillas of the various Eritrean liberation movements, *tegadelti* (masc. sing.: *tegadelai;* literally "struggler" but translated as "fighter"), which came into widespread use in the early 1970s when large numbers of Tigrinya-speaking youths joined the movement. Though it applies to all the nationalist guerrillas, the new "fighter culture" developed primarily in the EPLF. The young fighters rejected many traditional Eritrean attitudes concerning social status, gender inequality and religious segregation, and developed their own mix of Marxist idealism and secular nationalism that stressed self-sacrifice for the sake of the nation and one's comrades, self-reliance, self-improvement in EDUCATION and technical skills, group decision making, communal ownership of all material goods, and egalitarian fairness and self-discipline in all social interactions. Despite its innovations, the austere morality of the fighters also owed much to the heavily religious culture of rural Eritreans, who were impressed in particular by the justice and steadfastness of the fighters of the EPLF.

Fighter culture matured during the long years of isolation and constant warfare in the mountains of SAHEL, and by 1991 the fighters had their own code of behavior and traditions. Fighters also developed a distinctive personality, marked by a combination of self-confidence and seriousness, and even a uniform dress of plastic sandals (Arab.: *sheda),* tight shorts, military jacket, headscarf and white cotton blanket *(netsela)* looped over the shoulders. When they entered Asmara after liberation many fighters had no conception of how to use money or keep personal possessions, and they were appalled at the Western consumer-culture values and vices of their urban fellow citizens. An important element of the EPLF-dominated

government's transitional program has been to instill
some of its "fighter values" in the school-age generation
through education, NATIONAL SERVICE and media
emphasis on the sacrifices made by the MARTYRS of the
independence struggle.

Among rank-and-file fighters, however, there was
some difficulty in sustaining the spirit of sacrifice after
liberation, and the issues of continuing unpaid service by
fighters, DEMOBILIZATION, the fate of the 12,000 war-
handicapped fighters and the families of the close to
70,000 war-dead led to resentment among the veterans
who found they did not have the skills to easily integrate
into civilian society. These issues were suppressed until
the 1993 REFERENDUM, as fighters worked without pay to
revive the devastated country and staff the government.
But when ISAIAS AFWERKI announced that fighters would
continue to serve without pay, receiving only a small sum
of "pocket money" based on years in the field, a group of
disgruntled fighters led a mutiny (Tigrn.: Adma
Tegadelti) on May 20, 1993, in which commando and artillery units seized control of the airport, banks and government buildings in Asmara. Isaias met with fighters at
the stadium that evening and promised to come up with a
pay schedule and demobilization benefits for them by reducing other programs. In January 1994 fighters on military service began to receive salaries, but the mutiny seriously disturbed the government, which arrested 130
leaders and sentenced over 100 to prison, and began further programs to demobilize, compensate and rehabilitate
fighters *(see* DEMOBILIZATION; MAI HABAR).

FINANCE (Banking, Currency, Debt). Eritrea had a number
of currencies and financial regimes tied to the Italian and
British colonial ADMINISTRATIONs. At the time of FED-
ERATION (1952) the Ethiopian *birr* became the currency,
and Eritrea's national banks were linked to the state bank
of ETHIOPIA. The *birr* remained Eritrea's currency
through November 1997, when a national currency, the
"NAKFA," was introduced, initially convertible to *birr* at
a one-to-one rate. Although Eritrea pressed Ethiopia to

accept a dual-currency system for commercial exchanges between them, in which each country would accept the other's currency without conversion costs, this was not implemented.

The two most pressing issues in Eritrea's post-liberation financial development were relations with Ethiopia and with foreign lenders, led by the World Bank. In May 1991, when the EPLF formed the Provisional Government of Eritrea (PGE), it repudiated all debts owed by previous governments and nationalized the Ethiopian state banking system, forming the National Bank of Eritrea and the Commercial Bank of Eritrea. Until formal independence in 1993, foreign aid for reconstruction totaled less than $32 million, with half coming from non-governmental organizations, led by the CATHOLIC CHURCH, and half from bilateral loans. The European Community provided $72 million, half in FOOD AID, under its Lome Convention, to which Eritrea was admitted in May 1993. Negotiations with the World Bank were opened in 1993, and in March a $525 million credit was offered, with $147 million slated for a two year recovery and rehabilitation program. After further negotiations, in July 1994 Eritrea joined the World Bank organizations (IBRD, IDA, IMF), receiving a credit of $50 million for recovery, EDUCATION, ENERGY and port development.

In 1994 a new Investment Code was promulgated, with more liberalized provisions concerning taxation and profit repatriation. The National Bank was reorganized in 1996 under the direction of Tekie Beyene, an EPLF veteran and former ERA administrator. As of 1995, Eritrea's national debt totaled $75 million.

FISHING, Fisheries. Fishing is the traditional occupation of the people of the DENKEL coast and DAHLAK islands, who have used small wooden sailboats for many centuries, drying much of their catch for coastal trade and export to Arabia. The inshore fishing season runs from November to April, after which the fish move into deeper waters. The pearl fishery of the Dahlak islands also flourished since the first millennium B.C. During the Italian colonial period gas-powered boats and modern nets were introduced, and by the 1940s a small industry had developed with fish meal processing plants, a cannery, pearl and shell works and an ice plant in MASSAWA. By the mid-1950s the industry employed about 8,000, and in 1954 reached its high point with a catch of over 25,000 tons. The ARMED STRUGGLE destroyed the fishing industry. Nearly 80 percent of Eritrea's fishing families fled as REFUGEES, factory ships from the USSR and Poland depleted the fishery, and the infrastructure in Massawa was largely destroyed. The DERG's attempts to revive it as a state-controlled enterprise failed, and the total catch in the best year, 1980, was only 380 tons.

In 1991 the Eritrean government began rebuilding the industry as a means of improving food self-sufficiency and potential exports. Saleh Meki was appointed head of the Department of Marine Resources, charged with developing fisheries and marine TOURISM in an ecologically sound manner that would create sustained yields without impairing Eritrea's coral reefs and aquatic wildlife. Saleh also took over the EPLF's wartime aquaculture projects, in which salt-water fish-farming was developed around Mersa Teklai, on the SAHEL coast. During 1992-93 industry infrastructure was repaired and TIGRE-speaking former pastoralists were given training. Fresh fish began to be trucked to ASMARA, and a national campaign to encourage highlanders to eat fish, which was not part of their traditional diet, began. By 1993, when the Ministry of Marine Resources was formed, an ambitious program to develop a marine laboratory at HIRGHIGO and fresh fish exports was underway, as were freshwater aquaculture projects. In early 1993 a UNITED NATIONS Food and Agriculture Organization (FAO) project was negotiated providing $5.4 million to develop the fishing industry in SEMHAR. At the same time, a National Marine Park was designated to control development and exploitation around the Dahlak Islands and Massawa coast, including regulation of commercial fishing. Eritrea concluded agreements with EGYPT and YEMEN concerning fishing in its territorial waters, within which the Eritrean NAVY rigorously enforces fishing regulations. The Ministry of Marine Resources is currently led by PETROS SOLOMON.

FLAG. Eritrea's first flag was created at the outset of FEDERATION in 1952. It symbolized Eritreans' hopes that the UNITED NATIONS would guarantee their autonomy, as it looked very much like the UN flag, with olive branches encircling a six-leafed plant (representing Eritrea's six ADMINISTRATION divisions) on a sky-blue background. A new flag was adopted by the GOVERNMENT OF THE STATE OF ERITREA in 1993, which combined the EPLF's flag of interlocking green, red and blue triangles with the Federation flag's olive-and-plant emblem in gold, symbolizing the role of the EPLF in creating the new nation.

FOOD AID. Eritrea has been a net importer of cereals, the staple food of the population, from at least the beginning of ITALIAN COLONIALISM. Until the 1970s, most of this food came from northern ETHIOPIA and SUDAN, and particularly from the grain-surplus regions of TIGRAI. During the 1970s, the ARMED STRUGGLE and droughts interfered with these imports, and with internal AGRICULTURE as well, and by 1979 the population which had not fled the country as REFUGEES was increasingly dependent on foreign food aid.

In DERG-controlled areas foreign food aid was distributed in Food-for-Work Programs (FWP), administered through the Ethiopian Council of Churches and Catholic Relief Services, which were allowed to resume their operations along with other non-governmental organizations (NGOs) in 1980. The liberation fronts began to import food from Sudan in 1975, and the ERA started trucking in small international donations in 1976, but until the mid-1980s the cross-border operation met less than 15 percent of food needs in EPLF-controlled areas. During 1984 foreign food aid (much of it from the UNITED STATES) increased tremendously, with the Ethiopian government receiving $1 billion in 1985 alone. During the RED STAR CAMPAIGN some of this food aid began to be used to pay

the "Wheat Militia" (Tigrn.: Milisha Tsernai) that highland peasants were required to join to guard their villages
against EPLF attacks, and by 1985 reports indicated that a
portion of food aid was being diverted to feed the
Ethiopian army. In 1984 the ERA's cross-border operation
also began to receive large-scale food aid, coordinated
through the Sudan-based Emergency Relief Desk (ERD),
with the principal donor agency being the Lutheran World
Relief (LWR) agency, through which U.S. and European
Community (EC) donations were channeled, reaching over
$35 million during 1985.

   Food aid became a crucial factor in the Eritrean war
during the 1980s, as both sides used aid to support
civilian populations in areas under their control, and the
Derg attempted to deny aid to EPLF areas. During the 1984
FAMINE the Derg refused an EPLF proposal of safe passage
for food aid into the war zone, and in 1987 the EPLA
burned an Ethiopian convoy containing UN World Food
Program (WFP) trucks mixed with trucks carrying military supplies. Through ERA, the EPLF maintained good
relations with the ERD, which channeled growing EC and
U.S. food aid, with U.S. in-kind food aid to both the EPLF
and TPLF areas rising to almost $30 million in 1988 and
over $70 million in 1990. With the liberation of MAS-
SAWA, the principal port for Derg aid imports, a heated
dispute developed concerning importation of food aid under EPLF auspices. The Derg bombed food warehouses in
the port, and the population in its highland enclave lost
access to food aid except for small quantities brought in
by air (see AIRPORTS). On January 14, 1991, WFP food aid
resumed through Massawa, after an Ethiopian promise to
refrain from bombing in exchange for a portion of food aid
delivered through EPLA lines to ASMARA. A similar free
passage arrangement had begun in March 1990 to supply
food aid to central Ethiopia via ASSAB.

   At the time of liberation between 70 and 85 percent
of the Eritrean population was estimated to be dependent
on food aid. Both U.S. and EC food aid continued, as poor
harvests in 1991 and 1993 meant continued dependency,
although by June 1993 the number dependent on aid had

decreased to about 500,000. In 1995 food aid was still distributed to over 300,000 people through FWP and direct hand-outs, indicating a structural deficit in cereals that is expected to continue for the foreseeable future. But in 1995 aid donors, led by WFP and EC, began questioning Eritrean use of food aid to subsidize urban bread prices and NATIONAL SERVICE programs. In January 1996 the Eritrean government announced that it would monetize all donated grain and use the proceeds to subsidize jobs and public works programs, but food donors reacted by shutting off further grain supplies, provoking a crisis in which they insisted on control over delivery and pricing, while the Eritreans insisted on internal control over their chosen program. The stand-off lasted through September, when the U.S. relented (resuming distribution of its 1996-98 pledge of 86,000 metric tons), followed reluctantly by the EC at the end of the year. In 1997 the Eritrean-controlled, monetized food aid program was beginning to function, and was widely seen as a victory for Eritrea's policy of self-reliance even in a situation of dependency.

FORESTRY, FORESTS. Eritrea's forest cover has been reduced by about eighty percent in the last century. Highland forests of juniper, olive and African fig have all but disappeared except for a few areas of the SEMENAWI BAHRI, and lowland acacia, baobab and DUM PALM stands have been greatly reduced. Today, forest covers only 0.4 percent of Eritrea's land surface. Deforestation has led to widespread soil erosion, and has probably decreased Eritrea's rainfall. As firewood is Eritrea's main ENERGY source, forests have decreased in direct relation to POPULATION growth. The ARMED STRUGGLE further devastated already scanty forests, as soldiers collected firewood and used thousands of trees to reinforce their fortifications; while prolonged drought during the 1970s and 1980s killed many already weakened trees.

Reforestation projects were begun under ITALIAN COLONIALISM, when a Forest Guard was created to protect existing reserves and eucalyptus plantations. On the other hand, colonial entrepreneurs cut down much of the existing forest for fuel and building materials, and along the escarpment of northern AKELE GUZAI the juniper trees were cut and transported by cableway to the coast for export. The colonial forestry system broke down in the 1970s, and reforestation only began again on any significant scale in the 1980s, when the Derg oversaw large-scale terracing and tree planting under the terms of foreign-donated FOOD AID. The EPLF also undertook small-scale projects in its liberated zone, particularly in RORA Habab, where a pilot project using native olives and junipers was begun. The Derg's reforestation efforts (using the frequently unsuitable eucalyptus) were of limited success; but after liberation the EPLF's program was greatly expanded utilizing food-for-work programs, NATIONAL SERVICE workers, high school students on summer break, and even international volunteers. By 1997 a total of over 41 million seedlings had been planted.

FORO (Akele Guzai). Located at the foot of Zula dam on the HADAS River, the town of Foro developed from an Italian colonial "forto." The dam, which had been proposed several times, was finally built in 1961-63 to irrigate the alluvial plain behind Zula (*see* ADULIS), where the KEKIYA family and other entrepreneurs were introducing mechanized farming of cotton, sugar and grain. The village surrounding the old police post grew into a commercial town of several thousand with a mixed population of SAHO, TIGRE and TIGRINYA-speakers. The dam silted up within a decade, however, and farming declined. During the 1970s many residents fled from Ethiopian military operations against the ELF, and Foro changed hands a number of times. In 1986-88 it was occupied by an Ethiopian battalion, after which it was administered by the EPLF. Today Foro is an important administrative and market center, with a new clinic, school and the Agriculture Ministry's office for its Zula development project.

FOUR POWERS COMMISSION (1947-48). The Treaty of Paris (signed on February 10, 1947, coming into effect on September 15) ended hostilities between ITALY and the allied powers (BRITAIN, FRANCE, U.S., USSR) and gave the latter, known as the "Four Powers," responsibility for deciding Eritrea's political future. The Four Powers were divided over the future of Italy's colonies, with Britain and France interested in some form of settlement that would not jeopardize their own African colonies, the USSR primarily interested in supporting the pro-colonial Italian Communist Party, and the UNITED STATES supporting ETHIOPIAN claims to Eritrea. To help resolve their differences, the Four Powers created a Commission of Investigation to ascertain Eritrean opinion, which visited the colony from November 12, 1947, to January 3, 1948.

The BRITISH ADMINISTRATION had allowed POLITICAL PARTIES to form in early 1947 to organize public sentiment for the possible options of independence, union with Ethiopia or some form of trusteeship (generally Italian or British). These parties held rallies and presented petitions to the Four Powers Commission, several of which led to violence organized by pro-Ethiopian Unionists, notably at Teramni in SERAYE. In addition, 3,336 representatives of family and clan groupings were "elected" to present their people's views to the Commission. In the end, the Commission found Eritrean opinion quite divided, with about 45 percent supporting the pro-independence MUSLIM LEAGUE and LIBERAL PROGRESSIVE PARTY, 45 percent supporting the UNIONIST PARTY, and 10 percent various pro-Italy parties. The Four Powers Council of Ministers then used the Commission's report to support their own differing political positions on Eritrea's future, and when they could not reach agreement, on September 15, 1948, the Four Powers turned the matter over to the UNITED NATIONS, as stipulated in the Paris Treaty.

FUNJ (alt.: Fung). An empire founded around Sennar on the Blue Nile in the SUDAN by the Funj dynasty during the early 1500s. The Funj expanded their tributary rule into the western lowlands of Eritrea during the late 1500s through the NABTAB clan of the BENI 'AMER, but they were overthrown in 1821 by a military expedition from EGYPT.

FRANCE. French interest in Eritrea developed during the nineteenth century out of a combination of colonial rivalry with BRITAIN, the interests of French Catholic missionaries of the Lazzarist order, and individual French geographers and entrepreneurs who saw a port on Eritrea's coast as the means of gaining control over ETHIOPIA's foreign trade. After France had established a vice-consul at MASSAWA in 1840, various Ethiopian rulers saw the French as a possible alternative to the power of Britain or EGYPT on the coast, an interest which the adventurers d'Abadie, Combes and Lefebvre sought to promote. In 1842-43 the French attempted to purchase Anfile Bay on the DENKEL coast, but were unsuccessful; in 1845 French agents purchased EDD from an AFAR chief but never developed it; in 1859-60 the French supported "Agaw" NEGUSSIE in his struggle with Emperor Tewodros, and the former ceded ZULA Bay to the mission of Count Russell in exchange for arms, but Negussie's death ended the deal. During the 1860s the French, through their vice-consul Werner MUNZINGER, threatened to intervene to protect Eritrean Catholics from Tigrean persecution, but after 1884, the French concentrated on developing DJIBOUTI as their main entrepot for trade with central Ethiopia.

The French connection with Shewa (central Ethiopia), via Djibouti, precluded further interest in Eritrea, which the French conceded to ITALY. France supported Italian claims to Eritrea during the Four Powers' negotiations of 1948. The government was uncritical of HAILE SELASSIE I's policies in Eritrea and remained silent about the DERG's policies as well until 1981, when some critical remarks led to the expulsion of much of the French mission in Ethiopia. Thereafter, the government remained circumspect, protecting its Djiboutian interests, until the EPLF victory in 1991, when the Eritrean leaders accused France, apparently incorrectly, of supporting Afar irredentism. This diplomatic dispute was resolved in bilateral talks in December 1992, and in 1993 a French diplomatic presence was established through the Consul in Djibouti, followed in May 1994, by President ISAIAS AFWERKI's state visit to France in which a cooperation agreement and 22-million-franc aid package were signed.

- G -

GAAS. A leading Afar family of northern DENKEL, including the hereditary chiefs of Tio and parts of the BURE PENINSULA. Shaykh Musa Gaas, descendant of the patriarch Gaas Assa Mohamed Nakuda, mobilized northern Denkel in support of the MUSLIM LEAGUE during the 1940s, and members of the family supported the EPLF in Bure during the 1980s.

GASH River *see* MAREB River.

GASH-SETIT. A former provincial-level ADMINISTRATIVE DIVISION in the southwestern corner of what is now the Gash-Barka Region, extending from the northern drainages of the Gash River to the SETIT River in the south, and comprising most of the lands of the KUNAMA and NARA peoples, as well as those of BEJA and TIGRE-speakers along the Sudanese border in the west, and TIGRINYA-speakers along the border with the Adi-Abo district of TIGRAI in the east. The administrative division, with its headquarters at BARENTU, was first created as a Commissariati by the Italians in 1909, but returned to the control of AGORDAT in 1931, after which it remained a sub-division of the Western Province until 1975, when the DERG elevated it to *awraja* status in an attempt to cement the loyalty of the Kunama people.

The area saw the first battles of the ARMED STRUGGLE, and a number of Eritrean inter-ethnic clashes during the 1960s-70s. The DERG drove out the ELF in 1978, and held the area until the mid-1980s, when the EPLF established itself throughout the region, gaining complete control in 1988. After liberation IBRAHIM IDRIS TOTIL was appointed Governor, and a regional development association was formed. Much of Gash-Setit's population fled as REFUGEES to SUDAN during the war, and the province is

expected to absorb over 150,000 in the current REPATRI-
ATION process.

Gash-Setit has the richest farmland in Eritrea, including alluvial river valleys, the rainfed plains between
GULUJ and OM HAGER, and the irrigated cotton soil
around TESSENEI and ALI GHIDER. Pre-colonial AGRICUL-
TURE was stifled by the widespread presence of malaria,
but irrigated farming was begun in the 1920s by Italian
colonists, and was extended to rainfed tractor-farming of
sorghum and sesame along the Sudanese border in the late
1960s. Since liberation the Ministry of Agriculture has
focused its large-scale development projects on the
province, including the SETIT dam and Tessenei-Ali
Ghider projects. The TOKOMBIA area also has an important livestock market.

GASPARINI, Jacopo. The first Fascist governor of Eritrea,
from 1923-28, Gasparini was responsible for the development of the irrigated plantations around TESSENEI, and
remained president of the SIA development parastatal
until his death in Asmara in 1941.

GEBRE-MESKAL WOLDU, Fitwari (1907-1963). Early
Eritrean political leader and president of the MAHABER
FEQRI HAGER from its founding in 1941 to November
1946, when he was dismissed by pro-Ethiopian Unionist
forces, led by Col. Nega Haile Selassie, because of his
support for the compromise position of Federation with
Ethiopia advocated by WOLDE-AB WOLDE-MARIAM at the
WA'LA BET GHERGHIS. Gebre-Meskal was born in Akrur,
TSENADEGLE, in 1907 and served in the Italian colonial
ADMINISTRATION in Asmara, where he rose to the highest
rank available to Eritreans in the municipal government,
but in 1940 fled to SUDAN and joined the British and
Ethiopian forces, where he worked in the propaganda department, returning to Eritrea in 1941. He was appointed
secretary of the BRITISH ADMINISTRATION's Native Affairs Office in 1943, and was given a lucrative position as
agent for MELOTTI brewery from 1943-48, when he rejoined the UNIONIST PARTY's Hamasien branch, rising to

public office under the FEDERATION and obtaining appointment as Chief Justice of the Eritrean High Court in 1958.

GEBRE-YOHANNES TESFAMARIAM, Dej. Unionist leader and later advocate of peace negotiations with the nationalist guerrillas, Gebre-Yohannes was born in 1911, educated in MENDEFERA and joined the MAHABER FEQRI HAGER in 1941. He became secretary of the HAMASIEN branch of the UNIONIST PARTY in 1946 and vice-president in 1948. In 1951 he became editor of the newspaper *Etiopiya* and then Director of the Eritrean government's Press Department and later Minister of Public Works until 1962, when he was transferred to ADDIS ABABA and given a position on HAILE SELASSIE I's Advisory Council. In 1970 he led a group of Eritrean notables who protested the ONA massacre and met with the Emperor to propose peace negotiations with the ELF. In 1975 he resigned his position to protest the OM HAGER massacre, after which he was imprisoned by the DERG until 1982, when he retired to Asmara.

GEBRI (Tigrn.: "tribute"). A LAND tax in the TIGRINYA-speaking highlands that was customarily due to the Emperor of ETHIOPIA or the ruler of TIGRAI, but was usually paid to their local appointees (Tigrn.: Mislenie), or self-made lords (Shum-Gulti). Until the reign of Emperor YOHANNES IV, tribute was collected in kind, usually in grain; after which it was changed to cash. Gebri was assessed on the basis of MEDRI districts that included one or more GULTI subdistricts of several villages each. In most districts the village leaders (SHUMAGULLE), representing each ENDA group, would meet at the Gulti and MEDRI level to decide the distribution of the tribute sum by village, and the ENDA leaders would then divide their portion amongst their member families. Although this distribution was intended to be equitable according to soil fertility, abuses often occurred when powerful local lords arose, particularly in parts of SERAYE and HAMASIEN. The system continued in a modified form

under ITALIAN COLONIALISM, and was revised by HAILE
SELASSIE I during the FEDERATION, when he claimed
traditional Gebri, but then commuted its payment; it did
not end entirely until 1975, when the DERG and the liberation fronts abolished it, though the word is still often
used for land taxes.

GE'EZ. The liturgical language of the ORTHODOX CHURCH
and the name for the TIGRINYA writing system. Ge'ez developed as the language of the AKSUMITE empire, derived
from the merger of a Semitic SOUTH ARABIAN language
and one or more Cushitic languages, but there is some dispute as to whether it was the original root of all the
"Ethiopic" Semitic languages (including TIGRE, TIGRINYA
and AMHARIC) or simply a regional dialect that acquired
political predominance during the AKSUMITE period. In
any case, during the Aksumite period Ge'ez formed the
written language of the Eritrean region, utilizing a syllabary probably adapted from the "monumental" script of
the South Arabian writing system between the first and
fifth centuries A.D., although some recent scholarship
also points to earlier Nile Valley roots for the script.
        The earliest Ge'ez inscriptions date from the mid-
second century at MATARA and elsewhere in Akele Guzai,
which may be evidence for the theory that this was the
homeland of the Ag'azat people, who gave their name to the
language. The Ag'azat (S. Arab.: "emigrants") were probably a South Arabian group, who strongly influenced the
Akele Guzai-SHIMEZANA region from as early as the fifth
century B.C. and maintained a tributary relationship with
the rulers of Aksum, against whom they unsuccessfully
rebelled in the fifth and sixth centuries A.D. By the sixth
century, Ge'ez had replaced Greek as the literary language
of the empire, and as the Aksumites converted to Christianity it became the literary vehicle of the Church. The
Bible was translated into Ge'ez during the fifth-sixth
centuries and most of the literature produced in Eritrea
before the sixteenth century was written in Ge'ez, including the lives of saints (Tigrn.: *gedli,* lit.: "struggles") and
legal documents.

GENERAL COMMAND (ELF) *see* KIADA AL-AMA.

GHELEB (Senhit). The main settlement of the Bet Abrehe branch of the MENSA' people and the traditional seat of their KANTIBAI, Gheleb is set in a high round valley whose shield-like shape gives its name. In 1873 missionaries from SWEDEN settled in Gheleb with the permission of Kantibai Beamnet and developed a small SEM community including a school and clinic that distinguished Gheleb further as the most important Mensa' center through the Italian colonial period. The SEM built a junior high school during the 1940s, and the village had a mixed Muslim-Christian population of 2,000 before it was first attacked and burned by the Ethiopian army in late 1970. Much of its population fled to KEREN, while those who remained supported the ELF. Gheleb was again attacked by the Ethiopian army in March 1975 and in 1980, when many villagers were killed, after which most survivors fled to SUDAN. In May 1988, at the time of the SHE'EB massacre, Gheleb was cluster-bombed and the last of its population fled, after which it was on the front line between the Derg and EPLA until the end of the war. In 1995 its population was two hundred.

GHINDA (Semhar). An important agricultural and transport center on the road between ASMARA and MASSAWA, Ghinda has the mild climate and two rainy seasons that distinguish the mid-elevations of the SEMENAWI BAHRI. The area was inhabited by SAHO pastoralists before the Italians built a fort above the present town in 1889-90, establishing an administrative post on the key transport route that grew into the present town. The RAILROAD reached Ghinda in 1904, stimulating the growth of hotels and restaurants that still distinguish it, followed by Italian agricultural concessions that developed citrus and other crops, later expanded by Fratelli DE NADAI. An elementary school and Catholic mission were built, and during the Italian invasion of Ethiopia a hospital and military rest camp was constructed below the town, which were used by the British during the Second World War, but dismantled thereafter. In the 1960s an American Evangelical Mission hospital was built, which was re-opened in 1994.

During 1977-78 heavy fighting between the EPLF and the DERG occurred around the town, forcing much of its population to flee as REFUGEES. In late 1978 Ghinda was fortified as an Ethiopian garrison town, and although the EPLA overran Ghinda on October 17, 1985, in a diversionary attack, it was unable to liberate the town before the end of the war. During February to May 1990 heavy fighting occurred above DONGOLO, and thereafter the trenches below the town were known as the "Ghinda Front." On June 20, 1995, tens of thousands of Eritreans converged on the town for MARTYRS Day and the reburial of over one thousand Eritrean fighters who died on the front. Today Ghinda has a population of 15,000, including over 2,000 repatriated REFUGEES, and is a growing light industrial and ROAD TRANSPORT center, with warehouse facilities and railroad reconstruction increasing its economic importance.

GODA GUDI *see* GUNDET.

GOVERNMENT OF THE STATE OF ERITREA. The PROVISIONAL GOVERNMENT OF ERITREA (PGE) was superseded by Decree 37 of May 19, 1993, which created a three-branch government to oversee Eritrea's transition to Constitutional rule. The legislative branch was the new NATIONAL ASSEMBLY, which elected ISAIAS AFWERKI as State President on May 21 and on June 7 formed the executive branch or State Council from the Advisory Council of the former PGE ; while the judiciary remained the separate body formed in 1992 *(see* JUSTICE). After the EPLF's Third Congress, in March 1994, the State Council was reduced to the sixteen government Ministers appointed by the President, and the National Assembly was modified. Effective power remained in the hands of President Isaias and the EPLF/PFDJ leadership, who held the key Ministerial portfolios and half the seats on the National Assembly. This government is to remain in power until national elections are held in 1998 under Eritrea's new CONSTI-TUTION.

GULTI (Tigrn.: unit of communal tribute payment; land given in fief). A quasi-feudal system involving the right to collect tribute on land (GEBRI) overlay the various LAND TENURE systems in the Eritrean highlands until the Italian colonial period. The term *gulti* (from *gwelete:* "founder" or "settler") covers both the smallest unit of communal tribute assessment (usually comprising several contiguous villages) and the quasi-feudal right to collect tribute on land. This right to *gebri* was assigned to the local church and military aristocracy, in theory by the Emperor of ETHIOPIA, but often in fact by the lords of TIGRAI or the BAHRE NEGASHI. *Gulti* assignments are recorded from at least the thiteenth century to ORTHODOX CHURCH establishments, and later to local lords who provided military service and sometimes a portion of the tribute to their rulers. Initially, most of the *gulti* grants were held by monasteries, and the majority of the population paid its tribute directly to the local *shum gulti* (chief of the gulti district).

During the later eighteenth and early nineteenth centuries a number of gulti districts in SERAYE and HAMASIEN became permanent fiefs of local lords, who appropriated all tribute and began to form a hereditary caste known as *gultenya* (gulti-holders). On the other hand, most of AKELE GUZAI and the northern districts of Hamasien continued to pay their tribute directly to the representatives of the rulers of the MAREB MELLASH (whether Eritrean or Tigrean), through their *shum gulti* and *shum* MEDRI. The *gulti* system was complicated by continuous modification and restructuring by successive rulers, including the creation of a number of autonomous units (RISTI Gulti) which paid tribute directly to the local governor.

GULUJ (Gash-Setit). A market town and administrative post on the road between TESSENEI and OM HAGER, Guluj was founded as an Italian police post and developed into a town of several thousand during the tractor-farming boom of the 1960s. Its mixed population of ARABIC and TIGRE-speaking merchants and NARA, KUNAMA and TIGRINYA farmers largely supported the ELF during this period, and in 1967 the town was burned by the Ethiopian military, forcing most of the population to flee over the border into SUDAN as REFUGEES. The town was completely abandoned in 1975, except for a small Kunama and Nara settlement on its outskirts. Today the town center is still in ruins, but Guluj has a population of over two thousand, most of whom are repatriated refugees seeking work in the reviving agricultural economy of the southern GASH-SETIT plains.

GUNDET (Seraye). The district along the MAREB River valley between ADI QWALA and the border of TIGRAI. During the seventeenth through nineteenth centuries successive Ethiopian and Tigrean rulers settled military colonies in the district to protect their border and assure control of the route to the Eritrean coast, giving rise to a TIGRINYA-speaking population of mixed ancestry. The village of GODA GUDI in Gundet was fortified by EGYPT during its first invasion of the Eritrean highlands, and there on November 16-17, 1875, an Egyptian army of about three thousand, commanded by the Danish Col. Arendrup was defeated by a larger Tigrean army led by YOHANNES IV and Shalaqa ALULA, and aided by the Eritrean forces of WOLDE-MIKA'EL SOLOMUN.

GURA' (Akele Guzai). Situated in a wide valley nine kilometers southeast of DEKEMHARE, the village of Gura' was an important market center on the trade route from MAS-SAWA via the Alighede River to the Mareb River during the seventeenth to nineteenth centuries. It was the principal village of Eghela Hames district, and its settlers traced their origins to the Agne family of neighboring Korbaria. Several Tigrean rulers and BAHRE NEGASHIs made Gura' their temporary capital during expeditions in the highlands, and it was the site of two of the most important battles in recent Eritrean history. In 1876 an Egyptian army of 15,000, commanded by an American general and the son of Khedive Isma'il, encamped at Gura' during their second attempt to invade the highlands. On 7-9 March they were defeated by the larger Tigrean army of YOHANNES IV and Shalaqa (later Ras) ALULA, who forced the Egyptians to withdraw to the coast, ending their ambitions of controlling the highlands. Gura' was then used by Ras Alula as his headquarters when he became military governor of the MAREB MELLASH, and it was occupied by the BANDA of BAHTA HAGOS, representing ITALIAN COLONIALISM, in 1889.

The Italians left the village untouched until 1935, when they destroyed many houses and confiscated much of its prime land, Golgol Hames, for a military AIRPORT that was their main airbase during the invasion of Ethiopia. The airbase was converted into an Anglo-American aircraft repair and assembly center during 1942-43, when the UNITED STATES company of Johnson, Drake and Piper employed 2,000 Americans and an equal number of Eritrean and Italian workers. During 1944-45 the British dismantled the base, leaving only its concrete runway, which was used by U.S. aerial reconnaissance flights in the 1960s. On May 20, 1991, the final battle on the DEKEMHARE FRONT crossed the Gura' plain, where the EPLA defeated the DERG's forces in a violent tank battle.

- H -

HABAB. The most important of the three branches of the BET ASGHEDE, founded by Habte-Iyasu (Habtes) during the late seventeenth century. By the 1950s the Habab numbered some twenty-five thousand pastoralists living in the RORA Habab of SAHEL and migrating with their herds to the lower BARKA valley and coastal plains during the winter. Before colonial rule the Habab had an autonomous tribal government led by a KANTIBAI from the family of Habte-Iyasu, who enforced the power of the SHUMAGULLE class over their more numerous TIGRE-speaking Muslim serfs until the colonial period. The

Shumagulle were originally Christian, but converted to ISLAM in the early nineteenth century under the influence of the AD SHAYKH clan and later Egyptian governors, to whom the Habab paid tribute in return for military protection after 1865. In 1887 Kantibai Hamid put his people under Italian protection, but he and his brother were later arrested and died in prison, prompting his son, Kantibai Mahmoud, to lead the tribe over the border to Tokar, SUDAN, during 1891-92.

   After their return in 1892, the Italians allowed the Shumagulle to retain their privileges, but during the 1940s the anti-serf movement led by IBRAHIM SULTAN ALI eroded these, leading some of the Shumagulle to support HAILE SELASSIE I's rule, which promised to restore them. By the 1970s much of the tribe had fled to Sudan, and from 1979-88 some of the most devastating fighting of the ARMED STRUGGLE occurred on Habab land. The consequence of war, FAMINEs and the flight of REFUGEES was a leveling of the old social and economic divisions among the Habab, which accelerated in the Rora Habab under EPLF rule, as the area became a pilot project for rural reform and social restructuring, including women's property rights and literacy projects, an anti-female CIRCUMCISION campaign, a 460-hectare FORESTRY project, and experiments in rotational grazing. By 1994 there were eleven thousand Habab living on their mountain plateau above NAKFA.

HABESHA (Tigrn.: "Abyssinian"). A self-descriptive cultural definition today applied to members of the TIGRINYA ethno-linguistic group, as well as Tigrinya and AMHARIC-speaking Christians in ETHIOPIA. Habesha defines the culture that was produced by the fusion of Semitic and Cushitic elements in the Eritrean-Tigrean highlands and which flowered as an original civilization during the AKSUMITE period. The derivation of the word is disputed, but it was clearly used in ancient SOUTH ARABIA to describe the people of the Eritrean-Tigrean region. It is not the name of any known South Arabian tribal group, CONTI ROSSINI notwithstanding, nor of any

known group that existed on the African side of the Red
Sea. The name occurs in Sabean inscriptions describing
people from the Eritrea-Tigrai region as early as the first
century A.D., and South Arabian sources refer to the Aksumite empire as the "Kingdom of the Habeshat," a usage
that continues into medieval ARABIC texts describing the
Eritrean-Ethiopian region, from which the English appel-
lation "Abyssinia" derives.

HADAS River. A major drainage of eastern AKELE GUZAI,
running down a deep canyon from the ADI KAIYEH area to
the Gulf of ZULA. The river was dammed at FORO in the
1960s, and the EPLF built a temporary road up the canyon
during 1990 to serve the DEKEMHARE FRONT.

HADENDOWA *see* BEJA; BENI 'AMER; HEDAREB.

HADGU-AMBESSA *see* AD TEKLEZAN.

HAGER NAGRAN. Site of an ORTHODOX CHURCH
monastery founded in the sixth century, according to legend, by refugees from the massacre of Christians at Nagran (523 A.D.) in SOUTH ARABIA. Hager Nagran is located in the extreme north of the SAHEL mountains on the
border with SUDAN, near the plateaus of Hager Nish and
Hager Abai. The monastery prospered on the PILGRIMAGE
ROUTE to SUWAKIN   until the sixteenth century, when
Turkish rule and the rise of ISLAM in the area led to its
abandonment. Today the few remaining stones are used for
grinding by the BET ASGHEDE and others.

HAGAZ (Senhit). A village on the highway between KEREN
and AGORDAT with a mixed TIGRE and BILEN population.
Hagaz was the site of numerous guerrilla attacks and several civilian massacres during the ARMED STRUGGLE. It
was held by the ELF during 1977-78, and by the EPLF after 1988. On April 24, 1978, the ELF and EPLF agreed to
form a joint administration in a meeting there. Today it is
a growing market and transport center with an
agricultural development project nearby and a population

of over five thousand, including many repatriated
REFUGEES.

HAILE MENKERIOS. Currently Eritrean ambassador to
ETHIOPIA, Haile Menkerios is one of the inner circle of
original EPLF leaders. Born in HAMASIEN, Haile is a contemporary of ISAIAS AFWERKI, with whom he studied at
ADDIS ABABA University, after which he attended Bran-
deis and Harvard in the U.S., obtaining a doctorate in Education before joining the EPLF in the field in 1974. He was
elected to the first EPLF CENTRAL COMMITTEE and all
succeeding ones. He was appointed PGE representative to
Ethiopia in May 1991, becoming ambassador in 1993.

HAILE SELASSIE I (Emperor of Ethiopia, 1930-74). Born
Tafari Makonen in 1892, Haile Selassie was responsible
for uniting Eritrea with ETHIOPIA and Ethiopian policies
which led directly to the ARMED STRUGGLE for Eritrean
independence. Although his activities in pursuit of
Ethiopian sovereignty over Eritrea were largely carried
out through others, his ideas and decisions guided every
aspect of Ethiopian policy concerning Eritrea from May
1941, when he encouraged Eritreans residing in ADDIS
ABABA, including the five hundred he employed in his
government, to found the Ethiopia-Hamasien Society, dedicated to uniting Eritrea with what the society called its
"Mother Ethiopia." BRITAIN had used Haile Selassie's
name and prestige among Christian Eritreans in their war
effort against Italy, and had made some vague promises
concerning Eritrea's future links with Ethiopia which
were recalled by Ethiopians and their Eritrean supporters
in the MAHABER FEQRI HAGER (MFH) to buttress their
position, and during 1941-42 the Ethiopian government
financed a growing unity movement within the MFH.
    The Emperor used every strategy available to mobi-
lize Christian Eritreans in support of unification (*see*
UNIONIST PARTY), including the ORTHODOX CHURCH,
anti-Muslim chauvinism, anti-Italian racism and the
strong anticolonialism of Eritrean intellectuals, such as
GEBRE-MESKAL WOLDU and TEDLA BAIRU, who believed

that Ethiopian rule would mean freedom for both personal and societal advancement after years of European oppression. The Ethiopian campaign, which included a TIGRINYA newspaper, was particularly successful among the Eritrean POLICE, and other government employees.

In March 1946 the Emperor sent Col. Nega Haile Selassie to act as his Liaison Officer in Eritrea. Using Ethiopian funds, he set about organizing the pro-Ethiopian wing of the MFH into the Unionist Party. During 1947-50, when successive international commissions of investigation toured Eritrea, the emperor's agents organized a campaign of anti-independence, anti-Italian and anti-Muslim violence, that was intended to coerce Eritreans into supporting union and demonstrate to the outside world that only Ethiopian rule would be accepted by the people (*see* ANDENET; SHIFTA).

On the diplomatic front, the Ethiopian Foreign Minister, Aklilu Habte-Wold, worked tirelessly to convince the emperor's Western patrons, Britain and the UNITED STATES, to support Ethiopia's claims, but he was disappointed by the BEVIN-SFORZA PLAN and other deals which were made with no reference to Ethiopian wishes. By 1949 it was clear that pro-independence sentiments were growing among Eritreans, and the Ethiopian campaign of violence and assassination was stepped up, culminating in the intercommunal rioting in ASMARA of February, 1950. In late 1950 the emperor's strategy prevailed in the UN, as Ethiopian support of the United States in Korea, combined with destabilization in Eritrea and the rising importance of KAGNEW STATION, induced the U.S. to push through Eritrea's FEDERATION with Ethiopia.

The Emperor was not satisfied with an autonomous Eritrean state, which he saw as a potential challenge to his autocratic power, and in negotiations with Anze MATIENZO over the composition of the Federation, Aklilu Habte-Wold continually attempted to weaken Eritrea's autonomous institutions. The emperor's representative in Eritrea, ANDERGATCHEW MESSAI, and vice-representative, ASFAHA WOLDE-MIKA'EL, did everything they could to insure that Eritrea's institutions would come

under Ethiopian control during Federation, and after 1955
the emperor's campaign for complete unification moved
with increasing speed, culminating in ANNEXATION in
1962.

     After 1952, Haile Selassie visited Eritrea each Jan-
uary, dedicating new Orthodox Churches, dispensing honors, accepting petitions and meeting with Italian entrepreneurs, in whose businesses the imperial family held
important interests. The emperor's Eritrean policy during
the 1960s, carried out by ABIYE ABEBE and ASRATE
KASSA, concentrated on appeasing the Christian population in hopes of dividing them from their Muslim compatriots, who already largely supported the ARMED STRUG-
GLE for independence. In 1970 a harsher policy of repression began, advocated by Aklilu Habte-Wold and the
military. This further alienated the Christian community,
and by the time the emperor was deposed, in September
1974, the great majority Eritreans were united against
Ethiopian rule. Thus, Haile Selassie's Eritrean policy,
which he regarded as one of the great accomplishments of
his reign, was completely discredited.

HAILE   WOLDE-TENSA'E ("Diru'e"). Currently Minister
of Foreign Affairs, Haile-Mariam Wolde-Tensa'e (alt.:
Woldense) is one of the inner circle of original EPLF leaders and one of their leading ideologues. He was born in
HAMASIEN in 1946 and attended Prince Makonnen secondary school in Asmara until 1965, when he went with
ISAIAS AFWERKI to study engineering at ADDIS ABABA
University. In 1966 he left with Isaias to join the ELF,
where he was a member of the TRIPARTITE UNITY FORCES
and later the ALA group of the ELF-PLF. He headed the
political education department of the EPLF from June
1974 and sat on the front's CENTRAL COMMITTEE and
Political Bureau from their inception. During the 1980s
he headed the cadre school and Political Affairs Department of the front, and in September 1991 he was appointed
to the key Department of Economic Planning and Coordination, later transformed into the Ministry of Finance and
Development, which he headed until June, 1997.

HALAI *see* DIGSA.

HALENQA. A BEJA-speaking ethnic group in northwestern Eritrea, said to have migrated originally from SERAYE.

HAL-HAL (Senhit). A high plateau in northern SENHIT, located between the ANSEBA valley and the eastern drainages of the BARKA, and forming a strategic massif guarding the southern approaches of the SAHEL highlands. The area was on the ancient Christian PILGRIMAGE ROUTES and contains AKSUMITE and early Christian ruins around Aratukh. Today Hal-Hal is the northernmost settlement of the BILEN sub-tribe of Bet Tawqe, who moved into the area before the fifteenth century. Catholic missionaries visited Hal-Hal from the 1850s through 1872, when it came under the rule of EGYPT. During the period of ITALIAN COLONIALISM, a CATHOLIC CHURCH and administrative post were founded on the sloping plateau of Hal-Hal "Fisho" (It.: Officiale), followed by an agricultural concession and the growth of a small village and market center. By the 1960s the population was about ninety-five percent Muslim and five percent Christian.

The early ELF commander, OMER EZAZ, a native of Hal-Hal, raided its POLICE post several times and in 1967 a unit of COMMANDOS was stationed in the village. On September 5, 1968, Omer Ezaz's unit attacked the Commando base and suffered the worst ELF defeat of the 1960s, losing about seventy fighters including Omer and his lieutenant. The following day the Ethiopian army killed thirty villagers, stole most of their livestock and took the fighters' corpses to KEREN for public display. In 1970 the Commandos were withdrawn and the ELF controlled Hal-Hal until 1981, redistributing land from the Italian concession and forming a committee of elders. In 1981 the last fighting of the Second CIVIL WAR occurred in the area, after which the EPLF took over the administration, although their nearest military units were stationed at Molebso and Mai Walad.

From 1982 to 1991 Hal-Hal was the scene of some of the heaviest fighting of the war, beginning with the RED STAR CAMPAIGN and the 1983 military occupation of "Fisho," which the DERG transformed into an army corps base. During the AFABET battle the EPLA attacked the base and captured it in early April 1988, as part of its attempt to liberate KEREN. The Derg retook Hal-Hal "Fisho" in May, and by 1991 soldiers had completely stripped the area. During 1993-94 Hal-Hal was rebuilt as an administrative and market center. The road to Keren was reconstructed, the Catholic Secretariat built a clinic, school and church, returning REFUGEES built a mosque and shops, and a small reservoir was completed.

HALHALE (Seraye). A fertile plain and village between DEBARWA and Teramni, watered by the Mokh'aw Kolo mountains, which provide it with year-round grazing. From medieval times part of the plain was under Ethiopian imperial control or that of their Eritrean governors, who used it to pasture their livestock, and in the mid-eighteenth century it was transferred to the NA'IB of HIRGHIGO by Micha'el Suhul. The upper portions of the plain were farmed by the villagers of Adi Geda, but in 1892 the Italians confiscated the entire plain as state land and in the early 1900s agricultural concessions were established, fencing off the villagers' former lands and forcing them to work on Italian estates.

In 1938 the Halhale concession was acquired by Viscount Stefano MARAZZANI, who developed it as a modern, irrigated farm. During the 1940s the Marazzani concession became the most productive dairy farm in Eritrea, supplying most of ASMARA's milk products through the mid-1970s. Marazzani kept the concession until his death in the late 1960s, when his widow leased it to an Asmara lawyer, Gaetano Latilla. Latilla abandoned Halhale in late 1974, when the ELF allowed farmers from Adi Geda to take over the concession. In 1977 the front decided to operate it as a state farm using captured tractors, sparking a protest which led to the imprisonment of twenty villagers. The ELF lost the area in mid-1978, and the DERG redistributed the land to the villagers, retaining the roadside property as a military post and tree farm. After liberation, in 1993 the Eritrean government declared the former concession state property and attempted to repossess it for large-scale agricultural development, but met with serious protests from the four hundred families farming it. Today the government plans to develop a village-based cooperative to utilize its irrigation and dairy potential.

HAM *see* DEBRE LIBANOS of Shimezana.

HAMASIEN. Until 1995 the northernmost province of the central highlands, now largely part of the new Zoba Maakel (Central Region), Hamasien contains ASMARA and the historical districts of DEMBEZAN, DEQI TESHIM, KARNISHEM, the fertile slopes of the SEMENAWI BAHRI and the important villages of Adi Rasi, ADI NEFAS, AD TEKLEZAN, Embaderho, HAZZEGA, Himberti, Qwazien, Shiketi, TSAZZEGA, WOKI DUBA and ZAGHER, among others. Historically, the name "Hamasien" was used to describe much of present-day SERAYE as well, but by the nineteenth century the province's boundary was set at the Mokh'aw Kolo mountains, northwest of DEBARWA. A Portuguese map from 1630 refers to the highlands as the "Republic of Hamasien," indicating its independent political status under the House of TSAZZEGA, which dominated the province until the 1870s. Because of its central location on TRADE ROUTES from the coast and the ANSEBA valley, Hamasien's ruling families were the most powerful in Eritrea, and succeeding Tigrean and Italian rulers established their capital at Asmara. With the growth of this city, the history of Hamasien has largely become the history of Asmara, as outlying villages have been drawn into the urban economy and villagers have settled in the city. Italian entrepreneurs established industries and truck farms throughout the province to serve the metropolis, and today Hamasien contains about 80 percent of Eritrea's modern industries. Hamasien is also at the center of modern Eritrean politics and its dominant TIGRINYA culture, and much of the leadership of the present government, beginning with President ISAIAS AFWERKI, come from the province.

HAMID IDRIS AWATE (1911-1962). As the man who fired the first shots of the ARMED STRUGGLE, Hamid Idris Awate has been claimed by all Eritrea's liberation movements, but a complete account of his actions in 1960-62 has yet to be published. Hamid was born in 1911 to the Hafara clan of TIGRE-speaking agriculturists, a people of Nilotic origin settled east of TESSENEI and related to the ALGHEDEN, Bit Hama, ILLIT and SABDERAT, but linked politically to the BENI 'AMER. Hamid's mother was said to be NARA. Hamid joined the ITALIAN COLONIAL army as an ASCARI in the early 1930s, where he became literate in Italian. He deserted after the Italian defeat in the western lowlands in early 1941 and in 1942 he joined the SHIFTA band of Ali "Mumtaz" (Ali Muhamed Idris) in cattle-raiding and border warfare between the Beni 'Amer and the Sudanese Hadendowa and later the Wolqaiti of TIGRAI. He surrendered to the BRITISH ADMINISTRATION in 1951, and retired to Geset to farm, where he was a respected community leader and poet.

   During 1960, both the ELM and IDRIS MOHAMED ADEM were interested in Hamid Idris as a potential military leader. But it was Sayedna MOHAMED IBN DAWD IBN MUSTAFA, who actually met him in April 1961 near Gerset and asked him to lead an ELF cell and consider organizing a guerrilla force. Hamid was interested in the proposal, but told Sayedna Mohamed the ELF first needed a strong organization and modern arms. Nonetheless, Hamid went to AGORDAT and requested that the provincial administration supply him with arms to fight Wolqaiti cattle-raiders. In August 1961, as the ELF and ELM were waging a propaganda battle against each other, the Eritrean POLICE began to suspect him of antigovernment activities. A TIGRINYA Christian friend of Hamid's in police intelligence informed him of an impending raid on his home, and he gathered up his followers and fled to Mount Adal, between Agordat and Tessenei, where he was pursued by a police anti-shifta unit and involved in a gun battle on September 1, 1961. Hamid Idris's small band of eleven men armed with old Italian rifles grew during late 1961 to early 1962, as several Eritrean members of the SUDAN DEFENSE FORCE (SDF) joined him, forming the core of what became the ELF army. But Hamid Idris took ill and died near Haikota in June 1962. His remains were reburied at Haikota and a statue erected in his honor on September 1, 1994 in a ceremony attended by about ten thousand people.

HANISH ISLANDS. An uninhabited archipelago lying sixty miles off the Eritrean coast and twenty-five miles from YEMEN, whose sovereignty was never settled after it was relinquished by TURKEY in 1923. The Italian colonial government administered the islands from MASSAWA until 1941, after which BRITAIN maintained lighthouses on them from Aden until 1967. Both Yemen and Ethiopia claimed them in the 1970s, when Eritrean FIGHTERS used them as a base. This led both Yemen and Eritrea to claim them, along with the neighboring Zukur Islands, in 1995. The competing claims escalated into an armed conflict during December 15-18, when the Eritrean army gained control of Hanish Kebir. On June 21, 1996, both nations agreed to arbitrate the dispute under the supervision of the UNITED NATIONS and World Court. In October they agreed on procedures for selecting arbitrators, who began proceedings in London in April 1997.

HARAKAT *see* ERITREAN LIBERATION MOVEMENT (ELM).

HAREGOT ABAI (alt.: Abay). A leading Unionist politician and Mayor of ASMARA, Haregot was born in Asmara in 1909 to Bahre-Negashi Abai Habtezion, the chief of Asmara's "native quarter." He was educated in MENDE-FERA and served the Italian government in Asmara from 1924-41, after which he joined the MAHABER FEQRI HAGER and founded a bus company that eventually dominated city transport. He was an Assistant-Secretary of the Unionist Party, vice-president of its HAMASIEN branch, and was elected to the first ASSEMBLY in 1952, rising to

head the Department of Law and Justice in the Eritrean
government in 1954. In 1962 he became Mayor of Asmara
and presided over the paving of the Mai Bela sewer and
other public works projects. He later became Minister of
State for Eritrea in the Ethiopian Prime Minister's office.
During the 1940s, Haregot was administrator of the main
ORTHODOX CHURCH in Asmara, Kidisti Mariam, and oversaw much of its contemporary architecture. Haregot's son,
Seyoum, was educated in ADDIS ABABA and rose to
prominence in the government of HAILE SELASSIE I,
becoming a full cabinet minister in 1969. The family lost
their positions during the Ethiopian revolution.

HASO (alt.: Hazu). A SAHO tribe inhabiting the eastern
foothills of AKELE GUZAI from IRAFAILE south to the
Ethiopian border. They are pastoralists who have traditionally fought to protect their pastures from the neighboring AFAR and Ethiopian (Saho-speaking) Irob. They
are divided into ten historical clans under a tribal chief
or "Ona."

HAYLU TEWOLDE-MEDHIN, Dej. (c. 1805-77). Last
ruler of the House of TSAZZEGA, Dej. Haylu's career epit-
omized the unstable, personalized politics of the Eritrean
highlands in the nineteenth century. Haylu deposed his
father in 1832/33 as lord of the MAREB MELLASH, but
submitted to Dej. WUBE in 1835, who recognized him in
his position as ruler of the highlands until 1840, when he
imprisoned him for fifteen years on Amba Tesen in
TIGRAI, substituting his more malleable brother, Aite
Alula, as governor of Mareb Mellash. Emperor Tewodros
freed Haylu in 1855 and reinstated him as governor of
HAMASIEN. He fought off a challenge from his arch-rival
and nemesis, WOLDE-MIKA'EL SOLOMUN of HAZZEGA, in
1857, and the attempt of "Agaw" NEGUSSIE to control the
highlands in 1858-60. Haylu retained his position, but
once again fought Wolde-Mika'el in 1865-66, and in 1868-
69 failed to acknowledge the rise of YOHANNES IV (Kasa
Mertcha) in time to avoid his arrest and brief replacement
by Wolde-Mika'el, after which both he and his rival were

given alternating positions of power and enforced residence at the imperial court. When Wolde-Mika'el joined the Egyptians in late 1875, Haylu returned to full power, which he held until his rival killed him at WOKI DUBA in 1877.

HAZ-HAZ (Asmara). A red hill in northern ASMARA, comprising the colonial Amba Galliano district. Following the battle of BET MAK'A in 1878, where Ras WOLDE-MIKA'EL SOLOMUN defeated Ras Bairu, the latter's soldiers were captured on the hill, hence its name (Tigrn.: "catch-catch"). Haz-Haz was the site of an Italian officer's club and military clinic that was converted to a police station and women's prison under the DERG. Today the women's prison has been converted to a maternity hospital.

HAZAMO. The arid plains along the middle MAREB River valley, separating AKELE GUZAI from SERAYE. The area has been a grazing ground for SAHO pastoralists and TIGRINYA farmers from SHIMEZANA for many centuries, and occasional disputes over grazing lands have provoked numerous armed clashes in the area, leading to inter-ethnic fighting in the 1940s and clashes between ELF-supported Saho and Ethiopian-supported Tigrinya BANDAs in the 1960s. The area was held by the ELF through August 1978, when the DERG sent a mechanized column from TIGRAI through Hazamo (*see* MAI AINI). The EPLF occupied the area during 1980-81, and in 1982 instituted land reform benefiting poor farmers. Tsorona, on the road to Tigrai, developed as an important EPLF administrative center and was bombed in 1990. Since liberation, new schools and clinics have been built in the formerly remote area.

HAZZEGA (Hamasien). Together with TSAZZEGA, Hazzega is home to one of the two branches of the descendants of Tesfazion who formed the hereditary ruling dynasty of HAMASIEN and most of the MAREB MELLASH until 1879. Located in DEQI TESHIM, Hazzega was the native village of Tesfazion, descendant of the legendary Aite-Shum, who

ruled Hamasien in the 1630s. Tesfazion's elder sons remained in Hazzega and his two younger sons founded
Tsazzega. After their father's death the junior branch rose
to power, but the senior branch always retained a claim to
the governorship of Hamasien. Too weak to enforce their
claim themselves, the House (ENDA) of Hazzega turned to
outside powers for support, beginning with KANTIBAI
Kelata's bid for support from Ras Mika'el Suhul of TIGRAI,
who briefly put him in power (1768-70), followed by his
nephew Kantibai Zerai and Aite Solomun, who contested
for power with the rulers of Tsazzega in an increasingly
bitter blood feud that culminated in the rise of Hazzega's
WOLDE-MIKA'EL SOLOMUN. Ras Wolde-Mika'el's brief
success ended with the fall of both Houses, first to Tigrean rule, and then to the Italians. Today Hazzega is a
small village of about two thousand; it was held by the ELF
during 1974-77 and by the EPLF in 1978, when the DERG
broke through Eritrean lines at neighboring ADI YAQOB.

HEALTH CARE. Traditional Eritrean health care practices
varied among ethnic groups, but they generally included
three types: household or village common knowledge concerning wounds and illnesses that involved bone setting,
wound binding and herbal remidies; more specialized and
often spiritually medicated healing involving practitioners who burned, cut and prescribed herbal and magical
remidies for their clients; and specialized women who
served as midwives. Although this traditional medicine
was often effective, it was also at times counterproductive,
and the common belief in the efficacy of cutting and
burning treatments was, and still is, widespread among
much of the population.

     Western medicine was largely introduced by Euro-
pean missionaries in the late nineteenth century, and by
ITALIAN COLONIALISM in the early twentieth. Although
most Italian medical facilities were intended to serve the
European population, clinics were also opened for the Eritrean population, beginning with ASCARIs and colonial
civil servants, and spreading by the 1930s to the main
towns. During the invasion of Ethiopia and the Italian

immigration that followed it, both military and civilian hospitals were expanded in MASSAWA, GHINDA and AS-MARA, where a private Italian community hospital was also built. After the Second World War the BRITISH AD-MINISTRATION's Health Department closed military hospitals at Massawa and Ghinda, but upgraded some Eritrean clinics. An Eritrean Health Department was created in 1952, and took over operation of the rudimentary colonial urban-based health system.

During the 1950s the first Eritrean doctors received medical training overseas, and in the 1960s a number of Eritreans graduated from the medical school in ADDIS ABABA. In 1965 an Eritrean nurse/dresser training facility was opened in Asmara with aid from the Point 4 program of the UNITED STATES. In the 1960s a number of clinics were opened in smaller towns, staffed by Eritrean dressers or foreign missionaries, such as the American Evangelical hospital in Ghinda (1966) and the Lalmba hospital in Keren (1970). During the 1970s health care services moved into rural Eritrea on a limited scale under both the DERG and, particularly, the EPLF.

The EPLF health care system made the first attempt to integrate Eritrean traditional medicine with Western medicine, and trained hundreds of "barefoot doctors" to serve the rural population of the liberated areas. The Health Department was established in 1975 under Dr. Nerayo Tekle Mika'el (*see* ERA), and focused on training village health workers and traditional birth attendants (TBAs). Mobile clinics were established and in 1976 a central hospital was created at OROTA. The difficulty and expense of acquiring medicines abroad led to the construction of small-scale pharmaceutical plants in the 1980s, beginning with an intravenous solution plant built with Belgian help in 1983. By the mid-1980s there were over a thousand barefoot doctors, and scores of highly trained surgeons, doctors, nurses and technicians staffing six regional hospitals as well as the central hospital-laboratory complex, where in 1984 open-heart surgery was performed. In the same period an eye surgery and lens implant unit was created with Australian aid. War injuries also necessitated the creation of an artificial limb factory at Arareb, and rehabilitation facilities, which were situated at the EPLF rear-base in Port Sudan.

In 1991 the EPLF Health Department took over the entire Eritrean health care system, including the decrepit facilities under Ethiopian control, which had been used primarily as military hospitals. Excluding the EPLF field hospitals, which were dismantled, the health system contained eight hospitals, four health centers (clinics) and forty-five health stations (dispensaries). This system was in disrepair, understaffed (one doctor to 48,000 people) and in addition to FAMINE victims it had to care for 60,000 war disabled. The EPLF developed rehabilitation facilities for 12,000 disabled fighters in Asmara and at MAI HABAR, and moved to integrate the Ethiopian and EPLF health care systems in a new national Ministry of Health, led by Dr. Haile Mitz'un. The task of integration was difficult and further complicated by the Ministry's takeover of a number of private hospitals.

By 1994 the Ministry was responsible for seventeen hospitals, including four main hospitals in Asmara which receive country-wide referrals, 32 health centers and 120 health stations. In 1992 the nurse training program was reopened and graduated its first class, but Eritrea remained underserved, with a ratio of one doctor per 28,000 and one nurse per 8,393. Health statistics reflect this with infant mortality estimated in 1991 at 135 per 1,000 live births, life expectancy 46 years and a frightening increase in AIDS cases, which had spread primarily through PROSTITUTION during the Derg period and infected a confirmed 1,732 people by 1995, with an estimated 60,000 HIV carriers, 80 percent of whom reside in Asmara. SEBHAT EPHREM served temporarily as Minister of Health in 1994-95 to improve the Ministry's performance, and in June 1997 Saleh Meki was appointed Minister.

HEDAREB. One of Eritrea's nine linguistically defined nationalities, the Hedareb include those sub-tribes of the BENI 'AMER people who have retained use of the BEJA language, To-Bedawi, also known as "Hedareb." They

include those sub-tribes related to the Sudanese
Hadendowa, such as the Hashish, the LABAT and
HALENQA, and smaller groups like the Ad Ali, Ad Nazi,
Ad Sala, Ad Tawle, Hassal, Sheinab, and Sinkat Keinab.
Today the Hedareb nationality is a somewhat artificial
concept, as most To-Bedawi speakers are bilingual in
TIGRE, and many men also speak ARABIC. The Beja ele-
ments of their culture are shared by most BENI 'AMER,
although the Hedareb groups have historically been more
resistant to Islamic orthodoxy.

HERUI TEDLA BAIRU (alt.: Hirouy). Son of the first Eritrean Chief Executive, TEDLA BAIRU, Herui was a leading
figure in the radical wing of the ELF during the 1970s. He
attended university in London during the 1960s and was
recruited into the ELF in 1969, where he joined the LA-
BOR PARTY. Following in his father's footsteps, he was
elected vice-chairman of the REVOLUTIONARY COUNCIL
in 1971, in a move designed by Muslim leaders to placate
the growing TIGRINYA/Christian element within the front.
Herui participated in the decision to liquidate the EPLF
in 1972, but represented the socially progressive ideas
and ethnically defined Tigrinya/Christian constituency
which remained in the ELF during the first CIVIL WAR. He
lost his vice-chairmanship in 1975, however, after he attempted to broker a unity agreement with the EPLF.
Thereafter, he led the increasingly alienated
Tigrinya/Christian elements that produced the FALUL
movement. He never reconciled himself with the EPLF,
however, and after leaving the ELF in June 1977, he
founded his own Eritrean Democratic Movement (EDM),
which received support from IRAQ in 1979. Herui attempted to form an umbrella nationalist organization
modeled on the PLO, which would unite all the nationalist
fronts, but his group was increasingly marginalized (*see*
ELF FACTIONS), receiving TPLF support during the late
1980s and joining forces with the anti-EPLF elements of
SAGHEM after 1990. Herui left the EDM and returned to
Eritrea after liberation.

HEZBAWI   GUNBAR (Tigrn.: "People's Front") *see* ER-
ITREAN PEOPLE'S LIBERATION FRONT and PEOPLE'S
FRONT FOR DEMOCRACY AND JUSTICE.

HEZBAWI   SERAWIT (Tigrn.: "People's Army") *see* ER-
ITREAN PEOPLE'S LIBERATION ARMY.

HEWETT   TREATY (1884). Signed between Emperor
YOHANNES IV of ETHIOPIA and Admiral Sir William
Hewett, representing BRITAIN, on June 3, 1884 at ADWA
in TIGRAI. This treaty gave British recognition to Yohannes's claim to sovereignty over most of present-day
Eritrea, with the exception of MASSAWA, which the
British undertook to occupy as a free port. British
recognition was exchanged for Yohannes's military aid
against the Sudanese Mahdists, particularly to enable an
Egyptian garrison to evacuate KASSALA. Although the
garrison surrendered before it could be relieved, the
treaty did produce Ras ALULA's 1885 expedition into
Western Eritrea. The British, however, allowed ITALY to
occupy Massawa, abrogating the treaty, in the same year.

HIRGHIGO (Semhar; alt.: Harkiko, Hargigo, etc.). Located on
the mainland southwest of MASSAWA, Hirghigo was
founded in the fifteenth century by BELEW immigrants
whose leading family formed the dynasty of the NA'IBs.
Hirghigo became the seaward terminus of the Eritrean caravan trade, with a flourishing market and a heterogeneous
population of TIGRE-speakers, ASAWORTA Sahos, ARA-
BIC-speaking merchants and others. Because of its location at the foot of the mountains, Hirghigo supplied Massawa with most of its drinking water, and due to its
fresher climate many merchants located their permanent
homes there.
     The town suffered from the decline in the Na'ib's
power during the nineteenth century, as it was sacked by
Dej. WUBE in 1843/44, then by the Egyptians, who burned
it in 1847, and seized and fortified it in 1865. The Italians took it in 1885, and its commercial importance
declined with the development of the RAILROAD to AS-

MARA. But Hirghigo remained the seat of the Muslim coastal elite into the twentieth century, and during the 1940s its KEKIYA secondary school was an intellectual center of the emerging nationalist movement, producing some of the leading figures of the ARMED STRUGGLE, including IBRAHIM AFA, OSMAN SALEH SABBE and RAMADAN MOHAMED NUR. Consequently, the DERG targeted the town, beginning with a terrible massacre in 1975, which forced most of its surviving population to flee as REFUGEES, and ending with its total destruction in 1976. The site was abandoned until liberation, and in 1994 a master plan for rebuilding the town was created, including ambitious plans for a FISHING school and Marine Research Center. In 1997 construction of a major power plant was begun near the town.

H U D M O (pl. *hadamu*). The traditional house of the TIGRINYA highlands. Rectangular, built on a post-and-beam frame of tree trunks, with stone walls and earth roof. The first row of posts forms a porch, the entry room is an animal barn, separated from the living quarters by an interior wall. The living quarters are often further partitioned and plastered in mud with built-in seats, cupboards and a woodstove.

HUMED MOHAMED KARIKARI. The highest-ranking AFAR in the EPLF, Humed, a native of SUDOHA ILA, served on the CENTRAL COMMITTEE and commanded the Eritrean NAVY during the war. He was governor of DENKEL during 1994-95 and in October 1996 was reappointed commander of the Navy.

- I -

IBRAHIM AFA (d. 1985). Born the son of a poor waterseller in HIRGHIGO, Ibrahim Afa rose to become the military leader of the EPLF. He attended KEKIYA school until the eighth grade, when he left to join the Ethiopian NAVY. He rose to be a non-commissioned officer in the Marine COMMANDOS before deserting to join the ELF in

1967. He went to Cuba for further military training in 1968, after which he became a unit leader in Zone 4, where he sided with the TRIPARTITE UNITY FORCES and joined the PLF faction led by RAMADAN MOHAMED NUR. Like Ramadan, Ibrahim supported ISAIAS AFWERKI's leadership of the emerging EPLF during the struggles of the early 1970s, and emerged as the front's leading military commander by 1975, when he was appointed to the three person Military Committee, acting as its *de facto* "chief of staff" until his death. He was elected to both the CENTRAL COMMITEE and Political Committee of the EPLF at its First Congress. Ibrahim Afa was killed in an Ethiopian counterattack in night fighting around BARENTU in 1985, but his death was so demoralizing that the EPLF refused to acknowledge it until the Second and Unity Congress of 1987. Because of this silence, a number of rumors were circulated by the enemies of the EPLF that Ibrahim had been removed in an internal purge, but this could not be farther from the truth. He was perhaps Isaias's most trusted comrade, and one of the few times Isaias was ever seen to cry was when he received news of Ibrahim's untimely death.

IBRAHIM IDRIS TOTIL. A leading figure in the ELF and the Unity Movement of the 1980s, Ibrahim Totil was born to a NARA family in the late 1940s and attended secondary school in SUDAN, where he joined the ELF in 1967. He served as a political organizer in the front's offices in KASSALA and Wad Medani, and was one of the founding members of the Marxist-oriented LABOR PARTY. In 1971 he was elected to the Executive Committee, where he emerged, with AZIEN YASSIN, as a leading ideologue of the secular left within the mainstream ELF. After the Second CIVIL WAR, his secularism led him to clash with ABDALLAH IDRIS, who briefly arrested him in 1982, and in 1983 Totil joined the SAGHEM movement, forming the ELF-Central Leadership in 1985, which merged completely with the EPLF in 1987. Totil served in the front's political department until liberation, when he was appointed

Governor of SEMHAR province, making the transition to Administrator of the Northern Red Sea Region in 1995.

IBRAHIM SULTAN ALI (1909-1987). Leading nationalist politician of the 1940s-50s and founder of the MUSLIM LEAGUE. Ibrahim Sultan was born in KEREN, where he studied in Islamic and Italian colonial schools, joining the Eritrean RAILROAD where he worked as a chief conductor during 1922-26. He served the Italian administration in its Muslim Native Affairs section from 1926-41, rising to head its Eritrean staff, and continued in this position under the BRITISH ADMINISTRATION until 1943, when his critiques of European racism forced his retirement to TESSENEI, where he founded a creamery. His involvement in politics began with his founding role in the MAHABER FEQRI HAGER (MFH) in 1941, and during 1943-45 he organized the revolt of TIGRE serfs against their SHUMAG-ULLE lords, laying the foundation for a new political movement, the Muslim League, which elected him Secretary-General in December, 1946. As head of the Muslim League, Ibrahim worked with the British to see all the serfs emancipated by 1949, and he presented the views of Muslim Eritreans to the Commissions of Investigation of the FOUR POWERS and UNITED NATIONS, attending the Lake Success session of the UN in 1949, where he was instrumental in forming the INDEPENDENCE BLOC together with WOLDE-AB WOLDE-MARIAM and others.

Ibrahim attempted to dominate Muslim politics, however, incurring the animosity of other aspiring leaders and contributing to the destruction of the League in 1950, when ALI MOHAMED MUSA REDAI led most of the Beni 'Amer and other western tribes out of the organization and into the MUSLIM LEAGUE OF THE WESTERN PROVINCE. Unlike Ali Musa and others, Ibrahim refused to compromise on either the territorial integrity of Eritrea or its future independence, but he accepted the FEDERATION when it came, and was elected to the first ASSEMBLY in 1952, where he led the opposition to TEDLA BAIRU's UNIONIST PARTY, conspiring with pro-Ethiopian forces to bring Tedla's fall in 1955. This move, however, brought

Ethiopian control and Ibrahim's exclusion from the second
Assembly in 1956, after which he participated in efforts
to reinvolve the UN in Eritrea's affairs to block Ethiopian
ANNEXATION.

Ibrahim left Eritrea in 1959 for CAIRO, where he
joined the growing exile group. But his attempts to dominate exile politics failed, and though he remained a symbolic figure and made numerous speeches and petitions on
behalf of the Eritrean cause, he alienated many of his potential colleagues in both the ELM and ELF. After initially
failing to work with either Wolde-Ab or the ELM, in 1962
he helped them petition the UN in New York, and eventually joined the opposition Unity Movement in the late
1960s. By the 1970s he was completely marginalized, but
his status was rehabilitated after 1982, when he joined
the EPLF's call for a national united front, sending a taped
message that was played at the EPLF's Second Congress in
1987. He died shortly thereafter, on September 1, 1987,
and was eulogized by Wolde-Ab, with whom he has taken
his place as one of the "father figures" of the Eritrean nation.

IDRIS MOHAMED ADEM. Leading figure in the early nationalist movement and founder of the ELF, Idris Mohammed Adem was born into the DAGA subtribe of the
BENI 'AMER in AGORDAT in 1921. He attended an ARABIC
secondary school in Gedaref, SUDAN, and returned to
Agordat with the BRITISH ADMINISTRATION in 1941 to
serve as official secretary for the Beni 'Amer DIGLAL.
Idris Adem wrote for the Arabic language edition of the
Eritrean Weekly News, and his early politics favored the
partition schemes of the British and, later, the MUSLIM
LEAGUE OF THE WESTERN PROVINCE. He was elected to
the Eritrean ASSEMBLY in 1952, and in 1955 joined forces
with IBRAHIM SULTAN ALI and others to secure the
ouster of TEDLA BAIRU and ALI MOHAMED MUSA REDAI,
replacing the latter as President of the Assembly on July
26.

After this Idris Adem became an increasingly militant nationalist leader, fighting for an independent

electoral commission, which led to his removal from office in June 1956, and petitioning the UNITED NATIONS, which led to his house arrest in 1957. In March 1959, together with Ibrahim Sultan, Idris fled to Sudan, but not after first establishing contacts with HAMID IDRIS AWATE, Sayedna MOHAMED IBN DAWD IBN MUSTAFA and others who later formed the ELF network in western Eritrea. In CAIRO, Idris canvassed support for the idea of starting an armed rebellion against Ethiopian rule. He distrusted the already existing ERITREAN LIBERATION MOVEMENT, particularly because of its socialist and secular ideology, and he derided the strategies of Ibrahim, WOLDE-AB WOLDE-MARIAM and others who focused on the UN. Instead, Idris worked with student activists and fellow Muslims from western Eritrea to form the core of a new movement, the ERITREAN LIBERATION FRONT. Even after OSMAN SALEH SABBE joined the front, Idris remained the leading figure on its SUPREME COUNCIL. As the front grew he became the patron of its Beni 'Amer and western units, coalesced into Zone 1, providing them with arms and supplies through his connections in the Arab world.

Idris maintained his power even after internal dissent began in 1967, and in 1971 he was elected Chairman of the REVOLUTIONARY COUNCIL. But his drive for personal control, and his hard-line stance against leftist and Christian dissidents led directly to the outbreak of CIVIL WAR in 1972. With the rise of a new generation of leaders, Idris was increasingly isolated, and he was not re-elected in 1975, although his son Ibrahim led an ISLAMIST faction in the younger leadership. Idris continued to work as a fund-raiser in the Arab world, and was involved in the many attempts by SAUDI ARABIA to build an Islamist organization among the more conservative ELF FACTIONS during 1982-85. As of 1996, he continues to live in Jeddah.

IDRIS OSMAN GALADEWOS. Founding member and one of three original leaders of the ELF SUPREME COUNCIL, Idris Galadewos was born in 1934 at Hami-el-Mal near

Keren to a merchant family of BET JUK origin. In 1938 his
father moved to ALI GHIDER, where Idris attended the
Arabic elementary school, moving to Keren for middle
school. In 1951 he went to CAIRO on a secondary school
scholarship, entering Cairo University in 1956, where he
studied law through 1962. In 1959 he participated in
founding the Eritrean Student Union, and was involved in
discussions with the ELM. With several other students he
formulated an alternative political strategy calling for
immediate ARMED STRUGGLE in Eritrea and in 1960 he
helped IDRIS MOHAMED ADEM form the ERITREAN LIB-
ERATION FRONT (ELF).

Galadewos was elected Secretary of the ELF by its
founding group, and in 1962 joined the SUPREME COUN-
CIL. As the ELF split along ethnic lines during the mid-
1960s, Galadewos became the patron of OMER EZAZ's
BILEN faction, based in Zone 2. He also sponsored the
creation of Zone 5, recognizing the political importance of
the Christian highlanders. With the breakup of the ZONAL
COMMANDS his power declined, although he was elected to
the REVOLUTIONARY COUNCIL in 1971. He was not re-
elected in 1975, but he continued to serve as ELF representative in Cairo through 1981, and attempted to reunite
the ELF FACTIONS in the 1980s, serving in the leadership
of the United Organization (ELF-UO) after 1986. In 1992
he led the ELF-UO back to Eritrea, where he served as a
REFERENDUM Commissioner and then on the Constitutional Commission.

ILENI HAGOS (c. 1805-51). An important figure in the
history of HAZZEGA, Ileni was the daughter of Aite Hagos,
KANTIBAI of ZAGHER, and married Solomon Tewoldemed-
hin, Kantibai of Hazzega around 1815-20. She is remembered as a woman with a strong but vengeful personality,
whose tragic story epitomizes the nineteenth century
blood-feuds of the TIGRINYA highlands. She was the
mother of WOLDE-MIKA'EL SOLOMUN, and on the death of
her husband in 1837/38 she was left to defend her son's
political rights to the Shumet of HAMASIEN. In 1840,
when Dej. HAYLU TEWOLDE-MEDHIN of TSAZZEGA was

imprisoned by WUBE, her agent went to the ruler of TIGRAI and successfully argued for the Shumet to be restored to her young son. Dej. Haylu's son was deposed and Ileni served as her son's regent. Rule by a woman was unprecedented in the KEBESSA, and sparked widespread opposition; but Wube's Tigrean military governor helped impose Ileni's authority.

In 1841 Wube's troops left and a war broke out between Ileni and the House of Tsazzega, led by Aite Alula. Hazzega was defeated, but Alula allowed Ileni to rule Minabe-Zerai. She became unpopular, however, due to her onerous taxes and an ongoing quarrel with Kantibai Wolde-Gaber of DEMBEZAN. In 1842/43 she was deposed by Aite Gebrai, brother-in-law of Wolde-Gaber and in 1850/51, Ileni took revenge on Wolde-Gaber when he inadvertently appeared in Hazzega and was murdered by her sons, who fled to Tigrai, leaving their mother and their own infant sons with their relative, the Kantibai of KARNISHEM. But the forces of Tsazzega and Hazzega marched on Karnishem and took Ileni and her grandchildren to the new Kantibai of Dembezan, Wolde-Gaber's brother Gilwet, who tortured and murdered them. Ileni's sons then returned, killed Gilwet and burned AD TEKLEZAN in 1855. The blood feud was finally ended by the marriage of Wolde-Mika'el's daughter, Teru, with the nephew of Kantibai Gilwet.

ILLIT. A small Nilotic-speaking group related to the KUNAMA, living in western GASH-SETIT.

INDEPENDENCE BLOC (1949-50). A united front of pro-independence Eritrean POLITICAL PARTIES was formed at the UNITED NATIONS by representatives of the MUSLIM LEAGUE, Pro-ITALY and Italo-Eritrean parties in May 1949. The group came together with the support of ITALY in the aftermath of the defeat of the BEVIN-SFORZA PLAN. When they returned to Eritrea, on June 26, they formed the Independence Bloc together with the LIBERAL PROGRESSIVE PARTY (LPP) and WOLDE-AB WOLDE-MARIAM's Independent Eritrea Party. The Bloc called for immediate independence, and represented a clear majority of the Eritrean population, as many previous UNIONIST PARTY supporters defected to it. The power of the Bloc alarmed HAILE SELASSIE I and his Unionist organization unleashed a terrorist campaign against the Bloc, culminating in the ASMARA riots of February, 1950. After this the Bloc disintegrated, due to the manipulations of the Ethiopians and BRITISH ADMINISTRATION, as well as the unpopularity in the highlands of overt Italian support for the Bloc. It was dissolved in December 1950, but most of its members from the remnants of the original Muslim League and LPP together with the smaller parties, formed the ERITREAN DEMOCRATIC FRONT in January 1951 and contested the elections for the first ASSEMBLY where they continued to form a loose anti-Unionist coalition, the "Independent Federalists," through 1956.

INDUSTRY. Traditional Eritrean industries included small-scale mining, metal production, woodworking and weaving, but it was not until the advent of ITALIAN COLONIALISM that modern industries developed. Outside the SALT mining, ENERGY and transport sectors, where industrial production began in the mid-1900s, the first Italian industries were established in the 1920s to process raw materials for export, such as the DUM PALM button factory in KEREN and several tanneries. With the massive influx of Italian nationals after 1935, demand for local food and beverage manufacture, metal fabrication and repair, construction materials and other small industries increased tremendously, and Italian entrepreneurs opened numerous small factories and workshops, particularly to serve the military and ROAD TRANSPORT sectors, in ASMARA, DEKEMHARE and MASSAWA. Industrialization received another boost during 1941-44, when the BRITISH ADMINISTRATION encouraged local self-sufficiency and regional export production, and Italian entrepreneurs responded by opening food processing, chemical, glass, ceramic and shoe factories to supply local markets, ETHIOPIA and the Red Sea region. Almost all these new industries were located in Asmara, and this concentration only increased over the next forty years.

The 1942-45 war boom created modern Eritrea's industrial base, but after 1946 regional markets were lost to overseas competition, while political insecurity, combined with Italian emigration, produced a prolonged depression. After 1952 new industries were developed, principally by the ITALIAN POPULATION, to serve the markets of Ethiopia, including meat, fruit and vegetable canning, particularly on the DE NADAI estates, and textile production in Asmara, beginning with the BARAT-TOLO factory in 1956, and Ethio-Textiles Share Company in the 1960s. Already established Italian industries, such as the MELOTTI brewery, SAVA glass company and many others continued and even expanded their production. But all these industries failed to offset the decline in other sectors of the manufacturing and transport economy, as many factories closed or were moved to ADDIS ABABA and Kenya.

In 1975 all large and medium scale industries, including all those owned by foreigners and the imperial family, were nationalized by the DERG. Industrial production declined dramatically as the ARMED STRUGGLE intensified around the main industrial towns and industrial infrastructure was destroyed or removed by both the Ethiopian military and nationalist forces. Although some workshops were reconstructed in EPLF-held areas of SA-HEL, the Derg held the industrial towns, and during 1981-85 made some attempt to revive Eritrean industries, particularly to serve the war effort. But sabotage, lack of spare parts and raw materials shortages led to a continuing decline, which reached bottom in 1990, when industrial production virtually ceased and some factories were stripped for removal to Ethiopia.

In 1991 the PROVISIONAL GOVERNMENT OF ER-ITREA took over forty-two large to medium-sized state industries (90 percent in Asmara), including the Asmara Brewery (formerly Melotti), Asmara Textiles (formerly Barattolo) and Red Sea Textiles, Lalmba sack factory, AMAP match and chemical factory, Deluxe Shoes, the ceramic factory (formerly Tabacchi) and glass factory (formerly SAVA), as well as several sweater knitting and soap factories, the salt works in Massawa and ASSAB, and the PETROLEUM refinery. Some 644 small private workshops also existed, and two EPLF factories were transferred to Asmara and MENDEFERA. In 1992/93 the government undertook a program to privatize many state industries, but the initial investment code, combined with decrepit and outdated equipment, failed to attract capital. A revised investment code and improvements in some enterprises are hoped to lead to the privatization of about one-third of state factories before the end of the 1990s. A few industries, including the brewery, match factory and glass factory, have seen great rises in productivity as demand in local and regional markets has increased, and in 1997 soap and shoe factories were sold to private investors. Plans for attracting electronics and other light industries are also underway in the Ministry of Trade and Industry, directed since June 1997 by ALI SAID AB-DELLA.

IRAFAILE. Located at the base of the Gulf of ZULA, Irafaile is the administrative center for the sub-province of the same name, which includes the coastal lowlands from the mountains of Alid to BA'DA. Originally part of AKELE GUZAI, this division was included in the Northern Red Sea Administrative Region in 1995. Irafaile's name, meaning "elephant pasture" in SAHO, signifies the wildlife that abounded in this area before the twentieth century. Today about 27,000 Saho and AFAR pastoralists live in the sub-province, and the village boasts a new clinic and administrative center.

IRAQ. After the Ba'athist coup of 1968 Iraq began supplying small-scale military assistance and training to the ELF, but never approached the aid levels of Syria. Iraqi agents, however, attempted to meddle in the internal affairs of the Eritrean nationalist movement on numerous occasions, beginning in 1969 when they tried to build a base of support for a Ba'athist pan-Arabist movement in the ELF as a corollary to a similar attempt within the Sudanese military. Iraq contacted former Syrian and Iraqi trainees in the ELF and supported their moves against the KIADA AL-AMA in 1970, helping to precipitate the split of OSMAN SALEH SABBE and the ELF-PLF forces from the ELF. During the ensuing CIVIL WAR Iraq apparently sent discreet military aid to both sides, and this dual policy continued in the mid-1970s, with ELF Chairman AHMED NASSER visiting Baghdad in 1976 and Iraqi observers attending the EPLF First Congress in 1977. The EPLF maintained an office in Baghdad, but relations became increasingly strained as Iraq tried to broker a unity agreement between Sabbe's rump ELF-PLF and the ELF during 1978-79. In 1979 Iraq encouraged a rift in the ELF-PLF leading to the formation of the ELF-PLF Revolutionary Command, and after 1981 maneuvered among the various ELF FACTIONS, eventually supporting the ELF-RC. The Gulf War, followed by the EPLF victory, ended Iraqi influence in Eritrea. As of 1996 no ambassadors have been exchanged, although Iraq has recognized Eritrea and informal contacts are common.

ISAIAS AFWERKI. President of Eritrea and leader of the EPLF since its inception, Isaias' political vision has dominated the Eritrean nationalist movement and the new state since the 1970s. Isaias Afwerki was born January 2, 1946, in the Aba Shi'aul district of ASMARA. His father, whose native village was Salot, just outside the city, was a minor functionary in the state Tobacco Monopoly. His mother was descended from Tigrean immigrants from the Enderta area. Isaias attended Prince Makonnen secondary school, where he was involved in militantly nationalist STUDENT ORGANIZATIONS in the early 1960s. He graduated in 1965 and began studying Engineering at HSI University in ADDIS ABABA during 1965/66.

In September 1966 Isaias left University to the join the ELF, traveling through Asmara to SUDAN. In 1967 he was sent to CHINA and in 1968 he became Deputy Division Commander with political responsibilities for Zone 5, comprising his native HAMASIEN. He was a leading figure in the ESLAH reform movement, the TRIPARTITE UNITY FORCES and the TIGRINYA/Christian group which withdrew to ALA in 1970, where Isaias drafted a scathing critique of the ELF leadership in his 1971 statement of purpose, "We and Our Objectives," which formed the charter of the emerging EPLF. Isaias led his group into an alliance of convenience with OSMAN SALEH SABBE's ELF-PLF, but remained critical of Sabbe, eventually breaking with him to form the EPLF in 1975.

Together with a tight-knit group of associates, including ALI SAID ABDELLA, IBRAHIM AFA, PETROS SOLOMON, RAMADAN MOHAMED NUR and others, Isaias staved off attacks from the left (see MENKA) and right during the first CIVIL WAR, and led the formation of the EPLF in 1974-75. He served on both the political and military committees of the EPLF; but he preferred a collective to a personalist leadership style, and was elected Vice-Secretary General at the EPLF's First Congress in 1977. In 1987 his pre-eminent role was publicly acknowledged when he was elected Secretary-General, and in 1991 Isaias became Secretary-General of the PROVISIONAL GOVERNMENT OF ERITREA. In April 1993, he assumed the office of President, and in 1994 he was elected Secretary-General of the PEOPLE'S FRONT FOR DEMOCRACY AND JUSTICE (PFDJ).

Although Isaias was an unpretentious leader, sharing the Spartan life of other FIGHTERS in the SAHEL, he proved an effective international diplomat beginning with a tour of Europe and the UNITED STATES in 1989. In his 1993 speeches to the Organization of African Unity (June 28) and UNITED NATIONS (Sept. 30), his emphasis on self-reliance and blunt criticism of corruption in Africa marked him as a new voice in international politics.

As of 1997 Isaias' political position is unassailable, as he combines the powers of chief executive and Secretary-General of the only legal political party. He is at the center of most government decision-making, but has also tried to make himself available to the public on a routine basis, although his political style is not that of a populist. His intellectual brilliance, forthrightness, mastery of detail and unswerving dedication to social justice and national unity mark him as a remarkable leader both in Eritrea and abroad. Isaias' relative youth and good health, despite a 1993 relapse of cerebral malaria (*see* ISRAEL), indicate that he will dominate Eritrean politics for many years to come.

ISLAM. The Eritrean region has been associated with the Muslim religion since the days of Muhamed, when some of his earliest followers took refuge in the AKSUMITE Empire. But Islam only developed as an indigenous religion in the ninth century, when Arab merchants and immigrants introduced it to the DAHLAK islands and coastal areas, where it began to spread amongst the AFAR and SAHO peoples by the eleventh century, and among the BEJA and BELEW by the thirteenth. The number of Muslims among Eritrea's ethnic groups greatly increased during the 1530s, when Imam AHMED AL-GHAZALI ("Gragn") ruled the region and actively persecuted Christians. During this period the JIBERTI communities of the highlands took shape, and under the succeeding period of Turkish rule over the coastal lowlands Islam continued to spread among TIGRE and BEJA-speaking people. But for many previously animist peoples, conversion to Islam was quite nominal before the nineteenth century, and a syncretistic blend of traditional beliefs and a much-debased Islam remained common among many BENI 'AMER and other tribes.

      Beginning with Shaykh al-Amin ibn Hamad (see AD SHAYKH) in the early nineteenth century, and continuing with the MIRGHANIYYA Sufi order, a series of religious reformers purified Islamic practices and converted new groups among lowland Eritreans. Reform efforts were furthered by the rule of EGYPT from the 1840s through 1885, by which time almost all non-KEBESSA ethnic groups had converted to Islam with the exception of the KUNAMA and some BILEN. Centers of Islamic study developed during this period around AGORDAT, KEREN and MASSAWA, and Eritrean students began to travel to CAIRO to study at Al-Azhar University. During the 1880s/90s, Eritrean

Muslims, organized by the pro-Egyptian Mirghaniyya
order and other local sects, fought against the Sudanese
Mahdiyya, and Italian colonialists consequently viewed
Eritrean Islam as an ally in their wars against both
Mahdists and Ethiopian Christians.

The Muslim lowland peoples generally accepted
Italian rule, and in return the Italians supported Muslim
traditional ruling families and Islamic institutions with
monetary subventions and political privileges. The Shari'a
courts of Massawa were funded and upgraded in the 1890s,
and in 1900 the ASMARA Friday Mosque and an adjoining
Islamic Institution were built, with the latter housing
Shari'a courts and the offices of the Beni Awkaf, responsible for collecting and distributing Islamic charity. The
office of Mufti was created to supervise these institutions,
further integrating them into the state apparatus. In 1940
Shaykh Ibrahim el-Muktar Ahmed Ibn Omer, who studied
at Al-Azhar University in CAIRO, was appointed Mufti,
but on his death in 1969 Governor ASRATE KASSA refused
to appoint any of the Muslim community's nominees for
Mufti, and this policy continued under the DERG. Under
the BRITISH ADMINISTRATION, Shaykh Ibrahim was instrumental in expanding institutions of Islamic EDUCA-
TION, helping found the Egyptian-funded King Farouk
school in ASMARA in 1943, as well as other schools in
MENDEFERA, Massawa and Keren. Until 1952, the policies
of both Italian and British administrations facilitated the
spread of Islamic schools with ARABIC curriculums, and
allowed Muslims to rise in both business and state employment. Consequently, Islam, and the Mirghaniyya order
in particular, became a bulwark of colonial rule. The
number of Muslims increased from about 175,000 in 1905
to 312,000 in 1931 and 528,000 in 1948, and they were
consistently a narrow majority of the Eritrean population
before 1952.

The position of Islam in Eritrea suffered a decline
under Ethiopian rule, as the new administration favored
Christian Unionists. This discrimination increased as the
ARMED STRUGGLE developed with an initial base of primarily Muslim support, and Muslims made up the majority

of Eritreans who fled the country as REFUGEES. Since liberation, the government has reestablished Muslim institutions, including the office of Mufti, Shari'a courts, and
regional Islamic councils (Mejlis al-Awkaf). Census data
on religious affiliation is currently unavailable, but ob-
servation and refugee statistics seem to indicate that
Muslims no longer comprise a majority of the population
inside the country, although this may change if full
refugee REPATRIATION is achieved. This perception, when
combined with the history of divisive colonial religious
policies and the rise of a militant ISLAMIST movement in
the region has produced distrust of government policies
among some of the Muslim refugee population.

ISLAMIC JIHAD MOVEMENT *see* JIHAD.

ISLAMIST Movements (Pan-Islamism). Islamist ideology,
which favors the creation of a state based on Islamic law
and institutions, such as exists in Iran, is a recent development in Eritrean politics, but its political roots can be
traced back to the Pan-ARABISM and Muslim-oriented
propaganda of IDRIS MOHAMED ADEM and OSMAN SALEH
SABBE in the ELF during the 1960s. With the emergence of
a powerful Christian element in the nationalist movement
during the early 1970s, a reactionary Muslim group in the
ELF began to espouse an increasingly anti-Christian, Islamist political program, influenced no doubt by the rise
of Islamism in the Arab world and Iran. The leading figure
in this group was Ibrahim, son of Idris M. Adem, who was
imprisoned in 1978 by the mainstream leadership. Islamism reemerged with greater force after the ELF defeat
in 1981, when SAUDI ARABIA moved to support an Islamist program to reunite the more conservative ELF FAC-
TIONS. Out of this developed the JIHAD movement, with
its specifically Islamist political program. Since the
seizure of the Sudanese state by Islamist forces in 1989,
Islamism has developed as an increasingly threatening
opposition ideology to the secular nationalist program of
the current Eritrean government. Its appeal among Eritrean Muslims outside of the REFUGEE communities of

SUDAN and some Arab states appears to be limited; but a few Islamist religious figures were arrested in the lowland areas during 1995, following guerrilla actions by the Jihad Movement.

ISRAEL. Israel has been deeply involved in Eritrean affairs since the beginning of the ARMED STRUGGLE, during which Israel consistently supported Ethiopian control over Eritrea with arms and military training. Israel and Ethiopia shared a common fear of Pan-ARABISM, and in 1965 the UNITED STATES encouraged Israel to begin training Ethiopian security forces and the Eritrean COMMANDOS. By 1966 the Israeli military team numbered about one hundred. Israel also invested in the Eritrean economy, setting up Eritrea's largest meat canning operation under its parastatal INCODE company, as well as textiles, FISHING and other industries.

Following the Ethiopian revolution, Israeli military aid continued, with Israeli instructors training the DERG's first new divisions. Even after the Derg broke with the U.S., recognized the PLO and established ties with radical Arab states, secret Israeli aid continued because both governments shared an interest in suppressing Eritrean nationalism. In 1983 Israeli aid increased as the Ethiopians tied the emigration of their Jewish population, the Falashas, to obtaining $20 million in military aid, including napalm and cluster bombs. These supplies continued intermittently through 1991, and were greatly expanded in the last days of the war, as Israel arranged the airlift of 14,000 remaining Falashas from ADDIS ABABA. The Derg attempted to turn over the DAHLAK island naval base to Israel in April, but the end of the war came before this was arranged.

Despite this history, following liberation Israel moved quickly to shore up its position in Eritrea, once again with U.S. help. On February 5, 1992, the Israeli ambassador to Ethiopia visited Asmara to discuss relations, returning again in August. As the Eritrean government grew increasingly concerned about relations with the SUDAN and ISLAMIST political opponents, an opening to

Israel was arranged, culminating in President ISAIAS AFWERKI being airlifted to Israel by a U.S. military plane on January 6, 1993, for treatment of cerebral malaria. Isaias stayed through January 15, and some political negotiations seem to have taken place because an Israeli representative appeared in Asmara in February. These moves caused consternation among many Arab countries, but were not unpopular in Eritrea. Full diplomatic relations were established following the REFERENDUM, and on October 28, 1993, an Israeli ambassador arrived to open an official embassy. By this time several technical aid programs were underway, and these have been expanded in the field of AGRICULTURE, were Israel provides over forty technicians and material assistance for water conservation and irrigation projects.

ITALIAN COLONIALISM (1882-1941). ITALY created the modern territorial entity of Eritrea through a period of colonial rule spanning sixty years. This rule may be divided into three phases: (1) Territorial Expansion from 1882-96; (2) Consolidation from 1897-1931, in which Italian rule was modeled on the "classical" European colonial empires of the period; (3) Fascist Expansion from 1932-41, in which Eritrea became the main base for Italian conquest and exploitation of ETHIOPIA.

Beginning with Italian attempts to acquire territory around ASSAB in 1869, Italy's interest in Eritrea was focused on dominating the trade of Ethiopia, first by controlling its coastal entrepots, then by expanding into the northern highlands. Italian activities were encouraged by BRITAIN, which hoped Italy would prove a cooperative sub-imperial power capable of filling the political vacuum occasioned by EGYPT's withdrawal from the region. The first Italian colonial ADMINISTRATION was established at Assab in 1882, and on February 5, 1885, the Italian navy seized MASSAWA. Over the next year they occupied the central coast and extended treaties of protection to many lowland tribes including the BENI 'AMER, BILEN and HABAB. Italian occupation was generally welcomed by Muslim lowlanders, who saw it as a form of protection

from Tigrean raids and the expansionist policies of
YOHANNES IV. Many TIGRINYA/Christian military leaders
also saw the Italians as allies against Tigrean rule, including ABERRA KASA, BAHTA HAGOS, HADGU-
AMBESSA, Berembras KAFLE-YESUS and others, who
joined the Italians as leaders of irregular soldiers in
BANDA units that were armed and paid by Italy.

Yohannes IV refused to accept the Italian occupation,
and in January 1887 attacked their fort at SA'ATI,
destroying an Italian column at DOGALI. This defeat
ironically propelled further Italian expansion, fueled by
domestic calls for revenge. War was declared, 20,000
troops were dispatched to Eritrea, and diplomatic
initiatives were launched to secure an alliance with
Menelik of Shewa (*see* ETHIOPIA). In May 1888, General
Baldisserra took command, and in 1889 Italy signed the
Treaty of Wichale with Menelik, now Emperor of Ethiopia,
which recognized Italian possession of most of eastern
Eritrea. In August, Baldisserra occupied ASMARA, and
Italian rule was quickly extended to the MAREB-BELESA-
Mai Muna line in the highlands (*see* BORDERS).

On January 1, 1890, the Italian government created
the Colony of Eritrea, and set about securing their regime
against attacks from Tigreans, Sudanese Mahdists and internal rebellion. A dispute over the Treaty of Wichale led
to a falling out with Menelik, which the Italians countered
with an attempt to win Tigrean support in 1891 (*s e e*
TIGRAI). For the next five years the Italian government,
led by Crispi, pursued a policy of demographic colonization in the highlands, while fighting a series of wars
against the Mahdists to secure the Western lowlands (*s e e*
AGORDAT). Crispi hoped to settle thousands of Italian
peasants in agricultural colonies that would redirect Italian emigration to Italian-controlled territory. But colonial
seizure of KEBESSA lands, many of which had been depopulated by FAMINE, combined with the arrest of highland Banda leaders, produced Bahta Hagos' revolt in 1895,
followed by a Tigrean invasion and the events leading up
to the Battle of ADWA in March 1896, where Italian ambitions to conquer northern Ethiopia were crushed. Many

of the colonists who had settled in Eritrea fled, and plans for agricultural colonization of the highlands were largely abandoned.

After the Treaty of ADDIS ABABA ended war with Ethiopia, Italian colonial policy entered a "Phase of Consolidation," which lasted roughly until 1932, and was marked by an emphasis on developing Eritrea as a stable base for the economic exploitation of northern Ethiopian COMMERCE, recruitment of colonial soldiers (*see* ASCARI), and the development of plantation agriculture in the lowlands (see ALI GHIDIR; CASCIANI; DE ROSSI; TESSENEI). Colonial BORDERS were delimited with neighboring states, a system of "direct" rule was imposed in the highlands, replacing local notables with salaried colonial chiefs (Tigrn.: Mislenie), while in the lowlands "indirect" rule was maintained through the retention of the tribal ruling classes (*see* NABTAB; SHUMAGULLE) as salaried chiefs and the subvention of Islamic legal institutions. A series of administrative divisions were created, including provincial divisions *(commissariati)* and smaller districts *(residenze)*.

Most of these institutions and policies were implemented during the governorship of Ferdinando MARTINI (1897-1907), and they continued in effect after the Fascists came to power in 1922. They produced a dependent colonial economy closely linked to Italy (*see* COMMERCE), while Italian colonial expenditures, which generally exceeded Eritrea's revenue, financed administrative and economic infrastructure (including the RAILROAD, ROAD TRANSPORT and lowland irrigation) and rudimentary social services. Although this infrastructure was intended to serve Italian settlers and capital, it nonetheless laid the foundations for the integration of the modern Eritrean nation, despite the fact that few opportunities were available to Eritreans, with their access to modern EDUCATION severely restricted, and only the lowest levels of the colonial civil service available to a few former soldiers. Until the 1930s, Italian policy essentially froze in place existing Eritrean social structures, imposing over them a colonial superstructure in which Eritreans participated primarily as soldiers (*see* ASCARI). But tax burdens were not onerous, the POPULATION grew significantly and a local (almost entirely Muslim) merchant class developed.

This situation changed in 1932, when Mussolini's Fascist government began to plan the invasion of Ethiopia, using Eritrea as its primary base. The resurgence of Italian imperialism harked back to the first phase of Italian colonialism, including Mussolini's call for revenge for the humiliating Adwa debacle of 1896, and a renewed emphasis on demographic colonization of the Eritrean and Ethiopian highlands. Transport and military infrastructure were upgraded, Eritrean military conscription was introduced, new administrative divisions were created to merge smaller ethnic groups in a more rationalized bureaucracy, and protestant missionaries were expelled because of their supposed Ethiopian sympathies. These projects all accelerated tremendously in January 1935, when the Fascist general and Minister of Colonies, Emilio De Bono (1866-1944), was appointed High Commissioner of Italian East Africa to oversee "whirlwind" preparations for the invasion of Ethiopia, including modern motor roads, the creation of the new town of DEKEMHARE and the world's longest aerial cableway *(teleferica)* from Massawa to Asmara.

In October, De Bono led the invasion of Ethiopia; but in November he was replaced by Marshall Badoglio, who captured Addis Ababa in May, 1936. Eritrea's borders were expanded to include TIGRAI and the ITALIAN POPULATION mushroomed as tens of thousands of "nationals" poured into the colony. Over 60,000 remained after the war boom ended in 1937, largely in Asmara and Dekemhare, where they created a modern urban economy, heavily subsidized by the Italian state. A new generation of entrepreneurs laid the foundations for Eritrean INDUSTRY during the late 1930s, first by supplying the Italian community with food, shelter and transport, and then expanding into export manufacturing and agriculture during the 1940s.

During 1935-41, Fascist race laws were imposed and colonial towns and public facilities were strictly segregated between "natives" and Europeans. But the massive influx of Italian urban settlers and the development of an urbanized industrial economy had a profound social and cultural impact on Eritrean highland society, and particularly Asmara, that has lasted into the present. Italian colonial rule ended in April 1941, when BRITAIN conquered the colony. But the social and economic structures created by Italian colonialism persisted for many years under the ensuing BRITISH ADMINISTRATION, while the influence of Italian settlers and Italian culture persisted even longer.

ITALIAN POPULATION. The first Italian settlers came as missionaries in the mid-nineteenth century (*see* ITALY). From 1885-1900 MASSAWA housed the majority of Italians, despite its climate, after which ASMARA consistently housed over two-thirds of the colonists. The growth of the civilian population, including state officials, was slow in the early colonial period, reaching 585 in 1892, 3,949 in 1905, and about 4,700 in 1931. In 1935 began a massive increase, expanding to roughly 65,000 by 1939, as workers, administrators, Fascist party operatives, entrepreneurs and demobilized soldiers poured into the colony or returned to Eritrea from unstable conditions in Ethiopia. During the late 1930s, Asmara's average monthly Italian population rose from roughly 30,000 to over 50,000, and it was estimated at 55,000 in 1941 when the city was occupied by BRITAIN. Italian settlers created entirely new, European cities and towns during this period, and though they were officially separated from Eritreans by Fascist race policies, there was actually a great deal of interaction through employment and the social institution of *madamato* or concubinage, in which many Italian single men (the majority of new immigrants) lived with Eritrean women, producing a mixed-race population who largely associated themselves with Italian culture.

During 1941-42, the Italian population, including prisoners-of-war, actually increased as Italians were removed from Ethiopia; but the repatriation of over 10,000 civilians and 20,000 prisoners in 1943-44 left a population of some 40,000 by 1945. Many Italians were now involved in commerce, industry and agricultural development, all of which were encouraged by the British, while the numbers in state employment declined from 12,000 in 1947 to only 350 in 1952 as the British prepared for FEDERATION with Ethiopia. But fear of anti-Italian violence (*see* SHIFTA), Ethiopian rule and growing unemployment created an Italian exodus that reduced the population to 18,000 by 1952 and 10,000 by 1960. The remaining Italian community consisted of a few large industrialists and agricultural concessionaires, who commanded the heights of the Eritrean economy through personal connections with HAILE SELASSIE I, and an aging group of small business owners (some with mixed-race children) who were concentrated in Asmara. By 1970, less than 5,000 remained, and in early 1975 came a final exodus, as the ARMED STRUGGLE intensified and the DERG nationalized all Italian businesses. Only a few score very elderly Italian settlers remain in Asmara today, but the legacy of Italian settlement for highland urban Eritrea has been tremendous, exemplified by the Italian vocabulary that laces modern TIGRINYA, Italian tastes in food (such as pasta and capucino), dress (including the latest Roman fashions), leisure activities (bars, soccer football, bicycle racing) and urban architecture.

ITALY. Italian interest in the Eritrean region dates back to the fourteenth century, when CATHOLIC CHURCH chroniclers recorded information about the region, partially based on Italian merchants' accounts. Church interest was maintained through the nineteenth century, when Italian missionaries participated in attempts to establish the Catholic church in the region, including Giustino DE JACOBIS, Giuseppe Sapeto and Giovanni Stella (1821-69), with the latter two playing leading roles in the Italian acquisition of land and concessions at ASSAB (1869) and KEREN, respectively. After 1882, Italy's relation with Eritrea was one of direct colonization which lasted through 1941.

Italian government claims to Eritrea were formally relinquished in the Peace Treaty signed with the FOUR POWERS on February 10, 1947, after which the Italian government, led by its still extant Ministry of Colonies, attempted to gain a UN trusteeship over the territory. Italian ambitions for Eritrea were pursued by Count Sforza, who negotiated the BEVIN-SFORZA PLAN at the UNITED NATIONS, and in Eritrea by subsidizing various local Italian organizations, led by the Casa degli Italiani and CRIE, as well as two Eritrean POLITICAL PARTIES: the Pro-Italy Party, made up of veteran colonial soldiers (ASCARI) who hoped to regain their pensions; and the Italo-Eritrean Party, composed of the descendants of mixed-race marriages. With the defeat of the Bevin-Sforza plan in May 1949, Italy switched to support of immediate independence for Eritrea, which it hoped to dominate. Italy encouraged the formation of the INDEPENDENCE BLOC, and the Italian liaison officer in Eritrea, Count Di Gropello, dispensed large subventions to potential supporters. But the Italian strategy backfired, as Unionists were able to play on strong anti-Italian sentiments in the highlands. After the UN decided on FEDERATION in 1950, the Italian government tried to repair its relations with Ethiopia, establishing formal relations in 1951, and paying war reparations. Thereafter, Italian policy was essentially privatized, following the business interests of local Italian capital. Italy failed to raise the issue of Eritrea's ANNEXATION at the UN, and Italian businessmen developed close personal relations with HAILE SELASSIE I, which benefited the Ethiopian regime in Eritrea.

This policy continued during the DERG period, as Italy supplied commercial capital and development aid to Ethiopia, while it refused to accept most Eritrean political refugees. During the 1970s the EPLF opened an office and information center in Rome, and the Bologna cultural festival was begun (1971), but the Eritrean community in the former colonial metropole amounted to only 5,000 by 1991. Only in 1988, after the AFABET victory, did Italy move away from support of the Derg and attempt to establish good relations with the EPLF.

The obvious opportunism of Italian policy, together with the history of corruption in its aid programs, made the EPLF skeptical of Italian offers of assistance in the post-liberation period. Bi-lateral relations were discussed in Asmara in December 1992, but the Eritrean government rejected a $60 million loan offer for RAILROAD reconstruction and another for rebuilding Asmara's water system because they were tied to Italian contractors. Nonetheless, Italy extended immediate diplomatic recognition after the REFERENDUM, and by 1995, Italy was Eritrea's second largest donor of aid, totaling $50 million, after a long-term cooperation agreement was signed in March. By May 1997, when President Isaias made a state visit to Italy, Italian capital represented the largest foreign investment in Eritrea.

-J -

JANGEREN. A small tribal group associated with the BILEN, but originating from the Ad Sawra tribe of SAHEL. They live between HAL-HAL and the ANSEBA River valley, where the road passes through a narrow canyon known as Bab Jangeren. The Jangeren were administratively attached to the Bet Tarqe in 1932, and follow Bilen customary law. Their home saw heavy fighting in the ARMED STRUGGLE, and most Jangeren fled as REFUGEES in the 1970s. From 1988-91, Bab Jangeren was on the front lines and many villages were destroyed.

JEBBAH *see* ERITREAN LIBERATION FRONT (ELF).

JIBERTI (alt.: Jabarti). The name used to describe TIGRINYA-speaking Muslims living in the KEBESSA. The name comes from similar usage among AMHARIC and Tigrinya speakers in ETHIOPIA, and seems to originate in an ARABIC term meaning "the elect (of God)" that may have been associated with immigrants from Arabia to the Zeila area (ancient Adal) sometime before the fourteenth century. The present Jiberti population in Eritrea seem to originate from local converts to Islam during the period of

AHMED AL-GHAZALI ("Gragn"), the descendants of Muslim merchants, and Tigrean Jiberti immigrants. Traditionally, most Jiberti people were engaged in COMMERCE or artisanal occupations (particularly weaving), and in pre-colonial times were largely barred from land ownership. But in SERAYE and AKELE GUZAI there are a number of villages where Jiberti own and farm land. The Jiberti are often described as being more devout Muslims than their lowland coreligionists, and are particularly well-represented among religious scholars.

JIHAD (Eritrean Islamic Jihad; Arab.: "Holy Struggle"). A political movement advocating the creation of an Islamic Eritrean state founded on Muslim religious law, and dedicated to violent overthrow of the EPLF/PFDJ secular government. The Eritrean Islamic Jihad (a.k.a. Eritrean Islamic Liberation Front) was formed at a meeting in Gedaref, Sudan, in 1988 by a number of smaller organizations whose origins may be traced to the ISLAMIST tendency in the former ELF, the influence of SAUDI ARABIA on ELF FACTIONS in the early 1980s and, particularly, the support of SUDAN's National Islamic Front (NIF). Among the Jihad leadership were Mohamed Arafa and Hamid Turkiye, while members included Islamist-oriented fighters from various former-ELF factions, a number of students from KEREN's Bet Juk Islamic Institute who had attended Medina University in Saudi Arabia, and some of whom had fought as *mujahideen* ("holy warriors") in Afghanistan during the 1980s. During the ARMED STRUGGLE the Jihad viewed the EPLF, not Ethiopia, as their principle enemy, concentrating their ideological attacks on EPLF social programs and particularly women's liberation. With Sudanese NIF and Muslim Brotherhood support they recruited fighters among young Eritrean REFUGEES.

In 1989 Jihad launched a guerrilla campaign against the EPLF along the border with Western Eritrea, planting land mines and ambushing isolated units. Full-scale fighting occurred in August inside Sudanese territory, and again in December 1991 around SAWA in BARKA.

EPLF attempts to negotiate with Jihad led to a split in the leadership in August 1993, with Hamid Turkiye forming the Democratic Movement for the Liberation of Eritrea. Turkiye's guerrillas, supported by non-Eritrean *mu-jahideen,* fought the EPLF at Adi Harko in Barka in December 1993, and Jihad attacks on isolated vehicles have continued in western Eritrea and even SENHIT during 1995-97. The Jihad has little support among Eritrean Muslims, and the Eritrean government has accused the Sudanese NIF, since December 1993, of being the main instigator of its activities, leading directly to a virtual state of war between Eritrea and Sudan.

JUSTICE (Court System). Eritrea's justice system is founded on a patchwork of laws representing the nation's complex history. At the family and village level many issues are still settled by recourse to traditional laws. In the KEBESSA traditional laws are based on the customary laws of various descent groups (*see* ADKEME MELEGA; DEQI MINAB; LOGGO), which were codified in written documents during the fifteenth through seventeenth centuries and enforced by village councils (*see* ENDA; SHUMAG-ULLE) and local judges *(danya).* In the lowlands and northern highlands tribal customary laws were enforced by tribal leaders (*see* DIGLAL; NABTAB; SHUMAGULLE), and during the nineteenth century, as ISLAM spread, Muslim religious law *(shari'a)* was enforced by religious leaders (shayks) and later by appointed judges *(cadi)* under the rule of EGYPT and ITALIAN COLONIALISM.

Italian colonialists retained traditional and religious law for family and property disputes among Eritreans, but imposed another level of colonial civil law for capital crimes and disputes between Eritreans and Italians, while the Italian civil code was applied to Italian nationals. This two-tiered legal system was retained by the BRITISH ADMINISTRATION with some modifications until 1950, when a series of administrative proclamations gave Eritreans numerous civil rights and equal status with Italian nationals, paving the way for the election of Eritrea's first ASSEMBLY and its first CONSTITUTION, which remained the foundation of Eritrean law during the FEDERATION with ETHIOPIA. Eritrea's first Chief Justice was a Briton, Sir James Shearer, who attempted to defend Eritrea's autonomous legal system from encroachment under HAILE SELASSIE I's Ethiopian government. In 1960 the Ethiopian Criminal Code was adopted, and Shearer resigned. In 1962 Eritrea came under Ethiopian law, although the civil code remained ambiguous.

In 1975 the DERG altered Ethiopian law to facilitate radical social and economic restructuring, and many aspects of customary law were in principle abolished where they upheld economic, social and gender inequality. The ELF and EPLF instituted the same types of changes in customary law in the areas they controlled, and under the EPLF in the 1980s these were developed into a new justice system that combined local customary law with the fronts' principles of social justice, and particularly worked to overturn women's inequality in matters of property and marriage, as well as the privileges of traditional elites. EPLF administrators dispensed justice until 1991, when a new Eritrean justice system was created, relying on a combination of extant Ethiopian civil codes, customary law and the new principles established in the liberated zones. Local judges were appointed in the summer of 1991, and in October a new Supreme Court was formed, headed by a woman of Muslim background, Fozia Hashim. In May 1993 an independent judiciary was established and Fozia, a CENTRAL COMMITTEE member, was appointed Minister of Justice, responsible for revising Eritrea's legal codes to rationalize them and bring them into conformity with the principles of constitutional law outlined in the EPLF National Charter (for enforcement of laws *see* POLICE; PRISONS).

- K -

KAFLE-YESUS, Berembras *see* AREZA; ITALIAN COLONIALISM.

KAGNEW   STATION (Asmara). In January 1942 the
UNITED STATES' Army Signal Corps took over the ITAL-
IAN naval radio station (Radio Marina) in ASMARA, which
covered a small area above the city center. By 1950 this
communication facility was   serving U.S. forces in the Indian Ocean and providing unobstructed monitoring of
radio communication in the central USSR. The strategic
value of the Radio Marina base was a major issue in the
U.S. decision to support HAILE SELASSIE I's claim to Eritrea at the UNITED NATIONS. In 1950 the Emperor reinforced his American support by sending the Ethiopian
Kagnew Battalion to join U.S. forces in Korea. In May 1953
the U.S. secured a 25-year lease on the base, which was
expanded to include a large tract of land on the road to
Asmara airport and   named Kagnew Station.

Over the years many military barracks, officers
houses and recreational facilities were constructed, while
increasingly sophisticated electronic equipment was installed. The U.S. paid rental fees and local contracts of
some $4-6 million per year for the base, much of which
went into the Asmara economy. In addition, the substantial U.S. military aid given to Ethiopia during 1953-75
was seen as indirect "rental" payments for the base. In the
mid-1960s Kagnew housed 1,700 Americans and employed
some 1,100 Eritreans and Ethiopians. A high point of over
3,000 U.S. military and civilian personnel was reached in
1971, when radio, television, radar and radio telescope
equipment was operating at the base. But in 1973 the
opening of the U.S. base on Diego Garcia Island in the
Indian Ocean and improved satellite communication made
Kagnew Station obsolete, while the Eritrean ARMED
STRUGGLE made it increasingly untenable. Personnel were
sharply reduced, and by early 1977, when the base was
closed, there were only thirty-five Americans left.

In March 1977 the DERG took over the base and converted it into a headquarters and supply base for their
Eritrean OFFENSIVES. Russian officers were housed there
under tight security from early 1978, but on September
22 the main ammunition dump at Kagnew exploded and
burned for five days. The barracks and other facilities

deteriorated under the Derg, and in 1991 they were taken over by the EPLF as housing for fighters working in Asmara. Kagnew was renamed Maskar (Tigrn.: "camp") DENDEN and closed to civilian entry, which allowed many aspects of the EPLF's communal "fighter culture" to continue there through the mid-1990s.

KALEB. The most important ruler of the AKSUMITE Empire during the Christian period, Kaleb reigned from around 514/17 A.D. to somewhere between 530 and 550. He is remembered for his devotion to the ORTHODOX CHURCH and his conquest of SOUTH ARABIA. In 525 he sent a fleet from ADULIS to defeat the Jewish ruler of Himyar, who had massacred Arabian Christians at Nagran (*see* HAGER NAGRAN). A HABESHA garrison remained in South Arabia which eventually formed an independent state and fought several wars against Mecca just before the Prophet Mohammed's birth.

KANTIBAI. Traditional title of district political leaders among many TIGRE and TIGRINYA groups. Used for the office of city mayor during 1952-91.

KARNISHEM (Hamasien). The district just north of ASMARA, including the villages of ADI NEFAS, BELEZA, Embaderho (its historic center) and ZAGHER.

KARORA (Sahel). Karora developed as a colonial customs post on the road from ALGHEDEN to Tokar, SUDAN. During the 1960s it held a military garrison, and on January 5, 1977, it was the first town liberated by the EPLF, who held it until January 1979 and again after 1988. Today it is a frontier post and refugee REPATRIATION center.

KASSALA (Sudan). A large eastern Sudanese town situated close to the Eritrean border at TESSENEI, Kassala has had an important place in Eritrean history since it was fortified by EGYPT in 1840 and used as a base to raid, tax and then administer western Eritrea. Kassala became the center of the influential MIRGHANIYYA Sufi order in the

mid-nineteenth century and was besieged and captured by
Osman Diqna's BEJA warriors during the Sudanese
Mahdiyya (*see* HEWETT TREATY). ITALIAN COLONIAL
forces occupied Kassala from July 1894 to December 1897
as part of their war against the Mahdists, and Italy initially claimed the area, including the GASH and BARKA
river deltas, only relinquishing them in BORDER agreements with BRITAIN after the Battle of ADWA. Italy again
occupied Kassala from July 1940 to January 1941, and
during the 1950s Kassala became a center for Eritrean
Muslims fleeing Ethiopian control over western Eritrea.
The town remained a market center for western Barka
through the 1960s, when it became a center of ELF activities. Many Eritrean REFUGEES settled in Kassala and its
surrounding area after 1967, swelling to some 150,000 by
the mid-1980s, with about 75,000 in Kassala town, where
Eritreans continue to comprise about one-third of the
population in the mid-1990s.

KEBESSA (Tigrn.: "highlands"). Eritrea's central high-
lands, comprising the historic provinces of AKELE GUZAI,
HAMASIEN and SERAYE, and synonymous with the
TIGRINYA-speaking Orthodox Christian cultural area.

KEKIYA (merchant family). A leading clan of the BELEW
people of HIRGHIGO, descended in part from holders of the
Turkish military rank of Kakiya, the Kekiyas were already well-established in the MASSAWA economy when
the Italian army hired Mohamed ("Ahmed") Kekiya in
1885 to supply them with livestock. Ahmed's sons prospered under Italian rule, and Saleh Ahmed expanded into
ETHIOPIA during the Italian occupation. In 1944 Saleh
founded a five hundred-student ARABIC school at
Hirghigo, and in 1946 he obtained an agricultural concession at ZULA from the BRITISH ADMINISTRATION. He
was elected vice-president of the UNIONIST PARTY in December 1946, and Unionist representative for Zula and
Hirghigo in 1952. Although Saleh remained close to HAILE
SELASSIE I's regime, his brother Osman was involved in
the Eritrean nationalist movement during the 1950s, and

his son Hassan became a leading businessman in SUDAN during the 1970s, where he worked for the EPLF, providing banking, supply and transport services for the front. Today Hassan's family business dominates Eritrea's import trade, while another family member, Saleh Idris Kekiya, is Minister of Transport and Communications.

KEREN (Senhit). Third largest city of Eritrea, Keren is the urban center for the SENHIT area and the ANSEBA Administrative Region. The town is located in a bowl surrounded by granite mountains at the junction of ancient TRADE ROUTES connecting the BILEN region with the Western lowlands, KEBESSA and coast. When the Italian missionary and agricultural pioneer, Giovanni Stella, visited the area in 1851 Keren village had a Bilen population of about two thousand. Stella returned in 1855 and established a farm nearby, marrying into a Bilen family. Despite Stella's protests, the area suffered from Egyptian and Tigrean raids until 1872, when Werner MUNZINGER, who had also lived in Keren during 1854-61, garrisoned it with Egyptian troops and constructed the fort on Senhit Hill that still dominates the town. Munzinger connected the town to Massawa with a road and telegraph, and established a tobacco plantation with Greek capital. The Egyptians withdrew in 1885, and the fort came under Tigrean control until 1888, when it was seized by KAFLE-YESUS's BANDA. In June 1889 the Italian army occupied Keren and developed it as an administrative and market center with a growing Bilen Catholic population and important Muslim religious institutions (*see* BET JUK). Italian agricultural concessions were developed around the town, and by the early 1930s it had a population of almost 3,000, including 200 Italians.

During the Second World War the mountainous western approaches to the town were fortified and from February 3 to March 26, 1941, the Italian colonial army tried to stop the British invasion of Eritrea on these heights. The battle was extremely brutal, with thousands of soldiers killed on both sides, including many Eritrean ASCARI. During the succeeding BRITISH ADMINISTRATION, Keren acquired a secondary school and became a center for the MUSLIM LEAGUE and pro-Independence political forces. The agricultural economy prospered through the 1960s, and a hospital was built by an American NGO; but as the ARMED STRUGGLE intensified the town witnessed increasingly brutal Ethiopian military actions, with the bodies of fighters often hung on the streets. By 1977 Keren was surrounded by the EPLF, which liberated it on July 8 after a five day battle. The town became the unofficial capital of EPLF-liberated Eritrea, and hosted meetings of the front's mass organizations during 1978; but on November 26 the EPLF evacuated Keren during its STRATEGIC WITHDRAWAL, and much of the town's population fled as REFUGEES.

Keren was then transformed into a garrison and supply center for the DERG's OFFENSIVES in Northern Eritrea, and many TIGREANS and TIGRINYA-speakers moved in as workers and entrepreneurs. After the Battle of AFABET, Keren became the headquarters of the Ethiopian army in the north, and on April 1, 1988, the EPLA began an offensive from HAL-HAL that pushed to Mt. Lalmba on the outskirts of the town. On May 10-11 the Eritreans attempted to capture Keren, but were stopped by Ethiopian counterattacks which pushed them back to a new front-line encircling Keren from the mountain passes in the west to MES-HALIT in the north and the MENSA' mountains in the east. In March 1989 the DERG tried to break out, but failed, and after this the front stabilized until the war ended. After liberation, many former residents repatriated from Sudan, and by 1996 the town's population was 54,000. Today, the town's schools, hospital, and water supply have been reconstructed and plans are underway for light industrial development.

KERKEBET (Barka). Village and administrative post at the confluence of the BARKA and Kerkebet rivers, currently located in the ANSEBA Administrative Region. Originally a BENI 'AMER seasonal camp, because of its remoteness the site was often raided by the ELF during the 1960s and later used by the liberation fronts as a meeting area.

Today the PFDJ is supporting the development of irrigated farming along the Barka in the Kerkebet area.

KHATMIYYA *see* MIRGHANIYYA.

KIADA AL-AMA, ELF (Arab.: "General Command"). The General Command was formed in the ELF's reorganization at the ADOBAHA meeting in 1969 and provided the leadership of the Front through the First National Congress in 1971. Twenty of the thirty-eight seats on the Kiada al-Ama were held by conservative supporters of IDRIS MOHAMED ADEM, while only nine seats were held by reformists, allowing the Military and Security committees to persecute reformist and Christian elements, which led directly to the disintegration of the Front in 1970, the formation of the ELF-PLF and the first CIVIL WAR.

KOHAITO (Akele Guzai). The plateau between the KUMALIE and HADAS river canyons, containing extensive archaeologiacal sites from the pre-AKSUMITE and Aksumite periods that are probably synonymous with the town of Koloe cited in Greek texts. The plateau was settled by SAHO-speakers in the medieval period, and during the 1960s-70s served as a base for ELF operations. In 1975 an Ethiopian attack on the plateau was defeated, but in September 1977 the ELF lost many weapons and supplies as the DERG swept the plateau.

KUDO FELASI (Seraye; alt.: Godofelasi). A large village just outside MENDEFERA, Kudo Felasi was one of the main markets on the caravan route from TIGRAI to MASSAWA during the seventeen to nineteenth centuries. An Italian agricultural station was developed near the village in the 1890s, when large-scale colonial land alienation in the region provoked local resistance and eventually the abandonment of a European settler-colonization scheme. A military hospital was constructed at Kudo Felasi during the invasion of Ethiopia, and a school was built during the BRITISH ADMINISTRATION. The village was under ELF control in 1977-78, after which the DERG took over the hospital and school until the end of the ARMED STRUGGLE, after which they were rebuilt with aid from former American Peace Corps teachers.

KUFIT (Barka).   Site of an Egyptian frontier fort from 1852-57, located between AGORDAT and BARENTU. After the Egyptian withdrawal from BARKA in 1885, western Eritrea was invaded by a Sudanese Mahdist army led by Osman Diqna. Yohannes IV sent his general, Ras ALULA, with a Tigrean army and BENI 'AMER cavalry, to block the Mahdists, and on September 23, 1885, they met near Kufit. The Tigreans won a costly victory, and the Sudanese were driven back to KASSALA.

KUMALIE River (Akele Guzai). The Kumalie drainage cuts a spectacular gorge between the Amba Soira and KOHAITO plateaus, joining the HADAS above ZULA dam and providing an ancient TRADE ROUTE   from the coast around ADULIS to the highlands at Kaskase and SENAFE.

KUNAMA. Perhaps the oldest ethnic group in Eritrea, the Kunama, along with the smaller ILLIT, form their own distinct branch (Kunama-Illit) of the Nilo-Saharan language family. Together with the NARA, they are descendants of Nilotic people who occupied Western Eritrea (and perhaps the highlands) in prehistoric times. Their name means "those who I call people;" but the Kunama's neighbors generally have called them BAZA. They occupy the GASH-SETIT area of the Gash-Barka Administrative Region, and practice agriculture and livestock raising. Many Kunama maintain their ancient religion centered on a creator god, Anna, and a complex of local spirits, shamanistic ritual healers, and rain makers. The Kunama are distinctive in Eritrea because of their   egalitarian village councils and the high social status and property rights of women, which the present government upholds as a model for other Eritreans to follow. On the other hand, the Kunama have suffered a long history of prejudice and enslavement at the hands of their Muslim and Christian neighbors.

Slave-raids on the Kunama are recorded from the sixteenth century, and they increased under EGYPT in the nineteenth century. In 1861 Werner MUNZINGER visited the Kunama area and in 1866 missionaries from SWEDEN arrived. Both were welcomed as protectors from raids and exactions, but further Tigrean raids forced the Swedes to withdraw in 1870. ITALIAN COLONIALISM came during 1894-96, after which missionary activity resumed under both the Swedes and Catholic Capuchins. The Italians estimated the total Kunama population at only 15,000 in 1900, and by 1970 Ethiopian estimates put it at 40,000. Colonialism changed Kunama life as the Italians institutionalized the democratic social structure, imposing village and district chiefs, while missionaries converted some to Christianity and Islam spread even more rapidly. Market towns developed in BARENTU and TOKOMBIA, and many men found seasonal work on the plantations around TESSENEI or in Eastern SUDAN.

Poor relations with the Beni 'Amer, combined with the influence of the pro-Ethiopian Swedish mission, led Christian and traditionalist Kunama to support Ethiopian rule during the 1960s, and ELF units in turn raided Kunama settlements. In 1965 the Ethiopians recruited a Kunama militia, and the ELF never liberated Barentu due primarily to Kunama hostility. The DERG continued to court Kunama loyalty, while an already widespread, racist perception among non-Nilotic Eritreans (both Muslim and Christian) that the Kunama were somehow "not Eritrean" further alienated them from the nationalist fronts. Only when the EPLF entered the area in 1981, did the nationalists begin to gain some Kunama sympathy through village self-organization programs, social services and education. Kunama recruits helped the EPLF liberate Barentu in 1985, and by the late 1980s the Kunama were participating widely in the nationalist movement. Their acceptance of Eritrean nationality was affirmed by their near unanimous vote in the 1993 REFERENDUM. Today infrastructural improvement and plans for agricultural development in Gash-Setit are tying the Kunama more closely to the rest of Eritrea than they have ever been.

KUWAIT. During the early 1970s, Kuwaiti support for the ELF-PLF was cultivated by OSMAN SALEH SABBE through the JIBERTI financier Al-Amin Seraj, who maintained close ties with the ruling family. In the 1980s the EPLF was able to tap the same source, and since liberation Kuwait has given Eritrea significant financial assistance, especially for the development of electrical power. A Kuwaiti embassy was opened in June 1995.

- L -

LABAT. A subtribe of the BENI 'AMER, organized in two distinct sections, one around Agordat speaking TIGRE, and a second around TESSENEI speaking both Tigre and BEJA.

LABOR ORGANIZATIONS. Eritrean workers organized themselves from the 1940s onwards in pursuit of the interrelated goals of economic improvement and national independence. Although a wage-earning labor force developed during the 1930s, repressive Italian colonial policies and an ethnically divided workforce impeded early workers' organization. Until 1949, the BRITISH ADMINIS-TRATION (BA) also restricted Eritrean labor organization and upheld racially-defined labor codes that gave Italian workers wages and benefits far superior to those of Eritreans. The development of POLITICAL PARTIES gave workers a forum for their grievances, and the issue of equal pay and benefits for Eritreans became a political rallying point as the British moved towards decolonization. Muslim dockworkers in MASSAWA organized in 1948, and in the highlands the UNIONIST PARTY initially represented workers' demands. In 1949 dockworkers struck in Massawa, glassworkers struck in ASMARA, and during March-April Eritrean RAILROAD workers won a six week strike for equal benefits and "Eritreanization" of skilled employment.

During 1950-51, as the BA liberalized labor laws and "Eritreanized" the state sector, many workers organized shop unions and a series of strikes won them equality of pay and benefits. By the time of FEDERATION, Eritrean industrial and commercial workers had won most of their demands, and the BA's 1952 Labor Proclamation insured their right to organize and strike. To defend these gains, nationalist leader WOLDE-AB WOLDE-MARIAM helped organize a national Confederation of Free Eritrean Labor Unions in early 1952, and in December he was elected President, with Mohamed Seraj Abdu vice-president. The Confederation had 4,000 paid members and 6,000 more associates, and Wolde-Ab hoped it would form the foundation for a Labor Party dedicated to defending Eritrea's democratic institutions. But the Unionist-Ethiopian government set out immediately to destroy the Confederation, temporarily closing its offices after Wolde-Ab was wounded in early 1953, and then keeping the organization under constant POLICE surveillance. The Ethiopian state took over railroad and port facilities, and when these workers struck in 1954-56 they were brutally repressed.

The Confederation's young and nationalistic staff focused on getting the ASSEMBLY to enact a Labor Code to secure the rights instituted by the BA, which were opposed by the Unionist government. A battle developed over the issue that led the Confederation to call a General Strike in Asmara, Massawa and Keren from March 10-13, 1958. The General Strike was an important expression of Eritrean nationalist sentiment, and paralyzed the city until the Confederation's leaders were arrested and public demonstrations were broken with gunfire, reportedly leaving 9 dead and 535 injured. On May 13 a repressive Labor Code was passed, the Confederation was outlawed, and most of its leaders remained in prison, where they made connections with nationalist STUDENT ORGANIZATIONS, leading to the formation of the ELM.

Eritrean labor organizations remained officially "deregistered" and dormant until 1963, when the Confederation of Ethiopian Labor Unions (CELU), led by an Eritrean resident in ADDIS ABABA, began to press for their revival. In August 1964 an Eritrean branch of CELU was established, led by the powerful KAGNEW workers' union, and eventually representing some 10,000 workers in 56 shop unions. The interlocking interests of Italian employers and HAILE SELASSIE I's family made industrial actions difficult, and despite the dynamic leadership of Mesfin Abraha, brother of EPLF cadre "Woldenkiel" Abraha, during 1968-72, few advances were made. In the early 1970s Eritrean nationalism resurfaced in the unions, and some opened secret negotiations to affiliate independently with international labor organizations. The Ethiopian revolution transformed labor organizations, as the DERG nationalized industries and CELU became a battleground for competing revolutionary factions, eventually being replaced by the Derg's All-Ethiopian Trade Union (AETU), to which workers were compelled to belong.

Eritrean workers aided the liberation fronts in sabotage and intelligence operations as the ARMED STRUGGLE intensified, but Ethiopian repression also produced an exodus of workers to the fronts. The EPLF and ELF clandestine labor movements were virtually annihilated by the Derg during 1979-82. Consequently, the EPLF's National Union of Eritrean Workers (NUEW), founded in November 1979 in SAHEL, was essentially a support organization among workers in the Eritrean DIASPORA, soliciting contributions and organizing activities like the Bologna Festival (a cultural festival begun in 1975 in association with the EPLF's European workers' association annual meetings). Nonetheless, Ethiopian oppression sparked several strikes in Derg-controlled factories, including that by 3,000 workers at BARATTOLO Textiles in 1983. As INDUSTRIAL activity declined in the 1980s, the Eritrean workforce diminished, augmented by Tigrean immigrants.

After liberation, the NUEW organized Eritrean workers in shop unions, taking over the existing Ethiopian union structure, but under a new Labor Code enacted in December 1991 that protects workers' rights to organize. During 1992 NUEW organized the major industries and helped induce the government to decree a fifty percent salary increase. A founding congress of trade unions was held in November 1993, electing a central council, which in turn organized the NUEW's last congress in September 1994, where the nationalist political organization was transformed into the independent National Confederation of Eritrean Workers (NCEW). Despite this, the government clearly expects workers to refrain from actions that could harm economic reconstruction, despite an estimated fifty percent 1994 unemployment rate and low wages. The NCEW is particularly involved in obtaining job training aid from the ILO (which NUEW joined in June 1993), other international organizations and some European and North American national trade union confederations.

LABOR PARTY (ELF). A reformist political organization operating clandestinely inside the ELF from the late 1960s, and officially organized during 1971-77, when it dominated the front through its Executive Committee. Most ELF leaders of the 1970s belonged to it, including AB-DALLAH IDRIS, AHMED NASSER, AZIEN YASSIN, HERUI TEDLA BAIRU and IBRAHIM IDRIS TOTIL.

LAND CONFLICTS *see* DIGSA; HALHALE; TOR'A-TSE-NADEGLE WAR.

LAND LAWS. Eritrea's land laws developed historically out of the traditional LAND TENURE systems of specific localities, whose descent-based principles created continual litigation over claims traced back though both parental lines. Overlying these claims to use-rights was the theoretical "ownership" of all land in the pre-colonial KEBESSA and SENHIT by the Ethiopian emperor or his (often independent) subordinates (the Governor of TIGRAI or the BAHRE NEGASHI). This legal principle, apparently established in the SOUTH ARABIAN period, justified the collection of land taxes or "tribute" (GEBRI; GULTI). In the lowlands, land was held communally by tribal descent groups.

ITALAN COLONIALISM also asserted the state's ultimate authority over all land, and the Italians expropriated large tracts for colonization and development, including 483,000 hectares in the Kebessa during 1891-93.

The 1909 Ordinamento Agrario regularized land policy, curtailing further land alienation in the Kebessa (except for military purposes) and focusing on agricultural development in the lowlands, where all land below 350 meters in the east, and 750 meters in the west, was declared state land (It.: *terre demaniali*) susceptible to leasing for periods of twenty-five to fifty years to concessionaires. The Ordinamento was revised in 1926, and further land for military use was confiscated in the mid-1930s, but the law essentially remained in effect through the BRITISH ADMINISTRATION, which used it to alienate a further 10,000 hectares during 1942-44. Colonial policy also encouraged the adoption of DESA land tenure in the highlands.

After FEDERATION the Eritrean Land Tenure Act froze in place existing rural tenures, while HAILE SELASSIE I's imposition of Gebri (imperial tribute) for the first time since YOHANNES IV, provoked widespread opposition. In the lowlands *terre demaniale* laws remained in place and further concessions were leased both to foreigners and Eritreans. In 1975, both the DERG and the Eritrean liberation fronts introduced land laws designed to give land title to those who actually farmed it, although the legal principle behind this remained ultimate state control over land, exercised through politically-screened village assemblies. Both the Derg and the EPLF encouraged the further adoption of DESA tenure in the highlands, while lowland concessions were taken over as state farms.

During the 1980s, the EPLF experimented with various communal land tenure systems, but after liberation its new Land Commission, headed by Alemseged Tesfai, decided that all traditional tenures were hopelessly conflicted and impeded rational economic development, as thousands of old claims were revived, LAND CONFLICTS erupted into violence, and insecurity of tenure due to widespread litigation and periodic redistribution discouraged individual improvement of land or its use in capital formation. Instead, a comprehensive new Land Law, uniform to the entire country, was drafted during 1992-93. Inevitably, this law sought to find a compromise between the security provided by traditional communal tenures and the economic development potential of privatized property. The main tenets arrived at were: (1) exclusive state ownership of land, abolishing all traditional rights and tenures; (2) the right of all rural Eritreans to lease the use of farming/grazing land; (3) the right of all village residents to lease plots of land for housing; (4) the granting of lifetime leases on an individual basis (without gender bias) to the above mentioned people, with priority given to those who already work the land or live in proximity to it; (5) priority to descendants of leasees, but no direct inheritance of land; (6) the right to rent, mortgage or otherwise use leased land to raise capital; (7) the right of the state to dispose of all land not claimed and to acquire any land necessary for public projects through "compulsory purchase;" (8) the right of the state to revoke leases in cases of environmental abuse. These provisions were included in the Draft Land Law approved by the NATIONAL ASSEMBLY in March 1994; but the law is still in the process of implementation as regional Land Commission offices and a computerized national Land Registry are prepared.

LAND TENURE. Eritrea's traditional land tenure systems were all communal in nature, based on family, descent-group or tribal rights to land use. In the highlands, the most important communal tenure systems were known as DESA, RISTI (based on the ENDA descent group) and TSELMI. In the lowlands, land was held communally by tribes until the advent of ITALIAN COLONIALISM. A superstructure of LAND LAWS reserving tax and tribute rights (*see* GEBRI; GULTI; MEDRI) to the state and its designees overlay these tenure systems and shaped their organization during pre-colonial times. Traditional land tenure systems were abolished in 1994 by the Draft Land Law.

LANGUAGES *see* AFAR; AMHARIC; ARABIC; BILEN; EDUCATION; GE'EZ; HEDAREB; ITALIAN POPULATION; KUNAMA; NARA; PRESS; SAHO; TIGRE; TIGRINYA.

LAW (Legal Codes) *see* JUSTICE.

LIBERAL PROGRESSIVE PARTY (LPP). Founded Febru-
ary 18, 1947 in ADI KAYIEH, the LPP was the major
TIGRINYA/Christian political party supporting indepen-
dence during the 1940s. It was led by Ras TESSEMA AS-
BEROM and Seyoum Maascio, with a separate branch in
SERAYE. Locally the LPP was known as the "Eritrea for
Eritreans" (Tigrn.: Ertra n'Ertrawian) party, evincing its
roots in the pro-independence movement led by WOLDE-
AB WOLDE-MARIAM from 1945. The LPP's strongest following was in Ras Tessema's home district of AKELE
GUZAI; but the FOUR POWERS COMMISSION of 1947 reported it only represented 4.4 percent of the population.
This weak showing was probably due to the violent oppo-
sition of the UNIONIST PARTY, whose ANDENET terrorists
attacked LPP members throughout the KEBESSA. In 1949
the LPP joined the INDEPENDENCE BLOC, but during 1950
it disintegrated and Ras Tessema's son, ABRAHA
TESSEMA, led many of its members into the pro-FEDERA-
TION Liberal Unionist Party. It was dissolved in December
1950, but its remaining members, along with Wolde-Ab's
small Independent Eritrea Party and other members of the
Independence Bloc, formed the ERITREAN DEMOCRATIC
FRONT and contested the elections for the first
ASSEMBLY.

LITERATURE *see* ARABIC; PRESS; TIGRINYA.

LOCAL   GOVERNMENT. Eritrea's current system of local
government developed out of the People's Assemblies
(Tigrn.: Hezbawi Baito) organized by the EPLF in its liberated areas during the ARMED STRUGGLE. These assemblies represented the highest stage of a three-tiered system whose lower stages comprised, first, the People's
Committees (Hezbawi SHUMAGULLE) formed in newly liberated areas with strong EPLF oversight, and second, the
Challenge Committees (Shumagulle Bedeho) formed from
the People's Committee in elections once EPLF social re-

forms had begun. The People's Assemblies were democrat-
ically elected and incorporated the EPLF commitment to
social equality and women's rights. After liberation, the
People's Assembly model was applied to all Eritrea and
formed the foundation for a pyramidal system of indirect
elections that culminated at the national level. During
1992 local elections were held under EPLF supervision at
the sub-district and district level, and in the zobas
("zones") of the major cities. In January 1993 most of the
district-level committees elected provincial assemblies,
which then elected representatives to the NATIONAL AS-
SEMBLY in May. At each stage, a certain number of seats
were reserved for FIGHTERS, women and returning
REFUGEES. The People's Assemblies are responsible for
local laws, while appointees of the central government
carry out administrative functions.

LOGGO. A TIGRINYA-speaking descent group living in the
KEBESSA since ancient times and perhaps representing
some of the original population from the AKSUMITE period. The Loggo are divided between two widely separated
districts (ancient MEDRI): Loggo-Sarda, overlooking the
HAZAMO in southwestern AKELE GUZAI; and Loggo-
Chewa, between ADI BARO and ASMARA in HAMASIEN,
where their villages are mixed with those of the CHEWA,
against whom they fought during the fifteenth century.

-M -

MAHABER FEQRI HAGER (Tigrn.: "Society for Love of
Country"). The Mahaber Feqri Hager Ertra (MFH), often
called the "Patriotic Society," was formed May 5, 1941, in
ASMARA by Eritrea's leading intellectuals to protest
Italian attacks against them and call for the BRITISH AD-
MINISTRATION to implement its wartime promises that
Eritreans would have a say in deciding their political fu-
ture. Its founders included GEBRE-MESKAL WOLDU
(president), ABDULKADIR KABIRE (vice-president),
ABRAHA TESSEMA, IBRAHIM SULTAN ALI, MOHAMED
OMAR CADI and WOLDE-AB WOLDE-MARIAM, all of whom

agreed on an anti-colonial political program calling for an end to Italian privileges and economic domination, and Eritrean self-determination. But a rift soon emerged between those who believed Eritrea's future lay in some form of eventual independence and those who believed in unification with ETHIOPIA. The latter sentiment was reinforced by HAILE SELASSIE's patronage of the "Patriotic Society for the Reunification of Hamasien with Ethiopia," formed in ADDIS ABABA in May 1941 by Eritrean emigrés. This organization was purposefully confused with the MFH of Eritrea by Ethiopian propagandists, and its members worked with the Eritrean ORTHODOX CHURCH and TIGRINYA/Christian notables to create a cultural nationalist movement advocating union with Ethiopia.

By 1944, when the MFH supported an Eritrean POLICE strike, the coalition, which never formed an official political party because of British restrictions, was seriously divided between its pro-Unionist and pro-Independence wings, with the Unionists gaining the ascendancy and several Independents, including Ibrahim Sultan and Wolde-Ab leaving the organization to form their own movements. Nonetheless, it remained in existence as a forum for voicing a variety of Eritrean political aspirations until the WA'LA BET GHERGHIS meeting of November, 1946, where its old leadership and pro-Independence wing were forcibly ousted by pro-Ethiopian extremists led by TEDLA BAIRU, who then disingenuously claimed that the newly formed UNIONIST PARTY continued to represent the MFH. Despite the Unionists' continued use of the name among Tigrinya-speakers, the original MFH's existence may be said to have ended in December, 1946.

MAHMUD AHMED SHERIFO. Current Minister of Local Government, Mahmud Ahmed Mahmud Sherifo was born to a SAHO family from AKELE GUZAI and attended high school in ASMARA, from where he joined the ELF in 1967. He was a member of the TRIPARTITE UNITY FORCES and the original PLF led by RAMADAN MOHAMED NUR. He formed part of the original leadership of the EPLF, serving on the CENTRAL COMMITTEE. After liberation he was appointed Minister of Foreign Affairs, served as acting head of state in January 1994 while the president was hospitalized in ISRAEL, and in March became Minister of Local Government.

MAHMOUD DINAI. An early military leader in the ELF, Mahmoud was born into the Almada sub-tribe of the BENI 'AMER and joined the SUDAN DEFENSE FORCE in 1956, from where he was recruited into the ELF and went into the field in 1962. He rose to command Zone 1 in 1965, and was closely associated with IDRIS MOHAMED ADEM. His fortunes declined as the LABOR PARTY rose in the 1970s, and in 1978 he fled to join OSMAN SALEH SABBE's ELF-PLF, with which he remained associated through the 1980s.

MAHMOUD SAID NAWD. Founder of the ERITREAN LIB-ERATION MOVEMENT (ELM), Mahmoud Said Nawd was born in 1936 in RORA Habab, SAHEL the son of a Tokar cotton farmer. He attended school and worked in Port SUDAN from 1944-56, where he was involved in the anti-colonial movement led by the Sudanese Communist Party (SCP). In 1956 he returned to Eritrea specifically to make contact with the nationalist movement; but finding no party orga-nization he discussed forming one with IBRAHIM SULTAN ALI in 1957 and the SCP in 1958, both of whom opposed the idea. In 1959 he formed the ELM with other Eritreans in Port Sudan, and led it until 1970. In 1971, he joined OSMAN SALEH SABBE's emerging ELF-PLF and worked in the organization's Foreign Office until 1977, when he joined the EPLF as one of its representatives in the Middle East. From 1992-95 he served as governor of Sahel Province.

MAI AINI (Akele Guzai). A village at the intersection of the Adi Kayieh-Mendefera and Dekemhare roads, at the northern end of the HAZAMO plain. Its strategic position made it the site of an important battle in July 1978, when the EPLF tried to stop the advance of Ethiopian mecha-nized units from TIGRAI during the DERG's First

OFFENSIVE. EPLA units were overwhelmed and forced to abandon all of AKELE GUZAI in the first stage of the STRATEGIC WITHDRAWAL.

MAI DUMA (Seraye) *see* AREZA.

MAI HABAR (Hamasien). A wooded valley along a tributary of the Ali-Ghede River on the road from DEKEMHARE to Nefasit. In the 1940s an American missionary society established a sanitarium for lepers there, but left in 1975 when the clinic was nationalized by the DERG. It was taken over as an Ethiopian military base and was the scene of heavy fighting during September 1977. The base was overrun by EPLA forces in July 1985, but was retaken by the Ethiopians. After liberation the old sanitarium was converted into a rehabilitation center for disabled FIGHTERS. With donations raised from the Eritrean community and supplies from Norwegian Church Aid, a Disabled Technical Institute, with dorms, clinic, rehabilitation center and training workshops was built, opening on March 26, 1994. The vocational center was used as a transit camp for demobilizing disabled fighters in the summer of 1994, and on July 11 a group of them attempted to commandeer a bus to stage a protest in Asmara, but were fired on by EPLA security forces, killing three. Today the center is operating at full capacity.

MA'IKELE BAHRE (Tigrn.: "between the waters"). A twelfth to fourteenth century geographical term usually taken to mean the region between the MAREB River and the Red Sea ruled by a Christian governor owing allegiance to Ethiopian authorities. The term may also have applied to all the MEDRI BAHRE at times, including the territory of TIGRAI as far as the Takezze River.

MAI TSADA (Seraye). The highland district around ADI QWALA, known for its fertile soils and large precolonial GULTI and monastic landholdings.

M A R A Z Z A N I. An important Italian colonial family, de-cended from an early explorer of DENKEL, Viscount Ludovic Marazzani. His son, Filippo, served in the colonial army at ADWA and in the colonial administration; while Filippo's sons Stephano and Paolo (born at QWATIT in 1901-04) developed the HALHALE and Mai Zubo agricultural concessions outside DEBARWA.

M A R E B River. The largest river draining the central Eritrean highlands, the Mareb (Tigrn.: "west") forms much of the southern BORDER with Ethiopia, until it flows into the lowlands of GASH-SETIT province, where its name changes to the Gash. The river is seasonal, with its highest flow coming in July-September. Its waters provide irrigation for TESSENEI, ALI GHIDER, and across the Sudanese border north of KASSALA, where the river ends in a vast inland "delta" converted to cotton plantations in the 1900s.

M A R E B MELLASH (Tigrn.: "Beyond the Mareb"). A geographical term used to describe the KEBESSA region and, more broadly, central Eritrea (including parts of SEMHAR and SENHIT) from the sixteenth century onwards. The term is similar, but not exactly equivalent, to the earlier geographical term MA'IKELE BAHRE and the more broadly defined MEDRI BAHRE. Eritrean usage of the term added the idea "this side of the Mareb," and by the 17th century the term was equivalent to the territory claimed by the BAHRE NEGASHI. Its twentieth century usage generally refers only to the Kebessa.

M A R T I N I, Fernando (1841-1928). The most influential of Italian colonial governors, Martini ruled Eritrea from 1897-1907. He first visited the colony in 1891, as part of a parliamentary investigation committee, and staunchly supported the colony during the crisis of 1896. He formed the colony's first civil ADMINISTRATION in 1897, renouncing the disastrous policies of demographic colonization in the KEBESSA and military expansion in ETHIOPIA. Instead, he laid the administrative and legal foundations for the stable colonial state of the early twentieth century, moving the capital to ASMARA, initiating agricultural development in the lowlands, and implementing the policies of military recruitment, restricted EDUCATION and low taxes that were intended to insure Eritrean acquiescence. He published several major works on Italian colonialism, and after leaving Eritrea became a senator and Minister of State in Italy.

MARTYRS (Tigrn: *miswati).* Eritrean FIGHTERS who died in the ARMED STRUGGLE are respected as martyrs to the nationalist cause, and their sacrifice is constantly invoked to reinforce public support for Eritrean national unity and public service. During the war the concept of martyrdom was represented by powerful images of the blood of fallen fighters watering the plant of the new Eritrean nation, symbolized as a Red Flower cradling the children of an independent and peaceful future. This symbolism, combined with the very real loss of close to seventy thousand Eritrean young men and women during the war, had a powerful effect on mobilizing post-independence national solidarity behind the EPLF, and this heritage is one of the touchstones of the PFDJ, whose founding document cites the preservation of the memory of the martyr's sacrifices as one of the party's fundamental responsibilities.

During the war, the names of fallen fighters were withheld from their relatives, but in June 1992, after researching records extending back to the early ELF, the government announced the names of all known war dead. This provoked a national outpouring of grief in traditional wakes that lasted for over a week, culminating in national memorial services on June 20, the first Martyr's Day (a date chosen because it marked the bloodiest fighting of the 1982 RED STAR CAMPAIGN). Thereafter, Martyr's Day has been honored each year by pilgrimages often involving tens of thousands of people walking to the sites of various battles and reburying the dead with multi-denominational religious services, eulogies by surviving combatants and monuments (*see* ADI HAWESHA; ADI YAQOB; GHINDA).

MARYA (alt.: Maria). An important TIGRE-speaking tribe inhabiting northwestern SENHIT in the current ANSEBA Administrative Region. The Marya are divided into two sub-ribes, inhabiting separate RORA plateaus: the Marya Tselim ("Black Marya"), centered around OROTA, and the Marya Kaiyeh ("Red Marya"). They practice agro-PASTORALISM and were traditionally divided between TIGRE "serf" clans and aristocratic SHUMAGULLE clans who trace their origins to the same SAHO or Arab ancestor as the MENSA'. The Marya were originally Orthodox Christians, but during the 1600s-1800s they converted to ISLAM, beginning with the "serf" class and culminating in the Shumagulle class during 1820-35. During the 1960s the Marya supported the ELF, but in 1970 their leaders in the front, ABU TAYARA and Omer "Damer," disputed BENI 'AMER dominance and joined the ELF-PLF where they supported OSMAN SALEH SABBE's conservative faction. Most Marya fled as REFUGEES to SUDAN beginning in 1967 and accelerating during the heavy fighting in their region after 1978. Today they are returning to their lands, but disputes over grazing rights have provoked some conflicts with their BILEN neighbors.

MARYAM GHIMBI. ASMARA's most notorious political prison, used by the DERG from 1978-91 for the torture and execution of Eritrean civilians accused of collaborating with the liberation fronts. After liberation, from December 1991 to June 1992, it was opened to the public as a memorial to its victims, and then cleared for use as a municipal vehicle yard.

MASSAWA (Semhar). Second largest city and major port of central Eritrea, Massawa is the administrative center of the SEMHAR area and the current Northern Red Sea Region. The city originated on two islands, Massawa and Tawlud, on the northern shore of HIRGHIGO Bay. Massawa island, lying further offshore, was used by coastal traders since ancient times, and may be the BEJA port of Badi' cited by Al-Ya'qubi in the 9th century (Massawa is still referred

to as "Badé" in ARABIC, while it is called "Bats'e" in TI-
GRE and TIGRINYA).

By the eleventh century Massawa was the principle
entrepot of the Eritrean coast and was associated with the
rise of the Sultanate of the DAHLAK ISLANDS, which
controlled it through the fourteenth century, although it
was also claimed by the Ethiopian emperors AMDE SIYON
and ZARA YA'QOB, and regularly paid tribute to the Governors of TIGRAI. It had a mixed population of Arab and
Tigre merchants, among whom the BELEW families of
Hirghigo figured prominently due to their control over the
island's provisions, drinking water and the caravans and
TRADE ROUTES to the interior on which Massawa's COM-
MERCE depended. Massawa also developed as the center of
ISLAM in central Eritrea, with its Shari'a courts renowned
for their JUSTICE and its religious scholars spreading
their faith among the coastal population.

In the early sixteenth century Massawa became a
prize in the naval wars between Portugal and the Ottoman
Empire (*see* DAHLAK Archipelago). In 1557 it was decisively occupied by TURKEY, which garrisoned and fortified the island; but following the failure of Turkish attempts to occupy the highlands, the Turkish garrison became indigenized, while real political power shifted to the
Turks' Belew deputy, the NA'IB of Hirghigo. Petty struggles between the descendants of Turkish officers and the
Na'ibs dominated the port's politics through the eighteenth century, and its commerce and facilities declined
until 1809 when the Turks briefly reasserted direct authority, followed by occupation by EGYPT from 1813-23
and again in the 1840s. During this period the Na'ib lost
control of Massawa and the port again developed as a bastion of foreign commercial interests, including BRITAIN
and FRANCE from the 1840s.

As commerce expanded, the mainland around
Monkullo and Otumlo was settled by Massawa residents
seeking more secure water supplies and relief from the
stifling humidity of the island. A Turkish ban on stone
buildings on the mainland and continual raids during the
1840s-50s hampered this development, but after the

Egyptian take-over in 1865 the mainland was fortified, enabling merchants to build permanent residences and Protestant and Catholic missionaries to develop schools and other facilities in Monkullo. In 1872 the Egyptians appointed Werner MUNZINGER governor with instructions to improve the port as a base for further expansion into the interior. He built a water system from Monkullo to the islands, which were connected by a fortified causeway to the mainland in 1874. A governor's palace was built on Tewalud island in 1875/76, and though Egyptian plans for conquering the highlands died along with Munzinger, the city continued to be improved with multi-storied stone buildings.

ITALY's occupation of Massawa in February, 1885, accelerated the port's development. Docks, military quarters, commercial buildings and a hospital were added, and the suburbs were further fortified. Massawa served as Eritrea's official capital until 1900, and the Egyptian governor's palace was completely rebuilt with a Turkish-style dome and colonnaded porches. By 1893 the city had a population of 14,200 Eritreans and Arabs, and 2,200 Italians; but this shrank to only 5,400 Eritreans and Arabs, and 1,000 Italians by 1905. A SALT industry was developed in the tidal flats behind the Gherar peninsula, and Tewalud island was built-up as the RAILROAD's terminus. In 1921 much of the city was ruined by a powerful earthquake, and the port did not really recover until 1928, when harbor improvements were begun in preparation for war with ETHIOPIA.

The war of 1935-36 brought tremendous changes as improved ROAD TRANSPORT and a 71-kilometer aerial cableway connected Massawa to Asmara, while hundreds of thousands of tons of supplies and soldiers passed through the port. By 1938 the civilian population alone was over 15,000, including 4,000 Italians, and the mainland was being developed with a major electric power plant, fuel depots, a cement factory, hundreds of new Italian houses, and a naval base on the Abd el-Kader peninsula. By 1940 Massawa had the finest naval facilities on the African coast between Alexandria and Capetown, including floating drydocks, cranes, warehouses, barracks and a military AIRPORT. In 1941 the port was bombed by Britain, and in April most of the Italian navy was scuttled in the harbor. During 1942-43 British and American engineers worked feverishly with Eritrean crews to clear the harbor and utilize it as a naval repair base, but in 1944 the facilities were closed, and in 1945 the BRITISH ADMINISTRATION began selling off much of Massawa's infrastructure, including drydocks, cranes, harbor tenders, cement factory machinery, aerial cableway equipment, warehouses, and barracks.

This deconstruction, coupled with the development of ASSAB as the principle port for Ethiopia, produced an economic crisis that, combined with pro-Independence political movements, provoked a series of strikes during 1949-53. At the time of FEDERATION, in 1952, the Ethiopian state took over administration of the port, and in 1953 began issuing identity cards to dockworkers, reserving a proportion of jobs for Christians from the KEBESSA and Ethiopia. This led Muslim dockworkers to strike in January 1954, with support from much of the community; but Ethiopian military intervention crushed the strike. Massawa remained a center for anti-Ethiopian agitation, led by MOHAMED OMAR CADI through 1958, but the Ethiopian presence grew as their NAVY developed the Abd el-Kader peninsula base with U.S. aid and highland immigrants and Ethiopian officials settled in city, making up much of the increased population that by 1962 had grown to 21,300.

During the 1960s-70s, Ethiopian repression and economic discrimination produced an exodus of Massawa's Muslim population, reaching a climax in late 1977, with the first of the MASSAWA BATTLES. When the EPLA's siege was broken in 1978, Massawa was transformed into an Ethiopian garrison, and although EPLF guerrilla attacks on the naval base and fuel depot continued, setting spectacular fires in 1982 and 1986, the civilian population grew to about 60,000 in the mid-1980s, most of whom were Ethiopians. Massawa became the major port for FOOD AID to the FAMINE regions of Eritrea and Tigrai, and

many Tigreans came to work on the docks or provide services for the Ethiopian military. The population declined
again as the ARMED STRUGGLE intensified in northern
Semhar during 1989, and when the city was liberated after
the second Battle of Massawa it held only 30,000 residents.

The battle of January 1990, and subsequent
Ethiopian bombing, left the city and docks in ruins, the
oil depots gutted and the harbor blocked with sunken vessels, but by January 1991 the docks were partially
cleared and a UNITED NATIONS brokered agreement enabled food aid to begin arriving again. During 1992, 228
vessels unloaded 559,000 tons of cargo, most of it relief
supplies. This dropped to 386,000 tons in 1993, as warehouse facilities remained inadequate and a monsoon in
April ruined 6,000 tons of wheat. By 1994 the port was
being completely reconstructed under the direction of
Woldenkiel Abraha, head of the Ports Administration,
which moved its offices from Asmara to Massawa in May.
The fuel depot was repaired and expanded, as were the
hospital, government offices and a number of mainland industries. Some of the original population began to return
from abroad and the FISHING industry was redeveloped. In
1995 the railroad was reconstructed from Tewalud to the
suburbs, and the business district on Massawa island was
repaired.

MASSAWA, BATTLES (1977/78 and 1990). Massawa, because of its strategic importance, was the site of two of the
major battles of the ARMED STRUGGLE. The first began on
October 12-16, 1977, when EPLF forces led by PETROS
SOLOMON cut the road to ASMARA near Mai Atal. On December 9-10 the EPLA defeated an Ethiopian counterattack outside DOGALI and pushed the routed troops back to
the city's defensive perimeter. Then, on December 21-22,
the Eritreans overran all the mainland suburbs, driving
the DERG's forces onto the Abd-el Kader and Gherar pen-
ninsulas and the islands, where they were supported by
Ethiopian and USSR warships. On December 23 the EPLA
attempted a frontal assault on the peninsulas, with

FIGHTERS wading across the chest-deep evaporation ponds
of the Salina SALT works into a murderous fire that left
two hundred dead and four hundred wounded, the worst
losses yet suffered by the EPLA. Ethiopian jets and naval
artillery destroyed much of the mainland suburbs, and
most of the population fled or was killed. On December 31,
EPLA shells set the fuel depot on fire, burning 45 million
liters. The Eritreans pulled back for a long siege, but the
military balance turned against them and in July 1978
they made their STRATEGIC WITHDRAWAL from Semhar.

The Second Battle of Massawa was planned as a major
EPLA offensive, code-named "Fenkil," from March 1989,
when the EPLF Political Committee decided to abandon its
attempts to liberate KEREN and instead concentrate on
isolating Asmara from the sea. In January 1989, the Battle
of SEMENAWI BAHRI had proven that EPLA armor could
operate effectively on the coastal plains without air cover,
and had moved the front lines into northern Semhar,
within striking distance of the port. An offensive NAVY
was also developed during 1989, and in January 1990, the
EPLF secretly moved powerful forces into Semhar. At 1
AM on February 8 the Fenkil Offensive was launched,
cutting the Asmara road at Gattelai, pushing up the
mountains to DONGOLO and across the plain to Massawa.
By February 9 the EPLA was in the suburbs, and that
night Eritrean gunboats destroyed most of the Ethiopian
fleet. On February 10 the EPLA stormed the naval base,
securing all the mainland. A cease-fire was then negotiated in an attempt to save the civilian population and
avoid destruction of the islands; but the Derg refused to
allow the islands' garrison to surrender, and after defeating an Ethiopian attempt at seaborne reinforcement, on
February 16 the EPLA stormed the islands in a combined
land-sea assault covered by artillery fire that destroyed
much of western shore of the islands. Over 3,000 Eritrean
fighters died in the eight-day battle, and perhaps three
times as many Ethiopians.

The fighting was followed by a lull of several weeks
in which Ethiopian forces regrouped around GHINDA, but
in March the Derg began firing missiles into the city from

the DAHLAK islands and on April 3 started an air assault using cluster bombs and napalm that killed hundreds of civilians, destroyed much of the port infrastructure and burned large stores of FOOD AID. The heavy bombing ended by May, but further air raids in October and intermittent missile attacks continued to threaten the port and naval base until January 1991.

MATARA (Akele Guzai). A rock mountain just south of SENAFE, Amba Matara has been a holy site from ancient times. The name "Matara" was also given by nineteenth-century French travelers to ruins from the AKSUMITE and earlier periods that cluster on the adjoining plain, where a complex of stone mansions and churches was apparently destroyed by fire in the eighth century, contemporaneously with ADULIS. By the 1970s these were the most thoroughly excavated ruins in Eritrea, providing many insights into the region's ancient history (*see* ARCHAEOLOGY).

MATIENZO, Eduardo Anze. UNITED NATIONS High Commissioner for Eritrea, appointed under Resolution 390 A (V) on December 14, 1950, to implement the transition to FEDERATION. Matienzo, a Bolivian, arrived February 9 and immediately demanded the BRITISH ADMINISTRATION (BA) implement a serious anti-SHIFTA policy. He then organized the election of the first Eritrean ASSEMBLY and drafted a CONSTITUTION with input from the BA, ETHIOPIA and various Eritrean political leaders, including WOLDE-AB WOLDE-MARIAM. Matienzo took a firm stand for Eritrean autonomy, refusing to allow the Ethiopian Imperial Representative executive powers and insisting that the Assembly elect an independent Eritrean Chief Executive; but he was unable to resolve the problem of the Federal Government being essentially that of Emperor HAILE SELASSIE I. He left Eritrea immediately after Federation.

MEDICINE *see* HEALTH CARE.

MEDRI (Tigrn.: "land"). Derived from an ancient Sabean earth deity (Meder), the word Medri was used to designate the largest tribute-collection unit of the MAREB MELLASH during the fifteenth through nineteenth centuries. In the late 1800s there were 34 Medri, divided into 66 GULTI and over 800 villages. The Emperor of ETHIOPIA or, more often, the Governor of TIGRAI, would in theory assign a fixed tribute payment to each Medri, which the *shum medri* (administrative appointee) would divide among the constituent Gulti. The Medri formed tax districts in much of the KEBESSA under ITALIAN COLONIALISM, and continued to be the basic framework for subdistrict ADMINISTRATION until the 1995 administrative reform.

MEDRI BAHRE (Tigrn.: "Land of the Sea," i.e. coastal region). A common name for the central Eritrean region during the fifteenth to nineteenth centuries, its definition changes depending on the geographical position of the user. In ETHIOPIA it was once applied to the land from the Takezze River to the sea, thus including TIGRAI as well, but in the twentieth century it has meant the lands from the Mareb to the coast. An even narrower definition is used within Eritrea today to signify the eastern escarpment of the highlands, particularly from DEBRE BIZEN to the KUMALIE River, and the coastal plains of SEMHAR. Sometimes the term is shortened to just "Bahri."

MEKWENENTI (Tigrn.: "nobility"). The transgenerational elite families of the KEBESSA, such as the "Houses" of HAZZEGA and TSAZZEGA and the various district KANTIBAIs, were known by this title which implied the right to hold political office and GULTI positions.

MELOTTI. Luigi Melotti was an Italian industrialist who began his career in Eritrea with military construction contracts during 1935-37. In 1939 he founded an alcohol distillery in ASMARA, initially using DUM PALM fruit. In 1941 he built Eritrea's first brewery, and soon was exporting beer throughout the region. He also invested in Diego MIRENGHI's glass factory to insure bottle supplies.

After his death in 1946, his brother Rodolfo came to manage the business, but died in 1951 from a SHIFTA attack outside OM HAGER. His wife, Signora Melotti, continued to operate the business, which grew through the 1960s. She was known as generous to her employees and as a supporter of Eritrean independence. She left Eritrea when the DERG nationalized the company in 1975, changing the name to "Asmara," although locally the beer is still known as "Melotti." The company, employing six hundred workers, remains state-owned as of 1997 and is one of the few profit-making local industries, supplying Eritrea and exporting forty percent of its production.

MENDEFERA (Seraye). Eritrea's fifth largest urban center, Mendefera is today the administrative center of the Southern (Debub) Region. Known as Adi Ugri on all pre-1980s maps, Mendefera was originally a village near the Italian garrison of Adi Ugri, which was fortified in 1889 as the colonial headquarters for SERAYE. By 1905 it had a population of 2,800, including a hundred Italian civilians, and by 1931 it grew to over 5,000, boasting a secondary school and important Catholic institutions. During 1935-36 it became a ROAD TRANSPORT center and a number of small Italian industries were established. By 1962 the population was 11,500. In July 1977 the ELF liberated Mendefera, and shortly afterwards the central market was bombed by the DERG, which recaptured the town in July 1978. It remained in Ethiopian hands until 1991. Today the mayor is Dragon Haile Melekot, descendant of an important local family, who has overseen a campaign of infrastructural improvement and economic expansion with the support of the Eritrean government and, until 1996, the CATHOLIC CHURCH. Improvements include a new water system, shoe factory, garages, hospital, and power plant.

MENGISTU HAILE-MARIAM *see* DERG.

MENKA (Tigrn.: "bat" [animal]). A dissident political movement that developed in 1973 in the early PLF field forces of the ELF-PLF. It was led by Musie Tesfai-Mika'el,

and later joined by Tewolde Eyob, but most of its supporters were new recruits from student backgrounds who
called for radical democratic decision-making and Marxist social programs. Menka criticized ISAIAS AFWERKI
for centralizing control over the front, and he engaged
them in many public debates until mid-1974. Isaias
maintained the support of former-ELF veterans who real-
ized the dangers of a politically divided organization, including the Muslim PLF forces led by RAMADAN MO-
HAMED NUR, ALI SAID ABDELLA and IBRAHIM AFA. In
June a trial was held and in August 1974 at least five
Menka leaders were executed, including Musie and
Tewolde.

MENSA'. A small TIGRE-speaking ethnic group inhabiting
the mountain ridge between the upper ANSEBA Valley and
the coastal plain adjoining the SEMENAWI BAHRI. Traditionally the Mensa' were divided into a SHUMAGULLE
ruling caste and Tigre "serfs," with the ruling caste
claiming SAHO or Arab origins and divided into two clans,
with attached serfs, the Bet Abrehe and Bet Ishaqan. The
Mensa' were Orthodox Christians and their KANTIBAIs
were formally invested by the Ethiopian emperor or Governor of TIGRAI during the seventeenth to eighteenth
centuries. Nonetheless, during the nineteenth century
most of the Tigre "serfs" converted to ISLAM, followed by
the Shumagulle in the 1870s. But the Mensa' retain a syncretistic tolerance for both religions, with Muslims still
celebrating Orthodox feasts. In the late 1800s Protestant
missionaries began converting Bet Abrehe around GHELEB,
and under ITALIAN COLONIALISM the CATHOLIC CHURCH
converted many Bet Ishaqan around their center at
Mehlab. From 1970, the Mensa' suffered brutal Ethiopian
military attacks (*see* GHELEB), and many fled as
REFUGEES, while during 1988-91 the front lines around
KEREN cut directly through Mensa' land.

MERAGUZ (Seraye). A rich agricultural district southwest
of MENDEFERA with a large TIGRINYA Christian population.

MERET (Tigrn.: "district," "land"). The largest administrative division of the precolonial MAREB MELLASH. During the seventeenth to nineteenth centuries there were five Merets corresponding to the provinces of AKELE GUZAI, HAMASIEN and SERAYE, and the Western Seraye districts of DEQI TESFA and Deqi Melaga (*see* QOHAIN).

MERETTA SEMEBENE *see* AKELE GUZAI.

MES-HALIT (Senhit). A small TIGRE-speaking tribe inhabiting the area around the strategic pass of the same name that leads from the middle ANSEBA Valley to AFABET. Because it guards the northern entrance to KEREN, Mes-Halit pass was the site of several battles, including one between Free French and Italian troops during the Battle of Keren in March 1941, another during the EPLF's STRATEGIC WITHDRAWAL of November-December 1978, and a third following the Afabet battle of March 1988.

MESFIN HAGOS. One of the original leaders of the EPLF, Mesfin attended university in ADDIS ABABA in the early 1960s and joined the ELF in 1966. Along with ISAIAS AFWERKI, he was part of the initial group sent for training in CHINA, returning to be deputy commander of Zone 5. In 1970 he joined the original ELF-PLF group at SUDOHA ILA, then went north to join Isaias at ALA. In 1974 he was part of the five-man EPLF founding leadership, and served on the Political Committee through the Third Congress. He was a senior commander in the EPLA through liberation, leading it to victory on the DEKEMHARE FRONT in the final battle of the ARMED STRUGGLE, when he served as Chief of Staff. Popular with the FIGHTERS, he was appointed Minister of Defense after the short-lived mutiny of May, 1993, and then moved to his current position as Administrator of the Southern (Debub) Administrative Region.

MILITARY *see* ARMED STRUGGLE; ASCARI; DERG; ER-
ITREAN PEOPLE'S LIBERATION ARMY; ETHIOPIA; FIGHT-
ERS.

MINI-FERE. A SAHO tribe inhabiting the region between
SENAFE and IRAFAILE, the Mini-Fere trace their origins
to a fusion between Saho immigrants and a HABESHA military garrison. Today most   are Muslim pastoralists, but in
the past many were said to have been Christians, and
neighboring TIGRINYA groups have Mini-Fere ancestors.

MINING. Eritrea's mineral resources include Copper, Gold,
Iron, Manganese, Nickel-Chromium, PETROLEUM, Potash,
SALT and Silver. Obsidian was mined on the BURE peninsula since pre-historic times, and Egyptian trading expeditions exported it from at least the second millennium
B.C. Along with salt, gold has been the single most frequently   mined   mineral   in   Eritrea,   with   works   in
HAMASIEN dating back to the pre-AKSUMITE period. Eritrea's principal gold resources occur around ASMARA,
including sites at ADI NEFAS and Medri Zion (the latter
having been worked extensively in the medieval period),
and in GASH-SETIT from outside BARENTU (Basali,
Suzana) to the TOKOMBIA area (Augaro, Damishoba). All
these sites were worked by Italian miners during the
1930s-40s. During 1931-40, 21 mines produced 1700 kg
total, but declined thereafter. In 1953-62, 4 mines produced a total of 1100 kg, but were closed during the
ARMED STRUGGLE.
    Copper and silver traces were found alongside gold
deposits, and in the early 1970s a major deposit of extremely rich copper ore was located outside DEBARWA by
a Japanese company, which began production during
1973-74, but left after   ELF attacks. Major high-grade
iron ore deposits are located at Ghedem and Agametta in
direct proximity to the port of MASSAWA, but have not
been commercially exploited. Some of the world's finest
potash and manganese salts are located in the Col-
luli/Dalul area in northwestern DENKEL and across the
border in ETHIOPIA. These were mined from the First

World War onwards by an Italian company that built a railroad to Mersa Fatma to facilitate their export. Mining ended in 1960 when the lease expired, and has not been resumed.

In 1992 responsibility for developing Eritrea's mineral resources passed to the Department of Mines, formerly an EPLF department, which was merged in 1993 into the current Ministry of Energy and Mines, headed by Tesfai Gebreselassie. In 1994 foreign mining companies, including several from North America, began bidding for gold prospecting leases and in 1995 a new Mining Law clarified state ownership of all mineral resources and outlined tax incentives and profit repatriation rules for foreign investors. In 1996 two Canadian companies signed agreements for gold and silver prospecting in the Northern Red sea and Debub Regions, while other agreements are under negotiation.

MIRENGHI, Diego. Founder of the first glassworks in Eritrea in 1941, in association with the MELOTTI alcohol industry. In 1944 Mirenghi created the S.A. Vetreria di Asmara (SAVA) glassworks, utilizing local materials and training Eritrean glass workers. He moved his company to Kenya in 1951, taking many of his skilled workers with him, but the Asmara factory continued to operate under the control of Melotti, its major customer.

MIRGHANIYYA (Khatmiyya). A Muslim religious brotherhood (Arab.: *tariqa*) founded by Muhammad Uthman al-Mirghani (1793-1852), who was sent from Arabia by his teacher, Ahmed ibn Idris al-Fasi, to convert the BENI 'AMER in 1817. In 1837 al-Mirghani formed his own brotherhood, which he argued took precedence over all others, as it was the "seal" (Arab.: *khatm*) of all the brotherhoods, and was thus called the "Khatmiyya." Mirghani's sons spread the brotherhood throughout Northern SUDAN, working closely with Egyptian officials, and two of them won many converts in the Eritrean region: Al-Hasan (d. 1869), who settled at KASSALA (which became the seat of the Mirghaniyya order) converted the Beni

'Amer, HALENQA and HABAB to the sect; while Hashim
(d. 1899), who settled at MASSAWA in 1860 (where his
tomb at Otumlo remains an important shrine), converted
many ASAWORTA.

The Mirghaniyya opposed the Mahdiyya in Sudan,
and were supported by the Italian colonial government,
enabling them to spread throughout the north and west.
KEREN became the Mirghaniyya's center in Eritrea, led by
Seyid Abu-Bakr bin-Uthman and his son, Ja'afar. Although Seyid Abu-Bakr was formally elected President of
the MUSLIM LEAGUE, the Mirghaniyya did nothing to oppose Ethiopian rule after 1952, in keeping with their
heritage of cooperation with colonial authorities. The
sect's failure to support the nationalist movement led to
its marginalization during the ARMED STRUGGLE, particularly after 1975, when the leadership retreated to Kassala. Today, their moral authority in Eritrea has dwindled
to almost nothing.

MOHAMED ALI OMERO. Born into a HIRGHIGO merchant
family, Ali Omero attended the KEKIYA school until the
late 1950s, when he emigrated to CAIRO for further studies. He was involved in the Eritrean student movement
there and was among the early members of the ELF. In
1963 he was sent to Syria for military training, and rose
to command Zone 4 under the patronage of his former
teacher, OSMAN SALEH SABBE. When Sabbe split from the
ELF in 1970, Ali Omero led many reformist FIGHTERS to
SUDOHA ILA, where he was elected to the original leadership of the ELF-PLF. His close links to Osman Sabbe and
the old ELF hierarchy led to his removal from PLF leadership at another election in 1971, however, and he was excluded from the top ranks of the new EPLF, remaining a
battalion commander in the 1980s, though he eventually
sat on the CENTRAL COMMITTEE of the PFDJ and in
November 1993 was appointed ambassador to EGYPT.

MOHAMED IBN DAWD IBN MUSTAFA, Sayedna. A
crucial figure in the early development of the ELF,
Sayedna Mohamed (often referred to as Shaykh Mohamed

Dawd) was descended from a leading religious family of the FAIDAB sub-tribe of the BENI 'AMER, where his grandfather, Sayedna Mustafa, was a revered religious scholar. In late 1960 Sayedna Mohamed, a long acquaintance of IDRIS MOHAMED ADEM, was contacted by ELF organizers in KASSALA and began to establish a network of ELF cells among the Beni 'Amer around AGORDAT. In April 1961 he met with HAMID IDRIS AWATE near Geset and asked him to begin the ARMED STRUGGLE with ELF support, and in June again met him in Agordat. During this period, the ELF's criticism of the ELM exposed both organizations to Ethiopian intelligence and in July Sayedna Mohamed was put under house arrest in Agordat, ironically just after he had returned from a meeting at Felesab, near Ashier, where the date for launching the armed struggle had been decided. Subjected to continual Ethiopian harassment, in 1966 he finally fled to SUDAN, where he died in 1967.

MOHAMED OMAR CADI. A leading figure in the early nationalist movement, M. Omar Cadi was born in 1909 into the Bet Cadi clan of the ASAWORTA in FORO. From the 1930s he was involved in the meat canning industry in Massawa, and in 1941 was a founding member of the MAHABER FEQRI HAGER. He worked with WOLDE-AB WOLDE-MARIAM in an attempt to preserve the unity of the nationalist movement at the WA'LA BET GHERGHIS in 1946, after which he joined the MUSLIM LEAGUE. But in 1949 he led a group of MASSAWA merchants who opposed IBRAHIM SULTAN ALI out of the League, founding the Independent Muslim League of Massawa, which attempted to restore Muslim-Christian unity in Eritrea by proposing a compromise agreement for "conditional union" with Ethiopia that prefigured FEDERATION. He represented his party at the UNITED NATIONS in 1949-50, and published the newspaper *L'Unita*.

Omar Cadi's early espousal of Federation earned him a position as director of the UNIONIST paper *Unione e Progresso* in 1952, and a seat on the Federal Council. But when it became apparent that HAILE SELASSIE I was intent on dismantling the Federation, Omar Cadi led a series of legal challenges, filing a petition with the Eritrean Supreme Court in June 1956 against the legality of Eritrea's Second ASSEMBLY elections, and when this failed going to CAIRO where he prepared a petition for the UNITED NATIONS protesting the policies leading to Eritrea's ANNEXATION. In October 1957 the petition was presented in the form of a telegram signed by Eritrean notables, but Omar Cadi was convinced by Ethiopian officials to return to Eritrea where he was arrested in January 1958, sparking widespread protests. On April 30 he was sentenced by Ethiopian authorities to ten years imprisonment, but after annexation he was released and in 1969 was appointed mayor of Massawa. In 1975 he was imprisoned by the DERG, but was released in 1977. He then attempted to mediate the rift between the ELF and EPLF in 1979, and afterwards moved to SAUDI ARABIA, where he died.

MUNZINGER, Werner (1832-75). A Swiss-born freelance imperialist agent and scholar of Eritrean traditions, Werner Munzinger came to MASSAWA in 1853 in the employment of a CAIRO-based merchant firm. In 1854 he moved to KEREN, where he married a BILEN woman and lived until 1861, after which he served as guide for various European expeditions to the area. His knowledge of Eritrean customs and languages were gathered into his *Ostafrikanische Studien* in 1864, and led to his employment by various foreign powers, including FRANCE (1865-71), BRITAIN (1867-69) and eventually EGYPT (1871-75). He led the reconnaissance for Britain's 1868 Napier expedition and in 1871 was appointed Governor of Massawa by Egypt, which charged him with preparing the port as a base for conquering the rest of Eritrea. His improvements to the port and his home of Keren marked the beginning of colonial development in Eritrea, but he and his wife were killed in 1875 during an AFAR attack on the column of Egyptian troops he was leading through DENKEL.

MUSIC. Each of Eritrea's ethnic groups has its own distinctive traditional music, although similarities link them all, including the common use of a mono-rhythmic drum beat and the appreciation of distinctly high-pitched female voices. Among the TIGRE and TIGRINYA the traditional *krar* (a lyre-like instrument with five to seven strings) is widely used to accompany poetic ballads of love, war and praise. In the KEBESSA, a class of traditional praise-singers and itinerant musicians skilled in the use of the *wata* (a one-stringed fiddle) once existed, attaching themselves to patrons among the MEKWENENTI. From these *watista* developed the modern popular music of the highlands, beginning with recordings during the European colonial period and expanding markedly during the 1960s with the spread of local RADIO programs. These programs also highlighted the music of other ethnic groups, particularly the Tigre, whose vibrant traditional songs (with their martial beat accompanied by clashing swords) have always been popular in the highlands.

During the late 1950s cultural organizations were formed that popularized Eritrean nationalism through songs laced with metaphors and double-meanings. With the rise of the ELM and ELF, the nationalist content of popular music increased, until by the mid-1960s the radio and urban concerts echoed with songs like "Shigey Habumi" (Tigrn.: "give me my torch"). Because most Eritreans were illiterate, music was among the most effective tools for spreading national consciousness. But the actual development of the nationalist music of the 1970s was usually spontaneous, originating in the individual lyrics of a great variety of popular singers. After 1975, the nationalist musicians joined the liberation fronts, where they toured the liberated areas, or fled as REFUGEES. Both the ELF and EPLF created their own cultural troupes, but it was the EPLF which really harnessed popular music to its revolutionary program through an outpouring of cassette tapes that purposely drew on the musical traditions of every ethnic group to create a sense of national unity while extolling the heroic deeds of the FIGHTERS and the sacrifices of the MARTYRS.

The most notable EPLF band was the Red Flowers, formed in 1977. The band toured the liberated zones and Sudan, but in 1983 it was dispersed to fight the Ethiopian Seventh OFFENSIVE and many members died. Surviving members participated in other cultural troupes, some of which appeared at the famed Eritrean cultural Festival in Bologna during the 1980s. The appearance of many women singers in these cultural troops also emphasized the EPLF's policy of gender equality, and traditional love songs were replaced with lyrics expressing love of country. The nationalist genre, running from haunting ballads to stirring marches, became the mainstay of Eritrean music throughout the country and the DIASPORA during the 1980s, and since liberation it has remained the most commonly heard popular music. Since the DEMOBILIZA-TION of artists and musicians in 1994-95, many former EPLF singers have set-out on their own, including the all-women Shushan Band, the war-disabled fighters' group Haben and such popular singers as Ahmed Mansour, Fikhira, Tesfai Mahari, and Wedi Shaykh. The riveting KUNAMA singer, Dahab Fatinga, has given Kunama rhythm and dance a previously unknown national popularity, and the return of Yemane "Barya" Gebre-Meskal from twenty years exile in the Arab world was a major cultural event in 1994. Yemane "Barya's" untimely death in 1997 was widely mourned, for his songs, more than those of any other musician, represent the contemporary fusion of highland and lowland styles that is today creating a truly national Eritrean music and culture.

MUSLIM LEAGUE (Arab.: Rabita al-Islamiya). The most important independentist political party of the 1940s, the Muslim League was founded on December 4, 1946, in KEREN by IBRAHIM SULTAN ALI, who was elected its Secretary-General, while the head of the MIRGHANIYYA religious brotherhood became its titular President. The Muslim League developed out of a combination of Ibrahim's TIGRE serf-emancipation movement with the independence-oriented Muslim faction of the MAHABER FEQRI HAGER, led particularly by JIBERTI and SAHO from the central highlands. Ibrahim brought these groups together in an organization that sought to speak for all Muslims on the issue of Eritrea's future, resolving in January 1947 that Eritrea should not be partitioned, but should become independent, if necessary after a UNITED NATIONS trusteeship. This remained the League's platform until it disintegrated in 1950.

Despite its sectarian name and the presence of religious leaders, the League was by no means an ISLAMIST organization, and it envisioned a secular, democratic Eritrea as its goal, although its very existence symbolized the religious polarization of the 1940s. Ibrahim used the League to promote his campaign for serf-emancipation during 1947-49, and this brought the League into conflict with the traditional SHUMAGULLE aristocracy, who consequently supported the pro-Ethiopian UNIONIST PARTY, marking an initial split in Muslim ranks. Nonetheless, the League received the support of almost the entire Muslim population in 1947, receiving 40.5 percent of the indirect vote in the FOUR POWERS COMMISSION polling. This made its leadership a continuous target of Ethiopian-supported ANDENET terrorists, particularly after the League became the most important party in the INDEPENDENCE BLOC in 1949.

Ethiopian intimidation, combined with inter-tribal antagonisms and the abrasiveness of Ibrahim Sultan's domineering personality led to the disintegration of the League, as MOHAMED OMAR CADI formed the Independent Muslim League of Massawa and then ALI MOHAMED MUSA REDAI built the Muslim League of the Western Province, removing the League's single largest bloc of constituents. By December 1950, when Ibrahim participated in the peace meeting at Cinema Impero (see AS-MARA), the League had ceased to exist as an effective political party, and its remaining leaders ran for seats in the First ASSEMBLY as members of the ERITREAN DEMO-CRATIC FRONT.

MUSLIM LEAGUE OF THE WESTERN PROVINCE *see* ALI MOHAMED MUSA REDAI.

- N -

NABTAB. The ruling caste of the BENI 'AMER tribal confederacy from the seventeenth through twentieth centuries, whose members held economic and political privileges similar to those of the SHUMAGULLE aristocracies of the TIGRE tribes.

NA'IB (Arab.: "deputy"). The rulers of the SEMHAR area from the seventeenth through mid-nineteenth centuries, the Na'ibs were descended from the BELEW aristocracy of HIRGHIGO, whose leading family obtained appointment as local "deputy" of the Ottoman Turkish governor of MASSAWA sometime in the late sixteenth century. After TURKEY abandoned its attempt to conquer the highlands, the Na'ib emerged as the most powerful political figure on the central coast, with the right to collect tribute for the nominal Turkish government. The leading Belew families intermarried with the Turkish garrison in Massawa (*see* KEKIYA) and gained control over the port and trade routes to the highlands. This marked the political division of central Eritrea between the coast, controlled by the Na'ib, and the central highlands, controlled by the BAHRE NEGASHI.

A desultory struggle between these two sides, which also involved the rulers of TIGRAI and Northern ETHIOPIA, ensued for several centuries, with the two sides applying trade boycotts intermittently, such as Na'ib Musa bin 'Umri's blockade of the caravan trade in 1690, and Iyasu the Great's retaliatory blockade of food-supplies to Massawa. But the two sides also cooperated, and during the early 1700s, the Na'ib lent political and economic support to both Tigrean rulers and the House of TSAZZEGA, receiving in return valuable grazing lands and tribute rights along the caravan route through the KEBESSA, particularly around DIGSA, BET MAK'A and HALHALE. The high point of the Na'ib's power was during the late eighteenth century, when the dynasty completely controlled the external trade of the Eritrean and Tigrean highlands. The Na'ibs had almost no military force, how-

ever, and their power was due primarily to the weakness
of both the highlanders and the Turks during this period.

The dynasty itself was weakened by internal rivalries, as it divided into two rival families: the senior Bet
Hassen, based in Hirghigo, and the junior Bet Osman of
Monkullo. In the early 1800s the Turks and then EGYPT
took advantage of this rivalry to seize Massawa   and
weaken the Na'ibs' power, though the Na'ib remained in
control of the port's mainland suburbs until 1848. European agents also played on these family rivalries to gain
concessions, and in the 1840s the struggle with Egypt resumed, while the rising military power of the rulers of
Tigrai led to repeated raids on the coast that further
weakened the Na'ibs.   In 1848 the Egyptians imprisoned
the senior Na'ib of Hirghigo and set-up the junior family
as "puppet" rulers. Thereafter, the Na'ibs remained tribute collectors for succeeding Turkish and Egyptian
administrations, and in 1865 even this power was
terminated by the new Egyptian colonial administration.

Though they attempted to recoup their position several times during periods of Egyptian weakness, the
Na'ibs never recovered their political power, but they
welcomed ITALIAN COLONIALISM under which they were
able to develop their commercial interests around Massawa, while others played a leading role in Muslim religious affairs. The Na'ibs' descendants figured prominently in Semhar politics during the 1940s-50s, and retained some moral authority until the 1970s, when most
fled as refugees.

NAKFA. The administrative center of the RORA area of the
Northern Highlands, Nakfa was the symbolic "capital" of
liberated Eritrea from 1978-91. Its heroic defense by the
EPLF against repeated Ethiopian OFFENSIVES makes it a
powerful symbol of Eritrean nationalism. Located on a
high plateau between Rora HABAB and the Hedai River
valley, Nakfa has been settled since antiquity. An Italian
colonial post was established in the 1890s and the village
developed into the administrative and commercial center
of the Habab region, with a population of three hundred in

the late 1930s. It grew during the 1940s-50s, and HAILE
SELASSIE I funded the construction of a substantial
mosque in the early 1960s. But the town's police post
made it the site of early ELF attacks, and a military garrison was established in 1967. On March 23, 1977, the EPLF
captured the town after a siege of several months, marking
the beginning of the front's campaign to liberate Eritrean
towns.

     In December 1978, following the EPLF's STRATEGIC
WITHDRAWAL, the town became the last urban center under Eritrean control. By January 1979 the EPLA was defending the town from a trench line anchored on DEN-DEN
mountain, and through 1980 a series of bloody battles
took place as the DERG attempted to break this line. In
February-March 1982 the Ethiopians renewed their assault, bombing Nakfa into rubble but failing to break
through. For Eritreans, the defense of Nakfa took on the
same symbolic quality that Verdun held for the French in
the First World War, and today it symbolizes the sacrifices made by Eritrean freedom FIGHTERS. Consequently,
the name is used by numerous public schools, institutions, businesses and is the official name of Eritrea's new
currency (see FINANCE).

     After liberation in 1991, Nakfa became the provin-
cial capital of SAHEL, and significant public investment
was made in rebuilding the town and constructing a jet
airstrip nearby. The Third EPLF Congress was held there
in February 1994, but the administrative reorganization
of 1995 deprived Nakfa of its status as a provincial capital. Today it remains a regional administrative and commercial center with a growing population. The EPLF's
wartime workshops nearby have been converted into the
Winna Technical School, where NATIONAL SERVICE workers are recycling the tons of derelict military equipment
surrounding the town.

NARA. One of Eritrea's nine "nationalities," the Nara (also
known as BARYA) speak a Nilotic language distantly related to that of their neighbors, the KUNAMA. They practice sedentary agriculture in the Gash-Barka Region north

of BARENTU, and are one of the area's most ancient population groups. The conversion of Nara people from their
ethnic religion to ISLAM began under FUNJ domination in
the seventeenth century. By the nineteenth century the
Nara were largely Muslim, organized under their independent tribal leader, the Nazir. Conversion to Islam did not
save them from continual raids by their Muslim and
Christian neighbors, however, who often enslaved them,
giving their ethnic name Barya the connotation of "slave"
among neighboring peoples (*nara* means "clans"). Consequently, the Nara welcomed ITALIAN COLONIALISM,
which recognized their tribal administrative structure
and ended the raids. By this time the Nara were divided
into two major subtribes: the Mogreb in the west and Hig-
gir in the east. Religion linked the Nara more closely with
their Muslim neighbors, and they largely supported the
ELF in the 1960s-70s, unlike the Kunama. Much of the
population fled as REFUGEES after 1967, and today many
returnees are settling in the agricultural belt along the
Sudanese border, as well as in their former homes.

NATIONAL ASSEMBLY (Tigrn.: Hagerawi Baito; Arab.:
Majlis). Created by Proclamation 37 of the PROVISIONAL
GOVERNMENT OF ERITREA (PGE) on May 19, 1993, the
National Assembly is the legislative branch of the GOV-
ERNMENT OF THE STATE OF ERITREA. It outlines, debates, modifies and approves all legislation, votes on the
budget and elects the President. The first National Assembly was composed of the EPLF CENTRAL COMMITTEE
plus sixty representatives, half of whom comprised the
chair, secretary and one woman member from each of the
ten regional councils (see LOCAL GOVERNMENT), the
other thirty were appointed by the PGE Advisory Council
and were required to include ten women. In March 1994
the Assembly voted to restructure itself to include the
seventy-five members of the new Central Committee of the
PFDJ, together with seventy-five popularly elected members, including the thirty previous regional council members. In 1998 elections will be held for a democratically-

elected National Assembly under the provisions of Eritrea's new CONSTITUTION.

NATIONAL   SERVICE. The Provisional Government of Eritrea issued a decree on November 6, 1991, instituting a
National Service Program (NSP) in Eritrea, requiring all
Eritrean citizens age eighteen to forty to perform eighteen
months of national service, beginning with six months of
military training. The goals of the NSP were to create a reserve army capable of defending the country, to mobilize
the population for national reconstruction and to build a
unified sense of national identity through a common experience of service to the nation. Particular emphasis was
placed on replicating the experience of self-reliance and
self-sacrifice for the common good that enabled the EPLF
FIGHTERS to win the ARMED STRUGGLE for independence.
      It took several years to draw up plans, create the
necessary infrastructure and register citizens for the
program, although some returnees from the DIASPORA began serving in government ministries as early as 1991. On
March 16, 1994, NSP registration began, with the first
group being drawn from the urban youth of ASMARA and
the second from across the country. Although there was
initial resistance, a media campaign stressing the sacrifices already made by freedom fighters soon mobilized
public support. By August 1, 200,000 eligible recruits
had registered, and the first group of 10,000 left for the
new military training camp at SAWA in the BARKA region, where they learned military skills and immersed
themselves in the Spartan life of EPLF "fighter culture."
During the same summer, 35,000 high school students
were mobilized independently of the NSP to help in road
and agricultural reconstruction.
      The first round of military trainees graduated at
Sawa in December 1994 in a ceremony attended by the
President, which has become a political tradition. By mid-
1997, when the sixth round graduated, almost 100,000
young men and women had completed military training.
Following this training they are required to work in national reconstruction projects or government programs for

a further year. In November 1995 the NSP decree was amended to include citizens age forty to fifty in the national reserve army. Provisions were added to insure compliance by all citizens in the diaspora, while those in Eritrea who had not completed their NSP were required to post a 60,000 *birr* bond before leaving the country.

NAVY. The Eritrean navy developed out of ELF sea transport operations begun early in the ARMED STRUGGLE. Most of the initial personnel were fishermen from SEMHAR and the BURE PENINSULA. Many of them joined the ELF-PLF in the early 1970s, where they ran the maritime supply system that was crucial to the early development of the PLF and EPLF. This system used speedboats to ferry munitions and evacuate wounded via the HANISH ISLANDS and YEMEN, but it declined after the EPLF's break with OSMAN SALEH SABBE, although intercoastal transport from SUDAN to the SAHEL coast continued.

By the mid-1980s the EPLF's naval personnel were aging, and after the Second Congress in 1987 the front began training a new naval force for offensive operations. High-speed fiberglass boats were purchased in the Arab world and a training base was established at the remote Sudanese port of Aqiq, just north of the Eritrean border. HUMED MOHAMED KARIKARI was appointed commander, and by 1988 the new force began its first operations against targets around ASSAB and MASSAWA. These operations were planned to familiarize the navy with Ethiopian defenses, and on the night of February 9, 1990, they culminated in a spectacular assault on Massawa naval base, where nine Ethiopian warships were sunk, enabling the EPLA to capture the city. Further operations around Massawa and the DAHLAK Islands from camouflaged bases on the Bure peninsula continued through 1991, when the navy also supported the DENKEL CAMPAIGN.

At the end of the war the navy acquired most of the remaining resources of the Ethiopian navy, although some best vessels remained interned in DJIBOUTI. New high-speed patrol boats were added to the fleet that by 1995 contained approximately forty-five vessels. In 1994

Tewolde Kelati took over as naval commander, overseeing the training and equipment of a new, professional force that served with distinction in the brief battles around the Hanish Islands in 1995. In October 1996, Humed Karikari returned to command the navy.

NEGUSSIE, "Agaw." *see* FRANCE; TIGRAI; WUBE.

- O -

OBEL (Tigrn: "wilderness"). An important BENI 'AMER splinter group from the ELF during 1970-75. The name comes from a seasonal stream in SAHEL, where the group held its first meeting. There is another Obel river in western Seraye, a tributary of the MAREB. The Obel group formed around Adem Saleh, a Beni 'Amer ELF veteran and head of the Military Committee of the KIADA AL-AMA during 1969-70. The group represented a complex mix of personal ambitions and tribalist sentiments, including Beni 'Amer veterans who feared the decline of their ethnic power in the ELF, yet ironically allied themselves with the radical reformist and Christian fighters who created the EPLF. Despite their disaffection, the Obel group participated in the ELF's Awate Conference, and some of the rank-and-file attended the front's First National Congress. But, disappointed with the Congress' outcome, in December 1971 they denounced the new ELF leadership and formed the Eritrean Liberation Forces.

In January 1972 the Obel group joined OSMAN SALEH SABBE and PLF representatives in Beirut to form the ELF-PLF. The ELF responded with an attack on Obel forces in Barka on February 28, 1972, capturing its leaders, including Adem Saleh (imprisoned until 1975). The remnants of Obel joined with the PLF in the first CIVIL WAR, forming a joint military command in October 1972, but refusing a complete organizational merger. In mid-1972 the "Obeliyyun" were joined by ABU TAYARA's Marya group, and both these conservative forces criticized the PLF's Marxist political program. Obel's isolation led to their defeat by the ELF in early 1974, and on June 13,

1974, Osman Sabbe engineered the reunification of Obel's remnants with the ELF-PLF. Sabbe clearly hoped to use the conservative Muslim Obeliyyun to counter the radical PLF leadership, and in 1975-76 they sided with him in his dispute with EPLF leaders, after which Obeliyyun formed the backbone of his ELF-PLF "third force."

OFFENSIVES (Ethiopian). During 1978-85 the Ethiopian DERG launched a series of eight offensives against Eritrean nationalist guerrillas that were intended to destroy the nationalist movement forever. During this period of the ARMED STRUGGLE many Eritreans, and all the FIGHTERS of the EPLF, marked time itself in reference to these offensives, which came close to overwhelming the outnumbered and outgunned Eritrean forces, and provoked the most desperate and brutal fighting of the entire thirty year war. Consequently, an outline of these offensives, and the names used to describe them, are crucial to an understanding of modern Eritrea.

After receiving massive new arms supplies from the USSR, the Derg launched its First Offensive from bases in TIGRAI on June 11, 1978. The largest forces attacked the ELF through GASH-SETIT, and by July ELF units had been defeated from BARENTU to TESSENEI and were retreating beyond the BARKA into the mountains of SAHEL or across the border into SUDAN. A second Ethiopian force moved north from around Enticho into the HAZAMO plain, and after the EPLF's failure to stop them at MAI AINI and DEKEMHARE, the front abandoned AKELE GUZAI and MASSAWA during July. A new battle line was formed by ELF and EPLF units north of ASMARA, and the Derg's Second Offensive was launched against this line on November 20, 1978. The Ethiopians broke through at ADI YAQOB, provoking the EPLF's STRATEGIC WITHDRAWAL from Keren to NAKFA, covered by rear-guard actions at ELABERED, Kelhamet, Mai-Mide and Tselab. The Third Offensive began in January 1979, pushing EPLF and ELF units back to a trench line around Nakfa, where Ethiopian frontal assaults on DEN-DEN mountain were repulsed on February 6-9. A Fourth Offensive was then launched from

March 30 to April 11, in which the Derg tried to outflank
Eritrean positions by opening a new front around AL-
GHENA. This offensive was defeated with heavy losses on
both sides, and the Eritrean trench line was extended almost four hundred kilometers to the Sudanese border. In
an attempt to penetrate this line, a Fifth Offensive was
made during July 14-26, but again failed to break through
to Nakfa.

   After this, the Ethiopian military, which had lost
almost 25,000 soldiers in the first five offensives, regrouped and rearmed for a massive new multipronged effort to end the Eritrean rebellion in its largest offensive
of all, the Sixth Offensive or RED STAR CAMPAIGN of
early 1982. The failure of the Sixth Offensive marked the
beginning of a shift in the military balance, but two more
offensives were attempted by the Derg before the decisive
change in military fortunes occurred in 1988. On March
23, 1983, the Ethiopians launched a surprise attack on
EPLF lines around HAL-HAL. Unlike other offensives, this
Seventh Offensive was never publicized. Eritreans called
it the Selata (Tigrn.: "Stealth") Offensive, and only defeated it after heavy fighting that lasted through June. A
final Ethiopian offensive, code-named Red Sea, was made
during October 10-25, 1985, with massive frontal assaults
on Nakfa and an airborne flank attack north of Hal-Hal.
Altogether, according to EPLF records, the Ethiopian army
lost over 50,000 dead in these eight offensives.

OM HAGER (Gash-Setit). A market town and administrative
center located just north of the SETIT River, a few kilometers from the Sudanese and Ethiopian borders. Om Hager
developed as an Italian border post at the end of the
nineteenth century, and its market attracted a heterogeneous community of Sudanese Arabs, Beni 'Amer and
Muslim Bilen. In the late 1950s the town grew as commercial farming spread in the Setit valley and along the plain
between Om Hager and GULUJ. Tigrinya, Kunama, Nara and
Wolqaiti farm workers settled in the town, and the construction of an all-weather road and bridge across the
Setit in the late 1960s stimulated population growth to

about 30,000. The Muslim merchant community supported the ELF, and many were arrested in 1967, but the town continued to flourish until 1974, benefiting from the great boom in sesame production across the river in the Ethiopian region of Humera. The boom ended in 1974, when the Ethiopian revolution produced an anti-Derg opposition movement in Humera and increased ELF activity in Om Hager.

In August 1975, after ELF guerrillas demolished Humera's radio receivers, the Ethiopian military commander Shembel Belew, crossed the Setit at night and surrounded the town with 1,200 soldiers. They forced the people into fields beside the swollen torrent of Khor Bademit. Sudanese and Ethiopian citizens were allowed to leave, but the soldiers pushed some seven to eight thousand Eritreans against the river and machine-gunned them. Some two hundred and fifty died, including over a hundred who drowned as they fled across the river. The massacre would have been greater but for the intervention of Eritrean police COMMANDOS. After the massacre many residents fled to Sudan, while people from Humera looted the town, stripping its zinc roofs. In February 1976, the army returned and burned what remained.

Until 1982, only an Ethiopian military post remained on the town's site, and the population remained less than 1,000 until after Eritrea's liberation. Today Om Hager is again a regional market center with a population of about 5,000. The government has ambitious plans to develop it as a center for AGRICULTURE development projects employing repatriated REFUGEES, but the current tense relations with SUDAN have hurt its commercial sector, which has long been involved in cross-border smuggling of Eritrean manufactures and alcohol.

OMER (Hamed) **EZAZ.** A prominent ELF military leader during the 1960s, Omer Ezaz was born into a BILEN Bet Tawqe family in HAL-HAL and in 1946 joined the SUDAN DEFENSE FORCE (SDF) where he rose to the rank of corporal and served with the UN in the Congo. Like many SDF members he was involved with the ELM before joining the

ELF in 1961, where he was among the earliest guerrillas to go into the field, carrying arms to HAMID IDRIS AWATE. In 1962 he led a raid on the police station in Hal-Hal, and in 1965 he was appointed commander of Zone 2, including his native SENHIT region. As the ethnic division of the ELF progressed, Omer came to represent the small Bilen contingent, but he never completely agreed with the leadership's divisive policies, although he refused to join the reformist ESLAH movement at AREDAIB in 1968. In an apparent attempt to strengthen his independent bargaining position for the upcoming ANSEBA CONFERENCE, Omer led his two hundred men in an ill-prepared attack on HAL-HAL in August 1968, where his force was utterly routed and he died of wounds on August 12.

ONA (Senhit).   A BILEN village northwest of KEREN, Ona (Tigre: "ruins") was organized by the Ethiopian military as a "strategic hamlet" in 1967. When the ELF ambushed and killed the commander of the Second Division, General Teshome Ergetu, on November 21, 1970, near Keren, neighboring villages were subjected to brutal reprisals. On November 27, 120 people were machine-gunned in their mosque at Basik Dera, and on December 1, Ethiopian army units surrounded Ona, killing 625 and burning the village. Further massacres followed at ELABERED, GHELEB and elsewhere, producing an exodus of REFUGEES from rural SENHIT.

OROTA (alt.: Erota). A plateau controlled by the "Black" MARYA in east-central BARKA between the Dzara and KERKEBET drainages that was used as an early guerrilla base. The EPLF used the name as a code word for the valley in northern SAHEL where they established their central hospital after 1976.

ORTHODOX   CHURCH. The Eritrean Orthodox Church (ErOC) achieved de facto independence from the Ethiopian Orthodox Church in September 1992. The Church follows the ancient Monophysite Christian doctrine of the Ethiopian Orthodox and Egyptian Coptic churches, and until 1992 Eritrean Orthodox Christians, who form the vast majority of the Christian half of the population (in 1952 there were 459,000 Orthodox Christians out of a total Eritrean population of one million), were ecclesiastically subordinated to these institutions (the Patriarch of EGYPT appointed Ethiopia's archbishop until 1950). The Monophysite or *tewahdo* (Ge'ez: "union") doctrine that distinguishes these churches centers on belief in the unity of Christ, as opposed to the dual nature accepted by Western and Eastern Orthodox churches since the Council of Chalcedon (451 A.D.). To this doctrine are added specific practices that distinguish the Ethiopian Orthodox Church, including acceptance of certain scriptures, indigenous saints and a number of Judaic practices, including those associated with ritual cleanliness and food, liturgical dancing, veneration of the *tabot* ("ark") and adherence to the Sabbath.

Orthodox Christianity entered the Eritrean region in the early fourth century, when the Syrian missionary Frumentius joined the AKSUMITE court and converted the future ruler, EZANA, to his Monophysite beliefs. Frumentius became the first bishop of Aksum, and much of the early evangelization of the region occurred in central Eritrea and northern TIGRAI, furthered by the arrival of the Nine Saints (Ge'ez: Tsadkan; lit.: "white men") in the fifth century. The most important institutions of the early Church were its monasteries, the earliest in Eritrea being founded at DEBRE SINA and DEBRE LIBANOS. Other important religious establishments developed along the PILGRIMAGE ROUTES through the northern highlands, including the community at HAGER NAGRAN.

By the fourteenth century all the BILEN, TIGRINYA and TIGRE-speaking peoples were Orthodox Christians, as were many of the BELEW in the lowlands. During this period the Eritrean region was a center for a monastic revival that accompanied the preaching of EWOSTATEWOS and led to the founding of the great monasteries of DEBRE BIZEN, DEBRE MARYAM and DEBRE MERQOREWOS. In the fifteenth century these institutions received huge land grants from Ethiopian emperors anxious to appease the regionalist sentiments of the TIGRINYA-based Ewostatian movement. But during the 1500s ISLAM spread in the region, and by the mid-1800s Orthodox Christians were confined almost exclusively to the TIGRINYA-speaking population of the KEBESSA. Among Tigrinya Christians the Church dominated every aspect of social life through its laws, calendar and ownership of roughly one-third of all Kebessa land. The abbots of the great monasteries, and particularly Bizen, together with the Nebur-ed of Aksum (a combined ecclesiastical and civil officer), were the most important spiritual authorities in the region, and the Church provided the only EDUCATION available to Christians before the arrival of European missionaries.

From the 1600s onwards Orthodox resistance to repeated Roman Catholic missionary campaigns strengthened the Church's conservative traditions, and in the mid-1800s Ethiopian authorities (particularly YOHANNES IV) intervened to forcibly restore Orthodox practice. Under ITALIAN COLONIALISM the Church was initially suspected of supporting Italy's Ethiopian enemies, but Italian policy wooed the Eritrean clergy away from Ethiopian political connections through subventions. In 1937 the Fascists even replaced the Ethiopian Abuna ("Archbishop") in ADDIS ABABA with an Eritrean, Kyrilos, who installed pro-Italian prelates, such as the Bishop of Eritrea and Tigrai, Abuna Marqos.

During the 1940s, HAILE SELASSIE I was successful in using the Orthodox Church to develop popular support in the Kebessa for Eritrea's unification with Ethiopia. Abuna Marqos, who remained Bishop of Tigrai, threatened excommunication against those supporting independence, and parish priests mobilized their congregations in support of the UNIONIST PARTY. The campaign was largely successful, and after FEDERATION, the Emperor funded new churches and religious institutions. The leading role of the Church in Unionist politics continued under the priest DIMETROS GEBREMARIAM, who worked to modernize the Church's administrative and educational activities, but came into conflict with the conservative Marqos, who died in a car crash in 1961. After this, leadership of the

Eritrean Church reverted to its traditional representative, the Abbot of Debre Bizen.

After liberation in 1991 the Provisional Government pushed to separate the Eritrean Church from its Ethiopian parent, empowering the Abbot of Debre Bizen, Philippos, to act as Eritrean Archbishop. An EPLF supporter, Markarios, who had been ordained as bishop by the Coptic Patriarch in Egypt, was also pressed on Philippos as his aid, and for a time worked to modernize and democratize the Church, engendering the enmity of both Philippos and the conservative Eritrean hierarchy, while the Ethiopian parent Church decried Markarios' ordination in Egypt as illegal. This and other controversies stalled Eritrean attempts to negotiate their separation from the Ethiopian Church, but in September 1992 a compromise was found that allowed the ErOC de facto independence and dismissed the controversial Markarios. Archbishop Philippos's conservatism, and continuing connection with the Ethiopian Church, led to further controversies in 1993, and in November he was replaced under government pressure by the more liberal-minded and nationalist Yaqob, who had previously been Bishop of Gondar. In December the ErOC achieved legal independence and Markarios was restored to a position of responsibility. Five Eritrean dioceses were formed and direct relations with the Patriarchate of Alexandria were renewed to provide for religious instruction.

OSMAN SALEH SABBE (1932-87). Leading figure in the early Eritrean national liberation struggle and master of fundraising in the Arab world, Osman S. Sabbe was later condemned as a self-aggrandizing opportunist by both the ELF and EPLF. Sabbe was born to an ASAWORTA SAHO family in HIRGHIGO in 1932 and attended the KEKIYA school in the 1940s. In 1950-52 he trained as a teacher in ADDIS ABABA, where he made connections with the Ethiopian Muslim community. He taught at the Kekiya school from 1953-58, where he was instrumental in shaping the political consciousness of a generation of nationalist leaders that included AL-AMIN MOHAMED SAID, IBRAHIM AFA and RAMADAN MOHAMED NUR.

Sabbe viewed Eritrea as a nation divided between two communities, Muslim and Christian, with the Muslims connected by language and culture to the Arab world. His political ideas were colored by the secular pan-ARABISM of the period, rather than by any strong ISLAMIST beliefs, and although he was an anticommunist and was willing to use religion in appeals for political support, he was never particularly devout. Sabbe's hope for an independent Eritrea was through links with the Arab world, and his writings and speeches continually advocated this through a selective use of history. Sabbe encouraged his students to attend secondary school in CAIRO, and imported teaching materials from Egypt, which led to his arrest on charges of subversion in 1958. In 1958/59 he traveled to Addis where he attempted to organize an Ethiopian Muslim political movement, and continued his clandestine activities around MASSAWA until he left the country fearing another arrest in 1960.

Sabbe settled in Jeddah, SAUDI ARABIA, where he began fundraising for a book on Ethiopia's mistreatment of Eritrean Muslims and also made contact with the Embassy of SOMALIA. In the Fall of 1961 he was contacted by IDRIS MOHAMED ADEM and joined the ELF. Late in the year he traveled to Mogadishu where he courted and received Somali support for the ELF, including passports and funds for arms purchases. In December 1962 he went to Eritrea as the only outside member to participate in the first ELF military conference. In 1963 he joined Idris Adem and IDRIS OSMAN GALADEWOS in the ELF's external leadership, convincing the others to disband the Executive Committee in favor of a popular Congress which never took place. Instead, Sabbe became the third member of the self-appointed triumvirate (*see* SUPREME COUNCIL) that ran the front's foreign affairs, taking the title of General Secretary in 1965. Sabbe's astute use of pan-Arabist propaganda for fundraising and his connections with the field leadership made him the most dynamic of the three leaders, and he soon became a rival of Idris Adem. After the creation of the ZONAL COMMANDS, Sabbe's power base lay in the coastal Zone 3, which was also the locus of the growing ELF reform movement.

Though Sabbe apparently hoped to harness this movement to his own personal ambitions, he did not support its initial call for democratic elections. After the ADOBAHA meeting created a General Command (*see* KIADA AL-AMA) dominated by Adem's supporters, however, Sabbe developed links with the reformist TRIPARTITE UNITY FORCES and in 1970 broke with the General Command to form a rival ELF "General Secretariat." Using his Arab connections, Sabbe funded the movement of dissident FIGHTERS out of ELF territory and their reformation as the PLF at SUDOHA ILA in DENKEL. During 1971 Sabbe continued to support dissident factions, including OBEL, and in January 1972 sponsored the merger of three dissident groups into the ELF-PLF, whose Foreign Office he led through his General Secretariat. For this he was condemned by the ELF, provoking the First CIVIL WAR. Sabbe retained his position as Eritrea's leading spokesman in the Arab world, addressing the Islamic Foreign Ministers Conference in 1973, and he used his external resources to provide the ELF-PLF with automatic weapons and supplies via boat from Aden.

Although Sabbe's support was critical to the ELF-PLF's survival, his Arabist, and increasingly Islamist, political views were the antithesis of those of its radical field leadership (soon to form the EPLF). To counter the power of this leadership Sabbe backed the conservative Obel and ABU TAYARA groups. By 1975 the alliance of necessity that held the ELF-PLF together was disintegrating, and Sabbe struggled to retain his leadership position by negotiating a merger with the ELF without the field leadership's approval. This provoked a final break with the EPLF in March 1976, after which Sabbe attempted to create a "third force" from his few remaining conservative supporters. Although his military forces were inconsequential, he commanded enough diplomatic support to begin negotiations with the ELF, which produced further acrimony and splits within this front. By 1978, Sabbe was

condemned by all the Eritrean field forces, and his PLF-
RC was reduced to concocting lies about non-existent field
forces intended to retain its credibility among Arab supporters.

The destruction of the ELF in 1981 gave Sabbe a new
chance to play a leading role, and during 1982-86 he attempted to dominate the Unity Organization of conservative and Islamist-oriented ELF FACTIONS. His rivalry
with ABDALLAH IDRIS and others helped destroy this organization, however. After a serious car accident outside
Gedaref in March 1986, Sabbe was unable to continue his
leadership role, although his organization continued to
attract Arab donations, which were used particularly for
schools for Muslim REFUGEES in SUDAN. Osman Sabbe
died on April 6, 1987.

- P -

PASTORALISM (and Agro-Pastoralism). Rural Eritreans
rely on a mixture of agriculture and pastoralism (i.e.,
agro-pastoralism) in almost every region of the country.
In the highlands, many farmers move with their animals to
winter pastures at lower elevations where they also cultivate second crops in a cycle known as *sebekh-saghem*
(Tigrn.: "to seek pasture, to return to native village"; also
used to describe dry and wet seasons). In the lowlands
most people cultivate grain or gardens in addition to
livestock raising. Today, more animals are kept by highlanders than lowlanders. Nonetheless, the lowlands are
correctly seen as the predominant pastoral region, where
people such as the BENI 'AMER, HEDAREB and MARYA
rely in large part on their animal herds, while other TI-
GRE-speaking groups, and many AFAR and SAHO practice
agro-pastoralism.

Lowland agro-pastoralism is largely the product of
an arid environment that cannot sustain sedentary agriculture, and seasonal movements in search of grazing land
and stream-bed cultivation sites mark the lives of these
pastoral peoples. Livestock herds traditionally provided
insurance against droughts and other natural disasters, as

well as indispensable animal traction for agriculture. Since the turn of the century, when the Italians first introduced modern veterinary medicine, there has been a general increase in the animal population (total livestock was 1.1 million in 1905; 2.8 million in 1928; 2.2 million in 1938; 3.6 million in 1946; 7.2 million in 1992). But since the 1960s the combination of war, refugee flight, and widespread drought decimated Eritrea's lowland herds (war alone killed an estimated 350,000 animals). The population relying on pastoralism as its primary economic means has decreased from 36 percent during the BRITISH ADMINISTRATION to 6 percent in 1992.

The Eritrean government is currently grappling with the issue of restructuring the lowland pastoral economy to enable repatriated pastoralist REFUGEES to settle long enough to attend school, to have easier access to markets for their animals, and to adapt to the development of irrigated AGRICULTURE projects in some of their former grazing areas. There are indications that some of the traditional lowland pastoral economy will never regain its former shape, as repatriating refugees settle in new villages and a new generation follows other economic pursuits. But livestock production remains an important part of the economy, with animal exports, particularly to the Arab world, providing one of the few sources of foreign exchange in the years immediately following liberation.

PEASANTS' ORGANIZATIONS. Beginning in 1975, both the Ethiopian DERG and the EPLF attempted to organize rural Eritreans into peasants' associations as a means of increasing their political control and furthering their programs of economic redistribution and land reform. The Derg's program was implemented largely in the highlands between 1979 and 1985, and though it encountered some resistance, it was accepted in most villages as a means of continuing local control over land resources. The Ethiopians used Peasant Associations to organize Food-for-Work Programs, and also for the far less popular tasks of military conscription and militia service. The EPLF's peasant associations were developed during 1976-78 in the villages under their control, with the early association at ZAGHER providing a model. These associations oversaw more equitable land redistribution and attempted to arbitrate land conflicts. A congress of EPLF peasant representatives met at KEREN in March 1978 to form the National Union of Eritrean Peasants (NUEP). But with the EPLF's retreat to SAHEL later in the year, the NUEP became largely inactive, as the front controlled few agricultural villages. The NUEP became primarily a political organizing tool for developing LOCAL GOVERNMENT in liberated areas during the late 1980s, as the front abandoned its radical social reform program. In 1991 the NUEP was dismantled and its resources handed over to local village councils.

PEOPLE'S FRONT FOR DEMOCRACY AND JUSTICE (PFDJ; Tigrn.: Hezbawi Gunbar neDemocrasen Fetehen). Eritrea's ruling political party was formed at the Third Congress of the EPLF in February 1994 to replace the liberation front. Its initial membership and leadership were drawn entirely from the EPLF. ISAIAS AFWERKI was elected Chairman of its nineteen-member Executive Council, but many younger and less well-known fighters were elected to both its Executive and Central Councils (the latter has seventy-five members and replaces the EPLF's CENTRAL COMMITTEE). The Third Congress approved a National Charter outlining the basic principles of national unity, secular democracy and social and economic justice on which Eritrea's new CONSTITUTION will be built, and these principles, together with a series of specific Resolutions formed the political platform of the party. Many of the 1994 Resolutions pertained to the principles outlined in the Charter, but others underscored the PFDJ's commitment to care for former FIGHTERS and the poor.

Since its formation, the PFDJ has been opened to all Eritreans who wish to join it. Although its members currently form the Eritrean government, the PFDJ is constituted as an autonomous political party, and expects to contest elections with other national parties in the future. The PFDJ inherited many of the EPLF's assets, including

Red Sea Corporation and Trans-Horn Trucking, which are currently overseen by the PFDJ Economics Department, led by Hagos "Kisha" Gebrehiwet (*see* COMMERCE). Profits are used to fund rehabilitation programs and pension funds for disabled fighters and the families of MARTYRS.

PEOPLE'S LIBERATION FORCES (PLF; Tigrn.: Hezbawi Hailetat) *see* ELF-PLF; EPLF.

PETROLEUM. Eritrea's most important petroleum reserves seem to lie in what is known as the ZULA Tract: a block of coast and sea bottom stretching from the BURE PENINSULA and the Gulf of Zula to beyond the DAHLAK Archipelago. Oil seepage was noted at Zula in 1868, and during 1935-40 the Italian company AGIP drilled test wells in Dahlak, finding oil and gas. Drilling was resumed in the Dahlak tract during the 1960s, when Gulf, Mobil and Esso all acquired leases on the coast. During 1965-68 surveys proved that likely geological structures for oil reserves existed, and in 1967 one Mobil test well poured out 500,000 cubic meters of natural gas per day for fifty-five days. This prompted the Ethiopian government to sign an agreement with Shell Oil to exploit the coast in 1970, but the ARMED STRUGGLE precluded further exploration. The DERG negotiated contracts for exploration with Amoco, BP and IPCC (Canada), but these were never developed.

At liberation the Eritrean MINING department revoked BP's contract, but Amoco and IPCC kept theirs into 1994. Meanwhile, a 1992 survey showed 120,000 square kilometers of potential hydrocarbon acreage offshore from Dahlak to Zula. In November 1993 the government's Petroleum Operation Code was drafted, including high taxes, but low tariffs and royalties for exploration and recovery. In September 1994 the U.S.-based Andarko exploration company, an associate of Amoco with expertise in finding salt-dome formations containing petroleum, negotiated an exploration contract with the Ministry of Energy, Mining and Water Resources for the Zula Tract, and serious exploration began in 1996.

Petroleum refining at ASSAB, using oil from the
Persian Gulf, has been a major INDUSTRY since 1967, and
during the mid-1990s the refinery's production for the
Ethiopian market was Eritrea's only significant export. In
1995 the refinery had an annual   capacity of 800,000
metric tons.

PETROS   SOLOMON. Eritrea's current Minister of Marine
Resoucres, and a leading figure in the EPLF. Petros
Solomon was born in ASMARA in 1951 and attended high
school in both Asmara and ADDIS ABABA, where he
studied at the University before joining the EPLF in 1972.
A confidant of ISAIAS AFWERKI, Petros rose to become
one of the three members of the Military Committee in
1975, and from 1977-78 he commanded the Eastern Front
around MASSAWA. In 1977 he was elected to the Political
Bureau of the CENTRAL COMMITTEE, and as head of Mili-
tary Intelligence and Communications he served on the
Military Committee and General Staff through liberation.
In July 1992 Petros was appointed Minister of Defense, in
March 1994 he became Minister of Foreign Affairs, and in
June 1997 he moved to head the Ministry of Marine Resources. He is married with three children.

PILGRIMAGE   ROUTES. From the late AKSUMITE period
through the sixteenth century, and even beyond, a major
Orthodox Christian pilgrimage route ran from Northern
ETHIOPIA through SERAYE to ASMARA, and then along the
northern highlands through HAL-HAL, Rora HABAB,
HAGER NAGRAN and on to the port of SUWAKIN in SU-
DAN, where pilgrims embarked for Jerusalem, via EGYPT
or Aqaba. Muslim pilgrims also used this route at times,
but more commonly they embarked at MASSAWA for Jeddah and Mecca.

POLICE. The first Eritrean police forces were organized
under ITALIAN COLONIALISM, beginning with the all-European Carabinieri Reali. Other police forces developed
attached to a proliferation of colonial ministries and in-
spectorates. In the 1930s the Fascists added their own

all-European Polizia d'Africa Italiana, which engaged in a bitter rivalry with the Carabinieri. During 1941-44, the BRITISH ADMINISTRATION dismantled these forces and reorganized them into a single force staffed with British and Italian officers and Eritrean enlisted men. On February 5, 1944, 2,800 Eritrean policemen went on strike to protest the continued presence of Italian officers and a new uniform of shorts and sandals which they found undignified. The British accused pro-Ethiopian Unionists of fomenting the strike and replaced two hundred educated Christians with Muslim lowlanders. After this, the police force remained largely uninvolved in politics until FEDERATION. Italian officers were phased out and Eritreans trained to replace them. The British also formed a paramilitary police strike force to combat SHIFTA activities, known as 101 Force.

In 1952 the police came under the control of the Eritrean Chief Executive, TEDLA BAIRU, who retained a British police commissioner until his resignation in 1955 when the new Chief Executive appointed Tedla Ogbit as police commissioner. Tedla supported the pro-Ethiopian policies that led to ANNEXATION, and his deputy, Goitom Gebrezghi, police commander of ASMARA, was instrumental in suppressing the 1958 General Strike (see L A B O R ORGANIZATIONS). After annexation, Tedla, Goitom, and second-in-command, Zemariam Azazi, were flown to ADDIS ABABA and entertained by HAILE SELASSIE I. Nonetheless, Tedla Ogbit had a change of heart following annexation, and on June 11, 1963, was found shot to death in his office after he had apparently been involved in a plot to restore Eritrea's independent status. This plot was part of the larger ELM plan to infiltrate the Eritrean police and use them to carry out an anti-Ethiopian coup d'état. Though the plan never materialized, many Eritrean police were sympathetic to the nationalist movement. Immediately after Tedla's death, police headquarters was surrounded by Ethiopian troops and a number of leading Eritreans were detained. Zemariam Azazi replaced Tedla and was promoted to Brigadier-General.

General Zemariam worked to staff the police almost entirely with loyal TIGRINYA Christians, and in 1965 helped form the paramilitary Police COMMANDOS. But in 1968 he was replaced by a series of Amhara officers, beginning with Ardatchew Imechew. In 1974 leadership of the force was returned to the ranking Eritrean, General Goitom Gebrezghi, as part of the revolutionary Ethiopian DERG's early attempt to regain Eritrean support. But. the loyalty of the police was no longer assured, and following the Ethiopian Revolution the police and commandos frequently intervened to stop Ethiopian military abuses of Eritreans. In late 1974 many police began to desert to the liberation fronts, taking their arms with them in a trend that had begun as early as 1963. In January 1975 General Goitom fled to the Sudan through ELF lines, and in February much of the Eritrean police force and Commandos deserted to the nationalist guerrillas. After liberation EPLF FIGHTERS filled police functions, and in 1994 a new civil police force was inaugurated, composed of specially trained former fighters.

POLITICAL PARTIES. As of 1997, political parties outside the ruling PEOPLE'S FRONT FOR DEMOCRACY AND JUSTICE (PFDJ) have not been organized, although the new CONSTITUTION makes them legal. Before the present, Eritreans were legally entitled to organize political parties during only one period of their history, from January 1947 until the end of FEDERATION in November 1962. After 1958 this right was in reality severely curtailed. The period of greatest freedom and activity was under the BRITISH ADMINISTRATION from 1947-52, when the Independent Eritrea Party, LIBERAL PROGRESSIVE PARTY, MUSLIM LEAGUE, National Party, Pro-ITALY Party, UNIONIST PARTY and their multiple off-shoots, as well as the larger INDEPENDENCE BLOC and its successor, the ERITREAN DEMOCRATIC FRONT, were formed to contest the future of Eritrea and the elections for the first ASSEMBLY. These parties represented a tremendous diversity of political opinions and their activities often reinforced the fragmentation of the country along ethnic and religious lines. The rise of the Ethiopian-supported Unionist Party precluded any access to power for other parties after 1955, although a few independents did survive in the Assembly until 1960.

The liberation fronts were not political parties in the usual sense of the term, for their was no democratic legal structure for them to operate in. After liberation in 1991, the PROVISIONAL GOVERNMENT OF ERITREA specifically banned all political organizations outside the EPLF. In 1992 President ISAIAS AFWERKI even criticized the formation of provincial development associations in Barka and Senhit because of their "narrow provincial chauvinism." In its 1994 National Charter the EPLF leadership made clear it would not tolerate political parties organized along religious, regional or ethnic lines because these could reignite the divisions that historically weakened the country. The blanket right to organize contained in the CONSTITUTION may be restricted by the emphasis on "national unity" in other parts of the document, and the forthcoming Electoral Law is expected to contain rules to insure that all parties have a national, multiethnic basis.

POPULATION. As of 1997 there is no complete census of Eritrea's population. Estimates ranging from 2.5 to 3.5 million have been made based on projections from a complete census in 1931 and a partial census in 1952. Given comparable African growth rates from 1931, Eritrea should have a population of between 3.5 and 4 million. But since almost one million Eritreans lived outside the country (*see* DIASPORA; REFUGEES), and war and famine probably slowed population growth in the 1970s-80s, a figure of about 2.5 million residents is likely for the immediate post-war period. In 1997 government statistics on regional populations and refugee REPATRIATION give a total of about 2.8 million.

The first Italian colonial population estimate of 191,127 in 1893 was certainly an undercount, missing many areas of the west and north, and reflecting temporary emigration caused by the FAMINE of 1890. The 1905 census showed 274,944, again probably an undercount. The only really complete census ever taken, in 1931, gave a total of 596,013 Eritreans (52 percent Muslim and 47 percent Christian). The BRITISH ADMINISTRATION's indirect census of 1952 showed an increase in the Eritrean population to 1,031,000 (plus some 32,000 aliens). The Ethiopian administration's estimate in 1966 was 1,583,964.

Today the Eritrean Government is not involved in promoting population control. Popular wisdom holds that Eritrea needs to replace the people lost in the war, and currently the country has a high birth rate with over half the population estimated to be under eighteen years of age. Nonetheless, Planned Parenthood opened a healthcare center and two voluntary sterilization clinics in ASMARA in 1994.

PRESS (Newspapers and Literature). Until the nineteenth century, all literature in the Eritrean region was in the form of hand-copied manuscripts, most of which were religious or legal in character. The printing of GE'EZ began with British missionary society Bibles in 1810. Missionary tracts in ARABIC followed. The first printing press in the region was established by Catholic Lazzarists at MASSAWA during 1863-64, followed in 1879 by a Lazzarist press at KEREN. Protestant missionaries were particularly active in producing religious works in TIGRINYA, with the first dated to 1869. In 1885 the Swedish Evangelical Mission (SEM) established a press at Monkullo (Massawa) and began production in Tigrinya. Vernacular Bibles were opposed by the ORTHODOX CHURCH, and in 1880 YOHANNES IV ordered them all burned.

In 1890 Italian colonists at Massawa established the first commercial press and newspaper, *L'Eritreo*. In 1891 a second press was founded and published *Corriere eritreo*. In 1900 these presses and that of the Catholic mission were all transferred to ASMARA. By 1910 the SEM was printing religious tracts in a variety of local languages, and during 1912-15 published the first Tigrinya newspaper, *Melekete selam* ("Message of Peace"). Religious and educational literature in local languages increased through the 1930s, with eighty-six Tigrinya titles published between 1881 and 1940. The growth of the ITALIAN POPULATION in the 1930s spurred increased production of newspapers, journals, and business publications, sustaining four commercial printing presses, as well as those of the government and the churches. This continued into the 1940s, as the loosening of political restrictions under the BRITISH ADMINISTRATION allowed leftist and other papers to briefly flourish.

In 1941 the British Information Office began publishing the *Eritrean Weekly News,* and in 1943 added Arabic and Tigrinya versions, employing WOLDE-AB WOLDE-MARIAM to edit the Tigrinya *Semenawi Gazeta.* With the formation of POLITICAL PARTIES a number of other newspapers appeared in Amharic, Arabic and Tigrinya, including the UNIONIST PARTY's *Etiopiya* (Amh.) and *Hibret* (Tigrn.: "Union"); the MUSLIM LEAGUE's "Voice of Eritrea" publications, *Sawt al-Ertra* (Arab.) and *Dimitsi Ertra* (Tigr.); Wolde-Ab's *Hanti Ertra* ("One Eritrea"); and those of MOHAMED OMAR CADI. After FEDERATION the Unionist government acted swiftly to destroy the independent press, closing all rival local-language papers by 1954, including the *Semenawi gazeta.* The official *Il quotidiano eritreo, Zemen,* and *Etiopya* continued publication under government control, while four Italian newspapers survived until the early 1960s; including the Italian government-funded *Giornale dell'Eritrea* and the CATHOLIC CHURCH's *Veritas et vida,* both of which continued into the 1970s. *Hibret* was revived in 1963, and remained the largest Tigrinya paper through 1990.

The decades of the 1940s and 1950s also saw a flowering of Tigrinya-language literature (*see* TIGRINYA), but during the 1960s this declined under Ethiopian restrictions, and by the 1970s very little was being published in Eritrea beyond the government-controlled press. Outside the country the ELF began publishing political tracts in Arabic, English and other languages in the 1960s, and during the 1970s there was an outpouring of political

publications in the DIASPORA, including the revival of
Tigrinya language publications by the EPLF from 1971.
Many early nationalist publications were reproduced on
mimeograph machines, but as the fronts became more sophisticated they had much of their printing done in
Lebanon and Italy. In the late 1970s the EPLF developed
its own printing presses in SAHEL, and began publishing
a bi-weekly journal for Eritrean FIGHTERS, *Dimtsi Hafash*
("Voice of the Masses") and monthly news magazines including *Vanguard* and *Liberation* in Tigrinya, Arabic and
English. The range of local-language publications increased during the late 1980s, including the EPLF's
weekly newsmagazine, *Saghem* ("Return [to one's native
land]") and a number of historical and political books.

   After liberation, in 1992, the PGE began publishing
the newspaper *Hadas Ertra* ("New Eritrea") in Tigrinya
and Arabic, and in 1994 the English language weekly, *Eritrea Profile* was added. In addition to these government-
owned newspapers there are several religious weekly and
monthly publications in Tigrinya and Arabic, but no
commercial newspapers as of 1997. 1994 circulation
statistics for the government newspapers show a much
larger Tigrinya readership (200,000 per issue) than
Arabic (40,000) or English (14,400). A number of
Tigrinya and Arabic books have been produced locally
since 1992, but the old equipment at the Adulis, Dogali
and religious presses has impeded output. The completion
of a 15 million *birr* modern printing plant outside Asmara
in 1997 by the U.S.-based, Eritrean-owned, Red Sea Press
will greatly increase production of local language materials, including educational texts and journals. The new
CONSTITUTION guarantees freedom of the press and
"public access to information," and a press law has been
drafted ending government censorship, but the government
will retain the right to control foreign ownership and importation of printed matter. Enforcement of penalties for
libel and misinformation will be left to the courts.

PRISONS and PRISONERS OF WAR. Eritrea's modern prison
system was created by the Italian colonial administration,

which built prisons in ASMARA, KEREN, and MASSAWA in the 1890s, and sent political prisoners to bleak confinement at ASSAB or on Nocra Island in the DAHLAK Archipelago. The British used Eritrea's prisons to intern SHIFTA during the 1940s, and they were used by the Eritrean POLICE in the 1950s, when a maximum security prison was built at ADI QWALA. A great expansion of prisons began in the 1960s as the ARMED STRUGGLE developed, and after the DERG came to power new prisons were opened at EXPO, MARYAM GHIMBI and the Governor's Palace in Asmara, as well as other sites, where political prisoners were routinely tortured and executed. Captured Eritrean FIGHTERS were interned at SEMBEL military base in Asmara, and at Alem Bekagne ("End of the World") prison in ADDIS ABABA, where many were executed.

The liberation fronts also held political prisoners, including some of their own cadres, but for the EPLF the major issue was caring for Ethiopian prisoners of war (POWs). Although the EPLF captured tens of thousands of Ethiopian soldiers over the course of the war, the Derg refused to acknowledge their existence, and because the EPLF were not internationally recognized, the International Committee of the Red Cross (ICRC) provided no assistance. Consequently, the front was forced to feed and house the POWs on its own very meager resources. POWs were organized to produce their own food and conduct their own schools, but the EPLF's ultimate solution to the POW problem was to release most of them after conducting "political education" courses that frequently brought them to sympathize with the Eritrean cause. In November 1981 the EPLF proposed to release 3,000 POWs, but failed to obtain Ethiopian safe-passages for them or ICRC aid. They remained technically "free" but behind Eritrean lines. By 1985 the EPLF held 8,000 POWs, but still failed to obtain ICRC assistance. Finally, after the Battle of AFABET brought tens of thousands more, the EPLF began its own unilateral release of over 10,000 in December 1989, followed by 2,500 more in January 1990.

The released POWs faced further hardships, including imprisonment and reconscription when they returned

home, but the EPLF released 8,000 more in May 1990,
followed by over 30,000 in early 1991. Following liberation, during the summer and fall of 1991, the PGE released
86,000 more POWs, and in July 1992 the last 900 officers
were   turned over to the Transitional Government of
Ethiopia. Today the Eritrean police maintain jails in major
towns, and a number of quasi-political prisoners, including the leaders of the 1993 mutiny (*see* FIGHTERS) and
some former Eritrean members of the Ethiopian security
services charged with grave crimes, are held at Adi Qwala
prison. In Asmara, vagrants are also periodically rounded
up and given the choice of living in work camps or returning to their home villages.

PROSTITUTION. Courtesans and concubines have been a
part of   HABESHA culture for many centuries, and are
well documented in literature and popular songs. But the
development of paid urban prostitution was a phenomenon
of ITALIAN COLONIALISM, and particularly the 1930s,
when tens of thousands of single Italian men flooded
Eritrea's cities and rural Eritrean women found they
could earn money through more transitory forms of the already established institution of *madamato* (concubinage).
Prostitution flourished in the bars of the "native" quarters of major towns and particularly ASSAB, ASMARA and
MASSAWA throughout the war booms of 1935-45, and became an established aspect of urban life. It continued
through the 1960s, serving both local men and foreigners
(such as Americans at KAGNEW STATION), and then increased dramatically in the 1970s as the Ethiopian military garrison grew.
        By the 1980s Assab, Asmara and Massawa were
filled with prostitutes (Arab.: *shermuta;* Tigrn.: *mnzerma*
or *me'amn),* many of them migrants from TIGRAI. Bars, often owned by successful prostitutes, were the most common businesses in the garrison cities. After liberation the
EPLF acted swiftly to curtail widespread prostitution, de-
porting over two thousand Ethiopians and beginning a
public campaign associating it with the depravity of the
DERG period. The urban spread of AIDS (*see* HEALTH

CARE), primarily through prostitution, has been another major concern. Today, although prostitution is legal, practitioners are subject to government control and monthly health checks. In 1995 there were 1,500 prostitutes registered in Asmara (55 percent Eritrean and 45 percent Ethiopian), with the majority being TIGRINYA-speakers from rural areas.

PROTESTANT CHRISTIANITY (Tigrn.: Khenisha). Protestant Christianity entered the region in the early nineteenth century with missionaries bound for Ethiopia. Only in 1864 did Lutherans of the Swedish Evangelical Mission (SEM) establish themselves in Eritrea with the intention of converting the KUNAMA. The SEM founded a school at Monkullo (MASSAWA) in 1866 and worked with MUNZINGER to distribute Bibles in the KEBESSA, laying the foundations for the SEM community at TSAZZEGA. In 1872 other SEM missionaries established themselves at BELEZA and GHELEB, and during 1873-77 they were involved in controversies with the ORTHODOX CHURCH and local and Tigrean authorities in the Kebessa, culminating in the murder of one Swede and two Eritrean converts after the Battle of WOKI DUBA. The SEM then concentrated its energies on GHELEB in the MENSA' region, and on its school and PRESS at Monkullo until more favorable times arrived in the highlands with the Italian conquest.

In 1890 the SEM's Monkullo school was moved to Beleza, which became the center of their activities through the 1920s. By 1907 the SEM operated nine schools for Eritreans that offered the best EDUCATION available in the Italian period. An indigenous Protestant or "Khenisha" church developed with congregations in numerous villages, such as ADI NEFAS, as well as major towns. Because of their education, Protestants tended to figure prominently among Eritrea's early intelligentsia, with WOLDE-AB WOLDE-MARIAM being the most remarkable example. The Swedes' interest in educating Eritreans, and their support for HAILE SELASSIE I in Ethiopia, where they were also active, made them suspect to Italian authorities, and in 1932 the fascists began to harass them. In 1935, when Sweden supported Ethiopia against Italy, the SEM was expelled and its school system was administered by local Protestants under state control. Nonetheless, by 1952 there were sixteen thousand Eritrean Protestants.

The BRITISH ADMINISTRATION allowed the SEM to return along with a number of other Protestant sects during the 1940s, the most prominent coming from the UNITED STATES. American missionaries became increasingly involved in Eritrea during the 1950s and 1960s, including the American Evangelical Mission, which was involved in building schools and HEALTH CARE clinics primarily in lowland areas due to Haile Selassie's refusal to allow proselytization among Orthodox Christians. In ASMARA the Lutheran Church remained the most prominent sect, with its own neighborhood (Gheza Khenisha) and several churches. After a complete cessation of activities during 1975-91, Protestant missionaries are again active in Eritrea and the Khenisha population is increasing, particularly in urban areas. The Protestant churches are organized nationally under the umbrella of the Evangelical Churches of Eritrea.

PROVISIONAL GOVERNMENT OF ERITREA (PGE). The PGE was created in May 1991 by the EPLF's Executive Committee. Its legislative body was the EPLF CENTRAL COMMITTEE and its Secretary-General was ISAIAS AFWERKI. In May 1992 the Central Committee formalized this structure through its Proclamation 23, which created an Advisory Council of twenty-eight members, representing the heads of EPLF departments and the military, to serve as the PGE executive branch. The PGE ruled Eritrea until May 1993, when the GOVERNMENT OF THE STATE OF ERITREA was formed.

- Q -

QOHAIN (Seraye; alt.: Cohain). Comprising the lands in the bend of the MAREB River, west of GUNDET, Qohain is a remote and rugged region with strong historical links to TIGRAI. Its Orthodox monasteries and particularly the sanctuaries of DEBRE MARYAM and Debre Dehuhan (Enda Oninas) are some of the most venerated in Eritrea, and its population remains deeply attached to Orthodox traditions. During the mid-1960s HAILE SELASSIE I's government made use of these historical traditions to enlist Qohain peasants into an anti-ELF militia (BANDA), while ELF massacres of Christian peasants in 1967 reinforced the area's pro-Ethiopian loyalties. The "problem of Qohain" continued for the nationalists until the demise of the ELF, and it was only in 1984 that the EPLF began to operate in the area. To insure the area's integration into post-war Eritrea, the government constructed a new road linking the village of Mai Mene in the center of the district to the main ADI QWALA road at Enda Giorgis.

QWATIT (Akele Guzai; alt.: Cohatit). A large village on the road between MENDEFERA and ADI KAIYEH, Qwatit today has a population of about 30,000 and is developing as a market center. On January 13-14, 1895, an Italian colonial force defeated an attack on the town by the Tigrean army of Ras Mengesha.

- R -

RADIO. Radio broadcasting in Italian began during the colonial era, and an English-language station at KAGNEW STATION served ASMARA from the early 1960s. AMHARIC and TIGRINYA broadcasts began in the 1950s on government-controlled radio, and TIGRE broadcasts were added in the 1960s in an Ethiopian attempt to use local-language radio to counter the nationalist movement. ARABIC broadcasts began in the late 1960s under the direction of Abdurahman Abdella Siraj.

Nationalist political broadcasts were made into Eritrea from the Arab world beginning with WOLDE-AB WOLDE-MARIAM in 1956, and continued irregularly under the ELF, but an Eritrean-operated radio station was not created until the EPLF founded Dimtsi Hafash (Tigrn.: "Voice of the Masses") in January 1979. The station broadcast from a remote peak near HAGER NAGRAN and provided central Eritrea with EPLF contact after the STRATEGIC WITHDRAWAL. The station provided the largely illiterate rural population with its first exposure to many modern and nationalist ideas, developed at the Information Departments' office in Fah. In the mid-1980s service was expanded from Arabic, TIGRE and Tigrinya into AFAR, AMHARIC and KUNAMA. The signature sound of a Kalashnikov assault rifle opened the nightly news bulletin containing detailed war coverage. After liberation Dimtsi Hafash was moved to Asmara where it today remains Eritrea's only national radio station, providing news, music and educational programming in six of Eritrea's languages.

RABITA AL-ISLAMIYYA *see* MUSLIM LEAGUE.

RAILROAD. Eritrea's narrow-gauge rail system, today under reconstruction, once linked MASSAWA, ASMARA, KEREN and AGORDAT, extending a total of 216 miles (348 kilometers). The railroad was built by Eritrean and Italian laborers under Italian colonial direction, beginning with a purely military line connecting mainland Massawa with the fortress at SA'ATI in 1888. In 1895 this line was run across the causeway to Tewalid Island, where the main rail terminal was built, and work was begun on extending it into the highlands. After many delays caused by finance and terrain the line reached Mai Atal in 1901, GHINDA in 1904, Nefasit in 1910, and Asmara in 1911, where a major depot was built.

The extension of the line to Keren was not completed until 1922, after which plans were laid to push the line to TESSENEI and the Sudanese border, where the Italians hoped to gain the traffic from the KASSALA region. The line reached Agordat in 1928, and was extended a further nineteen miles to Bishia by 1932, when the project was abandoned because a competing (British) line had reached Tessenei via Kassala and Port Sudan. During the Second World War the BRITISH ADMINISTRATION tore up the line from Agordat to Bishia, and the link to Tessenei was maintained by a railroad-operated truck service. In the 1940s the railroad employed 1,500 people, including 1,325 Eritreans, and was the locus of one of Eritrea's earliest LABOR ORGANIZATIONS. In 1952 the Ethiopian state took over the line, despite a UN directive in favor of Eritrean control. Nonetheless, Eritreans made up most of the technical management by the late 1950s. Although the line's aging equipment and narrow gauge made it increasingly uncompetitive with ROAD TRANSPORT, in 1965 it still carried 446,000 passengers and 200,000 tons of freight. But during the 1960s the line became a target of guerrilla attacks, and in the early 1970s it was repeatedly sabotaged, leading to closure of the Keren-Agordat section. Finally, in 1976, service was discontinued and the workforce was pensioned off.

The rolling stock deteriorated in Asmara and Massawa, and much of the track was torn up by soldiers and used to reinforce fortifications during the ARMED STRUGGLE. By 1991 the line was almost completely destroyed. Nonetheless, in 1992 an Italian engineering firm was contracted to study rebuilding the line, but estimated it would cost $400 million. Instead, in 1994 the Ministry of Transportation organized NATIONAL SERVICE volunteers and others under the direction of retired railroad workers to rebuild the tracks from Massawa to Asmara using a large stock of new rails dating from the 1930s that were discovered on Tewalid Island. Railroad reconstruction became a material symbol of Eritrean self-reliance, and by December 1994 a commuter tram was running from the Massawa mainland to Tewalid Island. Over the following years the line has rebuilt into the mountains towards Asmara, reaching Ghinda in 1997.

RAMADAN MOHAMED NUR. An early member of the ELF and first Secretary-General of the EPLF, Ramadan M. Nur was born in HIRGHIGO in 1941 to a TIGRE-speaking merchant family. He attended KEKIYA school and in 1957 went to CAIRO for secondary school. In 1960 he and MOHAMED ALI OMERO were the first of their generation to join the ELF, and in 1963 Ramadan went with the first

group to receive military training in Syria. He rose to become political commissar of Zone 4 in 1965, and was one of
the original group of five sent for training in CHINA in
1967. He was involved in the ESLAH reform movement and
TRIPARTITE UNITY FORCES, and maintained ties with his
former teacher, OSMAN SALEH SABBE.

In 1970, Ramadan was among the founders of the PLF
at SUDOHA ILA, and in 1971 he was elected to lead the
PLF, after which he developed close links to the ALA
group led by his colleague from China, ISAIAS AFWERKI.
Together with Isaias and a few others, Ramadan created the
nucleus of what was to become the EPLF within the ELF-
PLF. At the front's First Congress in 1977 he was elected
Secretary-General, a position he held until 1987, when he
became vice-secretary general. Ramadan's self-effacing
humility and commitment to social revolution made him a
model of the EPLF's "fighter culture." After liberation he
served in a number of critical positions, including a brief
spell as governor of DENKEL in 1993, but at the EPLF's
Third Congress he announced his retirement from political life and in a stirring address reminded his colleagues
that they must pass on the leadership to younger generations and not cling too long to power.

RASHAIDA. One of Eritrea's nine "nationalities," the
Rashaida number about ten thousand today. They inhabit
the coastal plain from MASSAWA to the Sudanese border
and speak ARABIC. Most are pure Arabs, descended from
migrants who fled southern Hijaz in 1846 to escape the
rise of the Saudi Arabian state. They first settled on the
coast between SUWAKIN and Aqiq, but moved south into
Eritrea during the Mahdiyya. Today many live in Eastern
Sudan, particularly around KASSALA. The Rashaida are
divided between three main clans (Zinenu, Barasa and
Baratik), and through their practice of endogamy have
preserved their Arab culture and language, including the
embroidered black clothing of their veiled women. Primarily CAMEL herders and merchants, many Rashaida fled
to Sudan in the last fifteen years of war. Since liberation
the government is encouraging them to settle in permanent

locations, particularly around SHE'EB and Wed Ilu in northern Semhar, where 173 families settled in 1993, gaining access to clinics and schools.

RED STAR CAMPAIGN (Amh.: Wefri Keiyeh Kokhob). The Ethiopian military's 1982 Sixth OFFENSIVE was part of an elaborate, multi-faceted campaign, code-named "Red Star," by which the DERG intended to end the Eritrean rebellion forever. Preparation for the campaign began in 1980 under the new military governor, DAWIT WOLDE-GIORGIS, who planned to win the "hearts and minds" of Eritreans with social and economic development projects in the large area of the country that had returned to Ethiopian control in 1979. During 1981 about $50 million was spent on reconstructing damaged infrastructure, industries, public buildings and educational institutions, as well as on resettling and rehabilitating people from war-shattered areas. A similar sum was slated for 1982, but it fell victim to the failure of the Derg's military campaign.

   The main focus of the campaign was on defeating the EPLF. By early 1982 an army of over 100,000, supported by massive resources from the USSR, was deployed in Eritrea. Public pronouncements predicted the rebels' utter destruction. In January the Ethiopian dictator, Mengistu Haile Mariam, moved his office to Asmara to oversee operations, and on February 15, 1982, the Sixth Offensive was launched on three fronts: BARKA (where the Derg was quickly defeated), NAKFA and Northeast Sahel (around ALGHENA), where Ethiopian units even crossed into SUDAN around KARORA. The initial assaults involved an unprecedented use of air power and reports of poison gas, for which the EPLA had equipped FIGHTERS with homemade gas masks. Despite severe bombardments and high casualties among the outnumbered Eritreans, the Ethiopians failed to break through and heavy fighting continued into March, when the EPLA counterattacked. Further Ethiopian attacks were made on the Nakfa and Northeast Sahel fronts through June, but after the February failures, Mengistu returned to Ethiopia and the social campaign faded out. Total Ethiopian casualties were estimated by the EPLF at 33,000, while over 2,000 Eritreans died. Red Star marked the height of the Ethiopian military and political effort in Eritrea, and its defeat gave the EPLF great confidence, despite their serious losses.

REFERENDUM (1993). Eritrea's independence from ETHIOPIA was sanctioned by a national referendum held during April 23-25, 1993. The question posed was: "Do you approve Eritrea to become an independent, sovereign state?" and of the 1,102,410 Eritreans who voted, 99.8 percent answered "yes." All Eritrean citizens over eighteen, male and female, residing inside or outside Eritrea were eligible to vote, and almost all did. Only in Ethiopia and among the DIASPORA in the Middle East were there significant numbers who abstained.

The concept of holding a national vote on the question of Eritrea's political status was first raised by Eritrean nationalists in the 1940s, but was never pursued by the UNITED NATIONS. A formal proposal for a national referendum was made in November 1980 as part of the EPLF's seven-point plan to end the ARMED STRUGGLE, but was rejected by Ethiopia. The EPLF retained it as a basic component of their political platform, and in 1989 raised the idea in meetings with the DERG arranged by former U.S. President Carter. The proposal was again raised at the London Conference in May 1991, where it was accepted in principle by both the leaders of the new Ethiopian government and the UNITED STATES. On his return to Asmara, ISAIAS AFWERKI promised a referendum on independence within two years, and in July the new Ethiopian government formally supported the proposal. In December the Ethiopian president notified the UN that his country recognized the Eritrean people's right to determine their political future, clearing the way for Eritrea's recognition as a sovereign state following the referendum.

Preparations for holding the Referendum were made by a Referendum Commission, chaired by Dr. Amare Tekle, that was established by the PROVISIONAL GOVERNMENT OF ERITREA (PGE) in April 1992. The Commission obtained funding from the UNITED NATIONS, the U.S.

($350,000) and other countries beginning in July 1992. Citizens were registered, a computerized national role of voters was drawn up and then divided into electoral districts. Volunteers were recruited from Eritrea's schools and trained to man the polling places, which were built to a country-wide standard. Elaborate precautions were taken to insure an honest vote, and two teams of international observers (one from the UN) were invited to insure fairness. All reports indicated an entirely free and fair vote, but after thirty years of war the result was a foregone conclusion. Immediately after the results were announced on April 26, 1993, the Secretary-General of the PGE declared that Eritrea was an independent sovereign nation, although formal independence was not celebrated until May 24.

REFUGEES. Between 1967 and 1991 close to one million Eritreans fled their country to escape war and FAMINE. The vast majority of these refugees (over 700,000 total) settled in SUDAN, both in UNITED NATIONS-funded camps and around the cities and towns of the northeast. Many others formed a widespread DIASPORA in the Middle East, Europe, and North America (over 200,000). In addition, about 350,000 Eritreans were internally displaced by the war during 1976-78, and over 400,000 during 1988-91, when most of them found shelter in the camps of the ERITREAN RELIEF ASSOCIATION. Since liberation the REPATRIATION and resettlement of refugees has been a major preoccupation of the Eritrean government.

 Eritrean refugees fled in three major waves: (1) 1967-71; (2) 1975-80; (3) 1984-86. Refugee flight began in March 1967 with the first Ethiopian counter-insurgency campaigns in Western Eritrea, and by May 28,000 Muslim lowlanders had fled to Sudan. By 1971 there were 55,000 refugees (over 95 percent Muslim) in Sudan, most of whom settled around Gedaref and KASSALA or in agricultural villages along the Eritrean border. The second wave began in March 1975, and by May Ethiopian massacres had driven out 40,000 new refugees, raising the refugee population in Sudan to 85,500 by year's end and sending tens of thousands more to SAUDI ARABIA and other Middle Eastern countries. The heavy fighting of 1978-79 and the second CIVIL WAR of 1980-81 forced out most of the internally displaced, and by 1981 there were 419,000 refugees in Sudan.

From 1975 on the UN High Commission for Refugees (UNHCR) became increasingly involved in caring for refugees in Sudan. In an attempt to make them "self-supporting," during 1978-79 the Sudanese government, with UNHCR agreement, forcibly moved many refugees from urban areas and "transit camps" like Wad el-Hileau and Wad Sherife to agricultural settlements in the eastern interior including Abu Rakhim, Es-Suki, Qala en-Nahal and Um Rakuba, where they were expected to work on large mechanized farms. The second wave included large numbers of Christian TIGRINYA-speakers, tens of thousands of whom (including all the best educated) managed to gain refugee status in Europe and North America. The liberation fronts were active in organizing the refugees politically and often provided EDUCATION and internal justice for the communities. The internecine quarrels of the fronts, and particularly the ELF FACTIONS were fought among refugees in the Sudan; while the EPLF gained much of its financial support from the diaspora.

From mid-1984 through 1985 a third wave of refugees fled heavy fighting in the western lowlands and widespread famine. This wave included over 200,000 Tigreans from Northern Ethiopia, and by 1986 there were 772,000 Eritrean/Ethiopian refugees in Sudan. Although over 150,000 of the Tigreans repatriated in 1986-87, few Eritreans returned before 1991. At the end of the war there were an estimated 850,000 refugees outside the country, with probably over 600,000 resident in Sudan. Many had integrated themselves into the economies of their new homes, and their children were becoming dual citizens; but the great majority, including most of those in Sudan, hoped for REPATRIATION to Eritrea.

REPATRIATION. One of the most important issues facing Eritrea at the time of liberation was repatriation of the close to 850,000 refugees outside the country in 1991. While many of those in the DIASPORA in Western countries, the Middle East and Ethiopia had the resources to repatriate voluntarily if they wished (and the majority seemed to prefer to wait), about half a million of those resident in SUDAN were largely without resources and many lived in UNITED NATIONS High Commission for Refugees (UNHCR) funded camps. The PROVISIONAL GOVERNMENT OF ERITREA (PGE) immediately came under pressure from UNHCR to develop a program to repatriate refugees from the Sudanese camps, as well as self-settled refugees. But the lowland areas from which the great majority of these refugees had come had been severely damaged by the ARMED STRUGGLE, and the PGE had no resources to help reintegrate the refugees. Fearing that a large influx of refugees would seriously disrupt the social and economic fabric of the country if it was not properly planned and funded, the PGE created a Commission of Eritrean Refugee Affairs (CERA) to develop a plan for controlled refugee repatriation.

During 1992 several drafts were proposed and the PGE received much criticism from UNHCR and a number of Western NGOs for its failure to immediately undertake repatriation utilizing foreign NGOs. By December 1992 a final Eritrean proposal was drafted calling for a three-phase repatriation over three years covering some 450,000 refugees. The project was to be implemented solely by Eritrean agencies, and almost 90 percent of the refugees were scheduled to settle in the northern and western areas of the country (with the bulk scheduled for GASH-SETIT, Barka and Sahel), where the government would provide water, HEALTH CARE access, schools and temporary housing. The proposed minimum budget was $210 million. After further negotiations the UN accepted the plan, codenamed PROFERI, and created a UN Development Program (UNDP) mission to coordinate it. UNHCR, however, was only willing to fund transport and reception center costs, while the rest would be left to donor countries, NGOs and the government's own scanty resources.

A donor's meeting held in Geneva in July 1993 raised pledges of only $32 million, and in view of the limited resources available, a Pilot Program was developed to resettle 25,000 in nine sites. The Sudanese government added further difficulties, but in September 1994 an agreement was reached between Sudan and UNHCR, and in November the Pilot Program began. In the meantime 119,000 refugees had spontaneously repatriated by the end of 1994 according to CERA, with the majority settling in Gash-Setit, ASMARA, Sahel and SENHIT. Despite the break in diplomatic relations with Sudan and closure of the CERA office in KASSALA, by May 1995 almost 20,000 refugees had been repatriated in the Pilot Program and a number of lessons were learned concerning the siting and construction of new settlements.

The success of the Pilot Program increased donor interest in funding Phase One of PROFERI, which was scheduled for the 1995-96 dry season with a target of 100,000 refugees and a proposed budget of $76 million. As the Eritrean government entered a virtual state of war with Sudan, however, its ability to organize the outflux became increasingly difficult, and after members of the Islamic JIHAD infiltrated the returnees in late 1995 the government temporarily blocked further repatriation. As relations between the countries deteriorated, a wave of spontaneous returnees fled Sudanese harassment, and by July 1996 a total of over 165,000 refugees had repatriated, largely from Sudan, including 25,000 in PROFERI. By mid-1997 only an estimated 150,000 Eritrean refugees remained in Sudan. In 1996 the CERA and ERRA were merged to form the Eritrean Relief and Refugees Affairs Commission (ERRAC), responsible for the integrated repatriation of refugees. In May 1997, further clashes over refugee policy led to the expulsion of UNHCR's expatriate staff.

REVOLUTIONARY COUNCIL. Not to be confused with the earlier Revolutionary Command (1965-69), the Revolutionary Council (RC) was formed at the ELF's First National Congress in 1971. Intended to be the ruling body of the front, the RC's power was diminished by the formation of a parallel Executive Committee (*see* ELF). Nonetheless, the RC remained the more important of the two bodies until the demise of the front in 1981, after which its title was claimed by competing ELF FACTIONS.

RISTI. In its broadest sense *risti* means "use-rights" to village-controlled land in the KEBESSA. As such the word has an application in all traditional LAND TENURE systems, including DESA and TSELMI. But the word also denotes a specific type of land tenure in which use-rights are held by the ENDA group, who are descendants of the original settlers of the land. In this second sense, *risti* is used to denote the exclusive enda-based system of land tenure that was common to much of SERAYE and parts of other provinces before 1975.

A third use of the word is in conjunction with the concept of GULTI (right to land tax), and in precolonial times *risti-gulti* lands were those held in hereditary possession by powerful families or, more frequently, by monasteries and other institutions of the ORTHODOX CHURCH. By the nineteenth century, most of the non-Church *risti-gulti* lands paid their taxes directly to the Governor of TIGRAI or his local representatives, and this arrangement was preferred by their inhabitants because it gave them more control over tax collection.

ROAD TRANSPORT. Until the 1930s, Eritrea's road system was poorly developed and commerce relied largely on the RAILROAD or animal transport. The Italian invasion of ETHIOPIA, sparked the first highway construction program, beginning in January 1935, when 50,000 Italian laborers joined Eritrean road-building crews to construct a paved road from MASSAWA to ASMARA, and then to the Ethiopian border on two separate branches via AKELE GUZAI and SERAYE. When the cutoff from Nefasit to DEKEMHARE was completed in 1936, that town developed as the center of an Italian road transport industry that by

1938-40 employed 100,000 men and 7,000 heavy trucks to transport goods from the coast to ADDIS ABABA. In 1938 a road from ASSAB to Desse (Ethiopia) was also completed, which eventually made Assab the main port for Ethiopia's road transport industry. Italian entrepreneurs made fortunes in road contracting and trucking, and continued to dominate regional road transport through the 1960s. During the BRITISH ADMINISTRATION the truck fleet was reduced to 1,400, but in the 1950s/60s many new Fiats were added to the fleet. As the Italian drivers and mechanics who controlled the industry through the 1940s departed, Eritreans took their jobs and by the 1960s Eritrea was the center of road transport in the region (including Ethiopia and northeastern SUDAN) and Eritreans were the great majority of the region's truckers and mechanics.

The paved roads inherited from Italian colonialism were kept up through the period of HAILE SELASSIE I's reign, often with grants in aid from the UNITED STATES, and in the 1970s Eritrea had 600 kilometers of asphalt roads, 700 of all-weather gravel, and 4,500 of seasonal dirt. After 1975 the ARMED STRUGGLE seriously undermined Eritrean road transport, as the aging truck fleet was scattered to Ethiopia, the liberation fronts and Sudan, and military vehicles chewed up the roads. On the other hand, in the remote northern and western areas both the Ethiopian and Eritrean armies built hundreds of miles of new dirt roads, including the EPLF's hand-built Challenge Road linking its mountainous base area with Sudan. During the 1980s the EPLF developed a sophisticated trucking department, complete with repair shops and a growing fleet of Mercedes trucks used both by the front and by its ERA relief organization. These trucks, popularly known as *adetat* (Tigrn.: "our mothers"), brought a constant stream of supplies from Port Sudan to the Sahel and thence to many other areas of the country, traveling at night to avoid air attack.

At liberation in 1991 Eritrea had 3,845 kilometers of roads, including 807 paved, 840 gravel, 402 improved dirt, and 1,796 unimproved dirt. Many of these roads were in terrible disrepair, particularly the crucial trunk route from Massawa to Asmara and thence to KEREN and the west. The government allocated $27 million of its scarce resources to road reconstruction, beginning with the Massawa-Asmara and Asmara-Keren routes. By 1995 the Massawa-Keren sections had been completed, as well as many smaller roads, and work was beginning on the road from Keren to TESSENEI. A major new road is also being built to link Dekemhare to GASH-SETIT via MENDEFERA, AREZA, TOKOMBIA and BARENTU.

At the end of the war Eritrea had only 267 buses and interurban public transportation was limited, but by 1994 there were 767 private buses providing extensive service under an efficient government-regulated system. Trucking also was developed using the EPLF's aging fleet and a few private trucking companies. In 1992 the EPLF trucks were turned over to the PFDJ's Trans-Horn Trucking Company, which is now the major trucking company in the country. By 1994 it had a garage in Dekemhare with 400 employees, five mobile garages, 122 trucks, and 146 trailers.

RORA (Tigre: "high place"). The Rora region of Eritrea is in SAHEL, now divided between the ANSEBA and Northern Red Sea Administrative Regions. Commonly referred to as the Northern Highlands, the Rora mountains form a string of plateaus running parallel to the coast from northern SENHIT to the Sudanese border, averaging 2100 to 2700 meters in height. The plateaus have been used for agriculture and grazing since ancient times. From south to north the most important plateaus are: Rora Laba (or Kristan), Rora Endlal (or Massal), Rora BAQLA, Rora Maret, Rora Kaiyeh, Rora Tselim, and the Roras Hager Abbai and Hager Nish. The first three Roras together form the Rora HABAB.

- S -

SA'ATI (Semhar). Site of several important battles, Sa'ati is situated where the coastal plain behind MASSAWA begins to climb into the foothills on the route to ASMARA.

In October 1883, the troops of Ras ALULA annihilated an
Egyptian company which had occupied the site against
Alula's objections. This ended Egyptian pretensions in the
area and led to the HEWETT TREATY of 1884. In 1887 an
Italian colonial army reoccupied the site and on January
25, 1887 Alula's troops made a frontal assault on their
entrenched position, but suffered heavy losses. This induced Alula to change strategies and ambush an Italian
relief column at DOGALI the following night. The Italians
then built a fortress at Sa'ati linked by RAILROAD to
Massawa and held it against YOHANNES IV and an army of
80,000 in March 1888. During the colonial period Sa'ati
became a watering stop on the Massawa-Asmara railroad.
In 1974 the Ethiopian military reoccupied the Italian
fortifications, and fierce fighting occurred nearby during
the 1977 and 1990 EPLF assaults on Massawa.

SAB'A (Sabean) *see* SOUTH ARABIA.

SABDERAT. A small tribe bilingual in TIGRE and ARABIC
who live on the border with SUDAN opposite KASSALA
and north of TESSENEI. The village of the same name forms
the frontier post on the direct route from AGORDAT west
to Kassala which was built during the Italian colonial period, and was an important border crossing point for
REFUGEES from BARKA during the ARMED STRUGGLE.

SAGENEITI (Akele Guzai). A small town on the road from
DEKEMHARE to ADI KAIYEH, Sageneiti is the capital of
TSENADEGLE district and rose to prominence in the nineteenth century as the center of CATHOLIC CHURCH missionary work in AKELE GUZAI. It had a population of nine
hundred in 1875, and in 1883 a Catholic school was
founded there by Lazzarists. Because of its strategic position as the gateway to the central Eritrean plateau, the
Italian administration fortified the hills above the town
during the 1890s and made it an administrative center. It
was also the home of BAHTA HAGOS, and became headquarters of the BANDA forces in Akele Guzai commanded
by Bahta and an Italian lieutenant named, ironically,

Sanguinetti. The town grew as a colonial Residenza and by 1950 had a population of 3600. In the 1960s it became a base for Eritrean COMMANDOS and a locally recruited Christian banda. The Ethiopian army garrisoned the old Italian forts, but in July 1977 the town was liberated by the EPLF after a three-day battle. Sageneiti returned to the DERG a year later, and was retaken by the EPLF in a bloody battle on May 28, 1990. Today it is a district administrative center and benefits from renewed Italian Catholic investment in its schools.

SAGHEM (Tigrn.: "return to home"). The SAGHEM movement developed in 1983 among some ELF FACTIONS in Sudan who wished to return to Eritrea to fight in the ARMED STRUGGLE alongside the EPLF. On August 11, 1983, the secular nationalists grouped in the ELF-Central Council finalized a unity agreement with the EPLF enabling them to return to the field and fight alongside the front, but still maintain a separate organization with the understanding that a complete merger would eventually take place. Leading figures in this Saghem movement were IBRAHIM IDRIS TOTIL, who brought his NARA fighters with him to the field, Tewolde Gebre-Selassie and Zemhret Yohannes. Saghem was given a base area at Ghirghir and Totil was elected to head what was known as the ELF-Central Leadership (CL). In 1985 Saghem participated in the EPLF campaigns around BARENTU, but was divided by internal fighting. Totil's ELF-CL negotiated an agreement for full merger with the EPLF on November 22, 1986; but Tewolde Gebre-Selassie led a large minority who refused merger and formed what was known as the Eritrean Democratic Movement or Saghem Qetsel. While the ELF-CL joined the EPLF at the Second and Unity Congress in 1987, Tewolde's group returned to Sudan and from there joined the TIGREAN PEOPLE'S LIBERATION FRONT (TPLF) in TIGRAI, where they divided into two factions, Saghem Qetsel and the Democratic Movement for Liberation of Eritrea (DMLE), both of which remained in ETHIOPIA after liberation.

SAHEL (Arab.: "coast"). The former province in northeastern Eritrea which includes the northern highlands and coast, now part of the Northern Red Sea Administrative Region. In colonial times Sahel's administrative center was NAKFA, and it formed a remote and economically undeveloped area populated primarily by TIGRE-speaking pastoralists from the AD SHAYKH, BET ASGHEDE and the smaller Ad Mu'allim (noted Islamic scholars), Ad Sawra and BET MA'LA tribes. Its small harbors at Mersa Teklai and Mersa Gulbub were undeveloped. During the ARMED STRUGGLE the mountains of Sahel became the main base area for the guerrilla armies due to their remoteness, rugged terrain and proximity to SUDAN. Much of the war was fought in Sahel, including the terrible battles around AFABET, ALGHENA and Nakfa, and most of its population fled as refugees. The EPLF instituted some agricultural projects in the RORA areas, and the Ethiopian military built large bases on the plains, but this development did not make up for the tremendous damage incurred by the war. Since liberation the Eritrean government has been involved in reconstruction projects in the area, overseen from 1992 to 1995 by the veteran nationalist governor, MAHMOUD SAID NAWD. Besides the projects around Nakfa, a 500-unit refugee REPATRIATION center has been established at Mahimet, and a FISHING training center is operating at Mersa Gulbub.

SAHO. One of Eritrea's nine "nationalities," the Saho speak an Eastern Cushitic language closely related to AFAR. They seem to be a northern extension of the Afar people who moved along the eastern shore of the Gulf of ZULA and into the foothills of AKELE GUZAI during the ninth to twelfth centuries, A.D. They incorporated other ethnic groups from the remnants of the AKSUMITE EMPIRE, and by the fifteenth century had settled the eastern highlands of Akele Guzai as well, including the plateaus around KOHAITO and SENAFE, while others even crossed the MAREB into SERAYE. Some Saho groups also mixed with Arab immigrants around HIRGHIGO in SEMHAR, and the aristocratic castes of both the MARYA and MENSA' peoples trace their origins to the same Saho/Arab ancestor as several Saho subtribes. Originally pagan, the Saho are almost entirely Muslim today, and the few highland clans that are Orthodox Christians have largely been assimilated into the surrounding TIGRINYA-speaking culture. Most Saho are agro-pastoralists or merchants, but a few highland groups are settled farmers.

The Saho are divided from south to north into the following major sub-tribes: (1) Irob, mostly inhabiting the TIGRAI region of Agame; (2) MINI-FERE; (3) SENAFE; (4) DEBRI-MELA; (5) HASO; (6) ASAWORTA; (7) TOR'A. In 1933 the Italian ADMINISTRATION organized all the Saho into five tribes (2-6 above) under government-appointed chiefs, and placed the Tor'a and other smaller subtribes under the Asaworta. The British and Ethiopian administrations retained this system. By 1970, Saho-speakers numbered some 121,000, but during the early ARMED STUGGLE they suffered from Ethiopian military raids and internecine fighting with their Christian neighbors (the Saho largely supported the ELF under ABDELKRIM AHMED in the 1960s). By 1980 much of the population fled to SUDAN and SAUDI ARABIA as REFUGEES, and they have been slow to return.

SALEH AHMED IYAY. An important early nationalist leader, Saleh Iyay was born to a BILEN family in Keren and attended the Point Four technical school in ASMARA during the 1950s. He emigrated to Port SUDAN, where he met MAHMOUD SAID NAWD and in 1958 joined him in founding the ELM. In 1959 Saleh established ELM cells in AGORDAT and Keren, and he remained with the organization until its demise in 1965, after which he joined the ELF and worked in their foreign office. In 1970 he joined OSMAN SALEH SABBE in what became the foreign office of the ELF-PLF. He stayed with Sabbe after the initial split with the EPLF, and worked with various ELF FACTIONS in Sudan during the 1980s. He returned to Eritrea immediately after liberation, and in 1992 was appointed Governor of AKELE GUZAI, where he worked until the administrative reorganization of 1995.

SALT. Eritrea's most important mineral resource, salt has been mined and produced in the region since ancient times. The DENKEL depression contains large salt deposits straddling the border with Ethiopia that have traditionally been mined and transported to the highlands. The most important Eritrean deposits are around Dalul and BA'DA, and have historically been worked by the Dahimela AFAR. Along the coast the high saline content of the Red Sea and the heat of the environment make salt-evaporation more productive than almost anywhere in the world. Small-scale production by coastal Afars was used by the local FISHING population and exported to YEMEN since ancient times, but large-scale production only began under ITALIAN COLONIALISM.

    The Saline di MASSAWA company started production in 1905, followed by the Societe des Salines di ASSAB a few years later. Employing poorly-paid local labor, by the 1920s total production averaged 100,000 to 150,000 tons per year, with most of the exports going to India. This boom ended in 1927 when Ghandi forced the Indian government to impose stiff import duties, and thereafter most of the production went to Japan. Small-scale salt production by locals also continued around Assab and along the Denkel coast. In 1952 the Italian salt works were taken over by the Ethiopian state and in 1953 Eritrean workers struck unsuccessfully against Ethiopian management. Production was then mechanized, increasing the yield to over 100,000 tons per year at both Massawa and Assab and making salt Eritrea's single largest export earner. The Assab works were further modernized in the 1960s to supply the Ethiopian internal market, and continued to produce throughout the ARMED STRUGGLE, but the Massawa works, popularly known as "Salina," were seriously damaged in the MASSAWA BATTLES of late 1977, and were only partially repaired during 1980-81. After liberation a boom in local production by coastal Afars led to clashes over land rights around some salt pans, but the increase in industrial production after 1993 made it increasingly difficult for locals to compete. In 1994 the Assab plant was refurbished with new machinery and iodinization was added. Since liberation, salt has been Eritrea's single largest export income earner, with the bulk of production going to Ethiopia. As the state-owned salt works are refurbished, salt is also beginning to be sold again on the world market.

SAUDI ARABIA. Because of its proximity and spiritual importance to Eritrea's Muslim Population, Saudi Arabia, and particularly its port city of Jeddah, has long been linked with the Eritrean region. An Eritrean immigrant community developed in Jeddah in the 1950s, and in the 1960s the city was an important base for ELF diplomatic and fundraising activities. Saudi support for Eritrean nationalism declined as the ELF and EPLF turned to Marxism in the 1970s, but the Saudis encouraged the more conservative Muslim elements of the ELF FACTIONS and ELF-PLF to take an increasingly ISLAMIST political line after 1981.

Working with OSMAN SALEH SABBE, the Saudis sponsored a series of unity conferences, beginning at Jeddah in January 1983, that led to the short-lived United Organization. During this period the Saudis were deeply involved in SUDAN, and their Islamist policies led directly to the formation of the Eritrean Islamic JIHAD in 1987. Although they began to regret their support of Islamist political extremism in the late 1980s, they remained adamantly opposed to the EPLF, whose Jeddah offices they closed in 1985. Over 50,000 Muslim Eritrean REFUGEES settled in Saudi Arabia, with over 35,000 registered in Jeddah by 1993, including prominent former ELF leaders and much of the Muslim merchant community of MASSAWA.

In late 1992 the Saudis hosted the formation of an ELF "National Pact Alliance" in Jeddah, provoking ISAIAS AFWERKI to denounce Saudi Arabian interference in Eritrean affairs in his New Year's speech. The Saudis retaliated by closing the PGE diplomatic mission, expelling four Eritrean government representatives and threatening not to allow Eritrean residents to vote in the REFERENDUM on independence. The PGE refused to modify its criticism, and the Saudis relented in April, 1993, following the intervention of the head of the UNITED NATIONS' UNOVER mission. Reversing its policy, Saudi Arabia then recognized Eritrea, provided immediate relief aid for victims of a storm near Massawa, and in November 1994 pledged $35 million for ENERGY development. Predictably, in 1996 Saudi Arabia discreetly supported Eritrea in its dispute with YEMEN over the HANISH ISLANDS and in its campaign against the NIF government in Sudan.

SAWA (Barka). The Sawa River is a seasonal tributary of the BARKA, running northwards parallel with Sudanese border. Sawa "Forto" was an Italian colonial garrison and local administrative center, whose police post saw several ELF attacks in the 1960s, while the more remote Sawa valley was the site of both ELF and EPLF bases. In 1989 the area was chosen for an experimental, foreign-funded, "integrated development project" that attempted to transform the local population's economy from PASTORALISM to settled farming with ecologically disastrous results. In 1991 the EPLF dropped the project and people have returned to raising livestock.

Because of its proximity to the Sudanese border the area was also subject to Islamic JIHAD incursions, and in June 1991 a pitched battle was fought at Homib between the EPLA and Jihad. During March-June 1994 the NATIONAL SERVICE program built its military training camp near Sawa "Forto," catapulting Sawa into national prominence. The camp has dramatically changed the local economy, transforming Sawa into a center for southwestern Barka.

SEBHAT EPHREM. A leading figure in the EPLF, Sebhat Ephrem was born in Aksum, TIGRAI, to Eritrean parents from ASMARA in 1951. His father was a Protestant-educated schoolteacher and hospital administrator, and Sebhat attended the Evangelical Lutheran School in Asmara before going on to study pharmacology at the university in ADDIS ABABA. He left to join the EPLF in 1972, where he worked in the administration department. He had a gift for developing organizational systems, while his blend of intelligence and humor was well suited to EPLF "fighter culture." In 1977 he was elected to the Political Committee and appointed head of the Department of Public Administration. In 1986 he joined what became the General Staff, and Sebhat is credited as the leading strategist of the AFABET, MASSAWA and DEKEMHARE victories that won the ARMED STRUGGLE. After liberation Sebhat moved from one post to another, usually in an effort to bring his organizational skills to bear on the most important issues of the moment. He stayed with the army until June 1992, when he was appointed Governor (equivalent to mayor) of Asmara. He retained this position even when he was also appointed Minister of Health in March 1994, and after completing the reorganization of these two areas, in May 1995 he returned to the army to become Minister of Defense and Eritrea's first full General as the crisis with SUDAN became increasingly grave.

SEMBEL (Hamasien).   The historic name for the area around the present ASMARA AIRPORT. Sembel was expropriated for an Italian farm in the 1890s, and then developed as a military airport and barracks during the 1930s. The name was applied to the military complex used by the COMMANDOS and Ethiopian army from the 1960s, and to the military PRISON established there for captured Eritrean FIGHTERS. In February 1975 the Eritrean prison guards deserted, freeing their prisoners; and on July 15, 1977, the EPLF raided Sembel and freed 870 prisoners. The prison was filled again with fighters captured around ADI YAQOB and elsewhere, forty-five of whom were executed in 1984 after an EPLF raid on the neighboring airport.

After liberation Sembel barracks housed Eritrea's elite commando regiment. On Martyr's Day in 1984 a ceremony was held near Sembel to rebury 250 prisoners who had been executed there and elsewhere in Asmara. In 1995-96 a government-funded project constructed modern highrise apartments in the Sembel area, and the name is

now associated with urban development rather than exe-
cutions.

SEMENAWI BAHRI (Tigrn.: "Northern Seacoast"). The
northern Bahri lands lie along the escarpment that sepa-
rates HAMASIEN from the SEMHAR coastal plain, extending northward from GHINDA to the Debra Maar area on the
borders of MENSA'. This is the best-watered land in Eritrea, receiving both winter and summer rains. One of the
few remaining FORESTS in the country covers its slopes,
and during the Italian colonial period hillside farms
around Fil-Fil and Merara began to produce Eritrea's only
commercial coffee crop. The land is traditionally used
both by highland and lowland peoples for seasonal cultivation. As a meeting place of Eritrean cultures it was a
testing ground for the EPLF's multi-cultural social policies during 1975-78, when it formed an important base
area for the front, sheltering a hospital, garages and
schools until the STRATEGIC WITHDRAWAL. In 1988 the
DERG fortified the area, and on January 17-18, 1989, the
largest tank battle of the war was fought on the north
Semhar plain below the escarpment. Thirty-seven
Ethiopian tanks were destroyed and the EPLF moved its
lines to within striking distance of MASSAWA. Since liberation the commercial farms in the area are being redeveloped by former FIGHTERS.

SEMHAR. The former province comprising Eritrea's central
coast, now the southern part of Northern Red Sea Region.
Semhar extends from FORO north to the Lebka River, and
inland to the foothills of the highlands as far as GHINDA
and the SEMENAWI BAHRI. The administrative and commercial center of Semhar is MASSAWA, and before 1975
most of the region's population lived in the port and its
suburbs or HIRGHIGO. Outside these urban centers Semhar
is populated by agro-pastoralists from the ASAWORTA,
RASHAIDA and numerous TIGRE-speaking tribes, including the AFLENDA, BELEW, MES-HALIT and sections of the
AD SHAYKH and others. The road corridor from Massawa
to Ghinda forms the region's main axis, but commercial

farms have been developed on the river floodplains around Emberemi and SHE'EB. Since liberation, government reconstruction efforts have centered on the main road and port, but Hirghigo is scheduled for reconstruction as a FISHING center, while She'eb, Foro and the Semenawi Bahri are receiving agricultural development aid. In 1993 the province had a population of 77,000.

SENAFE (Akele Guzai). Named for a small SAHO sub-tribe who trace their ancestry to immigrants from San'a in YEMEN but are related to the neighboring MINI-FERE, the town of Senafe was a colonial creation. Before colonization the Senafe people lived in two villages near the present town, and their chief aided the British army which camped there in 1868. Although modern Senafe is located near the TIGRINYA village of MATARA and its adjoining ancient ruins, the town itself only developed after it was fortified by the Italian colonial army, which defeated a Tigrean force there in January 1895, following BAHTA HAGOS' revolt. A permanent garrison was established in 1902, followed by a vice-residenza. The town developed as a market and administrative center, and grew to 2,000 in the 1930s, when the main ASMARA-ADDIS ABABA highway was built through the town. The population remained stable through the 1960s, but increased again in the 1970s when it became an important Ethiopian military garrison. The Ethiopians held the town until May 1990, when the EPLF liberated it at the beginning of its AKELE GUZAI campaign. Today Senafe is a district administrative and market center with a military base on its outskirts.

SENHIT. The former province that includes the middle ANSEBA River valley and the highlands of the MENSA', BILEN and MARYA peoples, now largely within ANSEBA Administrative Region. Senhit is centered on KEREN, and its name comes from the hill in the center of the city on which the Egyptians built a fort in 1872. The region was an early center of European missionary activity and during the Italian colonial period plantations were developed along the Anseba River around ELABERED and Keren.

Senhit suffered extensive damage during the ARMED
STRUGGLE, as scores of villages were burned, peasants
massacred (notably at GHELEB and ONA) and much of the
population fled as REFUGEES. In the late 1980s some of
the heaviest fighting of the war occurred around HAL-HAL
and JANGEREN. Today the region is being rebuilt and re-
populated by repatriated refugees, while the government's
decentralization plans and reconstruction of the main
road linking Keren and Asmara have particularly spurred
the economy.

SERAYE (alt.: Serae; Serai). The historic southwestern
province of the KEBESSA highlands, including the plateau
north and west of the MAREB River (now part of the Debub
("Southern") Administrative Region) and the western district of DEQI TESFA. The capital and commercial center of
the region is MENDEFERA, and other important towns include ADI QWALA and AREZA. The name Seraye probably
derives from the "dark" forests which once covered the
plateau and contributed to its lack of urban and agricultural settlement during AKSUMITE times. But under these
forests the Seraye plateau from MAI TSADA and MERAGUZ
to Mendefera contained some of the richest farmland in
the highlands, and by the later medieval period it was
thickly populated along the important PILGRIMAGE and
TRADE ROUTES that ran through it from Aksum to the
ASMARA area. Trade sparked the development of a local
Muslim JIBERTI community, and by fifteenth century the
northern market town of DEBARWA had become the capital
of the MAREB MELLASH. During this period Ewostatian
monastic communities also settled Seraye's more remote
western districts, and today the region boasts twelve Orthodox monasteries.
     Seraye is populated by TIGRINYA-speaking peoples
from the DEQI MENAB and ADKEME MELEGA descent
groups, as well as smaller groups of immigrants from
TIGRAI in its southern districts of GUNDET and QOHAIN,
and a few SAHO pastoralists. It was more closely linked to
Tigrai than other parts of Eritrea during the precolonial
period, and because of its position between the regional

power centers of HAMASIEN and ADWA, it was the site of numerous battles. Long periods of external rule under Tigreans and Turks, agricultural surpluses and the concentration of church lands, combined to produce a less democratic political culture in Seraye than elsewhere in the highlands, and the power of local ruling families was reflected in its RISTI system of LAND TENURE, which privileged the founding families of the province.

Italian colonialists were interested in Seraye's agricultural and strategic potential, establishing a farm station at KUDO FELASI and military garrisons at Adi Qwala and ADI UGRI. Early colonial administrators extolled Seraye's climate, and it remained a prosperous agricultural region through the BRITISH ADMINISTRATION. Because of its close links with Tigrai and the Orthodox Church, Seraye was a bastion of the UNIONIST PARTY during the 1940s, and was less involved in the nationalist movement than other regions. Its western districts were the scene of fighting between Ethiopian-armed Christian peasants and the ELF in the 1960s, but in 1977 the ELF liberated much of the province, continuing the process of land reform (*see* DESA) begun by the DERG. The ELF recruited many young Christians into the front, and Seraye consequently never contributed as many FIGHTERS to the EPLF as other highland areas. The province was held by the Derg from 1978 until liberation in 1991, and escaped serious war damage. Since liberation the government has focused on developing its agricultural potential and many new businesses have opened around Mendefera.

SETIT River. Rising in ETHIOPIA and flowing through TIGRAI, where it is known as the Takezze, The Setit River forms the southwestern border of Eritrea from near Setona to OM HAGER. It is a major tributary of the Atbara, which provides seven percent of the total discharge of the Nile, and the claims of SUDAN and EGYPT to its water raise problems for Eritrean use of it. Nonetheless, the Setit is by far the best source for irrigation water and hydroelectricity in Eritrea, and in the 1930s the Italian colonial administration first proposed a dam at Setona, where a

deep rock gorge makes a superb reservoir site. After liberation the Eritrean government commissioned another
study which found no environmental or human displacement problems, and estimated construction costs at $300
million, to be shared equally by Eritrea and Ethiopia,
which would split the dam's water and ENERGY production. As of 1997 the project is seeking outside funding,
but Egyptian objections have raised difficulties. If built,
the dam will provide irrigation water for the potentially
rich AGRICULTURE of southwestern GASH-SETIT.

SHABIYYA *see* ERITREAN PEOPLE'S LIBERATION FRONT.

SHE'EB (Semhar). The name of both a tributary of the seasonal Laba River which flows across the coastal plain of
northern SEMHAR, and of a seasonal campsite near the
river inhabited by TIGRE-speaking pastoralists from the
AFLENDA and other tribes. This site, which had developed into an impoverished village by the 1980s, earned
notoriety on May 12, 1988, when Ethiopian soldiers massacred over four hundred civilians there, mostly women
and children. After liberation the government invested in
a development scheme around She'eb (the Wadi Project),
constructing micro-dams in the foothills of the escarpment and along the seasonal rivers to provide for irrigated
AGRICULTURE, and building schools, clinics and an agricultural station for the local population.

SHIFTA (Tigrn.: "bandit/rebel"). Shifta (plural: *shiftetet*)
appear throughout the precolonial history of the Eritrean
highlands, usually as political rebels who retreated to inaccessible areas and built up an armed following that
lived through banditry. This was a means for disgruntled
or ambitious leaders to assert their power against
Ethiopian and Tigrean central authorities, and in the
nineteenth century some of the most famous political
leaders of the highlands resorted to shifta activities
(shiftanet), including BAHTA HAGOS, Debab Araya and
WOLDE-MIKA'EL SOLOMUN.

ITALIAN COLONIALISM largely ended *shiftanet,* but during the BRITISH ADMINISTRATION (BA) it resumed for a number of reasons: (1) the change in colonial rule prompted the resumption of inter-ethnic disputes (*see* HAMID IDRIS AWATE; TOR'A-TSENADEGLE WAR); (2) highland TIGRINYA resentment against Italian land confiscation and discrimination in the Fascist period was vented in anti-Italian banditry and assassination; (3) weak British military and POLICE forces and the widespread availability of modern weapons cached during the disintegration of the Italian armies in 1941 facilitated the formation of shifta bands, often led by former ASCARI; (4) beginning in 1947 the Ethiopian government, represented by Col. Nega Haile Selassie, supported the recruitment of pro-Unionist shifta bands, providing them with arms and bases along the border in TIGRAI.

The *shiftanet* of the 1940s went through essentially three phases: First, during 1941-47 there were numerous attacks on individual Italians, including the early exploits of the Mosazghi brothers in AKELE GUZAI, and a series of inter-ethnic clashes, particularly between the BENI 'AMER and Hadendowa in the far west, all of which related to long-standing grievances and frequently involved demobilized and unemployed soldiers whose banditry might often be termed "proto-nationalist." In response, the British formed an anti-shifta police unit, but it was ineffective. Second, during 1947-50 the Ethiopian government organized some of the existing "proto-nationalist" Christian bandits and recruited new shifta bands to begin a rural terrorist campaign against the supporters of Eritrean independence, including Italians, in conjunction with the urban terrorism of ANDENET. The January 1948 attack on ELABERED signaled the beginning of this campaign, which reached its height from October 1949 through February 1950, when large-sale violence rocked ASMARA.

Third, during early 1951 *shiftanet* did not end despite the UNITED NATIONS decision to join Eritrea to Ethiopia, and actually increased to an average 130 incidents per month. The BA estimated two thousand *shiftetet* to be operating, about 35 percent of whom were now Muslim lowlanders. In early 1951 the UN High Commissioner, Anze MATIENZO, insisted the BA take firmer measures, and the end of rural violence came in the summer of 1951, after the intervention of Ethiopia, which cooperated with the British along the border and made a secret agreement to allow the most notorious *shiftetet* to take refuge on its territory. On June 16 the BA proclaimed a general amnesty for surrendering shifta, and after strengthening its military forces and imposing collective punishment on villages where shifta were based, over 1,300 *shiftetet* surrendered. This marked the end of large-scale *shiftanet* in Eritrea.

Some revival in *shiftanet* recurred in the mid-1950s, due to unemployment, frustration with Unionist political policies or, perhaps, further Ethiopian subterfuge. In 1955, Chief Executive TEDLA BAIRU reimposed BA emergency laws, but this only resulted in his political demise, and on July 23, 1955, HAILE SELASSIE I rescinded Tedla's emergency decree and offered a limited amnesty to remaining shifta. Although the Ethiopian administration later labeled nationalist guerrillas as "shifta" (or more frequently *wombede,* which has only criminal connotations), and early ELF guerrillas included some former *shiftetet* and drew on the shifta tradition for their tactics, the organization and political program of the FIGHTERS were a completely new phenomenon.

SHIMEZANA (Akele Guzai). The southernmost region of the AKELE GUZAI highlands, from the SENAFE area to the Ethiopian border. Although tradition claims that "Shimezana" was a younger brother of Akele and Guzai, thus linking the descent groups, the region also has strong traditional relations with neighboring Agame in TIGRAI. The ancient monasteries of Shimezana, including DEBRE LIBANOS, were administered by a MA'IKELE BAHRE appointed by the rulers of Lasta in the twelfth century, and during 1270-1328 the region was supposedly ruled by the governor of Enderta. During the medieval period much of the region was settled by SAHO people, some of whom

became Christians. Its monasteries, rugged terrain and remoteness, outside of the main road corridor to the
Ethiopian border, have made it a bastion of TIGRINYA and
ORTHODOX CHURCH traditions. Even today Shimezana has
had little modern development. Except for its eastern escarpment, it was largely controlled by Ethiopian military
forces during the ARMED STRUGGLE until its liberation
by the EPLF in April 1990.

SHIPPING. Eritrea's present shipping fleet was largely inherited from Ethiopia in 1991. In 1994 it included fourteen ships with a gross tonnage of 71,837. Two of these are
intercoastal oil tankers, that bring fuel from ASSAB to
MASSAWA. The others are cargo vessels, including a re-
frigerator and a livestock ship, both used for transport of
Eritrean products to SAUDI ARABIA, and one is a "Ro-Ro"
ferry.

SHUMAGULLE. The term for village leaders in both
TIGRINYA and TIGRE, it also signifies the council of elder
or ruling-caste men that once controlled village or clan
life in much of Eritrea. The term comes from *shum* (Tigrn.
and Tigre: "office holder"). In the KEBESSA, "shumagulle"
historically denoted the council of village leaders who
decided such matters as communal redistribution of LAND
TENURE and the individual allocation of GEBRI tax obligations. Among Tigre-speaking clans of the northern
highlands (HABAB, MARYA, MENSA' and some BILEN), and
in parts of SEMHAR, "shumagulle" also had a class connotation, designating an hereditary aristocracy to whom the
general population owed labor and customary obligations.
Today the Shumagulle are democratically-elected representatives at the lowest levels of LOCAL GOVERNMENT,
and may include young people and women. But the term
still carries the parallel meaning of an elderly, male and
respected community leader.

SLAVE TRADE and SLAVERY. The Eritrean coast served
throughout history as an embarkation point for slaves
captured throughout the Eritrean and Ethiopian regions.

As early as the fifteenth century B.C. there was a slave trade between the coast and EGYPT. Slavery was practiced in the AKSUMITE Empire and afterwards in the Eritrean highlands and along the coast. Most slaves in pre-colonial Eritrea were domestic servants, and many came from the Nilotic tribes of the southwest (*see* BARYA, KUNAMA, NARA), but many others came from what is today ETHIOPIA. Both Christian highlanders and the Muslim BENI 'AMER and BELEW tribes of the lowlands raided their weaker neighbors for slaves, and during the nineteenth century Egyptian expeditions also raided the BILEN. But more important than this local slave raiding or limited domestic slavery was the large export slave trade that developed from the southern Ethiopian highlands via Eritrean ports to the Arab world.

This slave trade, which was an important element of Eritrea's foreign COMMERCE from the sixteenth through mid-nineteenth centuries, focused on young women and children for use as domestic servants, concubines and a limited number of soldiers and eunuchs. By the nineteenth century, when good records become available, the majority of exported slaves were Oromo people who had been captured by Christian Ethiopian raiding parties. Most were sold in MASSAWA, where the NA'IB collected a tax of one Maria Theresa thaler (MTT) per slave and the port officials collected a further five MTTs. Records indicate an average export of 1,000 to 2,000 slaves per year before 1860, with specific reports showing 2,500 for 1845 and 1,100 for 1857. After prohibition in the early 1860s some 1,500 to 2,000 slaves were shipped from around Emberemi and HIRGHIGO, and in the early 1870s MUNZINGER still estimated the illegal trade at 1,000 per year. ITALIAN COLONIALISM ended domestic slavery and put a final stop to the slave trade, except for some very limited smuggling on the DENKEL coast through the 1890s.

SOMALIA. Because of similarities in its Italian colonization, BRITISH ADMINISTRATION (1941-50) and violent relations with ETHIOPIA, Somalia has been closely linked with modern Eritrea. Eritrean ASCARIs served in Somalia

under Italian rule, while after the Second World War
HAILE SELASSIE I claimed Somalia as part of Greater
Ethiopia. Somalia's political future was linked to that of
Eritrea in UNITED NATIONS negotiations leading to the
BEVIN-SFORZA PLAN, but after the plan's failure Somalia
was granted independence following a ten-year Italian
trusteeship, which then provided a precedent for unsuccessful Eritrean nationalist demands. Some political ana-
lysts claim that Haile Selassie refrained from annexing
Eritrea before 1960 because he still hoped to gain political control over Somalia when the UN-mandated trusteeship ended in that year. But when Somalia became independent its leaders immediately worked to establish links
with Eritrean nationalists, who they hoped would open a
"second front" to support their irredentist campaign to
wrest control of the Somali-inhabited region of Ogaden
from Ethiopia.

In the summer of 1960 Somali diplomats secretly
contacted IDRIS MOHAMED ADEM in Cairo and OSMAN
SALEH SABBE in ADDIS ABABA, offering them financial
and diplomatic support for the new ELF. Sabbe moved to
Somalia in late 1960, where he opened an ELF office and
obtained passports that allowed the ELF to move its first
arms supplies through Sudan. After their 1964 defeat in
the Ogaden, Somali support decreased, but they continued
their official links with both the ELF and later the ELF-
PLF through the mid-1970s. In 1977 the Somali invasion
of Ogadèn had a very negative outcome for Eritrean nationalists. Although it drained Ethiopian military resources and helped facilitate the "first liberation" of most
of Eritrea, it also impelled the USSR to switch its military
support to the DERG, and after quickly dispatching the
Somali forces in Ogaden, the new Soviet-equipped and advised army turned on Eritrea in 1978.

The EPLF never developed close relations with the
decaying regime of Siad Barre, but after liberation, Eritrean leaders took a renewed and now philanthropic interest in Somalia, offering to broker a peace initiative
between its warring factions and, in mid-1992, to send
peacekeeping troops there with international support.

After the UNITED STATES' attempt at peace-keeping slid into disaster, U.S. diplomats turned to Eritrea (and Ethiopia) to find a solution, and in June 1993 the Organization of African Unity appointed ISAIAS AFWERKI to mediate peace negotiations between the Somali factions, enabling the U.S. to extract its forces. As of 1996, Eritrea maintains contacts with several Somali factions and the autonomous government of Somaliland.

SOUTH ARABIA (Ancient Civilization). The ancient South Arabian civilization covered the present territory of YEMEN and parts of southern SAUDI ARABIA. By the eighsth century B.C. the Kingdom of Sab'a was the dominant power in the region. During this period of Sabean dominance (c. 700-300 B.C.), South Arabian merchants and immigrants had a strong influence on what is today Eritrea and TIGRAI, and this period, when historical civilization first emerged in the Eritrean region, is consequently known as the South Arabian (or Sabean) period. South Arabian contacts with the Eritrean region date back even further; some linguists say as early as the fourth millennium B.C., and ARCHAEOLOGY provides evidence from the thirteenth century B.C. Although the timing of the process is disputed, it is clear that South Arabian culture and language fused with the culture and language of Cushitic peoples already in the Eritrean-Tigrean region over a long period to produce the later AKSUMITE and HABESHA civilizations.

  According to the most recent scholarship, the highpoint of direct South Arabian immigration to the Eritrean coast seems to have been the eighth to sixth centuries B.C., after which a strongly South Arabian-influenced local culture developed in the Eritrea-Tigrai region, exemplified by archaeological evidence from the indigenous Kingdom of Da'amat which flourished sometime between the sixth and third centuries B.C. Da'amat's rulers used the Sabean political title of *mukharib* (priest-king) and appointed tax collectors known as *negasi*. Besides local gods, they worshipped the Sabean gods Aster (Venus), Almoqah (Moon), and Shams (Sun). They built with South Arabian-style stone architecture and used both the "cursive" and "monumental" forms of the South Arabian writing system, with the latter probably being modified to produce the contemporary GE'EZ writing system. Other indications of South Arabian influence are preserved in toponyms such as ANSEBA and ASSAB, and pervasive legends regarding the biblical Queen of Sab'a ("Sheba"), known locally as Azieb and said to be the mother, through a union with King Solomon, of Menelik I who brought with him from ancient Israel the mythical progenitors of the originary Habesha inhabitants of the KEBESSA.

After the fourth century B.C. direct South Arabian influence declined, even as Sab'a itself was conquered by rival Himyar, and archaeologists have posited the existence of an Intermediate Period (c. 300 B.C. - 100 A.D.) in which the continuing indigenization of South Arabian cultural elements took place, leading directly to the new Aksumite civilization.

STRATEGIC WITHDRAWAL (1978). The EPLF's 1978 retreat from most of central Eritrea during the ARMED STRUGGLE was explained at the time as a "strategic withdrawal" that followed Mao's long-term strategy for winning a guerrilla war. Outnumbered and outgunned by the DERG's new USSR-supplied armies, between July and December 1978 the EPLF withdrew from much of the territory it had liberated in the preceding two years. The withdrawal was orderly and managed to remove enough military and other equipment to sustain the EPLF during its grim years in SAHEL. The first withdrawal took place in July as the first of the Derg's OFFENSIVES swept through AKELE GUZAI. The EPLF retired from the province after rear-guard actions at MAI AINI and DEKEMHARE, and at the same time withdrew its forces from southern SEMHAR and abandoned its siege of MASSAWA, constructing a new defensive line from GHINDA and the SEMENAWI BAHRI through HAMASIEN north of ASMARA to the upper ANSEBA River.

The Ethiopian Second Offensive broke through this line at ADI YAQOB in November, forcing a hurried but

organized retreat from KEREN to the EPLF's Sahel base
area around NAKFA. Rear-guard actions at ELABERED,
Kelhamet, Mai-Mide and Tselab slowed the Ethiopian
advance long enough for all EPLF forces to retreat into the
Sahel redoubt before they could be cut-off by an Ethiopian
flanking attack along the coastal plain. The Strategic
Withdrawal enabled the EPLF to defend its base area
against all further assaults, and thus survive the most
difficult days of the war for independence.

STUDENT ORGANIZATIONS. From the late 1950s
through the early 1970s, Eritrean high school and university students were leading figures in the development
of the nationalist movement. Muslim students with nationalist sentiments generally left Eritrea to study in the
Arab world, and during the late 1950s formed an Eritrean
Students' Union in CAIRO, led in particular by Seid Hussein, that produced some of the founders of the ELF. Inside Eritrea, the first student political organizations were
organized around the anti-Ethiopian "Young Federalist"
movement in ASMARA, AGORDAT, KEREN and MASSAWA
during 1957. On May 9, students at Haile Selassie I Secondary School in Asmara, led by TUKU'E IHADOGO and
others, went on strike against the imposition of AMHARIC
as a language of instruction. Their imprisonment produced
a national student strike on May 22 and led to the first
student contacts with LABOR ORGANIZATIONS. Students
supported the 1958 General Strike in Asmara, and in 1959
Tuku'e was recruited into the ELM, which played a role in
organizing anti-Ethiopian student protests during 1960-
62.

    As Ethiopian plans for ANNEXATION progressed,
high school students marched in large numbers to protest
at the NATIONAL ASSEMBLY in September 1960, and again
in May 1962, when student strikes and demonstrations
spread across the country and were broken with brutal
POLICE repression. Further demonstrations followed annexation in early 1962, and in March 1965 over two thousand high school students were arrested in Asmara and
detained at SEMBEL camp. Student leaders during this

period included later EPLF-founders HAILE WOLDE-
TENSA'E (Diru'e), ISAIAS AFWERKI and Musie Tesfai-
Mika'el (*see* MENKA). After the 1965 demonstration,
direct links were made between Asmara students and the
ELF, and in the same year student-leader Kidane Kinfu
formed an ELF network at the university in ADDIS
ABABA, which drew in many future EPLF leaders.
Eritrean students also cultivated relations with Ethiopian
student radicals, particularly Tigreans, and it was out of
the University Students' Union of Addis Ababa (USUAA)
that contacts were made leading to later cooperation between the EPLF, EPRP and TIGREAN PEOPLE'S LIBERATION
FRONT. In 1966 a "General Union of Eritrean Students"
was formed in Asmara, but in 1967 the ELF network was
broken by defections and arrests.

Nationalist-oriented Eritrean student organizations
spread throughout the province and Ethiopia again during
1969, when Eritrean students marched from Bahar Dar to
Addis to protest their persecution by Ethiopian students
and faculty. Both the ELF and PLF recruited students
during the early 1970s through their underground student organizations, but because of its own former-student
leadership and more radical ideology the PLF was most
successful in gaining university students, including PET-
ROS SOLOMON and SEBHAT EPHREM. In 1972 many Eritrean students were expelled from university in Addis
and when they returned to Asmara they played an important role in politicizing high school and college students
there. During late 1974 and early 1975, tens of thousands
of Eritrean students joined the liberation fronts, forming
the core of the nationalist forces through the end of the
ARMED STRUGGLE.

In the overseas DIASPORA, the ELF founded another
"General Union of Eritrean Students" in Damascus in
1968. Ad hoc student organizations developed in a number
of European and North American countries in the early
1970s, and both ELF and EPLF sought to link these with
their own national student associations in the mid-1970s.
One of the most effective of these diaspora organizations
was the EPLF-affiliated Association of Eritrean Students

in North America (AESNA), formed in 1977 from the former Eritreans for Liberation in North America (EFLNA). The AESNA mobilized extensive support for the EPLF in the UNITED STATES, laying the groundwork for the EPLF's later sophisticated fundraising and information activities.

Inside Eritrea, the EPLF Association of Eritrean Students (AES) held its first congress in KEREN during May, 1978, which was attended by many delegates from the diaspora. But the AES was never able to really function inside Eritrea due to the disruption of EDUCATION and Ethiopian repression. Instead, following the EPLF's Second Congress in 1987 a National Union of Eritrean Youth (NUEY) was formed with a largely student leadership drawn from the diaspora in SUDAN and the Middle East. Its First Congress was held in 1989, when Muhyadin Shengeb was elected Secretary. In August 1994, a Second NUEY Congress was held, attended by three hundred delegates who decided to change the organization's name to the National Union of Eritrean Youth and Students (NUEYS) and incorporate many smaller student organizations. Although the NUEYS gets ten percent of its budget from the government, it is legally an independent organization. Today it has 35,000 members and is involved in organizing cultural, sporting and educational events, as well as information campaigns concerning social problems, such as female CIRCUMCISION.

SUDAN. Because of its long border with Eritrea and the close cultural contacts between eastern Sudanese and western Eritrean peoples, Sudan has always had an important place in Eritrean history. AKSUMITE traders used the routes through eastern Sudan to the Nile Valley, and in the fourth century Emperor EZANA conquered the Sudanese kingdom of Meroe. The BEJA peoples of Sudan were closely linked to the ancestors of today's BELEW, BENI 'AMER and HEDAREB. SUWAKIN was the major port on the Eritrean Christian PILGRIMAGE ROUTE to Jerusalem, and ISLAM entered western Eritrea largely through Arab immigrants to the Sudan. In the seventeenth century the

Sudanese FUNJ empire subjected the BARKA and northern GASH-SETIT regions (*see* NABTAB).

After 1840, EGYPT attempted to rule the western Eritrean lowlands from KASSALA, further linking Barka and Gash-Setit to the economy of eastern Sudan, while the spread of the Kassala-based MIRGHANIYYA Islamic sect reinforced these links. The conquest of eastern Sudan by the Mahdiyya in the 1880s broke these links, however, as the Beni 'Amer and other "Eritrean" tribes opposed the Mahdists (*see* KUFIT). This experience was critical in defining the colonial BORDERS between Sudan and Eritrea, as what were to become the "Eritrean" tribes supported Italian colonial forces against the Mahdists, while the British laid claim to Kassala for Sudan. Despite disputes over water rights on the Gash River, the Italians maintained good relations with British colonialists in Sudan until the Second World War, when Italy's defeat sparked a livestock-raiding war between the Sudanese Hadendowa and Eritrean Beni 'Amer through the mid-1940s.

During the 1940s Eritrea developed close links with eastern Sudan in anticipation of the BRITISH ADMINIS-TRATION's plan to annex Eritrea's western lowlands to Sudan (*see* BEVIN-SFORZA PLAN). During this period Eritrean Muslims joined the SUDAN DEFENSE FORCE (SDF), and Sudanese teachers were responsible for much of Eritrea's ARABIC school system, contributing to the immigration of Muslim Eritrean students to Sudan after FEDERATION. By the late 1950s Sudan was a center for Eritrean nationalist-oriented exiles, particularly in Kassala and Port Sudan, where the ERITREAN LIBERATION MOVEMENT (ELM) was formed by MAHMOUD SAID NAWD, who maintained close links with the Sudanese Communist Party (SCP). The ELF also began to operate in Sudan in 1960, and during 1961 obtained the support of Eritreans in the SDF. Under the conservative military regime of General Abbud, all Eritrean nationalist activities in Sudan were clandestine, although individual government officials were frequently supportive and Kassala became the ELF's logistical center.

With the overthrow of Abbud in October 1965, and the rise of sympathetic SCP and other politicians, the ELF was able to operate more openly. One factor in Sudanese politicians' support for the ELF was their strategy of using the Eritreans as a counter to Ethiopian support for the Southern Sudanese liberation movement, which the Ethiopians themselves continued to support in an attempt to pressure the Sudanese into expelling Eritrean organizations. This tit-for-tat relationship continued as the two conflicts grew in size, but Sudanese support for Eritrean nationalism was always arbitrary and tied to personal and local considerations. After 1967 large numbers of Eritrean REFUGEES fleeing into Sudan put further conflicting pressures on the Sudanese. Sudan also was the locus of many of the intrigues and internecine conflicts between Eritrean nationalists, which were often exploited by Sudanese authorities for their own purposes.

In May 1969 the Sudanese military returned to power under Jaafar Nimeiri, who was initially sympathetic to the ELF. But after a 1971 SCP coup attempt, he turned on the progressive forces that had supported Eritrean nationalism and negotiated an agreement with HAILE SELASSIE I in ADDIS ABABA in 1972, ending Sudanese support for Eri-trean rebels. Although it ended the Southern Sudanese civil war for ten years, the agreement only made life more difficult for the Eritrean fronts operating in Sudan, but did not halt their operations. By this time the Eritrean network in eastern Sudan, including a growing business community, was so deeply entrenched that local officials were unwilling to dislodge them; while with the collapse of Ethiopian forces in Eritrea during 1975-78, the rise of the procommunist DERG and a further massive influx of Eritrean refugees, relations between Sudan and the fronts resumed quite publicly. During this period the ELF supply network ran largely through Kassala, while the EPLF developed less important links to Port Sudan.

The apparent Ethiopian victory in 1979-80 and the collapse of the ELF led to a rapprochement between the Derg and Nimeiri, brokered in part by the USSR's Arab allies. In 1980 Nimeiri threatened to shut off supplies to the liberation fronts, and during 1981-83 the EPLF refrained from public activities, although it continued to operate in Sudan. Relations between Nimeiri and the fronts improved after 1983, as the Derg supported a renewed Southern Sudanese rebellion and the tit-for-tat policy was revived. Sudanese support for the EPLF grew even more after Nimeiri fell in 1985, and sympathetic civilian progressives returned to power. By the late 1980s the EPLF was operating offices and rehabilitation centers in major cities and a supply base at Suwakin, connected to SAHEL by truck transport, provided FOOD AID for the liberated areas. The EPLF refrained from carrying arms in Sudan, but otherwise was virtually autonomous in the area from Suwakin to Tokar and Eritrea's northeastern border.

In 1989 the new military government of Colonel Omer el-Beshir supported EPLF peace initiatives, but at the same time the government's ISLAMIST allies in the National Islamic Front (NIF), led by Hassan al-Turabi, provided clandestine direction for the Eritrean Islamic JIHAD's anti-EPLF campaign. In 1989 Sudanese military forces intervened in support of the Jihad during a battle with the EPLA on the border of Barka. The contradictions in Sudanese policy continued into the post-liberation period, when the government initially welcomed the EPLF victory, sending an official representative to Eritrea in December 1991 and closing the offices of all ELF FACTIONS in Sudan. In January 1992 Hassan al-Turabi was received with honors in Asmara, followed by official visits from President el-Beshir in March and August. Sudanese and Eri-trean leaders discussed bilateral cooperation and the REPATRIATION of refugees, and in 1993 Sudan recognized Eritrea immediately after the REFERENDUM. But continued NIF support for the Jihad, which staged guerrilla attacks inside Eritrea in December, led to increasing tensions, which were exacerbated by Hassan al-Turabi's call for a regional revolution to establish Islamic governments throughout the Horn of Africa.

Nonetheless, on August 12, 1994, the Eritrean and Sudanese governments signed a joint statement promising non-interference in each others' affairs and committing them to begin refugee repatriation. But in the following months the Eritrean government accused Sudan of complicity in smuggling Jihad guerrillas among the returning refugees, and on December 5, Eritrea broke diplomatic relations with Sudan. Reconciliation talks sponsored by YEMEN in late December failed, and Eritrea began to work with Ethiopia, Kenya and Uganda to form a regional anti-NIF front. In June 1995 the Eritrean PFDJ hosted a conference of all Sudanese opposition forces in Asmara, who agreed to form the National Democratic Alliance (NDA) front and launch an armed struggle against the NIF government of el-Beshir. This was followed by further conferences in Asmara in January and October 1996, and March 1997, by which time a virtual state of war existed between the two countries. In January 1997 the NDA opened an "Eastern Front" along the Sudan-Eritrea/Ethiopia border with Eritrean support, and in June the Eritrean government revealed a Sudanese assassination plot against President Isaias, while in July-August tensions were heightened by Sudanese air bombardment near the Eritrean border town of KARORA.

SUDAN DEFENSE FORCE (SDF). In 1941 the British military used Sudanese colonial troops from the SDF in its campaign to conquer Eritrea, and SDF units remained in Eritrea until 1946. In the Eritrean highlands, Christian resentment of the SDF presence was fanned into violence by Ethiopian-sponsored Unionists, and on August 28, 1946, SDF soldiers in ASMARA massacred forty-six Eritrean Christians and wounded sixty, after which they were withdrawn from the country. Nonetheless, during the 1940s a number of Muslim Eritreans joined the SDF, and recruitment continued into the 1950s, when Muslim men sought career opportunities outside Eritrea's increasingly Ethiopian-controlled administration.

Some of these Eritrean soldiers already had nationalist sympathies, and in 1959 they were contacted by the newly-formed ELM. But the ELM's failure to advocate an immediate ARMED STRUGGLE frustrated the soldiers,

and in late 1960 IDRIS MOHAMED ADEM and others successfully recruited nine Eritrean SDF soldiers into the
ELF, including Adem M. Hamed "Gindefel," OMER EZAZ,
Omer M. Ali "Damer," Mohamed Ali Idris "Abu Rigeila,"
Mohamed Abdallah "ABU TAYARA" and Taher Salem. After completing their service in the SDF, these ex-soldiers
formed the nucleus of the first group of FIGHTERS to go
into Eritrea in 1962, and were soon joined by nine more
ex-SDF soldiers, including MAHMOUD DINAI and Saleh
Heduq. During 1962-65 their military training was crucial to the ELF's development, and many served in the
early field leadership.

SUDOHA ILA (Denkel). ˙An AFAR village and well-site in
the mountains northwest of BEYLUL. During June 24 to
July 2, 1970, about seven hundred dissident ELF fighters
gathered there to form the PEOPLE'S LIBERATION FORCES
(PLF), electing MOHAMED ALI OMERO and MESFIN HAGOS
as their first leaders.

SUPREME COUNCIL (ELF). The ELF executive body reflected the personalized and undemocratic organization
that plagued the ELF in the 1960s. The Supreme Council
was a de facto organization that came into existence in
1963 when the original ELF Executive Committee failed to
develop and OSMAN SALEH SABBE's 1962 proposal for a
national congress was not accepted by other leaders. The
name "Supreme Council" derived from the usage of the Sudanese military government during this period, and it was
essentially a self-appointed triumvirate of IDRIS MO-
HAMED ADEM, IDRIS OSMAN GALADEWOS and Sabbe. It
represented only the external leadership, and by 1965 its
links to military forces inside Eritrea were strained. A
conference at KASSALA formalized the two bodies'
relationship and instituted the ZONAL COMMANDS, which
perpetuated the Supreme Council's personalized patronage
relationships with different ethnic groups.
    In 1967, as resentment against the triumvirate's
autocratic control over ELF finances and supplies grew,
the Council was expanded to formally include Taha Mo-

hamed Nur, Osman Idris Kheir, Ahmed Hassan and TEDLA
BAIRU, who was appointed without prior knowledge, apparently to placate Eritrean Christian sentiments. The
triumvirate continued to dominate the Council, but they
were themselves involved in a mutual power struggle. They
generally opposed reformist calls for meetings with the
internal military leadership in 1968-69, but also sought
to use the developing reform movement for their own ends.
At the ADOBAHA Conference in 1969 the new field leadership of the KIADA AL-AMA agreed to retain the
Supreme Council as the ELF's foreign office if it would
relinquish financial control, but when Idris Adem and
Sabbe attempted to thwart the agreement through separate
(and antagonistic) political machinations, the Council was
dissolved by the Kiada al-Ama in December.

SUWAKIN (alt. Suakin). The Red Sea port of Eastern SUDAN
until 1900, Suwakin served an important Orthodox Christian PILGRIMAGE ROUTE and COMMERCE with the northern highlands of Eritrea from the AKSUMITE period. It
was the capital of the Turkish province of HABESHA during the seventeenth to early nineteenth centuries, and its
governor held political control over MASSAWA. Suwakin
was held by BRITAIN during the wars of the Mahdiyya in
the 1880s-90s, and this began its commercial decline,
which was finalized by the construction of neighboring
Port Sudan in the early twentieth century. The port was
largely abandoned by the 1930s, but in the 1980s the
EPLF constructed a major supply base on the southern
shore of Suwakin Bay, which was operated in complete autonomy from the Sudanese government.

SWEDEN. The most important Swedish involvement in Eritrea was through the Swedish Evangelical Mission (SEM),
which began working in Eritrea in 1863 (*see* BELEZA; ED-
UCATION; GHELEB; KUNAMA; PRESS; PROTESTANT
CHRISTIANITY; WOLDE-AB WOLDE-MARIAM). The SEM
was expelled from Eritrea in 1935 by Italian authorities
due to Swedish support for ETHIOPIA, but returned after
1941. Many Eritrean students traveled to Sweden for

higher education, and a significant Eritrean DIASPORA community remains there through the present. In 1997 Sweden signed a $5.3 million aid accord with Eritrea.

- T -

TEDLA BAIRU Ogbit (1914-84). Eritrea's first Chief Executive and leader of the UNIONIST PARTY, Tedla Bairu was born in Gheremi, HAMASIEN. He attended the SEM school in ASMARA until 1926 and was one of the very few Eritreans to study in Italy, where he graduated from the Istituto Magistrale in Florence in 1933 (which may explain his fondness for the company of Italian women in later years). He was a teacher and then director of Italian "native" schools until 1940, ending this career in ADWA, where he was employed by the BRITISH ADMINISTRATION (BMA) as an interpreter in 1941. He served as a translator in the Asmara Native Affairs Office of the BMA until 1946, and was the first director of the *Semenawi gazetta* (*see* PRESS). Tedla was not in Asmara when the MAHABER FEQRI HAGER (MFH) was founded in May 1941, but he became involved in the organization upon his return to Eritrea.

Unlike WOLDE-AB WOLDE-MARIAM, whose career parallels that of Tedla's in many ways, Tedla Bairu did not support Eritrean independence, and instead became a vocal advocate of the pro-Ethiopian unionist cause. He left the BMA in late 1946, and at the WA'LA BET GHERGHIS in November he led the Unionist wing of the MFH in rejecting Wolde-Ab's proposed compromise. With Ethiopian support, Tedla replaced GEBRE-MESKAL WOLDU as Secretary-General of what became the Unionist Party in January 1947. Tedla led this organization through the 1940s, addressing various UNITED NATIONS bodies, editing the Unionist newspaper *Etiopiya* and mobilizing sectarian and regionalist interests for the Unionist cause. Described by his opponents as an "opportunist," Tedla's unwavering Unionist position and personal patronage network led to his unopposed election to the first ASSEMBLY for his home district of KARNISHEM in March, 1952. He was elected

President of the Assembly in April and became Eritrea's first Chief Executive in September, at the moment of FEDERATION.

During 1953 Tedla worked hand-in-hand with Ethiopian authorities to destroy Eritrea's independent institutions (*see* LABOR ORGANIZATIONS; PRESS). He refused to consult with the Assembly concerning the budget, and undermined the independence of the POLICE and judiciary. At the same time, Tedla tried to use Eritrea's autonomous institutions to develop an Eritrean power base for himself independent of Emperor HAILE SELASSIE I's government. He protested the arbitrary fixing of Eritrea's share of custom revenues by Ethiopia, and sought independent economic relationships with Italian capitalists. He came into conflict with the Emperor's representative, ANDERGATCHEW MESSAI, and by 1955 had alienated both his Ethiopian patrons and his Eritrean compatriots. In July he resorted to the imposition of a BMA emergency law suspending habeus corpus and closed the Assembly, citing a resurgence of SHIFTA activity. But this measure backfired, and on July 23, 1955, the Emperor forced his resignation. This was celebrated as a victory by Eritrean independents, but in reality Tedla's fall only further undermined Eritrean autonomy by destroying whatever independence the Unionist Party had maintained.

According some who knew him, Tedla already had become "disillusioned" with the Federation by 1955, and his ambiguous commitment to Eritrean autonomy led to his increasing support for the Eritrean nationalist movement in the 1960s. Nonetheless, Tedla accepted the Emperor's appointment as ambassador to SWEDEN, where he stayed until he defected to the ELF in 1967. In that year he was appointed to the SUPREME COUNCIL and made a number of nationalist radio broadcasts on behalf of the ELF and later OSMAN SALEH SABBE's General Secretariat, but his was purely a symbolic role. His son, HERUI TEDLA BAIRU, on the other hand, became very active in ELF politics. Tedla continued to live in Stockholm until his death in 1984.

TELEVISION. Eritrea's state-owned television station, ERI-TV, was set up in ASMARA with Canadian help in 1992 and began its first broadcasts in January 1993. Its programming, including news and cultural shows, is presented in ARABIC, TIGRINYA, and English.

TESSEMA ASBEROM, Ras. Born into the leading family of Ma'reba, AKELE GUZAI, in 1870, Ras Tessema expanded his family's power under ITALIAN COLONIALISM by supporting the Italians against his rival, BAHTA HAGOS (from neighboring SAGENEITI). He served in the ADWA campaign (1895-96) and was appointed chief of the northern Akele Guzai districts of Hadegti and later Eghela Hamus. He became famous for his dispensation of JUSTICE and particularly for his settlement of LAND CONFLICTS, including the bitter dispute between the districts of Robra and Deqi Admocom in which twelve people died in 1929, and the TOR'A-TSENADEGLE WAR. Together with his younger brother Berhe, he was the most powerful traditional chief in Akele Guzai.

In 1941 Ras Tessema was a founding member of the MAHABER FEQRI HAGER (MFH), and during the mid-1940s he supported the "TIGRAI/Tigrinya" policies floated by the BRITISH ADMINISTRATION, and then led the independence-oriented wing of the MFH, where he worked with WOLDE-AB WOLDE-MARIAM. He was appointed president of the Native Court of Akele Guzai in 1947, and in the same year became president of the LIBERAL PROGRESSIVE PARTY, which was largely run by his son, ABRAHA TESSEMA. As the leading senior statesman of the independence movement he was elected to the symbolic presidency of the INDEPENDENCE BLOC in 1949 and the Democratic Bloc which replaced it. In 1952 he was elected to the first Eritrean ASSEMBLY for the TSENADEGLE district, while his brother represented Ma'reba. His support for Eritrean autonomy led to his political eclipse, however, and he retired in 1956.

TESSENEI (Gash-Setit). The major town of western GASH-SETIT, Tessenei developed during the colonial period beside the GASH River where it flows into Sudan. In the early 1900s the site was picked for a diversion dam and reservoir to feed an irrigation system, and during the 1920s the village developed as an administrative center for the cotton plantations around neighboring ALI GHIDER. The Italian colonial Residenza was located in Tessenei after 1928, as were the offices of the SIA cotton company, a hospital, hotels, garages and workshops serving the colonial agricultural projects in the region. Eritrean workers and immigrants from ETHIOPIA and SUDAN settled in the town, which by 1938 had a population of about 1,800. The expansion of cotton growing and trade with the Sudan from the late 1940s onwards led to steady growth, and by 1962 the population was 12,000.

Because of its location across the border from KASSALA, Tessenei experienced numerous ELF raids in the 1960s and became the Ethiopian military headquarters for the region. The ELF liberated the town on May 5, 1977, and held it until July 23, 1978, when the DERG took it in their First OFFENSIVE. Although much of the population fled as REFUGEES, the Derg built the town into a major military base, using its small airstrip and hospital. It had a garrison of 3,000, 1,200 of whom were killed or captured when the EPLF liberated the town on January 15, 1984, capturing its fuel depots for their mechanized campaigns. Most of the population fled to Kassala during the heavy fighting and subsequent Ethiopian air raids, all of which severely damaged the town. On August 25, 1985, the EPLF abandoned Tessenei, and it was again held by the Derg until March 26, 1988, when the Ethiopians withdrew following their defeat at AFABET. The town was largely in ruins in 1991, although the resumption of COMMERCE with Sudan led to the development of hotels and shops. Reconstruction began in earnest with the government's investment in redeveloping cotton production at Ali Ghider. The airstrip, infrastructure and public buildings were repaired and by 1995 the population had grown to over 5,000. Today Tessenei is a sub-regional administrative center and contains customs and agricultural offices, as well as a nearby military base.

TIGRAI Province (Ethiopia). The northeastern province of
ETHIOPIA, Tigrai (alt.: Tigray, Tigre) shares a long border
with Eritrea and its TIGRINYA-speaking population
maintains strong historical ties with the people of the Eritrean KEBESSA. Northern Tigrai was the political center
of the AKSUMITE Empire, and after the development of
Orthodox Christianity, Aksum and its surrounding
monasteries became the spiritual center of the region.
These political and religious links to the highlands of
what is today central and northern Eritrea continued
through the nineteenth century, with the governor of
Tigrai (Tigrai Makonnen) often exercising direct political
control over central Eritrea (*see* BAHRE NEGASHI;
MA'IKELE BAHRE), while the Nebur-ed of Aksum held a
more limited ecclesiastical authority in the Kebessa. The
common language and culture of Tigrinya-speaking people
on both sides of the MAREB River was reinforced by continual population movement between the Eritrean and
Tigrai regions, with many Tigreans immigrating to the
Kebessa during the medieval period and again in the Italian colonial period.

Tigrean political control over portions of what is
now central Eritrea is documented from the thirteenth
century onwards, but during the early eighteenth century
this situation was briefly reversed when the "Eritrean"
House of TSAZZEGA held political power over northern
Tigrai. In the 1750s they lost this power to their former
counselor, Ras Mika'el "Sehul" who began the Tigrean
military subjugation of central Eritrea that lasted on-and-
off until 1889. During the Ethiopian Zemana Mesafent
("Era of Princes") the Tigrean rulers Ras Wolde-Sealssie,
Ras Sebagadis and Dejazmatch WUBE all imposed their
political control over central Eritrea with varying degrees
of success, often by exploiting the rivalry between
Tsazzega and HAZZEGA. The raids and atrocities inflicted
by Wube in particular left a legacy of hatred for Tigrean
rule throughout central Eritrea. Wube's heir, "Agaw" Negussie, attempted to retain control of the Kebessa but was
killed by the troops of Emperor Tewodros, leading to a

collapse of direct Tigrean control in the 1860s-70s, when EGYPT vied with Tigrean lords, such as Ras Araya and the future Emperor YOHANNES IV. The latter restored Tigrean rule, appointing his general, Ras ALULA, as military governor of central Eritrea in 1879. Alula's rule also left bitter memories of arbitrary and violent Tigrean rule, and in 1889 many Eritrean leaders supported the Italian occupation of the highlands.

During 1891-94 the Italians developed a "Politica Tigrina" strategy of supporting the ruler of Tigrai, Ras Men-gesha, against the Ethiopian Emperor Menelik II. In December 1891 Mengesha signed a secret treaty acknowledging Italian control over Eritrea, but he continued his relationship with Menelik, and when BAHTA HAGOS revolted against Italian rule he led his army into Eritrea in an attempt to reconquer the Kebessa, but was defeated in January 1895 at QWATIT and SENAFE. The Italians then attempted to conquer Tigrai, occupying Adwa, Adigrat and Makalle, but were driven north by Menelik and defeated at the Battle of ADWA. After this defeat the Italians largely abandoned their "Politica Tigrina," but continued to encourage Tigrinya linguistic development in Eritrea and the expansion of commercial ties with Tigrai, which they claimed as their exclusive economic sphere. In preparation for war with Ethiopia in 1932 the Fascists resumed their "Politica Tigrina" which culminated in the defection of Dej. Haile-Selassie Gugsa (hereditary lord of eastern Tigrai) when the Italians invaded Tigrai in 1935, and the annexation of Tigrai to the Governate of Eritrea in 1936 (followed by the Wolqait district of Begemder in 1939).

In 1942 Tigrai reverted to Ethiopia after a brief period of British military occupation, but the concept of an autonomous "Greater Tigrai," including the Tigrinya-speaking population of Eritrea, was kept alive by the BRITISH ADMINISTRATION in Eritrea and Eritrean notables such as Ras TESSEMA ASBEROM, while in Tigrai itself the idea of a "Tigrai/Tigrinya" state was part of the inspiration behind the Woyane revolt of 1943. The "Tigrai/Tigrinya" concept died in 1944, after Emperor HAILE SELASSIE I skillfully forced the British to accept his rule over the province and equally adeptly regained the loyalty of Tigrai's hereditary governor, Ras Mengesha. Thereafter, Tigrai served as a recruiting ground and base for the UNIONIST PARTY and pro-Ethiopian SHIFTA operating in Eritrea. But the heart of the "Tigrai/Tigrinya" concept of a shared cultural identity continued, and during the 1960s political links between highland Eritreans and Tigreans were renewed in Ethiopian STUDENT ORGANIZATIONS, and from these developed the close ties between the EPLF and TIGREAN PEOPLE'S LIBERATION FRONT.

Immigration in particular has linked the two Tigrinya-speaking regions since ancient times. Among many precolonial examples there is the settlement of western SERAYE by Tigreans associated with the medieval religious movement led by EWOSTATEWOS, the great intermixing of populations on both sides of the Mareb-Gash River, and the "Eritrean" (from western Seraye) ancestry of much of the population of Tigrai's Adi Abo district, between the Mareb and SETIT rivers. Since the colonial era began, Tigrean immigration into Eritrea has been greatest from the impoverished Agame region, which borders on SHIMEZANA in southern AKELE GUZAI. During the Italian and British administrations, Agame supplied much of Eritrea's casual urban labor, and the name "Agame" acquired a pejorative connotation among highland Eritreans. Agames and other Tigrean immigrants also made up much of the *makalay ailet* class (*see* ENDA) of landless rural laborers and tenant farmers, as well as seasonal agricultural workers on the lowland plantations of GASH-SETIT. During the 1940s, the tide of Tigrean immigration was so great that the British deported thousands of indigent immigrants, and into the 1970s Tigrean immigrants still made up a large proportion of the urban poor, many of whom survived by selling cactus fruit and other marginal activities.

The immigrants' frugal habits, however, combined with political favors from the Ethiopian authorities enabled many Tigreans to become entrepreneurs during the 1970s. After 1975, a renewed Tigrean immigration was encouraged by the DERG, and Tigrean factory workers and small business owners filled positions left empty by the flight of Eritrean nationalists and REFUGEES, while others became rich serving the Ethiopian military as contractors, bar maids and prostitutes. These new immigrants were resented by Eritreans, and many were deported or left voluntarily in 1991. Nonetheless, significant numbers of Tigreans have remained, and their position is aided by the close ties between the present Eritrean government and the Tigrean-dominated government of Ethiopia (*see* TIGREAN PEOPLE'S LIBERATION FRONT). In January 1992 immigrants in Asmara formed a mutual aid association, and although there have been some tensions between recent immigrants and native Eritreans, the general relationship between the two Tigrinya-speaking regions is extremely good. Buttressing this mutual respect is a shared past and mixed bloodlines that are highlighted by the Tigrean ancestry of notable nationalist leaders, including WOLDE-AB WOLDE-MARIAM and ISAIAS AFWERKI.

TIGRE (alt.: Tigray). Eritrea's second-most widely spoken language, Tigre is closer to ancient GE'EZ than its other Semitic relatives, TIGRINYA and AMHARIC. This has led some scholars to conjecture that Tigre developed out of the Cushitic-Semetic fusion in the Eritrean region which predated the AKSUMITE EMPIRE. Today's Tigre speakers are a mix of HABESHA peoples with later BEJA and Arab immigrants, but the language seems to have changed little since late Aksumite times. It is spoken today on the coastal plain north of the gulf of ZULA, in all the northern highlands and much of BARKA. Tigre-speaking ethnic groups, some of which are bilingual in ARABIC or Beja, include the AD SHAYKH, BENI' AMER, BET ASGHEDE, MARYA, MENSA', and the smaller SAHEL and SEMHAR tribes.

Among all these peoples a class division exists between an aristocratic clan of non-Tigre origin (*see* SHUMAGULLE) and the common people, who are usually referred to as "Tigre." The name therefore has also taken on connotations of "serf," because the commoners owed multiple labor obligations and dues to the aristocratic clans.

During the 1940s IBRAHIM SULTAN ALI began a "serf emancipation" movement that ended most of these semi-feudal obligations during 1947-49. The last of them were abolished by the liberation fronts in the 1970s.

Although most of the Tigre people belonged to the ORTHODOX CHURCH in the medieval period, by the late-1800s they had become uniformly Muslim (*see* ISLAM). The spread of Islam precluded the development of an indigenous Tigre literature until the 1970s, as   preference was given to ARABIC as the language of literature, religious instruction and education throughout the Tigre-speaking areas, despite Tigre's rich oral tradition of Muslim religious verses and commentaries. Consequently, it was Christian missionaries who first produced Tigre texts in both Arabic and Ge'ez scripts, beginning with the Swedish Evangelical Mission at GHELEB . European scholars, including missionaries, also took an interest in Tigre's extremely rich tradition of oral poetry and folk tales, some of which were collected and published by MUNZINGER, E. Littman and K. G. Roden, among others. In the early 1970s the ELF also started to collect Tigre oral traditions, followed by the more thorough mimeographed collections published by the EPLF in the 1980s.

The literary development of Tigre has been a politically contested issue since the 1940s, as most educated Tigre-speaking Muslims have been attached to the concept of Arabic as the proper language of formal education, and this idea was reinforced by the pan-Arabist politics of the early nationalist movement in the lowlands (*see* MUS-LIM LEAGUE; ERITREAN LIBERATION FRONT) and the long years that many Tigre-speakers spent as REFUGEES in Arabic-speaking countries during the ARMED STRUGGLE. Indeed, the Ethiopian government pioneered Tigre-language RADIO broadcasts in the 1960s in an attempt to counter Arab-oriented nationalist sentiments. In the 1970s it was the EPLF that introduced primary EDUCATION in Tigre rather than Arabic for Tigre native speakers, and although this was based on practical considerations (*see* EDUCATION), it also had a political component in that it ran counter to the ELF's pro-Arabic policies.

Because of the near-total illiteracy of its native speakers, the use of Tigre in radio broadcasts and popular MUSIC since the 1960s has probably had the greatest impact on the language's development and national acceptance. Particularly important were the singers Idris Amir and Al-Amin, who first brought Tigre music to urban Eritrea, where its powerful rhythms and haunting melodies made it popular among all linguistic groups. Since liberation the Eritrean government's educational program has given great impetus to the development of Tigre literature, including textbooks and collections of poetry, and we may expect a flowering of the language over the next decade.

TIGREAN PEOPLE'S LIBERATION FRONT (TPLF). The TPLF was founded in February 1975 by a group of students and peasants from Ethiopia's TIGRAI province. The front grew out of the Tigrean wing of Ethiopian STUDENT ORGANIZATIONS, some of whose more radical members had returned to Tigrai province from ADDIS ABABA in late 1974 to form a political movement initially known as the Tigrean National Organization. In need of training and logistical support, the Tigreans approached the ELF and EPLF for help. The ELF was uninterested, but the EPLF, after receiving assurances that the Tigreans supported Eritrea's right to self-determination, took about thirty fighters for training in January 1975. Around the same time the EPLF also took in a number of Ethiopian People's Revolutionary Party (EPRP) fighters for training, who included many Tigreans.

The EPLF's strategy of developing allies in northern Ethiopia turned out to be one of the most important in eventually winning Eritrean independence. The strategy naturally focused on the Tigreans because of their cultural ties with central Eritrea, but neither the TPLF or EPLF ever revived the "Tigrai/Tigrinya" ideas of the 1940s or in any way advocated the formation of state linking the TIGRINYA-speaking peoples of Tigrai and Eritrea (*see* TIGRAI). Instead, the TPLF advocated a democratic Ethiopia in which different nationalities would have regional autonomy and the right to self-determination. EPLF support was critical for the early TPLF, which held its first congress at its base in Agame in early 1976. During 1976-78 the TPLF fought not only the DERG but, more importantly, the conservative EDU, led by former Tigrean governor, Ras Seyoum Mengesha; the EPRP, which had established its own base in eastern Tigrai; and a rival Tigrean nationalist group supported by the ELF. After defeating these rivals, by mid-1978 the TPLF controlled Tigrai, and managed to survive the first Ethiopian OFFENSIVES against neighboring Eritrea, aiding the Eritrean fronts where possible.

In 1979 the TPLF held an organizational congress that reiterated its political program, and in March 1980 attacked a remnant of the EPRP which had established itself in Wolqait on the remote western borders of Tigrai. The ELF supported this EPRP group, but the TPLF defeated them and joined forces with the EPLF in the second Eritrean CIVIL WAR to attack the ELF in GASH-SETIT and help drive them out of Eritrea. The TPLF was the EPLF's only ally in its desperate struggle against the RED STAR CAMPAIGN, when some three thousand Tigreans who were training with the EPLF fought on the front lines in SAHEL, while TPLF units attacked Ethiopian convoys in Tigrai. In return the EPLF provided the TPLF transmission over its RADIO station, logistical support and training. The TPLF also took advantage of the Derg's preoccupation with Eritrea to consolidate its hold over most of the Tigrean countryside during 1980-85.

In March 1985 relations between the two fronts broke down, apparently due to EPLF criticism of the TPLF's political formula of ethnically-defined self-determination for Ethiopia's nationalities, as well as differences over military strategy and the TPLF's decision to evacuate hundreds of thousands of Tigrean REFUGEES to SUDAN during the 1984-85 FAMINE. After this break the TPLF leadership began a vocal attack on the USSR, adopting what they called the "Albanian" Marxist-Leninist line. The front also formed a political organization, the Marxist-Leninist League of Tigrai, which engaged in the type of arcane political debates and violent purges that had characterized the Ethiopian student movement a decade earlier, and which the EPLF was in the process of abandoning completely. Finally, the TPLF began to meddle in Eritrean internal conflicts, supporting several of the Christian splinter groups in SAGHEM.

The two fronts did not resume cooperation until after the EPLF victory at AFABET clarified the strategic situation. During April 20-24, 1988, the fronts' leadership met and resolved their political differences, agreeing to combine their resources and plan a joint military strategy against the DERG. They also became more deeply involved in supporting anti-Derg organizations in other parts of Ethiopia, particularly the Oromo Liberation Front and Ethiopian People's Democratic Movement (EPDM), which the TPLF eventually led in forming the umbrella Ethiopian Peoples' Revolutionary Democratic Front (EPRDF). The EPLF supplied artillery and armor to reinforce the TPLF in its major campaign to clear Tigrai of Ethiopian forces, culminating in the Battle of Shire during February 15-20, 1989. During August 3-5 the leadership of the fronts met again and planned their strategy for the final campaigns against the Derg, in which the TPLF/EPRDF moved south, supported again by EPLA heavy weapons, and eventually captured ADDIS ABABA simultaneously with the EPLF's liberation of Asmara. The TPLF Secretary-General, Meles Zenawi, then led the EPRDF in forming a new Ethiopian government, which supported Eritrea's right to hold a REFERENDUM on independence. Despite many potential problems, Meles Zenawi's government continues to maintain close relations with Eritrea as of 1997, and the ties developed between the two fronts during the war are maintained particularly at the level of military cooperation, security and a common diplomatic policy regarding SOMALIA, SUDAN, and other regional issues.

TIGRINYA (alt.: Tigrigna, Tigray). The most widely spoken Eritrean language and the mother tongue of the people of both the KEBESSA and TIGRAI province in Ethiopia. (The name "Tigrinya" is actually an Amharicism, and the

Tigrinya name for the language is Tigray; but because of confusion with the name of Eritrea's second most important language, TIGRE, "Tigrinya" is preferred). Tigrinya is a Semitic language, related to GE'EZ, Tigre, and more distantly, AMHARIC, and like them it contains many Cushitic elements.

The origins of Tigrinya are obscure, and there is today a debate as to whether the language is actually derived from GE'EZ, as commonly supposed, or developed simultaneously with Ge'ez and Tigre, perhaps in the Kebessa region during the AKSUMITE period. CONTI ROSSINI cites a thirteenth or fourteenth century set of landcharters from the monastery of Kuna Aba Mata (*see* D E B R E LIBANOS) as the oldest Tigrinya written documents, but these have disappeared. The first historical source mentioning Tigrinya as a language occurs only in the fifteenth century, and the oldest extant Tigrinya literature is a law code from LOGGO Sarda, dated to perhaps the early nineteenth century, although it seems to be a copy of a fifteenth century document. Before the twentieth century Tigrinya was essentially a vernacular of the common people, while the educated classes used Ge'ez and Amharic for writing (Tigrinya still contains many loan-words from these languages). Consequently, the development of Tigrinya as a written language stemmed primarily from the work of European missionaries at the end of the nineteenth century.

Protestant missionaries and Eritrean converts of the Swedish Evangelical Mission (SEM) were most active in developing the language. The SEM opened its first Tigrinya school in 1890 and had published twenty-five texts in the language by 1917. Most notable of SEM linguists was Tewolde-Medhin Gebre-Medhin (1860-1930), who translated much of the Bible and assisted J. Kolmodin in compiling an important collection of Eritrean folktales and oral history. Among early Catholics the most important linguist was Aba Yaqob Gebre-Yesus (1881-1961), who published Tigrinya grammars and religious texts in the 1920s. To these early efforts were added those of the

Orthodox monks of DEBRE BIZEN who published *Treasures of the Faith.*

The Italian colonial state also was interested in developing literary Tigrinya as an alternative to Amharic as part of its "Politica Tigrina" (*see* TIGRAI). In 1903 the first Tigrinya-Italian-Arabic dictionary was published by Hagos Tekeste, and in 1918 Francesco Da Bassano published a Tigrinya-Italian dictionary. By the 1940s the modern Tigrinya language was taking shape. In urban centers a new vernacular developed incorporating numerous Italian loan-words, while scholars like WOLDE-AB WOLDE-MARIAM worked to construct a literary language. In the 1940s the opening of Tigrinya-language schools (*see* EDUCATION) and a popular PRESS added much to the language's development, which continued with even greater impetus in the early years of FEDERATION, when Tigrinya became one of Eritrea's two official languages. In 1950 the first widely read Tigrinya novel was published, Aba Gebreyesus Hailu's *Hade Zanta* ("One Story") about an ASCARI in the Italo-Libyan wars. Works of history and literature continued into the 1960s, but with the official banning of Tigrinya from Eritrean schools and Ethiopian government support for Amharic, Tigrinya literature declined in the 1960s-70s.

After 1975 the EPLF worked to revive Tigrinya literature, publishing numerous political tracts and histories. In 1981 a Tigrinya-Arabic-English dictionary was completed at the front's research center in SAHEL, and during the 1980s Tigrinya folktales and oral histories were collected. The Tigrinya press continued in Asmara in the official newspaper *Hibret* ("Union"), and in 1984 the Derg allowed the municipality to establish another Tigrinya newspaper, *Dimtsi Asmare* ("Voice of Asmara"). In the 1980s, Abraham Negash conducted research on the history of the language at the UNIVERSITY OF ASMARA.

Since liberation there has been a great renaissance of Tigrinya literature, drama and music, led by former EPLF FIGHTERS who have formed cultural groups like the Mahaber Feqri Sene-Tebeb ("Art Lovers' Association"), which publishes the literary magazine *Candle* and

sponsors DRAMA. The historical works of Aba Yisak
Gebre-Yesus and the novels of Musa Aaron are popular,
along with an increasing number of works concerning the
ARMED STRUGGLE. The American Evangelical Mission has
published a Tigrinya-English grammar, and Amanuel
Sahle is preparing a new Tigrinya-English dictionary. In
education Tigrinya is taught in primary grades throughout the highlands and increasing numbers of textbooks are
available. Although Eritrea has avoided designating any
"official" national languages, Tigrinya is the most widely-
used language of commerce and government.

TOKOMBIA (Gash-Setit; alt.: Tucumbia, Dukumbya). An
important market center for the livestock trade of southeastern GASH-SETIT, Tokombia is located on the Gash
River in the heart of the KUNAMA area. It was the site of
numerous guerrilla raids during the early ARMED STRUG-
GLE, but remained in Ethiopian hands until October
1984, when the EPLF overran the Ethiopian garrison. The
DERG regained it in 1985, and it was not finally liberated
until April 1988. Today it is developing as a thriving
commercial and district administrative center, and plans
have been made to connect it to both BARENTU and AREZA
with all-weather roads.

TOR'A (alt.: Tero'a). The most northerly of the SAHO
tribes, the Tor'a ("grazers") inhabit the eastern escarpment of the central highlands from the HADAS River to the
SEMENAWI BAHRI area north of GHINDA. The Tor'a are
Muslim agro-pastoralists, most of whom are bilingual in
TIGRE. Their permanent camps are centered around
Agameda. During the colonial period they were divided
between two sub-tribes, the Bet Sarah, who were affiliated
with the ASAWORTA tribe as clients, and the Bet Muse,
who were bilingual in TIGRINYA and came under the political control of the chiefs of TSENADEGLE. Tensions between Tor'a pastoralists and Christian farmers over grazing land has led to several inter-ethnic conflicts, the most
recent being the TOR'A-TSENADEGLE WAR, which was
only settled in 1996. The Tor'a supported the ELF during

the early ARMED STRUGGLE, and many fled as REFUGEES in the 1970s.

TOR'A-TSENADEGLE WAR. The land conflict between the SAHO-speaking Muslim Tor'a and the TIGRINYA-speaking Christian peasants of TSENADEGLE was the most famous and bitter of many similar disputes between lowland pastoralists and highland agriculturists. Because of its ethno-religious overtones the Tor'a-Tsenadegle conflict was exploited by various political groups to divide the people of the region, and consequently symbolizes the volatile mixture of sectarian, ethnic and economic disputes that had to be overcome in the process of Eritrean nation-building. The dispute can be traced to the Italian colonial period, when Tor'a pastoralists refused to pay land taxes to Tsenadegle authorities for the use of mid-elevation land around Wa'alita, which Tsenadegle claimed. In 1914 a colonial court ordered the Tor'a to pay the tax, which they did until 1942. In that year the Tor'a petitioned the new BRITISH ADMINISTRATION (BMA) claiming the land was historically theirs, but in August 1946 the BMA decided in favor of Tsenadegle.

The BMA decision provoked serious fighting between the two groups on August 15. The British military intervened, imposing collective fines, but raids and ambushes continued between the two groups leaving about four dead. Both sides believed the BMA supported the other, and attempts to adjudicate the dispute in traditional courts failed. The violence was inflamed by the sectarian politics of the time, with the UNIONIST PARTY supporting Tsenadegle and the MUSLIM LEAGUE supporting the Tor'a. In April 1950 large-scale fighting again occurred, this time between armed SHIFTA bands, leaving over twenty dead around Agameda, and in June sixty Ethiopian-supported shifta arrived from TIGRAI to lead an attack around Miskile in which over sixty people died from both sides. Finally, in 1951 the British anti-shifta measures largely ended the fighting, though raiding continued between the two groups and the dispute was unresolved.

In the 1960s the ELF supported Tor'a claims while the Ethiopians armed a Tsenadegle BANDA in 1971, leading to renewed fighting. The development of the Christian wing of the ELF-PLF at nearby ALA gave the Tsenadegle their first positive relations with nationalist fighters, and in 1977 the Christian militia deserted to the EPLF when Tsenadegle was liberated. As the two fronts sought a unity agreement the Tor'a-Tsenadegle conflict became a major concern, and in March 1978 a joint ELF-EPLF commission brought seventy SHUMAGULLE from AKELE GUZAI together to settle the dispute, but no resolution was reached before the DERG's First Offensive overwhelmed the fronts. The dispute festered during the grim military occupation and FAMINES of the 1980s, and erupted again in May 1993 with fighting over firewood collection and grazing in Wa'alita. The EPLF attempted to separate the warring parties, but in June a man was killed, and in July top government officials intervened, led by RAMADAN MOHAMED NUR.

The government established provisional borders and the disputed lower Wa'alita area was designated neutral state land *(terre demaniale)* in which both sides could graze. But when Tsenadegle peasants attempted to go to their winter croplands around Agameda in October 1993 they were blocked by armed Tor'a, leading to further government intervention. In June 1994 renewed fighting killed three men near Serkat, and on July 20, ISAIAS AFWERKI met with the two group's leaders at DEKEMHARE, advising them that if they did not settle the conflict the government would permanently confiscate the land. Military units were stationed in the area and the antagonists were disarmed. Negotiations then began between the two communities and a complex resolution was eventually reached in which both parties gained access to the disputed lands on a rotational basis. The accord was celebrated in a formal ceremony at Silke in late April 1996, attended by 8,000 members of the two communities, government officials and President Isaias, who placed great emphasis on the symbolic importance for the entire nation of the resolution of this 84-year-old dispute.

TOURISM. Tourism first developed in Eritrea under the Fascist administration in the 1930s, when the state-owned CIAAO hotel chain and a detailed guidebook were created to popularize Italy's new African empire. HAILE SELASSIE I's government continued to promote tourism in the 1960s, particularly around MASSAWA, but the ARMED STRUGGLE ended it by the early 1970s. Today Eritrea's coral-lined Red Sea coast and ancient archaeological sites are among the resources which the government hopes will attract foreign tourists. To this end a Tourism Department was created in 1992, and in March 1994 was elevated to ministry status under the direction of Worku Tesfamikael, who was replaced by Ahmed Haj Ali in 1997. The ministry overseas promotional activities, the development of a resort complex on DAHLAK Island, scuba diving facilities, the government-owned hotel system (much of which is being privatized) and the government tourism office, which rents cars and guide services. During 1996 Eritrea had four thousand foreign visitors and tourism directly employed about three thousand.

TRADE ROUTES (Historical). From the SOUTH ARABIAN period through the AKSUMITE period Eritrea's most important commercial routes led from ADULIS to southern AKELE GUZAI and ETHIOPIA via the HADAS and KUMALIE river gorges. By the tenth century the route had shifted to the north, with the rise of MASSAWA, and climbed into the central highlands by several routes, from DIGSA in northern Akele Guzai, to ASMARA in HAMASIEN. By the fourteenth century, perhaps because of the inroads of the SAHO in Akele Guzai, the most important caravan route to Ethiopia ran through SERAYE, and Asmara became an important crossroads of this trade route with medieval PILGRIMAGE ROUTES. Routes of great antiquity but lesser importance ran from the KEBESSA to KEREN and then westwards through BARKA to the Nile Valley, and from the ASSAB area to central Ethiopia. Most goods were carried by donkey or mule in the highlands, and by CAMEL in the lowlands.

TRIPARTITE UNITY FORCES (Tigrn.: Hade Selestenya: Arab.: Wahed al-Salasiyya). A reformist movement in the ELF, the Tripartite Unity Forces were created at the ANSEBA Conference in September 1968, when members of the ESLAH reform movement brought together the leadership of ZONAL COMMANDS 3-5 to denounce the external leadership of the SUPREME COUNCIL and the tribalist politics of the leaders of Zones 1 and 2. The movement dissolved in 1970 as most of its members (including ISAIAS AFWERKI and RAMADAN MOHAMED NUR) left the ELF to form the constituent elements of what became the EPLF.

TSAZZEGA (Hamasien). The residence of the hereditary ruling family of HAMASIEN during the eighteenth to mid-nineteenth centuries, Tsazzega was founded in the early seventeenth century by the younger sons of Tesfazion Ate-Shum, ruler of Hamasien (*see* DEQI TESHIM; HAZZEGA). Tesfazion's son Habte-Sellasie ("Habsullus") and grandson, Gebre-Kristos, expanded the House of Tsazzega's power over most of the Eritrean highlands by the early eighteenth century, while the three sons of Gebre-Kristos (Tesfazion, Mamu, and Rase-Haymanot) extended their rule over northern TIGRAI and Wolqait as well during the 1730s. The highpoint of Tsazzega's power came under BAHRE NEGASHI Solomun (son of Tesfazion) in the 1740s, and is remembered as an era of peace and justice in the highlands. But Solomun's general, Mika'el "Sehul," usurped his rule in TIGRAI and briefly deposed his son, Bokru, in favor of the House of Hazzega, beginning a bitter feud that eventually destroyed both Houses.

Tsazzega retained power over Hamasien through the 1830s, despite challenges from Hazzega, but during the reign of Dej. HAYLU TEWOLDE-MEDHIN the fortunes of the village declined and it was twice burnt (1865, 1879) by Haylu's rival, WOLDE-MIKA'EL SOLUMUN of Hazzega. Haylu was succeeded by his grandson, ABERRA KASA, whose rebellion against ITALIAN COLONIALISM ended the political power of the House. Tsazzega's importance attracted Protestant missionaries to the village in 1872,

prompting Tigrean persecution of Tsazzega priests, and
the establishment of a Swedish Evangelical Mission school
after the Italian occupation. The mission school produced
some of Eritrea's post-war intellectuals, but all those with
education moved to nearby ASMARA. Because of its
proximity to this city, Tsazzega was held by the Ethiopians throughout the war. Today the population is about
4,600.

TSENADEGLE (Akele Guzai). The highland district of
AKELE GUZAI around SAGENEITI populated by TIGRINYA-
speaking Christian farmers. During the colonial period its
population was involved in a bitter conflict with neighboring Muslim pastoralists known as the TOR'A-TSE-
NADEGLE WAR.

TSELMI. A traditional form of RISTI land tenure in which
usufruct rights to land are passed from generation to generation within a family, rather than periodically redistributed as in the ENDA-based RISTI or DESA systems.
This system, the closest that exists to hereditary land
ownership in Eritrea, was confined to some districts of
SENHIT before the 1994 revision of LAND LAWS.

TUKU'E IHADOGO (alt.: Tukuh Yehadego). Student leader
and key figure in the ERITREAN LIBERATION MOVEMENT
(ELM), Tuku'e was born in Asmara around 1942. He attended high school at Haile Selassie I Secondary School,
where he was a leading figure in the 1957 student strike.
A famous football (soccer) player, he hit a police captain
with his head and was arrested. After graduating he
played with the Adulis Football Club and in December
1959 was recruited into the ELM when the team was playing in Port Sudan. He became a key ELM organizer in Asmara, where he worked for the Civil Aviation Authority,
and in late 1962 helped organize a protest against Eritrea's ANNEXATION, for which he was arrested but later
released by Police General Tedla Ogbit. He fled to SUDAN
where he worked with the ELM until its demise, and then
joined the ELF. Disillusioned by the assassination of his

colleagues Wolde Ghiday and Kidane Kinfu, in 1970 he joined OSMAN SALEH SABBE's organization, working in Aden and SUDAN. He was killed in an ELF ambush in 1971 while bringing supplies from Port Sudan to ELF-PLF fighters in SAHEL.

TURKEY (Ottoman Empire). The Turkish occupation of the Eritrean region during the sixteenth century marked the beginning of the series of colonial administrations which did so much to shape modern Eritrea. After conquering EGYPT in 1517, the Ottoman Turks defeated the Portuguese and other rivals in a long struggle for control of the Red Sea. The architect of Turkey's Red Sea empire was Ozdemur Pasha, who had served as governor of Hijaz (SAUDI ARABIA) and part of SUDAN before he conquered most of YEMEN in 1545-48. In 1555 he turned his energies to the Eritrean region, where he planned to create a new province.

In 1557 Ozdemur landed at MASSAWA, which he fortified together with HIRGHIGO, and then expanded into the northern highlands, linking his new conquests with the existing governate of SUWAKIN. In 1558 he marched into the KEBESSA with an army of one thousand men, but was defeated in TIGRAI by BAHRE NEGASHI YESH'AQ and retired to the coast. Ozdemur died in 1560, but the new province of HABESHA, governed from Suwakin, survived. In 1561 Bahre Negashi Yesh'aq invited the Turks back to the highlands, where they built a fortified capital at DEBARWA. They held HAMASIEN until 1567, when Yesh'aq again drove them out. They returned in the 1570s at Yesh'aq's invitation but in 1578 were decisively defeated by the Ethiopian Emperor Sarsa Dengel when they tried to invade TIGRAI. A final attempt was made in 1588 to invade the highlands in support of a rebel leader in Hamasien, but when this was defeated at the borders of Tigrai they retreated to their fortifications around Massawa and Hirghigo, which Sarsa Dengel failed to capture in 1589. This resulted in a political division of what is now Eritrea that lasted three hundred years, with the coastal lowlands claimed by a foreign colonial power (Turkey,

later EGYPT) and the central highlands claimed by the
rulers of Tigrai.

Massawa and the coastal region was administered by
a Turkish officer, the Kaimakam, appointed by the governor in Suwakin, which itself soon came under the administration of the governor of Hijaz. The Kaimakan commanded
a small Turkish garrison, but during the seventeenth
century the garrison was not replenished and instead
married into the local BELEW clans, becoming a self-per-
petuating aristocracy in Massawa. Real political power
passed to the Turkish appointed NA'IB of Hirghigo. During
the eighteenth century the fortifications fell into disrepair and commerce stagnated as the Ottoman Empire itself
declined.

In 1809 direct Turkish control of Massawa was
briefly restored before Egypt took control in 1813. Turkish administration was nominally restored in the 1820s,
but the Egyptians returned in the 1840s, by which time
Turkish rule was strongly influenced by BRITAIN and
FRANCE. In the 1850s the Sultan banned the SLAVE
TRADE at Massawa under European pressure and further
reduced the Na'ib's power by sending a new garrison, but
in 1865 Egypt obtained a permanent lease on the port. In-
terestingly, most Eritreans made no distinction between
the Turks and the Egyptians, whose military officers were
largely of similar (Balkan) origins. Both powers were referred to as "Turkiyya," and in the highlands the Gezat
Turkiyya (Tigrn.: "Turkish Period") is remembered as one
of disorder and injustice. The Turks retained their nominal claim to Eritrea even after Eritrea's occupation by
ITALY, and during the Italo-Turkish war of 1911-12, an
Italian fleet based at Massawa bombarded Yemeni ports
occupied by Turks. In 1923 the Turks formally renounced
their sovereignty over Eritrea and neighboring Red Sea
islands in the Treaty of Lausanne.

- U -

UNION OF SOVIET SOCIALIST REPUBLICS (USSR). The
Soviet Union had a long and contradiction-laden relation-

ship with Eritrean nationalism, beginning in the 1940s when Russian delegates on the FOUR POWERS COMMISSION first supported Eritrea's return to ITALY in hopes of gaining support for the Italian Communist Party in its domestic elections, then, a month later, supported a collective trusteeship. They maintained this latter proposal at the UNITED NATIONS, with the addition that ASSAB should be ceded to ETHIOPIA, and then, in 1950 switched to support for Eritrea's independence. Most of these changes seem to have derived from USSR assessments of their own international interests in their growing Cold War with the UNITED STATES. Consequently, as long as the U.S. maintained military bases in Eritrea, the Soviet Union gave some support to the movement for Eritrean independence. But a until the 1970s it did this discreetly through its Eastern European allies and SOMALIA, as it also maintained cordial relations with HAILE SELASSIE I's government, to which it extended $100 million in economic loans in 1959.

This ambiguous situation changed dramatically after the Ethiopian revolution brought to power the Marxist-oriented DERG. The Russians developed both a pragmatic and a romantic attachment to the new Ethiopian regime, which they saw as a key to their new expansionist African policy and in which they thought they saw parallels with their own revolutionary experience. In December 1976 the Derg negotiated a secret military agreement with the USSR, providing $385 million in arms contingent on Ethiopia's ouster of the U.S. For a short time the Russians believed they could bring together their clients, Somalia and South YEMEN (PDRY), Eritrean nationalists, and Ethiopia in a socialist-oriented regional federation. In March 1977 Fidel Castro toured the region with this proposal, but the plan was rejected by both the ELF and EPLF, as well as Somalia. Following this failure the USSR broke relations with Somalia, which had invaded Ethiopia's Ogaden region, while in May 1977 the Derg's leader, Mengistu Haile-Mariam, went to Moscow, where he was promised a further $500 million in arms.

During 1977-78 the ELF continued to praise the Soviet Union in an attempt to maintain good relations, and the EPLF refused to publicly criticize the USSR until after 1980. Both fronts clung to their own Marxist idealism and hoped the USSR would change its policy. Instead, the Soviet Union criticized the Eritreans as "secessionists" and agents of Western imperialism. From December 1977 through March 1978 the USSR supplied modern military equipment to Ethiopia including 400 tanks and 70 MiG fighter-bombers. The first Russian weapons and technicians showed up at the Battle of MASSAWA in late 1977, and following their defeat of the Somalis, the Russians turned on Eritrea in May 1978, leading the newly equipped Ethiopian army with an officer corps of over two hundred, including the commanding generals, and supplying pilots and technicians. The Soviets also brought in their allies, South Yemen, East Germany and Cuba to provide, respectively, combat, security, and logistical support. The result was the series of OFFENSIVES, which almost destroyed the ELF and drove the EPLF back to SAHEL.

The failure of the first five offensives to destroy the EPLF led the Russians to attempt other policies. One was the introduction of poison gas, which began in 1980, but was not widely used. Another was to open negotiations with the Eritrean fronts through Arab and East European allies. These were rejected by the EPLF and OSMAN SALEH SABBE, but the ELF pursued them as a means of regaining its position. In January, 1980, IDRIS OSMAN GALADEWOS met with Russian diplomats in Beirut, who proposed a limited Ethiopian-Eritrean federation, and from August to November, AHMED NASSER negotiated with the Derg, USSR and ITALIAN Communists, but failed to reach an agreement. Following this, the Soviets supported the Derg's multifaceted RED STAR CAMPAIGN, and by 1985 had shipped a total of $4 billion in arms to Ethiopia. In return the USSR received much of Ethiopia's hard currency earnings, over half of which still came from trade with the West, and the rights to use DAHLAK Island as a naval base.

The Derg's failure to defeat the EPLF and its increasing economic problems, highlighted by the 1984-85 FAMINE, led to a change of Soviet policy in 1985 under Gorbachev. By 1988 the USSR was highly critical of the Derg's "mechanistic" application of Marxist-Leninist ideas and particularly its disastrous collectivization program. The Battle of AFABET, where three Soviet officers were captured and one killed, also led the USSR to reassess its policies. Military aid began to be scaled back in 1989, but after the disasters of that year a team of top Russian generals visited Ethiopia and recommended one final military aid package in an attempt to stave off the Derg's collapse, probably to protect their massive investment in Ethiopia. In 1990 new arms shipments were sent via Assab, and by 1991 Ethiopia owed the USSR $8.6 billion for arms, which the post-Derg government repudiated. The collapse of the USSR simultaneously with that of the Derg was more than an irony of history, as it was the USSR that enabled the Derg to survive in its last decade. The arms supplied by the Soviet Union certainly lengthened the Eritrean war for independence, and vastly increased its brutality and devastation. Today Eritrea maintains diplomatic relations with the new Russian state, and neither government has raised the issue of war reparations.

UNIONIST PARTY. The political party that favored Eritrea's unification with ETHIOPIA and dominated the ensuing FEDERATION (1952-62). The Unionist Party's roots lay in the pro-Ethiopian wing of the early Eritrean nationalist organization, MAHABER FEQRI HAGER (MFH), from which most of its leadership was drawn, and whose name the party kept in its Tigrinya-language title (Mahaber Feqri Hager Ertra: Ertra mis Etiopiya). From 1941 the unionist wing of the original MFH had been funded and guided by HAILE SELASSIE I's Ethiopian government, whose strategy was to gain the support of the TIGRINYA-speaking Christian population of the KEBESSA by appealing to the historical and cultural links they shared with northern Ethiopia. The Emperor enlisted the ORTHODOX CHURCH, led by its Eritrean bishop, Abuna

Marqos, to gain support among rural Tigrinya/Christians, while in Asmara the unionists appealed to this community's resentments against the economically prosperous ITALIAN POPULATION and Muslim (frequently Arab) merchant community, both of which seemed to have the favor of the BRITISH ADMINISTRATION (BA).

Unionist members of the MFH helped instigate the 1944 POLICE strike, and in July 1946 their pro-Ethiopian demonstrations led to clashes with the BA, followed by anti-Arab rioting and the shooting deaths of four unionists by the SUDAN DEFENSE FORCE (SDF) garrison in early August, followed by the August 28 massacre of forty-six Christians. These events, combined with rural violence by anti-Italian SHIFTA and Muslim-Christian feuds such as the TOR'A-TSENADEGLE WAR, all brought the unionists growing support among TIGRINYA-speaking Christians. WOLDE-AB WOLDE-MARIAM's attempt to find a political compromise capable of reuniting Eritrea's divided population led to the WA'LA BET GHERGHIS conference of November, but this reconciliation attempt was derailed by an extreme Unionist "coup" that overthrew the more moderate MFH leadership (see GEBRE-MESKAL WOLDU) and replaced it with a new pro-Ethiopian leadership that included Honorary President Kidane-Mariam Gebre-Meskal, Vice-President Saleh KEKIYA, Secretary-General TEDLA BAIRU and Assistant-Secretary HAREGOT ABAI. These officers, led by the dynamic Tedla, officially registered the Unionist Party in Asmara on January 1, 1947.

The Unionists concentrated their political organization on the Christian population of the Kebessa, but they also gained the support a few Muslim JIBERTI merchants and members of the aristocratic classes of some lowland tribes. To keep their support they extolled existing cultural links to Ethiopia and reminded their constituents of the injustices of European colonial rule and past Muslim domination (see EGYPT; TURKEY) in publications like *Etiopiya,* the party newspaper. They also employed intimidation and terrorism, as well as monetary subsidies and offers of future political positions, to insure the highland population's loyalty as the FOUR POWERS COMMISSION and then the UNITED NATIONS (UN) commission of investigation toured the country. By 1947 they claimed the support of an estimated 44.8 percent of the population, including 71.6 percent in the Kebessa. During 1949, however, as they lost support to the INDEPENDENCE BLOC and feared a UN decision favoring Eritrean independence, they stepped up a campaign of violence that employed shifta brigands based in Tigrai and urban terrorism, culminating in the February 1950 rioting in Asmara that left forty-seven dead.

Once the decision on FEDERATION was made, the Unionist Party concentrated on gaining elected power in the Eritrean ASSEMBLY, where in 1952 they won thirty-two of sixty-eight seats, forming the largest party but not a majority. They gained control of the Assembly through an alliance with the MUSLIM LEAGUE OF THE WESTERN PROVINCE, and this enabled them to elect Tedla Bairu as Eritrean Chief Executive. The Unionists proceeded to monopolize the disposition of official positions and government jobs, which abounded during the Eritreanization of the Civil Service. Political patronage increased buttressed their popularity, but many Unionists also became attached to Eritrea's autonomous institutions, including the Chief Executive. This led to divisions in the party as Ethiopia pressed for complete unification. The Ethiopians took advantage of Tedla Bairu's unpopularity to remove him in 1955, and thereafter the party's leader, Keshi DIMETROS GEBREMARIAM, and the new Chief Executive, ASFAHA WOLDE-MIKA'EL, were mere creatures of the Ethiopian throne.

The elections of 1956 and 1960 returned ever larger Unionist majorities, but the party's leaders still had difficulty in obtaining an Assembly vote for complete ANNEXATION. When this was achieved in November 1962 what was left of the party was bought off with Ethiopian pensions and sinecures, after which it ceased to exist, as political parties were illegal in Haile Selassie's Ethiopia. Nonetheless, unionist politicians continued to dominate much of Eritrea's local government into the early 1970s, when many became disillusioned with Ethiopian rule and, ironically, turned to support Eritrean nationalism.

UNITED NATIONS. Eritrea has been called a "child," or better an "orphan," of the United Nations (UN) because its political future was decided by the international body in 1950. The "Eritrean Question" was put before the UN on September 15, 1948, following the failure of the Four Powers to arrive at a decision. Initially, Eritrea's future was tied to that of Italy's other African colonies: Libya and SOMALIA. At the Third General Assembly in 1949 BRITAIN and ITALY almost succeeded in partitioning Eritrea between ETHIOPIA and SUDAN under their BEVIN-SFORZA PLAN, but this was rejected because of a dispute over Libya. A number of Eritreans spoke before the General Assembly in May 1949, including IBRAHIM SULTAN ALI and TEDLA BAIRU.

After deciding the fate of Libya and Somalia, on November 21, 1949, a UN subcommittee decided to postpone the decision on Eritrea until the Fourth General Assembly and send a Committee of Investigation to the country, composed of representatives of Burma, Guatemala, Norway, Pakistan and South Africa. The Ethiopian government and UNIONIST PARTY stepped up their terrorist campaign before the Committee's arrival on February 12, 1950, and during February 21-23 ASMARA was wracked by severe intercommunal violence, prompting the UN committee to protest to the BRITISH ADMINISTRATION (BA), which in turn protested to Ethiopia. The committee's investigation was even more disorganized and less systematic than that of the Four Powers, and after leaving Eritrea (April 8) they drafted three separate reports. The Norwegian member recommended Eritrea's unification with Ethiopia; the Burmese and South African recommended a FEDERATION between the two; and the Pakistani and Guatemalan recommended independence after a ten-year trusteeship. The reports were submitted to the Interim Committee on Eritrea on July 13, but no decision could be reached because Italy, its Latin American supporters and a number of Muslim countries preferred independence, while the Western powers preferred union with Ethiopia.

The matter was then turned over to an Ad Hoc Political Committee where the UNITED STATES lobbied hard for Federation, which the Ethiopian government now supported. On November 26 the Ad Hoc committee adopted a largely U.S.-drafted resolution on Federation, which the Fifth General Assembly approved on December 2, 1950 (by 46 votes to 10), as UN Resolution 390 A (V). The BA was retained as the administering power, but a UN High Commissioner, Anze MATIENZO, was appointed to oversee the transition to Federation, which took place on September 15, 1952. The UN Federation scheme left Ethiopia with tremendous power (*see* FEDERATION), and no provisions were included for insuring that it did not violate the terms of the UN-drafted Federal Act, although Matienzo in his final report noted that the UN retained a general right to intervene as the UN resolution on Eritrea remained an "international instrument and, if violated, the General Assembly could be seized of the matter" (Final Report UNHC, ch. 2, p. 1).

The UN did create a Tribunal to oversee the disposition of former Italian parastatal companies. Eritrean nationalists submitted a number of petitions to this body, which sat in Asmara until June 1954, protesting Ethiopian encroachment on Eritrea's UN-mandated autonomy, but the Tribunal was not charged with these issues and failed to forward them to the Secretary-General. In 1957 MOHAMED OMAR CADI took a petition signed by prominent Eritreans to the UN General Assembly in New York, but received no response, and similar petitions made by Ibrahim Sultan in 1962, and IDRIS MOHAMED ADEM in 1963 had no effect. Eritrean attempts to lobby the UN during the 1960s-70s through sympathetic Arab countries were likewise blocked. During the 1980s, BEREKET HABTE-SELASSIE acted as the EPLF's representative to the UN, and although his arguments that UN resolutions dealing with decolonization could be applied to Eritrea were legally valid, the issue was never taken up.

It was only in 1991, after the new Ethiopian government agreed to support Eritrea's right to self-determination and wrote a letter to the UN Secretary-General to this
effect, that the UN turned its attention to Eritrea, approv-
ing a UN observer mission (UNOVER) to insure the valid-
ity of the Eritrean REFERENDUM. Eritrea joined the UN on
May 28, 1993, and on September 30, President ISAIAS
AFWERKI addressed the 48th General Assembly, remark-
ing:

> As I speak here today, I cannot help but re-
> member the appeals we sent year in and out to
> this Assembly ... describing the plight of our
> people and asking for legitimate sympathy,
> support and recognition. ... [but] the United
> Nations refused to raise its voice in the defense
> of a people whose future it had unjustly decided
> and whom it had pledged to protect.

Isaias went on to ask for increased international aid for
his war-torn country and other "marginalized" African
countries, but the UN High Commission for Refugees
(UNHCR) response to Eritrea's plea for massive aid for the
REPATRIATION of war REFUGEES was very limited.

On October 23, 1993, the UN Development Program
(UNDP) opened an office in Asmara intended to coordinate
a number of UN programs (FAO, UNHCR, UNICEF) to provide help with developing areas for refugee resettlement
and other tasks, but the controversies concerning repatriation and UN officials' criticisms of Eritrea's insistence on ultimate control over the programs led to a series
of disputes during 1993-94. These were overcome with the
acceptance of Eritrea's PROFERI repatriation plan, but as
relations with SUDAN deteriorated tensions again
mounted with UNHCR officials over screening repatriating
refugees from Sudan, and in May 1997 the entire UNHCR
foreign staff was expelled. Eritrea also has been a vocal
critic of the UN's failed policies in SOMALIA, Rwanda and
former Zaire (Congo). Outside the refugee sector relations
with UN agencies have been better. In April 1994, UNICEF

agreed to a four-year plan for aid in HEALTH CARE and EDUCATION, and other initiatives have followed.

UNITED STATES of America. The United States was instrumental in the 1950 UNITED NATIONS (UN) decision to Federate Eritrea with ETHIOPIA, and it supported HAILE SELASSIE I's control over Eritrea during 1953-74 with military and economic aid. American interest in Eritrea developed out of two quite different concerns. The primary one was to maintain access to military bases in Eritrea, the most important being the military communications base that the United States operated in ASMARA from 1942 onwards, which was renamed KAGNEW STATION in 1953 and remained a key component of U.S. Cold War strategies until 1973. In addition, the U.S. Navy also wanted to maintain access to port facilities at MASSAWA, which it had been using since 1941. The second concern of the United States during the 1940s to 1960s was to support Haile Selassie for political reasons having to do with his international stature as the leader of independent Africa and as an opponent of Fascism, colonialism and racism. These two interests converged in U.S. support for some form of unification between Eritrea and Ethiopia.

During the Four Powers discussions on Eritrea's future the United States largely followed BRITAIN's lead. Although they first proposed an international trusteeship, by 1948 U.S. delegates were proposing a partition plan that called for outright unification of DENKEL, AKELE GUZAI and SERAYE with Ethiopia and a trusteeship over the remaining area. At the UN in 1949 the U.S. supported Britain's BEVIN-SFORZA PLAN, but when this failed Americans began to lobby for FEDERATION as a compromise solution that would still give Ethiopia sovereignty over the increasingly valuable Eritrean military bases. U.S. support for Ethiopia was reinforced by Haile Selassie's offer of a battalion to serve in the Korean War, and following this, in the summer of 1950, the U.S. obtained British and Italian support for Federation, leading to the largely U.S.-drafted Federal Act being adopted by the UN in December.

Following Eritrea's federation with Ethiopia, the United States negotiated a 25-year lease on Kagnew Station and rights to use Massawa port in a Mutual Defense Assistance Agreement signed on May 22, 1953. In return for these facilities the U.S. was to pay rent on the bases and provide military training and equipment for a 30,000-man army. A U.S. Military Assistance Advisory Group (MAAG) arrived and the United States provided an average of $5 million in military aid per year during the 1950s. U.S. economic aid, increased purchase of Ethiopian exports and assistance in obtaining World Bank funds also followed. Because of the Kagnew base, much U.S. spending went into the Asmara economy, while aid projects like the Point 4 Technical School, Nursing School and U.S. Information Service Library benefited the city. In 1962 the first group of Peace Corps teachers arrived in Eritrea.

In 1960 a new agreement was negotiated increasing U.S. military aid to an average $10 million per year and providing for a 40,000-man army. In return, Haile Selassie supported the United States in the Congo, and in 1963 the United States obtained rights to use GURA' airfield for a military mapping project that later aided counter-insurgency operations against the ELF. As the conflict in Eritrea developed, and war with the Soviet-supported Somalis loomed, military aid was further increased, including a squadron of twelve F-5 jet fighter planes in 1964 and the first group of fifty-five U.S. counterinsurgency warfare specialists attached to MAAG specifically for operations in Eritrea. In 1965, the counterinsurgency team, code-named Delta, was increased to 164, but in 1966 was largely replaced by Israelis.

By the early 1970s the United States was concerned about the spread of the ARMED STRUGGLE in Eritrea, where ELF units had kidnapped U.S. personnel and sabotaged Kagnew. U.S. policy makers were disturbed by Haile Selassie's failure to restructure his autocratic government and the specter of political instability that loomed over his empire. In 1973 the US drastically cut back its Kagnew operations, and began to decrease its military aid to Ethiopia. But by 1974, when Haile Selassie was overthrown, the United States had given Ethiopia $253 million in military aid and $363 million in economic aid.

Despite its anti-U.S. rhetoric, the DERG continued to receive U.S. weapons during 1975-77, most of which ended up in Eritrea. Although direct aid decreased, the Derg purchased $100 million of military equipment in 1975, and in 1976 bought sixteen F-5Es for $72 million as well as other supplies. President Carter's condemnation of the Derg's human rights abuses and a secret agreement between the Derg and USSR led to U.S. withdrawal from Eritrea in early 1977 and a halt in U.S. weapons deliveries at the end of the year, but $1 million in "non-lethal" military equipment and $10 million in economic aid still was delivered to Ethiopia in 1978.

During the 1978-88 decade the United States criticized the USSR's support of the Derg's war in Eritrea, but made no attempt to aid Eritrean nationalists and continued to supply economic aid to Ethiopia through the International Development Agency and World Bank ($300 million during 1976-82). After FAMINE struck, the United States supplied Ethiopia with $270 billion in FOOD AID during 1984-88, about one-quarter of which went to Derg-controlled Eritrea. Although the United States also was beginning to supply large quantities of food aid to liberated Eritrea through the Lutheran World Relief Council during this period, and the EPLF had dropped its anti-Western rhetoric for a more pragmatic foreign policy, it was not until after the EPLF victory at AFABET that U.S. policy began to shift.

In April 1988, President Reagan condemned the Derg for its "policy of starvation" in TIGRAI and Eritrea, and in September 1989 former President Carter began a series of peace negotiations between EPLF and Derg representatives that had U.S. government blessing. The issue of food aid for the liberated zones was the opening wedge for this new diplomatic initiative, but there was clearly a new recognition among U.S. policy makers, led by Herman Cohen, that the EPLF and TPLF would soon be equal to the Derg, while the role of the USSR in the region was fast diminishing. In January 1990, U.S. Congressional staffers visited

liberated Eritrea and in February Cohen testified at a
Senate hearing that Eritreans had the right to self-determination, marking a complete change in U.S. policy. Immediately after this the EPLF was given access to U.S.
diplomats and established a mission in Washington, D.C.

In February 1991, ISAIAS AFWERKI visited Washington and discussed peace negotiations with Ethiopia. In
early May the Derg, EPLF and EPRDF (*see* TIGREAN PEO-
PLE'S LIBERATION FRONT) agreed to hold a peace conference in London, but when it took place during May 27-29
the Derg had already collapsed and instead the conference
was used to organize a U.S.-sanctioned transition to power
for the EPLF and EPRDF. United States support for the
1993 REFERENDUM helped smooth international acceptance of Eritrea's independence, and it marked a new and
increasingly close relationship between the United States
and EPLF. During the transition to independence the U.S.
provided food aid to sustain the population and the beginnings of a military aid program based on mutual interests in protecting the region against the spread of IS-
LAMIST movements based in SUDAN. Eritrea supported
the United States in the 1991 Gulf War against IRAQ, and
U.S. diplomacy was involved in the development of relations between Eritrea and ISRAEL, culminating in the U.S.
airlift of Isaias to Israel for emergency medical treatment
in 1993. Beginning in 1992, the United States was also
interested in obtaining Eritrean diplomatic aid in SOMA-
LIA, and in 1993 Eritrean intervention helped extricate
U.S. troops.

A U.S. representative was posted to Eritrea in August 1992, and after some heated discussions the former
U.S. consulate in Asmara was returned for use as a new
embassy, which opened immediately after the Referendum.
U.S. aid programs opened offices in the summer of 1993,
and in August a U.S. military mission visited to discuss
military aid and port visiting privileges. During Septem-
ber-October, President Isaias visited the United States
and held   diplomatic discussions concerning further bilateral ties as well as a public meeting with the large Eritrean DIASPORA community. During 1994, U.S. Navy

teams cleared wrecked ships from Massawa harbor and helped rebuild the hospital there, while on May 20 an agreement was signed to reestablish the Peace Corps in Eritrea, with the first group of twenty-five volunteers arriving in June 1995. In 1995 the U.S. Navy returned to help reconstruct some Massawa industries, while the United States pledged $13.2 million in development aid and a further $6.2 million in food aid. In September, 1996, the U.S. pledged a further $20 million in food aid through 1998. Today cooperation and development agreements in a number of fields link the United States and Eritrea, including the UNIVERSITY OF ASMARA and REFUGEE resettlement programs, while both military aid and diplomatic cooperation mark a joint policy to counter the National Islamic Front government in Sudan.

UNIVERSITY OF ASMARA. Eritrea's national university since 1992, the University of Asmara (UofA) was originally founded in 1958 as the Catholic College of Santa Famiglia on the grounds of an existing Catholic women's high school. The college was staffed by Italian teaching sisters and served the Eritrean middle class until 1967, when it was incorporated into the Ethiopian national university system as the University of Asmara. But it continued to be staffed largely by Catholic sisters, and until 1972 the language of instruction was Italian rather than English. The University had a mediocre reputation, and Eritrean students who could pass the entrance qualifications preferred to attend Haile Selassie I University in ADDIS ABABA or other Ethiopian technical colleges. The UofA's religious orientation and mediocrity was clearly preferred by the Ethiopian government, which had no intention of allowing the University to become a center of Eritrean intellectual activity or nationalism. Nonetheless, during 1972-74 many UofA students joined nationalist STUDENT ORGANIZATIONS, and in 1975 many left to join the liberation fronts rather than serve in the Derg's rural reform campaigns (*zemetcha*).

The University was largely closed during 1977-79, and reopened in 1980 as part of the Derg's educational system, which attempted to obliterate its Eritrean characteristics by replacing much of its teaching staff with Ethiopians and importing non-Eritrean students (75 percent by 1990). The University declined until its own staff described it as "a glorified high school," and in September 1990 its staff, students, books and equipment (computers, laboratories, etc.) were all transferred to Southern Ethiopia. When the EPLF arrived in 1991 all that was left were the buildings, which were used to provide extension courses for FIGHTERS, many of whom had left their studies in 1975. By 1992 a number of Eritrean and expatriate Catholic staff had returned, including Eritrean academics from other Ethiopian institutions, and in the fall the UofA began to offer its first regular classes. In the meantime the PGE government had taken a strong interest in rebuilding the University as the core of a national EDUCATION program designed to provide teachers for secondary schools and to increase Eritrea's self-sufficiency in technical and scientific fields. In 1992 an International Symposium brought together Eritrean DIASPORA academics and concerned foreigners to develop a long-term institutional plan.

Unfortunately, conflicts between staff and administration marred much of 1993, but in September a new president, Dr. Woldeab Yisak, was appointed and began implementing the International Symposium's recommendations and obtaining international support for academic development. UofA reopened in January 1994 with over eight hundred full-time day students and a larger number of night students (largely ex-fighters and government employees). Linkage programs were developed with various foreign universities to give Eritrean academics access to overseas training and provide funding, equipment and expatriate staff for the University. As of 1997, linkages include German and Australian university connections with Engineering; Norwegian and Finnish links with Education; Dutch and Italian links with Agriculture; American links with Archaeology, Law and Health; and Swedish links with Natural Sciences.

By 1996 the University had over twenty-five hundred full-time students, and in 1997 520 students graduated with bachelor's degrees. Problems still facing the University include the poor level of education among entering students; the small number of female students able to pass qualifying tests (only 11.7 percent of students in 1994/95); the overwhelming preponderance of TIGRINYA-speaking Christian students (over 90 percent of full-time students in 1993/94); and the continuing shortage of academic staff and equipment. But the enthusiasm of Eritreans for higher education, the high level of foreign interest, and the government's strong support, promise a bright future for the University.

- W -

WA'LA BET GHERGHIS (Tigrn.: "Bet Gherghis Meeting"). One of the key events in the development of Eritrean nationalist politics, the Bet Gherghis (alt.: Bet Giorgis) meeting was held during November 22-23, 1946, in the forested eastern suburb of ASMARA named for its ORTHODOX CHURCH dedicated to St. George. The meeting was organized during early November by ABDULKADIR KABIRE, GEBRE-MESKAL WOLDU, MOHAMED OMAR CADI, WOLDE-AB WOLDE-MARIAM, and other moderate leaders of the MAHABER FEQRI HAGER (MFH) nationalist front in an attempt to avoid the organization's permanent division into hostile pro-Independence and pro-Ethiopian UNIONIST factions following widespread sectarian violence (*see* TOR'A-TSENADEGLE WAR) and in anticipation of the BRITISH ADMINISTRATION's moves to legalize POLITICAL PARTIES. In a twelve-point draft submitted to the Wa'la, Wolde-Ab proposed to bring the two sides together with a compromise plan for "Conditional Union" (Tigrn.: *hibret bi woul'*) between Ethiopia and Eritrea, which in many respects prefigured their later FEDERATION.

Wolde-Ab's proposal was rejected by the pro-Ethiopian faction, led by Orthodox bishop Abuna Marqos, TEDLA BAIRU and the Ethiopian liaison officer, Colonel Nega Haile Selassie. The extreme Unionists favored "unconditional union" and on the night of November 22 organized a virtual coup against the moderate MFH leader Gebre-Meskal Woldu, replacing him with a pro-Ethiopian faction that formed the leadership of the new   UNIONIST PARTY. On November 23, Wolde-Ab and the moderates were confronted by the new leadership, supported by armed members of ANDENET, and Tedla Bairu launched a vicious personal attack on Wolde-Ab. The Wa'la then dispersed, with Tedla's supporters forming the Unionist Party and Independentists joining the MUSLIM LEAGUE or, a little later, the LIBERAL PROGRESSIVE PARTY.

WOKI DUBA (Hamasien). A small village in DEQI TESHIM district, today numbering about nine hundred people, Woki Duba has a tragic place in Eritrean history. On July 17, 1877, it was the site of the battle in which Ras WOLDE-MIKA'EL SOLOMUN defeated Dej. HAYLU TEWOLDE-MEDHIN of TSAZZEGA, killing him, his sons, and massacring a Swedish missionary and several others in the village church. A century later, during the ARMED STRUGGLE, Woki Duba was held jointly by the ELF and EPLF in October 1974, when it was the site of an important gathering of civilians and liberation forces during negotiations for a cease-fire in the First CIVIL WAR *(see* ZAGHER). But on February 2, 1975, during an engagement with the liberation fronts, the Ethiopian army massacred 103 villagers who had taken refuge in the church, prompting most of the villagers to flee to SUDAN as REFUGEES or join the EPLF.

WOLDE-AB   WOLDE-MARIAM (1905-1995). The leading TIGRINYA-speaking Christian figure in the early Eritrean nationalist movement, Wolde-Ab was born at Adi Zarna in SERAYE on April 27, 1905. His parents were immigrants from TIGRAI, his father from Adi Kelete near Aksum and his mother from Shire, but they had a relatively prosperous RISTI farm on which Wolde-Ab worked as a boy. His father sent Wolde-Ab and most of his eight siblings to the Swedish Evangelical Mission (SEM) school at MENDEFERA, where Wolde-Ab excelled and consequently attended the SEM seminary at BELEZA from 1926-30.

In 1931 Wolde-Ab was assigned to teach at the SEM school in Suzana, among the KUNAMA people, where he remained until 1935, when he returned to ASMARA to direct the SEM school system in Eritrea. During this period Wolde-Ab worked to regularize and popularize the writing of TIGRINYA, and in 1932 he published the first Tigrinya grammar, *Fidel tigrinya,* followed by his *Arki temheray* ("Students' Friend") in 1942, both of which became standard textbooks for the Eritrean school system through 1960. He remained director of SEM schools until 1942, when the BRITISH ADMINISTRATION enlisted him to direct and edit its Tigrinya-language newspaper, the *Semunawi gazetta,* published weekly by the British Information Service.

Wolde-Ab was already a leading Eritrean figure in the influential Protestant community, and the newspaper increased Wolde-Ab's political stature. He was a founding member of the MAHABER FEQRI HAGER (MFH), but unlike most Protestants, Wolde-Ab hesitated to support calls for Eritrea's unification with ETHIOPIA. His fears of Ethiopian domination were confirmed when he visited ADDIS ABABA in 1943, following his marriage to Aberash Yihdego. Although both he and his wife had many relatives in Addis, including leading members of the Protestant community of Mekane Yesus, Wolde-Ab was dismayed by the corruption and poverty of HAILE SELASSIE I's state. He returned to Eritrea determined to find an alternative political future involving independence, perhaps in some form of union with TIGRAI. Pan-Tigrean sentiments were encouraged by some British administrators and Ras TESSEMA ASBEROM, and in 1945 Wolde-Ab edited articles in the *Semunawi gazetta* supporting this policy.

By 1946, Wolde-Ab advocated a British trusteeship for Eritrea, followed by independence. But in October, as the MFH was splintering following intercommunal violence and Ethiopian support for a pro-Unionist faction, Wolde-Ab brought together both Muslim and Christian nationalists for the WA'LA BET GHERGHIS meeting, where he

advocated a conditional FEDERATION between Eritrea and
Ethiopia in an attempt to preserve the movement's unity.
After the failure of this compromise, and the founding of
other political parties, in February he co-founded the Eritrean LIBERAL PROGRESSIVE PARTY (LPP), but continued
to edit the *Semunawi gazetta* until 1948. His pro-independence stand, which he returned to following the Wa'la Bet
Gherghis failure, alienated Wolde-Ab from much of the
Christian community and made him the target of seven
Unionist assassination attempts during 1947-53, the first
two in June and July 1947. But Wolde-Ab continued to advocate Eritrean unity and independence, working closely
with ABDULKADIR KABIRE and IBRAHIM SULTAN ALI. In
1949 Wolde-Ab founded the Independent Eritrea Party
and joined the INDEPENDENCE BLOC, participating in the
delegation which argued Eritrea's case at the UNITED
NATIONS. In 1950 he became editor of the Bloc's Tigrinya
newspaper, *Hanti Ertra* ("One   Eritrea"), and   suffered
three more assassination attempts.

Following the UN decision to federate Eritrea and
Ethiopia, Wolde-Ab became vice-Secretary General of the
Eritrean Democratic Front, successor to the Independence
Bloc, and began working to create national LABOR ORGA-
NIZATIONS as a means of building a mass party capable of
resisting Ethiopian encroachment on Eritrean autonomy.
He suffered another attempt on his life in 1951, but con-
tinued to work for Eritrean autonomy under the new polit-
ical regime, authoring constitutional provisions safe-
guarding freedom of assembly and labor organization,
translating the new CONSTITUTION into Tigrinya, and in
November-December 1952 organizing the new Syndicate of
Free Eritrean Labor Unions, which elected him president.
Wolde-Ab represented a serious threat to Unionist and
Ethiopian domination, and in February 1953 he was attacked again, this time sustaining serious wounds which
left him hospitalized for five months. Nonetheless, he was
elected to the Eritrean ASSEMBLY in a by-election for his
Asmara district of Geza Khenisha, but his election was
annulled by TEDLA BAIRU. In the summer of 1953, under
intense political pressure, Wolde-Ab sought asylum in

EGYPT, leaving his wife and four young children in Eritrea.

In CAIRO he had difficulty continuing his political activity until 1956, when the Nasser government (*see* EGYPT) enabled him to make Tigrinya RADIO broadcasts into Eritrea for a few months beginning in early June. In 1957 he worked with MOHAMED OMAR CADI in a vain attempt to bring the Eritrean case to the UN's attention, but the sectarian politics of most of the Muslim exile community in Cairo left Wolde-Ab isolated until 1959. With the rise of the secular ERITREAN LIBERATION MOVEMENT (ELM), whose labor-oriented political program coincided with Wolde-Ab's own political vision, he returned to political activity, serving as the ELM's Cairo representative from 1961 through 1964, when he criticized the leaders' decision to send a separate military force into Eritrea in rivalry with the ELF. Wolde-Ab then participated in the Eritrean Unity Movement of the late 1960s along with MAHMOUD SAID NAWD, but his was a relatively isolated political voice until 1970, when OSMAN SALEH SABBE invited him to join the "foreign office" of the newly formed ELF-PLF. He remained associated with the foreign office, along with other prominent nationalists of earlier generations, until its demise in 1976, after which he was again isolated during the struggle between the ELF and EPLF.

The EPLF leadership, however, recognized Wolde-Ab, as well as Ibrahim Sultan, as heroic figures of the early nationalist movement, and during the late 1970s won Wolde-Ab over to their views on internal politics. In 1982 the EPLF assisted Wolde-Ab to move from Cairo to Rome, where he helped with EPLF public relations. In 1987 he returned to Eritrea for the first time to attend the Second and Unity Congress of the EPLF in SAHEL, making a moving speech on the need for national unity. His eulogy of Ibrahim Sultan a few months later reasserted Wolde-Ab's commitment to national unity, which he had made the cornerstone of his political career from the 1940s. In a 1983 interview he told this author, "I always said, 'I am not a Christian, I am not a highlander. I am an Eritrean.'"

Wolde-Ab rejoined his wife in Asmara following liberation, where he died May 15, 1995. His funeral was attended by the President and hundreds of thousands of
mourners, who all lauded the man who many see as the
"father" of both modern Eritrea and modern literary
Tigrinya.

WOLDE-MIKA'EL SOLOMUN, Ras (1823-1906). Leader
of the House of HAZZEGA in its power struggle with
TSAZZEGA, Ras Wolde-Mika'el ("Woldenkiel") spent much
of his life as a rebel SHIFTA in an attempt to maintain his
claim to local power caught between competing imperi-
alisms. He holds a controversial place in Eritrean history,
for he represents both the quest for independence in the
pre-colonial period, but at the same time his personal
ambition created many blood feuds, and his own cruelty
led to the destruction and depopulation of much of
HAMASIEN and Senhit. Wolde-Mika'el was born to Aite
Solomun, lord of Hazzega, and ILENI HAGOS, who struggled
to maintain power over Hamasien after her husband's
death. In 1850/51 Ileni's attempt, aided by Wolde-Mika'el
and his brother Merid, ended in disaster, and the brothers
fled to TIGRAI, returning in 1855 for revenge in their
blood feuds with DEMBEZAN and Tsazzega.

In 1856 they allied themselves with "Agaw" NE-
GUSSIE, nephew of Dej. WUBE, and Merid briefly ruled
HAMASIEN while his brother served as military leader in
continual battles with the forces of Tewodros and Dej.
HAYLU of TSAZZEGA. With Negussie's fall the brothers
lost power, Merid was imprisoned at Magdala, and in 1860
Wolde-Mika'el submitted to Dej. Haylu, receiving the
lordship of Minabe-Zerai (Hazzega) without its traditional
district of Ametsi. In 1864/65 the loss of Ametsi caused
Wolde-Mika'el to rebel against Haylu and burn his rival's
village, but in January 1866 he lost to Haylu in a battle at
ASMARA. Wolde-Mika'el then turned to the rising Tigrean
leader, Kassa Mertcha (YOHANNES IV) for aid, and in
1868, following BRITAIN's defeat of Tewodros, his alliance, sealed by marriage to Kassa's cousin, gained him
the lordship of Hamasien. Wolde-Mika'el's attempt to

break free of Kassa in 1869 led to his arrest, however, and he was retained at the new emperor's court for much of the period through 1875, while the Tigrean leader, Wagshum Gebru, governed the Eritrean highlands.

Wolde-Mika'el fought on Yohannes IV's side against EGYPT at the battle of GUNDET in 1875, but fell out with the Emperor over his general ALULA's confiscation of the seven hundred rifles Wolde-Mika'el's followers had captured. Wolde-Mika'el then turned to the Egyptians, who raised him to the rank of Ras in 1876, but after their defeat at GURA', Wolde-Mika'el retreated to HAL-HAL, raiding Ras Alula's governate of the MAREB MELLASH with an army that numbered some 7,000 highlanders, 3,000 armed with Egyptian-supplied rifles. In 1877 he retook control over Hamasien, killing Dej. Haylu at WOKI DUBA. Wolde-Mika'el established Hazzega as his administrative center, but his independent rule of the Mareb Mellash became a crucial diplomatic issue in negotiations between Egypt and Yohannes, with the former abandoning him in May 1878. In September, Alula returned with a Tigrean army and forced Wolde-Mika'el's submission, but allowed him to remain Ras of Hamasien until 1879, when he tricked him into coming unarmed to his camp at Gura', arrested him and sent him to Yohannes IV, who imprisoned him and his sons on Amba Selama in Tigrai.

Ras Alula kept him in prison even after Yohannes's death, but in 1891 Wolde-Mika'el escaped and was pardoned by Ras Mengesha, who hoped to use him in his struggle to regain the Mareb Mellash from Italian rule. He fought against the Italians at QWATIT and ADWA, but failed to receive the compensation he expected from Menelik II, and died in 1906 at Adwa with his family's fortunes unrestored.

WOMEN'S ORGANIZATIONS. One of the more profound social changes wrought by the nationalist movement has been the struggle to liberate women from the inferior status forced on them by the traditional laws and customs of all Eritrean ethnic groups except the KUNAMA. This struggle produced the Women's Organizations which first

developed in the liberation fronts during the 1970s, and
has been led largely by urban Eritreans whose access to
modern EDUCATION had inspired them to reject oppressive customs. The struggle for women's emancipation has
involved attempts to change both specific traditional legal
disabilities against women, and to change the even more
pervasive cultural norms which required women to remain
in a social position inferior to men.

The most important legal disabilities were those regarding the rights of marriage, divorce and inheritance. In
the traditional legal systems of both the highlands and
lowlands, among both Christians and Muslims, women's
marriages were arranged shortly after puberty by their
male guardians, were subject to the payment of dowries
and bride-prices, and involved the transfer of property,
whether land or animals, between males only, so that unmarried or divorced women were largely excluded form
property ownership. Among Muslim people divorces were
also legally difficult for women to obtain, while among all
traditional cultures the alternatives for unmarried women
were continued control by their father/guardian, extreme
poverty or PROSTITUTION. The primary function of women
in all societies was seen as the production of male heirs,
while both Christian and Muslim customs requiring a
woman's deference and subservience to male family members, seclusion or avoidance of male company in public
and widespread female CIRCUMCISION all reinforced wom-
en's legal disabilities and kept women from taking part in
family or community decisions or most aspects of public
life. And even when education did become more widely
available to women in the 1940s, the maxim of "education
for boys, marriage for girls" continued to prevail among
most families

In the 1950s increasing urbanization and access to
modern education produced the first generation of Eritreans to criticize the effects of women's inferior social status, but even the relatively progressive first Eritrean
CONSTITUTION (1952-62) reserved the right to vote to
men. During the 1950s the early nationalist movement
provided one opportunity for urban women to take part in

community political activities, and women were conspicuously involved in early student protests and labor strikes. Women's cells were organized by both the ELM and ELF, with the first ELF women's cell formed in 1963 in KASSALA. Women participated in sabotage and assassination activities carried out by male *fedayin* (urban guerrillas), often by luring Ethiopian military officers into traps using sexual enticements. But when women attempted to join ELF fighting units they were humiliated and rejected. Women did join the non-combatant departments of the front, however, and by the late 1960s there were hundreds involved in underground urban cells or working in ELF offices, HEALTH CARE clinics and education programs in Sudan.

During the 1960s, STUDENT ORGANIZATIONS began to discuss women's emancipation, and through the nationalist movements' student cells women came to the ELF and PLF during 1972-73 demanding to be given military training. In 1973 both fronts accepted their first women FIGHTERS, all of whom were students. Interviews given by the first women fighters reveal that the early EPLF (PLF) was more sensitive to integrating them into combat units, and by 1975 the front had decided to give women separate military training, while by the same year in the ELF women fighters complained of sexual harassment. The EPLF also recruited women's cells in towns and villages, and women participated in the same types of intelligence-gathering, sabotage and assassination activities as they had in support of ELF *fedayin*. These women's cells formed the foundation of the women's associations created by both fronts, including the General Union of Eritrean Women created by the ELF in 1975 and led by Ama Melakin, a BILEN graduate of CAIRO University. But in the ELF there was resistance to substantive women's participation from the many traditionally oriented Muslim men in the original leadership, and the front was never completely committed to supporting women's equality in the Western lowlands and SENHIT where its main base of support lay.

In contrast, the EPLF leadership viewed women's emancipation as a fundamental element of the social

revolution it was implementing in the rural areas of
Eritrea during 1975-78, and its Women's Association
members took an active part in village social and economic
reforms, while thousands of uneducated rural women
joined the front during the late 1970s, often to escape
patriarchal social controls. In 1978 the EPLF abolished
child and forced marriages in areas under its control,
guaranteeing women the right to divorce and equal rights
to family property, while political organizers and health
workers tried to change peoples attitudes concerning
customs such as seclusion and female circumcision.
Although many of these social programs were swept away
by the Ethiopian OFFENSIVES of the late 1970s, the
EPLF's commitment to women's emancipation was a key
element in its successful mobilization of the Eritrean
population in support of the nationalist movement, while
gender relations within the front itself provided a model
for a future egalitarian society.

In November 1979, the EPLF Women's Association
held a national congress in SAHEL and created the National Union of Eritrean Women (NUEWmn), covering the
DIASPORA community, Ethiopia (where many EPLF women
fighters were recruited) and its branches inside Eritrea.
ASKALU MENKERIOS was elected Chairwoman of the organization. Although she sat on the EPLF CENTRAL COM-
MITTEE (CC), women remained poorly represented in the
front's leadership (due to lack of education, according to
the front), with only six on the first CC and none on its
ruling Political Committee. But the number of women
fighters continued to increase during the 1980s, until by
liberation roughly 35 percent of the EPLF's 95,000 fighters were women, and women had risen from early positions
as squad leaders to become platoon commanders.

After liberation the struggle to emancipate women
became more complicated, despite the new government's
support for continuing reforms and national laws guaranteeing economic and political equality. Eritrean civilian
society remained largely attached to traditional attitudes
towards women's social status, and the alternative model
presented by EPLF fighter culture was somewhat eroded

by the disproportionate DEMOBILIZATION of women fighters, 20,000 of whom left the EPLA by 1995. The NUEWmn was also reorganized as an independent, non-governmental association in September 1992, when its 120,000 members (45,000 in Asmara) sent 509 delegates to its Fourth Congress.

Although the government initiated programs such as the reservation of seats for women at all levels of political representation and the application of NATIONAL SERVICE laws to women as well as men, other aspects of post-liberation Eritrea disturbed women's rights advocates, including the pressure on women fighters to return to traditional civilian roles, the increase of divorces among married fighters as relatives put pressure on men to have children and many women fighters found the years of brutal combat had left them sterile, and a general retreat from the activist social programs of the war years in rural areas where tradition was most deeply imbedded and over 95 percent of women remained illiterate. Confronting these issues, the NUEWmn was wracked by internal conflicts over whether its role should be that of a service organization an activist political movement. At the local level, however, there has been a resurgence of grass-roots women's organization around economic and cultural issues, while several groups of former women fighters organized their own self-help groups outside the NUEWmn, including the Women War Veteran's Association (BANA), whose 1,000 members established several successful cooperatives during 1995-96, before their organization was deregistered by the government for relying too heavily on foreign NGO funding. Although legal guarantees of women's rights are implied in Eritrea's new Constitution, the reality of the situation is that it takes many years to change deeply rooted cultural traditions, and only universal education and economic development will completely transform traditional attitudes.

WUBE Haile-Mariam, Dejazmach (c. 1800-1855). Ruler of Northern ETHIOPIA and central Eritrea from 1831 to 1855, Dej. Wube is still remembered in Eritrea for the cruelty of his raids and for his imposition of a Tigrean military government in the highlands. Beginning from his base in Simien, Wube conquered TIGRAI in 1831, and received the submission of HAYLU TEWOLDE-MEDHIN, lord of the MAREB MELLASH in 1832. Haylu rose against Wube in 1838/39 in alliance with Ras Ali of Ethiopia, but Wube defeated and imprisoned him. He then imposed a military government on the Eritrean highlands through the 1840s, using a policy of divide-and-rule that set AKELE GUZAI against SERAYE, TSAZZEGA against HAZZEGA, and the highlands against the lowlands, leaving a legacy of bitter feuds and warfare that divided Eritrea for a century.

In 1840 Wube raided SENHIT with Ras Haylu, deliberately dividing the MENSA' and BILEN Christian population of the upper ANSEBA from the KEBESSA highlands. In 1843/44 he conquered Akele Guzai and imposed a military governor (Tigrn.: *shum negarit*) on the central highlands, Blatta Kokobe, who installed an Ethiopian-style ADMINISTRATION. To obtain arms, Dej. Wube tried to establish direct relations with Europe via MASSAWA. He made diplomatic overtures to BRITAIN and FRANCE during 1841-49, and he repeatedly raided SEMHAR to control the NA'IBs and forestall occupation by EGYPT. His last raid was in 1850 against SENHIT and BARKA, again to block Egyptian expansion, and to seize KUNAMA and BILEN slaves. His power then declined as he struggled with the aspiring Emperor Tewodros, who defeated and killed him in 1855. His nephew, "Agaw" Negussie, rebelled against Tewodros and gained control over parts of the Eritrean highlands in 1858-59, attempting to revive Wube's alliance with France, but was killed in 1860.

- Y -

YEMEN. The peoples of the Arabian and Eritrean shores of the Red Sea have maintained close relations since ancient times (*see* SOUTH ARABIA). From at least 700 B.C., immigrants from what is today Yemen settled on the Eritrean coast and central highlands, while HABESHA people from the Eritrean region also settled and mixed with the population of the Tehama coastal region of Yemen. Yemeni and AFAR fishermen have both fished around the islands and along the two coasts since ancient times, while many coastal Eritrean Muslim tribes claim Yemeni Arab ancestors. During the tenth to twelfth centuries A.D., Yemeni rulers struggled with a local dynasty for control of the DAHLAK islands, and during the sixteenth to seventeenth centuries Ottoman TURKEY ruled both Yemen and coastal Eritrea. In the early nineteenth century the South Yemeni port of Aden was occupied by BRITAIN, which used it as a commercial base for the region, and Yemeni merchants settled in Eritrea in growing numbers. By the mid-twentieth century Yemeni Arabs were the largest non-Italian foreign community in Eritrea. After 1923, when Turkey renounced sovereignty over North Yemen and Red Sea islands, ITALY attempted repeatedly to acquire a protectorate over North Yemen. Italian missions (using Eritrean interpreters) were sent to the North Yemeni capital of San'a during 1930-34, but Fascist attempts at intimidation were countered by British support for North Yemeni independence.

In 1967, after a long anti-colonial struggle, the British colony of Aden became the independent People's Democratic Republic of Yemen (PDRY) and its leftist government became a key supporter of the Eritrean liberation fronts. During the same period the Ethiopian government harassed Yemeni residents of Eritrea, who dominated the middle-levels of commerce and were accused of supporting the ELF. During 1968, thousands of Yemenis were expelled from Eritrea following Ethiopian-incited riots against them in ASMARA. This increased South Yemeni support for Eritrean nationalists, and particularly OSMAN SALEH SABBE. During 1970-76 the PDRY allowed the ELF-PLF to use Aden and islands in the Red Sea claimed by both Yemen and Ethiopia (*see* HANISH ISLANDS) as bases for a NAVY supply operation that ferried arms, supplies and wounded fighters across the Red Sea. But in 1977 the PDRY broke its relations with Eritrean nationalists under pressure from the USSR, and during 1978-82 several thousand South Yemeni soldiers supported the Ethiopian

OFFENSIVES in Eritrea, where they piloted combat planes, drove tanks, operated artillery and supplied technical support.

PDRY support for the DERG declined in the late 1980s, as the USSR withdrew financial support and the PDRY began to negotiate unification with conservative North Yemen. In May 1990 the two countries were united as the Republic of Yemen, which established diplomatic relations with Eritrea after 1991 and recognized the new government soon after the 1993 REFERENDUM. Despite professions of friendship and important commercial links, the two new countries have had several disputes regarding the Red Sea. The first, concerning Yemeni FISHING in Eritrean waters, was settled by an agreement signed November 14, 1994. The second, concerning the HANISH ISLANDS, led to a brief war in December 1995, but has since been submitted to international arbitration.

YESH'AQ, Bahre Negashi (alt.: Isaq). The Tigrean-born ruler of the Eritrean KEBESSA during the tumultuous sixteenth century, Bahre Negashi Yesh'aq's career epitomizes the pre-colonial struggle of central Eritrean political leaders to maintain their autonomy when caught between foreign powers on the coast and Ethiopian rulers in the interior (for a comparison, see WOLDE-MIKA'EL SOLOMUN). Yesh'aq was appointed BAHRE NEGASHI of TIGRAI and the MAREB MELLASH sometime before 1520, when the Portuguese Alvarez expedition met him at his capital of DEBARWA. Yesh'aq led Tigrean and Kebessan resistance to the Muslim armies of Imam AHMED AL-GHAZALI ("Gragn") during the 1530s, but was driven into hiding. In 1541 he allied with the Portuguese expeditionary force led by Cristavao da Gama to defeat Ahmed Gragn's troops in AKELE GUZAI, and he participated in Emperor Galadewos' campaigns that overthrew Ahmed Gragn's rule.

In 1558 Yesh'aq defeated Ottoman TURKEY's first invasion of the highlands, but in 1559 he rebelled against the new Emperor Minas. Following his defeat by Minas in Adi-Abo and failure to gain Portugese support, Yesh'aq in

1560/61 allied with the Turks, whom he invited into the Kebessa. When the new Emperor Sarsa Dengel (Melek Seged) came to power in 1563, Yesh'aq attempted to play him against the Turks to retain his control over Tigrai and parts of the Kebessa, and in 1567 he drove the Turks out of Debarwa. But Sarsa Dengel's attempts to subjugate him turned him back to the Turks in 1578, when both he and the Turkish pasha were killed in battle against the Emperor's army at Adi Qoro, Tigrai.

YOHANNES IV (Emperor, 1872-89). The Tigrean-born military leader Kasa Mirtcha rose to power in TIGRAI and the Eritrean KEBESSA during the late 1860s, receiving crucial arms supplies from BRITAIN's Napier expedition in return for his support against Emperor Tewodros in 1868. He was crowned YOHANNES IV, Emperor of ETHIOPIA, in early 1872 following the defeat of his rival Tekle-Giorgis at ADWA in July, 1871. During the mid-1870s he struggled to control the Kebessa by playing the rival Houses of HAZZEGA and TSAZZEGA against each other and defeating two Egyptian invasions. After Ras WOLDE-MIKA'EL SOLOMUN killed Yohannes's military governor of the Kebessa, Bairu, in 1878, Yohannes appointed his leading general, Ras ALULA, as military governor of the Eritrean MAREB MELLASH in 1879. Alula ruled central Eritrea for Yohannes until 1889, and participated in Yohannes's expansion into the KEREN region following the 1884 HEWETT TREATY with Britain, which recognized Yohannes's control over most of modern Eritrea except MASSAWA. Alula also led Yohannes's successful defense of his Eritrean holdings against the Egyptians (*see* GUNDET; GURA'), the Mahdists (*see* KUFIT) and ITALY (*see* DOGALI; SA'ATI). Yohannes was killed March 10, 1889, at the Battle of Metemma fighting the Sudanese Mahdiyya, soon after which his successor, Menelik II of Shewa, approved the Italian occupation of central Eritrea.

- Z -

ZAGHER (Hamasien). An important site for nationalist political conferences in the mid-1970s and a "model village" for early EPLF social reforms, Zagher and its sister village Woki (often linked as Woki-Zagher) is located in the KARNISHEM district just north of ASMARA, on the edge of the SEMENAWI BAHRI escarpment. The village was founded in the fifteenth century by TIGRINYA-speaking Christians, whose three ENDA groups traditionally oversaw periodic redistribution of village land. By the 1960s Zagher had a population of about three thousand, but the land redistribution system had broken-down and much of the best land had fallen into the hands of the descendants of Italian-appointed colonial chiefs who collaborated with the Ethiopian government.

The ELF made little impact on the area, but in 1974 the emerging EPLF established a base at Solomuna, directly below Zagher, and the village became the site of clashes between the ELF and EPLF as the rival fronts moved into the highlands around Asmara. In August 1974 a clash between guerrilla patrols escalated into a series of pitched battles between the EPLF based in Woki and the ELF in Zagher. In September the villagers intervened, pleading with the FIGHTERS to negotiate a cease-fire. Because the CIVIL WAR between the two fronts was raging across Eritrea, the Zagher negotiations soon attracted civilians from all the highlands anxious to stop the fighting, including the Catholic prelate of Asmara, Aba Fissehatzion. During October an estimated 30,000 civilians, largely from Asmara, converged on the village urging the fronts to make a peace settlement, and on October 13 a cease-fire was signed, ending the first civil war.

The EPLF remained in control of Woki-Zagher, and during 1975 it became the front's headquarters in the KEBESSA. On November 12, 1975, a meeting was held at the village where EPLF leaders decided to reject the merger plan proposed by OSMAN SALEH SABBE with the ELF (*see* ELF-PLF), and on April 21, 1977, the first negotiations leading to a unity pact between the EPLF and

ELF occurred at Zagher. The EPLF presence also led to sweeping social reforms in the village as EPLF cadres organized the villagers according to their wealth and helped the poor majority to oust the wealthy former colonial appointees and redistribute their land. Zagher's new village council (*see* LOCAL GOVERNMENT) then became a model for EPLF reforms in other villages.

This ended in November 1978, when the DERG retook the village and many EPLF activists fled with the front to SAHEL. The Derg attempted to win over the villagers with its own reforms and social programs, but when some of the wealthier villagers cooperated with the Ethiopians in an attempt to recoup their position they were assassinated by EPLF commandos and the Derg turned increasingly to repression. This, combined with FAMINE in 1984-86 and a military garrison during 1988-91, caused much of the population to flee. By 1991 the remaining villagers were reduced to living on FOOD AID and the "model village" was a remote memory. But the villagers formed a new council, built a school and community center, and by 1993 agricultural outreach programs were improving crops and Woki-Zagher was experiencing a revival similar to that throughout rural Hamasien.

ZARA YA'QOB (Emperor, 1434-68). The most powerful Emperor of ETHIOPIA in the late medieval period, Zara Ya'qob's reign marked the highpoint of "Solomonic" (Amhara) political control over the central Eritrean region. Early in his reign, Zara Ya'qob led military campaigns in TIGRAI and the KEBESSA and strengthened his direct political control through the settlement of military colonies (*see* CHEWA) in the highlands. He reasserted Ethiopian control over the coast around MASSAWA, where his administration undertook harbor improvements at Gerar and created a new naval force. In 1450 his settlement of the ORTHODOX CHURCH's schism in favor of the followers of EWOSTATEWOS, combined with his large land grants to leading monasteries in the Eritrean highlands (*see* DEBRE BIZEN), appeased the regionalist religious movement that had threatened to detach the TIGRINYA-

seaking areas from the AMHARIC-speaking south. Zara
Ya'qob created the new governate of the BAHRE NEGASHI
to rule central Eritrea and northern Tigrai, and much of
the administrative system of the MAREB MELLASH dates
from his reign. This system lasted until the 1520s, when
the conquests of Imam AHMED AL-GHAZALI ("Gragn") and
the inroads of Ottoman TURKEY eroded Solomonic power in
the region.

ZELAMBESSA (Akele Guzai). A village lying between the
SHIMEZANA district of AKELE GUZAI and TIGRAI (*see*
BORDERS), its lands were split between Eritrea and
Ethiopia in 1991. Italian colonial forces fortified the main
track from Tigrai, and customs posts and a roadside village grew up as the trunk route from Ethiopia to ASMARA
developed. The fortifications were taken over by the
Ethiopian military in 1952, and the roadside village became an administrative post that was eventually associated with the governorship of Tigrai following Eritrea's
ANNEXATION. The older village remained under Eritrean
administrative control, however, and this situation has
produced a dispute between Eritrea and Ethiopia over
control of the roadside village and customs post, which the
Ethiopian government retained after 1993, but appears to
be on Eritrean land.
    In 1976, Zelambessa was also the site of the defeat,
verging on a massacre, of the "Peasant Red Army" recruited by the DERG in a vain attempt to use a traditional
Ethiopian mass levy of untrained farmers to overwhelm
liberation forces in Eritrea. A few thousand peasants from
Wello camped on the Zelambessa plateau in late May, in
preparation for an invasion of Shimezana, but they were
routed with an estimated 1,500 casualties by a combined
dawn attack of Eritrean and Tigrean fighters, after which
the Peasant Army campaign collapsed.

ZERO SCHOOL. The EPLF's school for war orphans and the
children of FIGHTERS, Zero School was founded at Adi Zero
in the SEMENAWI BAHRI with ninety students in 1976.
The school was moved to SAHEL during the STRATEGIC

WITHDRAWAL and in 1982 was settled in camouflaged buildings along a valley in the Arareb area (code named "OROTA"). The school provided innovative teaching for a growing number of students, pioneering new TIGRINYA texts developed by the EPLF's EDUCATION department. Despite its camouflage, the school was bombed on several occasions, including an attack in 1984 the killed six children. As the students grew, higher grades were added and in 1989 the new junior school was moved to NAKFA. By 1991, when the school closed, it had 3,000 students from first to eighth grade. The experience of EPLF children's education provided at Zero School has now been incorporated into national education programs, where many former Zero teachers work.

ZONAL COMMANDS (ELF). In May 1965 the ELF SUPREME COUNCIL reorganized the front's military forces in Eritrea into four "zones" modeled on the Wilayat (Arab.: "administrative district") of the Algerian revolution. The zones were intended to provide more effective organization for the fighting forces, but they contained the seeds of division as they were organized along existing ethnic/regional lines. Zone 1 covered the western lowlands of BARKA and GASH-SETIT, and its commander, MAHMOUD DINAI, and deputy, Saleh Hamid Idris, were members of the dominant BENI 'AMER tribe; Zone 2 covered SENHIT, whose main ethnic groups were reflected in the commander, OMER EZAZ of the BILEN, and deputy commander, Mohamed Omer Adem of the MARYA; Zone 3 was intended to cover the KEBESSA and its escarpments, but because of a lack of Christian support the zone became de facto a SAHO zone, as reflected in its commander, ABDELKRIM AHMED, and deputy, Hamid Saleh; Zone 4 covered the coast from SAHEL and SEMHAR to DENKEL, but was centered around MASSAWA, as reflected in its commander, MOHAMED ALI OMERO, and deputy, Abdallah Barih.

   Although the new zones led to an expansion of ELF activity during 1965-67, they also reinforced the personal power of the Supreme Council, whose three dominant figures patronized their specific zones of origin

by providing outside military supplies, training and
funds directly to zone commanders in return for their
political support. IDRIS M. ADEM supported Zone 1, IDRIS
OSMAN GALADEWOS supported Zone 2, and OSMAN
SALEH SABBE supported Zone 4, while Zone 3 was left with
no patronage and consequently became the weakest zone.
In an attempt to remedy the problems of Zone 3 and
recruit more TIGRINYA/Christians into the front, the
Supreme Council in 1966 formed a fifth "Christian" zone
around ASMARA and the central Kebessa, whose first
commander was Wolde Kahsai, a Christian unit leader
from Zone 3.

The military successes of the zonal system and particularly the extension of ELF recruitment into the
Kebessa under the new Zone 5 alarmed the administration
of HAILE SELASSIE I and prompted the first major
Ethiopian counter-insurgency campaign in 1967. But in
the campaign's aftermath the inter-ethnic tensions within
the system came to head when the Muslim deputy commander of Zone 5, Osman Hishal, executed twenty-seven
Christian fighters whom he accused of dereliction of duty,
leading to the defection of Wolde Kahsai to the Ethiopians
along with nineteen other Christians. This incident combined with the problems of patronage politics and ethnic
division within the zonal system led in 1967 to the creation of the ESLAH reform movement.

In an attempt to remedy some of the zonal system's
problems, the ELF leadership appointed "political commissars" to each of the zones with responsibility for improving the fighters' sense of commitment to a national
struggle, rather than narrow ethnic interests. The commissars were the five fighters initially trained in CHINA,
and included Musa Hamid Hashim (Zone 1), Mohamed
Cheikhi (Zone 2), RAMADAN MOHAMED NUR (Zone 4) and
ISAIAS AFWERKI (Zone 5). But conflicts between the
commissars and zone commanders added to the growth of
the reform movement, which finally succeeded in a partial
reorganization of the zonal commands at the ADOBAHA
meeting in 1969, when Zones 1 and 2 became "Sectors" 1
and 2, while Zones 3, 4, and 5, led by the TRIPARTITE

UNITY FORCES, were merged into Sector 3. This modified
zonal system remained in effect until early 1972, despite
the defection of most of Sector 3 and elements of the other
two sectors to the ELF-PLF during 1970-71. In February
1972 the old system was finally scrapped when ABDAL-
LAH IDRIS reorganized ELF military forces into twelve
sectors of one battalion each, which proved far more effective in prosecuting the ARMED STRUGGLE.

ZULA (Akele Guzai) *see* ADULIS; FORO.

BIBLIOGRAPHY

Note on Using the Bibliography

This bibliography is organized along historical lines, with all relevant materials from a particular period grouped together. The category "Economics" includes agriculture, commerce, industry, mining, etc.; "Social Issues" includes subjects such as health, refugees, social services, women's rights, etc. In addition to books and articles, I have included a few outstanding manuscripts and documents (note that unpublished dissertations from U.S. universities can be obtained in book form from University Microfilms, Ann Arbor, Michigan). I have not included newspaper (daily or weekly) articles, although these are a particularly important source for the last two decades. Especially useful are articles by Dan Connell in the *Guardian* (New York) and *Christian Science Monitor,* as well as reports in the *New York Times, Washington Post,* and *Le Monde.* Current information is available through the government's weekly, *Eritrea Profile,* and the "dehai" newsgroup on-line at: *dehai@thames.stanford.edu.* Because of the scarcity of English-language material on most Eritrean subjects, I have included many foreign-language sources, as well as general works on Ethiopia where they contain important material on Eritrea. The most useful sources are marked with an asterisk (*), and where the content is not obvious, I have added brief explanations in brackets.

All Eritrean and Ethiopian authors are listed by their first name; well-known Arabic sources are entered by the commonly used surname, and indexed to European-language translations where available.

ABBREVIATIONS AND ACRONYMS

AAU	Addis Ababa University (formerly Haile Selassie I University).
ACISE	*Atti del Convegno Internazionale di Studi Ethiopici.*
AE	*Annales d'Ethiopie.*
A.H.	After Hejira (Muslim calendar, c. 620 years behind Gregorian).
Amh.	Amharic language.
Asm.	Asmara.
ASMAE	Archivo Storico dello Ministero degli Affari Esteri (Rome).
ASMAI	Archivo Storico dello Ministero degli Affari Interno
AVA	Apostolic Vicarate of Asmara.
Boll.	*Bolletino (del/della).*
BSAC	*Bulletin de la Société d'Archéologie Classique.*
CNRS	Centre National de la Recherche Scientifique.
Colon.	*Colonial.*
CSCO	*Corpus Scriptorum Christianorum Orientalium.*
CISE	*Congresso Internazionale di Studi Etiopici.*
E.C.	Ethiopian Calendar (7-8 years behind Gregorian).
ed.	edited by.
EFLNA	Eritreans for Liberation in North America.
EPLF	Eritrean People's Liberation Front.
Erit.	*Eritrea.*
ESR	*Eritrean Studies Review* (Lawrenceville, New Jersey).
Eth.	*Ethiopia.*
Geo.	*Geography/Geografica.*
GSAI	*Giornale della Società Asiatica Italiana* (Florence).
Hist.	*History.*
IACI	Istituto Agricolo Coloniale Italiano (Florence).

IC	*L'Illustrazione Coloniale.*
ICES	*International Conference of Ethiopian Studies.*
IJAHS	*International Journal of African Historical Studies.*
J.	*Journal of.*
JA	*Journal Asiatique.*
JAH	*Journal of African History.*
JES	*Journal of Ethiopian Studies.*
JMAS	*Journal of Modern African Studies.*
JRAS	*Journal of the Royal Asiatic Society.*
JSS	*Journal of Semitic Studies.*
mimeo.	mimeograph.
MRAL	*Memorie della Reale Academia dei Lincei.*
PCL	Pavoni Center Library (Asmara).
P.	Press.
Proc.	*Proceedings of.*
QSE	*Quaderni di Studi Etiopici* (Asmara).
Rass.	*Rassegna (di).*
Rev.	*Review of.*
RFHO	*Revue Française d'Histoire d'Outre-Mer.*
RICE	Research and Information Center on Eritrea.
Riv.	*Rivista di.*
RRAL	*Rendiconti della Reale Academia dei Lincei.*
RSAI	*Rassegna Sociale dell'Africa Italiana.*
RSE	*Rassegna di Studi Etiopici.*
RSO	*Rassegna di Studi Orientali.*
ser.	series.
SNR	*Sudan Notes and Records* (Khartoum).
Soc.	*Society/Società.*
Tigrn.	Tigrinya language.
trans.	translated by.
UNESCO	United Nations Educational, Scientific, and Cultural Organization.
Univ.	University.
v.	volume(s).
ZA	*Zeitschrift für Assyriologie.*
ZDMG	*Zeitschrift der Deutschen Morganländischen Gesellschaft.*

ARCHIVAL RESOURCES

Because published works on Eritrea are scanty, I have included this guide to available archival resources, listed alphabetically by the country in which they are located.

Egypt

Cairo: The Egyptian National Archives from the Khedival period contain useful sources, particularly for the reign of Isma'il (1863-79), where correspondence between Egyptian governors in Massawa and Ras Wolde-Mika'el Solomun is preserved. For a guide to archival sources see: G. Douin, *Histoire du regne du Khédive Ismail,* v. 3, *L'empire africain* (1936-41).

Eritrea

Asmara houses many collections of archives, although some are disorganized and difficult to access. The most important holdings of the archives are described here:

1. The Center for Research and Documentation has a nearly complete collection of EPLF official publications from the war years, material from other parts of the national-ist movement, collections of interviews and oral histo-ries, and many books and articles concerning Eritrea from the former RICE collection. In addition, the Center has audio collections including interviews with na-tionalist leaders and an almost complete collection of Dimtsi Hafash radio broadcasts. It also houses a growing collection of rare manuscripts dating back to the fifteenth century, including religious texts, land charters, and genealogies.

2. The Ministry of Local Government's archive holds over 4,000 pages of oral histories collected from every Eritrean ethnic group by the EPLF during the 1980s.

3. The Ministry of Justice's archive holds court records covering thousands of land disputes, as well as criminal cases dating to the Italian colonial era.

4. The Islamic Institute Library houses Shari'a court records from Massawa dating to the late 1700s.

5. The former Biblioteca Italiana, which contained many useful materials on the Italian colonial period, was sold piecemeal to private individuals during the 1950s; the Museo Fernando Martini was closed in 1977 and most of its valuable archaeological collection is now in the National Museum (*see* G. Oman, *La necropoli islamica di Dahlak Kebir,* v. 2, for a catalog of Arabic inscriptions).

6. The Pavoni Center Library (PCL), located in a Catholic orphanage in Asmara and directed by Brother Ezio Tonini, contains an extremely useful collection, including some of the Biblioteca Italiana materials.

7. The archives of the (Roman Catholic) Apostolic Vicarate of Asmara (AVA) contain a very valuable collection of early letters and reports dating from the 1860s onward.

France

Paris: The archives of the Ministère des Affaires Etrangères (MAE) contain valuable correspondence from vice consuls in Massawa from the 1840s onward. The archives of the Maison Lazariste contain the extremely detailed reports and correspondence of the French Lazarist mission in Eritrea (1839-94), many of which have been published in the *Annales de la Congrégation de la Mission.*

Italy

Italian archives should provide the richest source on Eritrea's colonial history (1869-1941), but they are, unfortunately, poorly organized and incomplete. The various archives in which Eritrean materials are distributed are listed below. Materials on Eritrea began to be collected in the Ministry of Defense in 1885, but in the 1890s new archives began to be placed in the Ministry of Foreign Affairs. In 1913 the Ministry of Colonies was created, and most records were kept in its archival collection through 1942-43, when the ministry was dissolved and what remained of its archives were transferred back to the Ministry of Foreign Affairs. However, certain files were lost or destroyed. All 1935-40 "daily reports" from the AOI were shipped to Italy and disappeared, while those from 1940-41 were destroyed. To make matters worse, surviving 1935-41 documents, plus a number of earlier ones, were removed from the ASMAE archives by a special committee for documentation created in 1958 to prepare a history of Italy's African colonies, and many were never returned. Those that were returned are in a separate ASMAE file. The committee's work was never completed, and of the sixteen volumes published, only the first two (*see* Carlo Giulio, *L'Italia in Africa.* V. 1, *Ser. Storica: Etiopia-Mar Rosso*) refer to Eritrea through 1887.

Italian archives (located in Rome unless otherwise noted):

1. Ministry of Defense and Ministry of Marine (Ministero della Difensa and Ministero della Marina): early colonial materials (to 1913) and *ascari,* including service in 1911-32 Libyan war.

2. State Archives (Archivo dello Stàto): best for 1890-1913 period; Crispi and Martini materials; "Truppi Africani" in Eritrea, Libya, Ethiopia.

3. Chamber of Deputies Library (Biblioteca della Camera di Deputato): *Libre verde* cover the 1880s/90s.

4. Historical Archive of the Ministry of Foreign Affairs
   (Archivo Storico dello Ministero degli Affari Esteri):
   material from 1890s-1913 and refiled materials from
   defunct Ministry of Colonies (1913-42). Files: ASMAI
   (domestic); ASMAE (foreign); Archivo Eritreo; Archivo
   Etiopio; miscellaneous.

5. Overseas Agricultural Institute (Istituto Agronimo per
   l'Oltremare): agricultural reports and other data from
   1913 through 1952 (Florence).

6. African Institute (Istituto Africano): The former Istituto
   Italo-Africano, its holdings include all Italian colonial
   journals and newspapers.

Sweden

Stockholm: The Swedish National Archives contain a
complete collection of Swedish Evangelical Mission (SEM)
materials.

Turkey

Istanbul: According to Gengiz Orhonlu three sets of
archives dating from the Ottoman period contain information on Eritrea:

1. Archive of Prime Minister's Office (Basbakanlik Arsir
   Genel Mudurlugu) contains: "Divani Huayun Muhimme"
   Register covering 1553-1906 (Eritrean materials in
   1553-1720).

2. Archive of Topkapi Palace Museum (Tokapi Sarayi Muzei
   arsivi).

3. Archive of Ministry of Foreign Affairs (Harciciye
   nezareti arsivi).

London: The Public Records Office (PRO) contains a rich collection of reports and secret memos from the British Administration of Eritrea (1941-52). Most are in the Foreign Office (FO) 371 series. For a listing of many of the most useful materials see the bibliographies of: Jordan Gebre-Medhin, *Peasants and Nationalism in Eritrea;* Killion, T., "Workers, Capital and the State in the Ethiopian Region"; Okbazghi Yohannes, *Eritrea: A Pawn in World Politics.* The British Library's Oriental Printed Books and Manuscripts Collection also contains useful Eritrean materials, particularly among the Gordon Papers, Moffit Collection.

Oxford University holds two collections containing valuable materials on Eritrea:

1. Trevaskis Papers and Captured Italian Documents (034383-4): St. Anthony's College.

2. Newbold's File (Griffith Institute): Portfolio 2 contains a history of the Habab and genealogical lists compiled by Sir Douglas Newbold, C. H. Thompson, and Hassan Kantibai Mahmud (1932).

United Nations

New York: UN archives contain a wealth of reports and all the proceedings from the debates of 1947-50 regarding Eritrea and the implementation of the federation with Ethiopia (1951-52).

United States

Washington, D.C.: The National Archives contain declassified Department of State diplomatic and consular reports on Eritrea from 1942 through the early 1970s, some of which are also contained in published microfiche collections. A number of Congressional reports and Department of Defense reports on Ethiopia are also pertinent to Eritrea. For a good introduction to available material see the bibliographies of: Ellingson, Lloyd, "Eritrea: Separatism and Ir-

For a good introduction to available material see the bibliographies of: Ellingson, Lloyd, "Eritrea: Separatism and Irredentism;" Killion, T., "Workers, Capital and the State in the Ethiopian Region."

I. GENERAL WORKS

1. Bibliographic and Reference

Ahmed, Hussein. "The Historiography of Islam in Ethiopia." *J. Islamic Studies*, 3, 1 (1992) pp. 15-46.

Baldrati, I. *Note ecologiche sulla colonia Eritrea* (Pisa: 1928).

Bartoli, A. "Le isole Dahlac nel Mar Rosso." *Africa italiana*, v. 7/8 (1939).

Consociazione Turistica Italiana. *Guida dell'Africa Orientale Italiana* (Milan: Off. Fotolitografiche, 1938).*

Conti Rossini, Carlo. "Documenti Arabi per la storia dell'Etiopia." *MRAL*, ser. 6, no. 4 (1931).

_____. "Publicazione etiopiche dal 1926 al 1945." *RSE*, v. 4 (1945).

Dainelli, Giotto. "Le regioni climatiche della colonia Eritrea." *Riv. geo. italiana*, v. 4 (1909).

Dainelli, G., and O. Marinelli. *Risultati scientifici di un viaggio nella colonia Eritrea* (Florence: 1912).

Dainelli, G., and Mori. "Bibliografia geografica della colonia Eritrea: Anni 1891-1906." *Riv. geo.*, v. 4-5 (1907).

De Magistris, L. F. "Sul clima della colonia Eritrea." *Boll. soc. geo. italiana*, ser. 3, no. 8 (1895).

Eredia, F. "Le precipitazioni acquee nella colonia Eritrea." *Riv. delle colonie italiane* (1929).

Fantoli, A. "Bibliografia meteorologica delle colonie italiane." *Rass. econ. delle colonie*, v. 20 (1932).

Fumagalli, G. *Bibliografia etiopica* (Milan: 1893).

Getahun Dilebo. "Historical Origins and Development of the Eritrean Problem, 1889-1962." *Current Bibliography on African Affairs*, v. 7 (1974) pp. 221-44.

Great Britain. *Handbook on Eritrea* (London: H.M. Stationary Off., 1920).

Habtu Ghebre-Ab. *Ethiopia and Eritrea: A Documentary Study* (Lawrenceville, N.J.: Red Sea P., 1993).

Kassahun Checole. "Eritrea: A Preliminary Bibliography." *Africana Journal,* v. 6 (1975).

Kidane Tekle, and Alazar Hagos. *Atlas of Eritrea* (Stockholm: Dogali P., 1991).

Marcus, Harold. *The Modern History of Ethiopia and the Horn of Africa: A Selected and Annotated Bibliography.* (Stanford: Hoover Institution P., 1972).

Massara, E. "La regione fra Gasc e Setit." *IC,* v. 2 (1921).

Mohr, P. *The Geology of Ethiopia* [Eritrea] (Asmara: 1962).

Mulazzani, A. *Geo. della colonia Eritrea,* 2 v. (Florence: 1903-4).

Paice, Edward. *Guide to Eritrea* (Bucks, England: Bradt Publications, 1994).

Papstein, Robert. *Eritrea: A Tourist Guide* (Lawrenceville, N.J.: Red Sea P., 1995).

Parenzan, P. "Il litoral eritreo." *L'Africa Italiana* (1932).

Pollera, Alberto. *Piccola bibliografia dell'A.O. con speciale riguardo all'Eritrea e paesi confinanti* (Asmara: Governor of Eritrea, 1963).

Puglisi, Giuseppe. *Chi e? dell'Eritrea, 1952: Dizionario biografico* (Asmara: Agenzia Regina, 1952).*

RICE. *Bibliography on Eritrea* (Rome: RICE, 1982).*

Roberts, A. D. "Documentation on Ethiopia and Eritrea." *J. Documentation,* v. 1 (1946).

Sergew Hable Sellassie. *Bibliography of Ancient and Medieval Ethiopian History* (Addis Ababa: AAUP, 1969).*

Simon, J. "Bibliographie éthiopienne, 1946-51." *Orientalia,* v. 21 (1952).

Ullendorf, E., and S. Wright. *Catalogue of Ethiopian Manuscripts in the Cambridge Univ. Library* (Cambridge: Cambridge Univ. P., 1961).

Varley, D. H. *A Bibliography of Italian Colonisation in Africa with a Section on Abyssinia* (London: Dawsons, 1970).

Vitale, C. S. *Bibliography on the Climate of Ethiopia; Including the Province of Eritrea* (Silver Springs, Md.: U.S. Dept. of Commerce, 1968).

Wright, W. *Catalogue of the Ethiopic Manuscripts in the British Museum* (London: 1877).

2. History

Abir, Mordechai. *Ethiopia and the Red Sea: The Rise and Decline of the Solomonic Dynasty and Moslem-European Rivalry in the Region* (Jerusalem: 1980).

Adane Taye. *A Historical Survey of State Education in Eritrea* (Asmara: EMPDA, 1992).

Bairu Tafla. "Interdependence through Independence: The Challenges of Eritrean Historiography." In *New Trends in Ethiopian Studies,* v. 1, ed. H. Marcus (Lawrenceville, N.J.: Red Sea P., 1994).

Basset, Rene. *Etudes sur l'histoire de l'Ethiopie* (Paris: 1882).

Beguinot, F. *La cronaca abbreviata d'Abissinia* (Rome: 1901).

Blundell, Weld. *The Royal Chronicle of Abyssinia* (Oxford: Oxford Univ. P., 1922).

Cahsai Berhane, and E. Cahsai-Williamson *Erythrée: Un peuple en marche* (Paris: 1985).

Conti Rossini, Carlo. *Etiopia e genti di Etiopia* (Rome: 1937).
_____. "Schizzo etnico e storico delle popolazione eritree." In *L'Eritrea economica,* ed. F. Martini (Rome: Istituto Geo. de Agostini, 1913).*

Coulbeaux, J. B. *Histoire politique et religieuse de l'Abyssinie depuis les temps les plus reculés jusqu'à l'avènement de Menelick II,* 2 v. (Paris: 1929).

Flohn, H., and S. Nicholson. "Climatic Fluctuations in the Arid Belt of the 'Old World' since the Last Glacial Maximum." In *Paleoecology of Africa and the Surrounding Islands,* ed. E. M. van Zinderen Bakker et al. (Rotterdam: 1980).

Greenfield, R. "Pre-Colonial and Colonial History." In *Behind the War in Eritrea,* ed. Davidson, et al. (Nottingham: Spokesman, 1980).

Guebre Selassie. *Chronique du règne de Menelik II* [contains much useful information on early history, despite misleading title], trans. M. de Coppet (Paris: 1930).

Gilkes, P. "Eritrea: Historiography and Methodology." *African Affairs,* v. 99 (1991).

Killion, Tom. "The Eritrean Economy in Historical Perspective." *ESR,* 1, no. 1 (1996).

Kotler, Neil G. "History of Eritrea." (MS, Asmara: HSIU, 1966; in PCL).

Lapiso G. Delibo. *Ye-iteyopiya gejem ye-hezbena ye-mengest tarek* [Ethio-centric arguments on Eritrea's history] (Amh.: "The Long History of the People and Government of Ethiopia"; Addis Ababa: 1989-90).

Longrigg, Stephen H. *A Short History of Eritrea* (Oxford: Clarendon P., 1945).*

Mika'el Hasama Rakka. *Zanta Ertra* (Tigrn.: "History of Eritrea": Karlsruhe, Germany: 1986).

Muhammad Utman Abubakr. *Tarikh Eritriya ardan wa shaaban* (Arab.: "History of Eritrean Land and People"; Asmara: Asmara P.P., 1995).

Othman Saleh Sabby. *The History of Eritrea,* trans. Muhamad Fawaz al-Azem (Beirut: Dar Al-Masirah, n.d. [1974]).

Pankhurst, Richard. "Ethiopia and the Red Sea and Gulf of Aden Ports in the Nineteenth and Twentieth Centuries." *Ethiopian Observer,* v. 9 (1964).

————. *Economic History of Ethiopia, 1800-1935.* (Addis Ababa: Artistic P.P., 1968).

Perini, Ruffillo (and Gabre-Yesus). *Di qua dal Mareb (Mareb-mellasc')* [Tigrinya oral traditions and "feudal" geography] (Florence: Tipografia Cooperativa, 1905).*

Tewolde Beyene. "Introduction to the History of Eritrea: A Course Outline." (Univ. of Asmara, 1992. Mimeographed).

Trimingham, J. S. *Islam in Ethiopia* (London: Oxford Univ. P., 1954).*

Ullendorf, Edward. *The Ethiopians* (London: Oxford Univ. P., 1960).

Yesehaq Yusief. *Zanta ketema Asmera* (Tigrn.: "History of Asmara City"; Asmara: 1993).

3. Ethnography, Folklore and Customary Laws

Abdulkader Saleh Mohammed. *Die socio-economische bedingungen der nomadische Volksgruppen der Afar-Saho on Nord-Ost-Afrika* (Munster: Univ. of Munster/Westfale, Sociology Dept., 1984).

Airaghi, C., and S. Hidalgo. "Due escursioni nei Dembelas." *Boll. soc. geo. italiana* (1890).

Alemseged Tesfai. "Communal Land Ownership in Northern Ethiopia and Its Implications for Government Development Policies." Mimeo. no. 88 (Madison: Univ. of Wisconsin, Land Tenure Center, 1973).

Ambaye Zakarias. *Land Tenure in Eritrea* (Addis Ababa: 1966).

Beaton, A. C. "Tigre Folktales." *SNR*, v. 28 (1947).

Calciati, C., and L. Bracciani, eds. *Nel paese dei Cunama* (Milan: 1927).

Capomazza, I. "Cenni etnografici sulla popolazione dello Achelle-Guzai." *Boll. soc. africana d'Italia*, no. 9-11 (1908) and no. 1-2 (1909).

_____. "L'Assaorta Saho." *Boll. soc. africana d'Italia* (1910-11).

Castaldi, A. "Noterelle di etnografie eritree." *Boll. soc. africana d'Italia*, no. 29 (1910).

Cerulli, Enrico. "Note sui diritti consuetudinari dell'Eritrea." *Riv. coloniale* (1918).

Ciampi, Gabriele. "La popolazione dell'Eritrea." *Boll. soc. geo. italiana, serie XI*, 12 (1995): 487-524.

Conti Rossini, Carlo. "Sopra una tradizioni di Bilen." *GSAI*, v. 10 (1897).

_____. "Tradizione storiche dei Mensa." *GSAI*, v. 14 (1901).

_____. "I Loggo e la legge dei Loggo Sarda." *GSAI*, v. 17 (1904).

_____. "Studi su popolazione dell'Etiopia: La seconda migrazione Agau dell'Eritrea." *RSO*, v. 4 (1911-12).

_____. "Note sul Sahel eritreo." *RSO*, v. 6 (1914).

_____. *Principi di diritto consuetudinario dell'Eritrea* [history of highland Christian laws, and civil and religious institutions]. (Rome: 1916). *

_____. "I Cunama." *La terra e la vita*, v. 2 (1923).

_____. "Gult (Gulti)." *Nazionale dizionario italiano*, v. 6 (1938).

_____. "Lo statuto dello scioatte Anseba (Eritrea)." *Scritti giuridici in onore di Santi Romano* (Padua: 1939).

_____. "Medri." *Nazionale dizionario italiano*, v. 8 (1939).

_____. "Sulle calendrio astrologico degli Habab." *RSE*, v. 5 (1946).

_____. "Die Bedja." In *Afrika*, ed. H. von Bernatzik (Innsbruck: 1947).

Corso, R. "Il matriarcato dei Cunama della colonia Eritrea in rapporto con quello di altre popolazione dell'Africa." *La riv. di oriente*, v. 5-6 (1935).

D'Abbadie, A. "Sur le droit Bilen: A propos du livre de M. Werner Munzinger intitule 'Les moeurs et le droit des Bogos.'" *Bulletin soc. geo. de Paris* 2 (1866): 241-70, 470-86.

Duncanson, D. J. "Sir'at Adkeme Milaga: A Native Law Code of Eritrea." *Africa,* v. 19 (1949).

Ellero, G. "I Tacruri in Eritrea." *RSE* 6, no. 2 (1947).

Eritrean People's Liberation Front. "Tsebtseb afnawi qeyesa bahli Ertra: Metsna'ti beza'ba bahli beher Tegregna." [collection of Tigrinya oral traditions] (Tigrn. mimeo., 1981).

_____. "Afnawi medna'ti Bahli Ertra: 5. (1) Mesfenawi emneten lemdetaten mareten; (2) Besa't." [collection of oral traditions from various ethnic groups during Era of Princes] (Tigrn. mimeo., 1982).

_____. "Afnawi metsena'ti bahli Ertra: 1. Esrarhi abeyti; 2. Emegigba; 3. Ekedidnan selmaten." [collection of oral traditions from various ethnic groups] (Tigrn. mimeo., 1982).

_____. "Afnawi metsena'ti bahli Ertra: 4. Meten qetleten." [collection of oral traditions from various ethnic groups] (Tigrn. mimeo., 1982).

_____. "Metsena'ti beza'ba meslemnan krestenan ab hebret-seb Ertra." [collection of religious traditions] (Tigrn. mimeo., 1982).

Fiori, F. "Saggi musicale dell'Eritrea." *Boll. soc. geo. italiana,* v. 29 (1892).

Fleming, G. J. "Beni Amer Marriage Customs." *SNR* 2, no. 1 (1919).

Fragola, F. "La donna nella terra dei Danakil." *RSAI,* v. 4 (1941).

Gamba, P. "Genti dell'A.O.I.: Popolazione dell'Eritrea." *IC,* v. 1 (1939).

Garonne, V. "Su gli Atcheme-Melga: Cenni etnografici." *Boll. soc. geo. italiana,* v. 41 (1904).

Gebre-Yesus Abay. *Misarat alet hezbi Mereb Mellash* (Tigrn.: "Story of the People of the Mareb Mellash"; Asmara: 1961).

Gibello, Esilda. "Il matrimonio presso gli etiopici dell'Altopiano Eritreo." *Quaderni di studi etipici,* v. 1 (1980).

Goldsmith, J. H. "Marriage Customs among the Beni Amer Tribe." *SNR* 3, no. 4 (1920).

Grottanelli, V. L., and C. Massari. *I Baria, i Cunama e i Beni Amer* (Rome: Royal Italian Academy, 1943).

Hamilton. "The Halenga." *SNR,* v. 8 (1925).

Heuglin, T. von. "Das Gebiet der Beni-Amer und Habab." *Das Ausland,* v. 48 (1875).

Iwarson, J. "Islam in Eritrea and Abyssinia." *Moslem World,* v. 18 (Oct. 1928).

James, F. L. *The Wild Tribes of the Sudan* (London: 1883).

Kemink, Friderike. "The Tegrenna Customary Law Codes." *Paideuma,* v. 37 (1991).

Kolmodin, Johannes. *Traditions de Tsazzega et Hazzega.* (Upsala: Archives d'Etudes Orientales [v. 5], 1915).*

Lewis, I. M. *Peoples of the Horn of Africa: Somali, Afar and Saho* (London: International African Institute., 1955).

Loria, L. "Usi matromoniali assaortini." *Archivio di antropologia e etnologia* 66, no. 1-4 (1936).

Littman, Enno. *Publications of the Princeton Expedition to Abyssinia.* V. 2, *Tales, Customs and Dirges of the Tigre Tribes: English Translation* (Leyden: E. J. Brill, 1910).*

_____. "Bemerkungun uber den Islam in Nord-abessinien." *Der Islam,* v. 1 (1910).

Leslau, W. "Tigre Games." *RSE,* v. 17 (1961).

Marazzani Visconti Terzi, F. "Negli Habab." *Bolletino per l'agricoltura ed il commercio della colonia Eritrea* (Asmara: 1905).

Massara, E. "Islamismo e confraternita in Eritrea: i Morgani." *IC,* v. 8 (1921).

Michael Ghaber. *The Blin of Bogos* (Baghdad: M. Sarafian 1993).*

Munzinger, Werner. *Ueber die Sitten und das Recht der Bogos* (Winterthur: 1859).

_____. "Die Schohos und die Beduan bei Massaua." *Zeitschrift fur Allgemeine Erdkunde* 10 (1859): 89-110.

_____. *Ostrafrikanische Studen.* (Schaffhausen: 1864).*

Nadel, S. F. *Races and Tribes of Eritrea* (Asmara: BMA, 1943).*

_____. "Notes on Beni Amer Society." *SNR,* v. 26 (1945).

_____. "Land Tenure on the Eritrean Plateau." *Africa* 16, no. 1 (1946).

Naldini, E. "Escurzione alle Rore degli Habab ed all'Altopiano di Nacfa." *IACI* 10, no. 7 (1916).

Offeio, F. da. *Dall'Eritrea, lettere sui costumi abissini* (Rome: Tipografia la Vera Roma, 1904).

Odorizi, D. *Note storiche sulla religione mussulmana e sulle divisioni dell'Islam in Eritrea* (Asmara: Fioretti, 1916).

Pascale, Alberto. *Massua: Usi e costumi de' suoi indegini.* (Iride: Stabilimento Tipogafico, 1887).

Paul, A. "Notes on the Beni Amer." *SNR* 31, no. 3 (1950).

_____. *The Beja Tribes of Sudan* (Cambridge: Cambridge Univ. P., 1954).

Perini, R. "I resti e i gulti nell'Hamasien." *Nuova Antologia,* Mar. (1898).

Pollera, A. *Il regime della proprieta terriera in Etiopia e nella colonia Eritrea.* V. 12 (Rome: Ministero della Colonie, 1913).

_____. *I Baria ed i Cunama* (Rome: Royal Italian Geo. Soc., 1913).*

_____. *La donna in Etioipa* (Rome: Ministero della Colonie, 1922).

_____. *Le popolazioni indigene dell'Eritrea* (Bologna: Manuali Coloniale, 1935).

Roberti, F. *Gli Habab* (Rome: 1888).

Roden, K. G. *Le tribu dei Mensa: Storia, legge e costumi* (Stockholm: Evangeliska Fosterlands, 1913).*

Russell, F. F. "Eritrean Customary Law." *J. African Law* 3, no. 2 (1959).

Sarubbi, F. "Note sulle origini dei Beni Amer." *Riv. Colon. Italiane* (1934).

Savoia-Genova, E. di. "Consuetudini giuridiche del Serae." *RSE,* v. 7 (1948) and v. 11 (1953).

Schiller, A. A. "Customary Land Tenure among the Highland Peoples of Northern Ethiopia, a Bibliographic Essay." *African Law Studies.* no. 1 (1969).

Schweinfurth, G. "Consuetudini giuridiche del Serae." *RSE* (1948).

Seligman, C. G. "Notes on the History and Present Condition of the Beni Amer." *SNR,* 13, no. 2 (1970).

Tucci, G. "I Baria e i Cunama ed il problema del loro matriarcato." *Riv. Etnografica,* no. 3-4 (1927).

Venieri, L. "Sulla etnografica dei Saho." *Archivo per l'antropologia e l'etnologia* 65, no. 1-4 (1935).

Vitta, U. "Nei Maria." *Boll. soc. africana d'Italia,* v. 10 (1891).

Welmers, W. E. "Notes on the Structure of Saho." *Word* 8, no. 2 and 3 (1952).

Yassim M. Aberra. "Muslim Institutions in Ethiopia: The Asmara Awqaf." *J. Inst. of Muslim Minority Affairs,* 5, 1 (1983-84) pp. 203-23.

Zwemer, S. M. "Islam in Ethiopia and Eritrea." *Moslem World,* v. 26 (1936).

4. Languages and Literature

Abraham Negash. *Bibliography of Tigrinya Language Publications with Some Short Annotations* (Tigrn.; Asmara: Univ. of Asmara, 1983 E.C.).

Amanuel Sahle. "Tigrigna: Recent History and Development."
     Proc. 7th ICES (ed. S. Rubenson; Addis Ababa: 1984).*

Beaton, A. C., and A. Paul. *A Grammar and Vocabulary of the
     Tigre Language (as Spoken by the Beni Amer)* (Khartoum:
     1954).

Bender, M. L. ed. *Language in Ethiopia* (Oxford: Oxford Univ.
     P., 1976).

Bettini, L. "Gli idiomi parlati nella nostra colonia." *Boll.
     soc. geo. italiana,* v. 29 (1892).

Beurmann, M. von. *Vocabulary of the Tigre Language* (Halle:
     1868).

Camperio, M. *Manuale tigre-italiano* (Milan: Ulrico Hoepli,
     1894).

Candeo, G. "Vocabolario dancalo compilato in Assab e din-
     torni." *Boll. soc. africana d'Italia,* v. 12 (1893).

Capomazza, I. "L'Assaorta saho: vocabolario italiano, as-
     saorta-saho e assaorta-saho, italiano." *Boll. soc. africana
     d'Italia,* v. 29 (1910).

Castlenuovo del Zappa, G.-S. da. *Grammatica della lingua Cu-
     nama* (Asmara: 1938).

Cerulli, Enrico. *Storia della letteratura etiopica* (Milan:
     1956).*

Conti Rossini, Carlo. "Documenti per lo studio della lingua
     Tigre." *GSAI,* v. 16 (1903).

_____. "Raconti i conti bileni." *Actes du XIV Cong. Int.
     Orientalistes,* session 4, v. 2 (Algiers: 1905).

_____. "Schizzo del dialetto saho dell'Alta Assaorta in
     Eritrea." *RRAL,* ser. 5, v. 22 (1913).

_____. "Per la conoscenza della lingua cunama." *La
     terra e la vita,* v. 2 (1923).

_____. "Saggio sulla toponomatica dell'Eritrea tigrina."
     BSGI, ser. 7, v. 3, no. 10 (1938).

_____. *Lingua tigrigna* (Rome: Mondadori, 1940).*

_____. *Proverbi, tradizioni e canzoni tigrine* (Verbania:
     Ambrogio Airoldi, 1942).

Haile Gebre Kristos. "Poesia e canti popolari tigrini."
     Fourth CISE. V. 2 (Rome: 1974).

Jacob Ghebre-Ieusus, Aba. *Zenan tereten meslan nay
     qedemet* [Tigrn. popular poetry] (Tigrn.; Asmara: Ante-
     nati, 1941).

Kane, Thomas. "The Female Soldier in Tigrinya Literature."
In *New Trends in Ethiopian Studies,* v.1, ed. H. Marcus
(Lawrenceville, N.J.: Red Sea P., 1994).

Kolmodin, J.A. "Uber die 3 pers. masc. sing. perf. im Tigre."
Le monde oriental, v. 6 (1912).

Leslau, Wolf. *Documents Tigrigna* (Paris: C. Klincksieck,
1941).

_____. *Short Grammar of Tigre, dialect of Mensa* (New
Haven: Yale Univ. P., 1945).

_____. "Supplementary Observations on Tigre
grammar." *J. American Oriental Soc.,* v. 68 (1948).

_____. "Arabic Loanwords in Tigre."*Word,* v. 12 (1956).

_____. "Arabic Loanwords in Tigrigna." *J. American
Oriental Soc.,* v. 77 (1956).

_____. *An Annotated Bibliography of the Semitic Lan-
guages of Ethiopia* (The Hague: 1965).

Littman, E. "Das Verbum der Tigre-Sprache." *ZA,* v. 13
(1898).

Mason, John ed. *Tigrinya Grammar* (Ghinda and Philadelphia: American Evangelical Mission; 1994).

Mauro da Leonessa, P. *Grammatica analitica della lingua
tigray* (Rome: 1928).

Munzinger, W. "La langue tigre." *Rev. geo. internationale,* v.
9 (1884).

Musa Aron. *Mezgebe kalat smat ertrawyan* [Eritrean
personal names: Tigre and Tigrn.] (Toronto:1994).

Noldeke, T. "Tigre-Text." *ZA,* v. 24 (1910).

Palmer, F.R. "Relative clauses in Tigre." *Word,* v. 17 (1961).

_____. "Relative clauses in Tigrinya." *J. Semitic Stud-
ies,* v. 7 (1962).

Perbellini, A. M. "I meticci linguistici. del parlare italiano
con gli indigeni." *Etiopia* 1, no. 1 (1937): 49-50.

Savoia-Genova, E. di, and G. Simoncini. "Proverbi Tigrini."
RSE, v. 3 (1943).

Sundstrom, G. R. "Some Tigre texts with transliteration and
translation." *Le monde oriental,* v. 8 (1914).

Teferra Tsehaye and D. Beyl. "Personal Pronouns in
Tigrinya: A Socio-linguistic Study." *Ethiopianist Notes*
2, no. 3 (1978-79).

Thompson, E. David. "Kunama: Phonology and Noun Phrase." In *Nilo-Saharan Language Studies,* ed. L. Bender (East Lansing: Michigan State Univ. P., 1983).

Ullendorf, Edward. "A Tigrinya Language Council." *Africa,* v. 19 (1949).

_____. *The Semitic Langauges of Ethiopia* (London: 1955).

Vito, L. da. *Vocabolario della Lingua Tigrigna* (Rome: Casa editrice Italiana, 1893).

Winquist, C. *Sillabario nella Lingua Tigrinja* (Asmara: SEM; 1896)

Wolde-Ab Wolde-Mariam. *Fidel Tigrinya* [Tigrn. "Tigrinya Grammar"] (Asmara: SEM, 1932)

Yesehaq Gebre-Iyesus. *Tegra, tegray, tegrenya, tegre. enko tegra* (Tigrn.; Asmara: Franciscan P.P., 1993).

II. ANCIENT AND MEDIEVAL PERIOD (to c. 1520)

Alliot, A. "Pount-Pwane, l'Opone du geographe Ptolemée." *Revue d'égyptologie,* v. 8 (1951).

Altheim, F. and Ruth Stiehl. "Ezana von Aksum." *Klio,* v. 39 (1961).

_____. *Der Name Ezana: Festschrift fur Wilhelm Eilers.* (Wiesbaden: 1969).

Anfray, Francis. "La première campagne de fouilles a Matara après de Senafe (Nov. 1959 - Jan. 1960)." *AE,* v. 5 (1963).

_____. "Histoire de l'archeologie éthiopienne." *Tarik,* 1 (1963).

_____. "Notre connaissance du passé éthiopien d'après les recents travaux archeologiques." *Journal of Semitic Studies,* v. 9 (1964).

_____. "Chronique archeologique 1960-1964." *AE,* v. 6 (1965).

_____. "Matara." *Tarik,* v. 2 (1965).

_____. "Le musée archeologique d'Asmara." *RSE,* v. 21 (1966).

_____. "Matara." *AE,* v. 7 (1967).

_____. "Aspects de l'archeologie éthiopienne." *JAH*, v. 9 (1968).

_____. "La poterie de Matara. Esquisse typologique." *RSE*, v. 22 (1968).

_____. "Les rois d'Axoum d'après la numismatique." *JES*, 6 (1968).

_____. "L'archeologie d'Axoum en 1972." *Paideuma*, v. 18 (1972).

_____. "Deux villes axoumites: Adoulis et Matara." *Fourth CISE*, v.1 (Rome,1974): 752-65.*

_____. "The civilization of Aksum from the First to Seventh Century."In *General History of Africa*. V.2; *Ancient Civilizations of Africa*, ed. G. Mokhtar (Berkeley: UNESCO, 1981).

_____. *Eritrea: Preservation and Presentation of the Cultural Heritage* (Paris: UNESCO, Restricted Technical Report, 1994).

Anfray, F. and G. Annequin. "Matara: deuxieme, troisieme et quatrieme campagnes de fouilles." *AE*, v. 6 (1965).

Anfray, F., A.-J. Drewes and R. Schneider. *Recueil des inscriptions de l'Ethiopie des periodes preaxoumite et axoumite*, v. 1 (1991).

Anzani, A. "Numismatica axumita." *Rivista Italiana di Numismatica*, ser. 3, v. 3 (1926).

Arkell, A. J. "Four Occupation Sites at Agordat." *Kush*, v. 2 (1954).

Athanasius. *Historical Tracts*, trans. J.H. Newman (London; 1847). [* contains letter to Contantine with info. on Frumentius].

Basset, René. "Les inscriptions de l'Ile de Dahlak." *J A* (1893).

_____. "Numismatica e storia d'Etiopia." *JA*, no. 5-6 (1928-29).

Bausi, A., G. Lusini and I. Taddia. "Materiali di Studio dal Sara'e: le Istituzioni monastiche e la struttura della proprieta dondiaria" (MS, Rome: 1993).

Blanc, A.-C. "L'Industrie sur obsidienne des îles Dahlac (Mer Rouge)." *Actes du II Congres Panafricain de Prehistoire* (Algiers: 1952).

Bent, Theodore. *The Sacred City of the Ethiopians.* (London: 1893).

_____. "The Ancient Trade Route across Ethiopia." *Geo. Journal,* v. 2 (1893).

Brandt, S. A. "New Perspectives on the Origins of Food Production in Ethiopia." In *From Hunters to Farmers,* ed. J.D. Clark and S. Brandt (Berkeley: Univ. California P. 1984).

Budge, E. A. T. Wallis. *The Book of Saints of the Ethiopian Church.* (Cambridge: Cambridge Univ. P., 1928).

_____. *A History of Ethiopia, Nubia and Abyssinia,* 2 v. (London: 1928).

_____. *A History of Ethiopia,* v. 1 (Netherlands: Cosferhout N.B., 1966).

Caetani, L. *Annali dell'Islam* (Milan: 1905).

Calderini, A. "Documenti per la storia degli etiopi e loro rapporti col mondo romano." *Atti IV congresso di studi romani,* v. 2 (Rome: 1938).

Caquot, Andre. "L'inscription éthiopienne de Marib." *AE,* v. 6 (1965).

_____. "Arabe de Sud et Afrique. Examen d'une hypotèse recente." *AE,* v. 1 (1955).

Caquot, A. and P. Nautin. "Une nouvelle inscription grecque d'Ezana, roi d'Axoum." *JS* (1970).

Carpantier. *Martyrium sancti Arethae et sociorum in civitate Negran, Cum commentarium praevis. Acta Sanctorum,* v. 10 (Brussels: 1861).*

Cerulli, E. "Vestigia di antiche civilta in Eritrea e in Somalia." *Rass. italiana politica, letteraria e artistica* 35, no. 11 (1933).

_____. "L'Etiopia mediovale in alcuni brani di scrittori arabi." *RSE,* v. 3 (1943).

_____. "La Nubia cristiana, i Baria ed i Cunama, nel X secolo di. cristianità., secondo Ibn Hawqal, geografo arabo." *Annali dell'Istituto Universitario Orientale di Napoli. Nuova serie* 3 (Rome: 1949).

_____. "Ethiopia's Relations with the Muslim World." *General History of Africa.* V.3; *Africa from the Seventh to Eleventh Centuries,* ed. M. el Fasi (Berkeley: UNESCO, 1988).

Cervicek, P. "Rock Paintings of Laga Oda (Ethiopia)." *Paideuma*, v. 17 (1971).

Chabot, J. B., ed. *Chronicon Pseudo-Dionysiam vulgo dictam. (Corpus Scriptores Christianorum Orientalium. Scriptores syri, ser. 3*, v. 3 (Paris: 1933).*

Clark, J. D. "The Domestication Process in Sub-Saharan Africa with Special Reference to Ethiopia." *Cong. IX Union Internationale des Sciences Préhistoriques et Protohistoriques* (Nice: 1976).*

Contenson, Henri de. "Les premières rois d'Axoum d'après des découvertes recentes." *JA*, 248, fasc. 1 (1960).

_____. "Pre-Aksumite Culture." *General History of Africa*. V.2; *Ancient Civilizations of Africa*, ed. G. Mokhtar (Berkeley: UNESCO, 1981).

Conti Rossini, C. "L'iscrizione dell'obelisco presso Matara." *RRAL*, ser. 5, v. 5 (1896).

_____. "Il gadla Filipos ed il gadla Yohannes di Debre Bizen." *MAL*, ser. 5, v. 8 (1900). *

_____. "L'evangelo d'oro di Debra Libanos." *RRAL*, ser. 5, v. 10 (1901).

_____. "Gli atti di Abba Yonas." *RRAL*, ser. 5, v. 12 (1903)

_____. "Documenti per l'archeologia d'Eritrea nella bassa valle del Barca." *RRAL*, v. 12 (1903).

_____. "Vitae Sanctorum Indigenarum: Acta Marqore-wos." *CSCO: Scriptores Aethiopici*, v. 16-17 (Louvain: 1904).

_____. "Les listes des rois d'Aksum." *JA* (1909).

_____. "Sugli Habasat." *RRAL*, ser. 5, v. 15 (1909).*

_____. "Studi su popolazioni dell'Etiopia, IV: Antiche popolazione Nubia-Etiopiche." *RSO*, v. 6 (1913).

_____. "Documenti per l'archeologia eritrea nella bassa valle del Barca." *RRAL*, v. 12 (1913).

_____. "Expeditions et possessions des Habasat en Arabie." *JA* (1921).

_____. "Antiche rovine sulle rora Eritree." *RRAL*, ser. 5, v. 31 (1922).

_____. "Un codice illustrato eritreo del secolo XV." *Africa Italiana*, 1, no. 1 (1927).

_____. *Storia d'Etiopia* (Bergamo: Istituto Italiana d'Arti Grafiche, 1928).

_____. "L'iscrizione etiopica di Ham." *Atti della reale academia d'Italia* (Rome: 1939).

_____. "L'iscrizione etiopica di Ham." *RRAL, Atti*, ser. 7, v. 1 (1940).

_____. "Incisioni rupestri all'Haggher." *RSE* 3, no. 1 (1943).

_____. "Postille al 'Futuh al Habasah'." *Le Museon,* no. 59 (Brussels: 1946).

_____. "Gad ed il dio luna in Etiopia." *Studi e materali di storia delle religione* (Rome: 1947-48).

Cosmas Indicopleustes. *The Christian Topography of Cosmas, an Egyptian Monk.,* ed. and trans. J.W. McCrindle (London: 1897).*

_____. *The Christian Topography of Cosmas Indicopleustes,* ed. and trans. E.O. Winstedt (Cambridge: Cambridge Univ. P., 1909).

_____. *Cosmas Indicopleustes: Topographie chretienne,* trans. W. Wolska-Conus (Paris: 1968).

Crawford, O. G. S., ed. *Ethiopian Itineraries, c. 1400-1524,* Hakluyt, ser. 2, v. 59 (Cambridge: 1955).*

Cresti, F. "La Mosquée du Sayh Hammali à Massaoua." *Etudes Ethiopiennes,* v. 1 (Paris: Conference des Etudes Ethiopiennes, 1994)

Crowfoot, J. W. "Some Red Sea Ports in the Anglo-Egyptian Sudan." *Geo. J.* 27, no. 5 (1911).

Cuoq, J. *L'Islam en Ethiopie, Des Origines au XVIe siecle.*(Paris: 1981).

Dainelli, G., and O. Marinelli. "Le prime notizie sulle rovine di Cohaito nella colonia Eritrea." *Boll. soc. africana d'Italia,* v. 27 (1908).

Deramey, J. "Les inscriptions d'Adoulis et d'Axoum." *Revue de l'histoire des religions,* v. 24 (1891).

Desanges, J. "Une mention alterée d'Axoum dans l'exposition totius mundi et gentium." *AE,* 7(1967).

_____. "D'Axoum à l'Assam, aux portes de la Chine: le voyage de Scholasticus de Thebes (entre 360 et 500 apres J-C)." *Historia,*18, no. 5 (1969).

_____. *Recherches sur l'activité des Mediterranées aux confins de l'Afrique* (Rome: 1978).

Doresse, J. *Au Pays de la reine de Saba: L'Ethiopie antique et moderne.* (Paris: 1956).

_____. "La découverte d'Asbi-Dera. Nouveaux documents sur les rapports entre l'Egypte et l'Ethiopie à l'époque axoumite." *ACISE* (1959).

Drewes, A. J. *Inscriptions de l'Ethiopie Antique.* (Leiden: 1962).*

_____. "The Inscription from Dibdib in Eritrea." *Bibliotheca Orientalis,,* v. 11 (1954).

Drewes, A. and R. Schneider. "Origine et developpement de l'écriture éthiopi"nne jusqu'a l'epoque des inscriptions royales d'Axoum." *AE,* 10 (1976).

_____. *Recueille des Inscriptions Ethiopiennes d'Axoum,* v. 1-2 (Paris: 1992/3) *

Drouin, E. A. "Les listes royales éthiopiennes et leur autorité historique." *Revue Africaine,* Aug.-Oct. (Algiers: 1882).

Duncanson, D. J. "Girmaten: A New Archeological Site in Eritrea." *Antiquity,* v. 27 (1947).

_____. "Eritrean Rock Sculptures." *Man,* v. 52 (1952).

Ehret, C. F. "On the antiquity of agriculture in Ethiopia." *JAH,* v. 20 (1979).

Elgood, P. G. *The Ptolemies of Egypt* (Bristol: 1938).

Eusebius Pamphilus. *Ecclesiastical History,* ed. and trans. by K. Luke (London: 1927).

_____. *Vie de l'Empereur Constantin* (Paris: 1675).

Fattovich, Rudolfo. "Pre-Aksumite Civilization of Ethiopia: A Preliminary Review." *Proceedings of the Seminar for Arabian Studies,* v. 7 (1977).

_____. "Alcuni siti inediti dell'Eritre settentrionale." *Abbay,* v. 10 (Paris: CNRS, 1979).

_____. "I 'rilievi' rupestri di Daaro Caulos presso Asmara." *Annali dell'istituto universitario orientale,* v. 43 (1983).

_____. "Data for the History of the Ancient Peopling of the Northern Ethiopia-Sudanese Borderland." In *Proc. Seventh ICES,* ed. S. Rubenson (Addis Ababa: 1984).

_____. "Elementi per la Preistoria del Sudan Orientali e dell'Etiopia Settentionale." *Studi di Pal. in Onore di Salvatore M. Puglisi* (Rome: 1985).

_____. "Remarks on the late pre-history and early history of Northern Ethiopia." *Proc. Eighth ICES,* v. 1 (Addis Ababa: 1988).

_____. "Remarks on the Pre-Aksumite Period in Northern Ethiopia." *JES,* 13 (1990).

_____. "L'archaeologia del Mar Rosso: problemi e prospettive." *Abbay,* v. 14 (Paris: CNRS, 1991).

Franchini, V. "Pitture rupestri a Sullum Ba'atti." *RSE,* v. 10 (1951).

_____. "Pitture rupestri a Ba'atti Sullum nel Deghien." *RSE,* v. 11 (1952).

_____. "Stazioni litiche di superficie in Eritrea." *Il Bollettino,* v. 1 (Asmara: 1953).

_____. "Ritrovamenti Archeologici in Eritrea." *RSE,* v. 12 (1954).

_____. "Notizie su alcune Pitture ed Incisioni Rupestri recentimente ritrovate in Eritrea." *Atti del Convegno Int. di Studi Etiopici* (Rome: 1960).

_____. "Piturre rupestri e antichi resti architettonici dell'Akelle Guzai." *RSE,* v. 17 (1961).

_____. "Nuovi ritrovamenti di pitture rupestri e graffiti in Eritrea." *RSE,* v. 20 (1964).

Gallo, E. "La vecchia chiesa copta in Asmara." *Erythraea,* v. 2, Mar.-Apr. (1920).

Gaudio, A. "Quattro ritrovamenti archeologici e paleografici in Eritrea." *Il Bolletino,* v. 1 (Asm.: 1953).

Glaser, E. *Die Abessinien in Arabien und Afrika* (Munich: 1895).

_____. "Die altabessinische Inschrift von Matara." *ZDMG,* v. 50 (1896).

Graziosi, P. "Le pitture rupestri dell'Amba Focada (Eritrea)." *RSE,* v. 1 (1941).

_____. "Figure rupestri schematiche nell'Achelle Guzai." *Revista di scienze preistoriche,* v. 19 (1964).

_____. "New Discoveries of Rock Paintings in Ethiopia." *Antiquity,* 38 (1964).

Guidi, I. "Il Gadla Aragawi." *RRAL,* Atti, v. 2 (1896).

_____. *Storia della letteratura etiopica* (Rome: 1932).

Guillain, M. *Documents sur l'histoire, la geographie et le commerce de l'Afrique Orientale,* 2 v. (Paris: 1856).

Haberland, E. "The Horn of Africa." In *General History of Africa.* V. 5; *Africa from the Sixteenth to the Eighteenth Century,* ed. B. A. Ogot (Berkeley: UNESCO, 1992).

Halevy, J. "L'inscription éthiopienne de l'obelisque près de Matara." *Rev. Semetique,* v. 4 (1896).

_____. "Traces de l'influence indoparsie en Abyssinie." *Rev. Semitique,* v. 4 (1896).

Hamy. "Les Pays des Troglodytes." *L'Anthropologie,* v. 11 (1897).

Harden, J. M. *An Introduction to Ethiopic Christian Literature* (London: 1926)

Haughton, G. C. "Account of an ancient Arabic grave-stone found at Dahlac el-Kibeer near Massowah, Abyssinia." *Royal Asiatic Soc., Transactions,* v. 2 (1830).

Helidorus. *Aethiopica,* trans. M. Hadas (Ann Arbor: Univ. Michigan P., 1957).

Hirsch, B. "Cartographie et Itineraires: figures occidentales du nord de l'Ethiopie aux XVe et XVIe siècles." *Abbay,* 13 (1986-87).

Hourani, G. F. *Arab Seafaring in the Indian Ocean in Ancient and Medieval Times.* (Princeton: Univ. P.: 1951).

Hudud al-Alam. *The Regions of the World, A Persian Geographer, 982 A.D.,* trans. V. Minorsky (Oxford: Univ. P.: 1937).

Huntingford, G.B.W. *The Periplus of the Erythraen Sea* (London: Hakluyt Soc., 1980).*

Ibn-Hawkal. *Configuration de la Terre* [10th c. AD], trans. of *Kitab Surat al-Ard* by J.H. Kramers and G. Wiet (Paris and Beyreuth: 1964).*

Ibn-Ishaq. *Life of Mohammed,* ed. M. Edwards (London: 1964).

_____. *Serat Rasul Allah: Life of Muhammed,* trans. A. Guillaume (Oxford: Univ. P.: 1955).*

Ibn-Khaldun. *Yemen, Its Early Medieval History,* trans. H. C. Kay (London: 1892).

(Al-)Idrisi. *Geographie d'Edrisi,* trans. A. Jaubert (Paris: 1837).

Irvine, A. K. "On the Identity of the Habashat in the South Arabian Inscriptions." *JSS*, V. 10 (1965).

Jaeger, O. *Antiquities of North Ethiopia* (Stuttgart: 1965).

Jamme, A. *Sabean Inscriptions from Mahram Bilqis, Marib* (Baltimore: 1962).

Jones, Scott. "Archaeological and Environmental Observations in Rora Habab, Eritrea." *Azania*, v. 26 (1991).

Kammerer, Albert. *Essai sur l'Histoire antique d'Abyssinie; le Royaume d'Aksum et ses voisins d'Arabie et de Meroe* (Paris: 1928).

_____. *La Mer Rouge, l'Abyssinie et l'Arabie depuis l'Antiquite. V. 1: Les Pays de la Mer Erythree jusqu'a la fin du Moyen-Age* (Cairo: 1929).

Kirwan, L. P. "The Christian Topography and the Kingdom of Axum." *Geo. J.* 138, no. 2 (1972).

_____. "An Ethiopian-Sudanese Frontier Zone in Ancient History." *Geo. J.* 138, no. 4 (1972).

Kobishchanov, Yuri M. "The origin of Ethiopian literature." *Essays on African Cultures* (1966).

_____. "The sea voyages of ancient Ethiopians in the Indian Ocean." *Proc. Third ICES*, v. 1 (1966).

_____. *Axum.* (Philadelphia: Penn. State Univ. P.: 1979).

_____. "Aksum: political system, economics and culture, first to fourth century." In *General History of Africa. V. 2; Ancient Civilizations of Africa,* ed. G. Mokhtar (Berkeley: UNESCO, 1981).

Kramers, J. H. "L'Erythrée decrite dans une source arabe de Xe siècle.' *Atti del XIX Congresso Intern, degli Orientalisti* (Rome: 1935).

_____. "L'Erythrée au Xe siècle." *Analecta Orientalia,* v. 1 (Leiden: 1954).

Krebs, W. "Adulis—ein antiker Hafen am Roten Meer." *Altertum,* v. 15 (1969).

Littman, E., and Krencker, D. *Vorbericht der Deutsche Aksum-Expedition,* 5 (Berlin: 1913).

_____. "La leggenda del dragone del Aksum in lingua Tigrai." *RSE,* v. 6 (1947).

_____. "An old inscription from Berenice Road." *JRAS* (1954).

Lusini, Gianfrancesco. "Problèmes du mouvement eu-
stathéen." *Etudes Ethiopiennes,* v. 1 (Paris: Soc. française pour les études éthiopiennes, 1994).

MacDowell, D. W. "The early Western satraps and the date of
the Periplus." *Num. Cron.,* v. 4 (1964).

Malmusi, Benedetto. "Lapidi della necropoli musulmana di
Dahlak." *Memorie dell'Academia di Modena (sez. lettere),* ser. 2, no. 11 (1895) and *ibid.,* ser. 3, no. 2
(1898).

Manzi, L. *Il commercio in Etiopia, Nubia, Abissinia, Sudan,
etc. dai primordi alla dominazione Musulmana* (Rome:
1886).

(Al-)Maqrizi, Abu 'l-Abbas Ahmad b. 'Ali. *Historia regum
Islamiticorum in Abyssinia,* trans. and ed. Rinck
(Leyden: 1790).

_____. *Al-Ilmam bi akhbar man bi ard al-Habasha min
Muluk al-Islam* [c. 1435; Arab.] ed. G. Zaidan (Cairo:
1895).*

(Al-)Mas'udi. *Historical Encyclopedia entitled 'Meadows of
Gold and Mines of Gems,'* v. 1, trans. A. Sprenger (London: 1841).

_____. *Les Prairies d'or,* v. 3 [trans. of *Muruj;* 10th c.
A.D.], trans C. Barbier de Meynard and P. de Courteille
(Paris: 1864-77).*

Mathew, G. "The dating and Significance of the *Periplus of
the Erythrean Sea." East Africa and the Orient,* ed. H. N.
Chittick and R. Rotberg (London: 1976).

Milne, J. G. *A History of Egypt under Roman Rule* (London:
1924).

Mommsen, Th. *Eusebius: Historia ecclesiastica* 2, no. 2
(Leipzig: 1908).

Monneret de Villard. "Note sulle influenze asiatiche nel-
l'Africa Orientale." *RSO, no.* 17 (1938).

_____. "L'inscrizione etiopica di Ham e l'epigrafia
meroitica." *Aegyptus,* v. 20 (1940).

_____. *La Nubia romana* (Rome: 1941).

_____. "Problemi sulla storia religiosa del-
l'Abissinia." *RSAI, no.* 10 (1942).

_____. "Mose vescovo di Adulis." *Orientalia Cristiana
Periodica,* v. 13 (1947).

_____. "Aksum e i quattro rei del mondo." *Annali Lateranensi,* v. 12 (1948).

Mordini, A. "Un'antica porta in legno proveniente della chiesa di Gunaguna (Scimezana, Eritrea)." *RSO, no.* 19 (1940).

_____. "Un riparo sotto roccia con pitture rupestri nell'Amba Focada (Eritrea)." *RSE, no.* 1 (1941).

_____. "La chiesa di Baraknaha, nello Scimezana." *AE,* v. 4 (1961).

_____. "La reconnaissance et la preservation des anciennes eglises ethiopiennes." *Materiali per lo studio medioevo etiopico* (Rome: 1964).

Muir, W. *The Life of Mohammad from Original Sources* (Edinburgh: 1923).

Munro-Hay, Stuart. "A Tyranny of Sources: The history of Aksum from its Coinage." *NEAS* 3, no. 3 (1981-82).

_____. "The foreign trade of the Aksumite port of Adulis." *Azania, no.* 17 (1982).*

_____. *The Coinage of Aksum* (New Delhi: 1984).

_____. "Aksumite Chronology; some Reconsiderations." *Proc. Eighth ICES,* v. 2 (Addis Ababa: 1989).

_____. "The British Museum Excavations at Adulis, 1868." *Antiquaries J.,* 69, pt. 1 (1989).

_____. "The Rise and Fall of Aksum: Chronological Considerations." *JES,* 23 (1990).

Naville, E. *The Temple of Deir el-Bahri* [c. 1500 BC] (London: 1898).*

Negussie, Caroline. "Aksum and Matara: A Stratigraphic Comparison of Two Aksumite Towns." *New Trends in Ethiopian Studies,* v. 1 [12th ICES] ed. H. Marcus (Lawrenceville: Red Sea P., 1994).

Nikephorus Kallestus. *Historia Ecclesiastica* [4th-5th c.s AD]. In *Patrologiae Cursus Completus,* ser. *Graeca,* CXLVI, ed. J. P. Migne (Paris: n.d.).*

Oman, Giovanni. *La Necropoli Islamica di Dahlak Kebir (Mar Rosso),* v. 1-3 (Naples: 1976).*

Ouseley, W. *The Oriental Geography of Ebn Haukal, an Arabian Traveller of the 10th century* (London: 1800).

Palmer, J. "Periplus Maris Erythraei." *Classical Quarterly,* new ser. 1, no. 45 (1951).

Pankhurst, Richard. *An Introduction to the Economic History of Ethiopia, from Early Times to 1800.* (London: 1961).

_____. "Early Pharaonic Contacts with the Land of Punt." *QSE,* v. 5 (1984).

Paribeni, R. "Ricerche nel luogo dell'antica Adulis." *Monumenti Antichi pubblicati ... RRAL,* v. 18 (1907).

_____. "Etiope." *Enciclopedia Italiana dell'Arte Antica,* v. 3 (1960).

Perruchon, J. "Histoire des Guerres d'Amda Syon." *JA,* ser.8, v. 14 (1889).

_____. "Note pour l'histoire d'Ethiopie: Lettre adressée par le roi d'Ethiopie au roi Georges de Nubie sous le patriarcat de Philothée 981-1002 ou 1003." *Rev. Semetique,* 1 (1893).*

_____. *Les Chroniques de Zar'a Ya'eqob et de Ba'eda maryam* (Paris: 1893).

_____. "Vie de Cosmas, patriarche d'Alexandrie de 923 a 934." *Rev. Semetique,* v. 2 (1894).

Philostorgius. *The Ecclesiastical History* [4th-5th c.s A.D.] trans. E. Walford (London: 1875).*

Pigulevskaya, N. V. *Byzanz auf den Wegen nach indien: aus Geschichte des byzantinischen Handels mit dem Orient vom 4, bis 6 Jahrhundert* (Berlin: 1969).

Piva, A. "Una civilita scomparsa dell'Eritrea en gli scavi nelle regione di Cheren." *Nuova Antologia,* v.128 (1907).

Pirenne, J. *Paléographie des inscriptions sud-arabe* (Brussels: 1956).

_____. "Un problème clef pour la chronologie de l'Orient: La date du Periple de la mer Erythrée." *JA* (1961).

_____. "Arte Sabeo d'Etiopia." *Encyclopedia dell'Arte Antica,* v. 6 (Rome: 1965).

_____. "Le developpement de la navigation Egypte-Inde dans l'antiquité, sociétés et compagnies de commerce en Orient et dans l'Ocean Indien." *Coll. Internatl. Histoire Maritime, Actes 8e* (1970).

_____. "L'imbroglio de trois siecles de chronologie aksumite: IVe-VIe s." *Documents historiques de la civilisation éthiopienne,* v. 6 (Paris: CNRS, 1975).

_____. "The Chronology of Ancient South Arabia—Diversity of Opinion." In *Yemen,* ed. W. Daum (Innsbruck: 1987).

Pliny. *Natural History,* 11 v., trans. H. Rackman (Cambridge: Harvard Univ. P., 1938-62).

Polotsky, I., ed. *Mani, Kephalaia* (Stuttgart: 1940).

Polotsky, H. "Aramaic, Syriac and Ge'ez." *JSS,* v. 9 (1964).

Praetorius, Fr. "Ueber die Aethiopisch-Himjarischen Kreige." *ZDMG,* v. 24 (1870).

_____. "Der Name Adulis." *ZDMG,* v. 47 (1893).

Preaux, C. "Sur les communications de l'Ethiopie avec l'Egypte hellenistique." *Chronique d'Egypte,* v. 53 (1951).

Procopius. *History of the Wars,* 7 v. [6th-7th c.s AD] trans. of *De Bello Persico* by H.B. Ewing (Cambridge: Harvard Univ. P., 1914-40).*

Ptolemy, Claudius. *Geography of Claudius Ptolemy,* trans. E. Stevenson (New York: 1932).

Puglisi, G. "Le cisterne de Dahlak Kebir e di Adal." *Il Bolletino,* 1 (Asmara: 1953).

_____. "La necropoli de Desset el-Banaia ed una leggenda sul Cubbet es-Saladin." *Il Bolletino,* 2 (Asm.: 1957).

_____. "Alcuni vesitgi dell'isola di Dahlac Chebir e la leggenda dei Furs." *Proc. Third ICES,* v. 1 (1966).

Ricci, L. "Piccole note archaeologiche dell'Eritrea." *RSE,* v. 13 (1955).

_____. "Ritrovamenti archeologici in Eritrea II." *RSE,* v. 14 (1958).

_____. "Iscrizioni rupestri dell'Eritrea." *RSE,* v. 15-16 (1959-60).

_____. "Di due toponomi dell'Eritrea." *RSE,* v. 16 (1960).

_____. "Note marginali: La statuetta di bovino in bronzo da Zeban Kutur." *RSE,* v. 15 (1960).

Rossi, Etore. "Sulla storia delle isole Dahlak (Mar Rosso) nel medio evo." *Atti del 3 Congresso di Studi Coloniale* (Florence: 1937).

_____. "L'iscrizione epolcrale di Zain ul-Mulk figlia di un sultano di Dahlach (sec. XII) nel Museo di Treviso." *RSE* 3, no. 1 (1943).

Roubert, C. "Prospection et découvertes de documents préhistoriques en Dankalie." *Annales d'Ethiopie,* 8 (1970).

Rostovtzeff, M. "Foreign Commerce of Ptolemeic Egypt." *J. of Economic and Business History,* v. 4 (1932).

Rufinus, Tyranius. *Historia Ecclesiastica.* In *Patrologiae Cursus Competus:* ser. *Latina;* XXI, ed. J. P. Migne (Paris: n.d.).

_____. *Historia ecclesiastica* [4th-5th c.s A.D.] (Leipzig: 1908).*

Rundgren, F. "The root 'sft' in the Modern Ethiopic Languages (Tigre, Tigrina and Amharic) and Old Egyptian 'fty,' Coptic 'sft'." *Orientalia Suecana,* v. 2 (1953).

Ryckmans, G. *L'institutions monarchiques en Arabie Meridionale avant l'Islam* (Louvain: 1951).

_____. *Les Religions arabes preislamiques* (Louvain: 1951).

_____. *La persecution des Chretiens Himyarites au 6e siecle* (Istanbul: 1956).

_____. "Une 'éthiopienne' en Arabie." *AE,* v. 2 (1957).

Sauter, R. "L'arc et les panneaux sculptes de la vielle église d'Asmara." *RSE,* v. 23 (1969).

Sayce, A. "A Greek Inscription of a King (?) of Aksum found at Meroe." *Proc. of Soc. Biblical Archaeology,* v. 31 (1909).

Schiaparelli, E. "La geografia dell'Africa Orientale secondo le indicazioni dei monumenti egiziani." *RRAL,* ser. 5, v. 24 (1886).

Schneider, R. "Notes épigraphiques sur les découvertes de Matara." *AE,* v. 6 (1965).

_____. "Les débuts de l'histoire éthiopienne." *Documents historiques de la civilisation éthiopienne,* v. 7 (Paris: CNRS, 1970).

_____. "Deux Inscriptions Sud-Arabiques du Tigre." *Biblio. Orientalis* 30, no. 5-6 (1973).

_____. "Trois nouvelles inscriptions royales d'Axoum." *Fourth CISE,* v. 1 (Rome: 1974).*

_____. "Notes sur Filipos de Dabra Bizan et ses successeurs." *Annales d'Ethiopie,* v. 11 (1978).

_____. *Recueil des Innscriptions de l'Ethiopie des Periodes Pre-Axoumite et Axoumite,* 2 v. (Paris: 1992-93).*

Schoff, W. H., trans. *The Periplus of the Erythrean Sea* (London: 1912).

_____. "As to the date of the Periplus." *JRAS* (1917): 827-30.

Sergew Hable Sellassie. *Ancient and Medieval Ethiopian History to 1270*. (Addis Ababa: 1972).*

Shinnie, P. "The Fall of Meroe." *Kush,* v. 3 (1955).

_____. *Meroe* (London: 1967).

St. Martin, V. de. "Eclairecissements geographiques et historiques sur l'inscription d'Adulis." *JA*, ser. 6, v. 2 (1863).

Strabo. *The Geography of Strabo,* 8 v. ,ed. H. L. Jones (London: 1940).

Sundstrom, R. "Report of an Expedition to Adulis." *ZA,* v. 20, ed. E. Littmann (1907).

(Al-)Tabari. *Chronique,* 4 v. [8th-9th c.s A.D.] trans. M. H. Zotenberg (Paris: 1958).*

Tadesse Tamrat. *Church and State in Ethiopia, 1270-1527* (Oxford: Univ. P., 1972).*

_____. "The Horn of Africa: the Solomonids in Ethiopia and the States of the Horn of Africa." In *General History of Africa*. V. 4, *Africa from the Twelfth to the Sixteenth Century,* ed. D. T. Niane (Berkeley: UNESCO, 1984).

Tedeschi, Salvatore. "Profilio storico di Dayr as-Sultan." *JES* 2, no. 2 (1964).

_____. "Note storiche sulle isola Dahlak." *Proc. Third Internatl. Conference of Ethiopian Studies,* v.1 (1969).*

Tekle Tsadik Mekouria. *Yeityopia Tarik Axum Zagwe* [Amh.] (Addis Ababa: 1966-67).

_____. *L'Eglise d'Ethiopie* (Paris: 1967).

_____. "Christian Axum." In *General History of Africa*. V. 2; *Ancient Civilizations of Africa,* ed. G. Mokhtar (Berkeley: UNESCO, 1981).

_____. "The Horn of Africa." In *General History of Africa*. V. 3; *Africa from the Seventh to Eleventh Centuries,* ed. M. el Fasi (Berkeley: UNESCO, 1988).

Toussaint, A. *Histoire de l'ocean indien* (Paris: 1961).

Tringali, G. "Cenni sulle 'ona' di Asmara e dintorni." *AE,* v. 6 (1965).

_____. "Necropoli di Curbavaiechet (Asmara)." *JES*, 6 (1967).

_____. "Varieta di asce litiche in 'ona' dell'altopiano eritreo." *JES*, 7 (1969).

_____. "Necropoli di Cascase e oggetti sudarabici dell regione di Asmara (Eritrea)." *RSE*, v. 26 (1979).

_____. "Note su ritrivomenti archeologici in Eritrea." *RSE*, v. 28 (1981).

_____. "Orecchini in pietra ritrovati nella zona di Sembel-Cuscet (Asmara)." *QSE,*, v. 5 (1984).

_____. "Elenco commentato dei reporti archeologici custoditi nel Museo del Collegio 'La Salle' in Asmara." *QSE*, v. 6-7 (1985-86).

Turaiev, B., ed. *Vitae sanctorum Indigenorum: Acta S. Eustathii,* [Ewostatewos and Amde Siyon] "Scriptores Aethiopici," v. 15 (Paris: 1906).*

Ullendorf, E. "Note on the Introduction of Christianity into Ethiopia." *Africa,* 19 (1949).

_____. "The Obelisk of Matara." *JRAS* (1951).

_____. "Index of C. Conti Rossini's 'Storia d'Etiopia'." *RSE*, v. 18 (1962).

_____. *Ethiopia and the Bible* (London: 1967).

Vaccaro, F. *Le monete di Aksum* (Mantova: 1967).

Vigliardi-Micheli, A. "Le pitture rupestre di Carora (Nord Eritrea)." *Rev. di Scienze Prehistoriche*, v. 11 (1956).

Vincent, W. *The Periplus of the Erythrean Sea* (London: 1807).

Vicychl, W. "Egziabher, 'Dieu'." *AE*, v. 2 (1957).

_____. "Le titre de 'Roi de Rois'." *AE*, v. 2 (1957).

Wainwright, G. "Early Records of Iron in Abyssinia." *Man*, v. 30 (1947).

_____. "Early Foreign Trade in East Africa." *Man*, v. 30 (1947).

Wiet, H. G. "Les Relations Egypto-Abyssines sous les Sultans Mamluks." *BSAC*, v. 4 (1938).

_____. "Roitelets de Dahlak." *Bull. de l'institut de l'E-gypte*, v. 34 (1951-52).

Wissman, H. von. "Ancient History." *Le Museon*, 77 (1964).

Wissman, H., and C. Rathjens. "De Mari Erythraeo: Sonder-
druck aus der Lauten Sich." *Festschrift Stuttgarter Ge-
ographische Studien,* v. 69 (1957).

(Al-)Ya'qubi. *Historiae* [c. 872 A.D.; trans. of *Ta'rikh ibn
Wadih*] trans. T. Houtsma (1883).*

_____. "Kitab al-Buldan." [c. 892 A.D.] *Bibliotheca Ge-
ographorum Arabicorum,* v. 7, ed. De Goeje (1892).*

_____. *Les Pays,* trans. G. Wiet (Cairo: 1937).*

Yeshaq Gebre-Yesus. *Ferdu!* [Tigrn.: 'Judgement!'—on ancient
history of 'Ethiopian' region]. (Asm.: Franciscan P. P.;
1992).

Zaborski, A. "Notes on the Medieval History of the Beja
Tribes." *Folia orientali,* v. 7 (1965).

_____. "Some remarks concerning Ezana's inscriptions
and the Beja Tribes." *Folia orientali,* v. 9 (1967).

_____. "Some Eritrean place names in Arabic Medieval
Sources." *Folia orientali,* v. 12 (1970).

_____. "Beja and Tigre in the 9th and 10th c. Period."
Rocznik orientalistyczny 35, no. 1 (1972).

Zarins, Juris. "Obsidian and the Red Sea Trade: Prehistoric
Aspects." *Proceedings of Ninth Internatl. Congress of
Assocation of South Asian Archaeologists in Western
Europe* (Venice: 1988).

Zyhlarz, E. "Das Land Punt." *Zeitschaft der aegyptischen
Sprachen,* v. 32 (1942).

III. EARLY MODERN PERIOD
(c. 1520 to 1885)

Abdu Ali Habib. "History of Massawa: from early nineteenth
century to the coming of the Italians." (B.A. thesis;
AAU: 1973).

Abir, Mordechai. "Brokerage and Brokers in Ethiopia in the
First Half of the 19th Century." *JES,* 3 (1965).

_____. "Trade and Politics in the Ethiopian Region,
1830-1855." (Ph.D. diss.; Univ. of London: 1964).

_____. *Ethiopia: The Era of the Princes: The Challenge
of Islam and the Reunification of the Christian Empire,
1769-1855.* (London: Longmans, 1968).

Aleme Eshete. "Activities Politiques de la Mission Catholique (Lazariste) en Ethiopie (sous le règne de l'Empereur Johannes) 1868-1880." (MS; Paris: 1970).

_____. *La Mission Catholique Lazariste en Ethiopie* (Aix-en-Provence: Inst. d'Histoire des Pays d'Outre Mer: Etudes et Documents, v. 2, 1970).

Alvarez, Francisco. *The Prester John of the Indies: A Narrative of the Portugese Expedition to Abyssinia during the years 1520-1527,* v. 1-2, ed. and trans. C. F. Beckingham and G. W. B. Huntingford (London: Hakluyt Soc., 1961).

_____. *Carta das novas que vieram a el Rey nostro Senhor do descobrimento do Prese Joham* (Lisbon: 1521).

Annales de la Congregation de la Mission (Paris: Lazarist Mission, n.d. [1839-94]).

Annesley, G. *see* Valentia.

Aren, Gustav. *Evangelical Pioneers in Ethiopia: Origins of the Evangelical Church Mekane Yesus* (Stockholm: EFS Forlaget, 1978).

Baeteman, J. "Impressions de Voyage de France en Abyssinie." *Les Missions Catholiques* (Paris: 1922).

Bairu Tafla, ed. and trans. *A Chronicle of Emperor Yohannes: 1872-1889* (Wiesbaden: 1977).

Barros, Joao de. *Decada terceira da Asia* (Lisbon: 1628).

Beccari, C. *Rerum Aethiopicarum Scriptores Occidentales Inediti* [16th-17th c.s], v. 11 (Rome: 1911).*

_____. *Il Tigre descritto da un missionara gesuita del secolo XVII* [trans. of Emmanuel Barradas, "Do Reyno de Tigre" and *Tractatus tres historico-geographici,* c.1624-33] (Rome: 1912).*

_____. *Notizie e saggi di opere e documenti inediti riguardanti l'Etiopia* (Rome: 1913).

Bloss. "The Story of Suwakin." *SNR,* 19, no. 1 (1936) and 20, no. 2 (1937).

Bombaci, A. "Notizie sull Abissinia in fonti turche." *RSE,* no. 3 (1943).*

Bruce, James. *Travels to Discover the Source of the Nile* [1790], ed. C. F. Beckingham (Chicago: 1964).

Caulk, Richard. "Menilek and the Ethio-Egyptian War of 1875-76: a reconsideration of source material." *Rural Africana*, v. 11 (1970).

_____. "Yohannis IV, the Mahdists and the Colonial Partition of Northeast Africa." *Trans-African J. History* 1, v. 2 (1971).

_____. "Religion and the State in 19th Century Ethiopia." *J. of Eth. Studies*, v. 10 (1972).

_____. "Bad Men of the Borders: Shum and Shifta in Northern Ethiopia in the Nineteenth Century." *IJAHS* 17, no. 2 (1984).*

Chihab ed-Din (alt.: Shihab). *Histoire de le Conquete de l'Abyssinie, par Chihab ed-Din* [trans. of *Futuh al-Habasha* which covers Imam Ahmed 'Gragn' conquests, written c. 1559] trans. R. Basset (Paris: 1897).*

Combes, E., and M. Tamasier. *Voyage en Abyssinie, dans le pays des Galla, de Choa et d'Ifat,* [French in Denkel] v. 1 (Paris: 1838).*

Conti Rossini, C. "La guerra Turco-abissina del 1578." *Oriente Moderno,* v. 1 (1921-22), and v. 2 (1922-23).*

_____. "Portogallo ed Etiopia." *Accademia reale d'Italia* (Rome: 1940).

_____. "Joao Bermudez e la sua Relazione sull'Etiopia." *Academia de Sciecias de Lisboa* [3rd Congress] 4, no. 2 (Lisbon: 1941).

Coursac, J. de. *Le Regne de Yohannes depuis son Avenement jusqu'à ses Victoires de 1875 sur l'Armée Egyptienne* (Romans: 1926).

Crawford, O. G. S. *The Fung Kingdom of Sennar.* (Gloucester: 1951).

Cromer, Earl of. *Modern Egypt,* v. 3 (London: 1908).

Crummey, Donald. *Priests and Politicians: Protestant and Catholic Missions in Orthodox Ethiopia, 1830-1868* (Oxford: Univ. P., 1972).

_____. "Banditry and resistance: noble and peasant in nineteenth-century Ethiopia." In *Banditry, Rebellion and Social Protest in Africa,* ed. D. Crummey (Portsmouth: Heinemann, 1986).

Douin, George. *Histoire du Règne de Khedive Ismail, 1874-76.* V. 3, *L'Empire Africain,* parts 1-3 (Cairo: 1936, 1938, 1941).*

Dye, William. *Moslem Egypt and Christian Abyssinia* (New York: 1880).

Erlich, Haggai. "Alula, 'the Son of Qubi': A King's Man in Ethiopia, 1875-1897." *JAH* 15, no. 2 (1974).

_____. "1885 in Eritrea: The Year the Dervishes Were Cut Down." *Asian and African Studies,* v. 10 (1975).

_____. *Ethiopia and Eritrea During the Scramble for Africa: A Political Biography of Ras Alula* (East Lansing: Michigan State Univ. P., 1982).*

_____. *Ras Alula and the Scramble for Africa: A Political Biography* (Lawrenceville: Red Sea P., 1996).

Ferret, P. V. and J. G. Gallinier. *Voyage in Abyssinie* [French in Denkel] (Paris: 1847-48).

Gallina, F. "I Portoghesi a Massaua nei secoli XVI e XVII." *Boll. soc. geo. italiana* (1890).

Gebre-Yesus Abay. *Misarat alet hezbi Mereb Mellash* [Tigrn.: "Story of the People of the Mareb Mellash"] (Asmara: 1961).

Great Britain, House of Commons. *Correspondence Respecting Abyssinia, 1846-1868.* (London: 1868).*

Hotten, J. Camden. *Abyssinia and its People, or Life in the Land of Prester John.* (London: 1868).

Hozier, H. M. *The British Expedition to Abyssinia.* (London: 1869).

Holland, J. J., and H. M. Hozier. *Records of the Expedition to Abyssinia.* (London: 1870).

Issel, A. *Viaggio nel Mar Rosso e tra i Bogos* (Milan: 1872).

James, F. L. *The Wild Tribes of the Soudan* (London: 1883).

Kammerer, A. *Le Routier de Dom Joam de Castro* (Paris: 1936).

Keller-Zschokke, J. V. *Werner Munzinger Pascha, Sein Leben und Wirken* (Aarau: 1891).

Kennedy-Cooke, B. "The Red Sea Coast in 1540." *SNR* 16, no. 2 (1933).

Khazanov, A. M. "Portugal's Attempts at Colonizing Ethiopia in the 16th-17th Centuries." In *Etudes Ethiopiennes,* v. 1, ed.: C. Lepage (Paris: 1994).

Kolmodin, Johannes (with Bahta Tesfa-Hannes). *Zanta Haze-gen Tsazegen* [Tigrn. oral traditions; ed. introduction in French] (Upsala: 1912).

_____. *Traditions de Tsazzega et Hazzega*, 2 v. In series: *Archives d'Etudes Orientales* 5, no. 2 (Upsala: K.W. Appelberg, 1915).*

Lefebvre, T. *Voyage en Abyssinie execute pendant les an-nées 1839-43*, 6 v. (Paris: 1845-54).

Loring, W. W. *A Confederate Soldier in Egypt* (New York: 1884).

Ludolphus, Job. *A New History of Ethiopia*, trans. J. P. Gent (London: 1684).*

Malecot, Georges. "Les voyageurs français et les relations entre la France et l'Abyssinie de 1835 a 1870." *RFHO*, v. 58 (1971).

Mania, Enrico. "La donna hanno fondato l'Asmara." [oral traditions]*Sestante* 4, no. 2 (Asmara: 1968).*

Markham, Clements. *A History of the Abyssinian Expedition* (London: 1869).

Marston, Thomas E. *Britain's Imperial Role in the Red Sea Area 1800-1878* (Hamden, Conn.: 1961).

Massawa, Shari'a Court Records, v. 1-101. (MS.; Asmara: Islamic Institute Library).

Menges, J. "Am Rothen Meere: Massawa." *Aus Allen Welt-teilen*, v. 8 (1877): 182-85.

Mukhtar, Ibrahim. "Jame Akhbar Gazeret Badie." [Arabic] (MS.; Asmara: Islamic Institute Lib., n.d.).

Munzinger, Werner. "Les contrees limitrophes de l'Habesch." In *Nouvelles Annales des Voyages*, Apr. (1858).

_____. "Narrative of a Journey through the Afar Coun-try." *J. of the Royal Geo.Soc.*, v. 39 (1869).

_____. *Studi sull'Africa orientale* (Rome: 1890).

Orhanlu, Gengiz. "Turkish archival sources on Ethiopia." *Fourth CISE*, v. 1 (Rome: 1974).*

_____. *Osmanli Imparatorlugu' num guney si yaeti Habes eyalati* [Turkish] (Istanbul: 1974).

Pankhurst, R. K. P. "The Ethiopian Slave Trade in the Nine-teenth and early Twentieth Centuries." *JES*, 9 (1963).*

_____. "Ethiopia and the Red Sea and Gulf of Aden ports in the 19th and 20th centuries." *Ethiopia Observer,* no. 8 (1964).

_____. "The Trade of Northern Ethiopia in the Ninteenth and early Twentieth Centuries." *JES,* 2 (1964).

_____. "Tribute, Taxation and Government Revenues in Nineteenth and early Twentieth Century Ethiopia." *JES,* 7 (1968).

_____. "The Banyan or Indian Presence at Massawa, the Dahlak Islands and the Horn of Africa." *4eme Congress de la Assoc. Historique de l'Ocean Indien, Comm. Int. de l'Histoire Maritime* (St. Denis de la Reunion: 1972).

_____. "Some notes on the historical and economic geography of the Mesewa area (1520-1885)." *JES* 13, no. 1 (1979).

_____. *History of Ethiopian Cities and Towns, from the Middle Ages to the early 19th century* (Wiesbaden: 1982).

Parkyns, Mansfield. *Life in Abyssinia.* (London: 1968).

Piolet, J. B. *Les missions catholiques au XIX siecle* (Paris: n.d.).

Plowden, Walter. *Travels in Abyssinia and the Galla Country.* (London: 1868).

Portal, Gerald H. *My Mission to Abyssinia.* (London: 1892).

Ramm, A. "Great Britain and the planting of Italian Power in the Red Sea, 1868-1885." *English History Rev.* 59, May (1944).

Rassam, Hormuz. *Narrative of the British Mission.* (London: 1869).

Rubenson, Sven. *The Survival of Ethiopian Independence.* (London: Heinemann, 1976).*

Ruppell, W. P. S. E. *Reise in Abyssinia,* v.s 1-2 (Frankfurt: 1838-40).

Salt, Henry. *A Voyage to Abyssinia and Travels into the Interior of that Country* [1814] (London: Frank Cass; 1967).

Sapeto, G. *Viaggio e Missione Cattolica fra i Mensa, i Bogos e gli Habab* (Rome: 1857).*

(Stabilimento Tipografico dell'Opinone, ed.) *La Regione tra Massaua e Cassala: Note ed Appunti raccolti Consultando le Opere dei Vari Viaggiatori* (Rome: 1885).

Talhami, Ghada H. "Massawa under Khedive Ismail, 1865-79." *Proc. Fifth ICES* (Chicago: 1978).

Tedeschi, S. "Poncet and son voyage en Ethiopie." *JES*, 4 (1966).

Tellez, B. *The Travels of the Jesuits in Ethiopia* (London: 1710).

Thomas, H. *The Discovery of Abyssinia by the Portugese in 1520* (London: 1938).

Wylde, Augustus. *'83 to '87 in the Soudan: including the Hewett mission to King John* (London: 1887).*

_____. *Modern Abyssinia* [London: 1901] (Westport: 1970).

Valentia, Viscount [George Annesley]. *Voyages and Travels to India, Ceylon, the Red Sea, Abyssinia and Egypt, in the years 1802-06* (London: 1809).

Zewde Gabre-Sellassie. *Yohannes IV of Ethiopia: A Political Biography* (Oxford: Univ. P., 1975).*

IV. ITALIAN COLONIAL PERIOD (1885 to 1941)

1. History and Politics

Ambrosini, G. "Giuseppe Sapeto e l'origine della colonia Eritrea." *Boll. soc. geo. italiana*, no. 2-3 (1950).

Antinori, O. "La spedizione Italiani in Africa." *Boll. soc. geo. italiana*, no. 18 (1881).

Araia Tseggai. "Eritrean Women and Italian Soldiers: Status of Eritrean Women under Italian Rule." *J. Erit. Studies* 4, no. 1-2 (1989-90).

Ardemani, Ernesto. *Tre pagine gloriose nella storia militaire-civile-religiosa della colonia Eritrea* (Rome: 1901).

Aren, Gustav. *Evangelical Pioneers in Ethiopia: Origins of the Evangelical Church Mekane Yesus* [SEM] (Stockholm: EFS Forlaget, 1978).*

Arimondi, E. "The Italian Operations at Agordat: Notes and Documents." [trans.] *J. United Service Institution,* v. 38 (1894).

Badoglio, Pietro. *War in Abyssinia* (London: 1937).

Baer, G. *The Coming of the Italo-Ethiopian War* (Cambridge: Harvard Univ. P., 1967).

Baldacci, A. "Italian colonial expansion: Its origin, progress and difficulties." *United Empire,* 2 (1911).

Baldrati, I. "La palma dum della Colonia Eritrea." *Rass. Econ. Colon.* 19, no. 1 (Rome: 1931).

Baratieri, Oreste. *Memories d'Afrique: 1892-1896* (Paris: Delagrove, 1898).

_____. *Memorie d'Africa (1892-96)* (Milan/Rome: Fratelli Bocca, 1898).

Barbetta, R. *La colonizzazione dell'Eritrea* (Citta di Castello: 1913).

Bardi, P. M. *Dall'acquisto di Assab all'Impero Romano di Ethiopia* (Milano: 1936).

Battaglia, Roberto. *La prima guerra d'Africa* (Turin: 1958).

Battaglini, G. *Nel Turbino di una preparazione* (Rome: 1938).

Bel, Louis. "Diary" [In AVA, 4:6, fol. 88] (MS.; Asmara, n.d.).

Bizzoni, A. *L'Eritrea nel passto e nel presente* (Milan: 1897).

Bonichi, F. "La colonia agricola di Giovanni Stella e la sua storia." *Agric. Colon.* (1917).

Bovill, E. W. "Italy in Africa." *J. African Soc.,* v. 32 (1933).

Braukamper, Ulrich. "Frobenius as Political Agent: Journey to Eritrea in 1915." In *New Trends in Ethiopian Studies,* v. 1, ed. H. Marcus (Lawrenceville: Red Sea P., 1994).

Bravo, Gian Maria. "Africa bel suol d'amore. Sulla storia del colonialismo italiano." *Studi Storici,* v. 33 (1992).

Buscino, L. "A un anno dal Manifesto razzista." *RSAI* 2, no. 7 (Rome: 1939): 813-19.

Carrara, S. *La colonia Eritrea* (Torino: UTET; 1898).

Caruso, Cosimo. "Ricordi africani (1889-1896)." *Politica internazionale,*no. 42 (1938-39).

Castellano, Vitorio. "L'origini della colonia Eritrea e i tentativi di colonizzazione agricola." *Africa,* 7-8 (1947).

_____. "Considerazioni su alcuni fenomeni demografici della popolazione italiana dell'Eritrea dal 1882 al 1923." *Riv. italiana demografia e statistica,* no. 3 (1948): 386-417.

_____. "La popolazione italiana dell'Eritrea dal 1924 al 1940." *Riv. ital. demografia e statistica,* no. 4 (1948): 530-40.

Caulk, Richard. "'Black snake, white snake:' Bahta Hagos and his revolt against Italian overrule in Eritrea, 1894." In *Banditry, Rebellion and Social Protest in Africa,* ed. D. Crummey (Portsmouth: Heinemann, 1986).

Cerruti, G. E. "Colonizzazione dell'Eritrea." *Atti del 1o congesso geo. italiano* 2, no. 2 (Genoa: 1892).

Chesneau, M. "Les frontières de l'Ethiopie et de l'Erythrée." *La Geographie,* v. 7 (1903).

Ciotola, A. *L'opera sanitaria della colonia Eritrea* (Asmara: 1933).

Cipolla, A. "Le condizioni politiche ed ecomomiche dell'Eritrea rispetto a quelle dell'Etiopia." In *Eritrea economica,* ed. F. Martini (Rome: 1913).

Consociazione Turistica Italiana. *Guida dell'Africa Orientale Italiana* (Milan: 1938).*

Conti Rossini, C. "Il censimento delle popolazioni indigene della colonia Eritrea." *Riv. geo. italiana* (Florence: 1902).

_____. *Italia ed Etiopia: Dal tratto di Uccialli alla bataglia di Adua* (Rome: 1935).

Corni, G. *Problemi coloniali (Eritrea e Somalia)* (Milan: 1933).

Crispi, F. *Memoirs,* v. 1-3, ed.: T. Palamenghi-Crispi (London: 1912).

_____. *La prima guerra d'Africa* (Rome: 1914).

Dainelli, G. "The Italian Colonies." *Geo. Rev.* 19, no.3 (1929).

Dall'Ora, F. *Intendenza in A.O.* (Rome: 1937).

Da Maggiora, Gabriele. *Eritrea 1937-47: Decennio della missione dei frati minori cappuccini della provincia di Alessandria* (Rome: 1949).

Da Nembro, Metodio. *La missione dei minori capuccini in Eritrea (1894-1952)* (Capuccin Order: 1953).

De Bono, E. *Anno XIII: The Conquest of an Empire* (London: 1937).

Deherain, H. *La colonisation italienne dans l'Erythrée* (Paris: 1904).

De la Joinquiere, C. *Les Italiens en Erythrée* (Paris: 1895).

Del Bocca, Angelo. *Gli italiani in Africa Orientale,* v. 4 (Rome/Bari: Laterza, 1976-84).

_____. *The Ethiopian War* (Chicago: Univ. of Chicago P., 1969).

Della Valle, G. "La Dancalia e la sua esplorazione." *Riv. colon. Iialiane,* 9 (1935).

_____. "Leopoldo Franchetti e la colonazzazione dell'Eritrea." *Rass. italiana,* 194 (1934).

Dell'Istituto per gli studi di politica Internazionale. *L'Africa Orientale,* v. 2 (Milan: 1936).

Del Monte, Eugenio. "Genesi e sviluppo del meticciato in Eritrea." *Riv. colon.* 11, no. 7 (1937).

De Marco, R. *The Italianization of African Natives* [colonial education] (New York: 1943).*

Dini, Y.M.Y. *Nella Terra del Mar Rosso: Eritrea* (Milan: Jacca, 1971).

Evans, G. "The Battle of Keren." *History Today,* v. 16 (1966).

Ferraris, L. "La colonia eritrea." *Riv. colon.* (1920).

Franchetti, Leopoldo. *L'Italia e la sua colonia africana* (Citta di Castello: 1891).

_____. *Appendice alla relazione annuale sulla colonia Eritrea* (Rome: 1894).

Frobenius, Leo. *Erythraa: Lander und Zeiten des heiligen Konigsmords* (Berlin: Atlantis, 1931).

Gaddi, S. "I beni italiani in Eritrea." *Africa,* Mar. (1952).

Galliano, Giacomo. *La colonizzazione della Baia di Assab ed il governo* (Rome: 1884).

Gaslini, Mario dei. "I pionieri della Dancalia." *Riv. colon. italiane* (1931).

_____. *L'Italia sul Mar Rosso* (Milan: 1938).*

Giulio, Carlo. *L'Impressa di Massawa* (Rome: 1958).

_____. *L'Italia in Africa. V. 1, Ser. Storica: Etiopia-Mar Rosso (1857-1885)* (Rome: 1958).*

Goglia, Luigi. "Note sul razzismo coloniale fascista." *Storia Contemporanea* 19, no 6 (1988).

Great Britain (Foreign Office). *Peace Handbook.* V. 20, *Spanish and Italian Possessions: Independent States* (London: H.M. Stationary Office, 1920).

Greenlaw, R. R. "Eritrea." *Royal Air Force Quarterly,* v. 6 (1936).

Guebre Sellassie. *Chronique du Règne de Menelik II,* v. 1-2 (Paris: 1930-32).

Haneuse, J. *Notes sur l'Erythrée* (Paris: 1893).

Italy (Ministero degli Affari Esteri). *L'Africa italiana al parlamento nazionale, 1882-1905* (Rome: 1907).

Italy (Parliament). *Relazione general della R Commissione d'inchesta sul colonia Eritrea* (Rome: 1891).

————. *Libro verde: Avvenimenti d'Africa* (Rome: 1896).

————. *Relazione sulla colonia Eritrea* (Rome: 1913).

Iwarson, J. ,and A. Tron. *Notizie storiche e varie sulla missione evangelica svedese dell'Eritrea* [SEM] (Asmara: 1918).*

Jordan Gebre-Medhin. "European Colonial Rule and the Trasformation of Eritrean Rural Life." *Horn of Africa* 6, no. 2 (1983): 50-60.

Karpless, F. "The Italian Colonies." *Crown Colonies,* 4 (1934).

Leonard, Richard. "European Colonization and the Socio-Economic Integration of Eritrea." *The Eritrean Case* (Rome: RICE, 1982).

Lessona, A. "Italy and Africa." *Nineteenth Century,* no. 108 (1935).

Licata, G. B. *Assab e i Danachili* (Milan: 1885).

Loffredo, Renato. *Cheren: 31 gennaio-27 marzo 1941* (Milan: 1973).

Longworth, F. "Italy's New Red Sea Base: the possibilities of Assab." *Great Britain and the East,* 50, Feb. 24 (1938).

Macartney, M. H. "Young Italy in Old Africa." *Fortnightly Rev.,* no. 12 (1929).

Macartney, M. H., and P. Cremona. *Italy's Foreign and Colonial Policy, 1914-1937* (Oxford: Univ. P., 1948).

Malvezzi de' Medici, A, "Native Education in the Italian Colonies." *Educational Yearbook* (New York: Columbia Univ., Teachers' College; 1934).

Manassei, T. *Le prime colonie d'Italia: Eritrea e Soamlia* (Novara: 1912).

Mantegazza, V. *La guerra in Africa* (Florence: 1896).

————. *Gli italiani in Africa* (Florence: 1905).

Marescalchi, G. *Eritrea* (Milan: 1935).

Marinelli, G. "Le colonie Franchetti." *Riv. geo. italiana, v.* 3 (1898).

Martini, Fernando. *Nell'Affrica Italiana: Impressioni e recordi* (Milan: Fratelli Treves, 1895).*

————. *Cose Africane (da Saati ad Abba Garima)* (Milan: Fratelli Treves, 1896).

————. *Il Diario Eritrea, v.* 1-4 (Rome: 1946).*

Martini, Sebastiano. *La Baia d'Assab* (Florence: 1881).

Masturzi, G. "La colonia Eritrea." *L'Universo, v.* 5 (1926).

Matteoda, C. *L'accordo Gasparini-Sterry per l'utilizzazione delle acque del Gasc (12 Dic. 1924)* (Saluzzo: 1927).

Maydon, H. C. "Across Eritrea." *Geo. J.* 63, no. 1 (1924).

Melli, B. *La Colonia Eritrea* (Parma: 1900).

Messal, R. "L'armée coloniale Italienne." *Renseignments Coloniaux,* 39 (1930): 121-29.

Miege, J. C. *L'imperialisme italien de 1870 a nos jours* (Paris: SEDES, 1968).

Mondori, A. *L'Africa Orientale,*v. 1-2 (Milan: 1936).

Mondaini, G. "La politica indigena dell''talia coloniale." *Riv. colon., v.* 19 (1924).

Monile, F. *Africa Orientale* (Bologna: 1933).

Mori, A. *Legislazione della colonia Eritrea (1890-1912), v.* 1-7 (Rome: Ministry of Colonies, 1914).

————. "Il Mar Rosso ed i suoi problemi politico-economici." *La vie d'Italia e del mondo, v.* 7 (1936).

Nazari, V. *La Colonazzazione dell'Eritrea* (Casale: 1895).

Negri, L. *Massaua e ditorni.* (Valenza: 1887).

Nembro, Metodio da. *La missione minori cappucchini* (Rome: 1953).

Odirizzi, Dante. *Il commissariato regionale di Massaua al 1 gennaio 1910* (Asmara: 1911).

Offeio, Francesco da. *Dall'Eritrea* (Rome: 1904).

————. *I cappuccini nella colonia Eritrea: Ricordi* (Rome: 1910).

Orero, B. "Ricordi d'Africa." *Nuva Antologia,* Jan.-Feb. (Rome: 1901).

Paladino, G. "Documenti per la storia della colonia Eritrea." *L'Africa italiana, v.* 37 (1918).

Pankhurst, E. S. "Italy's African Rule." *Fortnightly Rev.,* Aug. (1941).

Pankhurst, R. "The foundations of education, printing, newspapers, book production, libraries and literacy in Ethiopia." *Eth. Observer* 6, no. 3 (1962).

————. "Italian settlement policy in Eritrea and its repercussions, 1889-96." In *Boston Univ. Papers in African History,* v. 1, ed.: J. Butler (Boston: Boston Univ. P.: 1964).

————. "The Great Ethiopian Famine of 1888-1892: A New Assessment." *J. Hist. of Medecine and Allied Sciences,* v. 21 (1966).

————. "The Textbooks of Itlaian Colonial Africa." *Eth. Observer* 11, no. 4 (1968).

————. "Fascist Racial Policies in Ethiopia, 1922-41." *Eth. Observer* 12, no. 4 (1969): 270-85.

————. "Italian and 'Native' labor during the Italian Fascist colonial occupation of Ethiopia, 1935-41." *Ghana Social Sciences J.* 2, no. 2 (1972).

————. "The History of Prostitution in Ethiopia." *JES* 12, no. 2 (1974) pp. 159-78.

————. *History of Ethiopian Cities and Towns, from the mid-19th century to 1935* (Stuttgart: Steiner Verlag, 1985).

Pantano, G. *Venti anni di vita africana* (Florence: 1932).

Paoli, Renato. *Nella colonia Eritrea: studi e viaggi* (Milan: Fratelli Treves, 1908).*

Pariani, A. *La Conquista dell'Impero* (Rome: 1938).

Pellenc, Capt. *Les italiens en Afrique* (Paris: 1897).

Pianavia-Vivaldi, Rosalia. *Tre anni in Eritrea* (Milan: L. F. Cogliati, 1901).*

Pollera, A. "La nuova Asmara." *Africana italiana, v.* 7/8 (1939).

Puglisi, Giuseppe. "Pionieri dell'Eritrea." *Africa,* 1 (1950).

————. *Chi e'? dell'Eritrea: Dizzionario Biografica, 1952* (Asmara: Agenzia Regina, 1952).*

Rainero, Roman. *I primi tentativi di colonizzazione agraria e di popolamento in Eritrea, 1890-95* (Milan: Marzorati, 1960).

————. *L'anticolonialismo italiano da Assab ad Adua* (Milan: Eitore. Comunita, 1971).

Ravizza. "Matrimoni misti e meticci nella colonia Eritrea." *Riv. d'Italia* 19, no. 2-IX (1916).

Reale Soc. Geo. Italiana. *L'Africa Orientale* (Bologna: 1935).

Reinisch, S. L. "Keren nei Bogos." *Boll. soc. geo italiana,* 26 (1889).

Renda, G. "La primogenita: l'Eritrea." *Riv. colon.* (1927).

Romadini, Massimo. "Da Massua ad Asmara: Ferdinando Martini in Eritrea nel 1891." *La Conoscenza dell'Asia e dell'Africa in Italia nei secoli XVIII e XIX* 3, no. 2 (Naples: Istituto Univ. Orientale, 1989).

Rossi, A. *L'Eritrea com' e oggi* (Rome: 1894).

Royal Institute of International Affairs. "The Italian Colonial Empire." *Information Papers,* no. 27 (1940).

Saint-Ives, G. "A travers l'Erythrée italienne." *L'Année geo.,* 2 (1902).

Saisi, P. "La popolazione italiana dell'Eritrea dal 1924 al 1940." *L'Universo,* 5 (1950).

Santagata, F. *La Colonia Eritrea nel Mar Rosso davanti 'all Abissinia* (Naples: 1935).

Sapelli, Alessandro. *Memorie d'Africa: 1883-1906* (Bologna: Zanichelli, 1935).

Sapeto, G. "Notizie sopra Assab." *Cosmos,* v. 4 (1877).

Sbacchi, Alberto. *Ethiopia under Mussolini: Fascism and the Colonial Experience* (London: Zed, 1985).

————. *Legacy of Bitterness: Ethiopia and Fascist Italy, 1935-41* (Lawrenceville: Red Sea P., 1996).

Sertoli Salis, R. *La giustizia indigena nelle colonie* (Padua: 1933).

Silani, Tomaso. *L'Africa Orientale Italiana* (Rome: 1933).

————, ed. *L'Impero (AOI)* [articles by leading colonial scholars and administrators] (Rome: 1937).*

Steer, G. *Caesar in Abyssinia* (Boston: 1937).

Stefanini, G. *I possedimenti italiani in Africa* (Florence: 1929).

Stjarne, P. "The Swedish Evangelical Mission in Ethiopia." *Ethiopia Observer,* 4 (1960).

Stroppa, F. "La situazione coloniale d'oggi e la politica rispetto agli indigeni." *Riv. colon., v.* 15 (1920).

Surdich, Francesco. "La donna dell'Africa Orientale nelle relazioni degli esploratori italiana (1870-1915)." Im *Miscellanea di storia delle esplorazioni,* v. 4 (Genova: 1979): 193-220.

_____. *L'esplorazione italiana dell'Africa* (Milan: 1982).

Taddia, Irma. "Sulla politica della terra nella colonia Eritrea, 1890-1950." *Riv. Storia Contemporanea,* 1 (1984).

_____. *L'Eritrea-Colonia, 1890-1952: Paesaggi, strutture, uomini del colonialismo* (Milano: 1986).*

Tate, H. R. "The Italian Colonial Empire." *J. Royal African Soc.* v. 40, Apr (1941).

Tadesse Beyene, Taddesse Tamrat and R. Pankhurst, ed. *The Centenary of Dogali* (Addis Ababa: 1988).

Tekeste Negash. "Resistance and Collaboration in Eritrea, 1882-1914." In *Proc. Seventh ICES,* ed. S. Rubenson (Addis Ababa: 1984).

_____. *No Medecine for the Bite of a White Snake: Notes on Nationalism and Resistance in Eritrea, 1890-1940* (Uppsala: 1986).

_____. *Italian Colonialism in Eritrea, 1882-1941: Policies, Praxis and Impact* (Uppsala: 1987).*

Thesiger, Wilfred. *A Life of My Choice* (Glasgow: 1987).

Traversi, L. *L'Italia e l'Etiopia* (Bologna: 1936).

Triulzi, Alessandro. "Ferdinando martini: immagini fotografiche e immagini coloniali." *Farestoria* 10, no. 17 (1991).

Villari, L. "The Italian Red Sea Colonies." *J. Central Asian Soc.,* v. 14 (1927).

Vitale, Massimo. "L'Opera dell'esercito." In *Africa Orientale 1868-1934,* v. 2, part 1, *Avvenimenti militari e impiego,* (Rome: 1962).

Wilberforce-Bell, H. "The Italian Colony of Eritrea." *J. Central Asian Soc.,* 10 (1923).

Yemane Mesghenna. *Italian Colonialism: A Case Study of Eritrea, 1869-1934: Motive, Praxis and Result* (Maryland: International Graphics, 1989).

Zaghi, Carlo. *L'Origini della Colonia Eritrea* (Bologna: L. Cappelli; 1934).*

————. "L'Italia e l'Etiopia alla Vigilia di Adua nei Dispacci Segreti di Luigi Capucci Contributo alla Biografia di un Grande Pioniere." *Gli Annali dell'Africa italiana* 4, no. 2 (1941).

Zammarano, V. Tadesco. *Le colonie italiane di diritto dominio* (Rome: 1930).

Zemhret Yohannes. *Mekhete antser Italieyawi megzieti ab Ertra* [Tigrn.: resistance to Italian rule] (Asmara: 1991).*

Zoli, C. "Il censimento della Dancalia meridionale." *Rass. econ. Cclon.* (1930).

Zoppi, V. "Problemi della politica indigena in Africa." *L'Oltremare,* no. 8, Dec. (1934).

2. Economy

Agricoltura coloniale. "L'agricoltura in Eritrea dal 1882 ad oggi." In no. 26 (1932).

Ajmone, E. "Sfruttiamo Tessenei!" *L'Oltremare,* 12 (1928).

Alamanni, E. Q. M. *La colonia Eritrea e i suoi commerci* (Torino: 1891).

Angelino, C. E. "Le ferrovie eritrée." In *L'A.O.I.,* ed. T. Silani (Rome: 1933).

Annali d'Africa italiana. "Il servizio veterinario in Eritrea." In v. 3, no. 1 (1940)"

Annaratone, C. "La camionabile Assab-Dessie." *L'Oltremare,* v. 3 (1929).

Arcangeli, A. *La camionale Mar Rosso-Altipiano eritreo (Massaua-Nefasit-Decamere)* (Rome: 1936).

Ardemani, E. *Colonia Eritrea: agricoltura, pastorizia e sottosuolo* (Turin: 1900).

Ascherson, P. "Bestiame e zooeconomia in colonia Eritrea." *Erythraea,* 3-4 (1920).

Aziza. "Per lo sviluppo dell'agricoltura in Eritrea."" *Boll. econ. dell'Erit.,* Sept. (1928).

Balbis, P. "La strada dell'Eritrea occidentale." In *L'Italia d'Oltremare* (1938).

Baldacci, L. "L'oro nell'Eritrea." *Boll. soc. africana d'Italia, v.* 16 (1897).

Baldrati, I. *Catalogo illustrativo della mostra agricola della colonia Eritrea* (Florence: Niccolai Editore, 1903)

_____. "L'agave sisalana." *Agric. Colon.* (1907).

_____. "Dei prodotti coloniale in rapporto ai bisogni della madre patria e specialmente della colura cotoniera." *Atti II congresso italiano all'Estero* (Rome: 1911).

_____. "Le condizioni agricole della valle del Barca." *Agric. colon.,* no. 5-6 (1911).

_____. "Le coltivazioni del caffe in Eritrea." *Agric. colon.,* no. 8 and 11 (1914).

_____. "La coltivazione del sesamo nella colonia Eritrea." *Riv. Colon.* 1, no. 2 (1906).

_____. *L'Eritrea sotto l'aspetto agricole* (Bologna: Cuppini, 1907).

_____. "La coltavazione del grano nell'Eritrea." *Boll. soc. africana d'Italia,* Sept.-Oct. (1911).

_____. "La palma dum della Colonia Eritrea." *Rass. econ. delle colonie, v.* 21 (1931).

_____. "Lo sviluppo dell'agricoltura in Eritrea nei 50 anni di occupazione italiana." *Riv. colon. italiana, v.* 6-7 (1933-34).

Baratieri, O. "Il commercio della madreperla a Massaua." *Boll. soc. africana d'Italia* Dec. (1894).

Bartolommei-Gioli, G. *La Colonizzazione agricola nella colonia Eritrea* (Florence: 1903).

_____. *L'agricoltura in Eritrea* (Rome: 1903).

_____. *Agricoltura e colonizzazione dell'Eritrea* (Rome: Ministry of Foreign Affairs, 1906).

Blessich, A. "Il commercio eritreo." *Boll. soc. africana d'Italia,* no. 6 (1897).

_____. "Il commercio di Massaua." *Boll. soc. africana d'Italia,* no. 17 (1898).

_____. "Il regime fondario della Colonia Eritrea." *Boll. soc. africana d'Italia, v.* 23 (1904).

Bologna, L. M. "Economie agricole eritrée." *Etiopia, v.* 7/8 (1938).

Bruno, A. "Il patrimonio forestale in Eritrea." *IC, v.* 7 (1934).

Brunori, B. "L'ordinamento forestale dell'Eritrea." *Atti III congresso di studi colon.,* v. 3 (Florence: 1937).

_____. "Sul problema forestale in Eritrea." *Riv. forestale italiano, v.* 8 (1939).

Calderni, V. "La camionabile Massaua-Decamere dal Mar Rosso all'altopianp eritreao." *Le Strade, v.* 19 (1937).

Carbonari, G. *Il tallero di Maria Teresa e la questione monetaria della Colonia Eritrea* (Rome: 1912).

Cardona, L. "Il mercato del bestiame in Asmara." *La Conquista della Terra, v.* 3 (1938).

Caroselli, F. G. "La nostra politica monetaria nella colonia Eritrea." *Atti nel primo congresso di studi colon.* (1936).

Ceriani, G. "Sulla irragazione della pianura di Tessenei e la coltivazione del cotone." *Boll. cotoniera* (1926): 555-6.

Cesari, C. "La prima colonia agricola italiana in Eritrea." *Etiopia, v.* 1 (1939).

Checchi, Michele. "Saline della costa Eritrea." *Riv. colon.* (1910).

_____. *Movimento commerciale della colonia Eritrea, 1885-1910* (Rome: 1911).

_____. "Del regime delle acque nell'Eritrea." *Atti II congresso degli italiani all'estero* (Rome: 1911).

_____, G. Giardi and G. Mori. *Ordinamento fondario della colonia Eritrea* (Asmara: 1908).

Chiaromonte, A. *Le grandi opere di valorizzazione agraria nell'Africa orientale italiana* (Florence: IACI, 1927).

Colletta, N. *Sulla utilizzione a scopo di irrigazione delle acque del fiume Gasc nella colonia Eritrea* (Rome: 1907).

Conti Rossini, C. "Api ed agricoltura in Eritrea." *Boll. soc. africana d'Italia, v.* 21 (1902).

Cortese, G. "Programa agricolo eritreo." *Riv. colon. italiane,* Oct. (1929).

506 Historical Dictionary of Eritrea

_____. "Vegetazione e piantie utili dell'Eritrea." *L'Oltremare, v.* 10 (1932).

_____. "Le attivita economiche dell'Eritrea." *L'Oltremare, v.* 11 (1932).

Cuomo, L. *Fauna e flora medica e industriale della colonia Eritrea* (Naples: 1898).

D'Aragona, S. "Le acque del Gasc." *IC, v.* 6 (1924).

De Benedictis, A. "Una grande opera compiuta: Tessenei." *La Terra, v.* 2 (1928).

De Ponti, G. "La coltivazione dell'agave nella colonia Eritrea." *Rass. econ. delle colon.* v. 9/10 (1930).

_____. "Possibilita minerarie in Eritrea." *L'Oltremare* (1932).

_____. "Il tabacco a Keren." *Boll. econ. Eritrea,* April (1935).

De Rossi, G. "L'agave in Eritrea." *L'Oltemare* (1930).

Dezani, S. "L'aloe della colonia Eritrea." *Boll. informazione dei ministero delle colonie* (1922).

Doria, T. "Le acque del Gasc in Eritrea e l'"rragazione." *IC, v.* 3 (1926).

_____. "Il nuovo ordinamento fondario della colonia Eritrea." *IC, v.* 2 (1927).

Ferretti, U. *I bovini eritrei e la produzione industriale de carne* (Rome: Centenari Eitore, 1908).

Filesi, T. *Colletivita e lavoro italiani in Eritrea* (Rome: 1961).

Fortunati G., and A. Casciani. *L'agave di sisal in Eritrea* (Rome: Fratelli Capaccini, 1909).

Garavaglia, A.C. "Il cotone in Eritrea." *Agric. colon.,* v. 1 (1924).

Giannattsio, V. "Sulla coltivazione dei tabacchi lenvantini in Eritrea." *Agric. colon.* (1936).

Governo dell'Eritrea. "La pesca nel Mar Rosso." *Boll. informazioni dei ministero delle colonie* (1921).

_____. "Le strade della colonia Eritrea." *Rass. econ. della colon.* (1930).

Gubellini, M. "Economia agraria indigena della zona costiera dell'Eritrea." *Agric. colon.,* v. 11 (1933).

Guidotti, R. "La coltivazione del cotone in Eritrea." *Boll. cotoniera,* no. 4-5 (1933-34).

_____. "Boschi e servizio forestale in Eritrea." *Rass. econ. delle colonie, v.* 22 (1934).

Infante, Eldo. *Rassegna tecnica delle eritree* (Asmara: 1947).

Introna, S. "I Minerali dell'A.O." *Africa,* 1*no.* 0/11 (1952).

Issel, A. "La pesca delle perle nel Mar Rosso." *L'Esplorazione commerciale, v.* 9 (1894).

Istituto Agricolo Coloniale Italiano. *L'Economia Eritrea* (Florence: IACI, 1932).*

_____. "Le communicazione ferroviarie." *Agric. colon., v.* 26 (1932).

Istituto Agronomico per l'A.I. *L'agricoltura nella colonia Eritrea e l'opera dell'Italia* (Florence: IACI, 1946).*

Istituto Coloniale Italiano. *Atti del secondo congresso degli italiani all'estero* (Rome: 1911).

Jamiceli, G. "Il porto di Assab." *Rass. d'oltremare,* no. 12 (1936) and no. 1-3 (1937).

Legnani, D. "L'oro in Eritrea." *LC, v.* 10 (1927).

Lessona, A. "Le ferrovie dell'Eritrea." *Gerarchia,* Sept. (1931).

Levi, C. "L'irrigazione nel bassopiano eritreo." *Riv. colon.* (1910).

Lischi, D. "Autarchia economica nell'Impero." *Rass. econ. dell'Africa italiana* (1937).

Maddalena, L. *Studi per le ricerche petrolifere nell'arcipelago delle isole Dahlak nel Mar Rosso* (Rome: 1937).

Mangano, G. "I prodotti della palma dum in Eritrea." *Boll. ministero delle colonie,* no. 12 (1914).

Marchi, E. *Studi sulla pastorizia della colonia Eritrea* [2nd edition, 1939] (Florence: IACI, 1910).*

Mari, A. "Il nuovo porto di Assab." *Africa italiana, v.* 7/8 (1939).

Martini, Fernando, ed. *L'Eritrea Economica* [detailed articles on every region] (Novara/Rome: Istituto Geo. Agostini, 1913).*

Massa, L. "Le piante da frutto coltivate in Eritrea." *Agric. colon., v.* 28 (1934).

Maugini, A. "Il distretto cotoneiro di Tessenei." *Atti III congresso di studi coloniale, v.* 8 (Florence: 1937).

Mazzochi-Alemann, N. "Il caffe nella colonia Eritrea." *Rass. econ. delle colonie*, v. 19 (1931).

Meschini, C. "La gomma arabica." *IC, v.* 10 (1935).

Miari De Cumani, G. "Assab porto dell'Impero." *Rass. econ. dell'A.I.* (1938).

Nobile, G., and L. Avetrani. *Progetto di irrigazione della pianura di Tessenei* (Rome: Tipografica Camera di Deputati, 1913).

Ninni, E. *Per la pesca in Libia, Eritrea e Somalia* (Venice: Officine Ferrari, 1921).

_____. *Relazione sulla campagna esploritiva della pesca nel Mar Rosso* (Rome: 1931).

Oderizzi, Dante. "Il commercio eritreo e il mercato etiopico." *Riv. colon.* (1906).

_____. "Della manodopera nelle nostre colonie: Eritrea." *Atti II congresso degli italiani all'estero* (Rome: 1911).

Ongaro, G. "Il problema del caffe in Eritrea." *L'Oltremare, v.* 8 (1934).

Ortolani, M. "Il commercio dell'Eritrea." *Riv. geo.* (1932).

_____. "Il porto di Massaua." *Riv. geo. italiana, v.* 4 1 (1934).

Papini, I. "Agricoltura indigena e colonazzazione in Eritrea e Somalia." *Africa*, no. 2 (1947).

Parazozoli, A. "La pesca del Mar Rosso." *L'Esplorazione commerciale* (1898).

Pedrazzi, O. "Centri e industrie della colonia Eritrea." *Riv. colon.* (1918).

Petazzi, E. "Il problema monetario della Colonia Eritrea." *Riv. d'Africa,* 1 (n.d.).

Pirani, A. "Mezzi di communicazione degli indigeni della colonia Eritrea." *Riv. colon. italiane* (1930).

Pollera, A. "Eritrea Agricola." *L'Italia colon.* (1933).

_____. "L'Eritrea e le sue superbe coltivazioni di caffe." *L'Italia colon.* (1934).

_____. "Il problema idrico in Eritrea." *Africa italiana, v.* 9/10 (1939).

Rava, Massimo. "Eritrea: lavori di Tessenei." *Boll. informazione economiche* (Rome: Ministry of Colonies, 1926).

Rossetti, C. "Il regime monetario delle Colonie Italiane." *Biblioteca di cultura colon.* 1 (1914).

Salvadei, G. "Il porto di Massaua.""*L'Oltremare* (1930).

_____. "Le communicazioni ferroviarie in Eritrei." *L'A-gricoltura colon.* (1932).

Salvadori, M. "Una grnde impresa industriale in Eritrea: le saline di Uachiro." *Riv. colon. italiano* (1931).

Santagara, F. "La istituzione di una casa di credito agrario in Eritrea." *Rass. econ. colon.* (1933).

Sarubbi, F. "I mercati indigeni in Eritrea." *R a s s. d'oltremare, v.* 3 (1937).

Spena, A. *Produzione mineraria dell'Eritrea* (Rome: 1938)

Taddia, Irma "Le trasformazioni della proprieta terriera nell'altopiano eritreo in periodo coloniale (1890-1950)." In *Africa come storia,* ed. A. Gentili, G. Mizzau, I. Taddia (Milan: 1980).

Tancredi, A. M. "Nel piano del sale." *Boll. soc. geo. italiana, v.* 48 (1911).

Tarantino, G. B. "Per la valorizzazione delle nostre colonie." *Riv. colonie italiane,* no. 4 (1930).

Tazzer, F. "Le risorse minerarie dell'Eritrea." *Africa italiana, v.* 7/8 (1939).

Tissi, E. "I terreni auriferi dell'Eritrea." *Rass. econ. delle colonie, v.* 21 (1933): 22-33.

Turi, T. "Il consorzio agrario cooperativo eritreo." *R i v. colon.* (1910).

U.S. Dept. of Commerce. *Eritrea, a Red Sea Colony of Increasing Interest to American Commerce* (Washington, D.C: U.S. Government, 1920).

_____. "Italian Colonial Development: Eritrea, Somaliland and Oltre Giuba." *Commerce Reports,* July 27 (Washington, D.C.: 1931).

Valori, F. "I porti dell'Eritrea." *Riv. politica econ.* (1938).

_____. "Produzioni eritree." *Africa italiana, v.* 7/8 (1939).

Zapponi, A. "L'ordinamento fondario della colonia Eritrea." [land laws] *Riv. d'Africa* (1911/12).

Zucco, G. "L'industria della pesca in Eritrea." *L'Oltremare* (1929).

V. MODERN PERIOD
(from 1941)

1. History and Politics

Abieto Tazaz and Semere G. "Unita' nazionale e nazionalismo eritreo: Difficolta' e contraddizioni di una lotta di liberazione." *Altrafrica,* 4/5 (Rome: 1977).
Abu Shanab, R. E. "The Eritrean Revolution." *Internat'l Rev. of Hist. and Political Science* 8, no. 4 (1971).
Abuetan, B. "Eritrea: United Nations Problem and Solution." *Middle Eastern Affairs* 2, no. 2 (1951).
Abdulrahman M. Babu. "The Eritrean Question in the Context of African Conflicts and Superpower Rivalries." *The Long Struggle of Eritrea* (Trenton: Red Sea P., 1988).
Alamin Mohamed Said. *Sewra Ertra* [Tigrn: "The Eritrean Revolution"] (Lawrenceville: Red Sea P., 1994).
Alazar Tesfa-Michael. *Eritrea Today: Fascist Oppression under Nose of British Military* (Woodford Green: 1946).
Alemseged Abbay. "The Trans-Mareb Past in the Present." *JMAS* 35, no. 2 (1997): 321-34.
Africa Watch (Alex de Waal). *Evil days: Thirty Years of War and Famine in Ethiopia* (New York: Human Rights Watch, 1991).
African-American Institute. *Eritrea: A Report on the Referendum on Independence, April 23-25* (Washington, D.C.: Africa-America Institute, 1994).
Amare Tekle. "The Creation of the Ethio-Eritrean Federation: A Case Study in Postwar International Relations (1945-1950)" (Ph.D. diss.; Univ. of Denver: 1964).
_____ (Referendum Commissioner). *Referendum '93: The Eritrean People Determine their Destiny* (Trenton: Red Sea P., 1993).
_____, ed.. *Eritrea and Ethiopia: From Conflict to Cooperation* (Lawrenceville: Red Sea P., 1994).
Andargachew Tiruneh. "Eritrea, Ethiopia and the Federation 1941-1952." *Northeast African Studies,* 3, no. 1 (1980-81).

Araia Tseggai. "The Case for Eritrean Independence." *Black Scholar* 7, June (1976): 20-27.

_____. "The History of the Eritrean Struggle."In *The Long Struggle of Eritrea,* ed.: L. Cliffe, et al (Trenton: Red Sea P., 1988).

Asgede Hagos. "Arabism: Ethiopia's Wartime Bogeyman in Eritrea." *ESR* 1, no. 1 (1996).

Asnake Ali. "Addis Zemen and the Eritrean Issue: A Review of Articles, 1941-47." In *New Trends in Ethiopian Studies,* v. 1, ed. H. Marcus (Lawrenceville: Red Sea P., 1994).

Association of Eritrean Students in North America (AESNA). *Selected Articles from 'Vanguard'* (New York: 1977).

_____. *In Defence of the Eritrean Revolution* (New York: 1978).

Barker, J. *Eritrea: 1941* (London: Faber, 1966).

Becker, G. H. *The Disposition of the Italian Colonies* (Geneva: 1952).

Bell, J. B. "Endemic Insurgency and International Order." *Orbis* 18, no. 2 (1974).

Bentwich, N. *Ethiopia, Eritrea and Somaliland* (London: Gollanz, 1945).

_____. "Ethiopia's federal union." *Quarterly Rev.,* no. 595, Jan. (1953).

Bereket Habte-Selassie. *Conflict and Intervention in the Horn of Africa* (New York: Monthly Review, 1980).*

_____. "Eritrea and the United Nations." *The Eritrean Case* (Rome: RICE, 1982).

_____. "From British Rule to Federation and Annexation." In *Behind the War in Eritrea,* ed.: B. Davidson et al (Nottingham: Spokesman, 1980).

_____. "Significance of the Second and Unification Congress of the EPLF and ELF (CL)." *J. Erit. Studies* 2, no. 1 (1987).

_____. *Eritrea and the United Nations and Other Essays* (Trenton: Red Sea P., 1989).

Biles, Peter. "Birth of a Nation." *Africa Report,* July/Aug. (1993).

Bimbi, Guido. "The National Liberation Struggle and the Liberation Fronts." *The Eritrean Case* (Rome: RICE; 1982).

Bitterlin, L. "Erythrée: une Palestine oubliée." *France-pays arabes,* Oct. (1975).

Bondestam, Lars. "External Involvement in Ethiopia and Eritrea." In *Behind the War in Eritrea* (Nottingham: Spokesman, 1980).

Boyce, F. "The internationalizing of internal war: Ethiopia, the Arabs and the case of Eritrea." *J. of International and Comparative Studies* 5, no. 3 (1972).

Butler, L. "Who is winning in Eritrea?" *New Africa,* Dec. (1988).

Calchi-Novati, Gianpaolo. *Il corno d'Africa nella storia e nella politica: Etiopia, Somalia e Eritrea fra nazionalismi, sottosviluppo e guerra* (Turin: S.E.I., 1994).

Campbell, John F. "Rambling Along the Red Sea: The Eritrean Question." *African Affairs,* v. 48 (1970).

_____. "Background to the Eritrean Conflict." *Africa Report,* May (1971): 19-20.

Caponi, L. "Questione agraria e questione nazionale en Eritrea, Etiopia e Somalia." *Altrafrica,* 1 (Rome: 1975)

Chaliand, Gerard. "The Horn of Africa's Dilemma." *Foreign Policy,* v. 30 (1978): 116-31.

_____, ed. *Guerrilla Strategies* (London: 1982).

Chiarelli, R. "Problemi politici e constituzionali dell'Eritrea di Ieri e di domani." *Altrafrica,* 1 (Rome: 1975).

Clapham, Christopher. *Transformation and Continuity in Revolutionary Ethiopia* (Cambridge: Univ. P., 1988).

_____. "The Political Economy of Conflict in the Horn of Africa." *Survival* 32, no. 5 (1990).

_____. "The Structure of Regional Conflict in the Horn of Africa." *Henok* 1, Aug. (1990).

Cliffe, Lionel, and B. Davidson, ed. *The Long Struggle of Eritrea for Independence and Constructive Peace* (Trenton: Red Sea P., 1988).*

_____. "Forging a Nation: the Eritrean Experience." *Third World Quarterly,* Oct. (1989).

Cobb, Charles. "Eritrea Wins the Peace." *National Geo.* 189, no. 6, June (1996): 82-105.

Connell, Dan. "The Battle for Massawa." *Sudanow,* Feb. [Khartoum] (1978).

_____. "Cubans Move into Eritrean Battle Front." *The Nation* 226, April (1978).

_____. "The Birth of an Eritrean Nation." *Horn of Africa* 3, no. 1 (1980).

_____. "The Changing Situation in Eritrea." In *Behind the War in Eritrea,* ed.: B. Davidson et al (Nottingham: Spokesman, 1980).

_____. "Eritrea: A Revolution in Process." *Monthly Review,* July/Aug. (1993): 1-26.

_____. *Against All Odds: A Chronicle of the Eritrean Revolution* (Trenton: Red Sea P., 1993).*

_____. "New Challenges in Postwar Eritrea." *ESR* 2, no. 1 (1997).

_____. "Report on Eritrea." Institute for Policy Studies: Wash. D.C. (1997).

Cora, G. "L'avvenire dell'Eritrea e dell'Etiopia." *Africa,* v. 5 (1948).

Cot, G. "Une lutte pour la vie." *Afrique-Asie,* Aug. 8 (1977).

Cumming, D. C. "The United Nations Disposal of Eritrea." *African Affairs* 52, no. 207 (1953).

_____. "British Stewardship of the Italian Colonies: an account rendered." *International Affairs* 29, Jan. (1953).

Daniel Kindie. "The Cold war Dimensions of the Eritrean Conflict 1946-1991." In *New Trends in Ethiopian Studies,* v. 1, ed.: H. Marcus (Lawrenceville: Red Sea P., 1994).

Davidson, Basil, L. Cliffe and Bereket H.-S., ed. *Behind the War in Eritrea* (Nottingham: Spokesman, 1980).*

Dawit Wolde Giorgis. *Red Tears; War, Famine and Revolution in Ethiopia* (Trenton: Red Sea P., 1989).*

Diamond, R. A. and D. Fouquet. "American Military Aid to Ethiopia and Eritrean Insurgency." *Africa Today,* v. 19 (1972): 37-43.

Dines, Mary. "The Ethiopian 'Red Terror'." "The Land, the People, the Revolution." In *Behind the War in Eritrea,* ed. B. Davidson et al (Nottingham: Spokesman, 1980).

_____. "Ethiopian Repression in Eritrea." In *The Eritrean Case* (Rome: RICE, 1982).

_____. "Ethiopian Violation of Human Rights in Eritrea." In *The Long Struggle of Eritrea,* ed. L. Cliffe et al (Trenton: Red Sea P., 1988).

"Documents: Six Memorable Unity Documents of the Eritrean Armed Struggle." *J. Erit. Studies* 5, no. 1 (1991).

Doornbos, Martin, et al. *Beyond the Conflict in the Horn* (Lawrenceville: Red Sea P., 1992).

Duffield, Mark, and J. Prendergast. *Without Troops or Tanks: Humanitarian Intervention in Ethiopia and Eritrea* (Lawrenceville: Red Sea P., 1994).

Dulles, J. F. "United States' Views on Former Italian Colonies." *U.S. Department of State Bulletin,* v. 20, April 17 (1949).

Dzurek, Daniel. "Eritrea-Yemen Dispute over the Hanish Islands." *Boundary and Security Bulletin* 4, no. 1 (Durham: Univ. of Durham, 1996).

_____. "The Hanish Islands Dispute." *ESR* 1, no. 2 (1996).

(The) Economist. "Italy's Former Colonies." June 28 (1947).

_____. "Italian Colonies." Aug. 28 (1948).

_____. "Ethiopia and Eritrea." Aug. 20 (1949).

Egyptian Soc. of International Law. "Eritrea: Constitution of 1955 (text)." *Federation in the Middle East* (Cairo: 1964).

Eisenloeffel, F., and I. Ronnback. *The Eritrean Durrah Odyssey: 1983* (Utrecht: Dutch Interchurch Aid, 1983).

Ellingson, Lloyd S. "The Emergence of Political Parties in Eritrea, 1941-50." *JAH* 18, no. 2 (1977).

_____. "The Origins of the Eritrean Liberation Movement." In *Proc. Fifth ICES,* ed. R. Hess (Chicago: 1979).

_____. "Eritrea: Separatism and Irredentism, 1941-1985." (Ph.D. diss.; Michigan State Univ.: 1986).*

EFLNA. *Revolution in Eritrea* (New York: 1975).

Eritrea, Governor-General [Aradom Tedla]. *Facts About Eritrea* (Asmara: Government P.P., 1964).

Eritrea, Provisional Government. "Birth of a Nation" Mimeograph (Asmara: 1993).

Eritrean Liberation Forces-People's Liberation Forces. "Eritrea: Victim of UN Decision and Ethiopian Aggression." Mimeograph (New York: [Dec. 3] 1971).

Eritrean Liberation Front. *United Nations Documents on Eritrea* (Beirut: n.d.).

_____. *The Federal Case of Eritrea with Ethiopia* (Damascus: n.d.).

_____. *Eritrea: History, Geography, Economy* (Damascus, n.d.).*

_____. *The Struggle of Eritrea* (Damascus: n.d.).*

_____. *The Eritrean Revolution: 16 years of armed struggle* (Beirut: 1977).

_____. *ELF: The National Revolutionary Vanguard of the Eritrean People* (ELF: 1978).

_____. *Eritrea: National Democratic Revolution versus Ethiopian Expansionism* (Beirut: 1979).

Eritrean People's Liberation Forces. "Nehnan Elamanan." [Tigrn.: "Our Struggle and its Goals"] ([Sweden;] Eritrean Students for Liberation/Europe, n.d. [1971]).*

Eritrean People's Liberation Front. "National Democratic Programme." [1st Congress] Mimeograph (1977).

_____. *The Eritrean Revolution: Sixteen Years of Armed Struggle* (Beirut: EPLF, 1977).

_____. *Memorandum: The Natonal Question in Eritrea* (Beirut: EPLF, 1978).

_____. *Hafeshawi politikawi temherti* [Tigrn.: "Study of Popular Politics"] (Bologna: EPLF, 1978).*

_____. *Selected Articles from EPLF Publications* (Rome: EPLF, 1982).

_____. *Ertran qelsan: kab tenti kesa'e 1941* [Tigrn.: "Eritrea's Struggle: Ancient Times to 1941"] (Sahel: 1987).

_____ . *Eritrea: Dawn After a Long Night* (EPLF Dept. of Information: [June] 1989).

_____. "Interview with WoldeAb WoldeMariam." *Sagem* 2, no. 10 [Tigrn.] 91990).

_____. *1961-1991: Nay 30 ametet helmi enkeghad* (Tigrn.: "30 years of armed struggle;" Asmara: 1991).

Erlich, Haggai. "The Eritrean Autonomy, 1952-62: Its Failure and Contribution to Further Escalation." In *Models of Autonomy,* ed. Y. Dinstein (New Brunswick: Rutgers Univ. P., 1981).

————. *The Struggle over Eritrea, 1962-1978* (Stanford: Stanford Univ. P., 1983).

————. "Tigre in Modern Ethiopian History." In *Proc. Seventh ICES,* ed. S. Rubenson (Addis Ababa: 1984).

Ethiopia, Government. "Reunion of Eritrea, Proclamation Order No. 27 of 1962." *Eth. Observer* 6, no. 4 (1962).

Ethiopia, Ministry of Foreign Affairs. *Eritrea Then and Now* (Addis Ababa: [May] 1976).

Ethiopia, Provisional Military Government. *Policy Declaration of the PMG to Solve the Problem in the Administrative Region of Eritrea in a Peaceful Way* (Addis Ababa: [May] 1976).

Eyassu Gayim. *The United Nations and Eritrea, 1948-1991 (Documents)* (Uppsala: Iustus Forlag, 1991).

————. *The Eritrean Question: The Conflict Between the Right of Self-determination and the Interests of States* (Uppsala: Iustus Forlag, 1993).*

Fabian Colonial Bureau. *The Fate Of Italy's Colonies* (London: H.M. Stationary Office, 1948).

Farer, Tom. *War Clouds over the Horn of Africa* (New York: Carnegie Endowment for International Peace, 1976).

Fasil Nahum. "Enigma of Eritrean Legislation." *J. Eth. Law,* 9, no. 1 (1973).

Fenet, Alain, Cao-Huy-Thuan and Tran-Van-Minh. *La question de l'Erythree: Droit international et politique des deux grands* (Paris: 1979).

Fenet, Alain. "The Eritrean People and the Principle of Self-Determination within the Framework of the United Nations." *The Eritrean Case* (Rome: RICE; 1982).

————. "The Right of the Eritrean People to Self-Determination." In *The Long Struggle of Eritrea,* ed. L. Cliffe, et al (Trenton: Red Sea P., 1988).

Fernyhough, Timothy. "Social mobility and dissident elites in Northern Ethiopia: The Role of Bandits, 1900-69." In *Banditry, Rebellion and Social Protest in Africa,* ed. D. Crummey (Portsmouth: Heinemann, 1986).

Firebrace, James. *Never Kneel Down: Drought, Development and Liberation in Eritrea* (Nottingham: Russell P., 1985).

Four Powers Commission. *Report of the Commission of Investigation of Former Italian Colonies.* V. 1, *Report on Eritrea* [with appendixes] (London: 1948).

Frankel, D. "Une défaite militaire." *Inprecor* 44, Feb. (1979).

Getachew Haile. "The Unity and Territorial Integrity of Ethiopia." *JMAS* 24, no. 3 (1986): 465-487.

Gilkes, Patrick. *The Dying Lion* (London: Julian Friedman, 1975).

_____. "Eritrea Could Stand Alone." *African Development* Apr. (1975).

_____. "Revolution and Military Strategy: The Ethiopian Army in the Ogaden and Eritrea, 1974-84." Presented to Eleventh ICES, Addis Ababa (MS.: 1991).

_____. "The Battle of Af Abet and Eritrean Independence." *Northeast African Studies* 2, no. 3 (1995)

Great Britain, Min. of Information. *The First to Freed* (London: H.M. Stationary Office, 1941).

_____. *Handbook for Eritrea* (Asmara: BMA, 1944).

Grimaldi, Fulvio. "The Eritrean Road to Unity?" *Middle East* 38, Dec. (1977).

_____. "The New Eritrea." *Sudanow* 2, Dec. (1977).

Hagag, Y. A., and R. Church. "Ethiopia, Eritrea and Somaliland." *Geo. Rev.* July (1953).

Halliday, F., and M. Molyneux. *The Ethiopian Revolution* (London: Zed, 1981).

Halliday, Fred. "The Fighting in Eritrea." *New Left Review,* 67 (1971).

Hanson, Mary. "Eritrea: The Hidden War in East Africa." *Pacific Research and World Empire Telegram* 1, Sept. (1969).

Hawley, F. "The Eritrean Referendum Overseas." *Africa Today* 40, no. 2 (1993).

Heiden, Linda. "The Eritrean Struggle for Independence." *Monthly Rev.,*30, no. 2 (1978).

Henze, Paul. "Arming the Horn 1960-1980." In *Proc. Seventh ICES,* ed. S. Rubenson (Addis Ababa: 1984).

_____. "Eritrea." In *The New Insurgencies: Anti-Communist Guerrillas in the Third World,* ed. M. Radu (New Brunswick: Transaction, 1990).

_____. "Ethiopia and Eritrea in Transition: The Impact of Ethnicity on Politics." In *New Trends in Ethiopian Studies,* v.2, ed. H. Marcus (Lawrenceville: Red Sea P., 1994).

Hubbell, Stephen. "Eritrea Nascent: The Next Fight for Independence." *The Nation,* May 31 (1993).

Hussey, E. R. "Eritrea Self-Governing." *African Affairs* 23, no. 213 (1954).

Islamic Review. "Eritrea's Bloc for Independence Sends Manifesto to British, Italian and Ethiopian Governments, 25 July, 1949." In v. 39, Oct. (1949).

Italian Affairs. "Italy and Eritrea." In v. 4, no. 1 (1955).

Iyob, Ruth. "Regional Hegemony: Domination and Resistance in the Horn of Africa." *J.MAS* 31, no. 2 (1993): 257-76.

_____. *The Eritrean Struggle for Independence: Domination, resistance, nationalism: 1941-93* (Cambridge: Cambridge Univ. P., 1995).*

Jevons, H. S. "Eritrea and Abyssinia." *The Spectator,* v. 175, Oct. 5 (1945).

Johnson, Deborah. "Media History of Eritrea." *ESR* 1, no. 1 (1996).

Johnson, T., and M. "Eritrea: The National Question and the Logic of Protracted Struggle." *African Affairs,* v. 80 (1981): 81-95.

Jordan Gebre-Medhin. *Peasants and Nationalism in Eritrea* (Trenton: Red Sea P., 1988).*

Kahsai Berhane. "A Political and Legal Analysis of the Red Sea Question." In [Mimeograph] "Working papers 7" (Trenton: n.d.).

Kaplan, R. D. *Surrender or Starve: The Wars Behind the Famine* (Boulder: Westview, 1988).

Keller, J. E. *Revolutionary Ethiopia: From Empire to People's Republic* (Bloomington: Indiana Univ. P., 1988).

_____. "Constitutionalism and the National Question in Africa: The Case of Eritrea." In *The Political Economy of Ethiopia,* ed. M. Ottaway (New York: 1990).

_____. "Eritrean Self-Determination Revisited." *Africa Today* 38, no. 2 (1991).

Kidane Mengesteab. "The Mesazgi brothers: Banditry in 1941-51 Eritrea." (MS. [B.A. thesis] Addis Ababa: AAU, n.d.)

Knutsson, Karl E. *Report from Eritrea* (Stockholm: I.W.G.I.A., 1971).

Kramer, Jack. "Hidden War in Eritrea." *Venture* 21, May (1969).

_____. "Africa's Hidden War." *Evergreen Rev.,* Dec. (1971).

Krylov, Alexander. "Islam and Nationalism: Two trends of the Separatist Movement in Ethiopia." *Northeast African Studies* 12, no. 2-3 (1990): 171-76.

Kutschera, Chris. *Erythrée/Eritrea* (Paris: EDIFRA, 1994).

Lefort, René. *Ethiopia: An Heretical Revolution?* (London: Zed, 1983).

Legum, Colin, and W. Lee. *Conflict in the Horn of Africa* (New York: 1977).

Lewis, I. M., ed. *Nationalism and Self-Determination in the Horn of Africa* (London: Ithaca P., 1983).*

Leonard, R. "Popular Participation in Liberation and Revolution." In *The Long Struggle of Eritrea,* ed. L. Cliffe et al (Trenton: Red Sea P., 1988).

Lobban, Richard. "Eritrean Liberation Front: A Close-up View." *Munger Africana Liberation Notes,* 13, Sept. (Pasadena: 1972).

_____. "The Eritrean War: Issues and Implications." *Canadian Journal of African Studies,* v. 10 (1976).

Lockheim, D. "Small war in Ethiopia." *World Politics,* Apr. 30 (1967).

Longrigg, S. H. "Disposal of Italian Africa." *International Affairs,* v. 21, July (1945).

_____. "Italy's Colonies." *The Spectator,* v. 127, July 27 (1945).

_____. "Disposal of Italian Africa." *International Affairs* 21, no. 3 (1945).

_____. "The Future of Eritrea." *African Affairs* 45, no. 180 (1946).

_____. "Eritrea: Present and Future." *United Empire,* Sept. (1946).

Machida, Robert. *Eritrea: The Struggle for Independence* (Trenton: Red Sea P., 1987).

Marcus, H. *Ethiopia, Great Britain and the United States, 1941-1974: The Politics of Empire* (Berkeley: Univ. of California P., 1983).

Marchal, Roland. "Guerre et famine: populations et guerrillas en Erythrée." *Communication au 12e congres international de sociologie* (Madrid: [July] 1990).

_____. "On Some Social aspects of the Conflicts in Eritrea and Sudan." In *Conflict in the Horn of Africa,* ed. Nzongola-Ntalaja (Atlanta: A.S.A., 1991)

_____. "La variante eritrea." *Politica internazionale,* v. 4 (1992).

_____. "Erythrée: l'an 01." *Politique africaine,* 50, June (1993).

_____. "Le refus de la revindication independantiste en Akkele-Guzai: le cas de Saganeiti." *Etudes éthiopiennes,* v. 1 (Paris: Soc. française pour les études éthiopiennes, 1994).

Marein, N. *Ethiopian Empire: Federation and Law* (Rotterdam: 1954).

Markakis, John. "Material and Social Aspects of National Conflict in the Horn of Africa." In *Proc. Seventh ICES,* ed. S. Rubenson (Addis Abeba: 1984).

_____. *National and Class Conflict in the Horn of Africa* [Ch.5] (Cambridge: Univ. P., 1987).*

_____. "The Nationalist Revolution in Eritrea." *JMAS* 26, no. 1 (1988).

_____. "Ethnic Conflict and the State in the Horn of Africa." In *Ethnicity and Conflict in the Horn of Africa* ed. K. Fukui and J. Markakis (London: Longmans, 1994).

Martin, D. "The war in Eritrea." *New Statesman,* Feb. 7 (1975).

Matatu, G. "Interview: Mohamed Said, Director of Information, ELF." *Africa* 44, April (1975).

McKay, V. "The Future of Italy's Colonies." *Foreign Policy Reports* 21, Jan. (1946).

Mekalh Harnet [pseudonym]. "Reflections on the Eritrean Revolution." *Horn of Africa* 6, no. 3 (1983/84): 3-15.

Meron, Theodor, and A. M. Pappas. "The Eritrean Autonomy: A Case Study of a Failure." In *Models of Autonomy,* ed. Y. Dinstein (New Brunswick: Transaction, 1981).

Mesfin Araya. "Eritrea, 1941-1952, The Failure of the Emergence of the Nation State: Towards a Clarification of the Eritrean Question in Ethiopia." (PhD. diss.; CUNY: 1988).

————. "The Eritrean Question: An Alternative Explanation." *JMAS* 28, no. 1 (1990).

Mesfin Gabriel. "Ethiopia Promises 'The Year of the Offensive'." *New African* 126, Feb. (1978).

Mohammed Usman Abubakr. *Tarik Eritrea al-Muwasir* [Arab.: "Contemporary Eritrean History"] (Cairo: 1994).

————. *Al-Haraka al-Tulabiyya al-Eritrea Wadawraha fi al-Thawra* [Arab.: "The Eritrean Student Movement's Participation in the Struggle"] (Cairo: 1994).

Morgan, E. "A geographical analysis of the Ethiopia-Eritrea conflict." *J. African Studies* 15, no. 4 (1977).

The Nation. "Former Italian Colonies." In v. 167, Sept. 18 (1948).

Neuberger, Benyamin. *National Self-Determination in Post-colonial Africa* (Boulder: Lynne Reiner, 1986).

Ngapit, Yves. "L'Erythrée et la question de l'unité africaine." *Peuples noirs, peuples africains* 2, no. 9 (1979).

Novati, Giampaolo. "Italy in the Triangle of Africa: Too many corners for half a power." *JMAS* 32, no. 3 (1994).

Nzongola-Ntalaja, Georges, ed. *Conflict in the Horn of Africa* (Atlanta: African Studies Association, 1991)

Okbazghi Yohannes. *Eritrea: A Pawn in World Politics* (Gainesville: Univ. of Florida P., 1991).*

————. "Eritrea: A Country in Transition." *Rev. of African Political Econ.,* v. 57 (1993).

Osman Saleh Sabbe. *The Roots of Eritrean Disagreements and How to Resolve Them* (Beirut: 1978).

————.*Juhudna min ajl al-Wakada* [Arab.: "Our Struggle for National Unity"] (Beirut: 1979).

_____. *Eritrea: The National Democratic Revolution ver-sus Ethiopian Expansionism* (Beirut: ELF, 1979).

Ottaway, Marina, and David. *Ethiopia: Empire in Revolution* (New York: Africana, 1978).

Ottaway, Marina. *Soviet and American Influence on the Horn of Africa* (New York: Africana, 1982).

_____. "Mediation in a Transitional Conflict: Eritrea." *Annals of American Acad. Political and Social Sciences, no.* 518 (1991): 69-81.

_____. "Nationalism Unbound: The Horn of Africa Revisited." *SAIS Rev.,* 2 (1992): 111-28.

Pankhurst, E. Sylvia. "Italian Colonies and Italian Poverty." *The Nation* 168, Mar. 26 (1949).

_____. "Reply to USSR Regarding the Italian Colonies." *The Nation,* May 8 (1949).

_____. *Eritrea on the Eve: The Past nad Future of Italy's 'First to be Freed'* (Woodford Green: Lailabela House, 1952).

_____. *Why Are We Destroying the Ethiopian Ports?* (London: Walighamstow, 1952).

Pankhurst, E. S., and R. K. P. *Ethiopia and Eritrea: The Last Phase of the Reunion Struggle (1941-52)* (Woodford Green: Lailabela House, 1953).

Papstein, Robert. *Eritrea: Revolution at Dusk* (Trenton: Red Sea P., 1991).

Pateman, Roy. "The Eritrean War." *Armed Forces and Society* 17, no. 1 (1990).

_____. "Liberté, Egalité, Fraternité: Aspects of the Er-itrean Revolution." *JMAS* 28, no. 3 (1990): 457-72.

_____. *Eritrea: Even the Stones are Burning* (Trenton: Red Sea P., 1990).*

_____. "Eritrea and Ethiopia: Strategies for Reconcilia-tion in the Horn of Africa." *Africa Today* 38, no. 2 (1991).

_____. "Eritrea Takes the World Stage." *Current History,* May (1994).

_____. "The Legacy of Eritrea's National Question." *Society* 33, no. 6 (1996).

Peninou, Jean Louis. "Les guerriers de la Mer Rouge." *Lib-eration,* Sept. 22-27 [Paris] (1975).

_____. "Eritrea: The Guerrillas of the Red Sea." Mimeograph. (New York: EFLNA, 1976).

Perham, M. *The Government of Ethiopia* (Evanston: Northwestern Univ. P., 1969).

Pliny the Middle-Aged. "Eclectic Notes on the Eritrean Liberation Front: E Pluribus Unum?" *Ethiopianist Notes* (East Lansing: Michigan State Univ., 1978).

Pool, David. *Eritrea: Africa's Longest War* (London: Anti-Slavery Soc. [Rept. 3], 1980).*

_____. "Eritrean Nationalism." In *Nationalism and Self-Determination in the Horn of Africa,* ed. I. M. Lewis (London: Ithaca P., 1983).

_____. "Eritrean Independence: The Legacy of the Derg and the Politics of Reconstruction." *African Affairs,* v. 92 (1992).

Poscia, Stefano. *Eritrea: Colonia Tradita* (Rome: Editore Associate, 1989).*

_____. "Aspettando il referendum nasce la nuova Eritrea." *Studi Piacenti,* v. 12 (1992): 133-51.

Prattico, Franco. "Viaggio nell'Eritrea in Fiamme." *Paese Sera* ,May 9 (1967).

Prunier, Gerard. "Atouts et faillesde l'Erythrée." *Le monde diplomatique,* Apr. (1993).

Rampone, Oscar. *Avvenne in Eritrea* (Milano: 1985).

Rasmuson, John, and M. Hoffman. *A History of Kagnew Station and American Forces in Eritrea* (Asmara: 1973).

Referendum Commission of Eritrea *see* Amare Tekle.

Remnek, Richard. "Soviet Policy in the Horn of Africa." In *The Soviet Union in the Third World: Successes and Failures,* ed.: R. Donaldson (London: 1981).

Research and Information Center on Eritrea. *Revolution in Eritrea: Eyewitness Reports* (Brussels: RICE, 1980).

Rivlin, B. *The United Nations and the Italian Colonies* (New York: 1950).

Robbs, P. "Battle for the Red Sea." *Africa Report,* Mar.-Apr. (1975).

Robinson, D. "War in Eritrea." *Contemporary Rev.,* 219, (1971): 1270.

Rodd, Lord Rennel. *British Military Administration of Occupied Territories in Africa (1941-47)* (London: H.M. Stationary Office, 1948).

Schiller, Arthur A. "Eritrea: Constitution and Federation with Ethiopia." *American J. Comparative Law,* 2 (1953).

Schroder, Gunter. [Interviews with early ELF fighters, 1987-89: unpublished] (MS., n.d.).

Schwab, Peter. "Israel's Weakened Position on the Horn of Africa." *New Outlook,*10, Apr. (1978).

Semere Haile. "The Roots of Ethiopia-Eritrea Conflict: The Erosion of the Federal Act." *J. Erit. Studies* 1, 1 (1986).

Sforza, Carlo (Count). "Italy's Position on the Former Colonies." *Vital Speeches,* v. 16, Oct. 15 (1949).

_____. *Cinque Anni a Palazzo Chiggi, La Politica Estera Italiana dal 1947 al 1951* (Rome: 1952).

Shepherd, G.W. "Free Eritrea: Linchpin for Stability and Peace on the Horn." *Africa Today* 40, no. 2 (1993).

Sherman, Richard. *Eritrea: The Unfinished Revolution* (New York: Praeger, 1980).*

_____. "The Rise of Eritrean Nationalism." *Northeast African Studies* 2, no. 1 (1980): 121-30.

Shumet Sishagne. "Notes on the Background to the Eritrean Problem: early 1950s-1960s." Mimeograph (Addis Ababa: AAU, Dept. of History, 1983).

_____. "Discord and Fragmentation in Eritrean Politics, 1941-1981." (Ph.D. diss.; Univ. of Illinois, Urbana: 1992).

Silberman, L. "Change and Conflict in the Horn of Africa." *Foreign Affairs* 37, no. 4 (1959).

Solomon Drar. *Ertrawyan komando, kiya 18 deqaiq* [Tigrn.] (Asmara: 1996).

Sorenson, John, and H. Adelman, ed. *African Refugees: Development Aid and Repatriation* (Boulder: Westview; 1994).

Sorenson, John. "Discourses on Eritrean National Identity." *JMAS* 29, no. 2 (1993).

_____. *Imagining Ethiopia: Struggles for History and Identity in the Horn of Africa* (New Brunswick: Rutgers Univ. P., 1993)"

Smith, J. A. C. "Human Rights in Eritrea." *Modern Law Rev.* 18, no. 5 (1955).

Spencer, John. *Ethiopia at Bay* (Algonac, Mich.: Reference, 1984).

Stafford, F. E. "The Ex-Italian Colonies." *International Affairs,* Jan. (1949).

Tahir Ibrahim Faidab. *Al-Haraka al-Eritrea wa masirataha al-tarikiya* [Arab.: "History of the Eritrean Liberation Movement"] (Beirut: Al-Shiuq P.P., 1994).

Tayew Geremew. "Rebellion in Eritrea—Who is Behind It? What are Its Aims?" *New Middle East* 31, Apr. (1971).

Taylor, Graham. "Ethiopia's Rebellion." *Africa Report,* Dec. (1969).

Tekeste Habtu. "The Role of the Eritrean Political Parties in the Establishment of the Federation between Ethiopia and Eritrea." (MS. [B.A. thesis]; Addis Ababa: AAU, 1968).

Tekeste Melake. "The Battle of Shire (Feb. 1989): A Turning Point in the Protracted War in Ethiopia." In *New Trends in Eth. Studies,* v.1, ed. H. Marcus (Lawrenceville; Red Sea P., 1994).

Tekeste Negash. *Eritrea and Ethiopia: The Federal Experience* (New Brunswick: Transaction, 1997).

Tekie Fessehatzion. "The International Dimensions of the Eritrean Question." *Horn of Africa,* 6, 2 (1983) pp. 7-30.

_____. "Eritrea: From Federation to Annexation, 1952-62." (Eritreans for Peace and Democracy [Working Paper No. 2], 1990).

_____. "The Eritrean Referendum of 1993." *ESR* 1, no. 1 (1996).

Tekle Mariam Woldemikael. "Political Mobilization and Nationalist Movements: The Case of the Eritrean People's Liberation Front." *Africa Today* 38, no. 2 (1991).

_____. "The Cultural Construction of Eritrean nationalist Movements." In *The Rising Tide of Cultural Pluralism,* ed. Crawford Young (Madison: Univ. of Michigan P., 1993).

_____. "Ethiopians and Eritreans." In *Refugees in America in the 1990s,* ed. D. Haines (Westport: Greenwood P., 1996).

Tesfatsion Medhanie. *Eritrea: Dynamics of a National Question* (Amsterdam: 1986).

_____. *Eritrea and Neighbours in the "New World Order"* (Bremen: Univ. of Bremen P., 1994).

Trevaskis, G. K. N. *Eritrea: A Colony in Transition* (Oxford: Oxford Univ. P., 1960).*

Tricontinental. "On the Shores of the Red Sea." no. 4-5 (Havana: 1968): 65-70.

Triulzi, A. "Le scelte della rivoluzione e la guerra in Eritrea." *Politica internazionale* 3, Mar. (1975).

Tronvoll, Kjeti. "The Eritrean Referendum: Peasant Voices." *ESR* 1, 1 (1996).

United Nations. "Resolution 390 A (5)." [Fifth Session] (New York: General Assembly Official Records, 1950).

_____. *Report of the Commission for Eritrea* [Supplement 8, (5) A/1285] (New York: General Assembly Official Records, 1950).

_____. *Progress Report of the Commissioner in Eritrea for 1951* [Doc. A/1959] (New York: General assembly Official Records, 1951).

_____. *Final Report of UN Commission in Eritrea* [Supplement 15, A/2188] (New York: General Assembly Official Records 1952).

_____. *Eritrea and the United Nations: Shaping a People's Destiny* (New York: 1953).

United States, Department of State: Office of Intelligence Research. "The Geographic Basis for a division of Eritrea between the Anglo-Egyptian Sudan and Ethiopia." Report 4493, Oct. 13 (1947).

_____. "Affinities of the Western Province of Eritrea with Adjacent Areas." Rept. 4996, Sept. 6 (1949).

_____. "The Capacity of Eritrea for Independence." Report 5311, July 11 (1950).

_____. "Implications of Federation for Ethiopia and Eritrea." Report 5595, Dec. 31 (1950).

_____. "The Ethiopia-Eritrea Federation: A Progress Report." Report 7130, Feb. 2 (1956).

Vigo, Anthony. "Between Two Worlds." *Africa Today,* Oct. (1965).

Warren, Herrick and Anita. "The U.S. Role in the Eritrean Conflict." *Africa Today* 23, Apr.-June (1976).

Wilson, R.C. "Eritrea: The present and future of a Yankee base." *Tricontinental* 71, Feb. [Havana] (1972).

Wise, E. F. "Future of Eritrea." *The Spectator,* v. 181, Dec. 3 (1948).

With, Peter A. "Politics and Liberation: the Eritrean Struggle 1961-86." (Ph.D. diss.; Univ. of Aarhus: 1987).

Wolde-Ab Wolde-Mariam. "Dalla federazione all'annessione: La lotta del popolo eritreo." *Altrafrica,* 1 (Rome: 1975).

Wolde-Yesus Ammar. *Eritrea: Root Causes of War and Refugees* (Baghdad: 1992).*

_____. "Role of Asmara Students in the Eritrean Nationalist Movement: 1958-68." *ESR* 2, no. 1 (1997).

Young, John. *Peasant Revolution in Ethiopia: The Tigray People's Liberation Front, 1975-91* (Cambridge: Univ. P., 1997).

Zafrulla Kahn. "The Future of the Former Italian Colonies." *Pakistan Horizons* 2, no. 3 (1949).

Zemhret Yohannes. "Nation-Building and Constitution-Making in Eritrea." *ESR* 1, no. 1 (1996).

Zewde Gebre Sellassie. *Eritrea and Ethiopia in the Context of the Red Sea and Africa* (Washington, D.C.: 1976).

2. Social Issues

Abeba Tesfagiorgis. *A Painful Season and a Stubborn Hope: The Odyssey of an Eritrean Mother* (Lawrenceville: Red Sea P., 1992).

Adane Taye. *An Historical Survey of State Education in Eritrea* (Asmara: 1992)

Ahmed Tahir Badouri. "Migration of Eritreans and the Government's Efforts to Repatriate Refugees from Sudan." *Eritrea Profile* 1, no. 42-45 (Asmara: 1994-95).

Allen, Tim, ed. *In Search of Cool Ground: War, Flight and Homecoming in Northeast Africa* (Lawrenceville: Red Sea P., 1996).*

Basalvik, Randi R. *Haile Selassie's Students: The Intellectual and Social Background to Revolution, 1952-77* (East Lansing: Michigan State Univ. P., 1985).

Bascom, Jonathan. "The Peasant Economy of Refugee Resettlement in Eastern Sudan." *Annals of the Association of American Geographers,* v. 83 (1993).

_____. "The dynamics of refugee repatriation: The case of Eritreans in Eastern Sudan." In *Population Migration and the Changing World Order,* ed. W. Gould and Findlay (London: J. Wiley and Sons, 1994).

_____. "Reconstituting Households and Reconstructing Home Areas: The Case of Eritrea." In *In Search of Cool Ground,* ed. T. Allen (Lawrenceville: Red Sea P., 1996).

Berhane Teklehaimanot. "Education in Eritrea during the European Colonial Period." *ESR* 1, no. 1 (1996).

Berhane Woldegabriel. "The Refugee Problem." *Sudanow* 2 July (1977).

Bulcha Mekuria. *Flight and Integration: Causes of Mass Exodus from Ethiopia and the Problems of Integration in the Sudan* (Uppsala: 1988).

Burgess, Doris. "Women at war: Eritrea." *Rev. of African Political Economy,* no. 45-46 (1989): 126-32.

Cliffe, Lionel. "The Impact of War and the Response to It in Different Agraian Systems in Eritrea." *Development and Change* 20, no. 3 (1989): 373-400.

Commission for Eritrean Refugee Affairs. *The Eritrean Refugee Problem: Issues and Challenges* (London: 1989).

Cowan, Nicole Ann. "Women in Eritrea: An Eyewitness Account." *Rev. of African Political Economy* no. 27/28 (1983): 143-55.

Dines, M. "The Social Transformation of Eritrean Society under the EPLF." In *The Eritrean Case* (Rome: RICE, 1982).

Downey, Hugh and Marty. *On Heart's Edge* [story of Lalmba Medical Relief Agency] (Arvada: Mikeren, 1996).

(The) Economist. "Eritrea: The Kitchen Calls." June 25 (1994).

Elias Habte-Sealassie. "Eritrean Refugees in Sudan." In *Beyond Conflict in the Horn* , ed. M. Doornbos, L. Cliffe, et al (London: J. Currey, 1992).

_____. "Homecoming in Eritrea." In *In Search of Cool Ground,* ed. T. Allen (Lawrenceville: Red Sea P., 1996).

EFLNA. *EPLF: Serving the Masses on the Medical Front* (New York: EFLNA, 1976).

_____. *EPLF: Serving the Masses on the Medical Front* (New York: EFLNA, 1978).

EPLF (Department of Education). "Education in the Liberated Areas." Mimeograph (1978).

Eritrean Relief Committee. *Eritrean Refugees in the Republic of Sudan* (Khartoum: ERC, 1980).

Eritrean Women's Association—Europe. *Women and Revolution in Eritrea* (Rome: EPLF, 1979).

Gabrehewet Nebarai "Eritrea: School Nutrition and Gardening Programme." *Eth. Observer* 4, no. 4 (1960).

Gaddi, S. "Liberta' di stampa in Eritrea." *Africa* 8, no. 10 (Rome: 1953).

Gaim Kibreab. *Refugees and Development in Africa: Case Study of Eritrea* (Trenton: Red Sea P., 1987).*

_____. *The Sudan, From Subsistence to Wage Labor: Refugee Settlements in the Central and Eastern Regions* (Trenton: Red Sea P., 1990).

_____. "Refugees in the Sudan: Unresolved Issues." In *African Refugees: Development Aid and Repatriation,* ed. Adelman and Sorenson (Boulder: Westview, 1994).

_____. "Left in Limbo: Prospects for Repatriation of Eritrean refugees from Sudan." In *In Search of Cool Ground,* ed. T. Allen (Lawrenceville: Red Sea P., 1996).

_____. *People on the Edge in the Horn of Africa* (Lawrenceville: Red Sea P., 1997).

Gottesman, Les. "Hermeneutics of Literacy During Eritrea's War of Independence." *ESR* 1, no. 2 (1996).

Grinker, Lori. "The Main Force: Women in Eritrea." *Ms. Magazine,* May/June (1992).

Grisman, C. S. "West Africans in Eritrea." *Nigerian Field* 20, no. 1 (1955).

Hodgin, Peter. "An Introduction to Eritrea's Ongoing Revolution: Women's Nationalist Mobilization and Gender Politics in Post-War Eritrea." *ESR* 2, 1 (1997).

Houtart, Francois. "The Social Revolution in Eritrea." In *Behind the War in Eritrea* (Nottingham: Spokesman, 1980).

_____. "Social Aspects of the Eritrean Revolution." *Race and Class,*22, no. 3 (1981).

Killion, T. "The Rebuiding of Asmara University and Eritrea's Educational Crisis." *Eritrean Studies Association Newsletter* 3 Apr. (1994).

Kok, Walter. "Self-Settled Refugees [in E. Sudan]." *J. Refugee Studies* 2, no. 4 (1989).

Kuhlman, T., and S. Ibrahim and W. Kok. *Refugees and Regional Development* [Eritreans in Sudan] (Amsterdam: Free Univ., Center for Development, 1987).

La Duke, Betty. *Africa: Womens' Art, Womens' Lives* [Ch. 7: "Eritrea: Artists/Fighters with New Visions."] (Lawrenceville: Red Sea P., 1997).

Marando, J. and RICE. *Life in Liberated Eritrea* (Rome: RICE, 1987).

Mayotte, Judy. "Disposable People? The Plight of Refugees." *Orbis,* no. 3 [Maryknoll, N.Y.] (1992).

Mottern, Nicholas. *Suffering Strong* [Eritrean women] (Trenton: Red Sea P., 1988).

Moussa, Helene. *Storm and Sanctuary: The Journey of Ethiopian and Eritrean Women Refugees* (Dundas, Ont.: Artemis, 1993).

National Union of Eritrean Women. *Women in the Eritrean Revolution: Eyewitness Reports* (1981).

Pateman, Roy. "Drought, Famine and Development." *The Long Struggle of Eritrea* (Trenton: Red Sea P., 1988).

Prendergast, John, and M. Duffield. "Public Welfare and the Politics of National Liberation in Ethiopia and Eritrea." In *New Trends in Ethiopian Studies,* v. 2, ed. H. Marcus (Lawrenceville: Red Sea P., 1994).

Puglisi, G. "La scuola in Eritrea ieri e oggi." *Affrica* 8, no. 3 and no. 5 (Rome: 1953).

Rentmeesters, Veronica. "Women and Development Planning." In *Emergent Eritrea,* ed. Gebre-Hiwet Tesfagiorgis (Trenton: Red sea P., 1993).

Silkin, Patricia. "Marriage and Social Change in the 'Liberated Zones' of Eritrea Controlled by the EPLF." Presented to Conference of the Review of African Political Economy (MS.; Liverpool: 1986).

_____. "New Marriage Laws and Social Change in the Liberated Areas of Eritrea." *International J. Sociology of Law* 12, no. 2 (1989): 147-63.

_____. "Changes in the Negotiation of Marriage in the Areas of Eritrea Administered by the EPLF." (MS.: [Masters of Philosophy-Anthropology]; University of London: 1989).

_____ [Trish Johnson]. "Eritrea: Women at War." *Spare Rib*, April (London: 1979).

Smith, Dolores. "My Name is Woman." [History of Asmara Univ.] *Proc. Ninth ICES* (1990): 469-80.

Styan, David. "Eritrea 1993: The End of the Beginning." [Refugees] In *In Search of Cool Ground*, ed. T. Allen (Lawrenceville: Red Sea P.; 1996).

Sullivan-Owomoyela, Joan. "New Wine in Old Bottles: Culturally Relevant Curriculum from Eritrea's Indigenous Education System." *ESR* 1, no. 2 (1996).

Terhas Hagos. "Women and the Eritrean Revolution." *Horn of Africa* 4, no. 2 (1981): 32-36.

Tesfa G. Gebremedhin. *Beyond Survival: The Economic Challenges of Agriculture and Development in Post-Independence Eritrea* (Lawrenceville: Red Sea P., 1996).

Teshome G. Wagaw. "Education in Eritrea, 1941-42." *Eth. J. Education* 6, no. 2 (1974).

U.S. Committee for Refugees [Hiram Ruiz]. *Beyond the Headlines: Refugees in the Horn of Africa* (Washington, DC: 1988).

Wilson, Amrit. *Women and the Eritrean Revolution: The Challenge Road* (Trenton: Red Sea P., 1991).

Yishaq Yusuf. *Hatsir zanta-hiwet memher Yishaq Tewolde Medhen: Qalsi metfe denqhwerna* [Tigrn.: "A Short Biography of Educator Yisaq Tewolde-Medhin: War on Illiteracy"] (Asmara: 1993).

3. Economy

African Business. "Donor Apathy Towards Eritrea Sets Dangerous Precedent." In Oct. no. (1994).

Altrafrica. "Lo statuto dell'unione sindicati liberi dei lavoratori eritrei." In no. 1 (Rome: 1975).

Araia Tseggai. "The Economic Viability of an Independent Eritrea." (Ph.D. diss.; Univ. of Nebraska: 1981).

_____. "Eritrea: The Socio-Economic Challenges of Independence." *Africa Toda,* 38, no. 2 (1991).

_____. "Development After Disaster." *J. of Business and Econ. Studies* 2, no. 2 (1992).

Asmara Chamber of Commerce. *Alphabetical list of firms in Asmara and surrounding areas* (Asmara: 1972).

Barnett, Tony. "Agriculture in the Eritrean Revolution." In *Behind the War in Eritrea,* ed. B. Davidson et al (Nottingham: Spokesman, 1980).

Bascom, Johnathan. "Border pastoralism in Eastern Sudan." *Geographical Rev.,* v. 82 (1992).

Berhane Woldemichael and Kamal Ibrahim and V. Boria. *Poverty in an Area of Plenty: A baseline study for development planning in the Zula Plain of Eritrea* (Asmara: Norwegian Church Aid, 1994).

Cerbella, Gino. *Eritrea 1959: La collettivita italiana nelle sue attivita economiche, sociali e culurali* (Asmara: Italian Consul General, 1959).

Cherian, K., ed. *Agric.ulture Industry and Commerce in Ethiopia and Eritrea: A Special Publication* (Asmara: 1957).

Collier, O. P. C. "The Eritrean Railways." *Railway Gazette* Sept. (London: 1949).

De Leone, E. "Industrie italiane in Eritrea." *Affrica,* v. 4 (1949).

E. P. E. [anonymous]. *Eritrea, anno 1952* [economic reports] (Asmara: 1952).

Ellsberg, E. *Under the Red Sea Sun* [US Navy in Massawa, 1942-43] (New York: 1946).

Eritrea, Dept. of Commerce and Industry. *Statistics of Industrial Production, 1962-65* (Asmara: 1965).

Eritrea, Governor-General [Aradom Tedla]. *Social and Economic Development of Eritrea since 1962* (Rome: 1966).

Eritrea, Government of the State of. *Macro-Policy* (Asmara: Government P. P., 1994).

"Eritrean Railways." *Ethiopian Observer* 3, no. 7 (1959).

Ethiopia, Ministry of Land Reform. *Report on Land Tenure Survey of Eritrea Province* (Addis Ababa: 1969).

Fiore, Giacinto. *200 pagine sull'Eritrea* (Asmara: 1950).

G. F. [anonymous]. "Le aziende Casciani in Eritrea." *Difesa Africana* no. 3/4 (1948).

Gaddi, S. "I beni italiani in Eritrea." *Affrica* ,Mar. (1952).

Gebre Tesfagiorgis, ed. *Emergent Eritrea: Challenges of Economic Development* (Lawrenceville: Red Sea P., 1993).*

Genuensis. "La vita industriale dell'Eritrea sotto l'occupazione britannica." *Italiani nel mondo,* v. 11 (1947).

Gherardi, D. "Preliminary geological survey of Eritrea." *Mining Magazine,* May-July (1951).

Gnarini, A., ed. *Guida Commerciale dell'Eritrea* (Asmara: 1946).

Gwynn, C. W. "Improvisation in Occupied Africa." *Fortnightly Rev.* 16 (1948): 982.

Hailu W. Emmanuel "Concession Agriculture in Eritrea." *Eth. Geo. J.,* v. 2 (1964).

————. "Major ports of Ethiopia: Aseb, Jibuti, Mesewa." *Eth. Geo. J.,* v. 3 (1965).

Holloway, M. L. "Eritrea: A Survey of the Country and its Mining Prospects." *Mining Magazine* , Aug. (1945).

————. "Salt Deposits of the Danakil Depression." *Mining Magazine,* Oct. (1945).

————. "Water Supply in Eritrea." *Water,* Nov. (1945).

Infante, E. *Economia Eritrea* [report on 7 years of British occupation] (Rome: 1948).

Italian Consulate General, Asmara. *Gli Italiani in Eritrea nel 1958* (Asmara: 1958).

Jones, D. "Some aspects of Eritrean Fruit Production." *SNR,* v. 46 (1965).

Jones, Scott. "Environment and Development in Eritrea." *Africa Today* 38, no. 2 (1991).

Kidane Mengisteab. "Rehabilitation of Degraded Land in Eritrea's Agricultural Policy." In *Emergent Eritrea,* ed. Gebre Tesfagiorgis (Trenton: Red Sea P., 1993).

Killion, T. "Workers, Capital and the State in the Ethiopian Region, 1919-1974." (Ph.D. diss.; Stanford Univ.: 1985).

————. "History of the Eritrean Labor Movement." *Demtsi Serahtegnatat* 1, no. 3 (Asm.: 1995).

_____. "Eritrean Workers' Organization and Early Nationalist Mobilization: 1948-58." *ESR* 2, no. 1 (1997).

McKay, V., and O. K. Ringwood. "Poverty of Resources in Italian Africa." *Foreign Policy Reports* 21, no. 20 (1946).

Means, R. "Employees Who May Not Strike." *J. Eth. Law* 4, no. 1 (1967).

_____. "The Eritrean Employment Act of 1958." *J. Eth. Law,* v. 5 (1968).

Misser, F. "Eritrea Seeks to Attract Foreign Investment." *African Business* (1992): 47.

Montanari, L. "Sulle strade dell'Eritrea." *Atti II convegno studi colon.* (Florence: 1947).

National Union of Eritrean Workers. *Tarik menqesqhas seretenyatat Ertra* [Tigrn.: "History of Eritrean Workers' Struggles"] (NUEW, 1981).

Orr, David. "Eritrea's Turn For Development." *Choices,* Sept. [UNDP] (1993): 4-11.

Papini, I. "La situazione dell'Eritrea nei suoi aspetti economici e politici." *Italiani nel mondo,* v. 2-5 (1946).

Puglisi, G. "Le pagine d'un libro contabile." *Africa* 5, no. 10 (1950).

_____. *Eritrea Tascabile* (Asmara: 1953).

Tomadini, E. *Annuario Economico Generale dell'Eritrea* (Asmara: 1947).

Tesfa G. Gebremedhin. "Constraints to a Viable Agricultural Development of Eritrea." *ESR* 1, no. 2 (1996).

Wayland, W. "Project 19." [U.S. at Gura' airbase] (MS.; Baltimore: 1944).

Yacob Fisseha. "Micro, Small and Medium Enterprises in Eritrea." *ESR* 1, no. 2 (1996).

ABOUT THE AUTHOR

TOM KILLION (B.A. University of California at Santa Cruz; Ph.D. Stanford University) is currently a lecturer in the Humanities Department at California State University, San Francisco and proprietor of the Quail Press in Santa Cruz. He has taught African History at Bowdoin College and the University of Asmara. Killion became interested in the Eritrean struggle for independence during the late 1970s, and began interviewing exiled nationalist leaders in Europe and northern Africa in the early 1980s while writing a doctoral dissertation on the Ethiopian labor movement. During 1987-88 he worked with Eritrean refugees at a camp in Eastern Sudan, and was an observer with the Eritrean guerrilla army at Afabet in March 1988. He has returned to Eritrea several times since 1991, including service as a referendum observer in 1993 and a year as a Fulbright scholar and lecturer at Asmara University in 1993-94. His research on economic and labor history in Ethiopia and Eritrea has been published in academic journals, while his contemporary reports have appeared frequently in the *Los Angeles Times*. Killion is now writing a general history of Eritrea. He is a member of the African Studies Association, American Historical Association and is currently president of the Eritrean Studies Association.